COMPREHENSIVE HANDBOOK OF
SOCIAL WORK
AND
SOCIAL WELFARE

Volume
4

COMPREHENSIVE HANDBOOK OF SOCIAL WORK AND SOCIAL WELFARE

SOCIAL POLICY AND POLICY PRACTICE

Volume Editor
Ira C. Colby

Editors-in-Chief
Karen M. Sowers   Catherine N. Dulmus

WILEY
John Wiley & Sons, Inc.

KH

Library of Congress Cataloging-in-Publication Data:

Comprehensive handbook of social work and social welfare /
    editors-in-chief, Karen M. Sowers and Catherine N. Dulmus.
        p.   cm.
    Includes bibliographical references.
    ISBN 978-0-471-76997-2 (cloth) Volume 1: The Profession of Social Work
    ISBN 978-0-471-76272-0 (cloth) Volume 2: Human Behavior in the Social Environment
    ISBN 978-0-471-76280-5 (cloth) Volume 3: Social Work Practice
    ISBN 978-0-471-76998-9 (cloth) Volume 4: Social Policy and Policy Practice
    ISBN 978-0-471-75222-6 (cloth) 4-Volume set
    1. Social service.   2. Social service—Practice.   3. Public welfare.   4. Social policy.
  I. Sowers, Karen M. (Karen Marlaine)   II. Dulmus, Catherine N.

    HV40.C66   2008
    361—dc22   2007026315

Printed in the United States of America.

10/5/09

There are two individuals who helped me over the years with my policy work. First, I go back to my first policy class at Virginia Commonwealth University School of Social Work, which was taught by Mrs. Charlotte Schrieberg. During my first year of studies, I had no idea what policy was or could do, but Mrs. Schriberg opened a door for me that I have never regretted going through. In thinking back to her two foundation year policy courses, I am reminded that I never got an A from her, but in retrospect it was not about the grade. It was about "knowing" and "doing." So to you, Mrs. Schrieberg, thank you for opening the door and influencing my life in a way that few have done.

And, of course, I again recognize my best friend and partner, Deborah Colby, an incredible social worker in her own right. For more than 35 years she has put up with my shenanigans and supported me in countless ways. She encourages my work, criticizes my "stuff" in an honest fashion, and has allowed me to grow as a person. I can only hope that this has been reciprocated in a similar manner.

Contents

SECTION IV   POLICY FORMULATION AND POSSIBILITIES

We challenged the chapter authors to not only provide an overview of specific content, but to feel free to raise controversial issues and debates within the profession. In the interest of intellectual freedom, many of our chapter authors have done just that in ways that are intriguing and thought provoking. It was our objective to be comprehensive but not encyclopedic. Readers wishing to obtain even greater specificity are encouraged to access works listed in the references for each chapter.

The *Handbook*'s focus on evidence should assist the reader with identifying opportunities to strengthen their own understanding of the amount of science that does or does not support our social work theory and practice. Social work researchers must expand the scientific evidence that supports social work theory and practice as well as informing policy, and enhance their functional scope to overcome the more than 10-year lag between research and practice. We are rightfully proud of our social work history, and its future will be driven by our success in demonstrating that as a profession we can achieve credible and verifiable outcomes across the spectrum of services that utilize our skills. As a profession, we must assure we value science so that even the most vulnerable populations receive the best available services.

We hope that you find this *Handbook* useful. We have endeavored to provide you, the reader and user, with a comprehensive work that will serve as a guide for your own work in this wonderful profession. We welcome your comments and suggestions.

KAREN M. SOWERS
CATHERINE N. DULMUS

Handbook Preface ───────────────

The profession of social work spans more than 100 years. Over this period, the profession has changed in scope and depth. Despite the varied functions and methods of our profession, it has always been committed to social justice and the promotion of well-being for all. The profession has made great strides and is experiencing a resurgence of energy, commitment, and advancement as we face new global realities and challenges and embrace new and innovative technologies.

In considering how the field of social work has evolved over the past century with the resulting explosion of new knowledge and technologies, it seemed imperative to create a resource (*Comprehensive Handbook of Social Work and Social Welfare*) that provides a manageable format of information for researchers, clinicians, educators, and students. Our editors at John Wiley & Sons, the volume editors (Ira Colby, William Rowe, Lisa Rapp-Paglicci, Bruce Thyer, and Barbara W. White) and we as editors-in-chief, developed this four-volume handbook to serve as a resource to the profession.

The *Comprehensive Handbook of Social Work and Social Welfare* includes four volumes (*The Profession of Social Work, Human Behavior in the Social Environment, Social Work Practice,* and *Social Policy and Policy Practice*). Each volume editor did an outstanding job of assembling the top social work scholars from around the globe to contribute chapters in their respective areas of expertise. We are enormously grateful to the chapter authors who have contributed their expert knowledge to this work. Each volume includes a Preface written by the respective volume editor(s) that provides a general overview to the volume. In developing the *Comprehensive Handbook,* we attempted to focus on evidence supporting our theoretical underpinnings and our practice interventions across multiple systems. Content was designed to explore areas critically and to present the best available knowledge impacting the well-being of social systems, organizations, individuals, families, groups, and communities. The content is contemporaneous and is reflective of demographic, social, political, and economic current and emerging trends. Authors have paid close attention to contextual factors that shape the profession and will have a future impact on practice. Our profession strives to understand the dimensions of human difference that we value and engage to ensure excellence in practice. These dimensions of diversity are multiple and include factors such as disability, religion, race, culture, sexual orientation, social class, and gender. Each of the volumes addresses how difference characterizes and shapes our profession and our daily practice. New knowledge, technology, and ideas that may have a bearing on contemporary and future social work practice are infused throughout each of the volumes.

Acknowledgments ———————————————————

An endeavor of this magnitude required the efforts of many people, and we are indebted to their unique and valuable contributions. First, we would like to thank Tracey Belmont, our initial editor at John Wiley & Sons, for recognizing the importance of this project to the profession of social work and for her commitment to making it a reality. It was Tracey's vision that allowed this project to get off the ground, and we are grateful to her. A special thanks to Lisa Gebo, our current editor at John Wiley & Sons, who provided us with expert guidance and technical support to see this project to fruition. Others to thank at John Wiley & Sons include Isabel Pratt and Sweta Gupta who assisted us with all aspects of the contractual and prepublication processes. They were invaluable in assisting with a project of this size, and we are grateful to them.

Most important, we would like to thank the volume editors and contributors who made this *Handbook* a reality. The volume editors did an excellent job of developing their respective volumes. We particularly thank them for their thoughtful selection and recruitment of chapter contributors. The contributor lists for each volume read like a "Who's Who" of social work scholars. We are pleased that each contributor recognized the importance of a seminal piece such as this *Handbook* for the profession of social work and willingly contributed their time and knowledge. We extend a special debt of gratitude to these eminent contributors from around the globe who so graciously and willingly shared their expertise with us. It is the work of these scholars that continues to move our profession forward.

K. M. S.
C. N. D.

Preface

While in the United Kingdom on a class trip, I received an e-mail from a colleague in Hong Kong who asked for a copy of a paper we had talked about during a recent visit to his city. Not able to access my computer files from my Blackberry, though I am sure there is a way to accommodate this simple transaction, I sent an e-mail to the paper's author, who lived in Norway. In turn she sent a copy of the paper to my Hong Kong colleague. The paper was waiting for him when he got to his office the next morning.

This entire process took less than 30 minutes, with the various e-mails traversing slightly more then 24,000 miles, or 38,700 kilometers. Just a few short years ago this would be unheard of and found only in science fiction movies. Today, in the twenty-first century, exchanges such as this are commonplace, ordinary, and unremarkable.

Yet for a moment, let's step back one generation, 20 years ago, to 1987, to revisit a very different experience.

- Multiple copies were duplicated on copy machines; a single copy resulted from carbon paper; and the mimeograph machine was an office staple.
- E-mail was an unknown commodity among the general population. Cell phones and pagers were limited in their distribution and used for the most part by physicians.
- Computer analysis was completed with IBM punch cards and computer card readers. Handheld calculators were the primary statistical analytic tool.
- The Compaq Portable III with 40 meg sold for $5,799 and included a 10" gas plasma screen. Microsoft introduced Windows 2.0 and MS DOS 3.3. The Mac SE initially sold for $2,900. The IBM PS/2 personal computer, with improved graphics, a 3.5-inch diskette drive, and chipsets, were added to the computer's motherboard.
- The Dow Jones Industrial Average, an accepted indicator of the strength of the American economy, closed at about 2,000 for the first time.
- President Ronald Reagan challenged Soviet Premier Mikhail Gorbachev, "If you seek peace, if you seek prosperity for the Soviet Union and Eastern Europe, if you seek liberalization . . . tear down this wall."
- The IBM Selectric typewriter, with its interchangeable typeball, offered a fast and creative mechanism to produce typed reports.

How the world has changed between 1987 and 2007, the publication year of this text. In 2007, the Dow Jones Average was above 12,000, the U.S. Congress authorized the construction of its own version of the Berlin Wall on the Texas-Mexico border to stop illegal immigration, cell phones are commonplace and multifunctional, the IBM Selectric typewriter is on display at the Smithsonian Museum of American History, and computer software programs conduct multiple levels of analysis faster and reference numerous tests of significance.

As we move into the twenty-first century, nearly instant access to information and the speed at which we transmit information have become commonplace. What once took days and weeks to accomplish now is completed in a matter of minutes and even seconds. The impact of distance and geographic borders is nearly nonexistent with the new means to communicate and share information.

Our global landscape is constantly changing. Between 1990 and 2006, 27 new countries were formed, with Montenegro being the most recent. Some of the new countries, such as the Czech Republic and Slovakia, came about through peaceful transactions; others, including Bosnia and East Timor, were sites of severe wars.

Global change took shape with five nations changing their names since the mid-1990s. The African nation of Zaire became the Democratic Republic of the Congo, Western Samoa became Samoa, and the Republic of Fiji is now the Republic of the Fiji Islands. Comoros became the Union of the Comoros Islands, and in 2003 Yugoslavia split into Serbia and Montenegro. As new nations formed, so too have many new governments moved into power, some peacefully, others through violent overthrow and war.

In 1987, the world population reached 5 billion people, 6.6 billion in 2006, and is estimated to reach 8 billion by 2028 (United Nations). The world as we know it in 2007 is far different from the world of only 20 years ago. We can only assume that 20 years hence, in 2027, the world will be very different from today.

This leads to my organizing assumption for this volume. Change is a constant in all our lives. Day in and day out we directly and indirectly experience change. And such change is formidable. Roth (1997, ix) writes in the *Encyclopedia of Social Issues:*

> The modern world . . . is a confusing place . . . the pace of social change has continually escalated . . . new discoveries . . . new technologies . . . new movements . . . new schools of political, philosophical, and social thought—all have combined to reshape the cultural landscape.

A primary way to effectively manage change in a positive, proactive manner that leads to global justice is through understanding the dynamic world of policy and its influences on our daily work.

Each year I teach a graduate foundation social welfare policy course, and one of the PowerPoint slides presented in our initial class reads as follows:

> "I want to learn how to do counseling."
> "Policy is plain BORING."
> "Policy doesn't have anything to do with individual, family, or group work!"
> "You know who teaches this course!!!"

The last comment is typically greeted with an uncomfortable laugh. Few students want to be in front of the dean! Over the years, I find that the majority of students want to learn about social work practice, in particular counseling and therapy, and initially view policy work as "just a required course." Yet by semester's end the students seem to make the connection between policy and practice, and many relish the opportunity to influence policy development. Though I wish this could be attributed to stellar course preparation and instruction, I defer to the idea that when given the opportunity to consider policy issues and concepts of social justice through a practice lens, students will recognize the importance of policy and its dynamic interplay with the lives of our clients as well as the community at large.

This text condenses experiences and observations from over 30 years of work. First, most social workers do not fully understand the nature of policy. I write this as an educator who feels that we have not done a good job of teaching about and analyzing the linkages between policy, practice, and social justice. Second, I firmly believe that sound policy grows from the direct interplay between practice and research. Collecting relevant information in a reliable and valid manner provides the evidence necessary to enhance social welfare policies. Third, social workers are in the best position to craft and advocate for creative, justice-based social policies. The practitioner experiences and observes in a very close, personal manner the negative impacts that social issues and injustice imprint on the lives of clients.

The contributors to this volume reflect a breadth and depth of experience that by itself is remarkable: a Nobel Peace laureate, the head of a major national foundation, distinguished faculty in both U.S. and international schools, and deans and directors of social work programs. Their works have influenced countless local, state, regional, national, and international policies. Through their individual efforts they have improved the lives of millions around the world.

This volume is not characteristic of the usual or standard policy textbook, nor should it be. There are scores of policy works available that cover current policies and related issues and introduce the reader to one or two models of analysis.

To be honest, I was a bit frustrated by my organization of the text. My initial frustration arose from trying to select topical areas to be included and excluded in a policy text—by itself, no easy task. No text can examine and envisage, let alone solve, the array of social issues that confront our communities. Thus, frustration number one was the Solomon-like decision to identify 20 areas for discussion knowing that many would be left out in this presentation. The subject areas were finally selected recognizing that each chapter deserved a much fuller discussion.

My second frustration grew from the text's organization. Originally I prearranged the chapters under four broad headings. But as the authors sent me their work, I moved away from the section approach. I was struck by what I was reading. The chapters, when read one after the next, possessed a natural flow and connectedness. The idea of sections seemed, at least to me, to disrupt the discourse. I shared this observation with colleagues, and although many understood my point, each and every one advised me to use sections. I realized that a book's format, though not a big deal for some, can become a major issue for others. We are all comfortable reading chapters organized around sections, as they give us a clear beginning and ending for content. Yet, in a compromise fashion, again recognizing that the policy process involves negotiation even with oneself, I agreed to the more traditional section format.

One of the unique opportunities in higher education is for so many gifted thinkers to put their ideas to paper for journal or text. Belief in the need to develop and contribute to the profession's knowledge base is worldwide and critical for us to remain relevant. This volume's authors reflect much needed multiple perspectives on social policy.

The authors were asked to reflect on their subject area within a post-9/11 context and to consider the subject within a global and technological world. They were asked to put forth ideas that would push the reader into new areas of thinking. The resulting chapters accomplish these purposes as the authors challenge us to look at issues and their influences in new ways. Parts of this work will make some uncomfortable, possibly angry, and some may question the value of the chapters. Others will grab on to the authors' ideas and embrace their perspectives. Although any author or editor would hope the reader finds the work the best of its kind, we realistically hope that this text helps you develop a fuller appreciation for the need and possibility to create a just society for people throughout the world.

So, what is it I trust the reader will pull from this volume? I hope you will be introduced to new concepts and ways of thinking about social issues and resulting social policies. If this holds true, then I am optimistic that you will be better skilled in and more knowledgeable about policy practice.

There is no need to belabor these points any further. Now is the time for you to read, consider, react, and advocate for proactive justice-based social policy. Social policy can be an instrument for positive change while supporting social work practice.

REFERENCE

Roth, J. K. (1997). *Encyclopedia of social issues* (Vol. 1). New York: Marshall Cavendish.

Contributors

Christopher W. Blackwell, PhD, ARNP-C
College of Nursing
University of Central Florida
Orlando, Florida

Ira C. Colby, DSW, ACSW, LCSW
Graduate College of Social Work
University of Houston
Houston, Texas

Enid Opal Cox, DSW
Graduate School of Social Work
University of Denver
Denver, Colorado

King Davis, PhD
Hogg Foundation for Mental Health
School of Social Work
University of Texas—Austin
Austin, Texas

Elizabeth DePoy, MSW, PhD
Center for Community Inclusion and
    Disability Studies
University of Maine
Orono, Maine

Sophia F. Dziegielewski, PhD, LISW
School of Social Work
University of Cincinnati
Cincinnati, Ohio

Rodney A. Ellis, PhD, CMSW
College of Social Work
University of Tennessee—Nashville
Nashville, Tennessee

Richard J. Gelles, PhD
Pennsylvania School of Social Policy
    and Practice
University of Pennsylvania
Philadelphia, Pennsylvania

Stephen French Gilson, MSW, PhD
School of Social Work
University of Maine
Orono, Maine

Richard Hoefer, PhD
School of Social Work
University of Texas—Austin
Austin, Texas

Bruce Jansson, PhD
School of Social Work
University of Southern California
Los Angeles, California

Howard Karger, PhD
School of Social Work and Applied
    Human Sciences
University of Queensland
Brisbane, Australia

Peter A. Kindle, MSW
Graduate College of Social Work
University of Houston
Houston, Texas

Sunil Kumar, PhD
Department of Social Policy
London School of Economics and
    Political Science
London, United Kingdom

Joseph Kin Fun Kwok, RSW, PhD, BBS, JP
Department of Applied Social Studies
City University of Hong Kong
Hong Kong, China

Robin Sakina Mama, PhD
Department of Social Work
Monmouth University
West Long Branch, New Jersey

Pamela J. Miller, MSW, PhD
School of Social Work
Portland State University
Portland, Oregon

Paul R. Raffoul, PhD
Graduate College of Social Work
University of Houston
Houston, Texas

Michael Reisch, MSW, PhD
School of Social Work
University of Michigan
Ann Arbor, Michigan

Gary Rosenberg, PhD
Department of Community and Preventative Medicine
Mount Sinai School of Medicine
New York, New York

Elizabeth A. Segal, PhD
School of Social Work
Arizona State University
Phoenix, Arizona

Carol Wilson Spigner, PhD
Pennsylvania School of Social Policy and Practice
University of Pennsylvania
Philadelphia, Pennsylvania

Stan Stojkovic, PhD
Helen Bader School of Social Welfare
University of Wisconsin—Milwaukee
Milwaukee, Wisconsin

Jody Williams
Nobel Peace Laureate
International Campaign to Ban Land Mines

Section I ——————————————————

POLICY AND JUSTICE: A GLOBAL IMPERATIVE

In years past, global or international discussions, if at all included in a text, were typically the last chapter, almost an "oh, by the way." But in today's world, a global perspective is foremost in our thinking. Every day the impact of global issues is felt by all people, from volatile oil prices that translate into roller-coaster gas prices to the war in the Mideast, which siphons off millions of dollars that otherwise could be spent on human service programs. Today's world is much smaller, and our neighborhood now extends to countries tens of thousands of miles away.

It is most appropriate to begin this volume with a chapter written by a remarkable individual, Jody Williams, who is the 1997 Nobel Peace Laureate. Spearheading an initiative by civil society, she helped bring together nations from around the world to sign a global treaty to ban land mines. Sadly, the United States, along with Iraq and Iran, remains among the few nations not to have joined the world in signing this treaty. Ms. Williams introduces this volume with a new paradigm that resonates very closely to the heart and soul of social work: human security. Clearly juxtaposing her proposal against the current U.S. federal program of homeland security, Williams sees justice and peace directly tied to the health and well-being of the global community. Human security is "the fundamental linchpin upon which rests all security" and reduces conflict if people's needs are met.

Robin Sakina Mama, PhD, is recognized for her international work, particularly with the promotion of social work in the United Nations. She brings to our attention the strong position that social workers have played and will continue to play on the global stage. International social work is not new to the profession, whose early efforts started shortly after World War I. Recognizing the importance of globalization, Mama writes, "Social work is also well prepared to work on policy that leads to solidarity and peace building among nations, which will have a direct impact on global social policy."

Joseph Kin Fun Kwok, PhD, provides a detailed discussion of social justice from an Asian perspective. Kwok explores the dimensions of justice with a detailed discussion of Asian policy and practice while noting particular challenges faced by human services. As does Mama, Kwok believes that social workers, based on their unique and diverse practice experiences, are in an excellent position to add their expertise in policy development.

Chapter 1

THE HUMAN SECURITY PARADIGM: PEACE WITH JUSTICE AND EQUALITY?

Jody Williams

At the end of the cold war, many people around the world spoke of their hope for a different world. Perhaps governments would consider bold new attempts to define national—and global—security in a now unipolar world. With the collapse of the Soviet Union and corresponding diminished threat, maybe standing armies and military budgets could be reduced, along with the number of nuclear weapons in silos and submarines and airplanes around the world. There was guarded optimism that perhaps war and militarization would no longer define the contours of our future. Maybe such changes could even spur a dramatic decrease in the global arms trade and conceivably result in a "peace dividend" to be used to resolve some of the intractable problems facing humankind. If such changes did occur, arguably the globe as a whole would be more secure.

But not everyone was contemplating peace dividends and a world full of new possibilities. A more sober view recognized that crafting a new approach to a changed and changing world would require deliberate and concerted efforts. Pessimists—some might call them "realists"—had little doubt that the sole remaining superpower would begin to seek new global enemies, in part because real threats exist, but also to justify its continued militarism as the United States contemplated how to react to—and, more important, how to consolidate—its unique position as the military, economic, and technological behemoth in the post–cold war world.

Now, faced with the emergence of new global powers such as China and India—nations requiring increased access to limited resources to fuel their economic growth—new tensions are arising and the world is experiencing an ever increasing divide between the global haves and have-nots. Throw into the mix the attacks on the United States of September 11, 2001, and the resulting declaration of "war" on "terror," and instead of a "brave new world" in the twenty-first century, we find ourselves sliding back into the bunker mentality of the cold war era. Or perhaps that mentality was never seriously challenged.

The post-9/11 world appears to be caught between terror and hope. In the current tension between terror and hope is also a struggle about how we as a global community define security. Will we continue to define security in terms of bigger weapons and more militarization, or will security be defined in terms of international law and human security? Will democracy, justice, and human rights continue to be eroded around the world to protect us from "terrorism," or can we step back from the collective brink and make hard and sober assessments of what framework will best ensure peace and justice and security in an increasingly globalizing world?

(RE)DEFINING SECURITY IN THE GLOBALIZED WORLD

Since the mid-1600s, power in the world has been defined almost exclusively by the military and economic might of individual, sovereign nation-states. In this Westphalian model, global stability—or peace—is maintained through a balance of power among these sovereign nations (O'Donnell, 2004). This security framework continues to dominate thinking even as we are increasingly coming to grips with the facts that in today's world, like it or not, there is not much that is not interconnected, there are now many factors that influence power among states, and many of those factors are transnational in character.

Globalization immediately brings to mind the seemingly effortless movement of capital and business around the world with little apparent regard for "sovereign borders." Economic globalization is seen by some as a positive force that will inevitably lead to the democratization of the planet. Others question the relationship between democratization and corporate entities that, largely lacking in accountability, have little apparent regard for workers' rights, the environment, or their impact on the social fabric of any particular country.

In the global economy, for example, today's corporations and even some individuals amass fortunes that can dwarf the entire budget of a nation—or an entire region of the world. The rules of the game of the global marketplace continue to evolve, and the worldwide reach of business calls into question the very relationship between the nation-state and such corporate entities. For many of us, it is these financial aspects we think of when the term "globalization" comes to mind, yet globalization is not confined to the economic sphere alone.

Other linkages are also increasing exponentially. The mass movement of people, coupled with 24-hour access to information, helps fuel a global marketplace of ideas and blurs the lines between what traditionally have been seen as domestic or international issues. As people, ideas, and images move with lightning speed around the world, the challenges grow for individual states to try to predict and manage the outcomes of such interactions. Security threats also have more serious global implications through this spread of knowledge and information.

Gone is the time when the state can effectively isolate its citizens and focus their concerns on domestic issues, while claiming sole purview over the international sphere. Often the domestic impact of foreign policy decisions has become too glaring for citizens to ignore. One horrific example, of course, is the September 11, 2001, terrorist attacks, which have roots in decades of U.S. foreign policy decisions toward the Middle East viewed as unfair by people in the region and that have fueled intense dislike and distrust of the country.

We are faced not only with war, terrorism, and armed violence around the world, but also with weapons proliferation, including weapons of mass destruction; global organized crime, including the trafficking of human beings, particularly women and children; perhaps irreversible destruction of our environment and the threats posed by global warming; widespread, pervasive poverty (this since time immemorial); and new and deadly diseases—to name but a few. Many actors influence both the evolution of the problems themselves and also possible responses to them. In addition to global business, international and regional institutions, as well as nongovernmental organizations (NGOs) and (transnational) civil society all have an impact on today's world.

With such a complex array of variables, it has become increasingly difficult for individual states to predict and manage the outcomes of many issues. Old concepts of state-based security in our global political and economic environment no longer offer long-term answers to today's global threats and challenges. Yet the resistance to meaningful analysis and discussion of what will bring us security—collectively and individually—is extremely strong and pervasive. Despite the resistance, discussion about what kind of security we should seek must take place.

HUMAN SECURITY: A NEW PARADIGM FOR GLOBAL SECURITY?

During the 1990s, some bold new initiatives provided collective solutions to various problems of global scope. One of those initiatives was the movement to ban antipersonnel land mines. The land mine campaign is important not only because it led to an international treaty in 1997 that, for the first time in history, eliminated a long and almost universally used conventional weapon. It also provided a successful model of government–civil society–international institution partnership that offered a concrete example of how the global community could work together to resolve common problems. Another successful, similar effort resulted in the creation of the International Criminal Court after 50 years of work to create an independent court to try war crimes and crimes against humanity.

Partly inspired by these efforts, the nucleus of a movement began to be explored that seeks to enhance global security not by increasing the number of weapons being developed, produced, and traded in an already overweaponized world, but by addressing "human security" needs as the fundamental linchpin upon which rests all security. Any number of governments, international institutions, and civil societies are exploring the framework as a distinctive concept for addressing global insecurities and are increasingly working to pursue policies that actively apply the human security framework.

One such effort grew out of discussions between Canada and Norway, expressly resulting from their work in the land mine ban movement. The Human Security Network was founded by a group of like-minded countries at a ministerial meeting in Norway on May 20, 1999. It seeks to apply a human security perspective to political processes that are aimed at the prevention or resolution of conflict as well as promoting peace and development. Ministers of the member countries have met annually since the Norway meeting to maintain a "dialogue on questions pertaining to human security" (Human Security Network, n.d.).

In 2000, an independent Commission on Human Security was launched at the UN Millennium Summit. The Commission describes human security as a framework that "encompasses human rights, good governance and access to economic opportunity, education and health care" (Commission on Human Security, 2003, p. 4). Human security is advanced (a) through protection, primarily the state-based responsibility to protect people from critical and pervasive threats, with institutions, civil society and nongovernmental actors, and the private sector also playing a key role in that protection; and (b) by empowering individuals and communities to develop their capabilities to make informed choices and to act on their own behalf (pp. 10–12). These elements together mean not only protecting people from threats, but also "creating political, social, environmental, economic, military and cultural systems that, when combined, give people the building blocks for survival, livelihood and dignity" (p. 4).

Thus at the core, human security policies seek to enhance both individual and societal security by promoting "freedom from want" and "freedom from fear." This concept has been underscored by observations of UN Secretary-General Kofi Annan that security, development, and human rights are interlinking elements of real security and that if all those elements are not advanced simultaneously, ultimately none will prevail.

Human security holds that in a globalized world, many actors can have an impact on outcomes, so means to address issues must be as broadly multilateral as possible. Dialogue, cross-cultural understanding, and conflict resolution enhance human security. Globalized relations, interaction, and communication enhance human security. The use of force is not scorned, but it is recognized as the absolute last resort, employed only if all other methods to resolve conflict have failed.

Part of the logic behind this thinking is that if the basic needs of the majority of the people of the world are met, providing them with a stake in and hope for their own future, the root causes of conflict are diminished. When a small minority has access to the majority of goods, services, and resources of the planet, those who have nothing have nothing to lose in giving up their lives on a suicide mission. Considering even a few of the commonly used statistics on poverty in today's world is numbing. The World Bank has defined the international poverty line as $1 to $2 a day.[1] In 2003, out of the developing world's 4.8 billion people, some 1.2 billion were living on $1 a day; another 2.8 billion were living on $2 a day (Infoplease, 2000–2007). In 2003, the richest fifth of the world's population received 85% of the total world income, while the poorest fifth received just 1.4% of the global income (Infoplease, 2000–2007).

As even George W. Bush—the world's strongest champion of a "muscular" approach to his war on terror—opined in a speech at the United Nations on September 14, 2005, we share a "moral duty" to fight not only terrorism but also the poverty, oppression, and hopelessness that give rise to it (Baker, 2005, p. A8). All the weapons in the world will not save us from angry and desperate people willing to fly airplanes into buildings to take the lives of thousands and sow the seeds of terror. The human security framework would sow seeds of hope by providing for socioeconomic justice and more equitable distribution of the world's resources.

NATIONAL SECURITY VERSUS HUMAN SECURITY

The national security "realists" have a very dim view of any meaningful debate about human security. It has been painted as a wishy-washy effort by "lesser powers"—read irrelevant—who do not have the military might or the "spine" to deal with real security issues. "Real" security is the purview of the individual, sovereign state based on nation-to-nation interaction. Utopian, unrealistic, idealistic—a concept not worthy of real discussion.

The human security framework is also criticized as being too vague and a catchall attempt to try to resolve all problems facing humanity rather than confine itself narrowly—therefore

---

[1] This is measured in 1993 purchasing power parity (PPP), which the Bank defines as "a method of measuring the relative purchasing power of different countries' currencies over the same types of goods and services. Because goods and services may cost more in one country than in another, PPP allows us to make more accurate comparisons of standards of living across countries" (Infoplease, 2000–2007).

effectively, of course—to real security issues. Critics of human security also imply that those who do support the framework see it as an either/or situation: Either you are for human security or you are for national security, but apparently they cannot coexist. And how could such a "vague" security framework possibly replace the centuries-old system of nation-states interacting through a delicate balance—or not—of a global chess match of power?

In this chess match, states with the most access to resources tend to dominate global politics and back that dominance with military might. Security, then, is as the ability of the state to advance and maintain its interests, generally at a cost to other states. Because security is state to state, realists also argue that national security is generally far too complex for the average citizen to understand, let alone have a voice in.

Admittedly, this view was shaken with the successes of the mine ban movement as well as the establishment of the ICC, but opponents of the Ottawa Process and government–civil society partnerships have sought to paint that process as a "one-off" success and return to "diplomacy as usual" in a state-based system. Even if some had been able to delude themselves in the immediate period after the fall of the Berlin Wall, the 9/11 attacks and ensuing war on terror should have dispelled all notions of a different kind of world after the fall of the Soviet Union.

Others argue that human security rhetoric is not matched with "concrete policy that makes a difference to the safety of people whose security is threatened" (Hataley & Nossal, 2004, p. 1). This argument seems to imply that the critical measure of a human security agenda is whether or not a state engages in humanitarian intervention to "ensure the safety of ordinary people in other places" (p. 3). Humanitarian intervention is a hotly debated issue in and of itself and is not, or should not be, the sole or even primary measure of a human security approach to global security.

For some, particularly U.S. neoconservatives, discussion of a human security framework is not just an attempt at an objective assessment of what really would make the world as a whole more secure, but should be seen for what it really is: an attack on American values. As one article states:

> This is a dramatic and fundamental distortion of the right to be secure. The effort to "broaden our view of what is meant by peace and security" obscures and runs counter to the long-standing right of nation-states to secure their own territories and populations from external threats—a principle upon which international legal traditions and treaty organizations such as the U.N. are based. The human security agenda has the potential to undermine not only the nation-state model on which the U.N. was founded, but also the principles of sovereignty, accountability, and national security that the United States holds as fundamental. (Carafano & Smith, 2006)

The human security framework is not an attack on the values of any nation. It is an attempt to respond to security needs in the dramatically different world of the twenty-first century. However, it is not primarily concerned with the security of the nation-state in isolation from the security of people inside and outside the confines of national boundaries. Terrorism, crime, and war are all examples of violence that destabilize the security of people. Their security is also affected by deprivation, whether it is the result of poverty or environmental pollution or disease and malnutrition or illiteracy or all of them combined. Piecemeal and scattershot responses to individual problems and crises will not address the root causes of violence and conflict or enhance global security. Because the human security framework looks at the myriad problems that have an impact on security, effectively enhancing security means attempting to take an integrated approach to addressing the problems.

Those who advocate that a human security agenda enhances the security of us all generally do not necessarily see human security and national security as mutually exclusive. The two, instead, can be complementary parts of a whole. But to meaningfully carry out a human security agenda would require, for example, significant reallocation of the billions and billions of dollars spent around the world annually on war, on "defense" and preparations for war, and for the equipment of war. All of the aspects described in the previous section must be pursued coherently for such a human security agenda to make sense and to change lives. Security, development and empowerment, and human rights are mutually reinforcing; and if all do not advance together, no one aspect will prevail ultimately. To make human security really work requires a major shift in policies, institutions, and choices about global resource allocation to address the basic needs of people everywhere rather than providing for the security of the relative few who make those policies and control those resources. This obviously is a huge challenge in today's world.

IS THERE A FUTURE FOR A HUMAN SECURITY FRAMEWORK?

The Role of Governments and International Institutions

Even if one accepts human security as a feasible approach to global security, why hasn't it had more traction? Considering the launch of the Human Security Network, it can convincingly be argued that the same governments that have promoted and sung the praises of the land mine ban movement and the civil society–government partnership that is its hallmark wanted to limit the reach of such partnerships. Though not likely wanting to return to status quo ante, when governments did meet in Oslo to discuss and launch the Network, NGO involvement even in the discussions about the concept was minimal at best.

In today's world of increasingly active and involved transnational civil society, trying to advance a new security agenda based on a top-down effort not built on an effective and broad government–civil society partnership seems doomed to limited success, if not failure. Given the long-standing relationship of many of the same NGOs with those governments and that the Network should want solid support from them on a human security agenda, the exclusion is hard to understand.

The Network appears to seek NGO involvement in events related to specific issues that it deems to be components of a human security agenda. However, there does not seem to be any mechanism for ongoing discussion and/or action between governments and NGOs/civil society to address the human security framework writ large. If advancing the framework must be done through broad and integrated responses to global problems, this fragmenting of issues and answers to them does not serve the human security agenda well, nor does an ad hoc approach to working with NGOs and civil society.

The situation appears much the same in the work on human security at the UN. Neither the UN's Commission on Human Security nor the subsequent Advisory Board on Human Security have either NGO/civil society involvement or even informal mechanisms for ongoing dialogue with them regarding this "people-centered" framework. For example, the report of a February 2006 workshop on human security organized by the government of Mexico in cooperation with the government of Japan seems to underscore this disconnect.

The section of the report titled "Civil Society and Human Security," states that the role of civil society in "making the concept of human security operative consists mainly in assuming the challenges of building human capacity through education and the promotion of renewed perceptions, as well as in pursuing new strategies to safeguard the security of people." The strategies put forward essentially refer to documenting abuses and promoting human rights and public security in the post-9/11 world (Report of the Workshop, 2006).

Although human rights is an area of intense work by civil society and NGOs, it is not the only issue of the broad human security agenda that NGOs address. If, as the Report of the Workshop (2006) says, the "concept of human security is a response to the needs of civil society throughout the world," surely civil society and NGOs have a much larger role to play than just dealing with various aspects of human rights.

The Role of Nongovernmental Organizations and Transnational Civil Society

But it is not just governments and international institutions that are at fault: Both NGOs and civil society in general have done little to connect the dots on human security and promote the agenda. Even though the words "human security" appear more frequently, the concept does not yet resonate for the general public—or even for many NGOs. Nongovernmental organizations must actively promote the concept of human security as the appropriate framework for global security in a globalized world. People must be educated to understand that by advancing human security, the security of the globe is advanced.

To raise awareness and advocate for this change, NGOs must identify their individual work as part of a larger human security agenda when reaching out to the broader public. Everyone must understand that protecting and promoting human rights is work that enhances human security. Efforts to advance sustainable development enhance human security. Every time the flow of weapons of war is limited or weapons are banned outright, human security is advanced. Involving women meaningfully in all aspects of conflict prevention and peace building and, in fact, in decision making in general is enhancing human security. Addressing poverty through debt repudiation, fair trade, and better aid—coupled with promoting good governance and tackling corruption—is enhancing human security.

Yet too often, opportunities are lost to make those connections. Too often, NGOs limit their own work and a broader ranging effectiveness by choosing to not make those connections. Every time those issues are de-linked, NGOs undercut collective efforts to promote a broader understanding and acceptance of a human security agenda as the framework to better prevent violent conflict. To effectively campaign and lobby, NGOs must find and use every opportunity to make the general public understand that our common security is increased by working together to meet the most basic needs of the majority of the planet—by working collectively to free women, men, and children from fear and to free them from want. By providing that majority with a stake in and hope for their own future, the root causes of conflict can be diminished. The opportunities to move away from reacting to violent conflict and toward its prevention are increased and, along with them, the development of a sustainable peace.

CONCLUSION

As stated in the introduction, the post-9/11 world appears to be caught between terror and hope. In this tension is also a struggle about how we as a global community define security. Will we continue to define security in terms of bigger weapons and more militarization, or will we define security in terms of international law and human security? Will democracy, justice, and human rights continue to be eroded around the world to protect us from "terrorism," or can we step back from the collective brink and make hard and sober assessments of what framework will best ensure peace and justice and security in an increasingly globalizing world?

To really begin to move the world away from a strictly national security view of global security, governments, international institutions, and NGOs alike must work consistently and collectively to change the global mind-set about what constitutes real global security and about what peace building really is—particularly in this post-9/11 world. A fundamental element of effective campaigning and advocacy to change that mind-set is setting the agenda. So far, it appears that neither governments nor NGOs have come anywhere close to setting an effective agenda to advance a clearly articulated human security framework and how it should be applied in today's world. Broad and deep and bold involvement by governments and NGOs and transnational civil society is also key to bringing about such change.

In his 2003 book, *War Is a Force That Gives Us Meaning*, Chris Hedges, a nonpacifist war correspondent for about 20 years, captures some of the difficulties inherent in changing the collective mind-set about violent conflict—and therefore how best to counter it. He writes:

> The effectiveness of the myths peddled in war is powerful. We often come to doubt our own perceptions. We hide these doubts, like troubled believers, sure that no one else feels them.... The myths have determined not only how we should speak but how we should think. The doubts we carry, the scenes we see that do not conform to the myth are hazy, difficult to express, unsettling.... We struggle uncomfortably with the jargon and clichés. But we have trouble expressing our discomfort because *the collective shout* [emphasis added] has made it hard for us to give words to our thoughts. This self-doubt is aided by the monstrosity of war. (p. 74)

As Hedges notes, the myths peddled in war are powerful. But perhaps the myths peddled *about* war are more so, particularly in the post-9/11 world. Moving beyond *the collective shout* that insists that if you want peace you must prepare for war is a huge challenge. Moving beyond *the collective myth* that creating a peaceful world is the fuzzy dream of human security idealists is a huge challenge. Governments and NGOs must work together to meet those challenges and raise our *collective awareness* about the rights and responsibilities of civil society in working to move beyond reacting to violence and toward actively setting the agenda to prevent it.

Finally, thinking about violence must be demystified. People can no longer hide behind the dismissal of violence with the commonly heard explanation that it is simply "human nature" to be violent. Violence is a choice—whether it is the choice of a man to beat the woman he supposedly loves, or the choice of one nation to invade another in the name of "freedom" or any other name, or the choice of terrorists of any stripe to attack civilian targets anywhere in the world to make their political point. *Violence is a choice.* The human security framework promotes the making of nonviolent choices to resolve conflicts. It is a feasible alternative to militarism and violence and war that can actively move the world beyond *the collective myth* that building peace is a fuzzy dream of utopian idealists.

A world increasingly dominated by the few, who give the impression of not caring much for the needs of the many, can only become increasingly insecure as the desperate and disenfranchised try to equalize the playing field. There is something wrong in a world that spends close to a trillion dollars on weapons and defense while spending a few billion on education globally. There is something profoundly unjust in a global economic system in which a handful of billionaires have more income than entire regions of the world.

Until the global community works together to address the common threats to human security posed by gross political, social, and economic inequalities we will not live in a secure world. But hope for a more secure world is not enough. Neither governments nor NGOs can abdicate their individual and collective responsibilities to participate in developing new strategies and policies to ensure our collective security. No one government, no one institution can possibly provide for the needs of us all. New coalitions must seek new solutions to seemingly intractable problems. Change will not happen overnight. But that should not be an excuse to not seek change.

REFERENCES

Baker, P. (2005, September 15). Bush, at U.N., links anti-poverty agenda to war on terrorism. *Washington Post*, p. A8.

Carafano, J. J., & Smith, J. A. (2006, September 1). *The muddled notion of "human security" at the U.N: A guide for U.S. policymakers* (Backgrounder #1966). Washington, DC: Heritage Foundation. Retrieved November 7, 2007, from www.heritage.org/Research/WorldwideFreedom/bg1966.cfm.

Commission on Human Security. (2003). *Human security now*. New York: Author. Retrieved November 7, 2007, from www.humansecurity-chs.org/finalreport/English/FinalReport.pdf.

Hataley, T. S., & Nossal, K. R. (2004, February). The limits of the human security agenda: The case of Canada's response to the Timor crisis. *Global Change, Peace and Security, 16*(1), 5–17. Retrieved November 7, 2007, from http://post.queensu.ca/~nossalk/papers/hataley-nossal_timor.pdf.

Hedges, C. (2003). *War is a force that gives us meaning*. New York: Simon & Schuster.

Human Security Network. (n.d.). *The network*. Retrieved November 7, 2007, from www.humansecuritynetwork.org/network-e.php.

Infoplease. (2000–2007). *Measuring global poverty*. Boston: Pearson Education. Retrieved November 7, 2007, from www.infoplease.com/ipa/A0908770.html.

O'Donnell, P. S. (2004). *Sovereignty past and present*. Retrieved November 7, 2007, from the International Consortium for the Advancement of Academic Publication web site, http://globalization.icaap.org/content/v4.1/odonnell.html.

Report of the Workshop on Human Security. (2006, March 24). 60th Session of the U.N. General Assembly, Agenda Item 120, Follow-up to the Outcome of the Millenium Summit; Letter dated March 27, 2006, from the Permanent Representatives of Japan and Mexico to the United Nations addressed to the Secretary General (Report of the Workshop on Human Security, organized by the Government of Mexico in cooperation with the Government of Japan, Mexico City, February 9 and 10, 2006), A/60/739.

Chapter 2

SOCIAL POLICY FROM A GLOBAL PERSPECTIVE

Robin Sakina Mama

Social workers are challenged every day to consider the global and international aspects of their practice. Many social workers now work with immigrants, refugees, and survivors of torture and trauma from other parts of the globe. Clients' residence status can help or hinder their treatment and access to service. Families are often dealing with adjustments to life in the United States while their relatives are struggling in another country. Detention centers that house new asylees or refugees have become a permanent part of our urban landscape.

International social work is not a new idea or a new field of practice. A number of social work professionals have been interested in understanding the international dimensions of social work practice since social work gained professional status (Findlay & McCormack, 2005). Social workers' involvement in international collaboration began after World War I, as evidenced by the establishment of several international organizations, such as the International Federation of Social Work and the International Association of Schools of Social Work (Healy, 2001). This involvement increased after World War II, as social workers became involved in rebuilding efforts after the war and with the United Nations. This involvement waxed and waned over the years but is now coming to the forefront as social workers realize that the idea that we work only within the boundaries of our own nation-state is no longer true. Influences beyond our borders are increasingly acknowledged as having a direct influence on local and national issues. The process underlying these changes is globalization (Findlay & McCormack, 2005).

GLOBALIZATION

It is not possible to discuss global social policy without first discussing globalization. Globalization has a complex definition, which social scientists have been researching for a number of years (Guillén, 2001). Most agree that globalization is a process (or set of processes; Hay, 2006) that encompass economic, political, and cultural dimensions. Other social scientists have defined globalization in a more detailed way so that it might be quantified empirically. For example, "Globalization is a process (or set of processes) that embodies a transformation in the spatial organization of social relations and transactions, generating transcontinental or inter-regional flows and networks of activity, interaction and power" (D. Held, as cited in C. Hay, 2006, p. 3). The forces that drive globalization include human migration, international trade, and the integration of financial markets.

Economic Dimensions of Globalization

Economically, globalization has been characterized by trade liberalization and increased international competition and investment, all driven by an increase in technological change. This increase in and dependence on technology cannot be easily dismissed. Developments in technology, in both computing and telecommunications, are changing the marketplace and the workforce. "Global E-commerce surged from 130.2 billion in 1999 to nearly 1.640 billion in 2003" ("Technology: Industrial Structure and Jobs," n.d., para 5). This surge in technology has created a knowledge economy, where access to information and the ability to use it creates productivity and prosperity. However, computer and technological access varies widely from country to country, with less developed countries lagging far behind. These gaps in access are called "digital divides" ("Digital Divides and Privacy and Security Concerns," n.d.), and they are beginning to reinforce national and international gaps in living standards. Digital divides occur in almost every country. The United States has made some progress in closing its digital divides. From 1997 to 2005, the proportion of U.S. adults with Internet access increased from 24% to 79%. Broadband usage in the United States has also increased; however, rural households still lag behind urban and suburban households by 14% to 16% (www.globalization101.org).

When these numbers are compared to international access to IT, the numbers of people in the world who have Internet access is much lower and is very unequal around the world. One way to examine access is to look at how much Internet access costs as a percentage of one's earned income. In many developing countries the cost of Internet access is a much larger proportion of income than in developed countries. For example, in the United States, Internet access is less than 1% of average monthly income, whereas in Nepal monthly Internet charges account for 270% of average monthly income (www.globalization101.org). The implications of this digital divide are significant, and a great deal of work at the United Nations has gone into narrowing this divide globally. The World Summit on the Information Society, held in Geneva in 2003 and Tunis in 2005, delineated several concrete steps toward closing the digital divide gap. The first of these recommendations is to meet basic needs, in terms of health care, clean water, food, sanitation, and the like. Access to information technology does little when one does not have food or clean water (Fors, 2003). A second important recommendation is to establish infrastructure and the need to be creative when developing IT infrastructure. Wireless technology is seen as one of the key ways to begin to provide access and infrastructure in developing countries (Fors, 2003; Sehrt, 2003).

Political Dimensions of Globalization

Politically, globalization has been characterized by American power and the influence of global institutions, such as the International Monetary Fund (IMF). Many believe that the recent rise in the influence of globalization has been brought about by the creation of new international organizations, such as the World Bank (WB), the IMF, and the World Trade Organization (WTO; Mama, 2004). These organizations seem to have had a homogenizing effect on the social and welfare policies of many countries and have created a " 'globalization of approaches', whereby a particular social, economic or political approach, judged beneficial by one of the cross-national organizations, is seen as appropriate for many countries regardless of cultural differences" (Findlay & McCormack, 2005, p. 233). The processes that these international organizations require countries to follow in order to qualify for aid are seen as undermining the capacity of countries to act autonomously, although there may be some facilitation of democratic procedures (Walby, 2000). Politically, globalization is not a uniform process; often resources are pitted against each other to satisfy international markets. For example, there can be calls for the state's protection of human rights at the same time that the country's welfare state erodes (Walby, 2000).

Cultural Dimensions of Globalization

Culturally, globalization has resulted in the dissemination of global ideas and values (McClelland & St. John, 2006). Some authors have suggested that the globalization of cultures and values has tended toward homogeneity, a process of "McDonaldization" of society, along with the processes of

> Ikea-isation, CNN-isation, Nike-isation and Survivor-isation. The same brand of clothing, the same home furniture, the same culinary taste, the same movies and shows, and the same news, debates and images of reality are found all across the globe ... in a short space of time we are now being nourished and nurtured by the same sources of mediating symbols. (Ahmadi, 2003, p. 16)

Ahmadi further suggests that this globalization of consciousness has the consequence of globalizing social problems, with an intensification of individualism as one component. The emphasis on individualism is a frightening aspect of globalization to those cultures that traditionally have focused on community and clan.

Cultural diversity and its role in globalization, especially of market products, is coming under scrutiny. How are cultural products different from other goods and services? The definitions of "culture" have evolved over time, initially referring only to "arts and literature" (Chan-Tibergian, 2006). After the World Conference on Cultural Policies in Mexico City in 1982, culture was "regarded as the set of distinctive spiritual, material, intellectual and emotional features of a society or social group, [that] ... encompasses, in addition to art and literature, lifestyles, ways of living together, value systems, traditions and beliefs" (United Nations Educational, Scientific and Cultural Organization [UNESCO], 2002, p. 18). These are significant changes, as the Permanent Forum on Indigenous Peoples takes these meanings to new levels in their fight for patents for cultural products or indigenous products.

Globalization as Process

Globalization is not a new phenomenon. Several processes of globalization have been operating simultaneously for many years: the globalization of economics, politics, knowledge, and culture (Ahmadi, 2003). This phenomenon, however, has challenged traditional social, political, and economic structures. Globalization has been brought about by cost reductions in transportation and communication, in addition to the dissolution of artificial barriers to trade, services, capital, and knowledge across borders (Mama, 2004).

There are many who would argue the benefits of globalization: open markets, positive competition, increased use of technology, and the potential to enrich many people, especially the poor. Globalization has reduced the sense of isolation felt by many in the developing world (but only those with the access to technology). The expansion and increased use of technology has provided access to knowledge and information that before was limited to only the wealthiest countries. Globalization has also increased the amount of interaction between people of different cultures. People from all over the world meet together to a much greater extent than they had in the past, and consequently begin to influence each other as well as understand each other. This global culture has led to the creation of new identities and new forms of literature, music, and art. There is now a very large global market for these creative industries, which figures to be around U.S. $800 billion per year (Chan-Tibergian, 2006, p. 92).

There are just as many critics of globalization as there are proponents. Globalization has not succeeded in reducing poverty, as was promised; in fact, the gap between the haves and the have-nots in developing countries is widening. The Center for Economic and Policy Research published in 2003 a "score card" on globalization from 1980 to 2000. Several facts from this comparison with the time period 1960 to 1980 are disturbing:

1. Life expectancy was reduced for four out of the five groups of countries examined, which cannot be explained by the AIDS pandemic.
2. [The rate in the] reduction of infant mortality was slower.
3. Progress in education slowed. (Weisbrot, Baker, Kraev, & Chen, 2003, 42)

Globalization has also not provided for stability in third world countries. Latin America and Asia are two good examples of how financial crises affect the entire global economy. In addition, globalization has had bad effects on the environment, with many poor countries using precious environmental resources in the name of development. The "sustainable development" movement is an attempt to preserve the environment while at the same time providing for development opportunities (Mama, 2004).

GLOBALIZATION AS IT RELATES TO POLICY

One often-used example of how globalization relates to social policy is the welfare state (Adelantado & Calderón, 2006; Brady, Beckgield, & Seeleib-Kaiser, 2005; Genschel, 2004; Wilson, 2006). Brady and his colleagues suggest that four theories of the relationship between globalization and the welfare state have emerged:

1. Globalization may cause an expansion of the welfare state.
2. Globalization may generate a crisis and retrenchment of the welfare state.
3. Globalization may have curvilinear effects and contribute to welfare state convergence.
4. Globalization may not affect the welfare state. (Brady et al., 2005, p. 922)

Taking each point separately, in the first theory, globalization causes an expansion of the welfare state by triggering political dynamics that result in generous welfare programs and corporatist labor market institutions. Some studies that support this theory have shown that trade openness significantly increases social welfare expenditures (Brady et al., 2005).

In the second theory, a crisis and retrenchment of the welfare state occurs as states undergo neoliberal restructuring to foster flexibility and competitiveness. The welfare state is reduced because of a need to be internationally competitive with a flexible labor force and austere fiscal policy (Brady et al., 2005). For example, the United States, Britain, New Zealand, Canada, and Australia have all adopted neoliberal approaches to social policy, which have had a direct effect on welfare spending. The neoliberal approach usually follows certain characteristics: tightened conditions of eligibility; extension of means testing; financial responsibility transferred to individuals, families, or employers; and a move away from simple provision of benefits for the unemployed (Findlay & McCormack, 2005, p. 233). In this case, globalization forces reductions in the welfare state because of the need for a flexible labor force to remain internationally competitive (Brady et al., 2005).

The third theory, globalization as convergence, contends that "globalization originally triggers an expansion of the welfare state with economic development. But at higher levels, globalization causes contractions in mature, generous, already developed welfare states" (Brady et al., 2005, p. 924). The curvilinear effects suggest that globalization forces a mean level of welfare effort by both high and low spenders.

Finally, there are a number of scholars that believe that globalization has an insignificant effect, if any, on the welfare state. According to Brady et al. (2005), these skeptics can be classified into four categories: those who believe that globalization has a contingent effect in certain circumstances, that welfare states reflect the "status quo" in affluent democracies, that "politics as usual" will drive the welfare state, and that deindustrialization drives welfare state expansion, not globalization.

Genschel (2004) offers one additional theory of globalization and policy: that globalization is a consequence of the problems with the welfare state, but can also be part of the welfare state's solution. This revisionist theory holds that the problems of the welfare state are self-inflicted, mostly due to high taxes and deductions that drain the economy, slowing the pace of economic growth. The interesting question in this argument is, How does globalization help save the welfare state? Genschel suggests that revisionists believe that the intensity of the feeling of crisis that comes from globalization will help sustain the welfare state. Globalization forces policy makers to reevaluate and then change policy. Revisionists also believe that as market integration deepens with globalization, countries will specialize in sectors in which they are competitive so that economic structures will diverge across countries and become more homogeneous within countries.

These theories indicate that there is significant concern as to how the forces of globalization affect social policy. These concerns raise another important issue concerning globalization and social policy: the ethics of globalization.

GLOBALIZATION AND ETHICS

The ethics of globalization ultimately centers around two questions: Who is globalization good for? and Who is it bad for? For those whose interests lie in the health and environmental movement, ethical principles such as autonomy, beneficence, nonmalfeasance, justice, utility, and stewardship are important to the discussion. For others, global ethics must support social equity and cultural diversity, as well as develop common global goals.

Global ethics are difficult to discuss without some thought given to the role of morality. But this further complicates the discussion, as one has to ask, Which morality? The morality of the Western democratic societies? Many people are looking to the religious communities of the world to provide answers to this question. In "Our Creative Diversity," published by the World Commission on Culture and Development, the UN, and UNESCO, the Commission lists several elements of a global civic culture that could provide the framework for a global ethical code, including human rights and responsibilities, the peaceful resolution of conflicts, democracy and civic governance, the protection of minorities, fairness in negotiation, and intergenerational equity (Pérez de Cuéllar, 1997).

Many are now calling for global ethics that emerge from a process of discussion and debate among global grassroots movements. These organizations proved to be quite powerful when they worked together to protest the WTO meetings in Seattle, Washington, and the campaign against the WB and the IMF. Their ability to join together across continents allowed for an understanding of shared values and objectives. The production of common statements of protest and organized actions begins to set the stage for discussion on global ethics. The question now is who will facilitate this process and take responsibility for the ensuing debate (Mama, 2004)?

GLOBALIZATION, POLICY, AND SOCIAL WORK PRACTICE

Social workers see the concerns of globalization played out in their professional work. Exploitation of a workforce that accepts low wages in one country affects the employment policies and labor market of another country. Sex tourism and exploitation of women and children in some parts of the world become a legal and public health concern in other places. Immigration, whether legal or illegal, has consequences for health and welfare systems, school systems, and legal systems as they attempt to help find homes for these immigrants or hinder them from residing in any one permanent place.

The first challenge for social work is to continue to raise the consciousness of the profession about these global linkages with social policy. Social workers need to be engaged at all levels of government in thinking about solutions and approaches to social problems that are different from past ideas. New welfare policies and new social work practices need to be created, especially those that aim to integrate the world's cultures in a productive and culturally sensitive way.

Globalization, even though it has the ability to exploit, can create opportunities for social justice:

> International social work can, via its extensive contacts and cooperation on core issues of social policy and social work, and by providing examples of alternative forms for organizing social welfare and for a fairer distribution of income among different groups, and furthermore, by disseminating the belief in the international conventions on human rights and the rights of specific groups, enhance the idea of democracy and human rights. (Ahmadi, 2003, p. 18)

Social work is also well prepared to work on policy that leads to solidarity and peace building among nations, which will have a direct impact on global social policy. The profession has the ability to take on global issues of poverty, women's rights, children's rights, and indigenous peoples' rights and can contribute to a global effort to support human values and ethics.

REFERENCES

Adelantado, J., & Calderón, E. (2006). Globalization and the welfare state: The same strategies for similar problems? *Journal of European Social Policy, 16*(4), 374–386.

Ahmadi, N. (2003). Globalisation of consciousness and new challenges for international social work. *International Journal of Social Welfare, 12*, 14–23.

Brady, D., Beckgield, J., & Seeleib-Kaiser, M. (2005). Economic globalization and the welfare state in affluent democracies, 1975–2001. *American Sociological Review, 70*(6), 921–948.

Chan-Tibergian, J. (2006). Cultural diversity as resistance to neoliberal globalization: The emergence of a global movement and convention. *Review of Education, 52*, 89–105.

Digital divides and privacy and security concerns. (n.d.). Retrieved February 11, 2007, from www.gloablization101.org/index.

Findlay, M., & McCormack, J. (2005). Globalisation and social work: A snapshot of Australian practitioners' views. *Australian Social Work, 58*(3), 231–243.

Fors, M. (2003). What the United Nations can do: Closing the digital divide. *UN Chronicle*. Retrieved February 13, 2007, from www.un.org/Pubs/chronical/2003/issue4/0403p31.asp.

Genschel, P. (2004). Globalization and the welfare state: A retrospective. *Journal of European Public Policy, 11*(4), 613–636.

Guillén, M. F. (2001). Is globalization civilizing, destructive, or feeble? A critique of five key debates in the social science literature. *Annual Review of Sociology, 27*, 235–260.

Hay, C. (2006). What's globalization got to do with it? Economic interdependence and the future of European welfare states. *Government and Opposition, 41*(1), 1–22.

Healy, L. M. (2001). *International social work: Professional action in an interdependent world.* Oxford: Oxford University Press.

Mama, R. (2004). *Ethics of globalization: Ethics* (Rev. ed.). Pasadena, CA: Salem Press.

McClelland, A., & St. John, S. (2006). Social policy responses to globalization in Australia and New Zealand, 1980–2005. *Australian Journal of Political Science, 41*(2), 177–191.

Pérez de Cuéllar, J. (1997). *Our creative diversity: Report to the World Commission on Culture and Diversity.* Paris: United Nations Educational, Scientific and Cultural Organization.

Sehrt, M. (2003). E-learning in the developing countries: Digital divide into digital opportunities. *UN Chronicle*. Retrieved February 13, 2007, from www.un.org/Pubs/chronical/2003/issue4/0403p31.asp.

Technology: Industrial structure and jobs. (n.d.). Retrieved February 11, 2007, from www.globalization101.org.

United Nations Educational, Scientific and Cultural Organization. (2002). *Universal declaration on cultural diversity. Cultural diversity series no. 1* (Document for the World Summit on Sustainable Development in Johannesburg). Paris: Author.

Walby, S. (2000). Gender, globalization, and democracy. *Gender and Development, 8*(1), 20–28.

Weisbrot, M., Baker, D., Kraev, E., & Chen, J. (2003). *The scorecard on globalization 1980–2000: Twenty years of diminished progress.* Washington, DC: Center for Economic and Policy Research.

Wilson, G. (2006). Local culture, globalization, and policy outcomes: An example from long-term care. *Global Social Policy, 6*(3), 288–303.

Chapter 3

SOCIAL JUSTICE FOR MARGINALIZED AND DISADVANTAGED GROUPS: ISSUES AND CHALLENGES FOR SOCIAL POLICIES IN ASIA

Joseph Kin Fun Kwok

The world has become wealthier over the past several decades, and we see more cars, electronic appliances, and high-rise buildings, particularly in cities in both developed and developing economies. However, the wealth is not spreading evenly. In some parts of the world, the number of poor people below the poverty line is increasing (United Nations Development Project [UNDP], 2003). The quality of life of people in cities is not actually improving when the number of people suffering from mental health challenges is increasing alarmingly. The past decades have also witnessed large-scale disasters, both man-made and natural, affecting huge numbers of people; frequent and large-scale social unrest, including racial conflicts and armed confrontations; and unprecedented terrorist activities, giving rise to the 9/11 attacks on the United States. Government changes in developing economies are frequent, and reports on social protests against government corruption are not uncommon.

People around the world are getting closer to each other, partly due to modern information communication technology and global media coverage, and partly due to increased cross-border activities. We see increased numbers of migrant workers and migrant brides in developed economies, and families with members spreading among countries, not to mention increased volumes of tourists. The global economy has also been moving toward more interaction and integration, with fewer and fewer barriers limiting the activities of multinational corporations.

All these developments have given rise to situations in which one country's problems can easily become challenging for many of its neighbors, if not to the region and the world. We are also moving closer to a scenario in which local challenges will require international solutions and international challenges will need initiatives and solutions at the local level.

The Asian region is one of the fastest developing regions in the world, and also a very active region in developing consensus policy mandates at national and regional levels to deal with old and emerging issues. Asia is particularly active in supporting policies and measures on people with disabilities. It was the first region to promulgate, through intergovernmental platforms hosted by United Nations Economic and Social Commission, a comprehensive policy mandate, the Asian and Pacific Decade of Disabled Persons 1993–2002, subsequently extended to the Biwako Millennium Framework 2003–2012. Asia also hosted in 2000 the first ever World Summit of International Non-Governmental Organizations of and for People with Disabilities, which jointly pronounced their commitment in pursuing an International Convention on the Rights of Persons with Disabilities.

Given the developments in Asia, this chapter examines social policy and social justice with a broad, multisectoral perspective, global and local, and treats them as evolving concepts. The chapter takes an inclusive and rights-based approach to these developments, as promoted by the United Nations and its special systems. Disability-concerned measures at national and regional levels are used to illustrate how issues and challenges are being tackled by different policies in Asia.

Social policy and social justice often appear as twin concepts. Social justice provides a general direction for the formulation of social policies. These two concepts, however, may be used and interpreted differently in different situations, different countries, and different cultures. A narrow perspective would restrict the application of the two concepts; an overly generalized perspective may provide little specificity for practice. Social policy and social justice in practice may give rise to varying interpretations and sometimes even opposing views, depending on the position of those affected, whether they are on the giving end or the receiving end of the policy. For example, a common and recurring question in societies today is, When it comes to a government's means-tested cash assistance to people in need, how much more assistance is justice and how much less is injustice? This question becomes more pragmatic and politicized when a government is facing economic hardship in finding new resources to meet its commitments and obligations. This is the kind of question faced by most cities in Asia for decades.

This chapter discusses the two concepts of social policy and social justice, drawing references from ancient Oriental philosophy and modern rights-based approaches. The Asian experiences in formulating social policy frameworks guiding regional and local actions are used as illustrations and related to the challenges faced by human services professionals.

SOCIAL JUSTICE: AN ASIAN PERSPECTIVE

Social justice is a relatively modern concept. One school refers to social justice as distributive justice, which is defined by Roemer (1996, p. 1) as "how a society or group should allocate its scarce resources or products among individuals with competing needs or claims." The United Nations (2006) approaches social justice from a human rights perspective and provides pivotal mandates for practices at the international and national levels.

Social justice is about human well-being. The concept may be recent, but its concerns are as old as our civilizations. In Chinese civilization, for example, debates about social policy and social justice are found in classical teachings of the ancient philosophers, whose works are still included in most Chinese schools and classes. Mencius (372–289 B.C.) was the outstanding Confucian sage of the Warring States period in China (475–221 B.C.). Mencius developed Confucius's doctrines on benevolence and applied them to the governance of an empire. His famous and often quoted teaching to a ruling king was:

> Do reverence to the elders in your own family and extend it to those in other families; show loving care to the young in your own family and extend it to those in other families—do this and you would find it as easy to rule the world as to roll something on the palm of your hand. (Mencius, 1999, Book 1, p. 19)

This ancient teaching of over two millennia ago provides a vivid illustration of how social policies should educate the powerful and the rich and shape the relationship between the governing and the governed. It is also about changing people's attitudes and behaviors and about sharing resources. Another of Mencius's famous teachings to the same king is also often quoted in modern times: "Why should Your Majesty have mentioned the word 'profit'? What counts is benevolence and righteousness. . . . If those above and those below snatch profit one from the other, the state will be endangered" (Book 1, p. 3). Social justice concerns more than material benefits. It extends to the complex relationships among different sectors of a society.

Some connections may be found between of the doctrine of benevolence of Confucius and Mencius and modern rights-based approaches promoted by the United Nations for humankind and people with special needs.

The application of justice to humankind is grounded solidly in the United Nations' 1948 Universal Declaration of Human Rights charter, which proclaimed that human rights are based on respect for the dignity and worth of all human beings and seek to ensure freedom from fear and want. The Universal Declaration is further elaborated by a number of important international conventions, in particular the eight "core" UN international rights treaties (see United Nations Treaties Database, 2000–2007): International Covenant on Civil and Political Rights; International Covenant on Economic, Social and Cultural rights; International Convention on the Elimination of All Forms of Racial Discrimination; Convention on the Elimination of All Forms of Discrimination against Women; Convention against Torture and Other Cruel, Inhuman or Degrading Treatment or Punishment; Convention on the Rights of the Child; International Convention on the Protection of the Rights of All Migrant Workers and Members of Their Families; and International Convention on the Rights of Persons with Disabilities (approved by the UN December 2006).

Human rights of all kinds, including economic, political, civil, cultural, and social, as promulgated by the UN are equally valid and important, but the obligations placed on stakeholders, in particular, member states of the UN, have different requirements. This is because of the recognition that a lack of resources can impede the realization of human rights. Some obligations are immediate, whereas others are progressive (see UN Committee on Economic, Social and Cultural Rights, 2006). Immediate state obligations to protect human rights are sanctioned by domestic and international law courts. Progressive state obligations are realized through social policies that either facilitate other stakeholders or meet directly those obligations. These are the domains where social justice shares a great many commonalities with those human rights permitting a progressive approach to obligations of governments and other stakeholders. This approach also requires a close interface between social policy and social justice through a human rights–based framework.

SOCIAL JUSTICE AND SOCIAL HARMONY

Fulfilling obligations to protect human rights is not the only goal of social justice. Governments of both developed and developing economies are often challenged by conflicting demands and interests from different sectors of a society. Providing social justice to one sector may not necessarily be just to the nonbenefiting sectors. Therefore, seeking social justice has been extended to include goals in realizing an ideal society that is prosperous, harmonious, and inclusive. China provides some good examples. One of the guiding principles of China's 11th Five-Year Plan (2006 to 2011) is to strengthen the construction of a harmonious society, which should be people-based, by resolving people's felt needs and practical problems, emphasizing coordinated economic and social development, creating employment, and speeding up the development of social services to promote whole-person development and strengthening social equality to allow all people to enjoy the fruits of reformed development (see Central People's Government of People's Republic of China, 2006). Social equity is China's official way of saying social justice, which is about the distribution of economic and social advancement for all people. Additionally, the plan's basic objective is to raise people's quality of life, economically and socially.

Five of the 11th Five-Year Plan's specific targets are worth noting here: (1) increasing medical coverage of rural cooperatives from 23.5% to over 80% (an annual increase of 56.5%); (2) increasing the number of people covered by old age insurance in towns and cities from 174 million to 223 million (a 5.1% annual increase); (3) creating new employment for towns and cities at the rate of 4.5 million employed every year; (4) increase average disposable income for residents of towns and cities from RMB10,493 to RMB13.390 (a 5% annual increase); and (5) increase average income of rural people from RMB3,255 to RMB4,150 (a 5% annual increase). The first two targets are mandatory, and the remaining three are indicative suggested targets.

Hong Kong, being a city known for blending the cultures of West and East, provides another interesting example of social justice policy making. The chief executive of the government of Hong Kong Special Administrative Region gave social justice a special heading in his 2005 annual policy address. His use of language also mirrors this crucible effect of cross-culturalization. Tsang (2005) writes that upholding social justice is the foundation of a harmonious society, in addition to the rule of law upheld by an independent judiciary, the free flow of information, a clean government, and a level playing field for business. Tsang is not specific about the contents of his social justice policy. In the full version of his policy address, he has included antidiscrimination legislative measures (e.g., Sex Discrimination Ordinance and Disability Discrimination Ordinance); the promotion of cultural diversity; equity in governance and a collaboration with NGOs to secure equal opportunities for all in society; preemployment measures, including a workplace attachment training allowance to encourage and equip young people to find work; and capacity-building programs to support women.

Mainland China's conception of social equity or social justice focuses on the distribution of economic and social advancement for all people. Hong Kong's version is more about antidiscrimination legislative measures, equity in governance, and equal opportunities for all people. The differences in emphasis and in focus in employing the concept of social justice or social equity in a government's high-level policy is to be expected. This leads us to a more complex question of how social policies can be developed to make a society conducive to social justice for all.

SOCIAL POLICY

Social policy, interpreted narrowly, refers to social welfare policies. Titmus (1974), who develops a comprehensive framework to analyze social policy as a subject of academic discipline, adopts such a narrow approach. Titmus (1976, 20) asserts:

> We are concerned with the study of a range of social needs and the functioning, in conditions of scarcity, of human organization, traditionally called social services or social welfare systems, to meet those needs. This complex area of social life lies outside or on the fringes of the so-called free market, the mechanisms of price and tests of profitability.

A broader connotation of social policy has become more predominant since the 1980s. The World Summit for Social Development 1995 (United Nations, 1995) set a good example in outlining a broad, multisectoral, and interdisciplinary approach to achieving actionable development goals. The 1995 World Summit stresses that policies and programs designed to achieve poverty eradication should include specific measures to foster social integration, including providing marginalized socioeconomic sectors and groups with equal access to opportunities.

However, the formulation of social polices and their effective implementation are subject to complex factors, including the government's politics, the nation's economy, and the global environment. Social policy as a practice is both an act and a science. As a science, there are various tools for and successful case illustrations of how a good social policy can be developed. As an art, it has no absolute formula for effective practice. Instead, it requires the sound judgment of those making the policies, leadership and capacity of those implementing the policies, and the support and collaboration of all stakeholders. Social policies dealing with social justice are not primarily about tangible services and redistribution of resources. It is also about educating those in power, those who are powerless, the haves and the have-nots. A well-argued and justified social policy may be poorly received and ineffective if concerned stakeholders do not own the policy, do not wish to follow its spirit and direction, do not wish to contribute to its implementation, and instead try all means to get the maximum profits from the policy and from not contributing to the goals of the policy.

Social policy can be studied along the following dimensions: purposes, actors and collaborators, target systems, target beneficiaries, procedures and measures, and interfacing and integrating with economic policies.

The purpose of a social policy may be general, such as improving people's quality of life and eliminating social inequalities through redistribution of resources. A social policy may include more specific measures, such as equal treatment of individuals and providing resources to those who cannot help themselves to meet their needs and become self-sufficient. Social policy may have short-term and long-term targets. Short-term targets often deal with critical situations that require immediate remedial action, such as massive unemployment of out-of-school youth. Long-term targets are often concerned with coordinated and sustainable development of a nation.

Actors of social policy may be governmental organizations, organizations that have a statutory role in enforcing legislation such as antidiscrimination legislation and in delivering public services, nongovernmental organizations, and the private sector. These actors may act on their own or together as collaborators.

The target systems of a social policy may refer to social welfare in a narrow approach or may include a wide array of social systems, such as health, education, housing, transport, and information communication. Target beneficiaries may be the wider society or a minority sector with special needs. Procedures and measures may be a governmental action agenda concerning fiscal policies, affirmative policies, legislative measures, and regulations.

Social policy in its broad interpretation has to be studied in relation to the economic policy of a government. This includes studies of the interfacing and integration of public and private sectors in meeting the purposes of a social policy.

In most societies, governmental social policies that have the clear purpose to address social justice are often targeting critical issues of national concern and often are highly politicized through media coverage. Such critical issues are mainly driven by massive major events such as armed confrontation within a nation or between nations, civil unrest as a result of protests against government corruption, racial confrontations, and uneven impacts of globalization. In other words, social disharmony, social exclusion, social unrest, people movements, and terrorist activities, which are common phenomena in today's societies, all have roots in the failure of governmental policies to achieve adequate social justice.

CRITICAL INCIDENTS AFFECTING THE ASIAN REGION IN RECENT DECADES

The Regional Financial Crisis

Regional turmoil started in May 1997, when currency speculators began their attack on the Thai baht. The baht fell on May 2, 1997, and the turmoil quickly spread to the Philippine peso, the Malaysian ringgit, the Indonesian rupiah, and the South Korean won. Within a short time these Asian currencies fell sharply, around 30% to 50%. Asian stock markets followed a similar pattern of free fall. The vicious cycle carried on as currency and stock market crashes dampened the confidence of domestic and foreign investors, who started further rounds of capital withdrawal. A few countries were able to rehabilitate themselves relatively quickly and graduated from loans and stringent measures from development agencies such as the IMF, which offered help during the crisis. All peoples have suffered from the financial crisis to varying degrees.

Hong Kong in Turmoil

Hong Kong provides an example with far-reaching implications for social policy studies. At the start of the financial turmoil, Hong Kong was fully engaged with the handover of sovereignty on July 1, 1997. Before the curtain was drawn on the handover funfairs and ceremonies, the Hong Kong financial markets were under siege by speculators. To defend the linked exchange rate of the Hong Kong dollar (U.S.$1:HK$7.8), the interests rates were raised to over 200%. Finally, the government went into the currency, stocks, and futures markets with U.S.$15.1 billion (HK$118 billion). The speculators were beaten off. An unexpected happy surprise, the government had by June 1999 made a paper profit of about U.S.$11.5 billion (HK$90 billion) from the financial incursion. Two years after the currency speculation battle, there was a drastic downturn in the Hong Kong economy, shown in the sharp fall of the GDP from 5.3 in 1997, to −5.3 in 1998, to −4.1 in January through March 1999 (Tsang, 1999). Rising unemployment became a major problem. The unemployment rate during March to May 1999 was 6.3%, and the underemployment rate was 2.9%. During that period, the size of the total labor force was provisionally estimated at 3,462,000, while the numbers of unemployed persons and underemployed persons were provisionally estimated at 216,000 and 103,000, respectively (Wong, 1999). Unemployment hit hardest the younger and older members of the workforce and those with lower education and skill levels. This was a great shock for a community that was used to an unemployment rate of between 2.5% and 3% for most of the previous 2 decades.

At the same time, wages were frozen or reduced. Property prices for residential units and offices fell by up to 50%. Undoubtedly, ordinary people were going through a very painful adjustment.

Long before the financial turmoil, Hong Kong had realized that high inflation for much of the 1990s, coupled with high property prices, had made Hong Kong noncompetitive. With such an open and externally oriented economy, Hong Kong was certain to face a correction; the question was when. The financial crisis made that adjustment process all the more fast and furious. Hong Kong was forced to reform itself so as to manage the downturn and return to the path of recovery.

Unfortunately, before any reforms took effect, the economic deterioration was further aggravated by the spread of severe and acute respiratory syndrome (SARS) in Asia in 2003, which practically crippled the travel, entertainment, and restaurant industries for nearly the whole of 2003.

The Hong Kong government was forced to undertake major reforms in its public policies in the direction of "small government and big market," covering all sectors, trimming spending, and devising new modes of providing public services; this required the involvement of the private sector and a new role for the government. Social polices made after the crisis have undoubtedly been subject to severe criticisms and protests from the grassroots and middle class, who have been hardest hit by such polices.

Hong Kong finally returned to a more stable and active economic recovery in 2004, largely due to the booming China economy and China's policy to allow solo tourists from Mainland China to Hong Kong.

Turmoil and Emerging Social Issues in Other Asian Countries

Over the past decade, quite a number of other countries in Asia have been facing challenges similar to those in Hong Kong and Thailand. Asia does not lack major natural disasters: the Kobe earthquake in 1995, the September 21, 2000, earthquake in Taiwan, the frequent massive flooding in China and Bangladesh, the unprecedented tsunami in December 2004. These and other natural disasters have caused large numbers of human causalities and losses in property and economic activity.

Asia also does not lack man-made disasters, including massive racial confrontations in Indonesia in 1998 targeting ethnic Chinese, frequent racial and religious conflicts, and armed confrontations in a number of countries, including Malaysia, Thailand, Timor, terrorist insurgents in the Philippines, and border confrontations.

Asia is not lacking in political upheavals, including people's movements in the Philippines, which toppled two presidents; people's movement in Nepal in 2006, giving rise to a new constitution and a new government; massive demonstrations against government corruption in Thailand and Taiwan in 2006; and a military coup in Thailand in September 2006, bringing Thailand back to military rule after 19 years of constitutional democracy.

Asia also feels the aftershocks from the 9/11 terrorist attacks on United States, not only because of the sudden shrinking of intercontinental travel, but also in the heightened alert of similar terrorist insurgents in the region. Terrorists' movements have been frequently reported in Southeast Asia, northwestern China, and middle Asia. The nuclear test conducted by North Korea in October 2006 raised security to an even higher priority among countries in Asia and the Pacific. Asian countries have since become more proactive in combating causes that breed extreme and confrontational ideologies and seeking closer collaborations in tackling terrorism worldwide. A wide array of short-term measures has been installed, including those concerning national security policies and measures. Long-term measures are being contemplated to target the cause of social conditions conducive to breeding extreme ideologies and social exclusion. As expected, a substantial portion of public revenue has been diverted to antiterrorism at the expense of social policy provisions.

On top of such critical issues, Asia has social issues of its own making, such as those concerning migrant workers from developing economies (e.g., Indonesia, Nepal, the Philippines, Sri Lanka, and Thailand) to developed economies (e.g., Hong Kong, Japan, Singapore, and Taiwan), cross-border marriages that split families (as in the case of Hong Kong), and an influx of large numbers of brides of different cultures (as in the case of Taiwan).

AN ASIAN PERSPECTIVE ON SOCIAL POLICY DEVELOPMENT

Social policy is influenced by complex factors, some of which were mentioned in the preceding paragraphs. Two other critical issues are state governance and poverty. Inefficiency and corruption are major concerns in state governance. The economic and social impacts of globalization, including those created by agreements made at the World Trade Organization, are more and more influencing national social polices, for example, those concerning migrant workers, cross-border marriages, sex trading, drug trafficking, free trade agreements on domestic employment, and employment in selected sectors of a society. For example, farmers in many rural areas in Asia are still making their living by small-scale and traditional farming and can hardly compete with their counterparts in Western rural societies.

Asia's challenges in recent decades have strongly supported the thesis that no single government can rely solely on its own polices and resources to handle domestic issues, the majority of which will have regional and international linkages. Not a single national social policy can steer and manage a society to achieve its intended goals in a rapidly changing environment. The making of social policies has to take into consideration unpredictable factors in creating conditions conducive to adapting to change, nurturing initiatives and a sense of ownership of all stakeholders, both within a country and across countries through regional collaborative platforms.

While social polices at the national level have to respond to national situations, a framework for policy mandates blessed with consensus among all nations in the region has proven effective in guiding national practices and regional collaborations through sharing capacity-building resources and good practices to make progresses toward common goals of social justice. This is an area in which the United Nations and its special systems, such as the International Labor Organization (ILO), UNICEF, and WHO, have been most effective in dealing with a range of critical emerging issues.

Disability issues offer good examples of a regional and international policy making process.

Social Policy and Social Justice for People with Disabilities

People with disabilities in the region are facing critical and severe situations. Based on the modest estimate of 1 in 10 adopted by WHO, the number of disabled people in Asia is already larger than the entire American population. About 80% of Asian people with disabilities live in rural or remote areas. Among the 900 million very poor people in the region, the disabled are among the most discriminated against and the most impoverished. Although comprehensive figures are hard to come by, there may be between 250 million and 300 million people with disabilities in the region, and close to 200 million have severe or moderate disabilities that need special services or assistance. It is estimated that 238 million people with disabilities in the region are of working age (Perry, 2002; United Nations Statistics Division, 2004). They are grossly underrepresented in the workforce. If they are employed, they tend to be underemployed or may work in informal settings where they lack protection with regard to security, safety, and decent wages. At the same time, people with disabilities often lack access to the very services and experiences that could lead to successful participation in the economic mainstream, such as vocational training, job opportunities, and credit for self-employment. It is therefore not surprising that the unemployment rate of people with disabilities in some countries is 40% to 80%. As an illustration of the magnitude of the challenges, China, in its 10th Five-Year Plan, reported that in 2003 alone, it created job opportunities for 268,000 disabled people in urban areas and increased the total number of employed disabled people in rural areas to 159 million.

Processes in Developing a Regional Policy Framework

Asia is a vast region, containing about 60% of the world's population, many living in rural and mountainous areas. Asia has some of the oldest civilizations and religions and some of the most advanced as well as poorest economies. Diversity and differences among governments and peoples of Asia are the norm rather than the exception. Poverty, armed confrontations, and natural disasters are among the main causes of disability. When it comes to disability concerns, there is a surprisingly strong sense of brotherhood and sisterhood as well as examples of deep collaboration among governments and peoples in Asia.

Immediately upon the close of the United Nations Decade of Disabled Persons 1983–1992, the UN Economic and Social Commission for Asia and the Pacific (ESCAP), with the unanimous approval of all its member governments, proclaimed the Asian and Pacific Decade of Disabled Persons 1993–2002, the first ever UN regional mandate of its kind, and a demonstration of a rather exceptional Asian solidarity and strong political will. In

2002, again with the unanimous approval of its members, ESCAP proclaimed the extension of the decade to 2003–2012 and the proclamation of the Biwako Millennium Framework (BMF) for compliance of its member governments. *The Biwako Millennium Framework: Toward an Inclusive, Barrier-Free and Rights-Based Society for Persons with Disabilities in Asia and the Pacific* (UN ESCAP, 2002), which was adopted at the high-level intergovernmental meeting in Japan in 2002, identifies seven priority areas, one of which is about training and employment of people with disabilities. Target 10 of this priority area states, "Recognizing the lack of formal job opportunities in many countries, Governments, international agencies, donors, NGOs and others in civil society must ensure that persons with disabilities and organizations of and for persons with disabilities have equitable access and are included in programs related to business development, entrepreneurship and credit distribution."

The NGOs in the region have been working very closely together in promoting the Asian and Pacific Decade. A Regional NGO Network for the Promotion of the Asian and Pacific Decade was founded in 1993 and reorganized in 2002 as the Asia Pacific Disability Forum, which comprises all major NGOs and international NGOs. One of its major activities was the annual campaigns for the Decade, which were held in rotation among its member countries. The involvement of major stakeholders of both governmental and nongovernmental sectors in the development and monitoring of the regional framework has proven to be useful in sensitizing governments to the needs of the disabled and supporting interventions at national and local levels.

Asian initiatives have been supportive of the global disability movement. In March 2000, the first International NGO World Summit was held in Beijing and unanimously committed to urge the United Nations to adopt an international convention on the rights of disabled persons. Since then some member states have taken the initiative in working within the UN systems to bring the convention's ideas to reality. Finally, after 6 years of an intensive drafting process, the International Convention on the Rights of Persons with Disabilities was adopted in August 2006 by the drafting UN Ad Hoc Committee, and a target for endorsement by the UN General Assembly was set for December 2006.

Asian stakeholders were among the most active players in the drafting process, including both governmental and nongovernmental representatives and organizations of persons with disabilities. The UN drafting process was open and inclusive, permitting active interventions from all interested and concerned NGOs. The Asian sector met regularly during the drafting period and involved stakeholder representatives, UN regional experts, and subject matter experts, and produced a number of important documents for the reference of the UN Ad Hoc Committee, including the often referenced Bangkok Recommendations 2003 (UN ESCAP, 2003).

The convention proclaimed its protected target population, the framework of rights items, the international monitoring and remedies system, and interstate meetings and conferences to promote the convention at national and local levels. It should be noted that the framework of rights items includes rights from various existing UN conventions, plus additional items specific to disability situations such as sign language and barrier-free access. This new convention will become the UN's eighth core human rights convention.

The convention drafting process is itself a significant process for raising awareness and building capacity for all stakeholders. The follow-up process of getting member states to become signatories to the convention further enhances awareness and commitment from high-level governmental bodies.

As far as Asia is concerned, the adoption of the international convention is a major step forward. The region will now be working on a twin track approach, involving all stakeholders in monitoring the implementation of the BMF and the convention at regional, national, and local levels (Takamine, 2003).

A discussion on a global rights-based disability framework will be less meaningful without references to specific policy frameworks that are comparable across the region. Following are some specific policy areas concerning employment of disabled people to illustrate the making of sound social policies at the national level. This is an area of priority concern of the regional BMF and the UN Convention.

Specific Measures Promoting Employment of People with Disabilities

Employment Quota Scheme

The first quota system in Asia to support employment of people with disabilities was set up by Japan as early as 1966. Now the employment quota scheme is a common feature in Asia, usually applying to medium (50 to 300) and large companies. The quota is 1% to 5% of a workforce, and the norm is 2% to 3%. Generally speaking, the quota system is regulated by legislation and may be combined with a levy on noncompliance (e.g., in China, Japan, Korea, Mongolia, Thailand, Vietnam). There is no levy system in some countries (e.g., Bangladesh and Sri Lanka for government only; Pakistan, India, and the Philippines for both government and private sector; Indonesia for private sector only; Perry, 2002). The levy is usually calculated on the market medium or minimum salary. The fund created from the levy is usually designated for use in support of the private sector to bring companies into compliance, to train people with disabilities, and to finance loans for self-employment.

The success of the quota system is dependent on the effectiveness and efficiency of the implementation agency. In Japan, the target of the quota and levy system has been extended over the years from people with physical challenges only to include people with intellectual challenges and people with psychiatric challenges (see Japan Organization for the Employment of the Elderly and Persons with Disabilities, 2006). However, the overall quota has seldom been fully filled because of the inadequate supply of people with disabilities who possess the required job skills (Matsui, 1998). As a result, the funds collected from the levy have grown rapidly, to the extent that the implementing agency is sitting on a rather large sum of unused money. This is perhaps one of the reasons why the implementing agency was given an expanded portfolio to cover the employment of old people since 2003.

In China, the local branches of the China Disabled Persons' Federation (CDPF) are given the authority to monitor the implementation of the quota and levy system, the details of which are determined by provincial and city governments in accordance with the laws promulgated by the central government (see Law of the People's Republic of China on the Protection of Disabled Persons, 1991). Some CDPF branches have reported success in creating job opportunities for people with disabilities, through their close liaison with and guidance offered to business concerns. Based on these successes, the CDPF has set a target of 85% employment rate for some urban localities.

In the case of the Philippines, although the Magna Carta for Disabled Persons (1992) provides for a quota system, the business sector's awareness of the law is low. A similar situation is reported in Vietnam, where a quota and levy system is provided for in Article 125 of the Labour Code, but the enforcement is uncertain and the fund is not operational.

Affirmative Action Policies Concerning Work Facilities for People with Disabilities

A number of Asian countries have established workshops that hire a relatively large proportion of people with disabilities. These facilities have different English names, such as sheltered workshops, social work centers, community workshops, welfare factories, supported employment, and disability-concerned enterprises. In the Philippines (Foundation for International Training, 2002) and India (*Law of India: The Persons with Disabilities [Equal Opportunities, Protection of Rights and Full Participation] Act,* 1995), for example, legislation gives workshops the exclusive rights to or priority in obtaining a limited range of public contracts; in South Korea (Republic of Korea, 2004), too, laws regulate such practices. These workshop facilities are the main providers of income-generating work for people with severe challenges. In some countries, sheltered workshops are generally considered welfare facilities, and people working there are treated more like trainees or welfare recipients and not workers under the normal legal definition. Welfare factories are more common in China and Vietnam, where they are owned and managed by the government and receive substantial tax exemptions and government subventions. In the 1970s and 1980s sheltered workshops in developed economies, such as Hong Kong, received substantial government funding to handle mainly labor-intensive, low-skilled work. Participants received day care services and earned very low wages.

In the 1990s, these facilities changed their mission and characteristics drastically. First, there was a drop in government funding. It is worthwhile to note as a comparison that government funding for sheltered workshops in developing countries has never been significant. Second, as low-skilled jobs in developed economies began moving to China, sheltered workshops faced rapid changes in market conditions.

In practice, the number of sheltered workshops in developed economies has been increasing over the past 2 decades due to the lack of employment opportunities for people with severe disabilities, especially those with mental retardation or psychiatric disabilities. In Japan, there are over 23,000 sheltered workshops serving 84,000 disabled people with over 25,000 staff members. The annual total subsidy of both local and national governments to sheltered workshops has increased to U.S.$500 million (Maruyama, 2003). The aim of these sheltered workshops is to assist their clients to obtain employment in the open labor market, but their annual placement rate in business and industry remains low at 2%. In the meantime, the workers' length of stay at sheltered workshops is increasing, with the majority staying for more than 5 years (Matsui, 1998). It is worthwhile to note that sheltered workshops in Japan have been given a new name: social work centers.

Japan also has a national network of small-scale community workshops for disabled people, the Japan Association of Community Workshops, which has a strong advocacy function. These workshops are mainly grassroots initiatives and are not supported by the central government. The national network has about 5,000 community workshops serving over 75,000 disabled people (Tateoka, 2003). The association is a very active member of Workability International and serves as its regional secretariat.

To cope with the changes, some workshops are expanding to include supported employment services for people with disabilities who could work in an open setting with support.

Others are moving into third sector services, including producing and marketing products with their own brand names. Still others are venturing into the business field either in partnership with a commercial partner or on their own brand names, without much change in the image of the workshop. The business venture approach has attracted much attention lately in some Asian countries' poverty alleviation programs, including those concerning disabled people.

A Missing Link between Social Policy and Social Justice: Social Capital Investment in Support of Persons with Disabilities

A human rights approach to social policy as discussed in preceding paragraphs demonstrates that social policy development requires a multisectoral and multidisciplinary approach, with due emphasis on processes and outcome and due attention to interfacing among interventions at international, regional, and national levels. Accordingly, a multistakeholder involvement and participation in the process is necessary. The lack of a gluing effect or social capital among all stakeholders is considered a critical factor leading to unsuccessful policy outcome. In areas of economic development projects, development assistances over past decades for less developed economies have returned mixed outcomes. Many projects have in fact failed in bringing sustainable social and economic improvements to disadvantaged sectors of a society. Development agencies have identified the lack of social capital as a critical cause. Indeed social capital as a critical factor in social policy has received increasing attention from leading global development agencies such as the World Bank and the Organization for Economic Cooperation and Development (OECD). The World Bank (2006) refers social capital to the institutions, relationships, and norms that shape the quality and quantity of a society's social interactions. Many projects in social capital for development work have received increasing attention from leading global organizations such as the World Bank and OECD. The World Bank (2006) considers social capital to be a major factor affecting the sustainability of its world poverty eradication programs. The OECD (2001) has extended its interest in human capital to include social capital and its impact on sustainable social development.

The Asian Development Bank (2004) has incorporated social capital as a critical factor in its poverty alleviation programs:

> When poverty is pronounced, social cohesion is often weak, and communities suffer from conflict, marginalization, and exclusion. In such cases, strong, proactive policies are required to reverse perceptions of social and psychological inferiority, to foster a sense of empowerment, and to create genuinely participatory institutions. Social capital and a more inclusive society can be promoted through antidiscrimination legislation, land reform, legal recognition of user groups, and accessible systems of justice. Specific measures may be required to provide suitable social services and equitable access to economic opportunity for ethnic minorities.

SOCIAL ENTERPRISE, SOCIAL CAPITAL

A social enterprise is primarily mission-driven, while surviving and progressing on self-sufficiency and market sustainability.

Kwok et al.* studied two organizations of persons with disabilities that engage in social enterprises, one from Manila and the other from Taipei. The following preliminary findings may offer some useful information for understanding the potentials of self-help organizations of persons with disabilities (SHOPs) in benefiting from social enterprises through social capital investment.

Affirmative Action Government Policies

In the Philippines, the government allocates 10% of its purchasing budget for chairs and tables of public schools to cooperatives of persons with disabilities. Cooperatives that meet the disability-related criteria and have the manufacturing capacity may bid for these government contracts. This policy strongly supports social enterprises.

The cooperatives of persons with disabilities are formally registered under the related cooperative ordinances. There is a central body, which is the national federation of cooperatives of persons with disabilities. The national body provides support to its local cooperatives in capacity building, including technical training and funding through development assistance from local and overseas funding bodies. The national body also has a plan to nurture and develop local cooperatives in all administrative areas of the Philippines.

The national body takes on the major task of negotiating with government departments responsible for the contracts for building school chairs and tables, in product design and research, in negotiating for raw materials supply, in negotiating for credit lines from development agencies and private organizations, in delivery of finished products, and in follow-up with government departments for payment. The national body works with local cooperatives that have the capacity to engage in the manufacturing work, in building manufacturing workshops, and in recruitment and training of disabled people to engage in business and manufacturing operations. The government contract does not guarantee profits, as the unit price of the restricted contract will be affected by mainstream tendering exercises which are highly competitive among large and major manufacturing firms. The national body has a major challenge in securing credit lines to support the operation, as government payment of such contracts is usually some months behind the delivery of goods.

The national body and local branches have been investing time and effort in building positive networks with political leaders, central government departments, development agencies and funding bodies that offer loans to businesses for development concerns, potential customers such as private colleges and schools, and other organizations of and for people with disabilities. The social networks developed by the selected organization cut across many sectors.

One successful local cooperative that has the capacity to engage in large-scale manufacturing contracts has demonstrated dedicated, committed leadership with the required business expertise. The cooperative's social networks with the government, the business community, and the civil society are highly functional. Its leaders have been recognized in several local and national award presentations. The social enterprise has received affirmative policy support from local government, at least in providing a low-cost workshop venue. Its products have received high commendations from customers. The cooperative's

*These discussions were based on preliminary findings of a study conducted by the author as principal investigator and supported by a research grant from of City University of Hong Kong, project number 7001571-640.

leaders, being alumni of local schools and colleges, have the informal networks to support their business marketing. The membership of the organization has gained both economic and social benefits from the social enterprises. Some of the profits from the enterprises are used to support community-based rehabilitation services through reaching out to other disabled people in need.

The national government has been publicizing its support for disabled people. The development agencies, such as development banks and NGO funding bodies, are also happy as the organization has achieved a good credit rating status.

In spite of the high quality of social capital that supports the social enterprise, the national and local bodies face challenges, and the business operation outlook is uncertain. First, the restricted tender portion of government contracts is unstable and short term, which cannot support long-term job provision for the employees of the organization. Second, the credit lines may not always be adequate, and those available still carry an interest rate that requires a very efficient business operation. Third, the trend of decentralization of government operations to regional levels has prevented the national body from engaging in contract tendering for its local branches, many of which do not have the required financial and technical capacity to engage in such manufacturing businesses.

To overcome the challenges and to pave the way for future development, the national body is lobbying the government to accept it as a bidder for the government's restricted tender. The national body is also considering a major campaign to set up a trust fund that will provide the financial credit support to its manufacturing arm.

Experiences of a Selected Organization from Taipei, Taiwan

In Taiwan, there is a mandatory employment quota system with a levy. Funds raised from the levy are used to provide subsidies to other organizations in terms of a wage subsidy to disabled employees over the quota. There is a further affirmative policy that provides income subsidies to disadvantaged groups in their initial job placement up to around 36 months, renewable every year subject to project performance appraisal. The government also allocates a small percentage of its purchase budget for products of sheltered workshops including those for people with disabilities.

The organization in Taipei was founded in the early 1980s by a highly respectable leader with a disability. It started with a small group of disabled people engaging in advocacy and has become one of the largest organizations of and for people with disabilities, with branches all over. It now has over 2,500 employees and operates a range of services, with a primary focus on people with disabilities. Large portions of its services are government contracts. The leaders are dedicated Christians, but the organization is not affiliated with any church groups. The organization has set up a social enterprise department to engage in a range of income-generating activities, which also provide job training and work to disabled employees. The range of activities includes special transport services, bottled water and stationery bearing the organization's name, a sheltered workshop cum enterprise, a cafeteria, insurance, and a call center.

Some business operations are government contracts, for example, the special transport service from a local government. It got the first contract awarded and from the contract income employed a good number of disabled drivers. The same contract, however, was awarded to a commercial firm when it was up for renewal because of bidding price consideration. The commercial firm's service quality was heavily criticized by disabled users, to the extent that the local government has pledged to review its contract bidding criteria and process in the next round.

One of the largest business operations of the organization is its sheltered workshop cum business. The workshop operates in partnership with some private companies in the manufacturing of wheelchairs and assistive devices. The workshop was built in the worst earthquake disaster area shortly after September 2000 with disaster relief funds from government and private donations, with the primary purpose of supporting the livelihoods of disaster victims.

The leaders and chief executives of the workshop, through their years of positive network relationships with political leaders, central and local governments, and the private sector, have been able to nurture a functional partnership with all parties to support the operation of the workshop, which has become one of the largest wheelchair manufacturing centers in Taiwan. Its major job orders come from charity sales, for example, from government contracts for wheelchairs needed for bilateral development projects, from private companies for children's wheelchairs for community service projects, and from fund-raising campaigns to involve college students in disability awareness projects involving the use of wheelchairs. The wheelchair project has acquired quality accreditation from international bodies and has entered the private market as a keen competitor. The wheelchair project is an organization-driven project and products are selling with the organization's own brand name. The wheelchair workshop benefits from related government policies that support accredited sheltered workshops, for example, income subsidy and job training of disabled employees, as well as subsidized social work staff.

The workshop also engages in business partnerships with interested private companies in marketing products that bear the brand name of the private partners. The organization is functioning as a service operator, receiving commissions to support the salaries of the employees, the majority of whom are disabled, and the business operation. The private partners are primarily interested in the high moral value of supporting disadvantaged and minority groups, and not so much concerned with monetary profits. The private partners believe that the high moral value of the organization and the involvement of disabled employees match well the mission of the company's products and support the healthy lifestyle being pursed by its employees, business partners, and customers. In this regard, the government's affirmative action policies in support of disabled employees through the levy funds of the employment quota scheme and special and time-limited grants to support the employment of disadvantaged social groups also benefit from the business networks and expertise in support of the operation. The private partners also provide a good source of volunteer support and charity fund-raising pools.

The realization of all these social enterprises is due to the vast social networks of the leaders and organizers, who have invested heavily in building social capital across governmental, private, and religious sectors. The leaders are appointed to influential committees of national and local governments. Its leaders, both paid and unpaid, have been recognized publicly for their contributions, and some have received outstanding national awards.

Like other businesses, and perhaps even more so, the NGO has to face a range of tough challenges to develop the sustainability of the social enterprises. The organization-driven wheelchair workshop, because of its space requirements, is facing high workshop rentals. Similar private businesses have already moved their manufacturing sites to Mainland China, where land and labor are much less costly. The organization's wheelchair workshop has to deal with factors of labor efficiency because of its high percentage of disabled employees, as well as other high operating costs. Although enjoying high brand name status and high product and service quality, the operation must employ more workers to meet the performance output requirement. To compete in the private market it must accept a price disadvantage, and its job orders from charities and restricted government contracts are unstable and do not offer a long-term solution. The profit margins of all these operations are still at low level, and sometimes even have to depend on donation support to balance the books.

Implications for Government Policy in Support of People with Disabilities

The two selected cases illustrate the dynamic interactions among government affirmative action policies, development agencies, NGO funding bodies, and the private sector, with the NGO social enterprises as the key players bridging and linking all interested and concerned sectors to develop and nurture social enterprises in support of organizations of people with disabilities. The impact of creating capacity-building and income-generating opportunities by the two NGOs to a great extent relies on their active social networks and trust relationships built across all sectors. The two organizations do not receive earmarked funding for their continued and sustainable development. Their future and further development is dependent on their own making. They both share a common wish to nurture a sustainable social enterprise that will in turn support the sustainable development of the organizations as a whole.

Social enterprises are primarily businesses, although they hold a high moral value. However, the high moral value is not a guarantee for running a successful and sustainable business. This high moral value may in some situations render social enterprises less competitive in a market economy that is subject to many competitive forces, including the global economy advocated by the World Trade Organization. Furthermore, NGOs that operate social enterprises may not have the capacity, such as the high-level physical, financial, and human capital, needed to respond proactively to rapidly changing market conditions.

Social capital investment therefore becomes more critical and strategic for organizations of persons with disabilities than for other kinds of businesses. With strong social capital, these organizations may be able to survive stormy market conditions. However, there needs to be an investment before they can generate positive social capital to support themselves. The investment has to come from within these organizations as well as from other stakeholders at the local, national, and globally regional levels.

Comprehensive and Proactive Support of Social Capital Development for People with Disabilities

At Local and National Levels

At the national level, government affirmative action policies in mandatory employment quota and levy programs, restricted tendering, and earmarked budgets are good practices that are worthy of replication in other areas of Asia. Such affirmative action will enhance disability awareness in the private sector and development agencies (governmental and nongovernmental) and stimulate interest in seeking or responding to invitations to create social enterprise partnerships. Support for continued and sustainable capacity building through government or government-directed public funding should be encouraged.

At the Regional Level

During this period of the Biwako Millennium Framework, it is timely to consider developing comprehensive and coordinated regional initiatives in building social capital to contribute to successful social enterprises. Regional Asia initiatives should be in the form of a tripartite platform for development, involving UN agencies, governments, and the private sector, with the primary purpose of supporting involvement in social enterprises.

The World Bank and the Asian Development Bank are major development agencies that have committed to a proactive social capital strategy for poverty alleviation in the context of achieving the UN Millennium Development Goals. The BMF has recognized social development as part of its overall agenda for action and brought in organizations of persons with disabilities as one of its policy targets. The ILO and the UN Food and Drug Organization, for example, are among the leading UN agencies with experience in developing disability-based tripartite business councils for development and income-generating projects. From the private business sector, many multinational corporations have already demonstrated a sound understanding of the principles and practice of diversity in their human resource management departments (Global Diversity Network, n.d.).

CONCLUSION

The Asian region and the world are facing rapid changes. Governments and peoples often have to face uncertainties caused by unpredictable political and economic forces. New issues emerge while old issues are becoming even more critical in the modern era. Professionals seeking social justice for disadvantaged sectors will have to equip themselves with enhanced capacity, flexibility, creativity, and innovation to be a major stakeholder in multisectoral, interdisciplinary social policy development in dealing with evolving complex situations.

The social work profession has a strategic role in working with people at all levels. It is therefore relevant to ask the profession if it is prepared to take a proactive role in the social policy making process of the new era. To do so, social work professionals may have to adopt a paradigm shift to equip themselves with broad helping perspectives and multiskills to prevail as partners of all sectors in the society and to engage in comprehensive policy-making processes in dealing with challenges of the modern times.

There are however indications that the social work profession is becoming marginalized by various mainstream sectors as it fails to get involved in new and alternative solutions to deal with challenges of welfare and economic transformation.

The social work profession began its mission by arguing that social welfare was not charity. The profession since then has adopted as its core practice the empowerment and well-being of individuals, groups, and communities. Social work is founded on social justice and guided by the call to nurture people's strengths and support human diversity. In

2003, the International Council on Social Welfare adopted a mission statement specifying that the Council aims

> to promote forms of social and economic development which aim to reduce poverty, hardship and vulnerability throughout the world, especially amongst disadvantaged people. It strives for recognition and protection of fundamental rights to food, shelter, education, health care and security. It believes that these rights are an essential foundation for freedom, justice and peace. It seeks also to advance equality of opportunity, freedom of self-expression and access to human services.

The International Association of Schools of Social Work (IASSW) and the International Federation of Social Workers (IFSW) support international social work that

> promotes social change, problem solving in human relationships and the empowerment and liberation of people to enhance well-being. Utilizing theories of human behavior and social systems, social work intervenes at the points where people interact with their environments. Principles of human rights and social justice are fundamental to social work. (Joint Committee of the IASSW and IFSW, 2002)

In line with this definition, the IASSW's discussion document on global qualifying standards for social work education and training identifies the following core purposes of social work:

- Facilitate the inclusion of marginalized, socially excluded, dispossessed, vulnerable and at-risk groups of people.
- Address and challenge barriers, inequalities and injustices that exist in society.
- Assist and mobilize individuals, families, groups and communities to enhance their well-being and their problem-solving capacities.
- Encourage people to engage in advocacy with regard to pertinent local, national, regional and/or international concerns.
- Advocate for, and/or with people, the formulation and targeted implementation of policies that are consistent with the ethical principles of the profession.
- Advocate for, and/or with people, changes in those structural conditions that maintain people in marginalized, dispossessed and vulnerable positions.
- Work toward the protection of people who are not in a position to do so themselves, for example children in need of care and persons experiencing mental illness or mental retardation within the parameters of accepted and ethically sound legislation.

A more careful analysis of the list of social work's core purposes explains why public misperception of social welfare still prevails. To some extent, the traditional conception of social work is still visible in the core purpose definition. Social work is defined in association primarily with and for people who are marginalized, at risk, or in need. Social workers are seen functioning primarily within the social services sector, with expertise focusing on helping skills and roles. Social work prides itself on its humanitarian values and dissociates itself from private market systems and values.

In the modern era, we are witnessing social workers functioning in many sectors of society, including the private sector. They have multiple skills and take on posts in a wide range of settings. They may be employed in formal caring systems, but their intervention extends into the private market and informal caring systems. They have a broader mandate to build a total caring system in the society.

Apparently, a change of paradigm of the social work profession is needed so that it will work in partnership with all sectors and all systems in society to deal with any challenges at the micro, meso, or macrolevels.

Social workers must pursue social policies grounded on a human rights perspective developed with the full participation of the society's relevant stakeholders by nurturing ownership and mutual support among all sectors, embracing multisectoral dimensions, and adopting interdisciplinary approaches. This is a formidable challenge. As mentioned in the beginning of this chapter, our ancient philosophers, two millenniums ago, already believed in, preached, and practiced educating kings, with absolute powers over their subjects, in sharing and caring, and their superiors and inferiors not to contend for profits. In modern time, our people have become more educated, our social systems and institutions have become better equipped, and the international and regional platforms are becoming more sensitized to human rights principles and values. With vision and perseverance and a paradigm shift in developing social policies that support disadvantaged sectors, the human services profession could make its due contribution to building a society that is inclusive, barrier free, and rights based.

REFERENCES

Ad Hoc Committee on a Comprehensive and Integral International Convention on the Protection and Promotion of the Rights and Dignity of Persons with Disabilities. (2006, August 14–25). *Draft convention on the rights of persons with disabilities and draft optional protocol.* Eighth session, New York. Advanced unedited version. Retrieved November 1, 2007, from www.un .org/esa/socdev/enable/rights/ahc8adart.htm.

Asian Development Bank. (2004). *Enhancing the fight against poverty in Asia and the Pacific: The poverty reduction strategy of the Asian Development Bank.* Retrieved September 7, 2006, from www.adb.org/Documents/Policies/Poverty_Reduction/2004/foreword.asp.

Central People's Government of People's Republic of China. (2006, March 16). *The National Economic and Social Development 11th Five Year Plan (2006–2011).* Retrieved October 8, 2006, from http://big5.gov.cn/gate/big5/www.gov.cn/ztzl/2006-03/16/content_228841_2.htm.

Foundation for International Training. (2002). *Identifying disability issues related to poverty reduction: Philippines country study.* Prepared for Asian Development Bank. Retrieved November 1, 2007, from www.adb.org/Documents/Conference/Disability_Development/phi.pdf.

Global Diversity Network. (n.d.). *Welcome to Global Diversity Network.* Home page. Retrieved September 11, 2006, from www.globaldiversitynetwork.com.

International Council on Social Welfare. (2003). *Mission statement.* Retrieved October 20, 2006, from http://www.icsw.org/.

Japan Organization for the Employment of the Elderly and Persons with Disabilities (2006). *Employment measures for persons with disabilities.* Retrieved October 22, 2006, from www.jeed.or.jp /english/supporting.html.

Joint Committee of the International Association of Schools of Social Work and International Federation of Social Workers. (2002). *Discussion document on global qualifying standards for social work education and training.* Retrieved October 22, 2006, from http://www.ifsw.org/GM-2002/GM-GStandards.htm.

Law of India: The Persons with Disabilities (Equal Opportunities, Protection of Rights and Full Participation) Act. (1995). (No. 1 of 1996). Retrieved on November 1, 2007, from http://www .disabilityindia.org/pwdacts.cfm.

Law of the People's Republic of China on the Protection of Disabled Persons. (1991). Retrieved on November 1, 2007, from http://www.gov.cn/banshi/2005-08/04/content_20235.htm.

Magna Carta for Disabled Persons (RA 7277): An Act Providing for the Rehabilitation, Self-Development, and Self-Reliance of Disabled Persons and Their Integration into the Mainstream of Society and for Other Purposes. Congress of the Philippines. (1992). Retrieved on November 1, 2007, from www.ncwdp.gov.ph/index.php?id1=46&id2=1&id3=6.

Maruyama, I. (2003, September). Promoting social employment of people with disabilities in Japan. In Eden Social Welfare Foundation (Ed.), *Proceedings of international conference on sheltered workplace, industry and environmental improvement for people with disabilities* (pp. 67–71). Taipei, Taiwan: Eden Social Welfare Foundation.

Matsui, R. (1998). An overview of the impact of employment quota system in Japan. *Asia Pacific Disability Rehabilitation Journal, 9*(1). Retrieved on November 1, 2007, from www.dinf.ne.jp/doc/english/asia/resource/apdrj/z13jo0100/z13jo0106.htm.

Mencius. (1999). Book 1 (Zhao Zhentao, Zhang Wenting, Zhou Dingzhi, Ying yi, & Yang Bojun, Trans.). In *Library of Chinese classics: Mencius* (pp. 1–25). Changsha, China: Hunan Peoples Publishing House.

Organization for Economic Cooperation and Development. (2001). *The well-being of nations: The role of human and social capital.* Paris: OECD.

Perry, D. A. (2002, October). *Situation of people with disabilities in the region: Disability issues in employment and social protection.* Paper presented at the Regional Workshop on Disability and Development, Asian Development Bank, ADB Headquarters, Manila, Philippines. Retrieved on November 1, 2007, from www.adb.org/Documents/Events/2002/Disability_Development/perry_paper.pdf.

Republic of Korea. (2004). Act on employment promotion and vocational rehabilitation for the disabled [Law No. 4219 of 13 January 1990]. In *Labor Laws of Korea* (pp. 623–645). Ministry of Labour, Republic of Korea.

Roemer, J. E. (1996). *Theories of distributive justice.* London: Harvard University Press.

Takamine, Y. (2003). *Disability issues in East Asia: Review and ways forward.* Retrieved October 22, 2006, from http://siteresources.worldbank.org/DISABILITY/Resources/Regions/East-Asia-Pacific/Disability_Issues_in_East_Asia_Takamine.pdf.

Tateoka, A. (2003, September). Japan association of community workshops for disabled persons. In Eden Social Welfare Foundation (Ed.), *Proceedings of International Conference on Sheltered Workplace, Industry and Environmental Improvement for People with Disabilities* (pp. 59–62). Taipei, Taiwan: Eden Social Welfare Foundation.

Titmus, R. M. (1974). *Social policy.* London: Allen & Unwin.

Titmus, R. M. (1976). *Commitment to welfare.* London: Allen & Unwin. (Original work published 1968)

Tsang, D. (1999, March 3). Speech of the financial secretary, Mr. Donald Tsang, moving the second reading of the Appropriation Bill 1999: "1999–2000 Budget: Onward with new strengths." Hong Kong SAR Government.

Tsang, D. (2005, October). *2005–2006 policy address by chief executive.* Retrieved October 8, 2006, from www.info.gov.hk/gia/general/200510/12/P200510120112.htm.

United Nations. (1995, March). *Report of the World Summit for Social Development, Copenhagen.* United Nations publication, Sales No. E.96.IV.8.

United Nations. (2000–2007) *United Nations Treaties Database.* Retrieved October 22, 2006, from http://untreaty.un.org/English/access.asp.

United Nations. (2006). *Social justice in an open world: The role of the United Nations.* New York: United Nations.

United Nations Committee on Economic, Social and Cultural Rights. (2006). *General comment no. 3.* Retrieved October 22, 2006, from www.ohchr.org/English/bodies/cescr/comments.htm.

United Nations Development Project. (2003). *Human development report 2003*. New York: Oxford University Press.

United Nations Economic and Social Commission for Asia and the Pacific. (2002). *Biwako Millennium Framework: Toward an inclusive, barrier-free and rights-based society for persons with disabilities in Asia and the Pacific*. Retrieved October 22, 2006, from http://www.unescap.org/esid/psis /disability/bmf/bmf.html.

United Nations Economic and Social Commission for Asia and the Pacific. (2003, June). *Bangkok recommendations on the elaboration of a comprehensive and integral international convention to promote and protect the rights and dignity of persons with disabilities*. Expert group meeting and seminar on an international convention to protect and promote the rights and dignity of persons with disabilities, Bangkok, Thailand. Retrieved October 24, 2006, from http://www.worldenable.net /bangkok2003/recommendations.htm.

United Nations Statistics Division. (2004). *Indicators on unemployment*. Available from http://unstats .un.org/unsd/demographic/products/socind/unempl.htm.

Wong, W. P. (1999). *Press release of Mr. Wong W. P., secretary for education and manpower, Tuesday, June 15, 1999*. Hong Kong, China.

World Bank. (2006). *Overview: Social capital*. Retrieved September 10, 2006, from http://web .worldbank.org/WBSITE/EXTERNAL/TOPICS/EXTSOCIALDEVELOPMENT/EXTTSOCIAL CAPITAL/0,,menuPK:401021~pagePK:149018~piPK:149093~theSitePK:401015,00.html.

Section II

THE CONTEXT OF POLICY: YESTERDAY, TODAY, AND TOMORROW

This section includes four chapters that together provide a national context for social welfare policy. There are any number of points to recognize and ideas to reflect upon when examining policy. Scores of books have been written focusing on any one of these many topical areas, but these four chapters succinctly tie together key ideas necessary for understanding and developing proactive social policy.

Bruce Jansson, PhD, is well recognized for his work in policy practice and understanding of the social work profession's history, as well as for his critical analysis of federal budget priorities from the New Deal to the present. Jansson creates the historical backdrop required for critical analysis. Rather than providing a simple chronicle overview, he challenges social historians and policy practitioners "to reconceptualize the evolution of the American welfare state by moving in new directions" and concludes that the future will be as capricious, if not more so, than the past. His assessment of history is insightful and offers a look not at all found in the traditional social work text.

Michael Reisch, PhD, is a noted scholar, in particular regarding issues related to the poor. Using a variety of economic data, Reisch analyzes the effects of major demographic transformations on social policy, with particular emphasis on immigration and internal migration, and concludes with a detailed discussion of these trends and their potential impact on future social policy in the United States. In a sobering fashion, one of Reisch's significant conclusions is that so-called safety net programs are particularly vulnerable as the population ages and the "economic and demographic effects of globalization mount."

Stan Stojkovic, PhD, is a well-known scholar in the field of criminal justice. He takes the reader through an analysis of the U.S. Patriot Act, which was enacted in 2001, and its numerous implications for social workers and the broader community. In particular, Stojkovic discusses the Act's activities and how they run counter to traditional democratic values. He also proposes that a separate system of justice that is secret, not accountable to the American people, and counters social work values is now in place. A profession that seeks justice, including procedural justice, will find Stojkovic's analysis troubling.

Ira Colby, DSW, has long been involved in political social work. His chapter explores the role of social welfare policy as a tool of social, economic, and political justice. He believes that practice informs policy and that social workers have accumulated a wealth of practice wisdom and evidence that has the potential to radically reshape social welfare policy. He proposes that social workers adopt a critical thinking model in policy practice and advocacy.

Chapter 4

RECONCEPTUALIZING THE EVOLUTION OF THE AMERICAN WELFARE STATE

Bruce Jansson

The American welfare state has become a pivotal feature of American society. It consumed more than 80% of the federal budget in 2007. It includes thousands of pages of regulations that govern the implementation of its many programs and that protect the public safety from environmental, housing, drug-related, and other hazards. It employs tens of thousands of persons.

Yet analyzing the welfare state's history poses daunting challenges for scholars. This chapter provides a survey of its development and poses questions for further research in its concluding section. I suggest that historians and social policy theorists need to reconceptualize the evolution of the American welfare state by moving in new directions.

SOME DAUNTING CHALLENGES FACING HISTORIANS OF THE AMERICAN WELFARE STATE

Before it is even possible to analyze the evolution of the American welfare state, key conceptual issues must be addressed. I discuss six of these challenges.

Expanding the Welfare State's Parameters

A number of scholars have defined the welfare state in relatively narrow terms as consisting primarily of those programs that focus on traditional social work concerns, such as mental health, welfare, maternal health, and child welfare programs (Axinn & Levin, 1982; Leiby, 1978; Trattner, 1979). I call these "the traditional histories" in subsequent discussion, which I contrast with my own history of the American welfare state (Jansson, 1988, 2005).

This relatively narrow definition risks ignoring considerable portions of the welfare state if we define it as including a wide range of policies that are relevant to the social, psychological, and economic well-being of citizens. Not only do they span a wide range of substantive issues, but they include tax policies that shape the distribution of wealth in the United States, budget policies that determine what policies receive priority, policies geared to preventive as well as curative goals, policies of all levels of government, and policies that shape interactions between public and private sectors.

The welfare state's substantive programs include a wide range of programs that address social and economic problems and needs of citizens, such as *institutions* that house persons with specific kinds of social problems or criminal offenses, including persons with mental problems, children who are orphaned or who are deemed to have been neglected or abused, and prisoners; means-tested *safety-net programs* for the poor (food stamps, Medicaid, Supplementary Security Income, Section 8 housing vouchers and subsidies); *universal social programs* (Medicare, Social Security, and unemployment insurance); *regulations* (food, drug, housing protections; civil rights laws for persons of color, women, mentally ill persons, persons with disabilities, the elderly, lesbian/gay/bisexual/transgender persons, and others); *protections for persons in specific organizations* such as work safety conditions for workers, safety and medical care for persons in mental institutions, nursing homes, and convalescent homes, and safety and care for children in child care and in their homes; *opportunity-enhancing programs* such as operations of educational programs and student scholarships, job training programs, the junior college system, land distribution, and economic development programs; *social and medical services* such as mental health, social service, and medical services; *preventive services* such as public health, early detection, outreach, sex education, and preschool programs; *cultural and recreational programs* such as libraries, Internet-access programs, public entertainment through public television, and public national, state, and county parks; and *family supplementing programs* such as child care, foster care, and adoptions programs. They include *community-building programs* such as creation of specific development zones in which businesses receive tax concessions to locate. They include local *zoning and land use policies* that influence where homeless persons can live and where halfway homes can be located. They include *criminal law,* which determines, for example, what drugs are criminalized and the penalties their use and distribution will incur. They include *civil law,* which determines, for example, grounds for divorce and obligations of divorced persons to each other and to their children. They include a large body of legal rules by local, state, and federal courts that shape the procedures and regulations of the American welfare state.

The American welfare state requires resources to operate its many programs, so its funding sources must be considered part of the welfare state. These include *government spending* (authorizations and appropriations of federal, state, and local governments); *government tax expenditures* (organizations' and persons' tax deductions, exclusions, deferrals, or tax credits when filing tax forms with federal and state governments with respect to mortgage interest deductions, corporate funding of employees' health insurance, funds placed in pension accounts by citizens, and citizens' charitable contributions); *tax credits* (child care tax credits and the Earned Income Tax Credit); *payroll taxes,* principally for Social Security, Medicare, and unemployment insurance; *consumer payments* such as out-of-pocket costs by enrollees in Medicare and Medicaid; and *private philanthropy* that includes a network of foundations and private donors that gave resources to an array of health and welfare institutions in 2007.

Traditional histories of the American welfare state emphasize curative programs established to help persons suffering from family, mental, income, health, and other problems, placing less emphasis on preventive preschool, education, and public health programs. In some eras, such as the nineteenth century, Americans pioneered land distribution and public education initiatives that were intended to promote opportunities for a wide range of citizens. Histories should not only chronicle these programs, but ask why they have failed to promote greater equality during specific eras—and why they were more effective in other eras, such as during the 4 decades after 1930 when social and economic inequality decreased compared to prior and subsequent periods.

Traditional histories focused on relationships of the welfare state with a relatively small number of vulnerable populations, such as women, persons of color, or welfare recipients. Yet many vulnerable populations have emerged during the American historical experience—and each of them is inextricably linked to the regulations and programs of the American welfare state. I have proposed five (often overlapping) groups that include at least 14 vulnerable populations: *economic vulnerable populations* (such as poor persons); *racial vulnerable populations* (such as African Americans, Latinos, Asian Americans, and Native Americans); *sociological vulnerable populations* placed in restrictive roles (such as women and the elderly); *nonconformist populations,* widely viewed as violating social norms (such as persons on welfare, gay men and lesbians, persons who have been incarcerated, mentally ill persons, and persons with physical disabilities); and *model vulnerable populations* (such as Jewish Americans and members of some White ethnic groups; Jansson, 2005.) To these groups might be added *immigrants* in specific eras, since members of different waves of immigrants have experienced—and continue to confront—profound prejudice, such as Irish Americans in the nineteenth century, Eastern Europeans and Italians from the Civil War to 1920, and Latinos in the contemporary period.

When discussing vulnerable populations, however, it is important not to ignore social class. Members of different waves of immigration, for example, were not only members of specific ethnic or racial groups, but often were relatively poor. European historians place far more emphasis on social class than do American historians and social scientists, who should devote more attention to disentangling the separate and combined influence of race and class in creating and sustaining such social problems as poverty, poor health, and mental illness (Kawachi, Daniels, & Robinson, 2005).

The American welfare state is possibly the most complex one in the world. Unlike those that are primarily funded directly by a central government, the American welfare state is shaped by the intersection of different levels of government and funding streams, courts, and not-for-profit, for-profit, and public entities. If we examine contemporary health policy in any major city, all of these factors determine the kinds and quality of medical services that low-income persons receive.

These complex jurisdictional arrangements are products of the unique way the American welfare state evolved from local to state to federal governments from the colonial era to the present. If the local and state agencies and programs *were* the American welfare state up to 1932 for all intents, the federal government *then* strengthened its role over the succeeding decades while often requiring states and localities to contribute fiscally and administratively to federal programs. The role of states became somewhat strengthened in the 1980s when many programs were devolved to them from the federal government during the presidency of Ronald Reagan.

Complex relationships exist as well among public, not-for-profit, and for-profit sectors. If not-for-profit agencies assumed major roles prior to the New Deal, they were relegated to lesser roles with the emergence of major government social spending during the New Deal and subsequently—but still remained an important feature of the welfare state through extensive contracts and grants from government agencies. Hardly existing before the New Deal, for-profit agencies grew rapidly in the 6 decades following the New Deal in medical, nursing home, child care, and other areas, often receiving considerable reimbursements and contracts from public agencies.

Courts have assumed a far larger role in shaping the American welfare state than in many other nations. The U.S. Constitution, with its various amendments and its Bill of Rights, is the source of many rulings concerning privacy, confidentiality, due process, relationships of federal and state governments, and fairness in the welfare state's myriad programs and regulations. Litigation is endemic to the American welfare state's evolution, both in historical eras and in the present.

Traditional histories of the American welfare state focused on the development of official programs and regulations. Yet many social needs have been met in American history not by public authorities but by an array of welfare state surrogates such as political machines in big eastern and midwestern cities (which provided jobs and welfare), private philanthropy, self-help groups, and faith-based initiatives such as the social welfare activities of Catholic and Protestant churches (Walch, 1993). Families themselves assumed major welfare functions, such as the extensive hiring of relatives and development of business enterprises by Jewish and Asian immigrant families.

It is important to understand the nature and extent of these welfare state surrogates because they often acted *as* a welfare state in the colonial era, in the nineteenth century when the United States hardly possessed an official welfare state, and, indeed, in the present. Even today, most persons with mental health problems, for example, use informal sources of care or simply do without care from any source (Davis, 2007).

The American welfare state interacted in complex ways with these nonpublic initiatives. In the early part of the nineteenth century, religious services were often mandated for inmates of poorhouses, mental asylums, and prisons. Sometimes public authorities funded not-for-profit subsidiaries of churches that refrained from proselytizing as they freely used public resources for their charity. More recently, the fundamentalist president George W. Bush has subsidized faith-based charities directly with (apparently) only vague requirements that they not proselytize—initiatives currently under review by the U.S. Supreme Court to see if they violate the constitutional separation of church and state.

Historians of the American welfare state need to be more attuned to the actual resources that were devoted to it. Some, such as Skocpol (1995), when discussing pensions for Civil War veterans and mothers' pensions in the progressive era, suggest that these were major policy initiatives when, in fact, they were supported by negligible resources. Even New Deal and Great Society initiatives were often backed by surprisingly small resources—with substantial allocations (aside from tax expenditures) only emerging in the 1970s (Jansson, 2001).

I contend that historians of the American welfare state's evolution need to markedly broaden its parameters. Indeed, we need multiple histories that focus on the evolution of various components of the American welfare state as well as histories that integrate these components into a unified analysis.

Placing the Welfare State in Its Full Context

If traditional histories risk unduly narrow parameters on the substantive content of the American welfare state, they tend as well not to analyze a range of contextual factors that have shaped its evolution. They correctly analyze such cultural factors as American punitive orientations toward poor persons and racism and the inheritance of poor-law traditions from Europe by early settlers, but place less emphasis on the role of the two major parties in supporting or opposing welfare reforms, the critical role of presidents, the role of military spending in constricting the domestic discretionary budget, special interests such as health insurance and drug companies, demographic factors, and immigration. The temperance, abolitionist, Know-Nothing, tenant farmer, and fundamentalist movements receive relatively little attention.

Nor did traditional histories aim to place the American welfare state in a comparative context. Why did it grow more slowly than European states in the wake of World War II, when Americans became relatively conservative even as Europeans were greatly increasing domestic spending? In what specific ways is the American welfare state unique?

The rapid globalizing of the world in recent decades, reflected in escalating movements of populations and capital across international boundaries, provides another reason for viewing the American welfare state in a global perspective. From the colonial period onward, Americans depended on immigration to provide them with a labor force sufficient to move the frontier westward and then to provide workers for its emerging industry in the wake of the Civil War. The nation's dependence on foreign capital in the nineteenth century was similar to the contemporary dependence of developing nations on capital inflows—and exacerbated economic volatility in the United States, with important repercussions for social policy. The depression of 1893, like many deep recessions that preceded it, provided the backdrop for the progressives' reform movement at the start of the twentieth century and was partly linked to the nation's primitive banking system and its reliance on other nations for capital.

Many major social problems in the United States are linked to globalization, such as losses in jobs, migration of populations into the United States from developing nations, and movement of cocaine and other drugs across national boundaries. If international treaties do not require American corporations that purchase or manufacture goods abroad to meet minimum wage and work safety conditions, companies will be tempted to place even more jobs abroad—and to continue to use the threat of movement of their operations abroad to force American workers to accept lower wages.

New histories of the American welfare need to devote more space to analyzing American social welfare initiatives abroad. How did the United States interact with the United Nations? How much foreign aid was funded in different eras, and how was it used? Why was the United States so tardy in committing resources to the global AIDS epidemic, even though the Central Intelligence Agency once called it the most serious threat to the national security of the United States? How did the United States gain control of the World Bank and the International Monetary Fund—and often use them to make developing nations cut domestic spending even when this policy undermined nations' efforts to address their social and economic problems (Stiglitz, 2002)?

Rethinking Which Time Periods to Prioritize

Historians also face the challenge of segmenting the welfare state's history into useful chronological segments. Traditional histories have used such periods as the colonial period, the civil war era, the progressive era, the New Deal, and the Great Society.

Selection of a relatively small number of eras risks ignoring key events, however. I supplemented them with periods of conflicting policy tendencies, such as when Democratic presidents confronted Republican congresses or when President Richard Nixon confronted a Democratic Congress, in such periods as 1945 to 1952, 1961 to 1963, 1969 to 1980, and 1992 to 2000. I also added conservative periods when relatively few social policies were adopted by the federal government and when some substantial policy pullbacks took place, such as 1868 to 1900 (the Gilded Age), 1920 to 1932 (with its three conservative presidents), 1941 to 1944 (when congressional conservatives ended the New Deal work programs), 1952 to 1960 (when President Dwight Eisenhower failed to propose new social programs, though he approved substantial augmentation of Social Security), 1980 to 1992 (when Presidents Ronald Reagan and George H. W. Bush cut back or rescinded social policies), and 2000 to 2008 (when President George W. Bush mostly focused on counterterrorism and the war with Iraq after the destruction of the World Trade Center as well as attacks on the Pentagon and a foiled attack on another target probably in the nation's capitol on September 11, 2001; Jansson, 2005).

My choice of these segments has merit for a chronological analysis of the evolution of the American welfare state, but a case can be made instead to identify key historical periods when important choices were made that shaped the nature of the American welfare state, including its formation, its relationship with important developments in the broader society (such as the frontier, the Civil War, the early period of industrialization, and urbanization), its development during societal crises such as depressions and wars, its relations with such nongovernmental entities such as corporations and religious institutions, and its relationships with state and local governments. Moreover, eras could be selected when the American welfare state made a strong push forward with respect to regulations, services, and programs that provided "hard" benefits of cash and food. They could also be selected because important issues or concepts emerged during them even if they were not fully realized, such as when President George W. Bush sought to privatize substantial portions of Medicare, Medicaid, and Social Security by using tax concessions to induce citizens to create private savings accounts to be used for pensions and health care.

These criteria suggest that eight segments were particularly critical to the construction of the American welfare state: the early formative period in the colonial era; the era of localism, morality, and frontier opportunity in the early and middle portions of the nineteenth century; the confluence of massive social problems and a primitive welfare state during and after the Civil War; the progressive era, when regulations first appeared; the New Deal and its immediate aftermath, when public policy developed nonmarket alternatives; the Great Society, when federal social services were greatly augmented; the 1970s, when funding priorities of the American welfare state markedly changed; and the 1980s through 2008 when Presidents Ronald Reagan and George W. Bush sought to retrench, devolve, and privatize the American welfare state. By contrast, policy developments from 1877 to 1900 and during the presidencies of Harry Truman, Dwight Eisenhower, George H. W. Bush, and Bill Clinton appear less important to the basic nature of the American welfare state, even if some important policies emerged during them.

EIGHT ERAS

I draw on the preceding discussion to suggest some ways that our understanding of developments in each of the eight eras might be advanced through new scholarship.

The Emergence of a Primitive Welfare State in the Colonial Period

A comparative perspective already illuminates discussion of the colonial period in traditional histories, particularly with respect to the importing of the Elizabethan Poor Laws to the colonies. Yet early European settlers to the colonies, principally from England and Germany, were more European than American in the period preceding the American Revolution (Wood, 1992), bringing to the colonies not just the Elizabethan Poor Laws, but many ideas drawn from societies that were evolving from feudal to capitalist nations and from state religions toward greater tolerance.

European immigrants who came to the colonies in the seventeenth and eighteenth centuries were imbued with conflicting tendencies because they experienced this period of transition in Europe (Jansson, 2005). They came from societies with a hierarchy of social statuses, social elitism, tolerance of the poor, deference, and localism that was characteristic of medieval society. Early colonial settlers were used to European societies in which virtually everything was tightly regulated, including the establishment of businesses in local towns, labor policies, and the location and expansion of towns. The policy known as mercantilism gave national authorities the right to support specific kinds of industries and to build infrastructure to facilitate economic growth. Local and state authorities could even regulate the price of bread—the commodity central to the diet of peasants. Even the ability of persons to migrate internally within societies was strictly regulated by laws of settlement.

Yet immigrants also came from societies where medieval policies and social arrangements that had prevailed in Europe for centuries were under sharp attack from intellectuals and business interests, not to mention peasants dispossessed from the land into urban areas.

If intellectuals espoused free markets, democratic systems of government, and deregulation, business interests attacked the taxes and regulations that were placed on them by central authorities—and both intellectuals and business interests often sought greater power for Parliament (in England) than for the monarchy.

Social policies in Europe were themselves embroiled in increasing controversy. Poor law institutions had a two-sided character. Sometimes they were implemented punitively, such as treating impoverished vagabonds harshly. Yet some poorhouses, possibly building on medieval notions that churches were places of nonjudgmental refuge that helped poor persons and vagabonds, were remarkably supportive of persons in need, even giving out clothing and food to broad numbers of persons (Snell, 1985).

The early settlers thus came to the American colonies with a curious mélange of concepts and practices. On the one hand, they had ideas akin to those passed down to them from feudal society; John Adams even wanted the American president to be called a monarch, and many of them did not want to rebel against England. Many viewed the governance of colonies by governors appointed by English monarchs as acceptable, as well as the many regulations established by these governors. On the other hand, many settlers were often deeply critical of medieval society and, in fact, wanted to create a utopian alternative based on widespread ownership of land, relatively free markets, toleration of religious sects, and relatively limited government, as the writings of Thomas Jefferson strongly suggest. As they neared the American Revolution in 1776, criticism of the Crown became more strident (Wood, 1992).

It is not surprising, then, that American social policy in the colonial period is not easy to characterize, unlike social policy in the nineteenth century, when relatively harsh views toward the poor and vagabonds emerged. The attention of the settlers was not, in any event, focused on social policy for poor persons, but on their grand experiment to construct a society in which preventive social policies would be paramount. As expressed by Jefferson and others, the colonists wanted to create a society dominated by small landowners in a rural society (Peterson, 1975). Colonial authorities and the land companies licensed by the Crown would sell vast tracts of land to these settlers, who would disperse onto this land, often in unsettled (save for Native Americans) areas.

If we broaden our definition of the welfare state to include such preventive programs, the heart of the colonial welfare state was not its small collection of poorhouses and prisons, but its land distribution policies and the involvement of many of its settlers in a market economy. Even indentured servants—a huge portion of the colonial population—intended to use their accumulated savings to purchase land, even if they continued a specific trade in rural towns.

The American Revolution reinforced the notion that Americans were creating a new kind of social order that would differ from the social strata and growing cities of European nations. Virtually everyone hoped to be an entrepreneur on small tracts of land, often coupling agriculture with small enterprises, such as making hats. If some Europeans still had reservations about the emerging capitalist order, Americans came mostly to assume that capitalism, entrepreneurship, and (land) speculation would lie at the heart of their society. Social classes would still exist, but most citizens (it was hoped) would live on the land in relative prosperity.

Considerable research suggests that the actual life of many settlers sharply diverged from this bucolic view (Nash, 1976). Many persons did *not* own land, including indentured servants, persons in growing towns, and laborers. Slaves and Native Americans hardly shared in Jefferson's utopia. Indeed, an American penchant for denial may itself have been a key facet of the emerging American culture that would forestall important social legislation in coming centuries.

Economic and geographic realities in the colonies also precluded the development of social programs. Aside from some large landowners, the bulk of the population was nearly destitute, whether on the frontier or in towns, and was in no position to pay considerable taxes (Sachs, 2005). The Crown confiscated much of their meager tax revenues before the Revolution. Having fought the American Revolution to evade taxation without representation, Americans showed an aversion to taxes in general from the outset of their republic. Desperate for resources to retire debt, to wage war against Native Americans, and to construct some public improvements, Washington and the Congress levied a tax on whiskey only to encounter a rebellion that Washington had to *personally* quell by leading federal troops into Pennsylvania (Smith, 1993).

Nor did federal and state governments possess the capability of developing substantial social programs. The Constitution gave the federal government specific enumerated powers that mostly related to establishing a currency, retaining a militia, conducting foreign policy, and regulating interstate commerce, but was mute on social welfare issues. (Several vague clauses, such as one that gave the federal government the power to advance "the general welfare" and a clause giving it the power to regulate interstate commerce, would later provide a foundation for social welfare functions, but mostly not until the progressive era and the 1930s.) Even as late as 1937, however, President Franklin Roosevelt feared the Supreme Court would nullify much of his New Deal on grounds that it lacked a constitutional basis. So paranoid were many citizens about *even* the limited constitutional power of the federal government that they insisted that a Bill of Rights be added to the Constitution to limit the power of the central government in 1791.

The disinclination to vest the federal government with significant power in domestic affairs was further accentuated by the growing chasm between Federalists like Washington, John Adams, and Alexander Hamilton on the one hand and the anti-Federalist Jefferson and his allies on the other hand (Smith, 1993). Jefferson and his allies won a landslide victory over Adams in 1800 that legitimized a weak central government equipped only to act on its narrow enumerated powers. The die was set for the next 132 years, during which the federal government would have a negligible role in social welfare policy, save for a brief period during and after the Civil War and for veterans and save for land distribution policies on the frontier. This striking eradication of governmental roles was in marked contrast to European societies, where central governments retained significant policy roles into the nineteenth century even if large welfare states did not emerge until just after World War II.

Even with only a relatively poor and small population, the emerging nation had powerful special interests in the colonial period. Huge cotton-selling firms in New York City had a vested interest in preserving slavery, which provided it with the material to send to England. Large landowners existed in many states, often exploiting their labor. Construction firms eagerly vied for contracts to build highways and canals in the developing nation.

Often lacking resources to purchase sufficient food and other goods, urban low-income populations sometimes rioted. Riots occurred in rural areas, too, as persons battled over the title to specific lands.

Nor were colonial leaders even remotely prepared to deal with egregious violations of human rights that were rampant with respect to slaves and Native Americans, not to mention women. Such rights as the freedom of speech and religion in the Bill of Rights, as well as the right to vote, were widely viewed as applicable only to White male citizens, not slaves, Native Americans, or women. The Constitution institutionalized slavery by mentioning it, directly or indirectly, more than 13 times, even declaring slaves to count as only three fifths of a person when computing how many representatives slave-holding states should have. Not wanting slave states to become a majority in the Congress, northern framers of the Constitution were able to forbid its extension into the still unsettled northwest territories, but no serious effort was made to forbid slavery itself—even if Congress finally ended the slave trade in 1808.

No longer protected by the Proclamation Line of 1763 that the British had established to place boundaries on White settlers' intrusion into their lands, Native Americans encountered an endless stream of settlers in succeeding decades who laid claim to their lands, receiving only delaying assistance from treaties with the federal government that "guaranteed" them land on the frontier—land often taken from them when yet another wave of settlers and treaties pushed them further westward.

Segregated not physically but in terms of their role in society, women were mostly expected to be mothers who would not intrude on male prerogatives in the professions, business, or government. Often rendered destitute because they could not even inherit property, women were relegated to a second-class status until well into the twentieth century.

It can be argued, then, that traditional histories, with their focus on Elizabethan Poor Laws, place too little emphasis on the many social welfare policies of the colonial period, including constitutional provisions, land distribution, slavery, confiscation of Native Americans' land, aversion to taxes, dislike of central government, and the conflict between Federalists and anti-Federalists led by Jefferson. The new nation was overwhelmingly rural, with few fiscal resources and with only primitive social welfare institutions, such as a few poorhouses and prisons. Unlike in European societies, Americans mostly did away with the policy functions of central governments as the views of Jefferson supplanted those of the Federalists—leaving the United States with a capitalist economy supplemented by only primitive roles for government.

Christian Morality and Frontier Opportunity, 1800 to 1860

Welfare and child welfare policies—the centerpieces of traditional histories—were also surpassed in size by land distribution policies and were part of a larger quest to impose Christian morality on the American public. With additional resources needed to construct the policies and with a hardening view toward destitute persons, the nation built many poorhouses in the early republic as it placed a negative construction on unemployed persons whom policy makers increasingly associated with the Irish and other immigrants in a pattern that would become even more marked in the later decades of the nineteenth century. In this era of institutions, many states also constructed mental institutions, sometimes at the behest of Dorothea Dix's monumental crusade to rescue the mentally ill from poorhouses.

The poorhouses and other institutions can also be viewed as part of a larger moral crusade to rescue the emerging, and very Christian, nation from sin. Indeed, as the work of Boyer (1978) suggests, Christian revivalism and morality pervaded the early republic. If Jefferson had idealized the emerging society as a society of small landowners who would lead upstanding lives, an array of persons added religion to this utopian concept. They would purge the nation of such sins as laziness, criminality, vagrancy, truancy, disobedience to parents, poor school performance, alcoholism, and (even) mental illness. Such moralists viewed virtually *every* social problem as a manifestation of immorality that could be prevented or arrested only by conversion to Christianity and the inculcation of good habits.

No better way could be found to inculcate morality—and even Christian morality—into persons with presumed social problems than institutions, where every second of their waking hours could be regulated. It was common in poorhouses and mental institutions of this era to begin and end the day with religious services—with hard work and discipline enforced for the remaining portions.

The endemic morality of this era found expression, too, in an array of community settings that often had a preventive focus. The Sunday school movement was a huge crusade to reach poor children in which thousands of middle-class volunteer teachers provided highly structured religious and moral instruction to as many as 400,000 low-income urban children by 1835 (Boyer, 1978). Convinced that "the very first drink is a long step toward Hell," temperance crusaders sought to restrict licenses to taverns, limit retail sales of alcohol, imprison sellers and users of alcohol, and persuade legislators in various states to declare alcohol an illegal substance. They successfully persuaded 13 states by the 1850s to prohibit the sale of alcohol (Tyrell, 1979).

Another interesting variation in applied morality took place when Charles Brace, who founded the private Children's Aid Society of New York, sought to rescue a growing population of street children (Mennel, 1973). Convinced that institutions deprived them of their innate creativity, he and his associates shipped more than 90,000 children to frontier families from 1853 to 1895, where he hoped they would learn the virtues of hard work. No less than other reformers, he sought to imbue these street children with virtues such as industriousness and personal discipline, only on the frontier rather than in institutions.

The linking of social problems with lack of morality was fraught with peril because many persons, then and now, develop myriad social problems not because they are amoral, but due to environmental, economic, physiological, sociological, developmental, familial, and other factors. When they are stigmatized with "bad character," they are probably less likely to surmount these problems than if given positive and, where possible, evidence-based assistance—or where empowerment strategies are used. The connection with *Christianity* also posed problems that would resurface in the contemporary period when efforts by the administration of George W. Bush to give resources to faith-based agencies and churches were challenged in the courts.

Even as America was waging a moral crusade against various perceived moral problems, it was also greatly expanding the social experiment it had begun in the colonial era: giving massive numbers of people opportunities to gain upward mobility. The nation expanded its relatively open-door policy to immigrants, mostly from Europe and Russia, by admitting millions of persons and made it relatively easy for them to obtain citizenship. It opened millions of acres of frontier lands for purchase at federal land auctions. It provided federal military protection to settlers from attacks by Native Americans. It tolerated the illegal squatting by many settlers on vacant but unpurchased land—and then enacted legislation on numerous occasions to allow many of them to purchase it (Rohrbough, 1968).

The United States launched yet another experiment when it implemented Jefferson's dream of universal free public education from the first through the eighth grade (before the Civil War) and then through high school (after the Civil War)—unprecedented policies in world history, with access to education still restricted to elites in most nations. White males were given the right to vote, including many immigrants from Europe.

The magnitude of these social experiments of massive immigration, relatively easy access to citizenship for Caucasian persons, distribution of vast lands on the frontier, access to public education, and the right (for White males) to vote were unprecedented in world history (Jansson, 2005). Many indigenous American citizens joined the westward movement, often selling their land to obtain funds to purchase land further west. These social experiments—arguably the heart of the American welfare state at that time—took place in a mostly agricultural society, even though small towns and cities grew in number.

The universal acceptance of capitalism as the way to organize the nation's economy, which had already emerged in the colonial period, was unique in world history, as bartering and semifeudal relationships still existed in much of the world. Americans had already subscribed to the notion of a (capitalist) footrace in which citizens, given land, education, and the vote, would create their own opportunities.

Much was wrong in this seeming paradise—and the society lacked the resources, institutions, or the will to do much about it (Sellers, 1991). Extreme poverty often existed on the frontier as settlers scrambled to survive winters and struggled to grow crops. Agricultural markets experienced booms and busts. Speculators often got special deals from federal land officers, allowing them to purchase huge holdings. Railroads were given extravagant amounts of free or cheap land in return for construction of lines heading west. Frontier life was often violent. A significant population of vagabonds emerged in the early republic who lacked land or other possessions. As parents headed west or succumbed to the epidemics that swept cities due to lack of sanitation and food inspections, large numbers of children fended for themselves on the streets—the harbinger of the homeless problem in later periods of American history (Halloran, 1989).

The human tragedies experienced by slaves and Native Americans in the colonial period vastly increased in the early republic. Far from remaining in the original southern states, plantation owners moved vast numbers of slaves westward to Mississippi, Louisiana, and Texas and aspired to new territories in areas that became the states of Missouri, Kansas, and Nebraska. Native Americans were removed from their lands on a massive scale and succumbed to diseases brought to them by settlers.

Nor did women's lot appreciably improve, despite the remarkable and prescient ideas and actions of such feminists as Susan B. Anthony and Elizabeth Cady Stanton. Unmarried women could work, but mostly as housekeepers or nannies. Married women remained constricted by the doctrine of "separate spheres" that relegated them to household chores and child rearing, leaving positions in business, agriculture, and the professions to White males (Harris, 1978).

Governments at local, state, and federal levels remained primitive by contemporary standards. Lacking a civil service, they were often corrupt. They lacked resources to tackle social problems, even had they wished to address them. Remarkably, Dorothea Dix convinced Congress to enact legislation to use some federal proceeds from federal land sales to help subsidize mental hospitals in various states—only to suffer a stinging veto from President Franklin Pierce in 1854, who declared:

> I cannot find any authority in the Constitution for making the federal government the great almoner of public charity throughout the United States. . . . Can it be controverted that the great mass of the business of government—that involved in the social relations . . . the mental and moral culture of men . . . the relief of the needy or otherwise unfortunate members of society—did not in practice remain with the States? (Axinn & Levin, 1982)

The Confluence of Massive Social and Economic Problems in the South, Southwest, and West with a Primitive Welfare State during and after the Civil War

When the framers legitimated slavery in the Constitution, they unwittingly set the stage for a civil war. Unable to ban slavery because they would have needed a two-thirds majority in Congress to amend the Constitution, northerners tolerated it—until southerners tried to create new slave-owning states in areas that became Nebraska and Kansas (Appleby, 1992). When Abraham Lincoln was elected president in 1860 on the platform of *not* allowing new states that allowed slavery, southerners feared that he might actually seek an end to slavery and bolted the Union by attacking a northern fort in South Carolina.

The resulting Civil War and its aftermath posed fundamental social welfare issues that the nation was ill-prepared to answer. If slavery was abolished, what would happen to the freed slaves in terms of their economic survival, not to mention other social and civil rights? How would the rights of African Americans be protected in the South? How would northerners prevent the reemergence of a White power structure in the South dedicated to oppressing African Americans?

Only the federal government possessed the resources, legal authority, and policing power to protect the freed slaves from southern Whites—and only the federal government could generate resources needed to educate and teach job skills to a slave population that had been systematically deprived of education and resources.

The president and Congress finally eradicated slavery with passage of the 13th Amendment to the Constitution in 1865. As important, the North occupied the South with a huge contingent of troops that clamped down on egregious acts of violence against African Americans. Empowered by the Military Reconstruction Act of 1867 to serve as the protector of civil rights, northern military forces allowed aggrieved African Americans to obtain redress from their former owners. It seemed, too, that the Freedman's Bureau, created in 1865 and lodged in the War Department, would be a vehicle for addressing some social and economic needs of the freed slaves. The legislation creating the Bureau even promised 40 acres of abandoned or confiscated land to every male refugee, and it was charged with providing education and welfare to freed slaves.

Events after the war soon proved, however, that the primitive welfare state of the nation, consisting mostly of scattered poorhouses and related institutions as well as a liberal land and immigration policy for Caucasian Europeans, was totally inadequate to the task of assisting freed slaves. In deep debt after the war, the federal government lacked needed resources. It also lacked the will to develop needed programs to help the freed slaves when Lincoln was succeeded by President Andrew Johnson, an unabashed southerner who tried to dissolve the Freedman's Bureau and who pardoned vast numbers of Confederate officials so that they could seek election to public office in southern states—even appointing many of them to the Freedman's Bureau.

Johnson's policies encouraged southern Whites to enact "Black Codes" in some jurisdictions that limited African Americans' right to free assembly and speech, even subjecting them to whipping for discourteous behavior.

When Johnson was replaced by General Ulysses Grant in 1866 in repudiation of Johnson's pro-South positions, the federal government became far more sympathetic to the rights of freed slaves. It enacted the 14th Amendment in 1868 which rescinded the constitutional provision that African Americans counted as only three fifths of a person, required that all citizens be given "equal protection" under the law, and stipulated that all people be accorded the protection of due process. The 15th Amendment in 1870 established universal suffrage of all adult males, and Civil Rights Acts enacted in 1870 and 1875 limited the ability of states to enforce discriminatory legislation and outlawed segregation in public facilities and schools. Congress even declared the infringement of the civil rights of people to be a federal offense in the Ku Klux Klan Act of 1872.

These laws protecting the civil rights of African Americans would prove ineffective, however, if they were not enforced either by the armed occupation of the South or by federal courts. Seething at their loss of power and often imbued with racism, many southern Whites had resorted to guerrilla warfare against African American leaders immediately after the Civil War and continued to fight even after the onslaught of federal legislation that protected the rights of freed slaves.

Ominously, the termination of the Freedman's Bureau in 1872 demonstrated that Congress and President Grant did not truly understand that the nation needed to supplement civil rights with programs that would address the social and economic needs of freed slaves. How could a mostly illiterate population with no resources, land, or equipment survive in the South without massive assistance? Indeed, an estimated one fourth of freed slaves died in the aftermath of the war from starvation, disease, or exposure.

In perhaps the most important event after the Civil War, northern Democrats who represented the interests of the White southern elite exacted a promise from northern Republicans to withdraw northern troops from the South in exchange for supporting Republican Rutherford Hayes when the vote in the Electoral College became stalemated. Without northern troops to protect them and lacking the weapons, resources, and organization of White southerners, African Americans were soon ousted from public offices and denied suffrage through the imposition of literacy tests and poll taxes. They were further intimidated by widespread public lynching. Southern legislatures soon enacted Jim Crow laws that undid protections of the civil rights legislation enacted after the Civil War. In a final insult, the Supreme Court chose not to heed the Civil Rights Acts of 1870 and 1875 in *Plessy v. Ferguson* (1896) when it ruled that an African American male could be required to sit in a separate railroad car, removed from the presence of Caucasians—setting the stage for the imposition of segregation in virtually every aspect of southern society, including public schools. In its ruling, moreover, the Court specified that civil rights could be enforced *only* with respect to the discriminatory acts of individuals rather than those of state and local governments, which legitimated the Jim Crow laws.

An array of factors worked in tandem to bring about these tragic results. Having never exercised *federal* power on a large scale prior to the Civil War, it is remarkable that a northern-dominated Congress was even able to enact sweeping civil rights legislation, or that it even approved and funded a military occupation of the South for 12 years after the war, or that it even created the Freedman's Bureau.

Lacking traditions to support and sustain large social programs, Americans were also imbued with views of the former slaves that discouraged positive assistance to them. Northerners often viewed African Americans' plight as resulting from their lack of morality, believing that slavery had made them a lazy and promiscuous people who would fare poorly in a freed condition *unless* they received moral education (Friedman, 1982). Indeed, the schools of the Freedman's Bureau focused on such education, much like the Sunday school movement of the antebellum period. If they mostly needed moral education, why give them practical skills, credit, land, equipment, horses, and housing needed to survive in rural regions? Possessing considerable racism, northerners did not support helping large numbers of freed slaves to move to northern cities to compete for the many jobs in the emerging industrial order. Nor did they confiscate sufficient lands of former slave owners to help former slaves, but allowed speculators and northerners to purchase most of the confiscated land rather than giving it to freed slaves. Nor did northerners even think to place large numbers of freed slaves on remaining federal lands on the frontier—partly because they coveted this land for themselves.

In similar fashion, the nation would prove unable to address the needs of large numbers of Spanish-speaking persons in the southwestern and western lands secured by the U.S. conquest of Mexico in 1848. While the United States agreed in the Treaty of Guadalupe Hidalgo to honor the civil rights of these persons, western settlers forced them from their land by intimidation and physical force, as well as through the courts, and kept them from voting. Latinos became low-paid workers for mining, ranching, and farming interests (McWilliams, 1968).

The Civil War and the conquest of Mexico created social, economic, and human rights problems that the nation lacked the ability to understand or to address. Rather than helping freed slaves and conquered peoples in the American Southwest and West, courts often undermined their rights. The nation desperately needed the social programs and regulations of an advanced welfare state to cope with these huge social and economic problems, but could only develop temporary and rudimentary remedies in the South and virtually none whatsoever in the Southwest and West.

The Regulatory Response of Progressives to Urban Problems

If the nation lacked the capability to address the major social problems of the South, Southwest, and West, it proved ill-prepared as well to deal with the problems of an urbanizing and industrializing society that evolved in the 4 decades following the Civil War. It primarily chose to address these problems through regulations rather than substantial social programs, but such regulations were, nonetheless, a major step toward the assertion of governmental powers to address social needs.

Traditional histories of the American welfare state place too much emphasis on the very small social programs created during the progressive era, such as mothers' pensions. In fact, by 1919 only 46,000 women were helped by the pensions (Gordon, 1994). Traditional histories fail to emphasize sufficiently the true innovation of the progressive era: the enactment of many regulations, particularly in local and state jurisdictions.

Facilitated by cheap labor from millions of immigrants as well as considerable foreign capital, the United States urbanized and industrialized in the wake of the Civil War at rates unprecedented in world history. Industrialists had virtually a monopoly on power. Unions hardly existed. Constrained by few regulations, industrialists subjected their workers to dangerous working conditions and meager wages. To forestall efforts by the government to control them and to obtain contracts to build the infrastructure of American cities, they bribed lawmakers at all levels of government. With virtually no social or economic programs other than an array of social welfare institutions and an emerging network of hospitals, the nation had virtually no strategy for addressing the victimization and problems of the industrial workforce that it had largely imported from abroad.

It is understandable that Americans instinctively resorted to *regulations* rather than social policies to address these social problems. Once enacted, they required few resources to implement at a time when the federal government devoted only 5.5% of its GDP to public spending, compared with 25.5% for France (Jansson, 2005). "Setting rules" was congruent with the moral culture of the United States, which often equated social ills with wrongdoing by landlords, industrialists, politicians, purveyors of spoiled food, and others—wrongdoing that could be curtailed if rules were established that prohibited specific actions, such as subjecting workers to fire hazards or selling contaminated food. The regulations also reflected actual experiences of most Americans with dangers imposed on them by the harmful actions of an array of powerful persons (Thelen, 1975).

In the so-called progressive era that extended roughly from 1900 to the American entry into World War I in 1917, Americans enacted a host of regulations at local, state, and federal levels. We take for granted regulations that place requirements on industry, landlords, employers, and institutions, such as safe working conditions, safe housing conditions, a minimum wage, and achievement standards for schools. We know that tens of thousands of pages of administrative regulations exist for federal and state programs. Civil rights protections exist for many vulnerable populations in federal and state jurisdictions. Many public service programs must have grievance procedures for those clients who believe they were treated unfairly. Companies must allow employees to decide by secret ballot if they wish to unionize. Large health systems must give advance notice of their intention to downsize operations or specific facilities and hold public hearings before acting.

Yet virtually no regulations existed in the United States in 1900—with dire consequences. Food was often tainted; housing was dilapidated and in danger of burning; workers were exposed to workplace dangers; women were involuntarily placed into prostitution; professions were unlicensed; workers were required to work 12 or more hours per day; and children were placed in employment. The civil rights of persons from many vulnerable populations were flagrantly violated. Persons who were injured at their place of employment often received no restitution.

The need for regulations was greater than during the pre–Civil War period because Americans no longer mostly lived on farms or in small towns due to the rapid industrialization of the United States between 1865 and 1900. Many of the 10 million immigrants who came to the United States between 1865 and 1890—and another 18 million who followed them in the next 30 years—worked in industrial settings. Their hours of work were unregulated, as was their pay. So unsafe were their machines that 35,000 workers died per year and 536,000 were injured per year in the progressive era (Weinstein, 1975). Now living in congested areas, citizens were more vulnerable to epidemics that were caused by lack of sanitation, such as cholera. Speculators built vast housing tracts that were unregulated by fire codes or other standards. Absent drug safety regulations, many persons died or were harmed by drugs.

The progressive movement was the first urban reform movement in the United States. Its leaders often were relatively affluent Caucasian persons during a period of relative prosperity. As exemplified by Theodore Roosevelt and Jane Addams, they were outraged by the political power and arrogance of so-called robber barons who had created huge industries and monopolies in the Gilded Age—only to often use their extraordinary resources to subjugate workers and to bribe politicians to give them lucrative concessions and to forestall regulations on their enterprises. While sometimes harboring prejudice toward immigrants, progressives were often disgusted by their sheer poverty, poor living conditions, and victimization by employers.

Progressives, too, were often motivated by Christian morality. They were inflamed by spectacular accounts by muckraking journalists of the greed of industrialists. Locked out of the professions and employment when married, many women found social reform a fulfilling activity.

Progressives came from both Democratic and Republican parties. Republican President Theodore Roosevelt, who took office in 1902 with the assassination of President William McKinley, courageously took on the corporate tycoons in his first term by siding with workers in some strikes and demanding dissolution of some monopolies. Reform continued when he was elected president in 1904; slowed when William Taft, a conservative Republican, was elected president in 1908; and resumed with the election of Democrat Woodrow Wilson in 1912 over Roosevelt, who ran that year as the nominee of the Progressive Party, a third party established in 1912 because Taft defeated Roosevelt in their competition to become the Republican presidential nominee.

While they focused on regulations, progressives also obtained some notable reforms that became precedents for subsequent reforms in the New Deal. They got many states to enact mothers' pensions for single (usually widowed) mothers and their children, but this welfare program was extremely small and poorly funded and granted benefits only to women deemed to be moral. They got workman's compensation enacted in most states so that injured workers received a payment rather than having to pursue lengthy litigation that usually was won by employers—but the payments were extremely low. They were able to establish a Children's Bureau in Washington, DC, but it mostly focused on research on the status of women and children.

Progressives did not, then, create a robust welfare state, but focused mostly on regulations. These regulations were hardly a panacea since governments often lacked the capacity and sometimes the will to implement them, particularly when special interests put adverse pressure on them. Nor were the regulations a substitute for major social programs that provide an array of benefits to persons.

Progressives mostly avoided the egregious violations of civil rights for persons of color across the nation. Indeed, many progressives, including Theodore Roosevelt, subscribed to the notion that African Americans possessed inferior intelligence compared to Anglo-Saxons (Dyer, 1980, pp. 21–44). African Americans were commonly lynched in the South, Latinos worked in extreme poverty in mostly agricultural and ranching areas after being displaced from the land by White settlers, and Asian Americans experienced marked prejudice in the West even as they developed ingenious irrigation systems for farming western lands. Women were finally granted the vote in 1920 with ratification of the 19th Amendment to the Constitution, but were mostly excluded from business, law, and other professions save for nursing, social work, and teaching at the secondary level.

As in the nineteenth century, then, the United States had only a primitive welfare state in the progressive era despite the enactment of important regulations. Historians need to place far more emphasis on the survival strategies of vulnerable populations in an era when they received scant assistance from local, state, or federal governments—save for an emerging set of regulations.

Addressing Destitution in the New Deal with Federal Social Programs

If progressives secured myriad regulations but enacted few social programs, reformers in the New Deal created many governmental social programs and some additional regulations. Unlike the progressive era, which was a time of relative prosperity, the New Deal was triggered by the catastrophe known as the Great Depression, which began with the stock market crash of 1929 but lasted for more than a decade, until an upsurge of military manufacturing restored economic growth by 1941 as the nation neared entry into World War II. So crushing was this depression—which often brought unemployment to rates of 25% of adult workers—that even conservatives had to support many of Franklin Roosevelt's initiatives to avert massive destitution and even starvation, as well as policies to help senior citizens cope with economic uncertainty.

No one could have guessed from the election of 1932 that Roosevelt would develop unprecedented reforms. He not only downplayed reforms in his campaign addresses, save for vague references to possible reforms, but he advocated cutting spending and balancing a federal budget in substantial deficit. He promised hope and unspecified innovation, but not much more. When he won the election with a landslide—as well as the election of 1936—he had a power base that proved instrumental to developing his reforms.

Roosevelt encountered substantial opposition to his reforms throughout the decade, but particularly from 1937 onward. Conservative southern Democrats controlled most congressional committees and teamed with conservative Republicans increasingly as the 1930s progressed. He was uncertain whether the Supreme Court would declare most of his reforms to be an unconstitutional exercise of federal authority until 1937, and then only after he threatened to pack the Court with liberal justices by getting Congress to allow him to add a new justice each time one failed to retire within 6 months of his 70th birthday. Because the nation only had a small federal income tax levied on the most affluent 5% of citizens and because federal excise and import taxes lagged during the Great Depression, federal revenues decreased from $4 billion to $2 billion in 1932—meaning Roosevelt had virtually no resources for social reforms. Trade unions, mostly limited in 1933 to skilled laborers, often had conservative leaders until their ranks were swelled by unskilled labor later in the decade.

It became immediately clear, however, that Roosevelt would not be a passive observer of the nation's misfortune. In the first year of his presidency he created many programs to help destitute and unemployed persons, including the Federal Emergency Relief Administration (FERA), a national welfare program for unemployed persons to be funded largely by the federal government, as well as its offshoot, the Civilian Works Administration (CWA), that would create mostly unskilled or semiskilled jobs with some of the FERA funds in the various states; in 1934, the CWA was replaced with the Works Progress Administration. He started the Public Works Administration to fund public works projects that required technical expertise, such as dams, airports, and flood-control projects. He started the Civilian Conservation Corps to provide jobs for young men in conservation projects. Later in the decade he established the National Youth Administration to subsidize the college education of youth and to establish a range of work projects for them.

He also sought to reform the economic system in his first year by establishing the Federal Deposit Insurance Corporation to protect banks from insolvency by insuring deposits, following this with the Security and Exchange Commission in 1934 to forestall undue speculation by investors and stockbrokers. He enacted the National Industrial Recovery Administration to avert the vicious circle of price slashing and laying off workers by getting business leaders in various economic sectors, such as steel, coal, and mining industries, to agree on process and to establish production quotas for each company. He established the Agricultural Adjustment Agency to accomplish similar goals in the agricultural sector, where thousands of farmers had gone bankrupt and often evicted sharecroppers and tenant farmers from their land. He enacted the Tennessee Valley Authority to stimulate economic development in a huge geographic area by initiating a network of dams and generating plants, selecting electricity to power cooperatives and towns, reforesting huge tracts, and building flood-control projects.

Roosevelt resorted to a clever strategy to fund these domestic initiatives. Having promised to balance the federal budget in his campaign of 1932, he found a way to appear *not* to increase deficits while increasing federal spending to fund his reforms. His solution was to divide the budget into "regular" and "emergency" portions, respectively funding the ongoing portions of the budget (such as the Post Office and other ongoing federal agencies) and his New Deal social programs (Jansson, 2001). He balanced the regular budget with great fanfare in 1933 by making draconian cuts in veterans' benefits and other ongoing programs, while funding the emergency budget by selling bonds to investors at home and abroad. These deficits, he argued, would only be temporary because his relief and work-relief programs would be terminated when the Great Depression lifted. This strategy allowed him to claim to be a fiscal conservative even while considerably increasing the national deficit. Even conservatives feared to oppose this ruse, however, because they realized that many persons in their districts were destitute and supported annual appropriations for New Deal programs nearly unanimously.

Roosevelt's reforms continued with the enactment of the Social Security Act in 1935, with its old-age pension program and unemployment insurance programs mostly funded by payroll deductions, as well as an assortment of means-tested welfare programs, including Aid to Dependent Children (ADC), changed to Aid to Families with Dependent Children(AFDC) in 1950, Old Age Assistance (OAA), and Aid to the Blind (AB, supplemented with Aid to the Disabled [AD] in 1950). (With enactment of these welfare programs, the FERA was terminated.) If Roosevelt portrayed his work-relief programs as temporary programs, he described the Social Security Act as a permanent reform—as well as the Fair Labor Standards Act of 1938, which established a national minimum wage, abolished child labor, and set maximum weekly hours of work. The New Deal also enacted the Wagner-Steagall Housing Act in 1937, which established a federal public housing program. In addition to these programs, the New Deal implemented an array of emergency food, medical, and housing programs that were widely viewed as temporary means to avert malnutrition, exposure, and disease.

Critics of the New Deal have correctly identified flaws and omissions in these various reforms, such as the failure to set national benefit standards for ADC, OAA, and AB or to set minimum wage standards for domestic workers or farm workers. When viewed from the perspective of preceding American history, however, Roosevelt's reforms are remarkable achievements. Whereas progressives had mostly focused on regulations, Roosevelt established the first major federally funded social programs in the United States—and supplemented them with an array of regulations over wages, union organizing, and prices.

As important as these reforms were, Roosevelt also created an ongoing power base that would prove instrumental in expanding the American welfare state during the rest of the twentieth century. If voting in national elections prior to 1932 had mostly been dictated by ethnicity and regional factors, it was considerably shaped by social class from 1932 up through the 1960s, with blue-collar Catholic and ethnic White voters disproportionately voting for Democratic candidates. African Americans, who had mostly voted Republican after the Civil War because the Republican Party led by Abraham Lincoln had abolished slavery, switched to the Democratic Party because Roosevelt helped many of them survive the Great Depression with his various work-relief and welfare initiatives. Jewish voters also aligned with the Democratic Party—an allegiance cemented when President Harry Truman strongly supported the establishment of Israel in the wake of World War II.

Roosevelt also brought organized labor into the Democrats' fold. He was at first critical of the militant tactics of unions supporting unskilled workers in the mining industry and automobile plants, such as the sit-down strikes of automobile workers. He gained their strong support, however, when he helped get the so-called Wagner Act passed in 1935, which placed the National Labor Relations Board in the Department of Labor and gave it the power to mandate and monitor elections of employees at specific companies. The bulk of campaign funds for Roosevelt's 1936 campaign came from organized labor. As many unions grew rapidly during the organizing of war industries in World War II, American unions became larger and more affluent, allowing them to become even larger contributors to Democratic candidates and the Democratic Party, as well as persuading many of their members to vote Democratic (Brody, 1980).

Americans' support for an enlarged American welfare state declined rapidly later in the decade, however. Many citizens came to view Roosevelt as seeking too much power in a nation that had only known a weak federal government. Republicans charged that he sought to create a kind of political machine that used work and welfare benefits to entice voters to support his regime. When he proposed to pack the Supreme Court in 1937 with liberal justices to avert vetoes of his domestic legislation, he inadvertently strengthened these fears.

His social reform movement was further slowed by the lifting of the Great Depression as preparations for World War II bolstered the economy. Roosevelt increasingly devoted his energies to war preparations. Once the nation was at war, conservatives aggressively attacked his work-relief programs on grounds that they no longer were essential. With his attention on the war effort and wanting a bipartisan coalition to wage it, Roosevelt did not oppose the termination of many of the New Deal's work and relief programs, with most of them rescinded by the end of 1942. Yet pension, unemployment, and welfare programs of the Social Security Act, Fair Labor Standards Act, public housing, and the Wagner Act remained as permanent elements of the American welfare state.

Roosevelt strengthened the power of the federal government in yet another important way during World War II. Although the federal income tax had been made constitutional in 1913, it collected hardly any revenue because it was restricted to only the most affluent 5% of the population in the New Deal (Leff, 1984). Desperately needing resources to finance the war, Roosevelt met a firestorm of opposition when he proposed extending the income tax to most Americans; 15 state legislatures threatened to rescind the 16th Amendment. He nonetheless got a broad-based federal income tax enacted, which became pivotal to the financing and subsequent growth of the American welfare state in succeeding decades.

The New Deal also initiated complex jurisdictional arrangements among local, state, and federal governments. While Social Security pensions were administered by the federal government, federal welfare and work-relief programs, as well as public housing programs, required states to contribute funds and to assume major administrative roles.

Although the New Deal created many programs that gave work and welfare to Americans, it failed to develop programs that gave them social and educational services—or civil rights, in the case of persons of color and other vulnerable populations. Intent on not angering southern Democrats who were a key part of his coalition and who chaired most congressional committees, Roosevelt blinked when it came to antilynching legislation even when it was favored by congressional liberals.

Important as work-relief and relief programs were during the New Deal, traditional histories overstate their size. Federal government spending in the New Deal consumed on average less than 10% of GDP as compared to about 20% in 2007—and the federal government collected revenues that totaled only 7.7% of GDP in 1941 as compared to roughly 20% in 2007 (Jansson, 2001). Only a small percentage of unemployed persons benefited from relief and work-relief programs. Historians should, therefore, place far more emphasis on survival strategies used by persons suffering from economic destitution in this era, since relatively few of them received major assistance during the worst economic catastrophe in American history. With unemployment rates sometimes soaring to 75%, survival strategies of persons of color deserve particular attention.

The Growth of Public Social Services and Personal Rights

The United States emerged from World War II with only a modest welfare state and minimal public investments in it. Domestic spending by the federal government was deeply cut by conservatives in the wake of World War II—and then fought a losing battle against military spending during the 1950s as the cold war escalated. (Military spending consumed roughly 75% of the federal government's budget in the 1950s.)

Medical and social services, as well as legislation to protect the civil rights of many vulnerable populations, were almost completely lacking from the welfare repertoire of the federal government, save for the medical programs of the Veterans Administration. The lack of medical services for retirees became an important issue in the 1960 presidential campaign between Democrat John Kennedy and Republican Richard Nixon since the federal government funded only the small, means-tested Kerr-Mills medical program for a small number of low-income retirees. Deciding not to enact national health insurance after World War II, the nation turned to employers to fund insurance for their employees voluntarily, but many of them decided not to provide it even when allowed to deduct its costs from corporate income taxes. Tens of millions of working Americans were left with no health insurance, and their ranks were swollen by retirees whose employer-provided health insurance lapsed when they retired.

Sensitized to mental health by the illness of his sister, Kennedy came to realize that many mentally ill persons lacked services in the community, particularly because many had been released from mental institutions due to the recent advent of psychotropic drugs. Increasing attention was also given the plight of low-income persons whose schools were often dilapidated and poorly staffed and who faced insensitive and fragmented services. Low-income children rarely received preschool education, unlike more affluent children who attended nongovernmental nursery schools. Sometimes displaced from jobs by technology, workers could rarely locate effective job training programs. Senior citizens lacked community services that might help them stay in their home rather than being forced into nursing homes or becoming a burden on their children.

Particularly in the South and Southwest, persons of color suffered flagrant violation of their civil rights in the 1950s. Disabled persons, gay men and lesbians, women, and Native Americans suffered discrimination in places of work and in their communities.

The civil rights movement provided the catalyst for many of the reforms of the 1960s as the Great Depression had catalyzed reforms in the 1930s. The White power structure opposed the growing grassroots civil rights movement led by Martin Luther King Jr. and others. As northerners watched violent reprisals against nonviolent demonstrations by African Americans in the South they became sensitized to the lack of personal rights of southern African Americans. They witnessed as well scores of uprisings in inner-city African American communities throughout the nation from 1964 through 1968.

Political developments also facilitated social reforms. When Vice President Lyndon Johnson succeeded President Kennedy after his assassination in late 1963, he pledged to enact legislation that Kennedy had proposed but failed to secure congressional approval for, including civil rights, antipoverty, and medical legislation. Johnson's landslide victory over Republican Barry Goldwater in 1964 gave him large Democratic majorities in Congress. He possessed prodigious political skills from his many years as Senate Majority Leader, and he wanted to establish a domestic legislative legacy that would exceed even Franklin Roosevelt's accomplishments.

Before he was assassinated, President Kennedy secured the enactment of the Manpower Development and Training Act of 1961 and the Mental Retardation and Community Mental Health Centers Act of 1964. President Johnson in his first year of office signed into legislation the Economic Opportunity Act (the so-called War on Poverty), the Food Stamps Act, and the Civil Rights Act of 1964.

With his strong majority in Congress, in his second year in office Johnson secured public health insurance for elderly persons (Medicare), a means-tested health program for poor persons of all ages (Medicaid), and the Elementary and Secondary Education Act; created the Department of Housing and Urban Development and expanded public and subsidized housing programs; and signed the Civil Rights Act of 1965 and the Older Americans Act, as well as many smaller measures.

However, Johnson's reform momentum was undermined by his own policies. He enacted the largest tax cut in the nation's history in 1964, which severely cut federal revenues—and had to promise congressional southern conservatives, in return for their support of this tax cut, not to incur deficits in the remaining years of his presidency. When he then chose to hugely increase troop commitments to the Vietnam War in 1965, he lacked resources to fund his Great Society and encountered growing opposition to reform from congressional conservatives who remembered his pledge not to incur deficits.

If Johnson inherited his reform coalition from President Franklin Roosevelt, he split that coalition in ways that would haunt liberals for the remainder of the twentieth century (Jansson, 2001). His involvement in the Vietnam War split Democrats into pro- and antiwar factions and accentuated the disillusionment of many White blue-collar Democrats in the North and White southern Democrats who had been uneasy with Johnson's civil rights legislation as well as the number of Great Society reforms that they often believed disproportionately and excessively helped persons of color. The term "White backlash" appeared as early as 1964 and described this growing alienation of many Democrats from their party, opening the door to the exodus of many of them to the Republican Party in the last 3 decades of the twentieth century.

Johnson suffered extraordinary political losses in the last 2 years of his presidency, putting an end to his reform momentum. Already angered by his reforms, conservatives of both parties fought to cut funding for his reforms and to prevent him from enacting additional ones. Facing almost certain defeat if he sought his party's nomination for another term in office, he allowed Vice President Hubert Humphrey to become the Democratic contender for the presidency in 1968.

Kennedy's and Johnson's contributions to the American welfare state were nonetheless substantial, not only by adding social and medical services to the American welfare state, but by extending civil rights to African Americans and to women, who were included in provisions of the 1964 Civil Rights Act. The civil rights legislation of 1964 and 1965 unleashed many civil rights measures in its wake. Women had already obtained partial coverage by the Equal Pay Act of 1963 and had obtained a ban on gender-based discrimination in Title VII of the Civil Rights Act of 1964, as well as a ruling by the Supreme Court in 1965 that overturned Connecticut's law making possession of contraceptives a crime. Women's advocacy groups persuaded President Johnson to include women in the scope of his 1965 executive order that required affirmative action programs to bring equal opportunity to persons of color in programs funded by federal, state, and local governments, establishing a precedent that the term *sex* or *gender* would appear whenever the phrase "race, creed, color, or national origin" appeared in legislation or executive orders.

The policy gains of African Americans directly extended to Latinos and Asian Americans, who were included in provisions banning discrimination on the basis of race, as well as efforts to deny them voting rights. The Chicano movement, led by Cesar Chavez and others, sought to empower Mexican agricultural laborers who had been excluded from provisions of the Wagner Act—finally getting legislation passed in California that gave them the right to vote to be unionized, often under the United Farm Workers. The Latino community was active in voter registration drives, efforts to pressure the Equal Employment Opportunity Commission to investigate job discrimination against Latinos, and efforts to extend the Civil Rights Act of 1965 to cover Latinos' voting rights.

Mobilization of disabled persons, gay men and lesbians, and senior citizens was also triggered in part by successes obtained by African Americans. The drive among gay men and lesbians intensified after the police raided the Stonewall Inn in Greenwich Village in 1969, setting off a riot. They wanted to change the diagnostic categories of the American Psychiatric Association, which defined homosexuality as a form of mental illness. They sought protections against job discrimination in schools and other places. They pressured local, state, and federal governments to combat the AIDS epidemic in the early and mid-1980s that initially focused on gay males in major American cities, with devastating consequences (D'Emilio, 1983). Through grassroots protests and with the assistance of Surgeon General C. Everett Koop, punitive and neglectful policies of the federal government gradually shifted toward AIDS treatment and prevention, even as increasing numbers of gay persons of color—as well as women in African American and Latino communities—contracted the disease. Gay men and lesbians had been routinely thrown out of the military forces prior to 1993, but finally obtained a compromise agreement in the administration of Bill Clinton that allowed them to remain in the military under a "Don't ask, don't tell" policy, which proved to be a discriminatory solution even if it allowed many closeted gays and lesbians to remain in the military. Gay men and lesbians fought to obtain court rulings and legislation in various states to allow them to form civil unions or marriages like heterosexual couples—unions that would not only legitimate their partnerships but give them various tax, insurance, and other benefits widely available to heterosexual couples. They sought antidiscrimination laws in local and state jurisdictions with respect to housing and jobs, with considerable success.

Partly influenced by a surge in disabled persons among veterans in the wake of the Vietnam War, leaders of the disability community obtained passage of the Rehabilitation Act of 1973, whose Section 504 prohibited discrimination against people with disabilities primarily in jobs funded with public funds. The Americans with Disabilities Act in 1990 went further, barring discrimination in all workplaces, housing, transportation systems, and public accommodations.

Often placed on reservations or living in extreme poverty in American cities, Native Americans benefited from Great Society policies that emphasized supports to their culture rather than assimilation; brought many social service, economic, and housing programs to their reservations; and sought tribal participation in their governance. The Indian Self-Determination and Education Assistance Act gave tribes the authority to assume responsibility for administering federal programs of the Departments of Interior and Health, Education, and Welfare.

With the Immigration Act of 1924, the United States shifted from a relatively open immigration policy to a closed and discriminatory one that gave preference to people from northern Europe as compared to Mexico, Central America, and Asia. Enactment of the Immigration Act of 1965 abolished these quotas by allowing annual admission of 170,000 immigrants from the Eastern Hemisphere and 120,000 from the Western Hemisphere in a "sharp ideological departure from the traditional view of America as a homogeneous white society" (Takaki, 1989, p. 419). Even more Asian and Central American immigrants were allowed after the Indochina Migration and Refugee Assistance Act of 1975 and the Refugee Act of 1980 were enacted.

So-called undocumented immigrants who worked in the United States for extended periods and paid taxes were often victimized by prejudice and deportation, even though they produced major economic benefits for agricultural, tourist, restaurant, and other industries and paid Social Security and other taxes. The Immigration Reform and Control Act of 1986 granted asylum to 3 million undocumented workers if they could prove they had worked in the United States for at least 3 years and levied penalties against employers who knowingly hired undocumented workers.

Millions of additional undocumented immigrants came to the United States in the 2 decades after 1986 due to the huge economic disparities between the United States and Mexico and developing nations. As many as 10 million of them spread across the nation in search of employment. They were often exploited by employers, lived in substandard housing, lacked access to health care aside from emergency rooms, and feared deportation. Large numbers perished as they sought to enter the United States across deserts on the southern border with Mexico. Mexican President Vicente Fox in 2001 and President George W. Bush in 2004 developed proposals to grant 3-year work visas to immigrants for hard-to-fill jobs and to provide amnesty for more immigrants, but were unable to persuade Congress to approve immigration reforms despite massive demonstrations in 2006 and 2007 by Latinos.

In addition to official policies, each of these vulnerable populations launched important consciousness-raising, empowerment, and advocacy projects. Women's groups, for example, worked to redress job discrimination, obtain more humane treatment of rape victims in local hospitals and courts, obtain funding for women's shelters, challenge specific instances of discrimination in places of work through lawsuits, get local and state laws to seek payments from divorced or absent fathers, and pass legislation to outlaw sexual harassment in workplaces. Women's advocacy groups and public interest attorneys had remarkable success in obtaining huge monetary damages from large corporations for failure to promote or reimburse women sufficiently compared to male employees.

The Great Society differed from the New Deal not only in the substantive content of its reforms, but in their intended permanency. Programs of the Great Society remained mostly intact in succeeding decades, even if their funding was slashed in conservative periods, such as during the Reagan presidency in the 1980s. Yet budget allocations to the Great Society were remarkably Spartan—and the expansion of social services and civil rights did not sufficiently address the economic needs of vulnerable populations.

The Rapid Expansion of Hard Benefits from 1968 through 1980

The portion of the American welfare state that was funded by entitlements and annual appropriations finally became a major priority for Americans in this period (Jansson, 2005). Expenditures rose from $158 billion in 1970 to $324 billion in 1980 (in 1980 dollars).

These increases in domestic spending took place, remarkably, during the conservative Republican presidencies of Nixon and Gerald Ford, as well as the conservative presidency of Democrat Jimmy Carter. Various factors led to this surprising result, including the Democrats' majorities in Congress throughout this period, the huge growth of Medicare and Medicaid, a small peace dividend when the Vietnam War ended, and the runaway inflation of the 1970s that swelled federal tax revenues. (Inflation pushed many persons into higher federal tax brackets even when their real wages did not increase.)

Increases in domestic spending occurred, moreover, due to the unusual politics of the Nixon presidency from 1968 until he left office in 1974. Determined not to let Democrats dominate the domestic agenda so that he could convert the Republicans from a minority to a majority party, Nixon resolved both to introduce his own domestic reforms and to claim partial credit for many reforms introduced by the Democrats.

Critical of the emphasis on social and medical services in the Great Society, Nixon wished to emphasize "hard benefits" that gave persons cash, in-kind benefits, and jobs, as well as transfers of federal revenues to states (Jansson, 2001).

Nixon startled the Congress when he proposed the Family Assistance Plan in 1969, a sweeping revision of welfare policy. Caught in a crossfire between liberals and conservatives, the plan was not enacted, but Congress approved passage of the Supplementary Security Program instead, which combined existing welfare programs for the elderly (OAA), the disabled (Aid to the Disabled), and the blind (Aid to the Blind) into a single program with national funding and administration. Although the Food Stamps Program had been enacted in 1964, it remained a relatively small program in the 1960s due to its cumbersome application process, its local eligibility policies, its optional adoption by states, and its partial funding by states. Nixon and the Congress nationalized the program, giving it uniform eligibility and benefits and making it a mandatory program for states. The president and Congress indexed Social Security benefits in 1972 so they would automatically rise with inflation. The Congress and President Ford enacted the Earned Income Tax Credit in 1975, which gave tax credits to intact families that earned beneath specified levels—tax credits and eligibility that were substantially increased in subsequent decades. The Congress enacted the Comprehensive Employment Training Act in 1973 that was reminiscent of some work-relief programs of the New Deal. Federal assistance for low-income housing doubled in the 1970s.

Nixon and the Congress also enacted federal sharing of revenues with states and local governments through the Local Fiscal Assistance Act of 1972. He hoped to devolve many federal programs to state and local governments, but was unable to persuade Congress to support most of his devolution proposals.

Some social service programs were adopted in the 1970s, including the Juvenile Justice and Delinquency Prevention Act of 1974, the Education for All Handicapped Children Act of 1975, and the Adoption Assistance and Child Welfare Act of 1980. The Occupational Safety and Health Act of 1970 was landmark legislation that propelled the federal government into oversight of the safety standards of industry.

Traditional histories of the American welfare state failed to give sufficient recognition to the size and scope of reforms of the 1970s as compared to the Great Society and the New Deal. They were at least as significant as these two prior eras—and far more significant when measured by the size of fiscal commitments to them. Although many gaps existed in the reforms of the 1970s, they gave the United States for the first time a system of safety-net programs for persons who lacked resources regardless of their age and sex. A single woman with preschool or school-age children could receive, for example, AFDC, food stamps, Medicaid, and subsidized housing.

Devolution of Federal Programs to the States and to Individuals in the Presidencies of Ronald Reagan and George W. Bush

The notion that the states and local governments should be the primary building blocks of the American welfare state has a long history. Due to political and constitutional barriers, the federal government emerged with a substantial social welfare role only in the New Deal—over 140 years after the republic was founded.

Often chafing when liberals succeeded in developing a substantial federal role, conservatives wanted to turn the clock back to times when states and local governments had been the predominant actors. They had three options: downsize federal social programs by cutting their funding, devolve federal social welfare programs back to state and local governments, or privatize the welfare state. If President Reagan led the devolution and retrenchment efforts, President George W. Bush made privatization his major goal.

Some accounts of social policy from 1981 through the present understandably emphasize the fragility of the American welfare state. Yet the American welfare state proved to be remarkably resilient—leaving many conservatives frustrated by their failure to gut it.

Reagan initiated fiscal and spending policies that placed extraordinary downward pressure on social spending. By getting huge tax cuts enacted and increases in military spending while not cutting entitlements (save for those that were means-tested, such as Medicaid and AFDC), Reagan created unprecedented peacetime deficits. He used these deficits to argue that the discretionary annual federal budget had to be severely cut—and he targeted an array of social programs that focused on poor persons for major cuts. He succeeded in cutting domestic discretionary spending by roughly 25% during his presidency (Jansson, 2001).

Determined to devolve many federal social welfare programs to the states, Reagan succeeded in getting Congress to eliminate 57 federal social programs (called "categorical programs" because the federal government dictated how they would be administered by the states) and to replace them with seven "block grants" in 1981. These gave states broad latitude in how they used these grants in such areas as social services; community services; alcohol, drug abuse, and mental health services; maternal and child health services; community development services; primary health services; and preventive health services.

Reagan was unable, however, to devolve entitlements, failing to persuade Congress to devolve food stamps to the states. Nor were such Republicans as House Speaker Newt Gingrich—and subsequently President George W. Bush—able to convince Congress to devolve Medicaid to the states. Unless conservatives could get entitlements devolved, which constituted the vast bulk of federal spending on social programs, their quest would remain substantially unfulfilled.

Partly because he believed that Reagan had not achieved sufficient retrenchment and devolution of the American welfare state, Gingrich led a conservative movement to achieve these goals. Engineering a Republican takeover of both Houses of Congress in 1994, Gingrich sought to force President Bill Clinton to make drastic cuts in social spending and to devolve Medicaid to the states. He, too, was frustrated in these goals. Not only did Clinton outmaneuver him, but he was deposed as speaker of the House by his fellow Republicans when Democrats made surprising gains in the congressional elections of 1998.

Conservatives were successful in obtaining the devolution and block-granting of AFDC when they persuaded Clinton to sign their version of the Personal Responsibility and Work Opportunities Act of 1996, which converted AFDC from an entitlement to the Temporary Assistance for Needy Families (TANF) block grant. Although Clinton, too, had espoused "changing welfare as we know it" in his presidential campaign of 1992, Republicans convinced him to sign a far more conservative version of TANF than he had originally wanted.

President George W. Bush aspired to downsize the welfare state in yet another way. Why not, he asked, privatize it by having citizens fund their own benefits with the help of tax concessions? The United States had long used the tax code to achieve social welfare aims. Immediately after the 16th Amendment to the Constitution was enacted in 1913 to allow the federal government to collect income taxes, the Congress voted so-called tax expenditures into existence. They allowed persons to deduct state and local taxes and mortgage interest payments from their gross income when calculating income subject to federal income taxes (Witte, 1985). Congress then enacted an array of deductions, exemptions, deferrals, and credits over the next 95 years. So huge were these tax deductions that just from 1975 through 2004, they cost the federal government $10.9 *trillion* dollars in lost tax revenues—*more than half* of the total federal revenues from individuals' income taxes in 2004 (Jansson, 2001). These various reductions in the normal taxes that individuals and corporations would pay are called *tax entitlements*.

Deductions of home mortgage payments, which totaled $53 billion in lost federal income in 2004, are by far the nation's largest subsidized housing program, greatly exceeding federal subsidies for rent of low-income persons or for the construction of public housing.

If the politics of federal programs subsidized through general revenues and payroll taxes are relatively public and controversial, the politics of tax expenditures are usually "subterranean" (Hacker, 2002). When the federal government failed to enact national health insurance after World War II, for example, insurance companies, corporations, and health interest groups persuaded Congress to allow corporations to deduct their cost of purchasing health care for their employees from their corporate income. Banks and investment companies persuaded Congress to give citizens tax incentives to establish private retirement accounts, whether Individual Retirement Accounts (IRAs) or Roth Retirement Accounts, on which they pay no taxes until they withdraw funds after retirement.

The Earned Income Tax Credit (EITC) is possibly the largest antipoverty program in the American welfare state. Enacted in 1975, it gives employed heads of low-income families a tax rebate. The federal government also subsidizes considerable numbers of low-income persons by not requiring them to pay federal income taxes if their income falls below specific levels.

When considered together—and with notable exceptions like the EITC—the American penchant for tax expenditures has proven to be highly inequitable (Jansson, 2001). Partly because they possess considerable taxable income as compared to less affluent persons, affluent Americans benefit disproportionately from many tax deductions. Renters do not benefit from home mortgage deductions. Low-income employees who work for employers who do not fund their health insurance receive no benefit from employers' tax deductions for costs of funding employees' health insurance. Persons who lack resources to pay into a retirement plan do not benefit from IRA and Roth tax deferrals and deductions.

Compared to most European nations, moreover, American tax rates favor relatively affluent persons, who pay about 35% on that portion of their income that exceeds $250,000; rates are often double this level in European nations. Taxes on capital gains are taxed in the United States only at a rate of 15% even though they are primarily realized by affluent persons selling investments. The greater income inequality in the United States compared to Europe, Canada, and Japan partly stems from the inequitable nature of American tax rates and tax expenditures.

Firmly believing that the creation of wealth benefits the entire society, President George W. Bush made tax cuts a centerpiece of his domestic policy. Immediately after taking office, he sought and obtained a $1.35 trillion tax cut—with roughly 40% of the tax cut's benefits going to the wealthiest 1% of the population. He achieved another $700 billion tax cut in 2003 that eliminated taxes on stock dividends, even though stocks are primarily owned by relatively affluent persons. He frequently argued in political speeches that citizens' income belonged to them rather than to government—implying that taxes should be cut even further.

If Nixon and Reagan favored devolving many federal programs to the states, Bush wanted to devolve some of them to individuals by promoting personal accounts with tax incentives. He wanted citizens to develop private retirement accounts (in place of Social Security) or health savings accounts (in place of Medicare and Medicaid) by not taxing funds that citizens placed in these accounts up to a specified annual amount.

Bush was unable to convince Congress that a radical structuring of the American welfare state was meritorious. Congress did enact his proposed tax cuts, but not his proposal to devolve much of the American welfare state to individuals or to convert Medicaid into a block grant. Congressional opposition to Bush's policies partly stemmed from their inequitable nature. Those persons who pay no or low federal income taxes would receive no or low tax benefits from placing personal funds into private accounts—even if they had sufficient resources to establish them in the first place. It would take most citizens years to build accounts of sufficient size to fund their retirement or major health costs—making it inequitable to end Social Security, Medicare, and Medicaid in the interim.

Strong Democratic gains in the congressional elections of 2006 made it even less likely that Bush's privatization policies would prevail. Yet both Reagan and Bush had articulated devolution, retrenchment, and privatization alternatives to the American welfare state that will likely resurface in coming decades, when conservatives again control the presidency or the Congress.

Rather than focus on retrenchment and devolution in the period 1981 through 2006, policy analysts ought to give greater emphasis to the *resilience* of the American welfare state. Overall domestic spending *increased* in this period, even if at a slower rate than in some preceding eras. Conservatives were unable to obtain the rollback in the American welfare state, and historians should analyze in more detail those defensive strategies that their opponents utilized to achieve this result.

TOPICS FOR FURTHER RESEARCH

Further historical research is needed to better understand how the welfare state has grown over the past 3 centuries. For an extraordinarily long period—from 1789 through 1933—the American welfare state existed in a primitive state when measured by aggregate expenditures, including both direct allocations of funds and tax expenditures. Indeed, many traditional histories and some historians risk exaggerating the actual importance of specific reforms—or the size of the American welfare state—by not examining actual resources devoted to them.

My brief analysis of eight eras suggests the American welfare state grew by a process of *accretion*. With the slate nearly wiped clean by 1800, Americans focused on residual institutions, welfare programs, land distribution, and public education. During important periods of American history, massive social problems overwhelmed the nation's primitive welfare state, such as during and after the Civil War—and arguably in the progressive and New Deal eras, when urbanization and a catastrophic depression created social problems that the nation addressed inadequately. By a process of accretion, the American welfare state gradually took form through regulations (the progressive era); substantial but mostly temporary federal work-relief and relief programs and permanent programs of the Social Security Act (the New Deal); social and medical services as well as civil rights (the Great Society); and resource and in-kind programs (the 1970s). Throughout the twentieth century, Americans gradually constructed an elaborate set of tax expenditures that supplemented direct expenditures, leading to combined spending that by the late 1970s was quite substantial in size and not that much lower than many European nations when measured as a percentage of GDP.

History suggests as well that the federal American welfare state grew in a series of spurts. The progressive era, New Deal, Great Society, and the 1970s produced growth spurts in regulations, work-relief and entitlement programs, social service and personal rights, and cash and in-kind programs. Less dramatic reforms occurred between these spurts, such as incremental expansion of Social Security, additional regulations, enactment of low-profile tax expenditures, enactment of small programs funded by the discretionary budget, and the extension of civil rights to groups such as the disabled. When considered in aggregate, these isolated reforms have considerable importance even if they were less dramatic than reforms during spurts.

As the American welfare state grew in and between spurts at the federal level, a similar process took place in the states. Some state spurts were linked to federal spurts because the federal government required the states to commit considerable resources or administrative effort to federal initiatives. Many New Deal and Great Society reforms required, for example, not only state fiscal contributions, but the creation of many new state-level administrative entities. States had to create state-level welfare and work-relief agencies in the New Deal and agencies to administer Medicaid in the Great Society.

When the federal government devolved many programs to the states during the Reagan presidency, it catalyzed a rapid growth of states' administrative capabilities because states now *had* to oversee 57 programs that had previously been overseen by the federal government. When the federal government allowed states to administer programs of the Occupational Safety and Health Administration in the early 1980s and when it converted AFDC into the TANF block grant in 1996, it similarly fostered a surge in the growth of state bureaucracies.

Social reforms also spurted when states had governors or legislative leaders with expansive agendas. When Pat Brown Sr. was governor of California from 1959 to 1967, for example, he persuaded the state legislature to fund massive increases in California's education and mental health programs, as well as its infrastructure. By contrast, far fewer reforms occurred during the tenures of many Republican governors, such as Reagan and George Deukmejian.

Policy spurts in states are limited in their size and number, however, by fiscal realities that confront states. When the federal government finally increased federal income tax to a substantial size during World War II and expanded it even further in succeeding decades, it effectively placed limits on states' fiscal resources, since their citizens would have objected to substantial taxing of their incomes from *both* state and federal governments. States remained heavily dependent, then, on lower sources of income, including property taxes and sales taxes, even if some states *did* tax incomes, though at far lower rates than the federal government. (Revenues of all states when aggregated totaled roughly half the size of federal revenues in 2000.) Elected officials in states were deterred from raising taxes too high, moreover, by the fear that many citizens and businesses would depart for states with lower taxes.

Those taxes that states and localities collected were often reserved for social welfare programs traditionally funded by them, including education, general relief, police, fire, infrastructure, and corrections. Their resources were preempted as well by required matching fund contributions for some federal programs; many states had to devote more than a quarter of their entire budget to their matching contributions to the Medicaid program in 2007. States had to implement some unfunded (or partially funded) federal mandates as well, such as mainstreaming developmentally and physically challenged children into the public schools, as required by federal law.

Expenditures for entitlements have been, by far, the largest portion of the American welfare state from the 1950s onward at the federal level—and expenditures for public education has dominated expenditures at the state level. By contrast, budget expenditures from the federal discretionary budget—determined each year by Congress and the president, unlike entitlements that are funded automatically to the level of claimed benefits in specific years—did not increase from 1978 to 2007 when calculated in inflation-adjusted dollars (Jansson, Dodd, & Smith, 2002). These federal discretionary funds finance block grants, child care, Section 8 public housing, mental health and substance abuse counseling, Head Start, and myriad other programs whose resources have been pinched by the combination of entitlement and military spending, as well as relatively low American income taxes. Many states, too, have crimped funding for an array of social service, health, public health, job training, and other programs due to the sheer size of education spending in their budgets—not to mention the costs of maintaining penal institutions.

Histories of the evolution of the American welfare state must account for the tension between its *reluctance* and its *resilience*. I identified a relatively full list of factors that I hypothesize promoted, singly and in tandem, reluctance, including various cultural, economic, political, legal, institutional, and social factors, as well as the extraordinary power of American conservatives and the late development of the American welfare state (Jansson, 2005). Many theorists implicate one or several factors, such as the weakness of class-based movements (Shalev, 1983); culture (Hartz, 1955); ideas of policy elites, organizational features of the state structure, and interest group pressures (Skocpol, 1995); manipulation of race by political elites (Edsall, 1991); or the role of corporate capitalists (Berkowitz &

McQuaid, 1980). In contrast, I hypothesize that multiple interacting factors have shaped the reluctance of the American welfare state.

Although compared to some welfare states in Europe the American welfare state has been reluctant, it has displayed remarkable resilience in the past 3 decades particularly in spending on entitlement programs. Just three of its programs (Social Security, Medicare, and Medicaid) grew from about 2% to 8% of GDP from 1960 to 2004—and are slated to grow at phenomenal rates in the next 3 decades as the boomers (persons born between 1946 and 1964) age. Indeed, the contemporary American welfare state is like a sprawling empire with legions of providers, complex relations with state and local governments, legislative and presidential allies and opponents, links with courts at all levels, and relations with governments and providers in foreign nations. When tax expenditures are included, Hacker (2002) contends that the American welfare state is not that different in its total size as a percentage of GDP from many European welfare states.

American scholars thus need to devote more research to analyzing why the American welfare state has grown so rapidly in the past 4 decades, and which parts of it have grown most rapidly. If federal entitlements and tax expenditures have grown rapidly, for example, federal domestic discretionary spending has hardly grown as a percentage of GDP from 1978 to the present (Jansson, 2001).

Social Security, Medicare, and Medicaid have grown rapidly partly because Americans have viewed their recipients as deserving and because so many Americans use them, including the friends and relatives of conservatives. The aging of the American population is certain to contribute to these programs' growth for pensions and health care and for nursing home care, which is largely funded by Medicaid. Americans' emphasis on medical technology has also fueled the growth of Medicare and Medicaid. Unless the United States enacts national health insurance, Medicaid will continue to grow rapidly since a substantial share of the medical costs of the 48 million uninsured persons (in 2007) is covered by Medicaid through its disproportionate-share program. As entitlements, moreover, these programs are automatically funded by Congress to the level of claimed benefits each year—immunizing them from cuts in annual budget battles.

Tax expenditures are highly popular as well because they disproportionately assist relatively affluent persons with their health, pension, housing, and other costs. Legislators like them because they can be expanded behind closed doors, unlike the public and controversial politics that usually accompany legislation to establish or expand social programs. When they want to cut federal spending, legislators typically focus on social programs rather than tax entitlements because they are more visible and more controversial.

The growth of the American welfare state has been facilitated by electoral policies and partisan politics. Legislators and presidents increase their popularity by claiming credit for social programs that have helped their constituents—even relatively conservative politicians who might otherwise want to cut American social spending for ideological reasons. It is not surprising, then, that Social Security has been called the "third rail" of American politics—to be cut only at significant political risk. Democrats have been the initiators of the overwhelming majority of new social programs in the United States in the past 4 decades, even though Republican moderates and idiosyncratic Republican presidents such as Nixon have lent their weight to social reforms.

Americans have placed considerable emphasis on opportunity-creating programs from the colonial period onward. It is not surprising, then, that Americans have developed a relatively robust junior college and college system even as they have evolved relatively harsh programs that address survival needs of low-income persons.

The links between interest groups and the financing of political campaigns means that large interest groups have more power in the United States than in many other nations. Mortgage interest tax deductions and tax incentives that promote retirement accounts such as IRAs have been strongly supported by real estate, banking, and mutual fund industries. The Food Stamps Program and the medical programs of the Veterans Administration have been strongly supported by agricultural interests and veterans groups such as the American Legion. Interest groups have the power not only to enact new programs, but to block those they dislike, as witnessed by the way health insurance companies assumed a key role in defeating Clinton's proposal for national health insurance.

Americans have had considerable empathy for groups widely perceived to be "deserving" from the colonial period onward, resulting in welfare programs for mothers, blind and disabled persons, retirees, temporarily unemployed persons, and victims of natural disasters.

Historians and policy analysts should also devote more attention to the tension between *retrenchment* and *resilience* in the American welfare state. Conservatives *did* fashion important cuts in the American welfare state from 1981 through 2006, yet overall social spending increased markedly in this period, suggesting the importance of policy momentum. Once enacted, social programs often foster their own growth, as their beneficiaries, as well as specific interest groups that form to protect them, oppose major cuts or termination even during intensely conservative periods (Pierson, 2000). Social Security expanded, for example, from a relatively small to a massive program as its benefits were successively extended to widows, dependent children, disabled persons, and children in college over many decades—just as Head Start expanded from serving low-income children to include children with developmental and physical challenges.

Policy momentum occurs as well in areas of group rights. Once women, Latinos, the disabled, and gay men and lesbians observed the important civil rights gains of African Americans in the mid-1960s, for example, they demanded similar protections for themselves.

The sheer size of the American welfare state is relatively inconsequential, however, if it fails to achieve important social objectives—whether in aggregate or in its specific programs or regulations. To what extent does it reduce inequality? To what extent does it not grant important rights to specific vulnerable populations? What gaps or omissions exist in its extension of rights and services to the American population? Which of its programs are based on faulty premises, thus doomed to fail? Which programs are ineffective? Which programs produce outcomes that are not sufficiently cost effective—or mostly wasteful? Which policies are inequitable (e.g., many tax deductions)?

WHERE NEXT?

The aging of the American population will require extraordinary expansion of not only Social Security and Medicare, but social services, home health, and nursing home care of the elderly population. The costs of these programs and services, when coupled with the extraordinary growth of the American national debt, will create a shortage of resources that can be met in three ways: increasing economic growth by importing younger immigrant workers, increasing taxes substantially, or cutting many other social programs. Each of these options will be controversial, suggesting volatile politics beginning sometime around 2016, when many of the so-called boomers reach age 65.

The American welfare state will likely have to increase its international reach in coming decades by seeking minimum wage, work safety, and antipollution requirements in treaties and trade policies. With many American workers earning only poverty-level wages, increasing efforts to level the playing field by requiring corporations in other nations to increase their wage scale is likely to occur—or a substantial American backlash against free trade will emerge.

Already spending roughly 15% of their GDP on health care in 2007, Americans will be hard-pressed to afford continuing escalation of medical costs in coming decades. None of the panaceas has worked, including managed care, competition between health plans, corporate provision of health care, reviews of physician practices, and advanced authorization for services—and it is unlikely that computerizing of medical records will substantially cut medical costs. Many experts agree that the relatively unrestrained use of medical technology by providers and consumers lies at the heart of cost escalation, but no strategies for containing it have proved successful.

High levels of inequality in the United States, which show no signs of dissipating, could eventually bring considerable domestic discontent and exacerbate such social problems as crime, poor health, and poor educational performance. No panaceas have yet emerged to bridge this chasm—and it remains uncertain what effects it will have on the nation's social, economic, and political systems. Although the United States has funded entitlements relatively generously, it has been excessively frugal in funding domestic discretionary spending that invests in low-income persons' education, health care, job training, and social services.

If the past is prologue, the American welfare state will again be put to the test as it addresses these coming issues. We can expect considerable controversy in coming decades between liberals and conservatives, red and blue states, and the two dominant political parties as contending factions put forward different approaches to coming challenges.

REFERENCES

Appleby, J. (1992). *Liberalism and Republicanism in the historical imagination*. Cambridge, MA: Harvard University Press.

Axinn, J., & Levin, H. (1982). *Social welfare: A history of the American response to need*. New York: Harper & Row.

Berkowitz, E., & McQuaid, K. (1980). *Creating the welfare state: The political economy of twentieth-century reform*. New York: Praeger.

Boyer, P. (1978). *Urban masses and moral order in America, 1920–1920*. Cambridge, MA: Harvard University Press.

Brody, D. (1980). *Workers in industrial America: Essays on the twentieth-century struggle*. New York: Oxford University Press.

Davis, K. (2007, April). The challenges posed by diversity to mental health policy. Unpublished lecture at the School of Social Work of the University of Southern California, Los Angeles.

D'Emilio, J. (1983). *Sexual politics, sexual communities: The making of a homosexual minority in the United States, 1940–1970*. Chicago: University of Chicago Press.

Dyer, T. (1980). *Theodore Roosevelt and the idea of race*. Baton Rouge: Louisiana University Press.

Edsall, T. (1991). *Chain reaction: The impact of race, rights, and taxes on American politics*. New York: Norton.

Friedman, L. (1982). *Gregarious saints: Self and community in American abolitionism*. Cambridge: Cambridge University Press.

Gordon, L. (1994). *Pitied but not entitled*. New York: Free Press.

Hacker, J. (2002). *The divided welfare state: The battle over public and private social benefits in the United States*. New York: Cambridge University Press.

Halloran, P. (1989). *Boston's wayward children: 1830–1930*. London: Associated University Presses.

Harris, B. (1978). *Beyond her sphere: Women and the professions in America*. Westport, CT: Greenwood Press.

Hartz, L. (1955). *The liberal tradition in America*. New York: Harcourt Brace.

Jansson, B. (1988). *The reluctant welfare state: A history of American social welfare policies*. Belmont, CA: Wadsworth.

Jansson, B. (2001). *The sixteen-trillion dollar mistake: How the U.S. bungled its national priorities from the New Deal to the present*. New York: Columbia University Press.

Jansson, B. (2005). *The reluctant welfare state: American social welfare policies—Past, present, and future*. Belmont, CA: Brooks/Cole.

Jansson, B., Dodd, S.-J., & Smith, S. (2002). Empowering domestic discretionary spending in federal budget deliberations. *Social Policy Journal, 1*(1), 5–18.

Kawachi, I., Daniels, N., & Robinson, D. (2005). Health disparities by race and class: Why both matter. *Health Affairs, 24*(2), 343–352.

Leff, M. (1984). *The limits of symbolic reform: The New Deal and taxation, 1933–1939*. Cambridge: Cambridge University Press.

Leiby, J. (1978). *A history of social welfare and social work in the United States*. New York: Columbia University Press.

McWilliams, C. (1968). *North from Mexico: The Spanish-speaking people of the United States*. New York: Greenwood Press.

Mennel, R. (1973). *Thorns and thistles: Juvenile delinquents in the United States, 1825–1940*. Hanover, NH: University Press of New England.

Nash, G. (1976). Social change and the growth of pre-revolutionary urban radicalism. In A. Young (Ed.), *The American Revolution: Explorations in the history of American radicalism* (pp. 11–30). De Kalb: Northern Illinois University Press.

Peterson, M. (1975). *Portable Thomas Jefferson*. New York: Viking Press.

Pierson, P. (2000). The new politics of the welfare state. In R. Goodwin & D. Mitchell (Eds.), *Foundations of the welfare state* (pp. 421–465). Northampton, MA: Elgar.

Rohrbough, M. (1968). *The land office business: The settlement and administration of American public lands, 1789–1837*. New York: Oxford University Press.

Sachs, J. (2005). *The end of poverty*. New York: Penguin Books.

Sellers, C. (1991). *The market revolution: Jacksonian America, 1815–1846*. New York: Oxford University Press.

Shalev, M. (1983). The social democratic model and beyond: Two generations of comparative research on the welfare state. *Comparative Social Research, 6*, 315–351.

Skocpol, T. (1995). *Social policy in the United States: Future possibilities in historical perspective*. Princeton, NJ: Princeton University Press.

Smith, R. (1993). *Patriarch: George Washington and the new American nation*. Boston: Houghton Mifflin.

Snell, K. (1985). *Annals of the laboring poor: Social change and agrarian England, 1660–1900*. Cambridge: Cambridge University Press.

Stiglitz, J. (2002). *Globalization and its discontents*. New York: Norton.

Takaki, R. (1989). *Strangers from a different shore*. Boston: Little, Brown.

Thelen, D. (1975). Not classes, but issues. In A. Mann (Ed.), *The progressive era: Major issues of interpretation* (pp. 4–42). Hindale, IL: Dryden Press.

Trattner, W. (1979). *From poor law to welfare state: A history of social welfare in America*. New York: Free Press.

Tyrell, I. (1979). *Sobering up: From temperance to prohibition in antebellum America, 1800–1862*. Westport, CT: Greenwood Press.

Walch, T. (Ed.). (1993). *Immigrant America: European ethnicity in the United States*. New York: Garland.

Weinstein, J. (1975). It's good for business. In A. Mann (Ed.), *The progressive era: Major issues of interpretation* (p. 112). Hindale, IL: Dryden Press.

Witte, J. (1985). *The politics and development of the federal income tax*. Madison: University of Wisconsin Press.

Wood, G. (1992). *The radicalism of the American revolution*. New York: Knopf.

Chapter 5

NOT BY THE NUMBERS ALONE: THE EFFECTS OF ECONOMIC AND DEMOGRAPHIC CHANGES ON SOCIAL POLICY

Michael Reisch

Since the nineteenth century, social policies in the United States have been shaped by rapid economic growth and social and demographic transformation, particularly the effects of industrialization, urbanization, immigration, and internal migration. These changes, which have altered the racial, ethnic, and religious makeup of U.S. society, have been compounded recently by the aging of the population, evolving gender roles, different conceptions of adolescence, and new cultural attitudes regarding marriage, parenting, the family, and sexual orientation. Some of these developments result from what Titmuss (1963) called the "diswelfares" of modern society, such as unemployment and underemployment, industrial accidents, and occupationally related illness. Others are the environmental by-products of unrestrained economic growth or the emergence of new cultural norms in an increasingly complex, multicultural society.

In response to these changes, the United States has developed a form of welfare capitalism, which consists of a patchwork of state and federal policies designed to create a floor on aggregate consumption, while reinforcing long-standing cultural values about work through the stigmatization of dependency (Axinn & Stern, 2008; Jansson, 2005; Katz, 2001; Patterson, 2001). Government funding for social policies has been limited, the locus of policy making has often been decentralized, and the private, nonprofit sector has played an important role in the provision of what remains a fragmented network of services. Social policies have been rationalized by certain underlying assumptions about the relationship of government to the market, the motivations for individual and collective behavior, and the goals of the social welfare system. Among these assumptions is that economic, demographic, social, and cultural issues arise from distinct sources and can therefore be addressed separately in the policy arena. Over the past several decades, however, such assumptions have been challenged or undermined by dramatic shifts in the global economy and an unprecedented transformation of the nation's population.

A major change has occurred, for example, in the scope of those issues that concern contemporary policy makers. It is now widely acknowledged that problems such as economic inequality, immigration, epidemic disease, and environmental degradation must be addressed in a cross-national context. Yet, our policy-making and policy implementation apparatus remains locked in anachronistic patterns (Ferrera, 2005). In addition, the devolution of policy making and implementation over the past quarter century has exacerbated the nation's inability to respond to such problems effectively and efficiently. If we cannot even formulate local or regional approaches to social and economic problems, how can we possibly begin to address them on a global scale?

ECONOMIC GLOBALIZATION

The most significant economic development during the past several decades has been economic globalization. Since the early 1970s, the global economic system has undergone revolutionary changes, which distinguish the world economy of today from the internationalization of commerce that has existed for millennia. The key features of this new global economy are the rapid mobility and liquidity of capital, the short-term nature of investments, the interlocking connections of national currency systems, the speed and growing importance of information transfer, the increased power of multinational corporations, the specialization of knowledge and production, and the declining influence of countervailing political forces to direct or control these processes. As a consequence of globalization, manufacturing and service industries are outsourced overseas, fewer workers with higher skills are needed to maintain corporate productivity rates, gender distinctions in the workplace have been blurred, and a seemingly intractable and widening gap in income, wealth, education, skills, and status has emerged between classes and races, both globally and in the United States (Deacon, 1999; Esping-Andersen, 2002; George, 1998; Penna, Paylor, & Washington, 2000; Pugh & Gould, 2000; Reisch, 2003).

These trends have multiple implications for social policy development, some of them direct and explicit (such as the need to improve the nation's educational system); others are more subtle and implied. For example, the domestic market has become a less significant source of corporate growth as a consequence of globalization (Jessop, 2002; Reisch & Gorin, 2001). This diminishes the importance of social policies, such as income transfer programs and wage/hour regulations, which over the past 75 years have been designed to maintain levels of consumption among Americans.

In a globalized economy, the efficiency of the corporate sector is increasingly predicated on lowering the costs of production, especially labor, and shifting the social costs of the market (such as pollution and health care) onto the public sector (Kapp, 1972). In this context, the attraction of overseas markets, the lure of cheap, unorganized labor, and the opportunity to exploit less restrictive or nonexistent occupational safety and environmental policies encourage and facilitate the transfer of corporate production and service delivery to sites abroad. Under the guise of promoting free trade and economic growth, the U.S. government has abetted such steps through its tax policies and the passage of treaties like the North American Free Trade Agreement (NAFTA). Thus, while corrective measures to ameliorate the social impact costs of globalization are now considered an indispensable aspect of the international economic system, it is widely recognized that these costs cannot be eliminated or significantly reduced without a major revision of the system itself. Ironically, the short-term goals of the global market system, expressed most powerfully in the United States, preclude the implementation of such corrective steps (Bergman & Lundberg, 2006; Deaton, 2003; Esping-Andersen, 2002; Jessop, 2002; Reisch, 2005).

These developments have also changed the nature of labor-management and corporate-community relationships, with consequences for those social policies that have traditionally provided workers and community residents with economic and social support. As recent contract negotiations in the auto and airline industries demonstrate, labor-management conflicts now focus increasingly on issues of givebacks, productivity demands, and job security rather than wage or benefit levels. Similarly, corporate-community relationships have been transformed by heightened interstate and intrastate competition for jobs. In an era of policy devolution and persistent state fiscal crisis, this has had devastating effects on the level of social provision states and localities can afford (Center on Budget and Policy Priorities, 2005; Holzer, Schanzenbach, Duncan, & Ludwig, 2007; Piven, 2002).

At a more fundamental level, the nature of property, property relations, and work itself has been changed by economic globalization. In other words, our assumptions about these fundamental building blocks of economic and social policies since the Industrial Revolution are far less valid today than they were even a few decades ago. For example, property is being transformed from cash, land, and other tangible commodities into credits. National and international economic and social policies now focus primarily on the protection of investors' property rights rather than the rights of the producers or consumers of wealth. Radical changes have also occurred in the nature of many occupations, the social basis of work, and the stability of employment (Blau, 1999; Esping-Andersen, 2002; Quigley, 2003; Wilson, 1996).

Economic globalization has been buttressed by an accompanying ideological rationale: that capitalist goals, values, and behaviors pervade the world economy and shape all major institutions and market mechanisms (George & Wilding, 2002; Piven, 2002). These changes appear in the language that guides policy discourse, in the distribution of power (both within the public domain and between the public and private sectors), and in views of politics itself (i.e., the process of determining and legitimating societal priorities). While there is certainly still wide variation in national economies, in most of the industrialized world policy making reflects the logic of maintaining a system of global capitalism. Its proponents assert that the transfer of national resources from production for domestic use to production for export is required to promote consistent economic development and to maintain a competitive edge in the global market.

Critics counter that an emphasis on foreign trade destabilizes long-standing institutions and community relationships, particularly in regions of the developing world with established, subsistence-model economies. Such effects are felt even in advanced economies such as the United States. In the past 3 decades, transnational corporations have destroyed local enterprises, precious natural resources have been privatized, social spending has been drastically reduced, taxation systems have become increasingly regressive, and both public and private debt burdens have soared (Deaton, 2003; Jessop, 2002; Pugh & Gould, 2000). The social impact of these developments has also been dramatic, most notably in those statistics that reflect negative social indicators, such as violent crime and neighborhood deterioration (Abe, 2001; Boushey, Brocht, Gundersen, & Bernstein, 2001; Chow, Johnson, & Austin, 2005; Holzer, Offner, & Sorensen, 2005; O'Conner, 2001).

Economic globalization has also revealed many of the anachronistic features of our policy-making system and the declining importance of political boundaries and allegiances. Simply put, national governments (to say nothing of state or local governments) lack the scope, speed of action, and institutional capacity to respond to economic, demographic, and social problems emanating from forces outside their span of control. The twentieth-century welfare state was founded on the belief that national governments could regulate the effects of national economies. Now that economies are transnational in scope, governments lack the authority and power (some suggest the will as well) to change their social policies in response (George & Wilding, 2002).

In addition, globalization has diminished the role of organized labor in struggles to maintain or expand the share of the social wage received by working people. Particularly in industrialized nations such as the United States, real wages have decreased since the mid-1970s and employment has become increasingly insecure. So-called lean production techniques, whose purpose is to enhance productivity and reduce labor costs, have led to such methods as on-time production, the substitution of unskilled for skilled workers, and outsourcing. These effects are now visible in the service sector as well, including health and mental health settings, universities, and child welfare agencies (McDonald, Harris, & Winterstein, 2003; Reisch & Gorin, 2001).

Globalization has also been closely linked to emerging demographic trends, including the mass movement of populations in search of employment, primarily from the global South to industrialized nations. In the United States, this has led to the perception of a crisis over immigration, particularly concerning undocumented immigrants. It has also exacerbated existing social and political conflicts, often along ethnic or racial lines. Some of the policy implications of these conflicts will be discussed next.

POVERTY, INEQUALITY, AND UNEMPLOYMENT

While proponents of globalization frequently tout its benefits for the nation's GNP, its economic impact has been uneven at best. Although median household income in the United States surpasses that of most industrialized nations, the United States has one of the highest poverty rates in the world (Center on Budget and Policy Priorities, 2005; Danziger & Gottschalk, 2004). Although the official poverty rate has remained fairly constant in recent years—fluctuating between 12% and 13%—the median income of American families has actually dropped since 2000 (Annie E. Casey Foundation, 2004; Bowles, Gintis, & Groves, 2005; Bureau of Labor Statistics, 2006; Mishel, Bernstein, & Allegretto, 2006; U.S. Census Bureau, 2006). The proportion of children in poverty in the United States continues to be about 20% (the highest in the industrialized world); the rate is over twice as high among African Americans and Latinos (Children's Defense Fund, 2006; Forum on Child and Family Statistics, 2006; U.S. Census Bureau, 2006). Poverty rates are also particularly high among recent immigrants, individuals with disabilities, people in rural areas (particularly in the South), and households headed by single women (Rainwater & Smeeding, 2003; Rank, 2004).

Child poverty in the United States increased between 2000 and 2004, a phenomenon directly related to the decline in purchasing power of the minimum wage and higher local unemployment rates. These children "consistently fare worse than children in more affluent families on measures of child well-being, family environment, and sociodemographic risk" (Loprest & Zedlewski, 2006, p. 1). They are nearly 3 times as likely to have fair or poor health and over twice as likely to have parents who report symptoms of poor mental health.

Research has shown that the expansion of employment opportunities alone is not sufficient to address these problems unless the jobs that are created pay what is now called a "living wage" (Andersson, Holzer, & Lane, 2005; Bowles et al., 2005; Cauthen & Lu, 2003; Skocpol, 2000). Child poverty is also a drain on the nation's economy. A recent study (Holzer et al., 2007, p. 1) concluded that "the costs to the U.S. associated with childhood poverty total about $500 billion per year, or the equivalent of nearly 4% of GDP."

There are several points about these data that make them even more striking. First, according to many scholars and policy analysts, the government's "absolute" measure of poverty, established in 1963, vastly understates the true extent of income need (Glennerster, 2002; National Research Council, 1995). Adjustments in the means by which we measure poverty would increase the current rate anywhere from 20% to nearly 100% (Iceland, 2003; Quigley, 2003).

Second, the gap between the poverty line and median family income has widened considerably over the past 4 decades, unlike in European nations, where a relative measure of poverty maintains a standard of 60% of median income (Rank, 2004). In addition, the U.S. method of determining poverty ignores the enormous socioeconomic changes that have occurred over the past 4 decades in consumption patterns, labor force participation, gender roles, household expenditures, regional shifts in the cost of living, and social policy developments in the areas of health, welfare, and education (Abramson, Tobin, & Vandergoot, 1995; Andersson et al., 2005; Boushey et al., 2001; Bowles et al., 2005; Caiazza, Shaw, & Werschkul, 2004; Cancian & Reed, 2001; Forum on Child and Family Statistics, 2006; Hertz, 2005; O'Conner, 2001; Patterson, 2001).

Finally, official poverty statistics reveal little about the depth, chronic nature, or likelihood of poverty across the life span. They also give no indication of the number of individuals and families who are living just above the official poverty line or of the lasting effects of extended spells of poverty. One ominous recent phenomenon is the stark increase in the percentage of low-income families in extreme poverty—that is, those having incomes 50% or less than the poverty line. The number of people living in intense poverty—those with family incomes below $11,000 per year—actually increased in the past several years, particularly among African Americans (U.S. Census Bureau, 2006).

Nearly half of all individuals counted as poor in the United States are now in such extreme or dire poverty (U.S. Department of Health and Human Services, 2004). Although the duration of poverty remains relatively short for most poor Americans, over 20% of poor individuals remain poor for 1 year or more (Iceland, 2003). African Americans, Latinos, and female-headed households are over 5 times more likely than Whites to experience chronic poverty (Borjas & Katz, 2005; Danziger & Gottschalk, 2004; Hertz, 2005; Holzer et al., 2005; Sanchez, 2006; U.S. Census Bureau, 2006).

The duration of poverty spells is compounded by the widespread experience of poverty among Americans. Rank (2004) presents startling data demonstrating that more than half of the U.S. population experiences an episode of poverty during their lifetime of 1 year or more, and over three fourths of the population experiences at least a year of near poverty. Even more striking is his finding that 91% of African Americans will experience poverty at some point in their life. Given our knowledge about the long-term effects of poverty on health, psychological development, and educational attainment, these figures belie the myth of prosperity and widespread well-being in the United States (Boushey et al., 2001; Campbell, Haveman, Sandefur, & Wolfe, 2005; Capps, Fix, Ost, Reardon-Anderson, &

Passel, 2004; Gershoff, 2003; Mishel et al., 2006). They also indicate the extent to which large numbers of the U.S. population, particularly in communities of color and immigrant communities, are at risk of a wide range of health, mental health, and social problems (Bean & Stevens, 2003; Capps et al. 2004; Case, Fertig, & Paxson, 2005; Corcoran, 2001; Dahl & Lochner, 2006; Deaton, 2003; Slack & Yoo, 2004).

Another major consequence of recent economic changes is the increase in structural unemployment and underemployment among workers in both developing and industrialized nations. Approximately one third of the global workforce is now unemployed or underemployed (i.e., earning below a living wage). This phenomenon is often masked in the United States by the means used to calculate the official unemployment rate, which has remained at about 5% for the past decade (Mishel et al., 2006). This statistic does not include individuals who are incarcerated, have never entered the workforce (e.g., impoverished inner-city adolescents), have given up looking for work, or are in the military. It also does not include workers who have shifted to part-time employment or taken jobs that pay significantly lower wages and lack health care and other fringe benefits (Andersson et al., 2005).

While U.S. poverty and unemployment statistics have varied little in recent years, key indicators of inequality worldwide have soared. Income inequality has nearly tripled in the past half century. The richest 20% of the world's population now produces nearly 85% of global GDP, while the poorest 20% produces less than 2% (Deaton, 2003; Jencks, 2002; Oxfam America, 2004).

These problems, however, are not limited to the global North-South dichotomy. There are disturbing and ominous developments in the United States as well. During the past generation the United States has become the most unequal of all industrialized nations and is more unequal today than at any time since World War II (Mishel et al., 2006; U.S. Census Bureau, 2006). A report published by the Economic Policy Institute and the Center on Budget and Policy Priorities (2006, p. 1) found that the "incomes of the country's richest families have climbed substantially during the past two decades, while middle and lower-income families have seen only modest increases." Despite the economic booms of the 1980s and 1990s, during the last quarter of the twentieth century the lower 60% of U.S. households experienced a decline in their share of all income, while the top 20% saw its share increase over 38%, and the top 1% increased its share by nearly 120%. As a potent symbol of this trend, between 1990 and 2000 CEO salaries increased 571%. They are now over 400 times that of an average worker (CBS.Marketwatch.com, 2007).

Looking beyond such symbols to the population as a whole, the top 1% of all U.S. households now has as much total disposable income as the bottom 40%. The richest 20% of families have average incomes 10 times as large as the poorest 20% (a gap that is one-third greater than in the late 1970s) and nearly 3 times as large as the middle 20%. Thus, despite the presence of aggregate GNP growth, "the triumph of the market has eroded most Americans' standard of living" (Blau, 1999, p. 22).

The long-term implications of these developments are dire. Today, half of all adults in the United States are at economic risk in terms of their levels of literacy and education. Over 47 million Americans lack health insurance and millions more have inadequate coverage. The infant mortality rate in the United States ranks 21st in the world. While in neighboring Mexico 90% of all children under 5 are immunized against childhood diseases, in some U.S. cities the rate is below 50%. As low-income families' economic well-being declines they "have a much harder time lifting themselves out of poverty and giving their children a decent start in life" (Children's Defense Fund, 2006, p. 3).

The primary reasons for increased income inequality are the erosion in wages for the 70% of the workforce who lack a college degree, the decline in the purchasing power of the minimum wage—which has not increased in a decade—and regressive trends in the overall burden of taxation. Another factor is the impact of new technology and deindustrialization, which have significantly reduced the number of unskilled and semiskilled entry-level jobs in the workforce, and created what is termed a "dual labor market" (Andersson et al., 2005; Borjas & Katz, 2005; Boushey et al., 2001; Bureau of Labor Statistics, 2006; Duncan, 1998; Holzer et al., 2005; Mishel et al., 2006). An additional factor is the impact of foreign competition, particularly from China and India, which is reflected in the burgeoning trade deficit and exacerbated by the outsourcing of both manufacturing and service jobs. Finally, the declining power of unions has made resistance to these developments more difficult and increased pressure on workers to renegotiate decades-old wage and benefit packages, as recent contract negotiations in the auto industry illustrate (Blau, 1999; Delgado, 1993).

The consequences of globalization, however, are not uniformly distributed in the United States. Certain regions have prospered even in times of economic stagnation, while others, like Michigan, remain mired in recession-like conditions. It is important, therefore, to distinguish between aggregate and distributional data when assessing the extent and nature of economic growth and change. There are also significant differences in poverty, unemployment, and welfare rates among and even within states, often based on the demographic differences of their populations (Annie E. Casey Foundation, 2004; Caiazza et al., 2004; Center on Budget and Policy Priorities, 2006).

Policy devolution has exacerbated these trends by reducing the role of the federal government in ameliorating these effects where they are most needed and making state governments responsible for addressing conditions they did not create. Many states and municipalities now confront the dilemma of responding to increased demands for social and health services in the face of eroding tax bases. Ironically, those states with chronic fiscal crises, such as Michigan, are precisely those that need the greatest infusion of resources to address the effects of globalization and demographic changes (Center on Budget and Policy Priorities, 2005).

In an analogous fashion, the same contradictory situation confronts families that are experiencing chronic poverty, low-wage work, and unemployment. Although the American dream of upward mobility has some validity, it has largely become a myth, especially for low-income and working-class Americans, who are disproportionately persons of color and immigrants. As educational attainment and job skills become increasingly important determinants of economic success in the global market, children from lower socioeconomic backgrounds face mounting obstacles due to the inadequacy of the schools most of them attend (Campbell et al., 2005; Capps et al., 2004; Dahl & Lochner, 2006; Forum on Child and Family Statistics, 2006; Gershoff, 2003).

Racial and class gaps in education, particularly in regard to workforce preparation at the secondary school level, create especially acute problems for African American, Latino, and American Indian youth. These problems are even more serious for the children of recent immigrants, documented or undocumented, and for children in single-parent female-headed households. African American and Latino children in these households are at greater risk for poverty and its social consequences because of their parents lower wages and higher rate of unemployment (Caiazza et al., 2004; Cancian & Reed, 2001; Case et al., 2005; Cauthen & Lu, 2003; Children's Defense Fund, 2006).

Thus, data on poverty and economic inequality in the United States are complicated further by the persistence of widespread racial inequality. Throughout U.S. history, race has played a significant role in the development of welfare policies (Brown, 1999; Jansson, 2005; Katz, 2001; Lieberman, 1998; Patterson, 2001). Even during periods of social reform, such as the Progressive Era, the 1930s, and the 1960s, persons of color faced discrimination in the application of eligibility standards and the distribution of social benefits; they also suffered the effects of White backlash against the modest gains they received. Over the past 40 years, the perpetuation of racial stereotypes in the mass media and the use of racial codes for partisan political purposes reduced public support for welfare programs as a whole (Clawson & Trice, 2000). In combination with persistent discrimination and the rollback of Affirmative Action programs, this has produced widening racial gaps in income and assets, which, in turn, result in growing racial disparities in health and education (Bowles et al., 2005; Brown, 1999; Bureau of Labor Statistics, 2006; Dahl & Lochner, 2006).

These developments, therefore, are not merely the consequence of uncontrollable global economic forces. They are also the result of conscious policy decisions made during the past quarter century. From the late 1950s through the 1970s, a full-time worker earning the minimum wage could maintain a family of three at or above the poverty level. Since 1981, however, because of the stagnation of minimum wage laws, the same worker's wages have been steadily below this level. The current value of the minimum wage in constant dollars is barely above what it was a half century ago (Bureau of Labor Statistics, 2006; Mishel et al., 2006).[1]

Today, because of the resistance of policy makers to the expansion of government-subsidized health care or health insurance, as illustrated by recent debates over the expansion of the federal children's health insurance (or S-Chip) program, the majority of working poor families with children lack health benefits. Since the passage of welfare reform in 1996, the proportion of families eligible for public assistance who are now receiving benefits dropped from 80% in 1996 to 48% in 2002 (Urban Institute, 2006). At the same time, the percentage of low-income single-parent families with an employed parent has increased 5% over the past 10 years. Efforts to reform welfare have also exacerbated the problem of children aging out of the foster care system and increased the cost of child welfare programs to states, which bear a disproportionate share of the fiscal burden (Annie E. Casey Foundation, 2004; Blank, 2002; Piven, 2002; Tumlin & Zimmerman, 2003).

DEMOGRAPHIC CHANGES: RACISM AND IMMIGRATION

In December 1880, at an informal meeting in New York City, the Committee on Immigration of the National Conference of Charities and Corrections concluded that there was an urgent need for "federal action to regulate immigration, supervise and protect immigrants, and to guard against the shipment to this country of criminals, and of lunatic, idiotic, crippled, and other infirm alien paupers" (Hoyt, 1881, p. 217). Similar attitudes about immigrants persisted throughout the early twentieth century. In a 1901 letter to Homer Folks, a national leader in the field of charities and child welfare, Prescott Hall, the secretary

---

[1]As this essay was being written, the U.S. House of Representatives passed the first increase in the federal minimum wage in over a decade, but it has not yet been implemented into law. It is noteworthy that since the 1990s, nearly 30 states have approved their own increases in the minimum wage.

of the Immigration Restriction League—whose board members included Robert Treat Paine and other leaders of the Charities Organization movement—asked for Folks's support of congressional legislation that would

exclude the more undesirable elements of our present immigration, . . . [specifically those who are] destitute of resources either in money or still more in ability and knowledge of the means to support [themselves]; [those who are] generally ignorant; [those who have] criminal tendencies; [those who are] adverse to country life and congregate in our city slums; [those who have] a low standard of living and little ambition to seek a better, and [those who have] no permanent interests in this country. (Hall, 1901)

Hall's language would not seem out of place today on some anti-immigration web sites.

During this period, policy makers focused on two primary concerns about immigrants: their impact on the nation's economy and their effect on a variety of social conditions, including crime and delinquency, public health, family life, and the demographic and cultural balance of the nation (Bowen, 1909; Fishberg, 1906; Hart, 1896; Hugo, 1912; Marshall, 1906; McMurtrie, 1909; Sanborn, 1886). Opinions on the former ranged widely, although there was widespread awareness that economic rather than political motivations were spurring mass immigration from Europe and Asia. In language strikingly similar to contemporary debates, proponents of immigration such as Phillip Garrett (1888, p. 188) argued, "It is surely conducive to the industrial well-being of the United States that a constant healthy flow of immigration should pour into this continent." Critics cited the threat of "industrial saturation," which would increase unemployment and depress wages, and an increase in undesirable interracial competition. Others commented on the danger of exploitation, particularly of young women and children (Coletti, 1912; Gates, 1909; Sulzberger, 1912; Taylor, 1913; U.S. Industrial Commission on Immigration and Education, 1901; Wald, 1909; Weyl, 1905).

Views about the social impact of unrestricted immigration reflected similar differences. Anti-immigration advocates spoke of the need "to rid ourselves of aliens who are a burden to our people or a menace to our peace and welfare" (Guenther, 1896, p. 305), cited the challenges of linguistic and cultural assimilation, and discussed the menace of growing numbers of "foreign quarters" in U.S. cities (Antwerp, 1890). Legislative proposals included deportation of immigrants who became dependents, tighter regulation of entry into the United States to screen out "convicts, lunatics, idiots, or others likely to become a public charge," and more stringent state residency laws (Gates, 1898; Hoyt, 1887; Hoyt, Sanborn, & Dana, 1886).

These attitudes about immigrants, particularly non-European immigrants, have persisted since colonial times. In the modern era, they have shaped restrictive federal legislation (most notably in 1882 and 1924), forced the repatriation of Mexican immigrants in the 1920s and 1930s, justified the incarceration of Japanese Americans during World War II, led to the passage of discriminatory state laws such as Proposition 187 in California, and spurred the current militarization of the U.S.-Mexico border. Even within the social welfare field, repeated concerns have been expressed about the alleged criminality of immigrants, their demands on the social service system, and, particularly in times of economic distress, their impact on the workforce (Barrabee, 1954; Bowler, 1931; Hopkins, 1932; Kohler, 1931; Lamb, 1942; Larned, 1930; MacCormack, 1934; Powell, 1943; Snyder, 1930; Warren, 1933). It was not until the post–World War II era that concerns about the quality of services to immigrants and migrants begun to be discussed in earnest (Douglass, 1955; Hoey, 1947; Rawley, 1948). These concerns recurred in the 1970s and 1980s in the aftermath of the Vietnam War, with an increased emphasis on improving the scope of programs addressing these issues (Blum, 1978, 1981; Finck, 1982–1983; Jones, 1981; Palmieri, 1980).

On the whole, however, U.S. policies have been fueled by persistent myths about the economic and social impact of immigrants. These include such myths as the following:

- *There are too many immigrants.* This myth is especially powerful when the immigrants are from different races, ethnicities, and religions and when the proportion of immigrants in urban areas equals or exceeds that of the native-born population. This situation existed in Chicago and New York at the turn of the twentieth century and is present today in New York, California, Florida, and Texas. This myth is often coupled with other myths, such as that most immigrants are poor and uneducated and are disproportionately involved in crime.

- *Immigrants take jobs from U.S. citizens and decrease the standard of living.* This myth is particularly prevalent today among low-income Whites and African Americans. It is usually most powerful during periods of economic insecurity or stagnation and in regions with high rates of poverty and unemployment.

- *The influx of immigrants will destroy the nation's cultural heritage and undermine its civilization.* The roots of this nativist sentiment go back at least as far as the creation of the Know-Nothing Party of the 1840s, perhaps even to the colonial period. At one time or another, the specter of cultural decline has been raised in the aftermath of Irish, Italian, Eastern European, Chinese, and Mexican immigration. Today, it is reflected in attacks on bilingual education, in support for "English-only" ballot initiatives, and in the anti-immigrant laws being debated in Congress.

- *Immigrants do not pay taxes—or pay insufficient taxes—and drain government resources by placing excessive demands on health and social services.* This myth persists despite numerous studies to the contrary and the discriminatory pattern of policy implementation toward immigrants (Borjas, 2002; Capps et al., 2004; Chow, Osterling, & Xu, 2005; Drachman, 1995; Foner, 1987; Jensen & Chitose, 1994; Muller, 1993; RAND Corporation, 2006; Tumlin & Zimmerman, 2003).

The persistence of these myths obscures many of the real issues that immigrants confront, such as increased juvenile delinquency among second-generation immigrant youth and the wide variation in the experiences, problems, and needs of different groups. Viewing all immigrants through the same lens also masks the role of race, regional, and religious differences among immigrants, even those from the same country (Bean & Stevens, 2003; Borjas, 2002; Capps et al., 2004; Carlson, 1994; Gold, 1989). In addition, myths about immigration make it harder to distinguish the effects of immigration and internal migration among both immigrants and the native-born population and to examine the relationship between these phenomena (Portes, 1990; Waldinger, 2001; Yang, 1995).

Historically, internal migration has occurred for several different reasons in patterns that are frequently repeated among different immigrant groups. One cause of migration is the natural resettlement process of immigrants from the coasts to the heartland, which occurs largely for economic reasons. A second cause is an intergenerational diaspora that coincides with broader trends in geographic and economic mobility in the United States. A third explanation is the migration of agricultural workers for employment, which is a cyclic and ongoing process. Finally, throughout U.S. history there have been periods of internal migration because of economic depression, agricultural failures, or political repression. These have included the Great Migration of African Americans in the early twentieth century, the movement of dustbowl "Okies" in the 1930s, and the influx of Puerto Ricans to the U.S. mainland in the 1950s (Takaki, 1994).

These periods of internal migration differ from the experiences of immigrants who came to the United States to flee political or religious persecution. Among the latter have been Germans in the mid-nineteenth century; Eastern European Jews in the late nineteenth and early twentieth centuries; Filipinos in the early twentieth century; Cubans in the 1920s, 1960s, and 1980s; German and Polish Jews in the 1930s and 1940s; Soviet Jews and Southeast Asians in the 1970s and 1980s; Central Americans in the 1980s; Haitians in the 1980s and 1990s; and Iraqis in the early twenty-first century (Waldinger, 2001; Takaki, 1994). Today, however, as a result of economic globalization, the lines between immigration and migration have been blurred, as have the distinctions between the economic, social, and political reasons for large population movements (Duncan, 1998; Ferrera, 2005; Penna et al., 2000).

Throughout U.S. history, immigrants and migrants have been at greater risk of poverty than native-born Americans. In recent decades, this trend has been exacerbated by the general decline in the wage scale, particularly for unskilled and semiskilled labor, changing occupational patterns, and cuts in public school funding and other social supports. Immigrants from Latin America and parts of the Caribbean are particularly vulnerable because of their lack of education and higher birthrates, although the poverty rate among Asian and Pacific Island immigrants is also higher than that of Whites (U.S. Census Bureau, 2006; Waldinger, 2001). These immigrants are increasingly concentrated not only in traditional coastal urban enclaves but also in heartland metropolises such as Minneapolis, Memphis, Denver, and Kansas City. Their presence has produced enhanced intergroup tensions and competition with other low-income communities and, in an era of policy devolution, has intensified pressures on local and state governments to create responsive social policies at the same time they are struggling with the realities of fiscal austerity (Abramovitz, 2005; Abramovitz, 2002; Center on Budget and Policy Priorities, 2005; Tumlin & Zimmerman, 2003).

As these changes have intensified the need for structural responses to the consequences of unregulated economic transformation, a variety of other demographic factors have made the policy and political environment increasingly complex. The following sociodemographic changes have taken on particular importance:

- *The aging of the population, especially the rapid increase in the so-called "old old" population (i.e., those over 85):* This already has had a dramatic impact on the cost of health care and has precipitated a fiscal "time bomb" in Medicare funding, which the nation's policy makers have, to date, failed to address (Social Security Administration, 2006). Less frequently discussed but no less significant consequences of this change have occurred in housing and employment patterns (e.g., for caretakers) and the stability of family systems.

- *The dramatic shifts in the racial and ethnic composition of the United States, particularly in large cities and major states such as California, Florida, Texas, and New York:* In several states and many large cities, former minorities are now the demographic, if not the political, majority (U.S. Census Bureau, 2006). This transformation underscores the existence of persistent disparities between population distribution and the distribution of resources, power, and status. It also alters intergroup dynamics and complicates growing intergroup tensions in unprecedented ways—that is, from a simple majority-minority racial/ethnic dichotomy to a complex network of interlocking alliances and conflicts.

• *Changing patterns of household size, including the growth of single-person households, particularly among women, and variations in these patterns among different ethnic groups and regions:* Significant variations in birth and mortality rates also have critical implications for social policy and will shape on what issues, in what areas, and through what means the United States will spend finite resources (Forum on Child and Family Statistics, 2006; U.S. Census Bureau, 2006).

• *The transformation of the family, including new gender roles, variations in family size by class, ethnicity, and religion, emerging patterns of intergenerational relationships and responsibilities, and new definitions of what constitutes a family:* These cultural and social changes have significant implications in such policy areas as health care, child welfare, and employment (Annie E. Casey Foundation, 2004; Children's Defense Fund, 2006; Forum on Child and Family Statistics, 2006).

• *The depopulation of certain regions of the country (e.g., rural areas, the plains) and the increased density of urban areas:* This trend is particularly important in an era of policy devolution (U.S. Census Bureau, 2006).

• *The economic decline of older, "inner-ring" suburbs, which are increasingly populated by persons of color, the elderly, and new immigrants:* Unless regional approaches to social and economic problems are developed, these communities will find it difficult to break out of their current downward spiral (Abramson et al., 1995; Massey & Denton, 1993).

• *Changing attitudes about sexual orientation, which affect social policies as wide ranging as legal definitions of marriage, laws regarding child custody and adoption, domestic partner benefits, and guardianship rights of nonmarried couples:* These issues have generated intense political and cultural controversy in the past decade and have been resolved differently (and through different means) in different parts of the nation.

IMPLICATIONS FOR SOCIAL POLICY

In combination, these profound economic and demographic changes raise several critical questions about the direction of U.S. social policy in the twenty-first century:

• Which groups should bear the social and economic costs of these changes?
• What values and goals will guide the development of future social policies?
• What roles should the public, nonprofit, and private sectors play in policy development and implementation to address these problems?

Developing answers to these questions is more difficult in the United States because of the unique way its social welfare system evolved. Unlike most other industrialized nations, social policies in the United States have been driven by pragmatic rather than ideological considerations (at least, until recently), and the nation has consistently relied more on the private sector and less on government than have its European counterparts (Axinn & Stern, 2008; Jansson, 2005; Katz, 2001; Patterson, 2001). U.S. social policies have tended to have more limited goals and a looser, more decentralized organizational structure. The United States also has confronted far greater demographic diversity than other industrialized nations. For the latter reason, some critics argue that in spite of its pragmatic appearances, U.S. policy choices were deliberately designed to maintain racial, gender, and class hierarchies (Brown, 1999; Lieberman, 1998; Piven, 2002; Quadagno, 1994; Reisch, 2005).

Nevertheless, since the nineteenth century there has been a gradual expansion of government intervention in the economy and society. The creation of publicly funded social policies in the twentieth century diminished somewhat the negative effects of the market by collectivizing what Kapp (1972) called the "social costs of private enterprise." Unlike in most European welfare states, however, U.S. social policies have focused primarily on reducing poverty rather than inequality, and such efforts have been modest, at best, even in periods of reform such as the 1930s and 1960s (Katz, 2001; Patterson, 2001).

There are several explanations for this so-called American exceptionalism that have implications for how the United States will respond to contemporary economic and demographic developments. One is the deep-seated American tendency to emphasize individualism and self-reliance and resist seeing problems or their solutions in group terms. Ironically, there has also been a contradictory tendency to attach labels to populations at risk that attribute their common condition to the possession or absence of particular cultural characteristics or behaviors. The "culture of poverty" thesis and the concept of a welfare "underclass" are just two examples of this phenomenon (Clawson & Trice, 2000; Quadagno, 1994). In combination, these tendencies have reinforced the values of dominant cultural groups and maintained the social and economic status quo. The relative weakness of working-class and left-wing political parties and the absence of sustained interracial social justice movements have also made it difficult for alternative policy proposals to obtain or sustain legitimacy (Reisch, 2005).

As a result of recent economic and demographic transformations, long-standing conflicts between charitable and social justice perspectives on social policy have now emerged in a different context. Throughout the twentieth century, social policy debates focused on the extent to which the government should establish rights or "entitlements," engage in institutionalized redistribution, or promote various forms of compensation or redress (Katz, 2001). These principles are now under attack by the logic of a world market system that regards social investment as an impediment to capital growth. A neoliberal post-Fordist regime has replaced the Keynesian-style system of social policies that first appeared in the 1930s. The new regime requires significant alterations in the institutional fabric of policy making to abet "the pursuit of a competitive edge in a global economy" (Jessop, 1999, p. 353). Consequently, in nearly all advanced welfare states, social policies are increasingly designed to enhance corporate rather than individual, family, or community well-being (McDonald et al., 2003; Taylor-Gooby, 2001). Piven (2002, p. 21) argues, however, that

what the American example actually suggests is not a model of a country adapting to globalization, but rather the impact of politics—class politics specifically, the impact of a business class moving to use public policy to shore up private profits.

WELFARE REFORM AS A POLICY ILLUSTRATION

For decades, proponents of so-called welfare reform inflated the costs of welfare programs and focused on a minority of recipients—African American adolescent mothers—to promote the myth of welfare failure. By creating a wedge issue based on symbolic appeals to racial and, to a lesser extent, gender bias, antiwelfare propagandists undermined the foundations of the U.S. welfare system itself. Many of the myths disseminated as facts at the height of the welfare reform debate reflected a deliberate misinterpretation about the nature of human need in modern industrial society. Over the past several decades, welfare reform can best be understood as the spearhead of a broader campaign to reduce government's role in addressing the economic and demographic problems generated or exacerbated by globalization (Abramovitz, 2005; Blank, 2002; Patterson, 2001; Reisch, 2003).

In this context, welfare reform has served several interrelated purposes. First, it helps lower the wage scale by increasing competition for unskilled jobs. This conforms to the logic of globalization by reducing the costs of production and making U.S. industries more competitive in the global market system. Second, it strengthens the drive for greater workforce discipline and compliance, particularly in the service sector of the economy. Third, it promotes a general reduction in the role of government, which has significant implications beyond the social welfare arena in such areas as trade, banking, and environmental regulations. Finally, by calling into question the legitimacy of welfare entitlements and government's effectiveness in administering social programs, it creates an enormous opportunity for the private sector to acquire new and vast resources of capital—the Social Security Trust Funds—as the recent political offensive by the Bush administration demonstrates (Reisch, 2003).

The effects of welfare reform, however, have been decidedly mixed. Its supporters point to the dramatic (nearly 50%) decline in welfare caseloads as evidence of success (Blank, 2002). Critics, however, argue that caseloads began to decline in the mid-1990s and continued to decrease throughout the decade due to economic growth. Further, they claim that the poverty rate is a better indicator of families' well-being and that it has not declined since 1996 (Children's Defense Fund, 2006). In addition, families on welfare are hardly well off: In 2001, the combined benefits of Temporary Assistance for Needy Families (TANF) and food stamps ranged from 37% to 71% of the poverty threshold (U.S. Department of Health and Human Services, 2004).

States have not kept track of former TANF recipients. There is no way to determine, therefore, whether they left welfare for employment or, if they did, whether they are still employed. Recent evidence indicates that many TANF recipients remain employed for only brief periods or are employed in low-wage jobs that often lack benefits. Others simply drop out of sight and are discouraged from reapplying for TANF because of the program's restrictions (Allen & Kirby, 2000; Borjas, 2002; Chow, Johnson, et al., 2005; Chow, Osterling, et al., 2005; Piven, 2002; Reisch, 2003; Tumlin & Zimmerman, 2003).

The consequences of welfare reform have been particularly severe for particular demographic segments of U.S. society. As a result of welfare reform, the myth that African Americans compose the largest portion of benefit recipients has become a reality. The 5-year time limit on benefits has had a disproportionate impact on persons of color, including those of Asian descent. Increasingly, low-income families (whether on or off welfare)

are concentrated in high-poverty neighborhoods, with deleterious effects on employment and educational opportunities, physical health and mental health status, and children's prospects for the future. Finally, the growth of anti-immigration sentiment in parts of the United States has led to an overall backlash against the provision of social welfare services to persons of color, including legal immigrants. These developments have planted the seeds for future conflict over the resolution of major policy issues.

CONCLUSION

The significance of welfare reform has not been confined to its effects on beneficiaries and their families. In an environment of economic globalization and increasing demographic complexity, such policy changes should also be assessed in regard to their impact on the underlying philosophy of U.S. social welfare; the respective roles of government, nonprofits, and the for-profit sector in twenty-first-century policy making; and the distribution of policy responsibilities among federal, state, and local governments. Welfare reform also illustrates the interlocking nature of economic and demographic changes. By terminating the entitlement to cash assistance and placing severe restrictions on the receipt of benefits, welfare reform undermines the concept of public aid that was at the core of the 1935 Social Security Act. This has increased the vulnerability of other entitlement programs, such as Old Age Assistance, Medicare, and Medicaid, to political and ideological attacks. The fate of these social safety net programs will be particularly critical in the years ahead as the population ages and the economic and demographic effects of globalization mount.

The confluence of these developments makes it clear that the United States can no longer separate debates over such issues as welfare, health care, and education from those over employment and immigration policy. By the mid-twenty-first century, the United States will have a growing population of elderly people, two thirds of them White, being supported by fewer workers, about half of whom will be persons of color. Not long after 2050, the majority of American workers will be persons of color, as will nearly 60% of the nation's children.

This contrast has profound implications for such issues as intergenerational responsibility and equity, the determination of funding priorities, and the management of social conflict in an increasingly diverse society. It creates hard fiscal choices in an era of chronic budget deficits. For example, should we spend finite health-care dollars today on the elderly or on children, their future benefactors?

Such questions have real-world implications. In less than 40 years, just to maintain Social Security benefits at their current levels, the United States will have to provide educational and social supports for today's children to enable them to earn an average wage that is 1.5 times more than at present. Without dramatic improvements in such supports, particularly for children of color, low-income children, and those from immigrant families, by the middle of the twenty-first century they will be economically worse off and unable to sustain our current health and income support systems for the elderly. As Martha Ozawa (1997) argued eloquently and prophetically a decade ago, unless current trends in social welfare spending are reversed, the United States is on a self-destructive econodemographic course that could transform the American dream into a nightmare.

REFERENCES

Abe, Y. (2001). Changes in gender and racial gaps in antisocial behavior: The NLSY97 versus the NLSY79. In R. Michael (Ed.), *Social awakening: Adolescent behavior as adulthood approaches* (pp. 339–378). New York: Russell Sage Foundation.

Abramovitz, M. (1999). *Regulating the lives of women: Social welfare policy from colonial times to the present* (2nd ed.). Boston: South End Press.

Abramovitz, M. (2002). *In jeopardy: The impact of welfare reform on nonprofit human service agencies in New York City.* New York: United Way of America.

Abramovitz, M. (2005). The largely untold story of welfare reform and the human services, *Social Work, 50*(2), 175–186.

Abramson, A., Tobin, M., & Vandergoot, M. (1995). The changing geography of metropolitan opportunity: The segregation of the poor in U.S. metropolitan areas, 1970–1990. *Housing Policy Debate, 6*(1), 45–72.

Allen, K., & Kirby, M. (2000). *Unfinished business: Why cities matter to welfare reform.* Washington, DC: Brookings Institution.

Andersson, F., Holzer, H. J., & Lane, J. I. (2005). *Moving up or moving on: Who advances in the low-wage labor market?* Washington, DC: Russell Sage Foundation.

Annie E. Casey Foundation. (2004). *City KIDS COUNT: Data on the well-being of children in large cities.* Baltimore: Author.

Antwerp, J. H. (1890). Report of the committee on immigration. In *Proceedings of the National Conference of Charities and Corrections* (pp. 279–281). Boston: Press of Geo H. Ellis.

Axinn, J., & Stern, M. (2008). *Social welfare: A history of the American response to need* (7th ed.). Boston: Allyn & Bacon.

Barrabee, P. (1954). How cultural factors affect family life. In *Proceedings of the National Conference of Social Work* (p. 17). Chicago: University of Chicago Press.

Bean, F. D., & Stevens, G. (2003). *America's newcomers and the dynamics of diversity.* New York: Russell Sage Foundation.

Bergman, L. R., & Lundberg, O. (2006). Perspectives on determinants of social welfare: Introduction and commentary. *International Journal of Social Welfare, 15*(1), 52–54, 549–552.

Blank, R. (2002). Evaluating welfare reform in the United States. *Journal of Economic Literature, 40*(4), 1105–1166.

Blau, J. (1999). *Illusions of prosperity: America's working families in an age of economic insecurity.* New York: Oxford University Press.

Blum, M. D. (1978). Service to immigrants in a multicultural society. In *Proceedings of the annual forum of the National Conference on Social Welfare* (pp. 216–233). New York: Columbia University Press.

Blum, M. D. (1981). Refugees and community tension. In *Proceedings of the annual forum of the National Conference on Social Welfare* (pp. 115–130). New York: Columbia University Press.

Borjas, G. (2002). *The impact of welfare reform on immigrant welfare use.* Washington, DC: Center for Immigrant Studies.

Borjas, G., & Katz, L. (2005). *The evolution of the Mexican-born workforce in the United States* (Working Paper No. 11281). Washington, DC: National Bureau of Economic Research.

Boushey, H., Brocht, C., Gundersen, B., & Bernstein, J. (2001). *Hardship in America: The real story of working families.* Washington, DC: Economic Policy Institute.

Bowen, J. T. (1909). The delinquent children of immigrant parents. In *Proceedings of the National Conference of Social Work* (pp. 255–260). Chicago: University of Chicago Press.

Bowler, A. (1931). Recent statistics on crime and the foreign born. In *Proceedings of the National Conference of Social Work* (pp. 479–494). Chicago: University of Chicago Press.

Bowles, S., Gintis, H., & Groves, M. (2005). Introduction. In S. Bowles, H. Gintis, & M. Groves (Eds.), *Unequal chances: Family background and economic success* (pp. 1–22). Princeton, NJ: Princeton University Press.

Brown, M. (1999). *Race, money, and the American welfare state*. Ithaca, NY: Cornell University Press.

Bureau of Labor Statistics. (2006, January). *Employment and earnings* (Report). Washington, DC: U.S. Government Printing Office.

Caiazza, A., Shaw, A., & Werschkul, M. (2004). *Women's economic status in the states: Wide disparities by race, ethnicity, and region*. Washington, DC: Institute for Women's Policy Research.

Campbell, M., Haveman, R., Sandefur, G., & Wolfe, B. (2005). Economic inequality and educational attainment across a generation. *Focus, 23*(3), 11–15.

Cancian, M., & Reed, D. (2001). Changes in family structure: Implications for poverty and related policy. In S. Danziger & R. Haveman (Eds.), *Understanding poverty* (pp. 69–96) Cambridge, MA: Harvard University Press.

Capps, R., Fix, M., Ost, J., Reardon-Anderson, J., & Passel, J. (2004). *The health and well-being of young children of immigrants*. Washington, DC: Urban Institute.

Carlson, A. W. (1994). America's new immigration: Characteristics, destinations, and impact, 1970–1989. *Social Science Journal, 31*(3), 213–236.

Case, A., Fertig, A., & Paxson, C. (2005). The lasting impact of childhood health and circumstance. *Journal of Health Economics, 24*(2), 365–389.

Cauthen, N., & Lu, H. (2003). *Employment alone is not enough for America's low-income children and families living at the edge* (Research Brief No. 1). New York: National Center for Children in Poverty.

CBS.Marketwatch.com. (March 21, 2001). CEO salaries increased nearly 600% in last decade. Retrieved March 21, 2007, from www.CBS.Marketwatch.com.

Center on Budget and Policy Priorities. (2005, August 30). *Economic recovery failed to benefit much of the population in 2004* (Report). Washington, DC: Author.

Center on Budget and Policy Priorities. (2006, January 26). *Income inequality grew across the country over the past two decades* (Report). Washington, DC: Author.

Children's Defense Fund. (2006). *Statistics on child poverty in the United States*. Washington, DC: Author.

Chow, J. C., Johnson, M. A., & Austin, M. J. (2005). The status of low-income neighborhoods in the post-welfare environment: Mapping the relationship between poverty and place. *Journal of Health and Social Policy, 21*(1), 1–32.

Chow, J. C., Osterling, K. L., & Xu, Q. (2005). The risk of timing out: Welfare-to-work services to Asian immigrants and refugees. *AAPI Nexus, 3*(2), 85–104.

Clawson, R., & Trice, R. (2000). Poverty as we know it: Media portrayals of the poor. *Public Opinion Quarterly, 64*(4), 53–64.

Coletti, U. (1912). The Italian immigrant. In *Proceedings of the National Conference on Social Work* (pp. 249–254). Chicago: University of Chicago Press.

Corcoran, M. (2001). Mobility, persistence, and the consequences of child poverty for children: Child and adult outcomes. In S. Danziger & R. Haveman (Eds.), *Understanding poverty* (pp. 127–161). Cambridge, MA: Harvard University Press.

Dahl, G., & Lochner, L. (2006). *The impact of family income on child achievement* (Working Paper No. 11279).Washington, DC: National Bureau of Economic Research.

Danziger, S., & Gottschalk, P. (2004). *Diverging fortunes: Trends in poverty and inequality*. New York: Russell Sage Foundation.

Deacon, B. (1999, January). *Towards a socially responsible globalization: International actors and discourses* (Occasional Paper). Helsinki, Finland: Global and Social Policy Programme.

Deaton, A. (2003). Health, inequality and economic development. *Journal of Economic Literature*, *41*(1), 113–158.

Delgado, H. L. (1993). *New immigrants, old unions: Organizing the undocumented workers in Los Angeles*. Philadelphia: Temple University Press.

Douglass, J. H. (1955). Migration. In *Proceedings of the National Conference on Social Welfare* (pp. 160–173). New York: Columbia University Press.

Drachman, D. (1995). Immigration statuses and their influence on service provision, access, and use. *Social Work*, *40*(2), 188–197.

Duncan, L. (1998). *The role of immigrant labor in a changing economy*. Retrieved March 15, 2005, from http://www.nelp.org/docUploads/duncan%2Epdf.

Esping-Andersen, G. (with Gallie, D., Hemerijck, A., & Myles, J.). (2002). *Why we need a new welfare state*. New York: Oxford University Press.

Ferrera, M. (2005). *The boundaries of welfare: European integration and the new spatial politics of social protection*. New York: Oxford University Press.

Finck, J. (1982–1983). Voting with their feet: Secondary migrations of Indochinese refugees. In *Proceedings of the annual forum of the National Conference on Social Welfare* (pp. 101–107)). New York: Columbia University Press.

Fishberg, M. (1906). Ethnic factors in immigration: A critical view. In *Proceedings of the National Conference of Social Work* (pp. 304–314). Chicago: University of Chicago Press.

Foner, N. (1987). *New immigrants in New York*. New York: Columbia University Press.

Forum on Child and Family Statistics. (2006). *America's children in brief: Key national indicators of well-being*. Washington, DC: Federal Interagency Forum on Child and Family Statistics.

Garrett, P. (1888). Immigration to the United States: Report of the Committee on Immigration. In *Proceedings of the National Conference of Charities and Corrections* (pp. 185–192). Boston: Press of Geo H. Ellis.

Gates, W. A. (1898). Alien and non-resident dependents in Minnesota. In *Proceedings of the National Conference of Charities and Corrections* (pp. 276–282). Boston: Press of Geo H. Ellis.

Gates, W. A. (1909). Oriental immigration on the Pacific Coast. In *Proceedings of the National Conference of Social Work* (pp. 230–232). Chicago: University of Chicago Press.

George, V. (1998). Political ideology, globalization, and welfare futures in Europe. *Journal of Social Policy*, *27*(1), 17–36.

George, V., & Wilding, P. (2002). *Globalization and human welfare*. New York: Palgrave.

Gershoff, E. (2003). *Low income and hardship among America's kindergartners*. New York: National Center for Children in Poverty.

Glennerster, H. (2002). United States poverty studies and poverty measurement: The past twenty-five years. *Social Service Review*, *79*(1), 83–107.

Gold, S. (1989). Differential adjustment among new immigrant family members. *Journal of Contemporary Ethnography*, *17*(4), 408–434.

Guenther, R. (1896). United States legislation respecting immigration. In *Proceedings of the National Conference of Charities and Corrections* (pp. 302–307). Boston: George H. Ellis.

Hall, P. F. (1901, October 19). *Letter to Homer Folks* [Letter, one page]. Boston: Immigration Restriction League.

Hart, H. (1896). Immigration and crime. In *Proceedings of the National Conference of Charities and Corrections* (pp. 307–313). Boston: George H. Ellis.

Hertz, T. (2005). Rags, riches, and race: The intergenerational economic mobility of Black and White families in the United States. In S. Bowles, S. Gintis, & M. O. Groves (Eds.), *Unequal chances: Family background and economic success* (pp. 165–191). Princeton, NJ: Princeton University Press.

Hoey, J. M. (1947). Adequate public social services for migrants. In *Proceedings of the National Conference on Social Welfare* (pp. 163–175). New York: Columbia University Press.

Holzer, H. J., Offner, P., & Sorensen, E. (2005). Declining employment among young Black men: The role of incarceration and child support. *Journal of Policy Analysis and Management, 24(2),* 329–350.

Holzer, H. J., Schanzenbach, D. W., Duncan, G. J., & Ludwig, J. (2007, January 24). *The economic costs of poverty in the United States: Subsequent effects of children growing up poor* [Report]. Washington, DC: Center for American Progress.

Hopkins, E. (1932). The police and the immigrant. In *Proceedings of the National Conference of Social Work* (pp. 509–519). Chicago: University of Chicago Press.

Hoyt, C. S. (1881). Report on immigration. In *Proceedings of the Conference of Charities and Corrections* (pp. 217–218). Boston: A. Williams & Company.

Hoyt, C. S. (1887). Alien paupers, insane, and criminals in New York. In *Proceedings of the National Conference of Charities and Corrections* (pp. 197–206). Boston: Press of Geo H. Ellis.

Hoyt, C. S., Sanborn, F. B., & Dana, M. (1886). Report of the standing committee on immigration and migration. In *Proceedings of the National Conference of Charities and Corrections* (pp. 251–252). Boston: Press of Geo H. Ellis.

Hugo, E. (1912). Desertion of wives and children by emigrants to America. In *Proceedings of the National Conference of Social Work* (pp. 257–260). Chicago: University of Chicago Press.

Iceland, J. (2003). Why poverty remains high: The role of income growth, economic inequality, and changes in family structure, 1949–1999. *Demography, 40*(3), 499–519.

Jansson, B. (2005). *The reluctant welfare state* (5th ed.). Pacific Grove, CA: Brooks/Cole.

Jencks, C. (2002). Does inequality matter? *Daedalus, 131*(1), 49–65.

Jensen, L., & Chitose, Y. (1994). Today's second generation: Evidence from the 1990 U.S. census. *International Migration Review, 28*(4), 714–735.

Jessop, B. (1999). The changing governance of welfare: Recent trends in its primary functions, scale, and modes of coordination. *Social Policy and Administration, 33,* 348–359.

Jessop, B. (2002). *The future of the capitalist state.* Cambridge, England: Polity Press.

Jones, J. M. (1981). Thursday's children: Foster home services for Cuban refugees. In *Proceedings of the National Conference on Social Welfare* (pp. 131–139). New York: Columbia University Press.

Kapp, J. W. (1972). *The social costs of private enterprise.* New York: Schocken.

Katz, M. (2001). *The price of citizenship: Redefining the American welfare state.* New York: Henry Holt.

Kohler, M. (1931). Enforcing our deportation laws. In *Proceedings of the National Conference of Social Work* (pp. 495–505). Chicago: University of Chicago Press.

Lamb, R. (1942). Mass relocation of aliens. In *Proceedings of the National Conference on Social Work* (pp. 186–194). New York: Columbia University Press.

Larned, R. (1930). The tangled threads of migrant family problems. In *Proceedings of the National Conference of Social Work* (pp. 469–477). Chicago: University of Chicago Press.

Lieberman, R. (1998). *Shifting the color line: Race and the American welfare state.* Cambridge, MA: Harvard University Press.

Loprest, P., & Zedlewski, S. (2006). *The changing role of welfare in the lives of low-income families with children.* Washington, DC: Urban Institute.

MacCormack, D. W. (1934). The New Deal for the alien. In *Proceedings of the National Conference of Social Work* (pp. 465–472). Chicago: University of Chicago Press.

Marshall, L. C. (1906). Race effects of immigration. In *Proceedings of the National Conference of Social Work* (pp. 314–324). Chicago: University of Chicago Press.

Massey, D. S., & Denton, N. A. (1993). *American apartheid: Segregation and the making of the underclass.* Cambridge, MA: Harvard University Press.

McDonald, C., Harris, J., & Winterstein, R. (2003). Contingent on context? Social work in Australia, Britain, and the USA. *British Journal of Social Work, 33,* 191–208.

McMurtrie, D. C. (1909). The immigrant and public health. In *Proceedings of the National Conference of Social Work* (pp. 247–250). Chicago: University of Chicago Press.

Mishel, L., Bernstein, J., & Allegretto, S. (2006). *The state of working America, 2006–2007*. Ithaca, NY: ILR Press.

Muller, T. (1993). *Immigrants and the American city*. New York: New York University Press.

National Research Council. (1995). *Measuring poverty*. Washington, DC: National Academy Press.

O'Conner, A. (2001). Understanding inequality in the late twentieth-century metropolis: New perspectives on the enduring racial divide. In A. O'Conner, C. Tilly, & L. D. Bobo (Eds.), *Urban inequality: Evidence from four cities* (pp. 1–33). New York: Russell Sage Foundation.

Oxfam America. (2004). *Like machines in the fields: Workers without rights in American agriculture—Trading away our rights: Women working in global supply chains*. Retrieved February 9, 2005, from http://www.oxfamamerica.org/pdfs/labor_report_04.pdf.

Ozawa, M. (1997). Demographic changes and social welfare. In M. Reisch & E. Gambrill (Eds.), *Social work in the 21st century* (pp. 8–27). Thousand Oaks, CA: Pine Forge Press.

Palmieri, V. H. (1980). International and domestic policies regarding refugees. In *Proceedings of the annual forum of the National Conference on Social Welfare* (pp. 121–124)). New York: Columbia University Press.

Patterson, J. (2001). *America's struggle against poverty in the 20th century*. Cambridge, MA: Harvard University Press.

Penna, S., Paylor, I., & Washington, J. (2000). Globalization, social exclusion, and the possibilities for global social work and welfare. *European Journal of Social Work*, *3*(2), 109–122.

Piven, F. F. (2002). Welfare policy and American politics. In F. F. Piven, J. Acker, M. Hallock, & S. Morgen (Eds.), *Work, welfare and politics: Confronting poverty in the wake of welfare reform* (pp. 19–33). Eugene: University of Oregon Press.

Portes, A. (1990). *Immigrant America: A portrait*. Berkeley: University of California Press.

Powell, J. (1943). America's refugees: Exodus and diaspora. In *Proceedings of the National Conference of Social Work* (pp. 301–309). New York: Columbia University Press.

Pugh, R., & Gould, N. (2000). Globalization, social work, and social welfare. *European Journal of Social Work*, *3*(2), 123–138.

Quadagno, J. (1994). *The color of welfare: How racism undermined the war on poverty*. New York: Oxford University Press.

Quigley, W. (2003). *Ending poverty as we know it*. Philadelphia: Temple University Press.

Rainwater, L., & Smeeding, T. M. (2003). *Poor kids in a rich country: America's children in comparative perspective*. New York: Russell Sage Foundation.

RAND Corporation. (2006). *Small fraction of spending on health goes to undocumented immigrants*. Retrieved November 30, 2006, from http://content.healthaffairs.org/current.shtml.

Rank, M. R. (2004). *One nation underprivileged: Why American poverty affects us all*. New York: Oxford University Press.

Rawley, C. (1948). Adjustment of Jewish displaced persons in an American community. In *Proceedings of the National Conference of Social Work* (pp. 317–323) Chicago: University of Chicago Press.

Reisch, M. (2003). Welfare reform, globalization, and the transformation of the welfare state. In M. R. Gonzalez (Ed.), *Community organization and social policy: A compendium* (2nd ed.). San Juan, Puerto Rico: Editorial Edil (in Spanish).

Reisch, M. (2005). American exceptionalism and critical social work: A retrospective and prospective analysis. In I. Ferguson, M. Lavalette, & E. Whitmore (Eds.), *Globalisation, global justice and social work* (pp. 157–171). London: Routledge.

Reisch, M., & Gorin, S. (2001). The nature of work and the future of the social work profession. *Social Work*, *46*(1), 9–19.

Sanborn, F. B. (1886). Migration and immigration. In *Proceedings of the National Conference of Charities and Corrections* (pp. 253–259). Boston. Geo II. Ellis.

Sanchez, M. (2006, October 22). *For Hispanics, poverty is relative* [Report]. Washington, DC: Inter-American Development Bank.

Skocpol, T. (2000). *The missing middle: Working families and the future of American social policy.* New York: Norton.

Slack, K., & Yoo, J. (2004, November). *Food hardships and child behavior problems among low income children* (Discussion Paper No. 1290–04). Madison, WI: Institute for Research on Poverty.

Snyder, P. F. (1930). Social considerations in deportability: The legal background and new legislation. In *Proceedings of the National Conference of Social Work* (pp. 495–501). Chicago: University of Chicago Press.

Social Security Administration. (2006). *Fast facts and figures about Social Security.* Washington, DC: Office of Policy, Office of Research, Evaluation, and Statistics.

Sulzberger, C. L. (1912). Immigration. In *Proceedings of the National Conference of Social Work* (pp. 239–249). Chicago: University of Chicago Press.

Takaki, R. (1994). *From distant shores: Perspectives on race and ethnicity in America.* New York: Oxford University Press.

Taylor, G. (1913). Distribution and assimilation of immigrants: Report for the committee. In *Proceedings of the National Conference of Social Work* (pp. 26–36). Chicago: University of Chicago Press.

Taylor-Gooby, P. (2001). *The politics of welfare in Europe, in welfare states under pressure.* London: Sage.

Titmuss, R. M. (1963). *Essays on the welfare state.* Boston: Beacon Press.

Tumlin, K. C., & Zimmerman, W. (2003). *Immigrants and TANF: A look at immigrant welfare recipients in three cities.* Washington, DC: Urban Institute.

Urban Institute. (2006, July). *Government work supports and low-income families: Facts and figures* (Report). Washington, DC: Author.

U.S. Census Bureau. (2006). *Poverty in the United States.* Washington, DC: U.S. Government Printing Office.

U.S. Department of Health and Human Services. (2004). *TANF recipients and their families.* Washington, DC: U.S. Government Printing Office.

U.S. Industrial Commission on Immigration and Education. (1901). *Report of the Commission* (Vol. 15, pp. 319–322). Washington, DC: U.S. Government Printing Office.

Wald, L. P. (1909). The immigrant young girl. In *Proceedings of the National Conference of Social Work* (pp. 261–265). Chicago: University of Chicago Press.

Waldinger, R. (Ed.). (2001). *Strangers at the gates: New immigrants in urban America.* Berkeley: University of California Press.

Warren, G. (1933). Assistance to aliens in America. In *Proceedings of the National Conference of Social Work* (pp. 578–589). Chicago: University of Chicago Press.

Weyl, W. E. (1905). Immigration and industrial saturation. In *Proceedings of the National Conference of Social Work* (pp. 363–375). Chicago: University of Chicago Press.

Wilson, W. J. (1996). *When work disappears: The world of the new urban poor.* New York: Knopf.

Yang, P. (1995). *Post 1965 immigration to the United States.* Westport, CT: Praeger.

Chapter 6 ————————————————————————

THE U.S. PATRIOT ACT: IMPLICATIONS FOR THE SOCIAL WORK PROFESSION

Stan Stojkovic

On September 11, 2001, the world changed forever. As two hijacked planes crashed into the twin towers of the World Trade Center and a third plane attacked the Pentagon in Washington, DC, the typical American was left with much fear and uncertainty as to the future. The post–terrorist attack investigation revealed that a small group of foreign terrorists, armed and financed by a terrorist network known as Al Qaeda, headed by a mastermind named Osama bin Laden, had begun their initial planning for the attack years before. In fact, the World Trade Center was attacked by fellow terrorist Ramzi Yousef in February 1993, and the tragedy of 9/11 was only one event in a long series of events intended to bring down the U.S. government and to fulfill a fatwa that demanded that all Muslims kill Americans in any location of the world because of American occupation in Islam's holy lands and aggression against Muslims (9/11 Commission, 2004).

In response, the U.S. Congress passed the Uniting and Strengthening America by Providing Appropriate Tools Required to Intercept and Obstruct Terrorism Act, commonly known as the U.S. Patriot Act, Public Law 107-56. The U.S. Patriot Act, passed with virtually no public debate and signed into law 6 weeks after the tragedy of 9/11, redefined the public's response to terrorism. In addition, the Act gave broad and sweeping powers to the federal government, through its various law enforcement agencies, to investigate, apprehend, and detain suspected terrorists. Similar acts and practices were created during times of strife in the country's past, such as the Alien Act of 1798, the suspension of habeas corpus by President Lincoln during the Civil War, and the Espionage Act of 1917. Yet the new powers outlined in the Patriot Act forced all social institutions to examine how they responded to the terrorist threat. Unlike previous attempts directed toward the nation's enemies, the Patriot Act was directed toward an unknown target: would-be terrorists.

With advancing technologies, terrorists have many tools to pursue bombings, kidnappings, and mass destruction. The 19 men, for example, who attacked the World Trade Center were from all over the world, and the extremists they worked for in planning the attack were headquartered in Afghanistan, an initial target of U.S. forces in response to the 9/11 tragedy. Yet questions still remain regarding homeland security and the ability of the federal government to prevent attacks and to pursue terrorists both in this country and around the world. The U.S. Patriot Act is designed, according to its supporters, to give law enforcement more effective weapons to address domestic terrorism and secure the homeland.

For the purposes of this paper, I show how the U.S. Patriot Act has changed the nature of the relationship between the federal government and the citizenry over the past 5 years. This change is most directly felt within the thousand of agencies that represent the criminal justice system. These organizations—police, prosecution, courts, and corrections—have all been directly or indirectly affected by the Act. The most significant change has occurred in law enforcement, especially federal law enforcement, where broad powers have been given to investigate, detect, apprehend, prosecute, and detain terrorists and other criminals. These changes have had a profound impact on the quality of life for Americans and aliens alike. Through our zeal to protect the homeland, we have passed laws and allowed criminal justice agencies to enter our lives in more invasive and insidious ways. Law enforcement agencies, like the terrorists they are pursuing, also have the power of modern technology at their fingertips. The ability to surveil and detect suspicious movements of criminals and terrorists is remarkably accurate and frightening at the same time. Cities across the country have adopted practices and employed technologies that allow government agencies to watch over citizens without their even knowing about it, outside of public review and possible criticism (American Civil Liberties Union [ACLU], 2003). Most important, with the passage of the U.S. Patriot Act we have created two systems of justice in this country: one that is transparent in its operations and one that is not.

The U.S. Patriot Act has led to the creation of a number of questionable practices in pursuit of terrorist suspects. I show how these practices, for all intents and purposes, have produced a subterranean system of justice that is antithetical to the core values of a democracy and the social work profession. Through the U.S. Patriot Act, the potential for abuse by government officials is very high, and the cost to average citizens is the liberty interest that we all have in a democracy. I contend that in the final analysis the U.S. Patriot Act has eroded fundamental freedoms that citizens have vis-à-vis their government and has not made us safe from terrorist attacks. I conclude with some thoughts on the impact of the Act on vulnerable populations, an audience that human service professionals deal with on a daily basis. This discussion focuses on what social work professionals can do to respond to the U.S. Patriot Act and to protect and advocate for those people for whom this law has had and will continue to have deleterious consequences.

SIGNIFICANT ACTIVITIES AND A NEW SYSTEM OF JUSTICE

The 324-page document that makes up the U.S. Patriot Act signed into law by President Bush on October 26, 2001, has many provisions that affect the law enforcement community. Much of the language of the Act provides specific direction to the Federal Bureau of Investigation. Section 215, for example, authorizes the director of the FBI to make application for the production of "any tangible things" for an investigation and serves as a supplement to the Foreign Intelligence Surveillance Act of 1978. Prior to the passage of the U.S. Patriot Act, the FBI could only obtain records, but under the current law they can seize any material that is pertinent to an investigation regarding "international terrorism or clandestine intelligence activities" (ACLU, 2003, p. 3). The U.S. Patriot Act has created a separate system of justice in this country based on activities that are outside public review. These activities include the detention of noncitizens, military tribunals, fingerprinting of immigrants, and domestic spying.

Detention of Noncitizens

One of the more frightening provisions of the U.S. Patriot Act is the ability of the government to detain noncitizens. Immediately following the September 11 attacks, the government began rounding up large numbers of immigrants, most of whom who were of Middle Eastern or South Asian origin. The ACLU (2003), along with other organizations, filed suit under the Freedom of Information Act to determine who these detainees were and the basis of their detention. To date, the government has not been forthcoming in providing a report on who these detainees are and what they are being charged with. In its zeal to seem responsive to terrorism, the government, through the Department of Justice, has embarked on a strategy that is nothing short of racial profiling, targeting largely young Middle Eastern and South Asian men.

The impact of this mass herding of suspected terrorists is not new in our history. Similar strategies were used by the government in the past, most notably during the era of the "Palmer raids." This name is derived from the infamous attorney general A. Mitchell Palmer, who used the raids against immigrants who were viewed as a threat to the social order. It is suspected that over 5,000 "Bolsheviks" were arrested, illegally detained with no charges brought against them, and in some cases deported for being suspected of violating the Espionage and Sedition Acts of 1917 and 1918. Most of the charges were later dropped and Palmer's efforts criticized (Powers, 1987). The current situation with young Middle Eastern and South Asian men post-9/11 is no different.

Attempts to understand the scope and magnitude of the detention of noncitizens are barely discernable. The only accounts are typically from journalists; very little research has been directed toward this topic. Operating under a siege mentality, the government has done what it always has done under difficult circumstances: arrest the usual suspects. In this case, the usual suspects are young Middle Eastern and South Asian men who, in a majority of instances, have broken no laws and have no interest in attacking the United States. The problems for law enforcement agencies in this detention process are numerous, particularly when they are asked to detain suspected terrorists as well as typical criminals. Some have even suggested that the increase in homeland security has drained local law enforcement budgets to a breaking point: "We've spent five years on homeland security. Now we need to focus on a little hometown security" (T. Barrett, quoted in Kingsbury, 2006, p. 34).

The consequences of this specious detention of noncitizens is that local law enforcement agencies, typically police and prosecution, are being asked to reorganize to focus on the activities of suspected terrorists at a time when resources are dwindling and local agencies have neither the time nor the inclination to investigate them. Additionally, these same law enforcement agencies are being asked to work with federal law enforcement agencies at a time when they are being criticized for racially profiling citizens, particularly African American and Hispanic citizens (Stojkovic, Kalinich, & Klofas, 2007). The end result is that usually nothing of substance gets accomplished; even when suspects are pursued in an earnest fashion, it is not clear that the detention of these noncitizens makes us safer. What we do know is that we have instituted through the U.S. Patriot Act actions that run counter to our existing laws and the laws of the international community.

Under the Patriot Act, the government can detain noncitizens for an indefinite "reasonable" period of time. In this country and according to the International Covenant on Civil and Political Rights (to which the United States is a signatory), the period of detention prior to being brought in front of a judge or magistrate is 48 hours or a few days; under the Patriot Act detention could be for months, and there have been cases in which people have been detained for months without access to a lawyer (Fainaru, 2002, as cited in ACLU, 2002). For most citizens such a practice strikes at the heart of our democracy, especially when there is no discernable benefit and when it actually makes things worse. In the first 5 years of its implementation, the U.S. Patriot Act and the provision to detain noncitizens has produced no demonstrable effects on the protection of the homeland or on the global war on terrorism. If anything, this activity has actually produced onerous and burdensome costs on law enforcement agencies and no actual increase in the safety of citizens. More pernicious, however, has been the effect of this activity on the quality of life for many persons, most of whom are foreign-born, immigrants, and come from Middle Eastern and South Asian countries.

Military Tribunals

One of the more disturbing activities emanating from the U.S. Patriot Act is the creation of military tribunals. In November 2001, President Bush as commander-in-chief granted himself unprecedented authority to create and operate military tribunals for suspected terrorists. These tribunals would be outside the purview and review of civilian courts. Suspected terrorists would be detained and, in some cases, defined as "enemy combatants," ultimately tried and convicted through the rubric of the military system of justice. The exact language of the presidential order also provides that ordinary rules of court procedure would not apply, for example, unanimity for jurors would be required only in capital cases, trials would be held in secret, and no review of the courts' actions would be allowed. Although these provisions of the U.S. Patriot Act do not apply to U.S. citizens, they do impact the over 18 million foreign-born legal residents of the United States (ACLU, 2003).

The infamous detention center at Guantánamo Bay, Cuba, is where some secret trials have been held, because if they were held in the United States suspects would have the right to habeas corpus review, a right inherent in our system of justice, as dictated by the U.S. Constitution. Yet, the presence of military tribunals abroad has brought much criticism from people all over the world. There is much debate at to whether military tribunals adequately protect the country or combat the war on terrorism. As with other legislation passed in the late 1990s and post-9/11, such as the Antiterrorism and Effective Death Penalty Act of 1996, the presumed benefits of these activities on terrorism or crime in general are suspect at best (Cole & Smith, 2007).

Moreover, the image of the United States as the longest running democracy has been tarnished by the presence of secret military tribunals. More often than not, suspects defined as terrorists or enemy combatants are neither, and as an intelligence-gathering tool detention facilities and the threat of facing a military tribunal have limited or no value. The questions of fundamental fairness and due process must be raised under such a secretive process. For those who work in the civilian court system, the notion of military tribunals and secretive processes are antithetical to our system of justice. This practice has raised the ire of both critics and citizens alike. How does a civilian system of justice survive when it has to operate parallel to a military system of justice that allows no review, limited due process, and no accountability?

Fingerprinting of Immigrants

While the civilian system of justice has spent the past decade trying to end the practice of racial profiling by criminal justice agencies, the federal government has created its own nefarious system of racial profiling by targeting men of Middle Eastern and South Asian decent and requiring them to submit to interrogations and fingerprinting. The obvious purpose is to have a record of who they are and what they are doing. No one has a problem with identifying would-be criminals and terrorists, but we don't allow people to do this outside the purview of the law and without rationale. In the civilian justice system, this is accomplished by having law enforcement agencies show probable cause that a crime has been committed or is about to be committed. Without this standard, no person can be pursued and ultimately arrested.

When tactics are used by law enforcement to investigate ordinary criminals without probable cause and subsequent arrests are made, the judiciary typically invalidates such arrests. It is well known that in many cases when such tactics are employed by law enforcement personnel there is usually a pretextual basis for the stop that cannot meet the probable cause standard. Again, this has been found to be a common practice among police who are conducting racial profiling among African Americans and Hispanic citizens (Engel & Calnon, 2004). A broken taillight, for example, becomes the pretext to justify a stop and ultimately a search of someone's car when there is no probable cause to stop him or her (see a fascinating description of this practice by theologian Cornell West, 1993).

The tragedy is that we are now practicing racial profiling with persons of Middle Eastern and South Asian origin, and we are doing so with impunity. Immediately following the 9/11 attacks, the federal government rounded up thousands of Middle Eastern and South Asian men with no cause, fingerprinted them, and provided no justification for their arrest and detention. The net result of such a practice was that ill will was engendered among young Middle Eastern and South Asian men and virtually nothing was gained to aid in the investigation of the 9/11 attacks nor credible information generated that would lead to other terrorist suspects (ACLU, 2002). With this practice, as with the other practices described, we are seeing the development of a separate system of justice that is beyond public review, where accountability is limited and injustices enhanced.

Domestic Spying

Prior to the passage of the U.S. Patriot Act, there was a clear distinction between intelligence agencies and traditional law enforcement. The Central Intelligence Agency, for example, was not allowed to conduct traditional law enforcement, nor was it allowed to employ intelligence-gathering strategies used in the foreign sector domestically. Yet Section 203 of the U.S. Patriot Act does allow for foreign intelligence information gathered as a result of a domestic investigation to be shared with the intelligence community. As expected, the definition of "foreign intelligence information" is very broad, and under such a broad rubric, the potential for abuse and harassment of ordinary citizens is very high. Coupled with eased restrictions on wiretaps and surveillance techniques, a system of justice has been created that is outside the domain of traditional public review and comment.

Former attorney general John Ashcroft rewrote sections of federal guidelines subsequent to the 9/11 attacks to provide broad powers to the FBI in the domestic spying arena. The original guidelines, written during the 1970s, were created to limit the activities of the CIA and FBI in the domestic spying arena and were a response to serious abuses by the government in its surveillance and harassment of civil rights leaders, such as Martin Luther King Jr., during the 1960s (ACLU, 2002). The new rules have broadened the powers of agencies such as the FBI to spy on ordinary citizens with very little oversight. Taken together, Sections 203, 206, 213, 216, 217, and 218 of the U.S. Patriot Act provide enormous power to governmental agencies to spy on U.S. citizens and to provide no or limited accounting or basis for such activity (Podesta, 2002). Additionally, in practice, we are seeing a separate system of justice evolving that is accountable only to managers and bureaucrats of the various agencies of the federal government and the executive branch of government. This type of system of justice is counter to the core values of a democracy, where transparency and openness are essential to good government.

THE U.S. PATRIOT ACT AND THE SOCIAL WORK PROFESSION

Although Congress acted in haste to pass the U.S. Patriot Act, it did do something that allowed for further review of the law once it was implemented by the various agencies of the federal government. The law had a sunset provision that allowed for greater review 4 years after its implementation. In the fall of 2005 and into early 2006, Congress did review many of the law's provisions and made some modifications to provide greater public oversight and protections of, primarily, First and Fourth Amendments rights of citizens. Yet critics argue that the U.S. Patriot Act Improvement and Reauthorization Act (HR 3199) does very little to curb the powers granted to federal law enforcement agencies such as the FBI, and the potential infringement of citizens' rights under the First and Fourth Amendments are still present. The ACLU has sued the FBI over the release of subscriber information by an Internet service provider. Although the government has acceded to the ACLU's demand that the provider not be forced to divulge sensitive information about its users, it still holds in place a gag order that does not allow providers to speak publicly about the order and does it through a national security letter (ACLU, 2006).

So, what does all this mean for the social work professional, and how does he or she deal with the consequences of the U.S. Patriot Act? There are some very clear steps that must be taken by the social work profession so that the harm of the aforementioned activities does not further threaten the vulnerable populations that we serve. These actions fall into three areas: advocacy, protection, and activism and reaffirmation.

Advocacy

The social work profession has had a long history of advocacy for those whom society has disregarded or abused. As social work professionals, we must work with others to address the abuses that the U.S. Patriot Act has created among vulnerable populations. The most glaring example of these has been how men and women of Middle Eastern and South Asian descent have been treated by the practices just described in the implementation of the Act. The social work profession has to continue to work with the victims of the U.S. Patriot Act. This means working with the legal community to petition the government when it is wrong and acting unjustly. It means speaking out against injustices and pursuing our traditional goal of social justice.

More important, it means sharing information with others and speaking out against the oppression of the minority by the majority under a specious law. The U.S. Patriot Act is in violation of the social work code of ethics that compels us to act against injustices and not practice any form of discrimination against someone based on national origin. This advocacy must be viewed as part of our mission and purpose as social workers. We cannot sit back idly while others are oppressed under the false pretense of security and safety, especially when we know that the implementation of the U.S. Patriot Act has not made us any more safe and has made us ultimately less free than we were prior to its implementation.

As a collective voice, we as social work professionals must join with other groups to support a dissenting view when it comes to the U.S. Patriot Act. The ACLU (2006) reports that over 400 communities and seven states have taken a stand demanding meaningful reform of the Act. Although Congress has been slow to react, there has been a groundswell of voices and professional organizations asking for changes in the law. As social workers, we should consider ourselves a part of the voice of dissent, since we have a long history of advocating for those who have no one to advocate for them. If we don't take on this advocacy role to change the U.S. Patriot Act, we not only violate our own code of ethics, but, more perniciously, we silently condone the mistreatment of vulnerable populations.

Protection

We must work with other like-minded organizations to protect vulnerable populations and victims of the U.S. Patriot Act. As we have done in the past with children who have been abused, women who have been battered, and the elderly who have mistreated, we must come to the assistance of those who need our aid in the wake of the implementation of the Act. The central thesis of this chapter is that two separate systems of justice were created as a result of the U.S. Patriot Act. This new clandestine system of justice has many victims. One of the more nefarious consequences of the sweeping powers of the Act is the misidentification or mislabeling of suspected terrorists and the mass rounding up of people who look like terrorists, for example, young Middle Eastern and South Asian men. Who protects these people against the ravages of the U.S. Patriot Act?

In many urban centers across this country, young Middle Eastern and South Asian men are being singled out for arrest, prosecution, and detention, with no ability to protect and advocate for themselves. Like the suspected Bolsheviks of the 1920s, the new bogeyman is the young Middle Eastern and South Asian male. Similar to his counterpart of the 1920s, he is being denied rights to an attorney, secretly detained and interrogated in unknown locations, tried in some cases, and sentenced to military prisons. We do not have accurate numbers on how many people are being placed in this secret system of justice because the government refuses to reveal the numbers. Who protects the potential victims of this abuse? Who comes to their aid when it looks like no one will? Again, the social work profession has a role in working with other professional associations to aid in the protection of these persons by demanding an accounting and, where appropriate, the opportunity to intervene.

The greatest protection is promoting greater visibility regarding the plight of persons being unjustly persecuted by the government. Chief Justice Oliver Wendell Holmes once stated that "sunlight is the greatest disinfectant." We need more sunlight on the workings of the government when implementing the U.S. Patriot Act. More people need to know what is going on under the name of democracy and freedom. As social workers we need to protect those who are being ensnarled in the government's web of bureaucracies created to enforce the provisions of the Patriot Act. The scope of this web reaches well beyond the domain of young Middle Eastern and South Asian men.

When the government is able is spy on its citizens, detain them without cause, fingerprint and interrogate them at will, and conduct secret military tribunals, it is a short leap to wiretapping homes, invading the privacy rights of citizens, conducting searches of homes, and chilling free speech. Through the various activities done under the authority of the U.S. Patriot Act, the government has made us all less free. For the social work field, predicated on informed choice, such a law is in opposition to everything we stand for as a profession dedicated to assisting others and promoting the greatest freedom allowable within the context of a democratic nation. If we don't protect the vulnerable, who will? The British philosopher Edmund Burke once stated, "The only thing necessary for the triumph of evil is that good men do nothing." Doing nothing is not a social work option when addressing the consequences of the U.S. Patriot Act.

Activism and Reaffirmation

Our best chance of addressing the wrongs of the U.S. Patriot Act is through good old-fashioned activism. We must become more involved in the political process and protect those vulnerable populations who are being targeted unjustly. This activism must be rooted in the belief that if people do not stand up and confront oppression, injustice, and abuse, all under the rubric of law, such practices will continue unabated. As a profession, social work has a long tradition of promoting the dignity of the individual vis-à-vis government-sponsored oppression and social justice. In our short glorious history, we have been called on to address wrongdoing when we see it and to affirm the principles on which this country and our professional code of ethics are based.

According to the preamble of the National Association of Social Workers (2006) code of ethics, we as social work professionals are committed to the core value of social justice. Social justice demands that we work with others to change the existing U.S. Patriot Act. As described in this chapter, numerous government activities have produced irreparable harm to individuals and provided them with minimal recourse to defend themselves against government agencies. As vulnerable populations, men and women of Middle Eastern and South Asian origin are being persecuted and unjustly labeled all under the notion of homeland security and rooting out suspected terrorists. The evidence is that the country is not safe against future terrorist attacks due to the creation of the U.S. Patriot Act. In fact, it may be hypothesized that we are actually less safe and less free simultaneously due to the Act.

Recent case law has attacked many of the premises and activities of the government under the U.S. Patriot Act. Take, for example, the case of *Doe I, II v. Gonzalez* (2006), in which the government sought to enforce a provision of the Act that compelled the divulging of information from Internet service providers regarding their subscribers' activities and, more nefariously, imposing a gag order that prevented providers from telling anyone that they had been served a national security letter. In September 2004, a district court struck down the U.S. Patriot Act provision that allowed the government to demand such information from Internet providers and declared the gag order rule unconstitutional. The situation, however, did not end there.

The government appealed the decision of the district court to the Second Circuit Court of Appeals, but before a decision could be issued, the U.S. Congress amended the specific provision of the U.S. Patriot Act to allow for greater judicial review when someone receives a national security letter. As a response, the FBI withdrew its national security letter, the second time it had done this when facing judicial review, and the appellate court sent the case back to the district court to rule on the constitutionality of the amended law. As we head into 2008, we will see more movement on this and other cases challenging the constitutionality of many provisions of the U.S. Patriot Act. The net effect of this decision is that the government no longer can issue national security letters (over 30,000 a year!) without allowing persons to whom the letters are directed to address particulars in open court. However, the pernicious gag order rule remains in effect.

This case demonstrates the potential abuse of power by the government under the auspices of the U.S. Patriot Act. Further legal developments will challenge the constitutionality of the Act. As social workers, we will have to work with others to check governmental actions that engender social injustice and oppression of vulnerable populations. To stay true to our mission and purpose, activism and reaffirmation of the social work values means that we speak truth to power and voice our opposition to any activity that further oppresses disadvantaged populations, especially actions that are done in our name as citizens and are wrongfully institutionalized through our laws.

CONCLUSION

The purpose of this chapter was to reveal the many practices that are being conducted by government officials under the aegis of the U.S. Patriot Act. I described these practices—detention of noncitizens, military tribunals, fingerprinting of immigrants, domestic spying—to show how a separate, secret system of criminal justice is evolving that is antithetical to the values and principles of a democracy and the social work profession. Such practices are damaging on many levels, as they are done under the authority of law. The U.S. Patriot Act, passed in the frenzied aftermath of 9/11, has changed the way the dispensation of justice is achieved in this country and the relationship that citizens have with their government.

As social work professionals, we have to recognize that we have a role and obligation to address and confront wrongful activities conducted under the authority granted by the U.S. Patriot Act. As advocates for the oppressed; protectors of freedom, fairness, and due process; and activists for change, we as a social work profession must align ourselves with other similarly minded organizations to protect these values and principles that are coming under attack by the government through the U.S. Patriot Act. We have always shown up when the vulnerable and oppressed needed us. They need us again to confront the evils and injustices pursued by a clandestine system of justice created by the U.S. Patriot Act.

In his book *Why We Can't Wait* (1964), the Reverend Martin Luther King Jr. defended peaceful protest and economic boycott by saying he could no longer wait for others to come forward and speak out against injustices toward vulnerable and oppressed populations. He could no longer wait for justice to happen; he decided to make justice happen. We as social work professionals must not wait for justice to happen in our current situation. We must remain ever vigilant to our mission and values of assisting those who have to carry the burden of government oppression as expressed through the U.S. Patriot Act. To do anything less would be inimical to our profession, the people we serve, and the democracy we cherish.

REFERENCES

Act Concerning Aliens, June 25, 1798, Ch. 58, Vol. 1, Statute 570.

American Civil Liberties Union. (2002). *Insatiable appetite: The government's demand for new and unnecessary powers after September 11—An ACLU report.* New York: Author.

American Civil Liberties Union. (2003). *Freedom under fire: Dissent in post-9/11 America.* New York: Author.

American Civil Liberties Union. (2006). FBI drops another Patriot Act demand but keeps gag on Internet service provider. Retrieved November 22, 2006, from www.aclu.org.

Anti-terrorism and Effective Death Penalty Act of 1996, April 24, 1996, Public Law 104-132, Vol. 110, Statute 1214.

Cole, G., & Smith, C. (2007). *The American system of criminal justice* (11th ed.). Belmont, CA: Wadsworth/Thompson.

Doe, I, II v. Gonzales, 05-0570-cv (L), 05-4896-cv (CON) (2006).

Engel, R., & Calnon, J. (2004). Examining the influence of drivers' characteristics during traffic stops with police: Results from a national survey. *Justice Quarterly, 21,* 49–90.

Espionage Act of 1917, June 15, 1917, Ch. 30, Vol. 40, Statute 217.

Espionage and Sedition Acts of 1917 and 1918, May 16, 1918, Ch. 75, Vol. 40, Statute 553.

Foreign Intelligence Service Act of 1978, Pub. Law No. 95-511, Vol. 92, Statute 1783.

King, M. L. Jr., (1964). *Why we can't wait.* New York: Harper & Row.

Kingsbury, K. (2006). The next crime wave. *Time, 168*(24), 70–77.

National Association of Social Workers. (2006). *Code of ethics of the National Association of Social Workers.* Washington, DC: Author.

9/11 Commission. (2004). *The 9/11 Commission report: Final report of the National Commission on Terrorist Attacks upon the United States* (Executive Summary). Washington, DC: General Accounting Office.

Podesta, J. (2002, Winter). USA Patriot Act: The good, the bad, and the sunset [Newsletter]. *Human Rights.*

Powers, R. (1987). *Secrecy and power: The life of J. Edgar Hoover.* New York: Free Press.

Stojkovic, S., Kalinich, D., & Klofas, J. (2007). *Criminal justice organizations: Administration and management* (4th ed.). Belmont, CA: Wadsworth/Thompson.

U.S. Patriot Act, Public Law, 107-56, Vol. 115, Statute 272.

U.S.A. Patriot Improvement and Reauthorization Act of 2005, H.R. 3199, 109th Congress.

West, C. (1993). *Race matters.* Boston: Beacon Press.

Chapter 7

SOCIAL WELFARE POLICY AS A FORM OF SOCIAL JUSTICE

Ira C. Colby

The core mission of the social work profession is the promotion of social, economic, and political justice for all people. Communities built on the principles of justice provide its members the opportunities to fully participate and share benefits in a fair and equitable manner. Though a noble ideal, the reality is very different, as disparities continue to plague people and nations around the world.

A case in point: In 1978, more than 130 nations met under the leadership of the World Health Organization (WHO) at the International Conference of Alma-Ata to address one global social issue: health care. Participants envisioned that by the year 2000 a global effort would result in health care for all people. The conference's report forthrightly stated, "Inequality in the health status of people, particularly between developed and developing countries, as well as within countries, is politically, socially, and economically unacceptable" (Declaration of Alma-Ata, 1978).

Over the following 3 decades some gaps closed, but the gulf in worldwide health care remains large and mandates continued changes in both policy and services in all regions of the world:

- The idea that more than 2 billion people worldwide face health threats every day is almost incomprehensible but most certainly unconscionable (WHO, 2007b, p. 10).
- According to UNAIDS (2006, p. 1), there are roughly 40 million people living with HIV—a staggering figure.
- Over half of all child deaths occur in children who are underweight (WHO, 2007b, p. 14).
- Just as unacceptable is that more than 345,000 people, mostly children, died from measles in 2005, even though effective immunization costs about 0.33 U.S. cents per dose and has been available for over 40 years (WHO, 2007a).
- In 2005, nearly half the people infected with the H5N1 virus died; the *New England Journal of Medicine* reported that significant roadblocks to understanding and controlling the virus remain (Osterholm, 2005).
- A World Bank Study estimates that an influenza pandemic would create severe worldwide economic losses of U.S.$800 billion (World Bank, 2005).

The human, economic, and societal costs of ill health are immense. Millions of people unnecessarily die prematurely from preventable and curable diseases. With relatively little cost, these people could live longer productive lives. But for them justice remains a foreign abstract. Data focusing on poverty, education, housing, life expectancy, and violence, among other indicators, reveal similar and equally disturbing trends that result in a common conclusion: True justice is far from being realized.

Social workers confront horrific problems on a daily basis that reflect the broad range of social issues that plague and threaten the lives of people and weaken our civil structures. Central to the social work profession's mission is its work with and on behalf of the most vulnerable, at-risk, and marginalized persons in our communities. Reamer (1993, p. 195) writes that social workers confront the most compelling issues of our time by working with these clients, and from these individual and collective experiences a unique perspective grows. Social workers are able to translate this practice wisdom into a powerful tool to influence public policy. Simply stated, practice informs policy by shaping its form and structure. By including policy practice in one's work, according to Hagen (2000, p. 555), social workers are able "to serve clients more effectively and to promote justice at all government levels."

Policy is a formal statement articulating rules and regulations that reflect values, beliefs, data, traditions, discussions, debates, and compromises of the body politic. Policy creates a community's context of justice in how it approaches the provision of social services. Public and private organizations and nonprofit and voluntary associations implement policies, which in turn are "experienced by individuals and families" (Jansson, 1999, p. 1). Similarly, policy is vital to the social worker because it specifies the type and level of service the practitioner is able to provide. Policy carries out multiple functions, ranging from crafting the broad framework in which a program or service evolves to detailing the available services.

Social welfare policies, which are a subset of the broader social policy arena, focus on issues that are controversial and the epicenter for many debates. Discussions on radio call-in shows and television panel shows are replete with welfare matters, ranging from immigration and border issues to the quality of health care for seniors. And the tone and controversies in these discussions are not new. Throughout American history, political leaders have staked out their positions relating to welfare:

- *Benjamin Franklin:* I am for doing good for the poor, but I differ in opinion about the means.... The more public provisions were made for the poor, the less they provided for themselves and the poorer they became.... On the contrary, the less that was done for them, the more they did for themselves. (n.d.)

- *President Franklin Roosevelt:* The Federal Government must and shall quit this business of relief. I am not willing that the vitality of our people be further sapped.... We must preserve not only the bodies of the unemployed from destitution but also their self-respect, their self-reliance and courage and determination. (n.d.)

- *President John F. Kennedy:* Welfare ... must be more than a salvage operation, picking up the debris from the wreckage of human lives. Its emphasis must be directed increasingly toward prevention and rehabilitation.... Poverty weakens individuals and nations. (Woolley & Peters, n.d.)

- *President Lyndon B. Johnson:* Unfortunately, many Americans live on the outskirts of hope—some because of their poverty, and some because of their color, and all too many because of both. Our task is to help replace their despair with opportunity. This administration today, here and now, declares unconditional war on poverty in America. I urge this Congress and all Americans to join with me in that effort (*Public Papers of the Presidents of the United States*, 1965).

- *President Ronald Reagan:* I have never questioned the need to take care of people who, through no fault of their own, can't provide for themselves. The rest of us have to do that. But I am against open-ended welfare programs that invite generation after generation of potentially productive people to remain on the dole; they deprive the able-bodied of the incentive to work and require productive people to support others who are physically and mentally able to work while prolonging an endless cycle of dependency that robs men and women of their dignity. (n.d.)

Many social workers and professional associations have been actively engaged in policy development and its advocacy to provide justice-based social welfare policies. As Haynes and Mickelson (2000, p. 2) write, "Although social workers have been influential in the political arena, politics has not consistently been a central arena for social work practice. Consequently, a historic and ongoing dynamic tension exists." A common refrain among social workers is "I just don't have the time for policy work." This is certainly understandable for the individual who is assigned a caseload of 30 clients in a public agency or in a setting that is underfinanced and underresourced. For some, the primacy of their work is the client's immediate situation, and time is not available to inform themselves about and advocate for justice-based social polices. There are others who feel that policy practice has little to do with their daily work; policy is viewed as irrelevant and with little connection to the client's life situation. This unfortunate perspective hinders the social work profession's efforts to create positive social change leading to a just society for all people. The growing practice wisdom and accumulating evidence goes untapped and, as a result, creates an unnecessary barrier for policy practice. For whatever reason, there are many trees that seem to get in the way, but the commonly held belief among social workers that policy work belongs elsewhere is a self-planted tree that must be cut down.

SOCIAL WELFARE POLICY DEFINED

There is no one overriding definition of social welfare policy that scholars, policy makers, or practitioners refer to on a consistent basis. The lack of one agreed upon definition results in frustration and a pessimistic perspective, such as that of Popple and Leighninger (1990, p. 26), who find the definition of welfare "difficult, confusing, and debated." On the other hand, there are numerous sources for definitions, the most common reference materials being the *Social Work Dictionary* (Barker, 2003) and various editions of the *Encyclopedia of Social Work* (see, e.g., Dear, 1995; Morris, 1986). Textbooks and journal articles also offer a variety of definitions. A sample of the various definitions illustrates the diversity, ranging from all-encompassing to narrowly focused descriptors:

- Social welfare policy is anything the government chooses to do, or not to do, that affects the quality of life of its people. (DiNitto & Dye, 1983, p. 2)
- The explicit or implicit standing plan that an organization or government uses as a guide for action. (Barker, 1995, p. 330)
- Establishes a specific set of program procedures (Baumheier & Schorr, 1977, p. 1453)
- Includes all public activities. (Zimmermann, 1979, p. 487)
- Considers resource distribution and its affect on "peoples' social well-being." (Dear, 1995, p. 2227)
- [Is] primarily understood as cash and in-kind payments to persons who need support because of physical or mental illness, poverty, age, disability, or other defined circumstances. (Chatterjee, 1966, p. 3)

- [A] pattern of relationships which develop in society to carry out mutual support function. (Gilbert & Specht, 1974, p. 5)

- Human concern for the well-being of individuals, families, groups, organizations, and communities. (Morales & Sheafor, 1989, p. 100)

- Collective interventions to meet certain needs of the individual and/or to serve the wider interests of society. (Titmus, 1959, p. 42)

- A system of social services and institutions, designed to aid individuals and groups to attain satisfying standards of life and health, and personal social relationships which permit them to develop their full capacities and promote their well-being in harmony with the needs of their families and community. (Friedlander, 1955, p. 140)

- A subset of social policy, which may be defined as the formal and consistent ordering of affairs. (Karger & Stoesz, 2004, p. 4)

- A nation's system of programs, benefits, and services that help people meet those social, economic, educational, and health needs that are fundamental to the maintenance of society. (Barker, 1995, p. 221)

These definitions reflect a specific philosophy or view of welfare. Close examination reveals three common themes:

1. Social welfare includes a variety of programs and services that result in some type of client-specific benefit.
2. Social welfare, defined as a system of programs and services, is designed to meet the needs of people. The needs to be addressed can be all-encompassing, including economic and social well-being, health, education, and overall quality of life, or they may be very restricted, targeting just one issue.
3. The outcome of social welfare policy is to improve the well-being of individuals, groups, and communities. Helping those client systems in time of need will later benefit society at large.

THE RELATIONSHIP BETWEEN JUSTICE THEORY AND SOCIAL WELFARE POLICY

All welfare policies are extensions of justice theories and reflect particular principles of the human condition. David Miller (2005) poses the central question related to justice and welfare:

> What constitutes a fair distribution of rights, resources and opportunities? Is it an equal distribution, in which case an equal distribution of what?...Or is it a distribution that gives each person what they deserve, or what they need? Or a distribution that gives everyone an adequate minimum of whatever it is that matters?

Miller's questions focus on *distributive justice,* that is, how benefits will be allocated to a community. Will they be equal, disproportional, or possibly need-based? The key issues in distributive justice are often framed by moral and legal positions, which can polarize groups to support or oppose a particular policy. The potential answers to Miller's queries rest within specific justice theories.

Reflecting an individual's, group's, or organization's values and beliefs, justice theories create a rationale to support particular policy initiatives. Recognizing and understanding the various, often competing justice theories is central in creating a successful policy change strategy. Such understanding requires the social work profession, as Morris writes (1986, p. 678), "to take into account not only its own beliefs and values, but those held by a large number of other nonadvocate citizens."

John Rawls's (1971) theory of justice most closely reflects the principles and beliefs of the social work profession. On the other hand, the core premise regarding resource distribution and property ownership expressed by Robert Nozick (1974) is counter to the profession's values.

Rawls (1971) believes that birth, status, and family are matters of chance, which should not influence or bias the benefits one accrues. True justice allows a society to rectify its inequities, with the end result yielding fairness to all its members. All social goods—liberty, power, opportunities, income, and wealth—are to be equally distributed only if the unequal distribution of these goods favors the least advantaged members of a community. Rawls contends that the inequality of opportunity is permissible if it is advantageous to those who have been set aside. For example, a university's admission criteria that benefits one racial or gender group over another is acceptable if that group has been or remains disadvantaged. Rawls's theory proposes a minmax approach that essentially maximizes the place of the least advantaged. Using a concept he calls the "veil of ignorance," Rawls reasons that a just policy can be written only by those who cannot know how the policy will impact themselves. For example, two people want the same piece of cake. One of them is asked to cut it so each of them may have a slice. Not knowing which slice he or she will receive, the person cutting the cake will probably make the slices as even as possible. To do otherwise could mean that he or she ends up with the smaller slice. The dual beliefs that a transaction's result should be for the greater good and that advantages and set-asides for those who have been marginalized are appropriate reflect core social work values.

In contrast, Nozick (1974) argues for a free-market libertarian model that advocates for individuals to be able to keep what they earn. Redistribution of social goods is not acceptable and violates the key premise that people should be able to retain the fruits of their labor. Taxation is not tolerable and forces workers to become slaves of the state, with a certain amount of their work-related benefits going to the state for its use. For Nozick, "the less government approach" is the best model. He asks, "If the state did not exist would it be necessary to invent it? Would one be needed, and would it have to be invented?" (p. 3) Libertarianism asserts that the state's role should be confined essentially to security and safety issues: police and fire protection, national defense, and the judicial system. Matters related to public education and social welfare, among others, are the responsibility of the private sector. Faith-based organizations, nonprofit social services, nongovernmental organizations, and private for-profit groups should provide welfare services. In a free-market model services would be structured to encourage efficiency and effectiveness and eliminate redundancy and fiscal waste. The government's role would be minimal at most, with individuals free to do as they wished with their own lives and property. No formal institution should interfere with an individual's control of his or her life; the role of the state is to protect from and retaliate against those who use force against an individual (Roth, 1997, pp. 958–959).

Rawls's (1971) theory supports the development of a progressive and active welfare state. Policies create a system of redistribution of resources and advantages for those historically and currently set aside. Nozick's (1974) minimalist approach provides for welfare only in terms of safety and security for the individual. The government should not be involved in meeting basic human needs or providing any system of support and care; these activities are left to the private, voluntary sectors.

SOCIAL WORK VALUES AND POLICY

The importance of policy for the social work profession is apparent in its organizing documents. From ethical codes of practice to accreditation standards, various national and international bodies clearly spell out the centrality of social policy in the curriculum. For example, through their respective accreditation protocols the American-based Council on Social Work Education (CSWE: 2001) and the International Association of Schools of Social Work (2007) each call on educators to steadfastly embrace and teach content around policy's central role.

The 2002 CWSE (2001, p. 7) Educational Policy and Accreditation Standards, the organizing document for baccalaureate and master's level social work education, notes that social work educational programs, though differing in "design, structure, and objectives," will prepare "social workers to formulate and influence social policies and social work services in diverse contexts." The National Association of Social Workers' (1999) Code of Ethics notes in its preamble, "Fundamental to social work is attention to the environmental forces that create, contribute to, and address problems in living" and "specifically directs its members in Standard 6.02 to facilitate informed participation by the public in shaping social policies and institutions."

Inclusion of social welfare policy in education and practice extends to social workers and programs around the world. Canadian social work education, for example, requires the study of Canadian welfare policy in accredited social work programs (Canadian Association of Schools of Social Work, 2004, p. 9); an "accredited social worker" in Australia must have knowledge of and ability in analysis and impact of policy development (Australian Association of Social Workers, 2004, p. 3); in 2004, the International Association of Schools of Social Work and the International Federation of Social Workers (2007, p. 7) adopted the "Global Standards for the Education and Training of the Social Work Profession," which includes social policy as a core area of study.

Worldwide, the promotion, development, and cultivation of effective policy in micro and macro arenas cross geographic borders and cultural divides. Social welfare policy is a powerful tool that can realize the aspirations of an entire society as well as the dreams and ideals embraced by a local community group, family, or individual.

Macro social welfare policy provides a framework and means to strengthen larger communities. As an instrument of change, social welfare policy can reduce or eliminate a particular issue that impacts at-risk and marginalized population groups, such as children, families, seniors, and people of color. Conversely, social policy may exacerbate or penalize a particular population group.

Micro social welfare policy directly influences the scope of work provided by the practitioner. Program eligibility, the form of services provided, a program's delivery structure, and funding mechanisms are outcomes of micro social welfare policy. Ineffective social policy creates frustrating practice obstacles. Typical of the barriers created by policy are eligibility criteria that limit client access to services, regulations that do not allow for case advocacy, and increased caseloads supported with minimal resources and time limits.

CONCEPTUAL FRAMEWORK FOR SOCIAL WELFARE

Social welfare policies are outgrowths of values, beliefs, and principles and vary in their commitments and range of services. For example, the primary public assistance program targeting poor families, Temporary Assistance to Needy Families (TANF), is time-limited and does not include full, comprehensive services. Social Security retirement, on the other hand, provides monthly retirement income that is based on the worker's lifelong financial contributions through payroll deductions. Essentially, TANF reflects the centuries-old belief that the poor cause their life situation and public assistance only reinforces their dependence on others. Retirees, on the other hand, who worked and contributed to the greater good through their payroll taxes, are able to make a just claim for retirement benefits.

The range of social welfare policies is best conceptualized through the classic work of Wilensky and Lebeaux (1965), *Industrial Society and Social Welfare,* in which they attempt to answer a basic question: Is social welfare a matter of giving assistance only in emergencies, or is it a frontline activity that society must provide? Their analysis includes two important concepts that continue to frame and influence social welfare discussions: residual social welfare and institutional welfare.

A cautionary note is in order. Not all programs and services are easily classified as one or the other; some programs have both institutional and residual attributes. The Head Start program, for example, is institutional in nature but is means-tested and restricted to a particular segment of the population. One solution is to expand the classic residual-institutional dichotomy to a residual-institutional continuum. A program's position on the continuum is determined by its eligibility criteria and the breadth and depth of its services.

The dichotomy between residual and institutional welfare imitates the inherent differences found in the justice theories expressed by Rawls and Nozick. Effective policy practice requires understanding and assessing the various justice theories that interact with and influence the development of a policy position.

Residual Welfare

Residual welfare views social welfare in narrow terms and typically includes only public assistance or policies related to the poor. Residual services carry a stigma, are time-limited, means-tested, and emergency-based, and are generally provided when all other forms of assistance are unavailable. Welfare services come into play only when all other systems have broken down or prove to be inadequate. Public assistance programs reflect the residual descriptions and include, among others, TANF, food stamps, Supplemental Security Income, General Assistance, and Medicaid.

The residual conception of social welfare rests on the individualistic notion that people are responsible for themselves and government intervenes only in times of crisis or emergency. Eligibility requires that people exhaust their own private resources, which may include assistance from the church, family members, friends, and employers, and requires people to prove their inability to provide for themselves and their families.

Social services are delivered only to people who meet certain defined criteria. The assessment procedure, commonly referred to as means testing, requires people to demonstrate that they do not have the financial ability to meet their specific needs. A residual program also mandates recertification for program participation, typically every 3 or 6 months. The recertification process is designed primarily to ensure that clients are still unable to meet their needs through private or personal sources.

People who receive residual services are generally viewed as being different from those who do need public services and are part of the majority group. They are viewed as failures because they do not emulate the ideals of rugged individualism, a cornerstone ideal of American society, which asserts that people take care of their own needs, are self-reliant, and work to provide for self and family. Clients in residual programs are often stereotyped by the larger society. They are often accused of making bad decisions, of requiring constant monitoring because of their inherent dishonesty, and of being lazy. In short, people in residual programs carry a stigma best described as blaming the victim, which Ryan (1976, p. 7) writes is applied to most social problems; people are perceived as "inferior, genetically defective, or morally unfit; the emphasis is on the intrinsic, even hereditary, defect."

Institutional Welfare

The second conception of social welfare described by Wilensky and Lebeaux (1965) is institutional social welfare. This definition is much more encompassing than the residual definition and extends to services that support all people. This framework recognizes the community's obligation to assist individual members because the problems are viewed, not as failures, but as part of life in modern society. Services go beyond immediate and basic need responses to emergencies. Assistance is provided well before people exhaust their own resources, and preventive and rehabilitative services are stressed.

An institutional program, as opposed to a residual program, is designed to meet the needs of all people. Eligibility is universal, no stigma is attached, and services are regular frontline programs in society. Institutional programs are so widely accepted in society that most are not viewed as social welfare programs at all. Social insurance programs, veterans programs, public education, food and drug regulations, and Medicare are institutional by nature.

Broadening the View of Social Welfare Policy

Richard Titmus (1965) argued that social welfare was much more than aid to the poor and in fact represented a broad system of support to the middle and upper classes. In his model, social welfare includes three separate but very distinct pieces: (1) fiscal welfare—tax benefits and supports for the middle and upper classes; (2) corporate welfare—tax benefits and supports for businesses; and (3) public welfare—assistance to the poor. Titmus ostensibly was arguing that social welfare reflects an institutional perspective.

Abramowitz (1983) applied the Titmus model to American social welfare and identified a "shadow welfare state" for the wealthy that parallels the social service system available to the poor. She concluded that poor and nonpoor alike benefit from government programs and tax laws that raise their disposable income. In other words, were it not for direct government support—whether through food stamps or a child care tax exemption—people would have fewer dollars to spend and to support themselves and their families. As with Titmus, Abramowitz extended social welfare well beyond services to the poor to encompass a wide range of programs and services that support the middle and upper classes.

The Titmus and Abramowitz position requires accepting the premise that corporate and fiscal welfare are the same as public welfare. If this position is accepted, then yes, all social welfare policies are institutional. The belief is that welfare, no matter its form, provides a subsidy that directly benefits the individual, with secondary benefits extending to the greater community. For example, home owners are able to claim a tax deduction for interest paid on home loans. The deduction encourages home ownership, for example, by lowering an individual's net taxable income, and supports the home building industry by encouraging the construction of new housing stock, which in turn requires suppliers to provide goods for the new construction. As more homes are built, more people are hired to build the homes, more supplies are needed, and the cycle continues. Rather than a tax deduction, the government just as easily could write a monthly or annual check to home owners to subsidize their housing. Titmus and Abramowitz would argue that the tax deduction is every bit a welfare expenditure, just as a Section 8 housing voucher is for the poor.

On the other hand, one could argue that corporate and fiscal welfare requires direct financial and work input from the recipient; that is, the benefit is determined by the amount and degree of effort invested by the individual. The argument continues that public welfare recipients are not required to make a similar contribution. This position reflects an equity and privilege model: What one receives is directly related to and proportional to what one contributes or invests. The resulting subsidy is a privilege extended only to those who participate in the program and supports the greater good. This position would argue that a home owner should receive a tax benefit because purchasing a home supports the greater good; conversely, Section 8 housing does not contribute to the greater good or a community's economic base.

CRAFTING JUSTICE-BASED POLICY

Policy practice, notes Jansson (1999, p. 10), allows the profession to promote its values and the well-being of clients, while at the same time countering opposition to proactive social welfare. The objective of policy practice is simple and straightforward: to change policy.

Haynes and Mickelson (2000, p. 23) write, "All social work is political." Although some may disagree with this assertion, there is no doubt that policy practice takes place within a political environment. Policies are made at the various levels of government, that is, local, state, and national, by boards of directors of nonprofit agencies and voluntary associations and CEOs of for-profit agencies. No matter the setting in which a policy emerges, it is the end result of a series of political decisions; who is included in and excluded from services, what services are provided, how the services are provided, and who provides the services reflect some of the political decisions that are addressed by policy. Given that policy is developed within a political environment, no one should be surprised that a policy is more often than not based on a political philosophy or ideology and disregards objective information and evidence. It is common for a policy to be organized around ambiguous evidence even though there has been a systematic review (Boaz & Pawson, 2005, p. 175). Such is the nature of the political process. The nagging question is: How can effective policy emerge if the political environment disregards objective evidence?

Critical Thinking

Critical thinking is the overarching skill set necessary for successful policy work. As Bok (2006, p. 67) notes, its development and refinement is one of the central purposes of higher education. Critical thinking is a systematic process that allows information to be considered and options to emerge in such a way that they result in clear policy. Defined as "reasonable and reflective thinking focused on deciding what to believe or do" (Fisher, 2001, p. 7), critical thinking creates and improves a current condition or situation. Logic and reasoning are cornerstones in the critical thinking process.

A policy position is the direct application of critical thinking. It requires analysis and organization of facts, developing opinions based on the facts, and the ability to argue the position and consider alternatives, all leading to the solving of specific problems. Paul and Elder (2007, p. 4) write that critical thinking is "self-directed, self-disciplined, self-monitored, and self-corrective." A rational and structured thinking process is important in organizing and distilling facts from myth and allows for clear, objective solutions to emerge.

Critical thinking allows and encourages essential questioning while systematically challenging one's own biases and beliefs. Philosophical and ideological positions are tested with the objective to discover new truths rather than to reinforce existing egocentric thinking. Paul and Elder (2007, p. 9) illustrate egocentric thinking with the following statements:

> It is true because I believe it.
>
> It is true because we believe it.
>
> It is true because I want to believe it.
>
> It is true because I have always believed it.
>
> It is true because it is in my self interest to believe it.

These egocentric statements rely on personal bias and prejudice. Policy that reflects this narrow laissez-faire thinking process only reinforces preconceived notions and hinders proactive change that is able to strengthen a community.

Critical thinking grows from evidence-based practice. The skilled practitioner recognizes that egocentric thinking is a common refrain, but by using practice evidence challenges the conventional position. Evidence and reasoning provide pathways to solutions. Injecting political considerations is necessary in the analysis, but it cannot become the primary reference point and driver in the process. A successful critical thinking process will yield a number of alternatives, some of which are better, stronger, and certainly more justice-oriented than others.

Traditional critical thinking methods are controlled processes that allow little room to impulsively react. Successful critical thinking must be flexible and allow for creative thinking, whose process is dynamic, vibrant, and intuitive. Flexibility, brainstorming, visioning, and metaphorical relationships are central in stimulating curiosity and furthering consideration of differing perspectives. Creative thinking balances the somewhat rigid critical thinking process by enabling a free flow of ideas and recognizing that some biases are impossible to disregard or subordinate.

Critical thinking is fraught with challenges. First and foremost is to recognize when one's personal views influence and color the collection and interpretation of evidence and lead to a series of foregone conclusions. Rawls (1971) proposed a veil of ignorance, which would shroud the person from all external variables and allow for an objective and fair result. Unfortunately, the human condition does not allow one to completely abdicate one's values and beliefs. Decisions, no matter how systematic, are not made in a valueless vacuum. Recognizing when one is disregarding evidence is paramount in critical thinking. The ability to minimize or set aside one's beliefs is most difficult but required.

A second challenge to critical thinking revolves around the collection of evidence. The World Wide Web opens the doors to a variety of data, information, and analyses of issues. The advantages of having so much information available, though many, can be overshadowed by the enticement of readily available information, and if left unattended, will result in faulty policy work. First and foremost, the reliability and validity of web sources must always be questioned; because information is posted on a web page does not mean it is legitimate. A second issue deals with information overload. The ease of information accessibility can be overwhelming. For example, Googling "social welfare policies in Texas" resulted in 1.12 million sites collected in .36 seconds. Critical thinking requires disciplined analysis of the Web, the ability to discern good information from bad, and ensuring that creativity is applied when seeking accurate, useful information.

A third challenge to critical thinking deals with process. Information must be assessed and distilled in a thoughtful and reflective manner in order for alternatives to emerge. First and foremost, the proposed policy must be justice-based and provide the maximum benefit for the community while advantaging those who are marginalized and set aside in a community. Achieving this objective requires time and simply cannot be rushed. Unfortunately, in today's world, time is considered a luxury and not valued as a requisite for work. Individuals are connected to their workplace 24/7; the written memo is virtually nonexistent, replaced by e-mails that can be sent from anywhere at any time of day or night; turnaround time for reports has been shortened due to the need for quick information. Successful critical thinking is threatened by the absence of process and the need for swift decisions.

CONCLUSION

Today's social problems are complex matters and impact all people, no matter their age, race, gender, ethnicity, or social status. These issues create significant barriers to creating just communities. But though the issues seem overwhelming, social concerns in one form or another will always be part of our landscape. This is not meant to be a pessimistic observation but reflects the unique aspects of the human condition. Roth (1997, p. xii) writes, "Social issues . . . would not exist if human beings knew everything, understood all the consequences of their actions, never made mistakes, always agreed with one another about what to do, and put exactly the right policies into practice."

Thomas Friedman (2005), in his work *The World Is Flat: A Brief History of the Twenty-first Century,* argues that the world is now more interconnected than at any time in its history. The lowering of trade and political barriers coupled with the technical advances of the digital revolution have made it possible to do business instantaneously with people anywhere in the world.

At this time the world's population is projected to be 6.58 billion (U.S. Census Bureau, 2007) in an estimated 228 nations (U.S. Census Bureau, IDB Release Notes, 2006), and, according to the 15th edition of *Ethnologue: Languages of the World*, there are 7,299 languages spoken around the world (as cited in Brown, 2006). The number of new nations, each with its own defining characteristics, beliefs, and traditions, will continue to grow. Between 1900 and 1950, approximately 1.2 countries were created each year; from 1950 to 1990, 2.2 nations were created each year; and in the 1990s, the number of new nations jumped to 3.1 annually (Enriquez, 2005).

No one can expect to gain even a rudimentary knowledge of the many nations of the world, each with its own language and culture. Nor can we foresee which cultures and languages will be important or exist in the middle of the twenty-first century. Similarly, no one can predict with steadfast assurance and accuracy future events in local, national, or international arenas.

Today we live in a different, more open world, with fewer borders that separate or minimize our interactions. No matter who we are or where we live, all people are touched by distant wars, terrorist threats, hurricanes, typhoons, tsunamis, Middle East oil shortages, narcotics trafficking, irreversible destruction of our environment coupled with the threats caused by global warming, widespread and pervasive poverty, new and deadly diseases, trade wars, and the daily threat posed by the growing world arsenal of nuclear weapons. All these events draw governments into new collaborative intergovernmental relationships. And all of these new patterns of behavior influence the development of social policy.

Stoesz (2000, p. 622) critically charged that the future is "bleak" for liberals unless they become "more versatile in [their] policy repertoire." The same could be said for conservatives and moderates. Stoesz is correct that to be relevant in the policy-making process social workers must incorporate a critical thinking, multidimensional approach that is firmly rooted in justice theory. Reliance on political, philosophical, or ideological dogma will only continue the broad and significant social and economic discrepancies that currently exist. Fair policy is achievable by the melding of practice wisdom with critical thinking guided by justice theory that mandates we promote the interests of the least advantaged.

REFERENCES

Abramowitz, M. (1983). Everyone is on welfare: "The role of redistribution in social policy" revisited. *Social Work, 28*(6), 440–445.

Australian Association of Social Workers. (2004). *Continuing professional educational policy*. Retrieved December 2, 2006, from www.aasw.asn.au/adobe/profdev/CPE_policy_2006.pdf.

Barker, R. (1995). *The social work dictionary* (3rd ed.). Washington, DC: National Association of Social Workers Press.

Barker, R. (2003). *The social work dictionary* (5th ed.). Washington, DC: National Association of Social Workers Press.

Baumheier, E. C., & Schorr, A. L. (1977). Social policy. In J. Turner (Ed.), *Encyclopedia of social work* (17th ed., pp. 1453–1463). Washington, DC: National Association of Social Workers Press.

Boaz, A., & Pawson, R. (2005). The perilous road from evidence to policy: Five journeys compared. *Journal of Social Policy, 34*, 175–194.

Bok, D. (2006). *Our underachieving colleges: A candid look at how much students learn and why they should be learning more*. Princeton, NJ: Princeton University Press.

Brown, K. (2006, March 16). Notes on the lists of languages. In K. Brown (Ed.), *Encyclopedia of languages & linguistics* (pp. 143–144). Retrieved November 27, 2007, from www.sciencedirect. com/science?_ob=ArticleURL&_udi=B7T84-4M3C3K0-WW&_rdoc=10&_hierId=1129000001 &_refWorkId=326&_fmt=full&_orig=na&_docanchor=&_idxType=GI&view=c&_ct=11 &_acct=C000050221&_version=1&_urlVersion=0&_userid=10&md5=f74dac071bd004ea 9878a0095bf3e001.

Canadian Association of Schools of Social Work. (2004). *CASSW standards for accreditation*. Ottawa, Ontario, Canada: Author.

Chatterjee, P. (1966). *Approaches to the welfare state*. Washington, DC: National Association of Social Workers Press.

Council on Social Work Education. (2001). *Educational policy and accreditation standards*. Alexandria, VA: Author.

Dear, R. B. (1995). Social welfare policy. In R. L. Edwards & J. G. Hobbs (Eds.), *Encyclopedia of social work* (19th ed., Vol. *3*, pp. 2226–2237). Washington, DC: National Association of Social Workers Press.

Declaration of Alma-Alta. (1978, September). *International Conference on Primary Health Care, Alma-Ata, USSR*. Retrieved December 4, 2006, from www.who.int/hpr/NPH/docs /declaration_almaata.pdf.

DiNitto, D., & Dye, T. (1983). *Social welfare politics and public policy* (2nd ed.). Englewood Cliffs, NJ: Prentice-Hall.

Enriquez, J. (2005). *The Untied States of America: Polarization, fracturing, and our future*. New York: Crown.

Fisher, A. (2001). *Critical thinking: An introduction*. New York: Cambridge University Press.

Franklin, B. (n.d.). *The Writings of Benjamin Franklin, London: 1757–1775* (Vols. 1–5). Retrieved November 5, 2006, from www.historycarper.com/resources/twobf3/price.htm.

Friedlander, W. (1955). *Introduction to social welfare*. New York: Prentice-Hall.

Friedman, T. L. (2005). *The world is flat: A brief history of the twenty-first century*. New York: Farrar, Straus and Giroux.

Gilbert, N., & Specht, H. (1974). *Dimensions of social welfare policy*. Englewood Cliffs, NJ: Prentice Hall.

Hagen, J. (2000). Critical perspectives on social welfare: Challenges and controversies. *Families in Society, 81*, 555–556.

Haynes, K., & Mickelson, J. (2000). *Affecting change: Social workers in the political arena* (4th ed.). Boston: Allyn & Bacon.

International Association of Schools of Social Work. (2007). *Global standards for the education and training of the social work profession*. Retrieved February 6, 2007, from www.iassw-aiets.org.

Jansson, B. (1999). *Becoming an effective policy advocate: From policy practice to social justice*. Pacific Grove, CA: Brooks/Cole.

Karger, H., & Stoesz, D. (2004). *American social welfare policy: A pluralist approach* (4th ed.). Boston: Allyn & Bacon.

Miller, D. (2005, November 26). *Justice and boundaries*. Speech presented at the Centre for the Study of Social Justice Conference, Nuffield College, Oxford.

Morales, A., & Sheafor, B. (1989). *Social work, a profession of many faces* (5th ed.). Boston: Allyn & Bacon.

Morris, R. (1986). Social welfare policy: Trends and issues. In A. Minahan (Ed.), *Encyclopedia of social work* (18th ed., Vol. *2*, pp. 664–681). Silver Spring, MD: National Association of Social Workers.

National Association of Social Workers. (1999). *Code of ethics of the National Association of Social Workers*. Washington, DC: Author.

Nozick, R. (1974). *Anarchy, state, and utopia*. New York: Basic Books.

Osterholm, M. T. (2005). Preparing for the next pandemic. *New England Journal of Medicine*, *352*(18), 1839–1842.

Paul, R., & Elder, L. (2007). *The miniature guide to critical thinking: Concepts and tools* (4th ed.). Dillon Beach, CA: Foundation for Critical Thinking.

Popple, P., & Leighninger, L. (1990). *Social work, social welfare, and American society*. Boston: Allyn & Bacon.

Public papers of the presidents of the United States. (1965). Lyndon B. Johnson, 1963–1964 (Vol. 1, entry 91, pp. 112–118). Washington, DC: U.S. Government Printing Office.

Rawls, J. (1971). *Theory of justice*. Cambridge, MA: Harvard University Press.

Reamer, F. (1993). *The philosophical foundations of social work*. New York: Columbia University Press.

Reagan, R. (n.d.). *RonaldReagan.com the official site*. Retrieved December 10, 2006, from www.ronaldreagan.com/secondterm.html.

Roosevelt, F. D. (n.d.). *State of the Union Address*. Retrieved November 5, 2006, from www.thisnation.com/library/sotu/1935fdr.html.

Roth, J. K. (1997). *Encyclopedia of social issues* (Vol. 4). New York: Marshall Cavendish.

Ryan, W. (1976). *Blaming the victim* (Rev. ed.). New York: Vintage Books.

Stoesz, D. (2000). Renaissance: Families in society. *Journal of Contemporary Human Services*, *81*(6), 621–628.

Titmus, R. (1959). *Essays on the welfare state*. New Haven, CT: Yale University Press.

Titmus, R. (1965). The role of redistribution in social policy. *Social Security Bulletin*, *28*(6), 34–55.

UNAIDS, Joint United Nations Programme on HIV/AIDS. (2006). *AIDS epidemic update*. Geneva, Switzerland: Author.

U.S. Census Bureau. (2006, August 24). *IDB release notes*. Retrieved December 4, 2006, from www.census.gov/ipc/www/idbr200608.html.

U.S. Census Bureau. (2007). *World POPClock projection*. Retrieved March 14, 2007, from www.census.gov/ipc/www/popclockworld.html.

Wilensky, H., & Lebeaux, C. (1965). *Industrial society and social welfare*. New York: Free Press.

Woolley, J., & Peters, G. (n.d.). *The American presidency project*. Santa Barbara: University of California (hosted), Gerhard Peters (database). Available from www.presidency.ucsb.edu/ws/?pid=8758/.

World Bank (2005, November 8). *Avian flu: Economic losses could top US$800 billion*. Retrieved December 4, 2006, from www.worldbank.org.

World Health Organization. (2007a). *Measles*. Retrieved February 1, 2007, from www.who.int/mediacentre/factsheets/fs286/en/.

World Health Organization. (2007b). *Working for health: An introduction to the World Health Organization*. Geneva, Switzerland: Author.

Zimmerman, S. L. (1979). Policy, social policy, and family policy. *Journal of Marriage and the Family*, *41*, 467–495.

Section III

POLICY TO PRACTICE AND PRACTICE TO POLICY

This section's chapters draw attention to policy vis-á-vis selected population groups and social issues. The section begins with a discussion of policy practice with a chapter by the well-known scholar Dr. Rodney Ellis. Ellis provides an overview of the policy practice processes, which he views as a series of sequential but overlapping stages, including preparing oneself, assembling a team, identifying, defining, and legitimizing the problem, selecting an approach for analysis, conducting the analysis, and evaluating the outcomes of the policy initiative. Ellis presents case vignettes and identifies specific, practical models of policy analysis and makes recommendations as to their appropriateness for different policy practice settings.

King Davis, PhD, director of the Hogg Foundation of Mental Health, discusses "new federalism" and the growing challenges faced in mental health. King believes that mental health care will remain a major financial and policy responsibility of state governments and underfinanced in almost all states. Among his many conclusions is the idea that "nationalization" of the mental health system would facilitate quality in breadth and depth of services. A proponent of a stronger role for the federal government in the provision of comprehensive mental health care, King raises key questions regarding the current status of underfunded mental health care in contrast to the growing need for services.

Enid Opal Cox, PhD, is a creative scholar in the field of gerontology. Dr. Cox's chapter begins with an overview of the nature and content of social policy and social services targeting older Americans, with attention to implications for social workers engaged in policy practice. She brings the reader through a lucid discussion of social and moral issues that impact policy development, with attention directed to policy trends of special concern to older adults, such as income, employment, and health.

Dr. Elizabeth DePoy and Dr. Stephen French Gilson, nationally recognized advocates for persons with disabilities, offer a thought-provoking chapter using explanatory legitimacy theory, in which they detail a critical analysis of contemporary disability policy. DePoy and Gilson conclude that legitimacy analysis creates universal rights, resources, and privileges on the basis of human description and need rather than on implicit, nomothetic, and essentialist assumptions about individual embodied worth. They challenge the professional community to rethink disability policy and other population categorical policies as being on a time continuum and to celebrate the diversity of ideas and bodies.

Two chapters focusing on health-care issues are written by authors from each coast. Pamela Miller, PhD, associate professor of social work at Portland State University, discusses a select group of policies that are relevant in today's practice context, though some may not be too familiar to the social work community. Miller argues that knowledge is needed for change, and the true motive behind exploration of these policies is to both frighten and inspire. Her concluding question encourages ongoing dialogue: "Should the focus [of policy change] be on something small, such as revamping a state's Medicaid policy, or large, such as redesigning the entire way health care is delivered? Should we continue the path of market reform of the identified problems or create new ways, outside of the private, for-profit sector, to handle our health crisis?"

Dr. Gary Rosenberg, professor of community medicine at Mount Sinai Hospital, initially presented his chapter at the opening plenary session of the 5th International Conference of Social Work in Health and Mental Health in Hong Kong. Rosenberg examines health care social work with an eye on the future, with specific attention directed to the significant challenges he believes social workers will have to confront and resolve if the profession is to remain relevant and effective. He discusses four hypotheses regarding the profession's future and contends that the use of transdisciplinary teams of social, behavioral, and biological researchers will work to add to the knowledge base of social work practice. Like Dr. Miller, he concludes with a series of questions that are central to the future of health-care social work.

Sunil Kumar, PhD, holds a lecture position at the London School of Economics in the Department of Social Policy. Dr. Kumar's work has focused on housing, in particular rental housing and the poor. His title, "Uban Housing Policy and Practice in the Developing World," sets the tone for an intriguing discussion. Kumar argues that there is a pressing need to focus on urban housing in developing nations, whose housing policies to date have been disjointed and fragmented. Dr. Kumar offers "out of the box" creative policy ideas around housing.

Richard Gelles, PhD, is a nationally known sociologist with expertise in child welfare, in particular permanency planning. Gelles and his coauthor Carol Wilson Spigner, DSW, pull no punches by confronting the social work profession and the social welfare system in general to confront what they believe is a failed system. Gelles and Spigner conclude that the government's attention to child welfare policy is infrequent with a system supported by minimal resources. Their prognosis challenges all policy makers when writing, "None of the federal legislative initiatives in the last 25 years has yielded significant improvements in achieving permanence for children in out-of-home care, assuring stable reunifications, or reducing the number of children waiting for adoption while also reducing adoption disruptions."

Sophia Dziegelewski, PhD, and Christopher Blackwell, PhD, provide a critical analysis of public funding of sectarian associations for HIV/AIDS programs. Their discussion examines several concerns that often emerge when religious-based organizations are responsible for care directed at the gay male population. Dziegelewski and Blackwell identify and discuss significant issues they feel result in negative perceptions and ideas about nonheterosexual behavior and intervention efforts with a strong focus on abstinence-only prevention strategies.

Chapter 8

POLICY PRACTICE

Rodney A. Ellis

Benjamin is a BSSW-level social worker who is employed as a case manager in a mental health treatment facility. He loves his work and has an excellent record of effective practice with his clients. He is concerned, however, about one aspect of his agency's operation. He has noticed that many clients have recently discontinued their treatment despite substantial improvement in their reported issues. Curious as to why this might be occurring, Benjamin made a few phone calls to clients who had recently dropped out of treatment. He was astounded to discover that four of the five people he called had stopped attending sessions because their state-provided supplemental income benefits had been cut. These former clients reported a simple choice: They could either not pay their rent or stop attending treatment sessions. They chose to take care of immediate necessities rather than their important, but less urgent, mental health needs.

Benjamin is disturbed that so many were leaving treatment, but he is even more disturbed that it was unnecessary that most of them do so. His agency had funding alternatives that would have allowed all the persons he called to remain in treatment. They had not taken advantage of those alternatives simply because they had not been aware of them. The agency had no means of assuring that the information was made available to them. Having discovered this problem, Benjamin resolves to find a way to solve it. Further, he wishes to institutionalize the solution so that it is certain to remain in place into the foreseeable future.

Alma is the executive director of the same agency at which Benjamin is a case manager. She is unaware that her agency's clients are withdrawing from services because of the income cutbacks. She is aware, however, that the cutbacks are occurring. Alma is a part of a local coalition of social service providers that is concerned about the conditions area residents have begun to face as a result of the cuts. A community needs assessments conducted after the changes revealed that the number of persons becoming homeless had increased, the rate of the referral of children into the child welfare system had nearly doubled, and community health experts were predicting a surge in emergency room treatment and hospitalizations. Further investigation showed that all these conditions could be traced, at least in part, to the loss of income many families have experienced. Several other effects have been reported in the community, including increased demand at food banks and a rising crime rate. No formal research has been conducted that could identify a link between these conditions and the cuts. There is, however, strong evidence from reports of residents that such a link exists. Further evidence is provided by the fact that these changes occurred in the wake of the cuts and have a logical relationship to them.

The coalition of agencies has been formed to study and address the problem. Its mission is to develop and implement a plan to get the cuts reversed and to assure a steady supply of supplemental income to the residents of their community and state. So far the coalition has met twice, collected available data about the cut and its effects, and drafted a mission statement to guide future activities. The statement is short, simple, and to the point: "The mission of the Supplemental Income Reinstatement Coalition is to restore the level of each program recipient's supplemental income to precut levels."

Both Benjamin and Alma face issues created by current social welfare policy. The problems have a common cause—the supplemental income cuts—but the manifestations of the issue and the levels at which they hope to address the issue are very different. Benjamin faces a problem at the agency level. It is a policy issue, more specifically, one caused by the absence of any effective policy to assure that an undesirable condition does not arise. He will probably find it relatively easy to identify a solution, gain access to decision makers, and persuade those decision makers to take steps to address the problem. Alma, on the other hand, faces a problem generated at a higher level and that affects many people in a variety of ways. Although ultimately the cause of the problems they want to address is the same, the scope and goals of their efforts will differ in significant ways.

Benjamin and Alma have chosen to engage in a very important social work activity: policy practice. Janssen (1999, p. 10) defines policy practice as "efforts to change policies in legislative, agency, and community settings, whether by establishing new policies, improving existing ones, or defeating the policy initiatives of other people." Despite the fact that many social workers express little interest in policy, their careers are intrinsically involved in social welfare policy. In fact, policy furnishes their careers. Problems are recognized by policy makers, policies are written, social programs are developed, and jobs are created—many filled by social workers.

In an ideal world policies would solve the problems they were intended to address. In reality this is sometimes not the case. Take, for example, Benjamin's discovery. Policies related to mental health treatment are working well. Policies to provide alternative funding for services also exist. There is, however, a problem in agency policy. No policy has been written to assure that clients are aware of the financial supports. In this case, policies such as those providing for mental health treatment fail because of the absence of other supportive policies.

Alma's group is hoping to address policy failure at a higher and broader level. The group has only recently begun to study the issue, but it appears that this body of policy worked well at one point. Changes in the social climate or political landscape have reduced its effectiveness.

The absence of policy and changes in the social or political situation are two of the many conditions that can cause or contribute to policy failure. Among the many others are poorly conceived policies, policies that fail to consider unintended consequences, policies that fail to consider the potential for disruption at other levels, and policies that are well-conceived but are not ultimately fundable (Ellis, 2003; Janssen, 1999). Further, some older social problems, such as poverty, have never been adequately addressed on a national scale, much less globally. Despite the ongoing problems faced by U.S. citizens, those problems often pale when compared to those of persons in other countries. New social problems also arise, prompted by events both national and international. The tragic events of 9/11 point to a clear need for new and innovative policies not only to prevent future tragedies, but also to provide support and assistance to victims should the preventive policies fail. Issues related to migration and immigration, refugeeism, and human rights issues also cry out for solutions crafted by the hands of social workers. The new responses must be "out of the box" in that they must look at problems globally rather than regionally or nationally. In the modern world very little happens in a national vacuum. Events in other countries and processes that cross international borders cause and exacerbate conditions within our own country. These increased pressures underscore the need for innovative solutions such as international exchanges of ideas, information, and problem-solving experts. Technological developments offer methods of communication, information transfer, and exchange of ideas that might otherwise be prohibitively costly or simply impossible. Social workers are among those at the table in some of the groups planning policy-directed interventions for these international issues. More social workers and more groups are needed as global change accelerates.

Hopefully, it is clear from this introductory discussion that social workers are, by the nature of their profession and position, inherently involved in social policy. In addition, they may engage in policy practice at many levels, from working to add a few lines to a policy and procedures manual to altering the laws that guide how nations interact. It is also important to recognize the unique contribution social workers often make to policy planning. First, social workers are often in a position to be among the first to recognize social problems. Those whose lives are directly affected by the problems are, of course, typically the first to recognize their presence. However, because of the direct communication with client groups social workers such as Benjamin have with persons in the community, these direct service workers may become aware of problems before any other group. A second reason a social work presence is important to the planning process is that it provides the opportunity to influence problem definition. Problem definition refers to the way policy makers interpret and explain a problem. Interpretation and explanation, in turn, influence the way a solution is formed. Consider, for example, problems experienced by persons in poverty. If, as many conservatives believe, it is possible for the impoverished to simply "pull themselves up by their bootstraps," policies should be written that provide for the most cursory of interventions. The vast majority of the responsibility for change would lie with poor people and their allegorical bootstraps. Social workers recognize that, while a portion of the responsibility for change lies with the individual, impoverished persons face a daunting gauntlet of barriers to change. They also know how to craft and implement solutions to many of those barriers. It seems unlikely that solutions to poverty on any scale, individual or global, are likely to occur without social work participation.

Yet another important reason for social workers to engage in policy practice is the clearly defined set of ethics and values they bring to the table. Policy-related discussions often bog down because the values of the participants are not clearly expressed. This is often seen when discussions degenerate to a point that one or both sides has stalled with no more logical arguments, simply saying something like "We must do it this way." What has often happened is that all effective arguments have been offered and countered, leaving participants with nothing more than their values as an argument. They may be unable to articulate those values because they have never sufficiently defined them. It may also be that participants recognize that to speak their values clearly would actually undermine their argument by revealing less than humanitarian assumptions or motives. By clearly defining their values, social workers can verbalize much of the core motivation for their argument. They also, thereby, earn the right to ask their opponents to verbalize theirs. The importance of the presence of a representative of such clear values and ethics in policy-related discussion is clear. Often, its only potential source is a social worker.

It is clear that effective policy practice is important to social workers, their clients, the profession, the nation, and the world. It is also clear that any social worker may be called to engage in policy practice at any time. This chapter is about effective policy practice. Although it was written primarily with practice within the United States in mind, much of it is applicable to international practice. The chapter discusses preparing for policy practice, identifying and defining the problem, assembling a policy practice team, selecting an approach, conducting an analysis, developing an action plan, and evaluating the outcomes of the activities. It is intended to provide a general understanding of the processes, techniques, and strategies of policy practice and to provide resources for gaining additional information and skill.

PREPARATION OF THE PRACTITIONER

The process of preparing for policy practice might be conceived as a series of stages. The first involves the acquisition of a specific set of knowledge and skills needed to interact, assess, plan interventions, and evaluate outcomes within the policy arena. Practitioners who have reached this point in their training are able to perform all the basic functions necessary to engage in policy practice and know how to acquire advanced knowledge, skills, and resources. Accredited BSSW and MSSW programs are designed to provide the basic knowledge and skills so that any graduate, however inadequate he or she may feel, has been taught the foundation of what he or she needs to know. The Council on Social Work Education (CSWE) refers to this foundational set of knowledge and skills as "generalist" because it allows the practitioner to work across multiple settings.

Generalist knowledge encompasses the theories and technique of successful professional intervention with clients and client systems. These theories and techniques are applied by practitioners as they interact with individuals, families, and groups in assessment, intervention planning, implementation of the selected intervention, and evaluation of the intervention's effectiveness. The theories and techniques utilize and are guided by scientifically supported principles of human behavior, including insight from social work researchers as well as those in psychology, sociology, medicine, political science, and public administration. Interventions are also structured and guided in accordance with social work ethics, values, and the profession's emphasis on cultural competence.

Generalist knowledge and skills can be applied across a variety of professional settings. For example, social workers in a clinical setting would use assessment skills, such as active listening, identifying client strengths, and identifying and understanding client relationships. Assessment might require knowledge of the theories of human development, psychopathology, and human motivation.

Although at first glance a social worker's efforts to change the way a law is written through interactions with a state legislature might seem very different from the work of a clinician, their tasks are, on closer examination, quite similar. For instance, a social worker engaging in policy practice might use active listening when interviewing various experts about current policy and its effects. Strengths-based assessment would be used with the population the policy was designed to benefit. Skills for analyzing interpersonal relationships would be used when assessing the relationships between stakeholders likely to support or oppose an initiative.

A policy practitioner equipped to practice at the generalist level would be able to facilitate policy change such as the one intended by Benjamin with minimal support from others. A presentation of findings to the executive committee of the agency might be all that would be required. On the other hand, a practitioner trying to produce changes in federal legislation might need to assemble a work group composed of persons with specialized knowledge and relationships to deal with the intricacies of practice at that level. For example, the practitioner might want to recruit a group member with knowledge and experience in utilizing a specific form of policy analysis to help lead the process. Still, the principle that generalist skills are a sufficient foundation for policy practice holds, even at the federal level. Generalist skills would be used to identify, recruit, retain, and encourage the required participation by group members.

The second stage of preparation for effective policy practice involves the development of advanced policy knowledge and skills. These are not typically available in BSSW programs (although some might be gained through unique internship experiences). They are, however, included in CSWE-accredited MSSW programs. They may also, of course, be obtained by dedicated practitioners who participate in seminars, readings, and interaction with more experienced professionals after they have received their degrees. Further, much of this knowledge and many of these skills can be developed while the practitioner is working. For example even if Alma did not have a strong working knowledge of a model of policy analysis, she could obtain books such as those by DiNitto and Cummins (2006) or Ellis (2003) and follow the procedures outlined therein. Advanced policy practice includes such components as mastery of at least one model of policy analysis, the ability to develop and implement a strategic plan to change policy, and a thorough knowledge of at least one major policy area.

The third stage of preparation includes knowledge of the people, issues, history, barriers, and political environment that exist within a specific policy arena. Considering Alma once again, despite having the basic knowledge and skills required for successful policy practice and having armed herself with the materials necessary to conduct an effective analysis, she may know little about the specifics of the persons, policies, and situations that have led to the supplemental income cuts. She can develop this knowledge as she proceeds with her analysis, but would do well to bring others into the coalition who already have this knowledge to help educate coalition members about the situations they will be facing.

Some practitioners may choose to advance to the fourth stage of preparation for policy practice. In the fourth stage practitioners become adept at advanced forms of evaluation, analysis, and assessment, such as cost-benefit analysis and forecasting (Ellis, 2003). Many of these tasks can be completed by specialists recruited to a team of practitioners. When funds are available, external experts may be hired to perform these analyses. For example, if Alma wanted to include a retrospective evaluation of the effectiveness of the income supplement cuts in her analysis she would have several alternatives. She might draw on her BSSW training supplemented by books on outcome evaluation. Alternatively, she might ask a professor trained in outcome evaluation to join her team. If no one was willing to do the work on a pro bono basis, she might determine whether funds were available to hire an expert to do the evaluation.

It is important to note that, although these four stages represent four distinct areas of competence, the lines between them are blurred. Practitioners do not necessarily obtain full proficiency at one level before progressing to the next. For example, a person with BSSW-level training might have lived and worked in a community for many years and might have obtained many of the proficiencies of level 3, but might lack the formal training and resources available at level 2. This practitioner might hastily seek education in these areas or might recruit team members who could bring that level of knowledge and skill to the table. The process of building a policy practice team is discussed next.

ASSEMBLING A TEAM

In a situation like Benjamin's no team may be necessary. He may be able to assemble the necessary data and undertake the required activities without any support from anyone else. Alma, however, is clearly in a position where the support of others would be beneficial, perhaps essential.

Team members should be recruited strategically. They may bring one of three essential components to the table. These components, the same as those required for any successful task group, are influence, competence, and motivation (Ellis, Crane Mallory, Gould, & Shatila, 2006).

Influence is the ability to directly affect the persons and forces involved in a change. In policy practice this may mean the capacity to access important stakeholders or to influence their opinions. It might also refer to someone who has resources, such as funding or personnel to support the effort. A policy practice work group may be highly skilled and very motivated, but without adequate power and resources it is unlikely to succeed.

Policy practice work groups must also contain members with competence. Competent members are those who have the essential knowledge and skills to perform the tasks required for policy analysis and planning. Persons with competence bring team-building skills, research skills, policy analysis skills, and action planning skills, as well as the ability to write and make public presentations effectively. In policy practice that crosses cultural or international borders, team members who understand those cultures and countries will be needed.

Motivation is also critical to a policy practice work group's success. Persons with motivation bring a strong desire for change to the group. Persons with influence and competence may be very motivated, but often motivation comes from those who do not have an official role in the process. Highly motivated people might be found among the persons who are directly experiencing the policy problem.

Policy practitioners must assess their work groups to determine the degree to which these three components exist and the ways they can be mobilized. When components are deficient or absent, new members should be recruited who can bring them to the table. This process of assessment and recruitment should be ongoing to assure that changes in group composition or in the policy environment do not negatively impact the group's effectiveness.

IDENTIFICATION, DEFINITION, AND LEGITIMIZATION OF THE PROBLEM

Policy practice may be viewed as a series of stages. Each stage includes the gathering of information about some aspect of the policy being considered for change. Although later stages may build on information gathered in earlier stages, the progression need not always be from one step to the next. The first and foundational stage, however, involves the identification, definition, and legitimization of the problem. It is important that most of the work at this stage be completed before a great deal of effort is expended on the other stages. Identification, definition, and legitimization assure that the problem is effectively recognized, carefully articulated, and appropriately acknowledged by persons with the power to make changes.

Identification refers to recognizing the presence of a problem. At this point the practitioner may not understand much about the problem but does recognize that people are affected by it. Benjamin reached the identification stage when he noticed an inordinate number of people who were not returning to receive services. Alma and her coalition have identified the problem of inadequate income and believe it to be the result of the income supplement cutbacks. They may, however, need some additional research to firmly establish that the cutbacks are the source of the problem.

When policy practitioners define a problem, they put it in writing. Although there is some disagreement between experts as to the exact content of the definition, four themes are commonly recognized: population, problem, perspectives, and policy (Ellis, 2003). A comprehensive problem statement, then, describes what population is affected, what its members lack and what prevents them from obtaining it (problem), the perspectives of those who experience the problem, and the policy that addresses, causes, or should address the problem.

Legitimization occurs when some authoritative policy-making body officially says that a problem exists. Although thousands might become homeless and foster care numbers might skyrocket, for the purposes of policy no problem exists until persons in power acknowledge it. So, in the case of Alma, if policy makers in her state have not recognized that the problem of inadequate income is impacting persons in their communities to the degree that it is, her work group must focus on bringing the problem to the attention of the legislators. Armed with a well-researched, well-articulated problem statement, they can also enhance the probability that the decision makers will perceive and define the problem as they do.

It is also important to understand the degree to which policy at each level of government influences the problem. Some problems are primarily addressed at a single level. For example, Social Security provides the primary body of policy for disability insurance. Other problems, such as child abuse, neglect, and abandonment, are addressed at multiple levels: federal, state, local, and agency. In some areas of policy, court decisions have also influenced the interpretation of policy, meaning that case law must also be considered in order to completely understand an area of policy. Practitioners must be certain they have collected and understand policy at every level to adequately formulate their definition. For example, although Alma's group appears to be dealing with a problem that has been primarily created at the state level, income maintenance policy also exists at the federal level and in some areas may be influenced locally as well. The group would need to know what responsibilities lie at which level and how the policy provisions interact between them.

Practitioners working in countries other than or in addition to the United States may find a political landscape that differs from the one described here. Levels of government that exist in the United States do not exist in many countries, for example. In some countries these levels might exist, but the distribution of responsibilities and power may vary. Where the structure of the government differs, practitioners should clearly identify the levels of government, assign them names, and list the responsibilities of each level in the specific area of policy being addressed. Strategies discussed in this book and in other resources can be adapted accordingly.

An additional important function of the problem statement is that it helps the group determine whether it is in agreement as to the nature of the problem. The problem statement will form the basis of all of the work the group does. It guides the way the problem is perceived, the area of policy selected for study, and the kinds of solutions that will be proposed. Obtaining agreement among the work group members is also important to assure that they remain united during the action phase of the initiative. Unity is critical to success, and constant, effective communication and shared understanding promote unity within the team.

Although a policy definition is drafted very early in the analysis process, it should be reviewed periodically to assure that information gained during research has not changed the group's understanding. When they discover that their understanding has changed, group members should adjust their definition accordingly.

SELECTING AN APPROACH

There are several approaches (often referred to as models) for conducting a policy analysis. Basically, the term "approach" or "model" refers to a method of collecting information about specific aspects of a body of policy. Those who analyze policy, meaning that they critically examine the aspects of the body of policy associated with their identified problem, are engaging in policy practice.

Dobelstein (1996) identified three general categories of policy analysis: *behavioral, incremental*, and *criteria-based*. Most forms of analysis fall into one of these three categories. Each has its own set of strengths and limitations, and each is, therefore, best used in different settings. Behavioral models use scientific methods and statistical analyses to identify and choose from among a group of alternatives. Incremental models identify several potential solutions, then piece together portions of those solutions to produce feasible alternatives. The final choice is made by weighing each alternative against the values of the public. This helps to determine both how useful and how acceptable each solution might be.

Approaches that are criteria-based share some of the characteristics of the behavioral and incremental models. As in the incremental model, several alternative solutions are identified in the initial steps. The solutions are then evaluated and ranked in the order of their level of acceptability to the public. Finally, the alternatives are evaluated using research methods common to behavioral models. The goal is to determine the cost, benefits, and feasibility of each alternative. A solution is then selected based on the values ranking and the research.

It is important to remember that one type of analysis may be more appropriate for one set of circumstances than for another. For example, behavioral methods are probably best suited for environments in which research reports are either already present or are readily funded, and where public norms and values are unlikely to have a strong impact on a decision. Incremental methods may be best for situations in which significant compromises between competing proposals can be anticipated and public values are expected to play a major role. Criteria-based approaches are likely to be more effective when a comprehensive approach is needed to address multiple aspects of the policy environment. For example, Benjamin can probably anticipate that the values of the persons operating his agency are similar to his own and that he will not face much opposition to his initiative. A behavioral approach in which he collects and analyzes a little more data and presents his findings to the executive board will probably be adequate for his situation. Alma's group, however, is likely to need a more comprehensive approach. They will need to collect relevant research and supplement it with some work of their own. Research alone is likely to be inadequate, however, because of the powerful and contradictory values that affect income maintenance policy (Ellwood, 1989). In this case a criteria-based method may be desirable.

Regardless of which type of analysis is selected, there are certain categories of information that must be collected and considered: (a) information about the history and current status of the problem and the policy that has been developed to address it, (b) identification of the norms and values of the voting public, (c) recognition of the political alliances that will support or oppose the proposal, (d) review of the current system of agencies that compose the service delivery system, (e) generation of a series of alternative solutions, (f) collection or production of appropriate professional analyses, and (g) examination of potential unintended consequences. Based on the analysis of some combination of these categories of information, a decision is made as to which alternative to recommend (Ellis, 2003).

Each of the three general types of policy analysis selects from among these categories of information, using some and ignoring or minimizing others. For example, a purely behavioral approach might not require information about the norms and values of the public or about political alliances, yet an incremental approach might consider this information vital. Each of the categories of analysis includes specific models, often named for the person who designed them. It is from these models that policy practitioners choose when they plan an analysis. Proficiency in one of them was a part of the second level of preparation for policy practice identified earlier in this chapter.

Some models also include action planning for change (Ellis, 2003). Others do not include this phase. This omission reflects the diversity of roles assumed by policy practitioners in various policy initiatives. At times the practitioner might be asked to perform an analysis only, with the person or organization commissioning the analysis making the decisions as to how to proceed. At other times the practitioner and his or her team might include action plan development and implementation as a part of their analysis.

CONDUCTING AN ANALYSIS

After a model has been selected, the practitioner or team must implement the analysis. In a team this can be accomplished by matching tasks to each member's area of proficiency. In Alma's group, for example, she may have recruited BSSWs or MSSWs who are particularly good at Internet and library research. These members might be selected for tasks such as identifying and obtaining copies of current policies at every level. High-level agency executives with many years working in the community might be asked to identify potential friends and foes of the proposal. A university professor might be asked to develop a plan for further study.

It is important that the individual tasks and responsibilities of each step of an analysis be identified, committed to writing, and assigned to team members with specific due dates and methods of reporting the results. In the previous section several categories of information that are used in policy analysis were identified. Practitioners must not only know what those categories are, but must be able to use strategies for obtaining accurate data for each.

Information about the History and Current Status of the Problem and Policy

One very effective strategy for accumulating information about the history and status of a policy is online resources. In the United States and many other countries there are web sites at federal, state (or territorial), and local levels from which information can be obtained. In Mexico, for example, practitioners might start at www.presidencia.gob.mx/. At the federal level in the United States, there are sites for each branch of the federal government. A good starting point for locating these is www.whitehouse.gov. Links from that site lead to web sites for the executive, legislative, and judicial branches. There are also sites for obtaining the actual policy documents, such as that of the Office of the Law Revision Counsel (http://uscode.house.gov/usc.htm) and for legislative information (http://thomas.loc.gov).

State and local governments also often have web sites that can be good sources for both policy and history. Most can be readily identified by using an Internet search engine with descriptor words such as the state's name and "government" or "state government." At all levels it is important to remember that policy documents may also exist within the executive branch of the respective governments. For instance, at the U.S. federal level presidential directives, executive orders, and administrative codes all contain policy.

Library research can provide useful information as well as hard copies of many policy documents. Recent documents and draft legislation may be difficult to obtain there because of the delay involved in getting the documents published and catalogued into government documents sections of local libraries. Still, for locating less recent documents and compiling information about the history of a policy area, U.S. public library government documents areas can be very helpful. The availability of such library information varies among countries, yet can be invaluable when it is accessed.

In many countries, including the United States, a great deal of information can be obtained from personal contact with government employees such as legislators, bureaucrats, and administrative staff. Such sources are often aware not only of the history of a policy area, but also of current trends and initiatives. Although higher level elected officials may be difficult to access, members of their staff are often very interested in providing information to those who ask. Their motivation may be varied. Some may hope that their friendly assistance will garner votes. Others may anticipate learning more about your initiative. Still others may simply wish to be helpful. Regardless of motivation, many will be very willing to talk.

Other good Internet resources include the web sites of special interest groups, news organizations, and other organizations that analyze or comment on social policy. Even very radical or oppositional sites can be important sources of information. These sites often offer perspectives not readily available in more traditional sites and may emphasize elements of policy neglected by those in current positions of power.

Another good source of information is textbooks and similar resources used for training in the chosen policy area. Many such documents review the history of policy and offer insight into the forces that have shaped it. Although the information may not be in depth, the texts may offer references that provide more comprehensive materials.

Identification of the Norms and Values of the Voting Public

The importance of the role of norms and values in policy making was described in earlier sections of this chapter. Proposals that run contrary to the predominant values of the voting public, or that cannot be made to appear consistent with those values, are likely to fail. Practitioners, then, must understand the values of the stakeholders (including the voting public), must be able to articulate those values, and must be able to explain their proposals in a way that persons with a variety of values will find attractive.

There are many sources from which stakeholder values can be identified. News reports, for example, often contain statements of the motivations of legislators, the comments of other public figures, and a few reactions from members of the general public. Although media sources often have significant limitations, they can often provide insight into the norms and values of many different stakeholders and stakeholder groups.

Published books and articles (other than publications from media sources) are another useful resource for identifying values. In some policy areas relevant values have been carefully and accurately documented. For example, in *Poor Support,* Elwood (1989) identified a group of opposing values that underlie income maintenance policy in the United States. Recognizing those values is critical to understanding the historical development of policy in this area and to planning successful initiatives. Popular books, textbooks, academic journals, and popular periodicals can also help practitioners identify and articulate norms and values.

One very simple way of determining the values of an individual or group is to ask them. Although some may try to mask oppositional positions with acceptable terminology, asking for a statement of position from an influential person or political group will usually provide useful information. The statement can also be compared to the past voting records, service records, or political activities of the individual or group in question should further clarification be desired.

The values of larger groups can often be identified through focus groups or surveys. Focus groups include experts who are likely to know the positions of other experts and members of the general population. Surveys might be sent directly to citizens, and their results tabulated and summarized for the policy practice work group.

However information about norms and values is collected, it is important that practitioners be thorough in gathering perspectives. Thoroughness may be a particular challenge when dealing with international issues because of the diversity of groups and complexity of perspectives that may be involved. For example, a practitioner working on policy changes to benefit Kurdish immigrants to the United States might be tempted to assume that a survey within a single federal relocation area would provide a representative sampling of norms and values. However, a quick Internet search would identify 10 or more political groups currently operating within Kurdistan. Many of these groups hold very different ideals. Practitioners who wish to understand the norms and values of the Kurdish people would need to have information about all these groups, information that might or might not be available in a single relocation area.

Recognition of the Political Alliances That Will Support or Oppose the Proposal

When analyzing policy it is critical to learn what individuals and groups are likely to support or oppose a proposal. A part of understanding this political landscape is knowing about the current political parties, identifying the existing political alliances, and becoming aware of any special groups that may be interested in the initiative's outcome.

Political parties are organized groups of people who share similar values and political ideals. They unite to select candidates who then compete with persons from other political parties for offices or positions within the government. In the United States there are two primary political parties: Democrats and Republicans. Historically, Republicans have held conservative values and Democrats have held liberal values, although in recent years the differences between the two have become far less pronounced. Other parties have come and gone, and some that currently exist don't always enter a candidate in elections. The U.S. system remains predominantly a two-party system.

Other countries may have only one political party or may have a great variety of parties emphasizing an assortment of values. Regardless of the number and philosophical position of the parties, it is important to know what each group believes as well as what position it is likely to take on the proposed initiative.

The political landscape is often filled with political alliances. These alliances may range from formal, collaborative enterprises with clear, written agreements, to informal arrangements made verbally between individuals and small groups. They may occur on either side of an issue or between political opponents. Alliances may be related to party loyalty or may have grown from an assortment of personal situations. Regardless of their nature and source, political alliances can be powerful influences in the political arena. In addition, they seem to exist in virtually every culture. Practitioners must identify them, must understand the basis for the alliances, and must plan strategies to deal with them effectively.

Review of the Current System of Agencies That Compose the Service Delivery System

Effective policy practice requires understanding how the intent of a policy or body of policy is operationalized and implemented. Most often this begins with a policy-making body (such as a legislature) and extends though government agencies that either fund, provide guidance and support for, or implement (or some combination of these three) other agencies, often private, who actually deliver the services. In the United States, these are typically either not-for-profit or for-profit agencies. In other countries they might be for-profit agencies or nongovernmental organizations (NGOs).

When past attempts have been made to address a social problem, yet the problem still exists, it is possible that something within the delivery system is either creating or contributing to the problem. In the example of Benjamin, the problem of inadequate income is not created within his agency, nor is the problem of inadequate service provision. But the failure of the agency to make its clients aware of funding alternatives does contribute to inadequate service provision.

Understanding the policy-making system allows the practitioner to determine the level at which a problem should be addressed. For example, although income maintenance policy is primarily a federal area in the United States, Alma's work group faces an unusual situation in which the state provided a supplement but then eliminated the supplement during budget cuts. Because the group probably has a greater probability of producing change at a state level and because the problem was generated at a state level, the group would probably do well to address it at that level.

Generation of Alternative Solutions

Policy practitioners must also generate alternative solutions. They may do this by devising their own solutions or by resurrecting solutions proposed by others in the past. The solutions may be broad and comprehensive or may offer an incremental approach, in which smaller aspects of the problem are addressed individually. Although a single solution will probably ultimately be offered, practitioners often find that generating a variety of possibilities from which they then choose is the most effective approach.

The information gathered during other portions of the analysis should be used both to inform the development of alternatives and to choose between them. The solution ultimately recommended should have a strong probability of being effective, be feasible to implement, and be desirable to a sufficient number of stakeholders to make its acceptance likely.

Collection or Production of Appropriate Professional Analyses

Many types of professional analyses are available to examine the performance of current policy and to predict how a new proposal is likely to perform. Options for professional analysis include program evaluation, needs assessment, cost-benefit analysis, forecasting, sensitivity analysis, allocation formulae, quick decision analysis, and political feasibility analysis (Ellis, 2003). A thorough discussion of these methods is beyond the scope of this chapter, and most require specialized training to conduct effectively. A careful search of available literature may yield a number of such analyses already in existence. Alternatively, policy practice work groups might hire an expert to conduct a professional analysis or recruit a group member who possesses the necessary knowledge and skill.

Examination of Potential Unintended Consequences

Whenever policy changes are enacted, there is the potential for unintended consequences to result. It seems unlikely, for instance, that the state legislators who approved the cuts in Alma's case study anticipated their devastating effects on other social service systems. A little forethought on the part of the policy makers might have prevented the current crisis.

Policy practice work groups can try to anticipate what they might not otherwise expect by using a variety of techniques. For example, they can brainstorm best- and worst-case scenarios or research the results of similar initiatives in their chosen policy area or in similar policy areas. Alternatively, they could ask other experts in the area what they might expect, using either individual interviews or focus groups.

Selection of an Alternative

If the practitioner or work group develops more than a single alternative solution, most situations will require that the one perceived to be the best is selected for proposal and support. The best alternative will be the one that is some mixture of the most likely to succeed, the most feasible, the most acceptable, and the least likely to produce undesirable consequences.

Practitioners may make this decision through informal discussion and evaluation or may develop a more formal method of scoring alternatives, such as the marginal numerical attributions used in criteria-based methods.

It is important to remember that a solution seen as best for one community or geographical area may not be best for another. This is particularly true when international issues are involved. Practitioners who are considering recommendations that will impact conditions in other countries need to remember that needs, values, support systems, and similar conditions are likely to vary between and within countries. International policy practice requires a thorough understanding of every area that will be affected.

Action Planning

In some situations practitioners may be asked only to analyze policy and provide a recommended solution or solutions. At other times they may need to develop a strategy for bringing the change to fruition. Although this might seem a daunting task, a similar process is included in any CSWE-accredited MSSW program in the form of strategic planning.

In strategic planning an overall mission statement is prepared, then goals, objectives, and tasks are identified. These goals, objectives, and tasks are, in fact, the steps that must be undertaken to accomplish the mission. When the tasks have been identified and articulated, each is assigned to an individual or a small group, and a date for completion and a means of reporting the results to the overall group are specified. The results are usually recorded either in log or matrix form to allow for easy tracking.

The capacities individual members bring to a policy analysis work group should be important considerations when tasks are assigned for the action plan. Persons who bring competence in public relations, advertising, and media relations should be involved in the completion of tasks of that nature. Those who bring influence may best be involved in contact with and persuasion of decision makers. The persons who excel in motivation may be the ones with the drive and persistence to prepare and distribute brochures, make multiple phone calls, and prepare and supervise mass mailings. Some group members may want to participate in more than one type of activity, but most should be encouraged to direct their primary efforts toward those activities in which they bring the greatest capacity.

EVALUATING THE OUTCOMES

Effective social work practice requires effective evaluation. This is as true for policy practice as it is for clinical work or program development. Only when outcome measures are chosen, variables are tracked, and the results are analyzed and reported can any practitioner know whether the goals he or she set out to meet have been accomplished.

Policy outcome evaluation uses one or more of the forms of professional analysis discussed earlier. Perhaps in most cases it involves an outcome evaluation design that looks at target conditions that existed before a new policy was introduced and compares them to those conditions after the policy has gone into effect. For example, Alma's group might track income, referrals to child welfare, homelessness, and medical service utilization rates. If income increased among the target client group and referrals to child welfare, homelessness, and medical service utilization among the target client group decreased, this might be seen as evidence that the team's policy intervention was effective.

CONCLUSION

This chapter has identified and described the primary processes involved in policy practice: (a) preparation of the practitioner, (b) assembling a team, (c) identification, definition, and legitimization of the problem, (d) selecting an approach for analysis, (f) conducting the analysis, and (g) evaluating the outcomes. The processes were presented primarily to address case studies based on conditions typical of the United States, but comments were included to make them more relevant to international policy practice where such comments were necessary.

REFERENCES

DiNitto, D. M., & Cummins, L. K. (2006). *Social welfare: Politics and public policy* (6th ed.). Boston: Allyn & Bacon.

Dobelstein, A. W. (1996). *Social welfare: Policy and analysis* (2nd ed.). Chicago: Nelson-Hall.

Ellis, R. A. (2003). *Impacting social policy: A practitioner's guide to analysis and action*. Pacific Grove, CA: Brooks Cole/Wadsworth.

Ellis, R. A., Crane Mallory, K., Gould, M. Y., & Shatila, S. L. (2006). *The macro practitioner's workbook: A step-by-step guide to effectiveness with organizations and communities*. Pacific Grove, CA: Brooks Cole/Wadsworth.

Elwood, D. T. (1989). *Poor support: Poverty in the American family*. New York: Basic Books.

Janssen, B. S. (1999). *Becoming an effective policy advocate: From policy practice to social justice*. Pacific Grove, CA: Brooks Cole/Wadsworth.

Chapter 9

NEW FEDERALISM, NEW FREEDOM, AND STATES' RIGHTS: THE UNCERTAIN AND FRAGMENTED DIRECTION OF PUBLIC MENTAL HEALTH POLICY IN THE UNITED STATES

King Davis

THE EPIDEMIOLOGY AND BURDEN OF MENTAL ILLNESS

Interest in the epidemiology, causation, and cost of mental illness is evident in numerous academic studies and government reports published in the United States over the past century. Although data and conclusions from many earlier studies were severely limited by subjective bias, they were used to formulate a narrow conceptual basis for mental health policy, planning, financing, control, and practice in the United States. State governments drafted mental health policies that resulted in long-term institutionalization, social control, segregation by race and disability, criminalization of the mentally ill, involuntary admissions, and the abrogation of constitutional rights (Babcock, 1895; Blanton, 1931; Carothers, 1940; Cartwright, 1851; Evarts, 1914; Faris & Dunham, 1939; Fischer, 1969; Gould, 1981; Grossack, 1963; Herrnstein & Murray, 1994; Hurd et al., 1916; D. D. Jackson, 1960; Jarvis, 1842, 1844; Keeler & Vitols, 1963; Kleiner & Parker, 1959; Kramer, Von Korff, & Kessler, 1980; Lidz & Lidz, 1949; Malzberg, 1940, 1953; McCandless, 1996; O'Malley, 1914; Pasamanick, 1959; Scott, 1997; Witmer, 1891). The federal government maintained a minimalist role in ameliorating these mental health concerns until the beginning of the twentieth century (Burnim, 2006; Mechanic, 1989; Rothman, 1970; U.S. Congress, 1946, 1980).

Over the past 2 decades, however, a series of more contemporary epidemiological studies and reports introduced alternative hypotheses and findings about the probable causes, distribution, treatment, burden, disparities, and costs of mental and physical illness in the United States and worldwide (Adebimpe, 1994; Andreasen, 1997; Chandra & Skinner, 2003; Epstein & Ayanian, 2001; Institute of Medicine, 2005; J. S. Jackson et al., 1996; Keppel, Pearcy, & Wagener, 2002; Kessler, 2005; Neighbors & Lumpkin, 1990; Plepys & Klein, 1995; Regier et al., 1993; Robins & Regier, 1991; Takeuchi & Cheung, 1998; U.S. Department of Health and Human Services, 1999, 2001; World Health Organization [WHO], 2001). In addition, more contemporary studies measure the financial resources invested in the system (sources, savings, distribution) and the economic losses from untreated mental illness (Altman & Levitt, 2002; Congressional Budget Office, 1999; Frank, 2006; Heldring, 2003; Institute of Medicine, 2005; Manderscheid & Henderson, 2001; Moscarelli, Rupp, & Sartorious, 1996; Mulligan, 2003; National Mental Health Association, 2001; Rice & Miller, 1996; Substance Abuse and Mental Health Services Administration [SAMHSA], 2006b; WHO, 2001; Unutzer, Schoenbaum, & Druss, 2006). Other studies and reports have focused more closely on assessing the functioning of the systems of services provided by state governments (National Alliance on Mental Illness, 2006).

A recent report by the WHO (2001) shows that close to 20% to 25% of the world's population of adults have a diagnosable mental illness. The total number of adults affected worldwide was close to 450 million persons, including 58 million over 18 years of age in the United States alone (National Institute of Mental Health, 2006b). Similar studies suggest that up to 21% of U.S. children have a disorder catalogued in the third edition of the *Diagnostic and Statistical Manual of Mental Disorders* (U.S. Department of Health and Human Services, 1999). Of those adults affected by mental disorders, about 6% to 8% have a diagnosis of severe illness (Schizophrenia, Major Depressive Disorder, or Bipolar Disorder), and close to 5% of children have a serious emotional disorder (National Institute of Mental Health, 2006b). These disorders occur at different rates in the population but with minimal variation by country of origin. For example, only 1.5% to 3% of the world's population develop Schizophrenia, although the overall burden of this illness is extreme. Close to 16% of the world's population develop clinical depression, and 7% develop Bipolar Disorder. Anxiety (13%) is the most frequently occurring disorder in children and substance abuse disorders (2%) the least frequent (U.S. Department of Health and Human Services, 1999). Recent replication studies in the United States support these data.

Kessler et al. (2005) sought to identify lifetime prevalence rates and age of onset in their U.S. replication study. Using the sample generated from the National Comorbidity Survey, they note that the lifetime prevalence of all disorders (not including Schizophrenia) in the United States is close to 46%. The highest overall prevalence per disorder was for Major Depressive Disorder at 17%, while alcoholism occurred at a rate of 13% and Phobic Disorder at 12.5%. When examined by class of disorders, anxiety ranked first at 29%, with substance abuse disorder at 25% and mood disorders at 21% of the U.S. population. The most surprising finding reported by Kessler et al. was the age of onset. Anxiety disorders occur at a median age of 11; substance abuse tends to occur at a median age of 20; and mood disorders at age 30. Kessler et al. also reported that women had a higher risk of developing both anxiety and mood disorders. African Americans and Hispanics were at lower risk of anxiety, mood, and substance abuse disorders, and all lower educated populations, regardless of race, were at greater risk of substance abuse.

Wang et al. (2005) examined the use of mental health services in the same nationally representative sample of 9,282 North Americans over a 12-month period. The researchers were interested in the extent to which the sample was differentiated by such factors as receipt of services by sector (general medicine, specialty care, and alternative medicine), number of visits during the year, and quality of treatment. In addition, the research explored the relationship between the use of services and race, gender, and income.

Overall, Wang et al. (2005) found that the majority of North Americans with mental disorders (60%) do not obtain services. In addition, the services they receive are often of poor quality (68%) and are not consistent with evidence-based practices. The median number of visits during the 12-month study period was only 3.0 per person. Compared to earlier studies, the researchers found that 41% of the sample obtained services during the year, whereas in 1990 only 25% of the sample obtained care, and 19% received care in a prior study in 1980. The chance of obtaining care increased based on the person being below age 60, "female, non-Hispanic white, and previously married; not having a low average family income; and not living in a rural area" (p. 632). Sociodemographic variables place limits on access to quality services but do not appear to increase substantially the rates of prevalence rates (U.S. Department of Health and Human Services, 2001; Wang et al., 2005).

Recent reports from WHO (2000, 2001, 2004) show the extent to which mental disorders contribute to a variety of major problems (described as burdens) for the individual, family, community, employer, and society in general. Some of the problems that accompany mental disorders include the following:

- *Long-term disability:* The WHO reports that mental disorders are among the major sources of disability throughout the world. Close to 15% of the disease burden stems from mental illness; 18.6% stems from cardiovascular disease (National Institute of Mental Health, 2006c; WHO, 2001, 2004). However, in the United States, Canada, and Western Europe, mental illness is the major source of disability in the age range 15 to 44 (New Freedom Commission on Mental Health, 2003b).

- *Productivity losses:* Part of the burden of mental disorders is the loss of wages and productivity. The National Mental Health Association (NMHA, 2001) found two major effects of mental disorders. In 1997, the NMHA reported a loss of over $100 billion in productivity associated with mental illness. The NMHA measured productivity losses as the annual number of days of lost employment. In 1997, the workforce in the United States lost over 1 billion days of work (NMHA, 2001); in 2000 losses from a single disorder (depression) accounted for 200 million lost days. Other job-related effects include a higher frequency of job termination either through resignation or firing ("National Survey," 2006). A key policy dilemma for persons with mental disabilities is the potential loss of coverage under the Americans with Disabilities Act once they begin treatment. The U.S. Supreme Court (*Albertsons, Inc. v. Kirkingburg,* 1999; *Murphy v. United Parcel Services,* 1999; *Sutton v. United Airlines, Inc.,* 1999) decided that whether or not a finding of disability is warranted is dependent on the effects of treatment or medication.

- *High unemployment rates:* The New Freedom Commission on Mental Health (2003b) found that unemployment rates for adults with serious mental illness exceeded 90%.

- *High suicide rates:* Suicide ranks as the 11th highest cause of death in the United States (National Institute of Mental Health, 2006a). In 2000, suicides took close to 30,000 lives at a rate of 11 per 100,000. Although suicides account for fewer than 2% of all deaths, the overall number is 5 times greater than the number of deaths from homicides. Of those persons who commit suicide, the greatest majority (90%) have a diagnosis of depression (National Institute of Mental Health, 2006a). There are marked differences in rates of suicide by such factors as sex, age, and race. Men are more successful in carrying out suicides, although women make more attempts. Whites generally commit suicides at significantly greater rates than other racial and ethnic groups. Suicide was the third highest cause of death for young adults and adolescents in 2000. Advanced age is also a risk factor for suicide, with older adults committing suicide at rates that are disproportionately higher than their numbers in the general population.

Epidemiological data from several contemporary studies offer a fundamentally different conceptual basis for future mental health policy, planning, and practice in the United States. More of these contemporary studies and reports support insurance, community-based care, culturally specific services, earlier intervention, evidence-based practices, integrating care across health and mental health sectors, utilization review, continued investment in research, use of technology, and increased involvement of consumers and families. However, over several decades, national concerns about lower quality of care, lack of human rights, unnecessary admissions, discrimination, high rates of death, and slow rates of innovation have increased frustration with the pace of change and the degree of involvement by the federal government in state mental health affairs. Unfortunately, unresolved differences over federalism, remnants of the states' rights philosophy, and inconsistent federal encroachment in state affairs have had the impact of introducing and maintaining high levels of uncertainty and destructive fragmentation (New Freedom Commission on Mental Health, 2003b) into mental health policy, planning, and service implementation in the United States. Unresolved differences between state and federal governments limit the ready adoption of newer epidemiological findings, conceptualizations, and evidence-based methods for managing mental disorders and their socioeconomic side effects.

In this chapter, the focus is on identifying and understanding the uncertain direction and fragmentation of mental health care policy in the United States. I also identify and discuss four processes utilized by the federal government to encroach on decisions heretofore under the aegis of state governments. The chapter concludes with a recommendation to nationalize the responsibility for mental health care as the basis for promoting a clear future public policy in the United States.

UNRESOLVED FEDERALISM IN MENTAL HEALTH POLICY

The history and climate of public mental health policy generally in the United States reflects long-term tension between the federal and state governments over the extent of power (federalism) each can exercise over specific areas of policy as well as the policy-making process (Drake, 1999; *McCulloch v. State of Maryland,* 1819). Federalism is defined as the actual "sharing of power between the states and the national government" (Close Up Foundation, 2006). Other authors describe federalism as the most "striking aspect of the American Constitution" ("Federalism," 2006), albeit unclear about how power sharing is decided, maintained, or evaluated. Descriptions of federalism underscore the importance of determining who makes policy and the various interests that propel the policy direction selected. State interests determined the direction of public mental health policy from the colonial period to the twenty-first century.

The U.S. Constitution is the primary document for defining the respective powers of the states and the federal government. Although the Constitution is explicit about the enumerated powers of the federal government vis-à-vis the states, it does not adequately address the extent to which the federal government has implied power (*Powers of the*

Federal Government, 2006). Nor is it clear from the Constitution what is the extent of powers reserved to the states. Chief Justice Marshall In *McCulloch v. Maryland* sought to clarify the multiple questions about enumerated powers as well as the implied powers of the federal government in this 1819 decision. In his opinion, Marshall reached the conclusion that not all powers of the federal government can be specified in the Constitution. The Court concluded, however, that an absence of specificity does not preclude Congress from creating legislation that is, by implication, congruent with the interests of the nation as a whole. In addition, Marshall's majority opinion gave supreme power to the federal government and the Congress where disputes arise over federalism (*McCulloch v. State of Maryland,* 1819).

The vague distribution of power between the federal and state governments continues to require Supreme Court interventions and reflect deep divisions over what constitutes an acceptable balance of power held by various levels of government (Drake, 1999; Hernandez & Pear, 2006). Although the *McCulloch v. Maryland* case focused on the ability of the federal government to establish a banking institution not subject to state tariffs, a variety of issues have fueled the long-term debate over federalism: slavery, voting rights by race and sex, school integration, death penalty, right to life, use of stem cells, equal protection, assisted suicide, gay marriage, and eminent domain.

Most efforts to resolve these disputes over federalism refer to the 10th Amendment to the Constitution and to precedents established by the *McCulloch* case (*McCulloch v. State of Maryland,* 1819). Based on interpretations of this amendment, states concluded that they have all those powers specifically guaranteed to them under the Constitution as well as those that are not specifically denied them (U.S. Congress, 1787). To some extent, states attempt to use the same theory of implied powers put forth by the Supreme Court in *McCulloch*. States also propose that they and not federal authorities govern the creation of public policy and determine what federal policies are binding on them.

Several alternative conceptualizations of federalism have evolved over the years. Boyd (2006) provides definitions of various forms of federalism as well as the periods in which a particular form emerged. In Table 9.1, Boyd's four chronological periods of federalism are expanded in this chapter to include key mental health issues, policy responses, and social justice issues associated with each different form of federalism.

Boyd (2006) defines the period 1700 to 1788 as prefederalism. During the prefederalism period, the loose federation of states promulgated the Articles of Confederation to define their relationships and the distribution of authority, power, and decision making. When Boyd's conceptualization of federalism is placed in the context of mental health policy, two categories of interest emerge (each of these categories is applied for each type of federalism). First, the major mental health policy problem during the period of prefederalism was the extent of untreated mental illness in the colonial population—irrespective of race, sex, legal status, and class. Second, the policy response to this issue was twofold. Colonies, starting with Virginia, imported the hospital-oriented policies and structures that were current in Europe. These formal policies and structures emerged to displace the more informal mechanisms of family caregiving and local community care that were prominent prior to 1750. During the prefederalism period, there were also a number of important social justice issues on the horizon. These included issues of citizenship, slavery, women's suffrage, poverty, securing the rights of Native Americans, and unemployment. In response to these issues the federal government passed a series of naturalization acts (Davis & Iron Cloud Two-Dogs, 2004; U.S. Congress, 1790) designed to specify who

Table 9.1   Mental Health and Changes in Federalism 1700–2006

Period	Key Mental Health Issue	Level of Federalism*	Policy Response	Social Justice Issues
1700–1788	Untreated mental illness	Prefederalism	State hospital Family caregiving Local responsibility Church involvement Almshouses	Slavery Citizenship Women's suffrage Poverty Native American rights
1789–1865 1865–1901	Increased demand for services	Dual federalism	Increased number of facilities Increased admissions Segregation by race and class State responsibility Pierce Veto	Reconstruction Voting rights Education Equal protection Employment Economic equality Segregation
1901–1960	Custodial care Access Readiness	Cooperative federalism	National Institute of Mental Health State mental health departments National study Psychological readiness for war Postwar mental health services	Migration Racial violence School integration Civil rights Voting rights World wars Poverty
1961–1968	Deinstitutionalization	Creative federalism	Community mental health Medicaid Medicare CRIPA Head Start War on poverty	Human rights Civil rights Poverty Homelessness Health disparities Vietnam War
1968–2006	Community mental health expansion Fragmentation	Contemporary federalism New federalism	HMO Act Omnibus Reconciliation Act Block grants Parity Managed care Transformation	Integrated care Human rights Access to services Evidence based Cultural competence Consumer involvement

*Based on *American Federalism, 1776 to 1997*, by E. Boyd, 2006, retrieved June 27, 2007, from http://usinfo .state.gov.usa/infousa/politics/states/federal.htm.

within the population qualified for citizenship, holding public office, and participation in voting. Local communities were expected to manage poverty and idleness in the population (Pumphrey & Pumphrey, 1961).

Boyd's (2006) second period extended from 1789 to 1901. He sees this as the first example of dual federalism. In dual federalism, there is extremely limited sharing or collaboration between the federal and state governments. Each form of government establishes its own power base and seeks to disempower the other. The key mental health issue during the first portion of this period (1789 to 1865) was the increased demand for hospital-based services. Many states had developed state hospitals, but these had quickly become overcrowded, eliminating almost all possibilities of effective treatment (Dain, 1964). The policy response was an effort by the states to build additional facilities, expand existing ones, and increase the number of admissions to the breaking point. Appeal by the states for federal assistance to acquire land to build additional hospitals was throttled when President Pierce (1854) vetoed the congressional legislation supporting the measure. The key social justice issues during this period were the federal effort to reconstruct the South following the end of the Civil War and the decision to override state interests by extending the right to citizenship and voting to African males (Davis & Iron Cloud Two-Dogs, 2004). In the second portion of the first dual federalism period, the major issues centered around such social justice concerns as equal protection under the law, voting rights for women, economic equality, out-migration of Native populations, immigration of Chinese men, and the rapid rise in hostility, discrimination, and segregation of former slaves.

Boyd (2006) describes the period from 1901 to 1960 as the first example of cooperative federalism. He defines this as a period in which there is a marked level of cooperation between the respective levels of government. Overt hostilities are lessened in favor of measures that increase the chances that both levels of government will achieve their aims. Boyd identified Theodore Roosevelt's New Nationalism, Wilson's New Freedom Program, the 16th Amendment, which allowed income taxes, and the New Deal as examples of this expanded cooperation between the federal and state governments. Boyd interpreted this as a period in which the states and the federal government came to an agreement on the balance between civil rights for African Americans and the remnants of states' rights. During the period of cooperative federalism, a prime issue in mental health was the high proportion of Americans who failed to enter the military because of low intelligence scores and the high rate of postwar psychiatric casualties (Berlien & Waggoner, 1966; Brill & Kupper, 1966). A secondary issue was the heightened awareness that care in state hospitals was increasingly custodial.

Caplan (1961) was instrumental in identifying the value of providing prevention, early intervention, and emergency services as a precursor to the development of community mental health. During the cooperative federalism period, Congress passed legislation creating the first national mental health study commission (U.S. Congress, 1946). Their report focused on the conditions in state hospitals that violated human rights and acceptable psychiatric care. In response to these mental health concerns, the National Institute of Mental Health (NIMH) was developed and most states created state departments of mental health.

A number of important social justice issues were evident during the period of cooperative federalism. Chief among these were school integration, immigration, migration of low-income Blacks from southern states, voting rights issues, access to Social Security, segregation in the military, and the continued presence of poverty and discrimination against women. Change in these social justice issues required considerable involvement by the federal courts, combined with civil rights demonstrations and advocacy by Lyndon Johnson and key congressional supports (U.S. Congress, 1964). Many of these issues were conceptualized as having important mental health implications (Allport, 1954; Arnoff, 1975;

Biegel, Milligan, Putnam, & Song, 1994; Brody, 1966; Byrd & Clayton, 2002; Cannon & Locke, 1977; Chandra & Skinner, 2003; Cross, Bazron, Dennis, & Isaacs, 1989; Grossack, 1963; Hansen, 1959; Neighbors, Jackson, Campbell, & Williams, 1989; U.S. Department of Health and Human Services, 2001; Zane, Takeuchi, & Young, 1994).

The shortest period of federalism takes place from 1961 to 1968. Boyd (2006) describes this period as creative federalism. Boyd sees Lyndon B. Johnson as the architect of creative federalism, as reflected in his Great Society programs. Johnson made a concerted effort to obtain legislation that would eliminate poverty. In addition, it was during his administration that Medicaid and Medicare were passed. Johnson also signed amendments to extend community mental health centers legislation. During the Johnson years, the key mental health policy issue was deinstitutionalization of residents from state mental hospitals. Community mental health legislation and the introduction of new medications were seen as the twin factors that would make deinstitutionalization occur, if not succeed. Johnson also used the power of his presidency to introduce federal legislation to break down barriers that remained at the state level (U.S. Congress, 1960, 1964, 1965a, 1965b, 1965c, 1968). He sought to resolve numerous social justice issues during the period. These included voting rights, homelessness, racial discrimination, unemployment, health disparities, and access to equal protection.

Boyd's (2006) final period of federalism occurs from 1968 through 2006, which he describes as the period of contemporary federalism. What distinguished this period were the multiple changes that occurred in relations between the federal and state branches of government. The impetus for contemporary federalism is the vast change in philosophical orientation and values between the individuals who became president. From 1968 to 2005, Johnson, Nixon, Ford, Carter, Reagan, Bush, and Clinton occupied the oval office. There were numerous differences in perceptions of federalism within this group. Johnson and Carter were similar in their orientation; Nixon, Ford, Reagan, and Bush sought to empower the states and weaken the federal hold on power. In this period, Carter sought to return to an expanded role of the federal government similar to Johnson's vision. However, when Carter lost the presidency, Reagan promptly curtailed his federal expansion plans. The most prominent mental health issue during this period was the continued fragmentation of vision, planning, and financing of care. Carter's commission documented these gaps at the beginning of the period, and Bush's commission reaffirmed their presence in almost the exact same terms. Throughout the period, the federal government took numerous positions on federalism and the mental health system. It was during this period that HMO legislation was passed with support and leadership from Nixon (1972) and Ted Kennedy (Ambrose, 1985). Reagan empowered the states through the Omnibus Reconciliation Act and his block grant program (Boyd, 2006; Thomas, 1998). Clinton assisted in the development of managed health care and parity, and Bush ushered in transformation of mental health care at the state level.

The vast differences in priorities, values, and goals of these administrations resulted in a constant pattern of expansion and contraction, uncertainty and fragmentation in mental health policy at the state level. States, community mental health centers, state hospitals, and insurers could not be certain about the direction that federal policy in mental health would take from one presidential administration to the next. No federal policy direction seemed permanent or funding assured for the long term. States may have found their value on states' rights and maintenance of state hospitals a source of security and certainty that was lacking in the numerous changes in federal perspective. The least amount of federal involvement and control of mental health may have been preferred at the state level (Breeden, 1976; Drake, 1999).

STATES' RIGHTS AND CONTROL OF MENTAL HEALTH POLICY

As early as 1765, state and local colonial governments developed myriad public policies and residential services for responding to and managing persons with mental illness (Baseler, 1998; Deutsch, 1949; Foucault, 1965; Grob, 1973; McCandless, 1996; Rothman, 1970). These initial state and local policies were designed to quell the colonists' intense fear of the mentally ill, offer respite to distressed family and religious caregivers, and reduce the terse news editorials that charged inaction and disinterest by colonial governments (Davis, 1998). An increasingly large segment of the public wanted immediate protection from a recent series of violent acts by men living in the community considered mentally ill and dangerous to others. In response to these publicized fears, the Virginia House of Burgesses passed legislation in 1763 to build the Public Hospital for Persons of Insane and Disordered Minds to treat mental illness in free White persons (Dain, 1964, 1968; *Public Hospital*, 2006). Simultaneously, the Virginia legislature empowered local governments to use coercive powers to force individuals into state institutions.

Passage of this hospital-oriented mental health policy, albeit a first in the American colonies, was not without considerable international precedent. Several European countries had relied on similar policies to segregate people with tuberculosis, leprosy, and other communicable diseases from the general population. Virginia's colonial government assumed that a similar segregationist policy would prove successful in managing persons with mental illness and restoring the fragile integrity of colonial society (Deutsch, 1949; Grob, 1994; Rothman, 1970). However, American asylums segregated persons with mental illness from the general population, their families, and communities for lengthy periods, sometimes for life. Such lengthy periods of segregation may have contributed to the development of stigma, disability, and difficulty integrating persons with mental illness back into their communities. Successful challenge of the long-term segregation of the mentally disabled did not occur until passage of the Americans with Disabilities Act in 1990 (U.S. Congress, 2005; *Albertsons, Inc. v. Kirkingburg,* 1999; *Murphy v. United Parcel Services,* 1999; *Sutton v. United Airlines, Inc.,* 1999).

Other colonial governments quickly replicated the hospital-oriented policies crafted in Virginia. In less than 50 years, almost all state governments had developed uncontested monopolies over the multiple domains of mental health care: policy development, inpatient services, management and oversight, and financial support. Prior to state monopolies in mental health, families provided the majority of long-term support for the mentally ill (Belknap, 1956; Deutsch, 1949; Hatfield, 1987).

State control of mental health policy resulted in the development, maintenance, and expansion of hundreds of fledgling mental hospitals that provided both economic and emotional security to the small agrarian communities in which they were located. Although these mental institutions were unable to cure or arrest mental illness, the economic and employment advantages of long lengths of stay and consistent rates of admissions brought major increases in state general fund dollars, staffing, authority, power, and influence well into the twentieth century. Institutionalized segregation of the mentally disabled became the de facto national policy in the United States for close to 200 years.

Until 1945, most mental hospital directors or superintendents reported directly to the governor of their state and had direct access to the money committees in the state legislature (Poen, 1979). In addition, state hospitals developed powerful lay boards of directors who petitioned state government on their behalf and on behalf of their employees. State facilities created jobs, sales, wealth, and votes at the local level. The federal government's direct involvement in state mental health policy came first in 1865 with passage of legislation creating the Freedman's Bureau and the requirement that states provide mental health treatment for former slaves (Virginia State Department of Mental Hygiene and Hospitals, 1960). However, federal intervention terminated quickly. Federal intervention in the mid-1800s resulted in the creation of state mental institutions segregated by race as well as disability.

In addition to passage of hospital-oriented mental health policies, colonial governments passed a series of related public policies to address poverty, communicable diseases, mental retardation, unemployment, crime, abandoned children, and dependent elderly (Rothman, 1970). Here too colonial governments relied increasingly on the building of isolated institutions that segregated afflicted persons from the community as a means of protection and social control. If needed, state governments could justify their control of public mental health and related problem areas through an interpretation of the 10th Amendment to the U.S. Constitution that gave them all of the rights explicitly articulated as well as those not specifically denied them (states' rights) in this historic document (U.S. Congress, 1787). States deftly used these interpretations to maintain almost total control of the public policy-making apparatus in mental health and related areas for over 200 years (Davis & Iron Cloud Two-Dogs, 2004). However, there were few efforts by the federal government to alter the course of mental health care or policy at the state level until near the end of the nineteenth century.

To the contrary, the federal government maintained a minimalist role in each of the domains of mental health, but particularly in the constructing of public policies and financing of hospital construction and staffing costs. The federal government conveniently saw the states as financially and programmatically responsible for the care of the mentally ill. The federal position was made clear as early as 1854, when President Pierce (1854) vetoed a Senate bill aimed at providing federal lands to the states to construct mental institutions. Pierce expressed concern that approval of the bill would soon extend federal support to the states for similar services and other indigent populations. He believed that extending this level of support to the states violated the U.S. Constitution. Specifically, the basis of the veto was Pierce's concern that the tenuous balance of power (federalism) between the federal and state governments was at risk.

However, after congressional and presidential action in 1945, the federal government became increasingly involved in creating national policy that focused specifically on harmful conditions in state hospitals. Until development of the Community Mental Health Centers Program in 1963 (Pub. L. 88-164), the federal government did not provide direct funding for mental health care at the state or local level. State general funds were the primary source of operating dollars for state hospitals and for support of some aftercare services from 1765 to 1965. Public Law 88-164 was unprecedented in that it authorized federal resources to support new outpatient and inpatient mental health (five essential) services by local nonprofit organizations (community mental health centers) that bypassed the state. Federal plans were to develop close to 2,500 community mental health centers that would eventually displace aging and overcrowded state mental hospitals. However, it was unclear what would happen to the economies in local communities once the state hospitals closed.

When Reagan and not Carter was elected president in 1980, federal plans to empower community mental health centers ended with fewer than 700 centers completed (Manderscheid & Henderson, 2001). Federal support of community mental health centers ended, although the centers that received construction grants had a legal obligation to continue providing services for 20 years. The community mental health centers policy established a federal precedent for involvement in the design, delivery, and evaluation of mental health services in the states. Later policies in Medicaid, Medicare, and constitutional standards of care (human rights) would permanently change the balance of power between the federal and state governments in mental health.

Part of the impetus for the minimalist position of the federal government in mental health was the unacceptable risk that states would rely on the federal treasury to provide support for state hospitals and other institutions. The risk for the states was the potential that acceptance of federal dollars would be followed by federal encroachment in what was interpreted as the sovereign right of each state to develop its unique policies in mental health, health, education, voting, and public accommodations (*Brown v. Topeka Board of Education,* 1954). The federal government was concerned that its involvement in the creation of state mental health policies and services would eventually result in these becoming fixed federal tax obligations. In addition to costs, the continued federal focus on conditions in state hospitals was a clear message that the federal government saw these facilities as ineffective and their harmful practices as eventually the basis for congressional action. However, it was unclear what constitutional basis the federal government would exercise to enable increased involvement in policy matters considered reserved to the states.

States' rights was a key southern political strategy in the early 1950s that sought to maintain the idea that "each state is sovereign and has the right to order its own affairs without interference from the federal government" (Scheffler, 1994, p. 109). Southern strategists (strict constructionists) saw states' rights as a legitimate philosophical basis for raising a number of questions about shared political powers: determining the appropriate distribution of decision-making power, the taxing power of each branch of government, whether slavery would continue in the southern states, and if not, whether there would be compensation for the immediate and long-term financial loss for slave owners (Althouse, 2001; Baker & Young, 2001; Drake, 1999; Browne, 1914). The more successfully the states' rights idea could be sold and adopted, the less power the federal government would have to intervene in key areas of civil rights, ostensibly protected under the Constitution of the United States. The essence of the states' rights strategy was the intent by the southern states to control the legal distribution of access to social institutions.

It was in part the failure of the southern states to demonstrate an ability or willingness to abide by the constitutional provisions of equal protection under the law in racial and disability areas that stimulated the federal government to encroach on responsibilities formerly monopolized by the states (Ennis & Siegel, 1973; U.S. Congress, 1980). In effect, states' rights was a seriously flawed strategy based primarily on an abrogation of constitutional rights of individuals and groups by race, social class, residency, income, and disability (Breeden, 1976; Drake, 1999; U.S. Congress, 2005). The long-term purported failure of the states to meet constitutional requirements in mental health raises the critical question of what, if any, constitutional authority the federal government holds in matters of mental health services. Do the repeated violations alleged to have taken place under the aegis of the states rise to such an egregious level that federal intervention is warranted?

FEDERAL ENCROACHMENT IN STATE MENTAL HEALTH POLICY AND SERVICES

Increased federal involvement in multiple domains of mental health is the most critical variable in determining the current status and future direction of public mental health care in the United States. Although the federal government avoided substantive financial, policy, and programmatic responsibility for state mental health systems for almost 2 centuries, the degree of federal involvement in mental health has expanded in direct response to the level of federalism espoused by each president and Congress since 1945. The monopoly formerly exercised by state mental health authorities, governors, and legislative bodies over mental health policy direction became diluted as the power of the federal government increased. From 1945 to 1980, federal power increased steadily as state control over mental health waned. Is this expansion in power over mental health a reflection of the implied powers of the Congress and in concert with the Constitution (*McCulloch v. State of Maryland,* 1819)? Once the state fails to carry out constitutional guarantees over a protracted period, is there an obligation on the part of the federal government to protect citizens against the state in matters of mental health, as in other areas (*Brown v. Topeka Board of Education,* 1954; *United States of America v. Morrison et al.,* 2000)? Does the finding that long-term institutionalization of the mentally disabled constitutes segregation obligate the federal government to take corrective action? Have the states failed in their constitutional obligation to provide safe mental health care to all citizens?

In response to persistent mental health problems (particularly harmful conditions in state hospitals), the federal government used four connected strategies (Table 9.2) to increase its enumerated power vis-à-vis the states: passage of a host of national mental health acts (public laws), application of findings from presidential commissions, new requirements based on financing and reimbursement policies, and federal lawsuits and court decisions.

National Mental Health Acts and Public Laws

From 1869 to 2003, the U.S. Congress passed numerous public laws aimed at correcting a wide variety of problems in public mental health care. Ten of these public laws are included in Table 9.2. President Pierce reinforced the minimalist federal role in mental health policy development in 1854. At that time, Pierce issued his now famous veto that prevented the federal government from donating land to states on which to build state mental hospitals. Pierce based his veto on the risk that federal support of state mental hospitals would be followed quickly by similar requests to support other services heretofore supported by state general funds. Substantive federal involvement in state matters of mental health came initially through the Bureau of Refugees, Freedmen, and Abandoned Lands in 1865. Congress, fearing a postslavery increase in mental illness, required southern states to establish mental institutions for former slaves. Soon after passage of this act, the state of

Table 9.2   Federal Strategies, Actions, and Outcomes

Federal Strategy	Specific Action	Outcomes
Mental health acts and public laws	Pierce veto of 1854	Precluded federal land for state hospitals
	Freedman's Act 1865	Required state hospital care for former slaves and Native Americans
	Mental Health Act 1946 (Pub. L. 79-487)	Created NIMH and single state mental health agency; subcommittee on race
	Mental Health Act 1955 (Pub. L. 84-142)	Created Joint Commission on Mental Health to study conditions in mental hospitals
	Mental Health Act 1963 (Pub. L. 88-164)	Created community mental health centers financed by federal revenue
	Mental Health Act 1965 (Pub. L. 89-105)	Extended prior legislation
	Mental Health Act 1980 (Pub. L. 96-416)	Allowed federal government to sue states to protect civil rights
	Mental Health Act 1981 (Pub. L. 97-35)	Rescinded community mental health centers; established block grants
	Mental Health Act 1987 (Pub. L. 99-319)	Protection and advocacy for the mentally ill; established human rights
	Mental Health Act 1998 (Pub. L. 100-77)	Housing assistance for homeless persons with mental illness
	Americans with Disabilities Act 1990 (Pub. L. 101-336)	Targeted barriers to the disabled; saw long-term hospitalization as segregation and discrimination
		Sought parity between health and mental health coverage in insurance
Presidential commissions and executive orders	Carter Commission	New legislation to expand federal support of mental health centers
	Bush Commission	Recommended transformation of mental health systems
Financing	Pub. L. 88-164 Medicaid Medicare	Monies for construction and staffing in community mental health centers; amended Social Security Act to provide federal payments to the states for medical and psychiatric care
	Omnibus Reconciliation Act (Pub. L. 97-35)	Provided monies to the states in block grant format
Judicial decisions, public laws, and class action suits	*Wyatt v. Stickney,* 1972	Established standards for services; rejected cost arguments of the states
	Pub. L. 96-416 (1980)	Allowed federal government to sue states for conditions in institutions that violate the Constitution
	Olmstead v. L.C., 1999	Reinforced the right to life in the community for the mentally disabled

Virginia passed legislation creating the first state mental hospital (Central Lunatic Asylum) exclusively for Africans in America (Brown, 1887; Denton, 1960; Drewry, 1916; Virginia State Department of Mental Hygiene and Hospitals, 1960). Within a few years, all of the southern and border states established mental hospitals segregated by race—as were many other public facilities up to 1968.

The National Mental Health Act of 1946 (U.S. Congress, 1946) was passed during the Truman administration following widespread national concerns about psychiatric disorders and lack of preparedness for war (Berlien & Waggoner, 1966; Brill & Kupper, 1966). In this Act, the federal government used its resources to encourage states to establish single departments of mental health. Prior to this Act, state hospitals reported directly to the governor of each state. The Mental Health Act of 1946 also created the National Institute of Mental Health and charged it with improving the mental health of the nation. Improvement was defined as increases in resources for research, training, enhanced diagnosis and treatment, and monetary assistance to the states. Part of the impetus for both actions was the research and eventual publication by Deutsch (1948) on the horrid conditions in state mental hospitals.

The Mental Health Study Act of 1955 (U.S. Congress, 1955) established the Joint Commission on Mental Health. The Joint Commission's major strategy was to study and evaluate the condition of state mental institutions and make recommendations to the president and Congress at its conclusion. Deutsch's 1948 publication provided the benchmark for a critical study of state hospital conditions. At the time the Joint Commission began its work in 1955, over 750,000 persons were warehoused in state mental institutions. The majority of these individuals would spend their lives in state institutions with limited opportunity for recovery, return to the community, or gainful employment. The stark and inhumane conditions exposed by the Joint Commission's report sparked national interest in deinstitutionalization and closure of state institutions (Joint Commission on Mental Illness and Health, 1961; Sharfstein, 2000; U.S. Congress, 1955).

This report chronicled the squalid and unsafe conditions in state hospitals throughout the United States and the absence of quality health or mental health care. These conditions were not unlike those found in community care earlier by Dorthea Dix (Gollaher, 1995) and thought to be ameliorated with the development of "humane" state hospitals. The Joint Commission found high rates of death in state institutions that lacked rudimentary medical care. However, the major impetus for deinstitutionalization was the need to find a more permanent means to limit the growth of state general funds. The Joint Commission's findings and recommendations did not result in actual federal policy until 8 years later, during the Kennedy administration. The Community Mental Health and Mental Retardation Construction Act (Pub. L. 99-164) contained many of the recommendations from the Joint Commission (U.S. Congress, 1955, 1963, 1965b). This public law energized the effort to develop community mental health centers but did not alter state operation of mental institutions.

Public Law 88-164 provided federal funding for the construction of buildings to house community mental health and mental retardation functions. Kennedy's novel approach to community mental health followed the recommendations of the Joint Commission's report as well as psychiatric experiences in World War II (Berlien & Waggoner, 1966; Brill & Kupper, 1966). In addition, community mental health practice was supported by new research on the benefits of newly discovered psychotropic drugs (Healy, 2002). Sharfstein

(2000, p. 616) points out that community mental health "emphasizes better access to high-quality care" based on the philosophical tenets of the movement in 1963. The federal government followed the construction grants with funding for staffing grants in 1967 (U.S. Congress, 1967). These staffing grants required community mental health centers to offer five essential services (outpatient, inpatient, consultation and education, day care, and emergency services) to a defined catchment area not to exceed 250,000 individuals. The construction and staffing grants also had the impact of shifting the locus of inpatient and outpatient care from state institutions to the nonprofit sector of the community. By the time the community mental health program officially ended in 1981, centers were to offer 15 services and be fiscally self-sustaining. The greater the number of discreet services provided, the greater the chances of providing quality treatment and prevention.

In its effort to improve quality of care at the community level, community mental health center legislation essentially bypassed states' rights tradition and the maintenance of state hospitals and created a totally new nonprofit infrastructure, only minimally under the direction of state governments. States could not supplant federal funding or discontinue their own existing fiscal commitments. Community mental health centers were an indirect federal effort to circumvent state control of mental health services and quality without the federal government assuming clinical responsibility for direct care for thousands of low-income, chronically ill individuals.

The public laws passed by Congress from 1945 to 1980 had an impact on the power of states in three areas. Federal mental health laws established standards of care that sought to hold states legally accountable. The federal government used these laws to establish alternative service structures financed by the federal treasury that had the potential effect of reducing utilization of state hospitals. Public laws passed over the past 50 years established clear guidelines to ensure that states did not violate or ignore constitutional or human rights of persons with mental disabilities. Where states were in violation of these laws, the federal government could sue the states and force compliance.

Increases in Federal Financing

Historically, states have exercised a monopoly, albeit burdensome, over of the mental health system through their control of mental health policies and the general funds that supported state hospitals. State control of inpatient services, where the majority of mental health episodes took place, gave states the maximum opportunity to determine the direction of mental health care and policy in the United States. As recently as 1969, the majority (80%) of mental health episodes took place in state and county mental hospital facilities, justifying the continued investment of scarce state general funds (Manderscheid & Henderson, 2001). States also contributed close to 85% of all the funding during this period. State funds provided direct support to state hospitals but, more important, were the major source of employment for those communities in which state hospitals were located. However, federal funding and reimbursement policies precipitated major changes in utilization of inpatient care and associated costs from 1969 to 2001. For example, in 1990 there were close to 750 state mental hospitals that consumed 40% of all mental health expenditures (SAMHSA, 2006b). However, by 2001, the number of state and county mental hospitals had declined to 229 and accounted for less than 25% of all inpatient services (SAMHSA, 2006b).

Historically, the federal government would not provide financial resources or reimburse states under Medicaid to offset the cost of operating state hospitals or freestanding private psychiatric inpatient services to persons between the ages of 21 and 64 (U.S. Congress, 1965a). The original Medicaid policy, as well as its numerous amendments, treats institutions for mental diseases differently from general hospitals with psychiatric units. Federal funding for persons with psychiatric disorders is available to support services for children (under age 21) in state mental institutions, for adults over age 65, and for adults 21 to 64 served in general hospital psychiatric units. Federal regulations governing reimbursements under Medicaid have helped shift an increasingly larger share of psychiatric treatment away from state mental institutions toward general hospitals with psychiatric units (Manderscheid & Henderson, 2001).

From 1991 to 2001, expenditures for mental health and substance abuse services increased from $60 billion to $104 billion (SAMHSA, 2006b). Of the total, mental health expenditures alone grew from $49 billion in 1991 to $85 billion by 2001. Expenditures for mental health grew at a slower rate per annum (5.7%) between 1991 and 2001 than the general health sector (6%). When controlled for inflation, national expenditures for mental health grew at 3.7% per annum versus 4.8% for overall health care (Mark, Coffey, Vandivort-Warren, Harwood, & King, 2005; SAMHSA, 2006b).

During the decade 1991 to 2001, the pattern of expenditures by state and federal governments moved in opposite directions. Overall, expenditures by states declined as a percentage of total national expenditures, while the federal share of overall expenditures for mental health grew substantially. In 1991, state and local governments accounted for 47% of all mental health expenditures, while the federal government accounted for 53%. By 2001, the state local share had declined to 37% and the federal share had ballooned to 63% of all mental health expenditures (Mark et al., 2005; SAMHSA, 2006b).

The growth in federal expenditures over the 10-year period has principally been restricted to offsetting the cost of medication and outpatient services—thus continuing the trend toward community services established by Kennedy and Carter. Payments to specialty inpatient facilities declined significantly over the period, paralleling the decline in number of inpatient beds, psychiatric episodes, and number of state hospitals (Manderscheid & Henderson, 2001; Mark et al., 2005; SAMHSA, 2006b; Wang et al., 2006).

Mark et al. (2005) examined the changes in federal financial participation in the funding of mental health care from 1991 to 2001. Of the $104 billion expended, close to 82% was spent for mental health care alone and only 7.6% for substance abuse care. When compared to total health care spending in the United States, behavioral health accounted for only 7.6% of the total. Of interest was the difference between the amounts of funding paid for by government agencies and that paid from private sources (insurance and out of pocket). The governmental share of total behavioral health care spending was approximately 65% versus 35% from these private sources. Of the federal share of behavioral health funding, close to 26% came through Medicaid (Pub. L. 88-197). Interestingly, state governments paid out an amount in behavioral health care (26%) that is roughly equal to that of the federal government. When total behavioral costs are calculated however, close to 37% is paid for by the states.

Several policy conclusions can be reached through examination of these decennial expenditures. First, it is clear that behavioral health care remains a policy (and service) responsibility of the federal and state governments and less of a responsibility in the private sector. For example, the overall share of total costs assumed by the government increased from 57% in 1991 to 63% by 2001. Beyond this conclusion, behavioral health care costs are borne by the government principally for low-income populations through Medicaid expenditures shared between the federal and state governments. However, when all expenditures are included, mental health and substance abuse service remains a primary responsibility of state governments increasingly dependent on federal funds.

What is equally clear is that the federal government establishes its policy agenda through the budget. Recent efforts by the federal government to reduce Medicaid funding for disabled populations appears to undercut the emphasis on recovery. A second conclusion is that government is increasingly supporting nonhospital services for persons with behavioral health problems. In 2001, close to 72% of all behavioral health care expenditures was for nonhospital care. Between 1991 and 2001, hospital care for behavioral health declined from 40% of total expenditures to 24%. A third major policy conclusion is that behavioral health care is increasingly being addressed through medication or prescription drugs, which accounted for the majority of cost increases over the decade. It is these marked changes in the actual amount of federal funding, combined with new regulations, that has allowed the federal government to exercise greater control of the state mental health infrastructure.

Presidential Commissions and Involvement in Mental Health Policy

In April 2002, President George W. Bush appointed a 15-member commission to "conduct a comprehensive study" of the mental health system in the United States (Bush, 2006; New Freedom Commission on Mental Health, 2006). Bush's executive order establishing the charge to the commission was similar in language and content to the first presidential mental health commission appointed by Carter in 1978 (Bush, 2006; Grob, 2005). On the surface, each president sought to catalogue the extent of problems in the existing system, improve the quality of mental health care, propose new policies, and offer solutions for controlling the escalating cost of care. The focus of this investigatory work by both presidential commissions was public mental health systems (facilities, centers, and clinics) historically managed by state mental health authorities. But Carter expected his commission to offer a variety of recommendations for meeting the needs of the underserved mentally ill through expanded federal support of nonprofit community mental health centers (Grob, 2005), whereas Bush wanted his commission to focus on newer concepts of transformation, rehabilitation, and recovery and their ties to employment. Bush's commission also sought to enlist the participation of families and consumers, state agencies, and federal organizations under the direction of the federal government (New Freedom Commission on Mental Health, 2003b). The activist role of the federal government proposed by the Bush commission's report was similar to that proposed by Carter but at clear political odds to Reagan's concept of New Federalism (Boyd, 2006; Stoesz & Karger, 1993). Under New Federalism, Reagan wanted states to regain greater control of resources, decisions, and policy making as the federal government's authority receded. To Reagan, Carter's policies inappropriately enhanced federal power and control at the expense of the southern states' rights agenda.

Beneath the surface, however, Carter and Bush, both former southern governors, understood that the complex labyrinth of state mental health could not change without effective new medications, fully funded community services, improved care in state hospitals, increased insurance coverage, and affordable housing for persons with mental illness. Kennedy came closer to public recognition of these dilemmas when he sought to increase the investments by the federal government following completion of the Joint Commission's report (Joint Commission on Mental Illness and Health, 1961; Kennedy, 2006b). What further distinguished Carter's and Bush's historic commissions was the different mental health policy context that birthed them. Carter's commission was established at a time when there was substantive support for expanding the number and financing of federal community mental health centers. At its conclusion, Carter's commission recommended new legislation to drive its findings and polices. However, Reagan rescinded Carter's Mental Health Centers Act within the first few weeks of his administration. Reagan interpreted Carter's policies as increasing federal power over the states and increasing the financial burden on government and business (Thomas, 1998).

Bush appointed his commission at a time when such values as increased privatization, recovery, disease management, religious involvement, evidence-based practice, and family participation were at their zenith. These values coincided with Bush's intent to "promote increased access to educational and employment opportunities for people with disabilities" (New Freedom Commission on Mental Health, 2003a, p. 1). Following completion of his commission, however, Bush did not actively press for new legislation or issue executive orders to implement its major findings or recommendations. Surprisingly, the Bush administration sought to reduce support from Medicaid and Medicare and reduce housing and health care for the mentally disabled. Consumer advocates found Bush's willingness to reduce existing Medicaid benefits and housing contrary to the recommendations of his commission and inimical to recovery.

One year after Bush appointed his New Freedom Commission they issued an extensive final report of their findings and recommendations (New Freedom Commission on Mental Health, 2003b). Not surprisingly, the Bush commission reported that mental health services in the United States were characterized by the following problems and obstacles:

- Fragmentation in services for children and adults and the aged
- Stigma that surrounds mental illnesses
- Unfair treatment and financial requirements placed on benefits in private insurance
- Numerous barriers that impede care
- High rates of unemployment and disability
- Disparities by race and class
- Limited access to treatment
- Discrepancies between evidence-based treatments and services available
- Mental health workforce lagging behind need
- Excess rates of suicide and limited suicide prevention
- Limited goals

These findings were not unlike those articulated by Carter's commission 24 years before (Carter, 2006; Grob, 2005) or those of the Joint Commission on Mental Health established by Congress in 1955 during the Eisenhower administration (Joint Commission on

Mental Illness and Health, 1961). It is important to identify and understand the factors that reinforce delay of new policy directions and maintain such uncertainty 50 years after the first comprehensive study of mental health care. Such an understanding may be valuable in helping drive the multiple recommendations in the Bush commission's report toward implementation (National Technical Assistance Center [NTAC], 2004; Substance Abuse and Mental Health Services Administration, 2005).

The Bush commission reviewed the previous studies, reports, and findings on mental health care (U.S. Department of Health and Human Services, 1999, 2001) and concluded that the answer to the long-term problems of fragmentation and poor quality of care required transformation of public and, to some extent, private mental health systems. Initially, it was unclear how the Bush administration and its commission defined transformation operationally. The commission defined transformation as a vision, a process, and an outcome (Anderson, 1994). However, the administration found Cebowski's (Power, 2004) definition more acceptable: Transformation is a highly complex and continuous process that seeks to create or anticipate the future. Furthermore, Cebowski indicated that transformation might entail creating new principles, sources of power, and structure, culture, policy, and programs.

To achieve its transformation goal, the federal government needed to provide incentives to overcome the inertia and resistance of the states. The federal government issued a Request for Proposal that provided $15 million over 5 years to each of seven states to support their transformation efforts (SAMHSA, 2006a). The amount provided per state represents a very small percentage of the annual budgets of these agencies and seems insufficient to bring about transformation. In addition to funding, the seven states obtained federal technical assistance in how to develop and implement comprehensive transformation plans. At the end of the first year of funding, the federal government suddenly stated that any future transformation efforts in other states would require funding via a state's existing block grant program. To reach this conceptual goal, the Bush commission identified and defined a complex series of specific concepts, goals, targets, strategies, analyses, forums, plans, and processes that would take place at the federal, state, and local level to achieve transformation (SAMHSA, 2005).

The Bush mental health commission report was the first since the Carter commission in 1981 and only the fifth effort by an American president (Truman, Eisenhower, Kennedy, and Carter) to make major policy recommendations to improve the quality of mental health care as a national priority. Each president sought substantive changes in the power relationship between the federal and state governments. Kennedy (2006a, 2006b, 2006c) outlined critical questions about these relationships and the implications for the mentally disabled if they were left unresolved.

The practical value of Truman's, Eisenhower's, Kennedy's, Carter's, and Bush's recommendations for changes in public mental health was severely limited by the continued presence of two unresolved historical public policy dilemmas. First, there is no agreement between the states and the national government on the acceptable level of federalism in mental health policy and related services. For close to two centuries, state governments controlled the mental health policy process and the delivery of services. The federal government was essentially kept at bay in a dual federalism position described by Boyd (2006). It was this power imbalance in mental health that the Kennedy administration questioned and identified as an impediment to developing new financial and services arrangements consistent with the recommendations of the Joint Commission on Mental Health. It was Kennedy's (2006b, 2006c) belief that improved quality at the state (hospital) level required increased federal pressure, legislation, and finances. Truman, Kennedy, Johnson, and Carter proposed an increase in the power of the federal government, but the nature of the power relationships between the state and federal governments remained unclear (Kennedy, 2006b).

The historical tension between the two levels of government remains significant and exacerbated by the frequent expansions and contractions and directional changes in federal and state policy.

Second, the states implemented their long-term monopoly on mental health care by investing the majority of their energy and resources into the construction, staffing, and maintenance of state mental hospitals. The shift toward community mental health services resulted from critical federal reports (Joint Commission on Mental Illness and Health, 1961), and human rights litigation (U.S. Congress, 1980), followed by legislative support of nonprofit organizations. Federal community mental health policy essentially bypassed the traditional state authority (U.S. Congress, 1963). Did the federal government have the authority to provide federal revenues to support alternative mental health services in the states but outside the aegis of state government? The Supreme Court's decision in *McCulloch* (*McCulloch v. State of Maryland,* 1819) supports the idea that federal intervention in mental health at the state level is consistent with the theory of implied power.

The New Freedom Commission report is similar in breath and quality to the Joint Commission's and the Carter commission's reports. The New Freedom Commission report was completed in 2003; however, all of its subreports have yet to be issued publicly. In addition, the implementation guidelines were issued in July 2005; however, no executive orders or legislation has followed. The New Freedom Commission report seems to be following a pattern similar to that of previous commissions and their findings in which policy action lags behind incisive analysis.

The New Freedom Commission report and the president's major goals are at best a set of indirect federal recommendations to state governors and legislators. However valuable, these federally generated goals do not carry the strength of public law or executive order and have no immediate enforcement powers. Conceptualizing the report and the president's goals as recommendations to the states means the federal government has to identify multiple incentives or sanctions to get states to share or exchange their long-term control of the mental health policy process and adopt new federal standards for practice. Neither of these tasks can be achieved without the expenditure of significant political and economic capital, both of which may be in shorter supply in the last 2 years of a weakened incumbent administration, where reelection is no longer a lever to entice compliance. What power does the federal government have that would be instrumental in increasing the chances that state governments will voluntarily adopt federal recommendations?

Federal Lawsuits and Judicial Cases against the States

Two federal court cases (*Olmstead v. L.C.,* 1999; *Wyatt v. Stickney,* 1971) and two public laws (Pub. L. 96-416, Civil Rights of Institutionalized Persons Act; Pub. L. 100-336, Americans with Disabilities Act) established similar federal quality standards for state mental health systems. These two judicial cases and two public laws also created a legal foundation for federal intervention and penalties when states fail to meet federal standards. Prior to these judicial and public law interventions, the federal government did not seek to force states to comply with any set of national standards of treatment or service.

However, *Wyatt v. Stickney* (1971) stands as one of the most important federal judicial decisions in the history of American mental health law. Wyatt was a psychiatric patient in Bryce State Hospital in Alabama and Stickney was the commissioner of mental health for the state. When Alabama sought to reduce its operating costs, it planned to decrease the number of staff and the overall staff-to-patient ratio. However, Wyatt, through his guardian, objected to this change by the state and argued that his constitutional right to effective treatment would be compromised if the ratio were changed. Furthermore, Wyatt argued that the long-term nature of his hospitalization amounted to involuntary confinement with very limited chance of his ever returning to the community. The reduction in staffing would therefore further decrease his chances of release from confinement.

The federal court agreed with Wyatt's argument and used his pleadings to build a consent decree that outlined the quality treatment standards the state of Alabama had to adopt. The list of requisite changes became the Wyatt standards and established a precedent for other state mental health systems.

Arguments between the federal government and the state in the *Wyatt* case took place over a 30-year period. The case was finally closed in 1993, when the courts agreed that Alabama had reached a reasonable degree of compliance with the agreed-upon standards of care. The *Wyatt* case was significant in the ongoing struggle between the federal and state government because it forced the state to adopt and meet specified standards. In addition, the case successfully countermanded the state's claim that a lack of funding was sufficient justification to maintain a status quo that violated human rights and constitutional guarantees.

The Civil Rights of Institutionalized Persons Act (CRIPA; U.S. Congress, 1980; Pub. L. 96-416) gave the Department of Justice the power to bring suit against the states for constitutional violations that took place in state facilities. The legal basis of Public Law 96-416 parallels the arguments made successfully in the *Wyatt v. Stickney* case in 1971. The Act concluded that residents of state (public) institutions maintain their constitutional rights while confined, and CRIPA does not permit states to ignore these rights. The rights identified in the Act include a right to treatment, a right to periodic evaluations, protection from abuse and harmful treatment, a right to medical care, and a right to return to the community. Where a state institution violates these rights, the Justice Department has the authority to conduct on-site evaluations and seek voluntary compliance with its findings and recommended changes. Where states are unwilling to abide by the findings, the Justice Department files charges and institutes court proceedings.

From 1980 to 2000, the U.S. Justice Department successfully sued 28 states for violations of CRIPA. This Act originally allowed federal intervention in protecting the constitutional rights of persons in prisons. However, the federal government expanded the purview of the Act to encompass the rights of persons with mental illness who were residents of state mental institutions. Recently, the Act was expanded to include an unprecedented community remedy: In Hawaii, the Department of Justice required the state mental health system to develop and implement a community services plan that would provide services outside the state hospital (Creamer, 2001; Gorman, 2006; Hanson-Mayer, 2006; Hawaii Department of Health, Adult Mental Health Division, 2005; Kobayashi, 2006; Minkoff, 2006).

The Americans with Disabilities Act (ADA) focuses on eliminating all barriers to persons with disabilities—mental as well as physical. The ADA concluded that confining "persons with disabilities in institutions constitutes unnecessary and illegal segregation" (U.S. Congress, 2005). To eliminate this segregation, the ADA required states, local governments, and employers to remove all barriers—behavioral and physical. Specifically, the ADA concluded that individuals with disabilities had a right to life in the community.

The second legal case of importance in mental health was *Olmstead v. L.C.*, filed in 1999. This case was heard in Georgia and was brought by two plaintiffs who were confined in the Georgia Regional Hospital Center. The plaintiffs alleged that they were being held in the state facilities in violation of the ADA and prior judgments in other cases. Furthermore, the plaintiffs claimed that the state had consistently failed to place them in a less restrictive community setting although they were found clinically eligible.

In response to the plaintiff's arguments, the state of Georgia sought to defend its actions based on funding shortages and potential harm to the state's programs or systems. In essence, the state sought to base its claim on the proposal that the accommodations sought by the plaintiffs was too costly. On appeal, the state's cost base defense was deemed worthy of examination, and the case was remanded back to the district court for review. The case was eventually heard by the U.S. Supreme Court. Justice Goldberg wrote the majority opinion for the court and asserted that states had an obligation under the ADA to provide placements in communities rather than in traditional state institutions. Although the court supported the rights of persons with mental illness, they also recognized the financial constraints placed on the states.

NATIONALIZATION: SOLVING THE RIDDLE OF FRAGMENTATION AND UNCERTAINTY

The multiple reports, studies, and congressional commissions completed over the past several decades reached very similar pessimistic conclusions about the status of mental health care in the United States. Overall, there seems to be minimal differences between the range of widespread problems noted in the 1946 report completed for President Truman, the Joint Commission Report in 1955, the Carter Commission in 1980, and those noted in the 2003 report from the Bush administration. The preponderance of the long-term epidemiological, economic, and services evidence confirms that the mental health system at the state level remains in substantial crisis, even failure. The laissez-faire American mental health policy of state-run systems, supported with inconsistent federal funding, has been far less than successful. Although some progress is evident in mental health care from one decade to another (Frank & Glied, 2006), few national models of effectiveness have been identified for widespread adoption. Progress in mental health, as noted by Kessler et al. (2005), Frank and Glied (2006) and Wang et al. (2006), has been slow, uneven, and met with limited enthusiasm (Frank & Morlock, 1997). Frank and Glied conclude that the traditional state mental health authority model of care is waning in strength, influence, and control, albeit at a slow pace. They base their conclusions on the significant reduction in state general funds compared to federal funds that support services at the state and local level.

As recently as 2003, the New Freedom Commission on Mental Health (2003b) documented the continued depth of fragmentation, uncertainty, disarray, and barriers to effective and cost-efficient services. The long-term reoccurring nature of these problems undoubtedly influenced the commission's critical recommendation to "transform" the entire system of care. Although stated more subtly in its report, the New Freedom Commission's recommendation for transformation aims principally at changing antiquated state (public) mental health systems—hospitals, community mental health programs, and their policies ("92 Million Dollars," 2006).

The oblique focus on state mental health systems in the commission's recommendation is apparent in that the only decisive action taken by the Bush administration following the report was the issuance of state transformation grants (SAMHSA, 2006a). Each of these grants went to individual states to the exclusion of either local governments or the private sector. Clearly, transformation is perceived by the federal government as an issue for state governments and seems to waken dormant questions about federalism, states' rights, constitutionality, finances, and the future direction of public mental health policy in the United States.

The New Freedom Commission's transformation recommendation raises three substantial questions about the depth of the state mental health crisis and the potential role of the federal government in managing such a change. First, has the quality of functioning of the American mental health system reached a point where the nation's productivity and stability are at risk? Affirmative responses to societal concern about these issues led to the establishment of state mental hospitals in the eighteenth century. Second, is the level of risk, human rights violations, or slow rate of change in state mental health services high enough to require direct federal intervention? Third, does the federal government have constitutional authority to intervene in mental health matters of state governments? Each of these questions has been answered affirmatively for decades.

The functioning of the mental health system is related to the risk of lowered productivity and economic instability. For example, Kessler et al.'s (2005) replication study found the lifetime rate of incidence of mental disorder in the U.S. population to be 45%. Their findings are buttressed by findings from Wang et al. (2005) that 68% of those persons who need mental health services in the United States are not obtaining them, and, when they do access services, there is a discrepancy between what is provided and the standard (evidence-based practices) in the field. The recent study by the National Alliance on Mental Illness found that the key variable in risk and cost is the extent to which depression is treated ("National Survey," 2006). Where treatment is either unavailable or provided poorly, cost of medical care increases substantially. In an earlier study, the NMHA (2001) estimated that untreated and poorly treated mental disorders cost the United States in excess of $100 billion a year in lost productivity. Other published works (Ettner, Frank, & Kessler, 1997; Stoudemire, Frank, & Hedemark, 1986; Timbe, Horvitz-Lennon, Frank, & Normand, 2006) show various linkages between economic, labor force, and psychiatric variables. Further evidence of the potential impact on the national economy is shown in the following long-term problems:

- Fragmentation in funding and policy direction
- Difficulty accessing service
- Disparities by race and class

- Lag in the application of innovation
- Low quality of services
- Failure to use evidence-based methodologies
- Most persons in need not seeking services
- Increased suicide rates
- High rates of comorbid conditions
- Inadequate number trained mental health workers in the workforce
- Conflict within levels of government
- Excessive cost
- Lowered productivity

Mental health care remains a major financial and policy responsibility of state governments, albeit underfinanced in almost all states. Although the day-to-day operations are under the aegis of state commissioners or directors, policy change rests with governors and legislators who appoint them and oversee the budgets of state mental health agencies. These agencies cannot pursue a policy direction unless it is supported by or is consistent with the state administration. Because of the highly politicized environment in which they operate, mental health systems are greatly constrained and slow to make substantive changes that will reduce local employment levels. The potential impact (elective risk) on governors and legislators seems to dictate a slow pace of change that could effectively thwart federal transformation goals. To install quality and transformation guidelines seems to dictate an alternative strategy to that used to initiate community mental health. Left to their own idiosyncrasies, states seem unable to sustain reform despite continued scandals, deaths, injuries, and federal intervention (Chang, 2006; Minkoff, 2006). States have not been able to provide consistent policy direction to solve the long-term crisis in mental health. The New Freedom Commission's report seems to affirm that solving the mental health crisis in America requires strategic federal intervention, financial support, and technical assistance (New Freedom Commission on Mental Health, 2003b; NTAC, 2004; Unutzer et al., 2006; personal communication from A. K. Power to H. Harbin, B. C. Edwards, H. Goldman, C. Koyanagi, S. Pires, L. Rosenberg, & L. Schwalbe, November 13, 2006).

Nationalization of state mental health systems offers such a strategy. Nationalization is a voluntary policy agreement between the federal and state governments in which control of the existing state system and its infrastructure are transferred to the U.S. government. As part of the voluntary agreement, states would be required to maintain their current level of expenditures, matched by an equal amount of federal funding. The federal government would manage all aspects of the existing system, including all facilities, community centers, and central offices. Day-to-day management of the system would be by the federal government and directors would be employees of SAMHSA. Policy and planning would be under the aegis of the federal government, with an expectation that such planning would aim at total transformation of the existing system of care. Nationalization of state mental health systems is proposed as a short-term (5- to 10-year) strategy for helping to resolve the political risks incurred by state-level actors and as a means of encouraging transformation.

The federal government could enter into a contractual relationship with the states to manage their mental health systems, create a collective future vision, develop statewide plans, and implement those plans. Nationalization would involve cost sharing by all levels of government and would allow the federal government to plan for the integration of health and mental health services. As part of nationalization, the federal government could develop, with the states, a planned closure of state facilities and the transfer of their responsibilities to the primary care sector. Transferring current inpatient services to the primary care sector would eliminate the fiscal constraints on institutions for mental disease and would immediately increase the potential quality of health care for persons with mental or addictive illnesses.

Over the past 45 years, there has been a gradual shift toward national control of public mental health systems. The shifts have come about through increases in federal funding, lawsuits against the states, expanded federal laws, and the introduction of new services concepts from federal reports and commissions. Clearly, the shift in responsibility and control has been to such an extent that public mental health systems are experiencing a decline in their authority and control. Nationalization is an unspoken reality. There is value in completing the nationalization of public mental health systems as a means of transforming mental health care in the United States, as proposed in the report of the New Freedom Commission on Mental Health (2003b).

Any proposal to increase federal authority over traditional state functions raises numerous concerns and questions. Obviously, such a proposal raises questions about appropriate levels of federalism, old issues that remain unresolved. States too will see such a proposal as an infringement of or encroachment on their sovereign right to make policy decisions. Others will question whether there is a constitutional basis for such federal action, although couched here in terms of voluntary agreement. Nationalization of public mental health care seems to be a necessary and vital policy strategy for the United States. The lifetime prevalence of mental disorders, escalating costs, and an annual loss of billions of dollars in productivity offer a compelling case that mental health care in the United States is in serious crisis, if not an epidemic. Equally compelling is the conclusion that state governments alone cannot resolve the crisis and thus reduce the human and economic losses. The economic, political, and employment value of maintaining state hospitals in small communities precludes an easy solution to the crisis. The crisis appears to be of such proportion and historical precedent that federal action is needed to redirect public policy toward the illusive goal of transformation.

REFERENCES

Adebimpe, V. R. (1994). Race, racism and epidemiological surveys. *Hospital and Community Psychiatry*, *45*, 27–31.

Albertsons, Inc. v. Kirkingburg, 527 U.S. 555, 143 F. 3rd. 1228 (1999).

Allport, G. W. (1954). *The nature of prejudice*. Cambridge, MA: Addison-Wesley.

Althouse, A. (2001). Why talking about "states' rights" cannot avoid the need for normative federalism analysis. *Duke Law Journal*, *51*, 363–376.

Altman, D. E., & Levitt, L. (2002). The sad history of health care cost containment as told in one chart. *Health Affairs*, *22*, 83–84.

Ambrose, S. E. (1985). *Nixon: The triumph of a politician—1962–1972*. (Vols. 1–2) New York: Simon & Schuster.

Anderson, C. (1994). *Black labor, White wealth: The search for power and economic justice*. Edgewood, MD: Duncan and Duncan.

Andreasen, N. C. (1997). Linking mind and brain in the study of mental illnesses: A project for a scientific psychopathology. *Science, 275*, 1586–1593.

Arnoff, F. (1975). Social consequences of policy toward mental illness. *Science, 188*, 1277–1281.

Babcock, J. W. (1895). The colored insane. In J. W. Babcock, (Ed.), *National Conference of Charities and Corrections* (pp. 184–186). Boston: National Conference of Charities and Corrections.

Baker, L. A., & Young, E. A. (2001). Federalism and the double standard of judicial review. *Duke Law Journal, 51*, 143–149.

Baseler, M. C. (1998). *Asylum for mankind: America, 1607–1800*. Ithaca, NY: Cornell University Press.

Belknap, I. (1956). *Human problems of a state mental hospital*. New York: McGraw-Hill.

Berlien, I. C., & Waggoner, R. W. (1966). Selection and induction. In R. S. Anderson, A. L. Glass, R. J. Bernucci, J. B. Coates, & L. Ahnfeldt (Eds.), *Neuropsychiatry in World War II* (pp. 153–188). Washington, DC: Department of the Army, Office of the Surgeon General.

Biegel, D. E., Milligan, S. E., Putnam, P. L., & Song, L. Y. (1994). Predictors of burden among lower socioeconomic status caregivers with chronic mental illness. *Community Mental Health Journal, 30*, 473–494.

Blanton, W. B. (1931). *Medicine in Virginia in the eighteenth century*. Richmond, VA: Garett and Massie.

Boyd, E. (2006). *American federalism, 1776 to 1997: Significant events*. Available from http://usinfo.state.gov.usa/infousa/politics/states/federal.htm.

Breeden, J. O. (1976). States rights medicine in the old South. *Journal of Southern History, 25*, 53–72.

Brill, N. Q., & Kupper, H. I. (1966). The psychiatric patient after discharge. In R. S. Anderson, A. J. Glass, R. J. Bernucci, J. B. Coates, & L. Ahnfeldt (Eds.), *Neuropsychiatry in World War II* (pp. 735–759). Washington, DC: Department of the Army, Office of the Surgeon General.

Brody, E. B. (1966). Psychiatry and prejudice. In S. Arieti (Ed.), *American handbook of psychiatry* (p. 3). New York: Basic Books.

Brown, G. O. (1887, August 9). *Letter to the Freedman's Bureau from General G.O. Brown requesting to rent (Bacon Tate's) land to establish Central State Hospital for African Americans* [Personal correspondence]. Richmond: Virginia State Archives.

Brown v. Topeka Board of Education, 347 U.S. 483 (1954).

Browne, F. F. (1914). *The every-day life of Abraham Lincoln*. New York: Murray.

Burnim, I. A. (2006). *The ADA's "integration mandate" should promote community services*. Available from www.bazelon.org/issues/disabilityrights/incourt/olmstead/ibtest.html.

Bush, G. W. (2006). *New Freedom Commission executive order*. Available from www.whitehouse.gov/news/releases/2002/04/200020429-2.html.

Byrd, W. M., & Clayton, L. A. (2002). *An American health dilemma: Race, medicine, and health care in the United States 1900–2000* (Vols. 1–2). New York: Routledge.

Cannon, M. S., & Locke, B. Z. (1977). Being Black is detrimental to one's mental health: Myth or reality? *Phylon, 38*, 408–428.

Caplan, G. (1961). *An approach to community mental health*. New York: Grune & Stratton.

Carothers, J. C. (1940). Some speculations on insanity in Africans and in general. *East African Medical Journal, 17*, 90–105.

Carter, J. (2006). *President Carter's Commission on Mental Health*. Available from www.presidency.ucsb.edu/ws/print.php?pid=6643/.

Cartwright, S. (1851). Report on the diseases and physical peculiarities of the Negro race. *New Orleans Medical Surgical Journal, 7*, 692–705.

Chandra, A., & Skinner, J. (2003). *Geography and racial health disparities*. Cambridge, MA: National Bureau of Economic Research.

Chang, K. (2006). *Twelfth report and recommendation to the U.S. District Court of Hawaii*. In United States of America v. State of Hawaii. Honolulu, HI: U.S. District Court.

Close Up Foundation. (2006). *Federalism*. Available from www.closeup.org/federal.htm.

Congressional Budget Office. (1999). *Economic and budget outlook: Fiscal years 2000–2009*. Washington, DC: Author.

Creamer, B. (2001). Federal court puts state hospital under the gun. *Honolulu Advertiser*. Available from www.honoluluadvertiser.com.

Cross, T. L., Bazron, B., Dennis, K., & Isaacs, M. (1989). *Toward a culturally competent system of care*. Washington, DC: Georgetown University Child Development Center.

Dain, N. (1964). *Concepts of insanity in the United States 1789–1865*. New Brunswick, NJ: Rutgers University Press.

Dain, N. (1968). *History of Eastern State Hospital*. Williamsburg, VA: Colonial Williamsburg Foundation.

Davis, K. (1998). Race, health status and managed health care. In F. L. Brisbane (Ed.), *Special collaborative edition CSAP cultural competence series* (pp. 145–163). Rockville, MD: Bureau of Primary Care, Center for Substance Abuse Prevention.

Davis, K., & Iron Cloud Two-Dogs, E. (2004). The color of social policy: Oppression of indigenous tribal populations and Africans in America. In K. Davis & T. Bent-Goodley (Eds.), *The color of social policy* (pp. 3–20). Alexandria, VA: Council on Social Work Education.

Denton, T. G. (1960). *Central State Hospital 1865–1960*. Richmond, VA: Department of Mental Hygiene and Hospitals.

Deutsch, A. (1948). *The shame of the states*. New York: Harcourt Brace.

Deutsch, A. (1949). *The mentally ill in America: A history of their care and treatment from colonial times* (2nd ed.). New York: Columbia University Press.

Drake, F. D. (1999). *States' rights and American federalism: A documentary history*. Westport, CT: Greenwood Press.

Drewry, W. F. (1916). *Central State Hospital*. (Vols. 1–3). Baltimore: Johns Hopkins University Press.

Ennis, B. J., & Siegel, L. (1973). *The rights of mental patients*. New York: Baron.

Epstein, A. M., & Ayanian, J. Z. (2001). Racial disparities in medical care. *New England Journal of Medicine, 344*, 1471–1473.

Ettner, S. L., Frank, R. G., & Kessler, R. C. (1997). The impact of psychiatric disorder on labor market outcomes. *Industrial and Labor Relations Review, 51*, 64–81.

Evarts, A. B. (1914). Dementia praecox in the colored race. *Psychoanalytic Review, 1*, 388–403.

Faris, R., & Dunham, H. W. (1939). *Mental disorders in urban areas*. Chicago: University of Chicago Press.

Federalism. (2006). *Pinkmonkey*. Available from www.pinkmonkey.com/studyguides/subjects/am_gov/chap2/a0200001.asp.

Fischer, J. (1969). Negroes, Whites and rates of mental illness: Reconsideration of a myth. *Psychiatry, 32*, 438–446.

Foucault, M. (1965). *Madness and civilization: A history of insanity in the age of reason* (R. Howard, Trans.). New York: Random House.

Frank, R. G. (2006, February 2). *Mental health care: Gains and gaps*. Unpublished Presentation to Grantmakers in Health Summit, San Francisco.

Frank, R. G., & Glied, S. (2006). *Better but not well*. Baltimore: Johns Hopkins University Press.

Frank, R. G., & Morlock, L. L. (1997). *Managing fragmented public mental health services*. New York: Milbank Memorial Fund.

Gollaher, D. (1995). *Voice for the mad: The life of Dorothea Dix*. New York: Free Press.

Gorman, P. G. (2006). *Final evaluation of the Adult Mental Health Division* (Report No. 7). In United States of America v. State of Hawaii. Honolulu, HI: U.S. District Court.

Gould, S. J. (1981). *The mismeasure of man*. New York: Norton.

Grob, G. N. (1973). *Mental institutions in America: Social policy to 1875*. New York: Free Press.

Grob, G. N. (1994). *The mad among us: A history of the care of America's mentally ill*. Cambridge, MA: Harvard University Press.

Grob, G. N. (2005). Public policy and mental illnesses: Jimmy Carter's Presidential Commission on Mental Health. *Milbank Quarterly, 83*, 425–456.

Grossack, M. M. (1963). *Mental health and segregation*. New York: Springer.

Hansen, C. F. (1959). Mental health aspects of desegregation. *Journal of the National Medical Association, 51*, 450–456.

Hanson-Mayer, G. (2006). *Final evaluation of the Adult Mental Health Division* (Report No. 12). In United States of America v. State of Hawaii. Honolulu, HI: U.S. District Court.

Hatfield, A. B. (1987). Families as caregivers: A historical perspective. In A. B. Hatfield & H. P. Lefley (Eds.), *Families of the mentally ill: Coping and adaptation* (pp. 3–29). New York: Guilford Press.

Hawaii Department of Health, Adult Mental Health Division. (2005). *Statewide comprehensive integrated service plan*. Honolulu, HI: Author.

Healy, D. (2002). *The creation of psychopharmacology*. Cambridge, MA: Harvard University Press.

Heldring, M. (2003, April 7). Mental health funding is part of cost effect reform: Health care reform. *Seattle Times*. p. 12.

Hernandez, R., & Pear, R. (2006, July 12). Once an enemy, health industry warms to Clinton. *New York Times*. p. 1.

Herrnstein, R. J., & Murray, C. (1994). *The bell curve: Intelligence and class structure in American life*. New York: Free Press.

Hurd, H. M., Drewry, W. F., Dewey, R., Pilgrim, C. W., Lumer, G. A., & Burgess, T. J. W. (1916). *The institutional care of the insane in the United States and Canada*. Baltimore: Johns Hopkins University Press.

Institute of Medicine. (2005). *Crossing the quality chasm: Adaptation for mental health and addictive disorders*. Washington, DC: Author.

Jackson, D. D. (1960). *The etiology of schizophrenia*. New York: Basic Books.

Jackson, J. S., Brown, T., Williams, D. W., Torres, M., Sellers, S., & Brown, K. (1996). Perceptions and experiences of racism and the physical and mental health status of African Americans: A thirteen-year national panel study. *Ethnicity and Disease, 6*, 132–147.

Jarvis, E. (1842). Statistics on insanity in the United States. *Boston Medicine and Surgery Journal, 27*, 116–121.

Jarvis, E. (1844). Insanity among the colored population of the free states. *American Journal of the Medical Sciences, 7*, 71–83.

Joint Commission on Mental Illness and Health. (1961). *Action for mental health*. New York: Science Editions.

Keeler, M. H., & Vitols, M. M. (1963). Migration and schizophrenia in North Carolina Negroes. *American Journal of Orthopsychiatry, 33*, 557.

Kennedy, J. F. (2006a). *Kennedy's remarks on proposed measures to combat mental illness and mental retardation*. Available from www.presidency.ucsb.edu/ws/pring.php?pid=9547/.

Kennedy, J. F. (2006b). *Letter to the Board of Commissioners of the District of Columbia*. Available from www.presidency.ucsb.edu/ws/print.php?pid=9563/.

Kennedy, J. F. (2006c). *Letter to Secretary Ribicoff concerning the role of the federal government in the field of mental health*. Available from www.presidency.ucsb.edu/ws/print.php?pid=8469/.

Keppel, K. G., Pearcy, J. N., & Wagener, D. K. (2002). *Trends in racial and ethnic-specific rates for the health status indicators: United States, 1990–1998* (Rep. No. 23). Hyattsville, MD: Centers for Disease Control and Prevention, National Center for Health Statistics.

Kessler, R. C., Berglund, P., Demler, O., Jin, R., Merikangas, L. R., & Walters, E. E. (2005). Lifetime prevalence and age-of-onset distributions of DSM-IV disorders in the national comorbidity survey replication. *Archives of General Psychiatry, 62*, 593–602.

Kleiner, R. J., & Parker, S. (1959). Migration and mental illness: A new look. *American Sociological Review, 24*, 687–690.

Kobayashi, K. (2006). State still lagging in mental health services. *Honolulu Advertiser*. Available from www.honoluluadvertiser.com.

Kramer, M., Von Korff, M., & Kessler, L. (1980). The lifetime prevalence of mental disorders: Estimation, uses and limitations. *Psychological Medicine, 10*, 429–436.

Lidz, R. W., & Lidz, T. (1949). The family environment of schizophrenic patients. *American Journal of Psychiatry, 106*, 332.

Malzberg, B. (1940). *Social and biological aspects of mental disease*. New York: State Hospital Press.

Malzberg, B. (1953). Mental diseases among Negroes in New York State, 1939–1941. *Mental Hygiene, 37*, 450–476.

Manderscheid, R. W., & Henderson, M. J. (2001). *Mental health, United States, 2000*. Washington, DC: Center for Mental Health Services.

Mark, T. L., Coffey, R. M., Vandivort-Warren, R., Harwood, H. J., & King, E. C. (2005). U.S. spending for mental health and substance abuse treatment, 1991–2001. *Health Affairs, 24*, 133–142.

McCandless, P. (1996). *Moonlight, magnolias, and madness: Insanity in South Carolina from the colonial period to the progressive era*. Chapel Hill: University of North Carolina Press.

McCulloch v. State of Maryland, 17 U.S. 316 (1819).

Mechanic, D. (1989). *Mental health and social policy* (3rd ed.). Englewood Cliffs, NJ: Prentice-Hall.

Minkoff, K. (2006). *Twelfth team evaluation of the Hawaii Adult Mental Health Division action* (Report No. 12). In United States of America v. State of Hawaii. Honolulu, HI: U.S. Federal District Court.

Moscarelli, M., Rupp, A., & Sartorious, N. (1996). *Handbook of mental health economics and health policy*. New York: Wiley.

Mulligan, K. (2003, January 3). Mental health system reform must start with funding. *Psychiatric News, 38*, 9.

Murphy v. United Parcel Services, 527 U.S. 516. 141 F. 3rd 1185 (1999).

National Alliance on Mental Illness. (2006). *Grading the states: A report on America's health care system for serious mental illness*. Alexandria, VA: Author.

National Institute of Mental Health. (2006a). *In harm's way: Suicide in America*. Available from www.nimh.nih.gov/publicat/harmsway.cfm.

National Institute of Mental Health. (2006b). *The impact of mental illness on society*. Available from www.nimh.nih.gov/publicat/burden.cfm.

National Institute of Mental Health. (2006c). *Statistics*. Available from www.nimh.nih.gov /HealthInformation/statisticsmenu.cfm.

National Mental Health Association. (2001). *Labor Day 2001 report: Untreated and mistreated mental illness and substance abuse costs U.S. $113 billion a year*. Alexandria, VA: Author.

National survey finds depression costs nearly tripled for individuals with limited access to care. (2006). *Houston Chronicle*. Available from www.chron.com/cs/CDA/printstory.mpl/conws/4038661/.

National Technical Assistance Center. (2004). Answering the challenge: Responses to the president's New Freedom Commission final report. *Network, 8*, 1–68.

Neighbors, H. W., Jackson, J., Campbell, L., & Williams, D. (1989). The influence of racial factors on psychiatric diagnosis: A review and suggestions for research. *Community Mental Health Journal, 25*, 301–311.

Neighbors, H. W., & Lumpkin, S. (1990). The epidemiology of mental disorder in the Black population. In D. S. Ruiz & J. P. Comer (Eds.), *Handbook of mental health and mental disorder among Black Americans* (pp. 55–70). New York: Greenwood Press.

New Freedom Commission on Mental Health. (2003a). *Achieving the promise: Transforming mental health care in America—Executive summary of final report* (Rep. No. DMS-03–3831). Rockville, MD: Department of Health and Human Services.

New Freedom Commission on Mental Health. (2003b). *Achieving the promise: Transforming mental health care in America—Final report* (Rep. No. SMA-03–3832). Rockville, MD: Department of Health and Human Services.

New Freedom Commission on Mental Health. (2006). *New Freedom Commission members*. Available from www.mentalhealthcommission.gov/minutes/Hune02.htm.

92 million dollars allocated for transformation grants. (2006). *Medical News Today*. Available from www.medicalnewstoday.com/medicalnews.php?newsid=31366/.

Nixon, R. M. (1972, March 2). *Health care: Request for action on 3 programs: Message to Congress on health care*. (Pub. L. No. 93-222). Washington, DC: Committee on Labor and Public Welfare.

Olmstead v. L.C., 527 U.S. 581 (1999).

O'Malley, M. (1914). Insanity in the colored race. *Journal of Insanity, 71*, 309–336.

Pasamanick, B. A. (1959). *The epidemiology of mental disorder*. Washington, DC: American Association for the Advancement of Science.

Pierce, F. (1854). *Franklin Pierce's 1854 veto*. Available from www.disabilitymuseum.org /lib/docs/682.htm?page=print/.

Plepys, C., & Klein, R. (1995). *Health status indicators: Differentials by race and Hispanic origin* (Rep. No. 10). Hyattsville, MD: Centers for Disease Control and Prevention, National Center for Health Statistics.

Poen, M. M. (1979). *Harry S. Truman versus the medical lobby: The genesis of Medicare*. Columbia: University of Missouri Press.

Power, A. K. (2004). *Mental health system transformation: Bridging science and service*. Bethesda, MD: National Institute of Mental Health.

Powers of the federal government. (2006). Street Law and the Supreme Court Historical Society. Available from www.landmarkcases.org.

Public hospital at Colonial Williamsburg. (2006). Colonial Williamsburg Foundation. Available from www.history.org/Almanack/places/hb/hbhos.cfm.

Pumphrey, R. E., & Pumphrey, M. W. (1961). *Heritage of American social work*. New York: Columbia University Press.

Regier, D. A., Farmer, M. E., Rae, D. S., Meyers, J. K., Kramer, M., Robins, L. N., et al. (1993). One-month prevalence of mental disorders in the United States and sociodemographic characteristics: The Epidemiologic Catchment Area study. *Acta Psychiatrica Scandinavica, 88*, 35–47.

Rice, D. P., & Miller, L. S. (1996). The economic burden of schizophrenia: Conceptual and methodological issues, and cost estimates. In M. Moscarelli, A. Rupp, & N. Sartorious (Eds.), *Handbook of mental health economics and health policy* (pp. 321–324). New York: Wiley.

Robins, L. N., & Regier, D. A. (1991). *Psychiatric disorders in America: The Epidemiological Catchment Area study*. New York: Free Press.

Rothman, D. (1970). *The discovery of the asylum*. Boston: Little, Brown.

Scheffler, R. M., & Miller, A. B. (1991). Differences in mental health service utilization among ethnic subpopulations. *International Journal of Law and Psychiatry, 14*, 363–376.

Scott, D. M. (1997). *Social policy and the image of the damaged Black psyche 1880–1996*. Chapel Hill: University of North Carolina Press.

Sharfstein, S. S. (2000). Whatever happened to community mental health? *Psychiatric Services, 51*, 61–620.

Stoesz, D., & Karger, H. J. (1993). Deconstructing welfare: The Reagan legacy and the welfare state. *Social Work, 38*, 619–628.

Stoudemire, A., Frank, R. G., & Hedemark, N. (1986). The economic burden of depression. *General Hospital Psychiatry, 8*, 387–394.

Substance Abuse and Mental Health Services Administration. (2005). *Transforming mental health care in America* (Rep. No. SMA-05-4060). Rockville, MD: U.S. Department of Health and Human Services.

Substance Abuse and Mental Health Services Administration. (2005). *Transforming mental health care in America: The federal action agenda: First steps* (Rep. No. SMA-05–4060). Rockville, MD: U.S. Department of Health and Human Services.

Substance Abuse and Mental Health Services Administration. (2006a). *Mental health transformation state incentives grant program*. Rockville, MD: Author. Available from www.samhsa.gov/matrix/mhst_ta.aspx.

Substance Abuse and Mental Health Services Administration. (2006b). *National expenditures for mental health services and substance abuse treatment 1991–2001*. Rockville, MD: Author. Available from www.samhsa.gov/spendingestimates/chapter 4.aspx.

Sutton v. United Airlines, Inc., 527 U.S. 471, 130 F. 3rd 893 (1999).

Takeuchi, D. T., & Cheung, M. K. (1998). Coercive and voluntary referrals: How ethnic minority adults get into mental health treatment. *Ethnicity and Health, 3*, 149–158.

Thomas, A. R. (1998). Ronald Reagan and the commitment of the mentally ill: Capital, interest groups, and the eclipse of social policy. *Electronic Journal of Sociology*. Retrieved June 27, 2007, from www.sociolkogy.org/content/vol003.004/thomas.html.

Timbe, J. W., Horvitz-Lennon, M., Frank, R. G., & Normand, S. L. T. (2006). A meta-analysis of labor supply effects of interventions for major depressive disorder. *Psychiatric Services, 57*, 212–218.

United States of America v. Morrison et al., 529 U.S. 598 (2000).

Unutzer, J., Schoenbaum, M., & Druss, B. (2006). Transforming mental health care at the interface with general medicine: Report for the President's New Freedom Commission for Mental Health. *Psychiatric Services, 57*, 37–47.

U.S. Congress. (1787, September 17). Constitution of the United States, 10th Amendment.

U.S. Congress. (1790, March 24). The Naturalization Act of 1790. 1 Stat.103-104.

U.S. Congress. (1946). The National Mental Health Act. Pub. L. 79-487.

U.S. Congress. (1955, July 28). Mental Health Study Act of 1955. Pub. L. 94-182, 487.

U.S. Congress. (1960). Civil Rights Act of 1960.

U.S. Congress. (1963). Mental Retardation Facilities and Community Mental Health Centers Construction Act of 1963. Pub. L. 88-164.

U.S. Congress. (1964). Civil Rights Act of 1964.

U.S. Congress. (1965a). Civil Rights Act of 1965, The Voting Rights Act of 1965.

U.S. Congress. (1965b, July 1). Hart-Celler Act (Immigration and Naturalization Act of 1965).

U.S. Congress. (1965c). *Medicaid: Institutions for mental diseases*. Pub. L. 89-197, 42 CFR 441.

U.S. Congress. (1967). Mental Health Amendments of 1967. Pub. L. 90-31.

U.S. Congress. (1968). Civil Rights Act of 1968: Fair Housing Act of 1968.

U.S. Congress. (1980). Civil Rights of Institutionalized Persons Act.

U.S. Congress. (2005). Americans with Disabilities Act.

U.S. Department of Health and Human Services. (1999). *Mental health: A report of the surgeon general*. Rockville, MD: U.S. Department of Health and Human Services, Substance Abuse and Mental Health Services Administration, and National Institute of Mental Health.

U.S. Department of Health and Human Services. (2001). *Mental health: Culture, race, and ethnicity—A supplement to mental health: A report of the surgeon general.* Rockville, MD: U.S. Department of Health and Human Services, Substance Abuse and Mental Health Services Administration, Center for Mental Health Services.

Virginia State Department of Mental Hygiene and Hospitals. (1960). *Central State Hospital, 1865–1960.* Richmond, VA: Author.

Wang, P. S., Demler, O., Olfson, M., Pincus, H. A., Wells, K. B., & Kessler, R. C. (2006). Changing profiles of service sectors used for mental health care in the United States. *American Journal of Psychiatry, 163,* 1187–1198.

Wang, P. S., Lane, M., Olfson, M., Pincus, H. A., Wells, K. B., & Kessler, R. C. (2005). Twelve-month use of mental health services in the United States. *Archives of General Psychiatry, 62,* 629–640.

Witmer, A. H. (1891). Insanity in the colored race in the United States. *Alienist and Neurologist, 12,* 19–30.

World Health Organization. (2000). *The world health report 2000: Health systems—Improving performance.* Geneva, Switzerland: Author.

World Health Organization. (2001). *The world health report 2001: Mental health—New understanding, new hope.* Geneva, Switzerland: Author.

World Health Organization. (2004). *The world health report 2002: Changing history.* Geneva, Switzerland: Author.

Wyatt v. Stickney 325 F. Supp 781 (M.D. Ala. 1971), 334 F. Supp. 1242 (M. D. Ala. 1971), 344 F. Supp. 373 (M.D. Ala. 1972) sub nom Wyatt v. Aderholt, 503 F. 2d 1305 (5th Cir. 1974). (1971).

Zane, N. W. S., Takeuchi, D. T., & Young, K. N. J. (1994). *Confronting critical health issues of Asian and Pacific Islander Americans.* Thousand Oaks, CA: Sage.

Chapter 10

AGING IN THE UNITED STATES: CHALLENGES TO SOCIAL POLICY AND POLICY PRACTICE

Enid Opal Cox

For decades gerontologists in the United States, Europe, Japan, and elsewhere, in economically advantaged capitalist and socialist countries, as well as gerontologists who were working with nongovernmental organizations such as Help Age International (Tout, 1989) and governmental organizations serving India, China, and other developing countries, have advocated for attention to the increasing numbers of older persons. These advocacy efforts have focused on both the needs of older adults as well as issues related to their societal roles. At the turn of the century, the dramatic increase in the number of older adults in countries around the world, the increasing percentage of national populations represented by those 65 and older, increased longevity, concerns about the dependency ratio, and, to a lesser extent, growing diversity within this older population—both worldwide and within national jurisdictions—have generated attention (Takamura, 2001; Wells & Taylor, 2001). Questions are being asked with greater frequency in the political arena concerning the potential social, economic, and political impact of these demographic changes.

In the United States, a recent profile of statistics regarding adults over 65 provides the following data:

- In 2004, there were 36.3 million adults 65 and over (12.4% of the total population); in 2030, there will be an estimated 71.5 million (approximately 20% of the total population; Administration on Aging [AoA], 2006).
- The 85+ population is expected to rise from 6.1 million in 2010 to 7.3 million in 2020 (AoA, 2006).
- In 2004, 18.1% of those 65+ were members of ethnic minority populations. Of these, 8.2% were African Americans; 6.0% persons of Hispanic origin; approximately 2.9% Asian or Pacific Islanders; and fewer than 1% American Indian or Native Alaskans (AoA, 2006).
- Projections for 2050 suggest that, of a total population of 65+ (80.1 million), 65 million will be White (non-Hispanic), 12.5% Hispanic, 8.4% African American, and 6.7% other ethnic populations (Hooyman & Kiyak, 2005).

The aging of America and countries around the world is a mark of success and a challenge:

> For most of recorded history, average life expectancy at birth was less than 30 years. By 1900, average life expectancy in the United States had reached nearly age 50, and by 2000 it had reached age 74 for men and 80 for women. These vast improvements can be traced to a wide array of nutritional and environmental factors as well as advances in medicine. Recent advances in medical care, particularly surrounding the detection and treatment of heart disease, have led to marked increases in life expectancy after 65. (Friedland & Summer, 2005, p. v)

On the one hand, we can expect increased longevity with better health; on the other hand, long life has meant increased years of disability and need for care for some elders, especially those over the age of 85.

Unfortunately, the political discourse is currently characterizing the aging population dynamic as a "crisis" around the world, often requiring the preferred neoliberal solution of social welfare cuts. Fears in the United States regarding public expenditures that support older Americans have been widely expressed, as resources directed to war and other economic conditions lead to increased national deficits.

In response to this crisis imagery, Friedland and Summer (2005) caution that society's future is not determined solely by demographic changes. In their analysis, the role of economic productivity, changes in health status and behaviors, changes in workforce participation of older adults, and related public policy decisions are identified as key determinants of the impact of aging on societies. A focus on these factors as well as population growth is important to advocates of policy that addresses aging societies.

The purpose of this chapter is to provide an overview of the nature and content of social policy and social services targeting older Americans, with attention to implications for social workers engaged in policy practice. The larger political and moral economy is briefly introduced as critical to the understanding of aging issues and policy in the United States. In addition, key content of policy and social and moral debate in the United States that has direct impact on policy development is explored. The specific policy overview and discussion section is limited to key policies and policy trends in selected areas of special concern to older adults, such as income, employment, health care, housing, transportation, and the resulting network of health and social services.

THE POLITICAL AND MORAL ECONOMY CONTEXT OF AGING SOCIETIES

Any exploration of the aging of societies and social policy and programs, developed in response to needs and/or strengths of older adults, requires recognition of the larger political, moral, and economic context (D. Cox & Pawar, 2006). McMichael (2000, p. xxxvii) notes, "We can no longer understand changes in our society without situating them globally." The resources, technology, policies, and interventions designed to meet human needs will increasingly be related to international impact on national political economies. The relative power of internationalization on policy decisions will be related to the depth of integration of economies through the globalization movement. Gerber (1999,

p. 9) offers the following definition of shallow and deep integration that suggests the potential power of this movement:

> Shallow integration is the elimination or reduction of tariffs, quotas, and other border-related barriers, such as customer procedures that restrict the flow of goods across borders. Deep integration is the elimination, reduction, or alteration of domestic polices when they have the unintended consequences of acting as trade barriers. Major examples include labor and environmental standards, investment regulation, the rules of fair competition between firms, and allowable forms of government support for private industry.

The trend toward deep integration is evident in the regulations of such institutions as the International Monetary Fund and the World Bank, coupled with regional trade alliances. Rapid development in technology, with respect to communication and other devices that facilitate international production systems, internationalization of the labor market, and intelligence, provide strong support for deep integration (Friedman, 2005).

Proponents of the rapid advance of globalization of a laissez-faire market system tout the ability of this process to raise the standard of living of countries with less-developed economies and suggest that this process is an inevitable change (Macarov, 2003). However, opponents warn of the current and future potential of this form of globalization of markets to increase poverty around the world in both industrialized and postindustrial nations and economically less-developed countries (Macarov, 2003).

Often using the rationale of international economic development, the United States, Europe, and Japan have adopted the politics of neoliberalism. This shift in philosophy, which promotes less government, less skepticism toward business, cooperation with the needs of a global laissez-faire market system, and a higher degree of individual responsibility for meeting human needs (especially in the United States), provided the framework for social welfare change during the 1980s and 1990s. During the second Bush administration, the United States has shifted into a framework of neoconservatism and cultural conservatism that promotes radical privatization of social welfare programs and stronger government regulation of social and moral values and issues, such as attacking the separation of government and religion (Hart, 2006). These shifts, coupled with government deficits (related to changing economic factors and military expenditures), have strong implications for present and future aging policy in the United States (Estes, 2001a; Gilbert & van Voorhis, 2003; Karger & Stoesz, 2005; Leonard, 1997).

The changes we see in social welfare programs in the United States and elsewhere are a product of the current process of internationalization of economies plus national political, social, and economic factors. Together, these elements are producing or promoting

- Deep cuts in social welfare programs
- Devolution (shifting responsibility to lower levels of government)
- Privatization of social programs (shifting responsibility to private for-profit and not-for-profit firms and organizations)
- Shifting of responsibility to individuals and families
- Deregulation

Social policy targeting older adults in the United States is being developed and modified in the context of these trends as well as other factors unique to the United States. The social construction of aging in the United States has taken directions that define the particular policy and service approaches that exist. Ongoing changes in the discourse concerning older adults will continue to have an important role in future policy. The following section provides a discussion of the political and moral economy of aging in the United States and other related social processes that provide the specific framework for aging policy.

CHANGING SOCIAL PERCEPTIONS, EXPECTATIONS, AND POLICIES

Inherent in the social change process are the social construction of issues and related discourses (Leonard, 1997). Robertson (1999, p. 81) stresses that the concept of moral economy is broader than the concepts of rights and needs in that it "is as much about our obligations to one another as it is about the claims we are entitled to make against each other." This section briefly reviews a few prevalent historical perceptions regarding the status of older adults. It also discusses selected dimensions of the current discourse regarding perceptions of older adults, including their social roles and issues related to resource allocation in an aging society. Other key factors, reflecting issues that have been raised regarding future policy targeting older adults, are also noted, including ageism and age discrimination, diversity within the aging population, and the potential of technological development. These factors provide the context for a number of specific policy areas affecting older adults in the United States and are strongly influenced by overall factors in the political economy described earlier.

The medicalization of aging, political and moral perceptions regarding the nature and appropriateness of roles of older adults, and perceptions of fair entitlement of older adults to public resources are particularly relevant to understanding the moral economy of aging in the United States. Rapid change in the political economy, coupled with the ongoing concern about population increase, has spurred an escalated attention to these aspects of aging. In turn, the social and moral context of aging has had strong impact on past policy in aging and will have important influence on future policy.

Medicalization of Aging

Perhaps the most powerful stranglehold on aging policy, the meaning of aging, and the status of older persons in the United States has been and continues to be the widely accepted social construction of aging as a medical problem. This view of aging presumes medical solutions to the issue of aging. Estes, Wallace, Linkins, and Binney (2001, p. 46) note, "The biomedical model emphasizes the etiology, clinical treatment and management of disease of the elderly as defined and treated by medical practitioners while giving marginal attention to the social and behavioral process and problems."

The power of the medical-industrial complex has not only guided social policy discourse and mobilized large percentages of government and private resources targeting older adults into the provision of health-care services and health-related research; it has also assured the dominance of the medical model in service provision. The medical model is essentially characterized by diagnosis and focus on illness, the expectancy that professionals will cure the illness, and compliance expectations by medical professionals (Ambrosino, Heffernan,

Shuttlesworth, & Ambrosino, 2005; Atchley & Barusch, 2004; Manning, 1998). This model has dominated the scope of sanctioned social work services and the nature of social work interventions available to older adults in an ever-expanding arena of settings. Its impact will be further addressed in the discussion regarding social services and social work policy practice.

Estes et al. (2001, p. 49) provide critical understanding of the role of the commodification of health care as another contextualizing factor contributing to the medical impact on aging policy. They define commodification as "the process of taking a good or service that has been produced and used, but not bought or sold, and turning it into an item that is exchanged for money." This process includes the shift of health care from the arena of social needs and rights to a source of private profit. Related to the issue of health care and profit is the complication of the increasing tendency to associate older adults with the overall problems of health care costs in the United States. Specifically, political commentary often blames older Americans for the high health-care expenditures of the public sector, without taking into consideration private sector factors involved in those high costs.

Older Adults, Status, Roles, and Resources

Historical reviews present a complex picture of the status of older adults over time in the United States. Status changes, in general, are primarily related to the labor market or economic productivity capacity of older persons in the context of overall changes associated with modernization, including factors such as (a) size of the labor pool, (b) physical demands of available work, (c) importance of experience as a factor in worker productivity, and (d) ability to adapt to new technology and workplace structures, such as larger bureaucracies (Barusch, 2006). It is important to note that social policy initiated on behalf of the elderly has often been in response to needs of the economy rather than the elders. For example, the Social Security Act (1935), passed into law in 1936, was initiated in large part to shrink the labor market in a time of great unemployment.

Fostered by the Industrial Revolution, many European countries began to institutionalize retirement through government pensions, with the United States following with the introduction of Social Security in 1935 (Moody, 2006). Many sociologists and historians have argued that, between 1950 and 1970, retirement was increasingly considered a widely accepted social process. Retirement became popularly viewed as a "natural" process, representing a reward for long periods of economic contribution or payment of deferred wages. Other observers have contended that retirement's strong development was due to its usefulness as a tool for business to control its labor pool. Retirement was also widely associated with the idea that ability to continue working was diminished for older workers (Moody, 2006; Phillipson, 1999).

Another area of the historical political and moral economy, strongly relevant to the elderly and social policy in the United States, has been the status of older Americans with respect to public assistance. Over time, older adults have enjoyed a position of lesser stigma with respect to need for and use of public resources. The poor elderly were among the "worthy poor," as documented by historical accounts of social welfare in England and the United States (Axinn & Stern, 2005; Day, 2003). However, this status did not guarantee adequate governmental support, as evidenced by consistently low levels of assistance, placement in poorhouses, and consistently high levels of poverty among older people in the

United States, which persisted through the 1950s (Applebaum & Payne, 2005; Day, 2003; Hudson, 2005).

Advocates for older adults in the 1930s were able to use this "worthy poor" status in addition to labor issues to facilitate the Social Security Act, passed into law in 1936, and the passage of several contextualizing policy initiatives during the 1960s and 1970s. Among these policy initiatives were Medicare and Medicaid (1965), and the Older Americans Act (1965). Additionally, other resources, including income, health and social services, employment, housing, and a wide variety of senior discounts, were initiated at all levels of government and by nongovernmental not-for-profit agencies (Binstock, 2004).

In the late 1970s the political tide had turned to neoliberal perspectives, and both the economic and health status of older adults showed improvement. Consequently, the long-accepted tenet of age as a key criterion for eligibility for social welfare began to come under scrutiny (Hudson, 1997).

Questions concerning both need and worthiness of older Americans became part of political discourse, and a number of political and academic knowledge-based movements or agendas were initiated during the 1980s and 1990s that challenged the social construction of aging and older adults. These activities generated important challenges that continue to linger in current political debate specific to older adults. Such challenges were fueled by the "crisis" concept of population aging in the United States, economic stagnation, war-related deficits, and popular acceptance of the assumption of powerlessness of national governments to make decisions that were not controlled by the dictates of competition in a global economy. Thus issues regarding the status of older adults with respect to (a) social welfare entitlements and other benefits, (b) changing role expectations, (c) attention to diversity in the aging population, (d) identifying the nature of ageism in the United States, and (e) attention to the potential role of technology were added to the political arena.

Changing Perceptions of Older Adults and Social Welfare

The need to quell the popularity of age-based programs fit both neoliberal and neoconservative agendas. An overall concern with increasing numbers of older adults (the aging of "baby boomers"), together with decreased public resources and increasing concern about Social Security, Medicare, and Medicaid costs, have provided a supportive environment for challenging the social construction of older Americans as a worthy group for collective support.

Social Welfare Worthiness of the Elderly

In the 1980s, a well-financed campaign was launched that sought to frame social welfare issues as a contest between the elderly and the young (Atchley & Barusch, 2004; E. O. Cox & Parsons, 1994). Popular media began to support a shift of perceptions of older adults from a "needy and worthy population" to a "greedy population." Stories and cartoons of extravagant recreational pursuits of retired persons flooded the popular press. One cartoon, for example, depicted elderly individuals traveling in a car with bumper stickers that said "We are spending our children's inheritance." "Wealth and waste" was the essence of the message concerning the status and morality of older adults (Stoller & Gibson, 2000).

A political movement supporting this perspective, the intergenerational equity movement initiated in the mid-1980s, gave organized political and policy articulation to creating the "old versus young debate" surrounding public policy support for older adults. Social Security and Medicare were obvious targets for this perspective. The older population was portrayed as taking too much from existing public resources and being the cause of the poverty of children in the United States (Minkler, 2006).

Overall, these efforts challenged both the need premise for public support of older adults and their assumed moral worthiness, which had been based primarily on economic and social contributions though lifelong work. The extent to which these efforts increased intergenerational conflict requires further investigation. However, the failure of neoconservative efforts to severely cut Social Security and Medicare to this point in time, the great amount of long-term care assistance provided by families to their elderly members, and the addition of drug benefits to Medicare raise questions about the effectiveness of this movement. Hudson (2005, p. 322) states that "although there remained no evidence that generational tensions had permeated the thinking of the general public, it became common if not accepted knowledge in policy circles that aging benefits had to be reined in." Additionally, few data have been gathered regarding the impact this propaganda has had on state, local, and not-for-profit resource decisions. In many arenas this issue may not be as dead as it is assumed to be by some gerontologists.

The effort to change the general image of older persons from a worthy population to a greedy population who represents a burden to children was in part responsible for efforts to counter this imagery. Two such efforts, largely initiated in academic circles, were the successful aging and the productive aging movements.

Successful Aging   Gerontologists, interested primarily in challenging negative or false perceptions of older adults and increasing the role potential in late life, worked to advance more positive images of this older group based on their research and advocacy interests. One such effort was the concept of successful aging, defined in a MacArthur Foundation study as a combination of (a) good physical heath, (b) high cognitive functioning, and (c) continuing participation in social activity at a high level (Rowe & Kahn, 1997). Although this image of optimum success for older adults drew considerable support, especially from the medical profession, criticisms were quick to follow. Such appraisals included the challenge that achievement of these criteria was based on middle-class values, including staying young and related structural opportunities. Class, cultural differences, and conditions over one's lifetime had not been considered in the definition of successful aging (Hooyman & Kiyak, 2005; Rowe & Kahn, 1997).

Productive Aging   The concept of productive aging was advanced in a similar attempt to focus attention on the facts that most elderly people are productive, society must provide structural access to valuable roles for older adults, and the opportunity to participate in valued roles enhances health and mental health (Caro, Bass, & Chen, 2006; Morrow-Howell, 2006). Caro et al. defined productive aging as follows: "Productive aging is any activity by an older individual that produces goods or services or develops the capacity to produce them, whether they are to be paid for or not" (p. 247). These scholars acknowledge that their definition differs from other definitions that have included activities of personal enrichment. Holstein (1999) calls attention to a fourth dimension of the productive aging discussion. Based on her analysis, the focus on productive aging as a movement "affirms a cultural ideal: It is good and desirable for U.S. culture to evaluate productivity as a ruling metaphor for a 'good' old age" (p. 359). This aspect of productive aging has resulted in criticisms similar to those of successful aging, especially regarding the way the advancement of this concept as a goal for late life relates to minority ethnic populations, women, and those with fewer economic resources and lifelong limited access to labor-market-related productivity (Holstein, 1999; Hooyman & Kiyak, 2005).

In the long run, even with many attempts to make productivity an inclusive term, the historical linkage of this term to market productivity is likely to prevail. The important goal of promoting productive aging, as an effort to increase knowledge about the contributions of older adults to society and the need to remove barriers to these contributions, may be offset by a politically inspired dictate to older adults that they must be engaged in productive market-related labor as their primary, socially acceptable role. This perception also justifies cuts in aging-related social welfare programs.

Challenge to the Social Institution Status of Retirement

Closely related to efforts to characterize older adults as healthy and able is the political-social movement to delegitimize the institution of retirement. As discussed earlier, retirement enjoyed increasing status as a social institution around the world from the 1950s through the 1980s, especially in economically developed societies. In the United States, for example, acceptance of retirement is indicated by a substantial change in the 65+ employed population, from 54.7% in 1950 (Moody, 2006) to 14.4% in 2004 (AoA, 2006). Even though there was a push for early retirement during the 1980s and somewhat during the 1990s, concurrently there was a growing concern about the economic feasibility of retirement. During the first decade of the twenty-first century, we are witnessing a challenge to the acceptability of retirement as a social institution. This challenge is based on the assumed better health and economic status and ability to work of older adults, fears about the ability of governments to continue their current levels of support of income and health care for older adults, and questions about the potential need for older adults in the labor force (Atchley & Barusch, 2004; Ghilarducci, 2006; Hudson, 1997; Moody, 2006).

Ageism and Age Discrimination

The nature and depth of ageism and age discrimination in the United States requires further study, but significant evidence exists to suggest the strong prevalence of many different forms and settings related to these two concepts (Atchley & Barusch, 2004; Butler, 2006; Cohen, 2001; Palmore, 2005). Studies also affirm that numerous older adults have internalized many of the cultural stereotypes held by other age groups. Historically, discrimination in employment has been the primary academic focus regarding age discrimination. The powerful imagery of "aging as progressive decline" provided support, in addition to economic factors, for the development of mandatory retirement beginning in the 1920s and has continued to be a factor in other decisions negatively impacting older workers (Butler, 2006; Novak, 2006).

A comprehensive report conducted in 2006 under the direction of Robert Butler has identified many forms of age discrimination in key areas of concern to older adults. The following examples of these findings illustrate their potential significance to aging-related policy:

- One to 3 million Americans age 65 and older have been abused by someone they depend on for care, and over 5 million are estimated to be victims of financial exploitation each year.
- Nine out of 10 nursing homes are inadequately staffed.
- Of workers 65 and over, 16.9% perceive that they experienced work-related discrimination in 2002.
- Only 10% of people age 65 and over receive appropriate screening tests for bone density, colorectal and prostate cancer, and glaucoma, despite their increased susceptibility to these conditions (Butler, 2006).

These examples represent only a few of those identified in the report and do not include the elaborate array of prejudicial attitudes (ageism), including (a) treatment in daily life of older adults as mentally disabled (e.g., asking younger individuals what the older customers they are accompanying want), (b) negative media portrayals, (c) the ignoring of ideas presented by older adults, and (d) forced societal disengagement (Atchley & Barusch, 2004). The increasing awareness of the comprehensiveness and complexity of age discrimination in the United States challenges issues related to the work and retirement agenda and efforts to provide older adults access to a range of meaningful roles in the postmodern social structure.

Recognition of Diversity in the Aging Population

Perhaps the most significant dimension of aging in the United States beyond demographics is the increasing diversity among older adults and its implications for public policy. The multiple facets of diversity within the older adult population, including class, age, sex, ethnicity, and health status, have become more widely recognized as critical factors in today's policy arenas (Dressel, Minkler, & Yen, 1999; Hudson, 1997; Torres-Gil, 2001). Age-based policy development during the 1960s and 1970s primarily utilized chronological age, usually 55, 60, 62, or 65, as the basis for eligibility for public resources. This universal approach was supplemented by a number of selective or means-based programs, such as Supplemental Security Insurance (SSI) and Medicaid.

As attention is called to the strengths and needs of different groups within the aging population, profound differences in the ability to meet basic needs will be identified. Estes (2001b, p. 13) notes that, from a political economy perspective, "social policy for the aged mirrors the structural arrangements in the U.S. society and the distribution of material, political, and symbolic resources within it." Advocates for older adults face an intensifying challenge to preserve universal programs, while at the same time meeting social justice mandates to assure that basic needs are met for all older adults. Questions regarding adequacy, appropriateness, and accessibility of social welfare provisions must be continually evaluated and addressed. In sum, it is evident that diversity within the aging population, as in society as a whole, will have a significant impact on social policy, especially within the confines of increasing globalization and neoconservative and/or neoliberal political approaches.

Potential Role of Technology

The future role of technology in the lives of older Americans has generated the interest of both the pubic and private for-profit sectors. The primary focus of development of technology for older adults has targeted issues of disability and frailty as well as assisting caregivers (Charness, 2005; SPRY [Setting Priorities for Retirement Years] Foundation, 2005; Takamura, 2001). Technology assistance for caregivers includes, for example, a wide range of monitoring devices, technological setups to allow virtual house calls, electronically linked systems for contact with emergency services, systems to allow more intense inter-action with care providers (including a variety of over-the-phone medication monitoring), and services that assist with a patient's physical self-care, such as advanced-capacity wheelchairs. The primary aim has been to facilitate institutional activities of daily living.

Some advocates suggest a much greater potential for technology in other aspects of older Americans' lives. Most important, they identify the need to enhance the knowledge and skills of older adults with respect to use of technology. In 2002, only 17% of adults over 50 used the Internet (Center for Research and Education on Aging and Technology Enhancement, 2002). The education of older adults, access to computers, and making computers more user-friendly represent significant challenges. However, the quest for independence in late life will continue to be strongly related to older adults' ability to access and use computers and other technological devices.

Coughlin and Lau (2006a) suggest an integrated approach to technological develop-ment targeting older adults, including the following areas of development: (a) health, (b) safety, (c) connectivity, (d) contribution, and (e) legacy. Health and safety interventions include those suggested earlier, whereas connectivity technology would encompass com-munications with a broader range of purposes, such as entertainment, transportation, and development of livable communities. Contribution and legacy technological development refer to education-, workplace-, and cognitive-enhancement technologies, as well as cross-generational learning enhancement.

The challenge to independence and privacy that may well come with increased surveillance is an issue that has been raised by many older adults as well as gerontologists. Surveillance capacity has greatly increased and can monitor almost every movement and activity in one's home or in an institution. Coughlin and Lau (2006b, p. 3) state the issue as follows:

> Although the potential benefits of these technology applications are many, the important question of privacy remains. How we can maintain independent lives while preserving our health and safety as we age is the essential tension in introducing and financing many innovations. Who decides: How is the data managed, to whom is it reported, and under what conditions? These are just a few of the questions raised by existing and emerging technologies in some homes today and in all our lives tomorrow.

These questions will have ongoing impact on policy decisions in many arenas of aging policy. The following section provides a brief overview of issues and policy trends in selected areas of aging policy and an overview and analysis of issues in health and social services in aging. The social issues and changes described will be important factors in social policy specific to the need of older adults.

OVERVIEW OF SELECTED POLICY AND SERVICES TARGETING OLDER ADULTS

From a political economy perspective, the interconnectedness of international, national, and local policy is evident. Indeed, an attempt to distinguish aging policy from general political and economic or social welfare policy requires constant awareness of this background. In addition, any overview of aging-related policy exposes an array of policy arenas too comprehensive for the boundaries of this chapter. The following is a discussion of selected policy areas that addresses specific common needs of older adults and selected key policies related to these areas. The policy areas selected are income, employment, health, housing, and transportation, as well as an overview of other supportive and social services, including the contribution of the Older Americans Act.

Current issues in aging policy in the United States reflect the trends, discussed earlier, of privatization, social welfare cuts, devolution, and deregulation. In addition, historical characteristics of U.S. social welfare provision, including shared responsibility among the federal government, state government, and private sector (for-profit and not-for-profit) as well as individual and family responsibility (emphasized to an ever-greater degree), have been made increasingly complex by these larger trends. This is discussed further in the overview of health and social services, outlined later in this section.

Income Issues in Late Life and Related Policies

Most older Americans are concerned about adequate income in late life. In fact, according to Ekerdt (2004), adults of all ages are becoming increasingly aware of the need to save for retirement, even to the detriment of other needs. Retirement income for older adults most frequently comes from four sources: Social Security, work, pensions, and savings, supplemented by means-tested programs such as Supplemental Security Insurance (SSI) for individuals with very low income and resources.

The relationship of these sources of income to need is complex. Income policy provides an example of Estes's (2001b) contention, noted earlier, that policy tends to reinforce life-long inequities. Higher income and social status throughout one's life span allow for higher accumulation of Social Security income, higher savings rates, and better employment opportunities before and after retirement age. Sources of income reported by older persons in 2003 include Social Security (90%), income from assets (56%), private pensions (30%), government employee pensions (14%), and earnings (23%). Of these sources, Social Security benefits accounted for 39% of the aggregate income of the older population; for one-third of these older adults, Social Security accounted for 90% or more of their income. Earnings accounted for 25% of this population's income, asset income 14%, and pensions 19%. Access to these sources of income is strongly influenced by class, sex, education, and ethnic status (Social Security Administration, 2004).

A critical look at statistics regarding income and need, especially cost of living, is required to guide future policy advocacy. Specific to those 65 and over, the 2006 federal poverty line is $9,800 for individuals and $13,200 for couples (U.S. Department of Health and Human Services, 2006). In 2004, 9.8% of this older population was reported at or below the poverty line, and another 16.7% was at or below 125% of the poverty line—$12,250 for individuals and $16,500 for couples. In 2004, the median income for older individuals was $21,102 for males and $12,080 for females (AoA, 2005). These income amounts have little meaning separated from the costs of basic need (housing, utilities, food, and medical expense not covered by other funds). Some estimates suggest that as many as one-third of American families have difficulty meeting daily needs. See, for example, Ehrenreich's (2002) publication regarding everyday needs.

Furthermore, there is great diversity with respect to the gravity of poverty and which population groups among adults 65+ are represented in poverty. For example, 5.8% of individuals over 65 have less than $5,000, 49.4% have less than $14,999, and over 30% of households headed by these older Americans have annual incomes under $24,999. Ethnic diversity in income distribution, related to elders with income below the poverty line, includes for example, 7.5% of Whites (non-Hispanic) compared to 23.9% of African Americans, 18.7% of Hispanic Americans, and 13.1% of Asian Americans over 65 (AoA, 2005). These statistics indicate that a large percentage of older persons have cause for serious concern about the adequacy of their late-life income. Need and income is also complicated by extremely high medical costs that can quickly decimate wealth.

Advocates for older adults facing income deficiencies have begun to engage more aggressively in comparisons of the U.S. poverty line to cost of living in regions throughout the United States. Future policy related to poverty among older adults will no doubt focus on this discrepancy and the need to advocate for acceptance of a livable poverty guideline.

Current debates surrounding income policy target Social Security reform, the changing nature of pension systems and pension stability, and concerns about a variety of issues related to employment. The specific policy debates related to these issues are strongly influenced by the neoliberal-neoconservative political perspectives described earlier.

Social Security Issues

Social Security is currently a primary target for reform, based on these competing political perspectives. Social Security was created in the vortex of the Depression of the 1930s among many conflicting political agendas, including the need to remove older adults from the labor market and the desperate poverty of a "deserving population." Today, this perspective has been challenged, as noted earlier, by such factors as changing images of older adults, their increasing number, and their better health and economic status. Social Security has been a primary factor in this improved economic status.

The political arena presents the status of Social Security as being in crisis, framing the issue as an intergenerational equity debate rather than reflecting intergenerational interdependence and current economic circumstances, including the increasing government deficit—largely a result of the war in Iraq. Fueled by a neoconservative political perspective, opponents of Social Security in its present form have initiated proposals based on various degrees of privatization. Schieber (1997), for example, suggests a strategy that would allow a portion of Social Security taxes to be placed in individual investment accounts, while preserving a basic flat rate benefit ($410, in 1996-adjusted dollars), to be earned with 10 years of covered earnings. Politically, many supporters are concerned that this quasi-privatization approach will eradicate the social principle of government responsibility as well as a sense of mutual support inherent in the current system.

Opponents of basic changes in Social Security disagree with drastic predictions of the oncoming fiscal crisis in the program and suggest a number of moderate reforms, such as increasing the age of eligibility for full entitlement, basing the amount of entitlement on 38 years rather than 35 years of contribution, making small increases in payroll taxes, and increasing the percentage of Social Security benefits that are taxed (see, e.g., Bush, 2005; Herd, 2005; Schulz, 2001).

It is also important to note that this current policy debate regarding Social Security has taken the focus away from the issue of basic adequacy of the program for meeting the income needs of older adults—a guiding emphasis in the Social Security reforms of the 1970s and early 1980s. Increasing diversity among older adults will require that policy be modified to better meet the needs of these populations (e.g., women and populations with lower life expectancy) and the increasing progressive redistribution for low-income populations.

Supplemental Security Insurance, a public assistance program, was initiated in 1974 to provide a minimum income for the elderly, blind, and disabled persons with very limited income and assets ($2,000 for individuals, $3,000 for couples, in 2004). The 2006 income levels for eligibility are $603 for individuals and $903 for an eligible individual with an eligible spouse (Social Security Administration, 2005). Approximately 20% of SSI payments go to older adults (Applebaum & Payne, 2005). Cost containment, adequacy, changes in eligibility requirements to exclude individuals with alcohol or drug disability, ongoing immigrant status issues, and a very uncoordinated administration are the primary policy issues surrounding this program.

Private Pension Issues

In response to current economic changes, many private pension plans are facing challenges. For example, workers from several major corporations who had pension plans based on profit sharing have seen their pensions devastated by stock devaluations, mergers, and other changes. Workers owning 401-K and similar plans have also seen pension losses due to stock downturns. These problems have raised serious concerns among many older adults and occur at a time when public and private pension systems are changing from defined benefit plans, usually backed by the Pension Benefit Guaranty Corporation, to defined contribution plans, which increase personal risk for employees and pensioners. Defined benefit plans promise a specific amount of income at retirement, usually dependent on salary and years of service. Defined contribution plans are individual accounts composed of contributions from either the worker or the employer or both. The employee is then responsible for the outcomes of investment of these funds.

Public policy issues related to the government's role in monitoring these plans include, for example, lack of limits on profit-sharing systems, the high risk placed on employees, and the existence of fraud and other illegal practices. Related issues are the ever-changing government tax policy regarding pre- versus posttax saving opportunities for 401-K-type pension funds and individual retirement accounts (IRAs); taxing of pensions; and concerns about portability, inflation protection, and coverage of dependents.

Employment Issues

To address income issues of older adults, a wide range of employment issues must be addressed, such as age-based layoffs and age-based discrimination in training opportunities, promotion, and hiring. Among ways to remove the barriers to employment of older workers are the following two strategies: (1) provision of adequate research and administrative support to improve implementation of the Age Discrimination and Employment Act (ADEA) objectives and (2) resources to initiate innovative ways to retain older workers, such as the development of flexible- and/or reduced-hour systems, appropriate technology training, and continued support of current federal and state older workers' programs (Barnett, 2005; Butler, 2006; Hooyman & Kiyak, 2005).

Health Policy Issues

Health care is a primary concern of older Americans. Medicare, initiated in 1965 as a federal health-care insurance program for adults 65 and over, as well as some younger disabled persons, currently provides core coverage of hospital care; short-term rehabilitative nursing home care; home health and hospice care (part A); and supplemental medical insurance, a voluntary component (part B) of physicians' care.

Despite this very important program, most poor and middle-income older adults are deeply concerned about either ongoing uncovered costs of late-life health care or the potential cost of long-term institutional care in nursing homes or intensive in-home care services. Current costs of nursing home care range from $54,000 to over $72,000 per year, whereas the median wealth (with exception of home equity) of older adults, by income quartile from lowest to highest income, is estimated at $3,500, $29,532, $78,213, $124,733, and $328,432 (Social Security Administration, 2004).

Key areas of health policy of special concern to older adults are limitations and changes in Medicare, Medicaid, and long-term care resources and services. Policy debates in these arenas have overlapping, complementary, and different issues related to heath care and older adults. Both Medicare and Medicaid provide some resources for long-term care. Medicaid costs for nursing home care are of great concern.

Medicare Issues

Medicare policy concerns have historically included the fit between the chronic illnesses that are common among older adults and an acute medical model care system that is oriented toward curing acute illnesses through hospitalization, emergency care, surgical care, drugs, short-term intervention in physicians' offices, and so on. A number of changes have occurred aimed at this mismatch, including expansion of the program to include increased home health care (Hooyman & Kiyak, 2005). However, from a social work perspective, these changes fall far short of financial support for a social model of care. In addition, severe limitations on Medicare-funded home care continue to inhibit adequate psychosocial community services. Examples of such limitations are the requirement that eligible recipients of care be strictly homebound and that specific nursing care, physical therapy, and/or occupational therapy be a prerequisite for social services and the continuation thereof.

In addition to this ongoing core issue, there are an increasing number of policy issues surrounding Medicare: (a) political concerns about the increasing costs of the overall program; (b) increased pressure for privatization of the program as a whole and in part; (c) ever-increasing premiums, deductibles, and cuts in coverage (as cost-saving strategies); (d) mental health parity; (e) a variety of issues concerning access and quality related to the contracting of health maintenance organizations; (f) early discharge from hospitals related to prospective cost-containment strategies; (g) lack of coverage for dental and eye care; and (h) issues regarding structure, access, and adequacy of the Medical Prescription and Drug Act of 2003.

Medicaid Issues

Medicaid was initiated in 1965 to provide health care for low-income Americans and is funded by a combination of federal and state monies. States have a range of authority over program access and included services. Policy issues include (a) political concerns about rising costs (especially nursing home costs for older adults who either were initially eligible for Medicaid or spend down to eligibility, often due to loss of resources, mostly through nursing home costs); (b) cuts in eligibility of special populations, such as elderly immigrants and individuals with alcohol and/or drug addictions; and (c) concerns related to limited coverage and quality, similar to issues facing Medicare.

Long-Term Care Policy Issues

Issues surrounding long-term care policy encompass both long-term institutional care in nursing homes and intensive in-home care services that involve community-based long-term care. Such issues include (a) lack of a national policy that provides financial support for older adults requiring nursing home care and/or community-based care; (b) the ongoing struggle for resources between institutional and community-based long-term care; (c) the extremely high cost of care; (d) the critical shortage of care providers; (e) competency, training, and supervision of care providers; (f) the need to expand support for family and personal caregivers; (g) the need to support a wide range of institutional care supports, including the ongoing struggle between patients' rights and institutional monitoring functions; (h) the need to expand prevention and health-promotion interventions as well as other social and community interventions; and (i) the high cost and scant coverage of existing private, long-term care insurance policies (Hooyman & Kiyak, 2005).

Housing Policy Issues

Libson (2006, p. 9) writes, "A crisis exists for older Americans who need affordable housing and the crisis is getting worse." Among the challenging housing policy issues for older adults are (a) ongoing cuts in federal support for building affordable housing, (b) limited affordable housing vouchers and other forms of rental supplements since the 1980s, (c) the difficulty of relying on state and local affordable housing development, (d) increasing costs of rentals (including loss of existing affordable housing through mortgage maturation of federally financed building projects and related changes), and (e) lack of resources to sustain and renovate existing housing (Libson, 2006).

Clearly, the cost of housing is a significant challenge for many older Americans. According to the AoA (2005, p. 11):

> Of the 21.6 million households headed by older persons in 2003, the following situations existed: (a) 80% were owners and 20% renters, (b) median year of construction of the housing was 1965, (c) almost 73% of older homeowners owned their homes free and clear, and (d) the median values of this housing was $122,790.

In light of these statistics, issues surrounding maintenance and repair have become critical, in addition to those related to availability of appropriate housing and the cost of purchase or rental. Other salient issues pertaining to housing are associated with the linkage to potential health and social services and neighborhood and location considerations, such as transportation availability, safety of walking and shopping, nearness of supportive relationships, and unsympathetic or hostile neighbors.

A wide range of senior housing units have been developed by private and governmental resources during the past 25 years, leading to the development of an array of supportive services, both in housing settings and the community (e.g., food services, personal care and medication assistance, and housekeeping services; Wilson, 2005–2006). This expansion of senior-specific housing has also raised policy issues concerning age-segregated versus intergenerational housing settings, affordability, and level of monitoring (especially as health-related services become involved).

Transportation Issues

Policymakers do not consistently give much attention to transportation issues of older adults; however, this issue ranked third among concerns of delegates attending the 2005 White House Conference on Aging (Hudson, 2006). Transportation policy issues range from concerns about the abilities of older drivers and lack of public transportation (especially in suburban areas) to availability of special transportation programs to meet health and shopping needs. Again, the mix between public- and private-sector roles is central to many policy arguments as regards increasing costs, safety concerns, liability as a barrier to volunteer services, and the possible future role of technology.

Common Policy Directions

This brief look at selected policy issues affecting older adults demonstrates the interrelatedness of these policy areas and illustrates common trends. Such trends include (a) the predominant concern with cost, (b) cuts in programs or failure to keep up with increasing needs, (c) the need for attention to diverse circumstances of older adults, and (d) overall dominance of the medical model in resource allocation. These trends continue to have strong impact on income, housing, transportation, medical benefits, and other resources allocated to older adults in the United States.

Neoconservative solutions are proposed across policy areas, and the realities of need and lack of attention to special populations are not well-articulated on current politically accepted policy agendas. Policy that strongly supports older adults' strengths and targets ageism (including age discrimination) is not emphasized. Leaders in the gerontological community note the decline in effective advocacy for older adults' issues and strongly support the need to re-create effective advocacy approaches to assure quality of life for older adults in the United States (Rother, 2004; Stone, 2004).

Older Americans Act

The Older Americans Act (OAA) was passed in 1965. It established the following national objectives for all older Americans:

- An adequate income in retirement
- The best possible physical and mental health
- Suitable housing
- Full restorative services for those needing institutional care
- A broad range of community-based services
- Employment opportunities without discrimination
- Retirement in health and dignity, after years of contribution to the economy
- Access to participation in civic, cultural, educational, and training opportunities
- Access to a range of community-based supportive services
- Freedom, independence, and free exercise of individual initiative in planning and managing their own lives
- Participation in decision making regarding services
- Immediate benefit of aging-related research

These objectives have provided substantial support to advocacy efforts in ensuing decades.

Through grants to states and community programs, the OAA provides for the establishment and funding of a wide range of home- and community-based services under Title III. Multipurpose senior centers, congregate and home-delivered meals, case management, protective services, telephone reassurance, and caregiver support are among many more programs and services that have been funded. Title VII of this Act provides for state-administered ombudsman programs to assure residents' rights in nursing homes, assisted living facilities, boarding homes (with some limitations depending on the state), and elder abuse programs. Other titles of the Act fund separate programs for Native American reservations, employment programs, and research and training projects.

In addition, the OAA provides for the establishment of the AoA, currently located in the Department of Health and Human Services, charged with the responsibility of carrying out the core responsibilities of planning, advocacy, and mobilization of priority and innovative programs and services for older Americans related to these objectives. Furthermore, the AoA established an aging network, consisting of state offices on aging and, in most states, a number of regional agencies on aging. (Please refer to National Association of Area Agencies on Aging, 2006.)

Choices for Independence is an AoA-sponsored initiative that was included in the 2006 OAA reauthorization proposal. This initiative provides strong support and financial resources to states for expansion of consumer-directed care approaches to community-based, long-term care. Choices for Independence provides an example of the AoA approach to influencing health and social services and could provide opportunities for social work practitioners who are committed to empowerment and strengths practice models (Kunkel & Nelson, 2005).

It is important to note that AoA programs were never designed or funded at a level to meet the needs of all older adults, but rather to act as a catalyst for state and local development in addressing these needs. Great diversity exists in the programs that are available at local levels. Since initiated, AoA services have retained universal eligibility for programs; however, in recent decades, they have begun to target those most in need (income-based). Furthermore, in recent years, more focus has been given to medically related services. Overall, OAA represents a powerful tool in maintaining focus on the special needs and contributions of older adults. The leadership provided through the aging network has expanded and maintained this focus throughout the country during radically changing political eras.

Title XX Services

In the late 1950s and into the 1960s, social workers working in county departments of public assistance were able to provide a broad range of social services, including protective services and casework (case management) services regarding long-term, care-related issues that encompassed advocacy, education, finding resources, and work with elders and their families. However, since the mid-1970s, as noted earlier, aging services have primarily focused on medical approaches, funded through Medicare and Medicaid. Currently, Title XX of the Social Security Act provides a number of community-based social service programs. However, this program has lost funding over the years, and services for the elderly have been especially cut. Presently, most county departments of social service provide case management (often contracted to private providers), adult protective services, and a few other services to older adults with very limited income.

Characteristics of the Health and Social Service Delivery System

These overall policies and diverse programs for older adults have resulted in a service delivery system with the following characteristics:

- Change from entitlements to charity approaches or work requirements
- Predominance of medical model programs and services
- Services provided by one level of joint efforts or two or more levels of government, with increasing eligibility requirements and cuts in provisions
- Services provided by for-profit and not-for-profit organizations (funded by a variety of foundations and other charitable efforts, government contracts, and fees for service), with little coordination and leaving many gaps in service
- Categorical assistance versus universal programs that restrict access
- Complex and changing eligibility requirements designed to limit access

- Strong political focus on privatization strategies and cuts in social welfare
- Diversity in programs available, depending on geographical location
- Lack of attention to special needs and strengths of ethnic/cultural minorities, older women, those with least resources, and other diverse populations, as well as to the development of cultural competence in program planning and among providers

A comprehensive review of service delivery issues is not possible in the scope of this chapter to address the many issues facing health and social service design and implementation, or areas of concern such as rural versus urban concerns, the breadth of caregiver and care-receiver concerns, and other critical issues. However, the overall reinforcement of class differences and the increasing bipolarization of income and opportunity, noted by Estes (2001b), and the ongoing processes noted earlier relative to the globalization of the economy, plus U.S. economic circumstances, all suggest that turbulent times are ahead. New ways of meeting needs, forms of intervention, and a refocus on issues of social justice are among the directions we must pursue.

IMPLICATIONS FOR SOCIAL WORK POLICY PRACTITIONERS

The dynamic interface of international and national political and moral economies, the aging of societies around the world, and the ongoing struggle to address human needs and social justice raise many challenges and opportunities for social workers engaged in policy practice. The struggle to secure resources, protect the environment, and develop the necessary political power to achieve these goals will require new knowledge, skills, and strong commitment. History and current status suggest that special focus will be required to assure equity of older adults as this process evolves.

The social work profession has placed little emphasis on the older population during most of its history (Rosen & Zlotnik, 2001; Takamura, 2001). Recent efforts sponsored by the John A. Hartford Foundation and other contributors have resulted in increased attention to aging in social work education, faculty development, and research (Rosen & Zlotnik, 2001). However, a significant emphasis of this movement supports physical and mental health-related development. The potential for social work to assume leadership and expand interventions necessary to more fully address the many issues facing older adults will require expansion of these boundaries.

Several definitions can be found for social work-related policy practice. Jansson (1999, p. 10) defines policy practice as "efforts to change polices in legislative, agency and community settings whether by establishing new polices, improving existing ones, or defeating the policy initiatives of other people." Barusch (2006) emphasizes a wide variety of strategies that focus on assessment, analysis, and empowerment, such as advocacy, negotiation, compromise, coalition building and maintaining, and persuasive strategies. A challenge not fully addressed in most reviews of policy practice is the need for more knowledge about both micro- and macro-economics. The policy practice suggestions presented next are compatible with this broader range of activities and are inclusive of Jansson's arenas of focus, as well as use of an international perspective and facilitation of opportunity for social work.

Key Directions for a Policy Practice Agenda

Although numerous gerontological policy practice issues that require attention have been identified, only the following few overall recommendations for a social work policy practice agenda are presented here:

- Expand the political economy perspective of policy analysis and development of social welfare approaches and advocacy to include an international context.
- Work with coalitions to maintain and improve existing benefits for older adults, such as Social Security, Medicare, Medicaid, and OAA benefits.
- Work with members of oppressed populations within the older adult population to define strengths and needs and create culturally acceptable policy, including adequate resources.
- Develop a strong role in framing the debates concerning older adult policy.
- Create partnerships with older adults, their advocates, and mass-based organizations serving older adult agendas.
- Provide policy support to establish social work practice in critical arenas beyond medical and mental health model settings.
- Provide policy support for new models of practice and innovative interventions in all arenas of gerontological practice.
- Focus on adequate training and resources to apply state-of-the-art technology to policy practice efforts.

International Focus

Knowledge about national and international political-economy issues is increasingly related directly to social welfare issues at the national and local levels. Social workers need to be not only aware of current trends in the internationalization of economies and apparent outcomes, but also well informed about alternative visions and critiques of these directions. To provide leadership in addressing rationales for social welfare cuts, labor market changes, and other economic factors, social workers must be confident of their knowledge of economic issues and the range of alternatives. Moreover, gaining a comprehensive knowledge of social welfare policies and program strategies around the world, especially in aging-related areas, will become ever more important as various countries find creative ways to address long-term care needs and better integrate older adults into society.

Maintaining Existing Entitlements and Addressing Issues of Diversity

The future presents challenging agendas for advocates supporting the needs of older adults. In the context of increasing demand and diminishing resources, the struggle to maintain existing entitlements and other key programs, as well as identify and find ways to meet the needs of populations not adequately served by these programs, will encourage old and new debates regarding universal versus selective government provision. Long-time inequities will have to be addressed, and social justice strategies may be politically placed in competition with preservation of middle-class older adults. Leadership in policy action will require strong commitment and skills (Binstock, 2004).

Framing Debates Concerning Older Adult Policy

Selected current issues in aging-related policy, and the surrounding debates and assumptions concerning the nature of older adults and the political economy, have been discussed. Active assertions and remnants of these moral economy discourses, such as (a) the struggle to present a balanced perspective of older adults that includes strengths, contributions, and needs through the active and productive aging movements; (b) a focus on older adults as the cause of high medical costs; (c) a focus on intergenerational inequities rather than interdependence; and (d) the medicalization of aging, all continue to provide parameters of the discussion concerning aging in society and strongly affect policy issues and advocacy efforts.

Observing the changing political paradigms in the United States, Lakoff (2004) raises the issue of the critical need for reframing and proactive framing of current discourse to develop more progressive politics. He urges an aggressive participation in framing policy debate and suggests one example of a progressive think tank, the Rock Ridge Institute (2006), that is at work in this process.

Leonard (1997) provides comprehensive examples of the power of popular discourse in impacting and supporting social welfare and social policy in postmodern times. He recommends widespread efforts to develop a critical consciousness and multiple coalitions supporting an emancipatory project that promotes social justice as well as a political economy supportive of human need. Social work policy practitioners will need ever-increasing knowledge and skills in communication strategies and related technology as well as organizing and coalition-building skills to be effective participants in such a task.

Partnering with Older Adults, Other Advocates, and Mass-Based Organizations

Social work policy practitioners have knowledge and skills for organizing and developing partnerships with elderly and intergenerational constituencies to participate in the policy process. Additionally, partnerships can be developed with a wide range of existing membership-based senior organizations and related intergenerational groups, including organized associations representing ethnic minority elders, older women, and large membership organizations, such as the American Association of Retired Persons (AARP), Generations United, Health United States, and the Alliance for Retired Americans (ARA). These organizations, in addition to the many special interest groups addressing income, housing, and medical issues of older adults (e.g., the American Association of Homes and Services for the Aging [AHSA]), have well-funded research and policy advocacy components (Stone, 2004).

Social workers in policy practice must increase representation both in professional positions within these organizations and as members of boards and committees that govern policy activity. Such exposure will benefit the leadership capacity of the social work profession in gerontology.

Expanding Arenas of Social Work Practice in Gerontology

Policy practice targeting governments, private foundations, and organizations and agencies can be a major contributor to the development of opportunities for expansion of social work interventions in a wide variety of new settings and in settings in which social work is poorly represented. In addition to the development of more diverse settings, opportunities for implementation of new models of practice and practice approaches that are not often supported in existing settings must be supported in both new and existing social work settings. For example, promoting a better balance between medical and social services in nursing homes, hospitals, in-home care, and assisted-living facilities requires legislative support.

Today, aging newsletters are raising questions about older adults' willingness to be "cases" or "managed." A number of current practice models emphasize the strengths and resiliency of older adults, as well as acknowledging their capacity and current efforts as they continue to contribute to society (E. O. Cox & Chapin, 2001; Greene & Cohen, 2005; Silverstone, 2005). These models suggest the necessity of forming consultative partnerships in addressing late-life issues.

The development of settings that promote efficacy-building and partnership approaches to intervention can greatly enhance the partnerships with older adults critical to social action and policy change. Of particular note are (a) empowerment-oriented models that facilitate social action as an integral part of intervention outcomes, even those targeting elderly who require significant care to meet daily needs (E. O. Cox & Parsons, 1994; Gutierrez, Parsons, & Cox, 1998), and (b) community development interventions (Austin, Camp, Flux, McClelland, & Sieppert, 2005; Rosalynn Carter Institute for Caregiving, 2004). Policies and programs that focus on consumer-directed care (AoA, 2005), care-net development, self-care, naturally occurring retirement communities, health promotion, and a wide variety of senior volunteer programs also present opportunities for expansion of linkages and partnerships with older adults who can provide support for policy issues and efforts to frame policy discourse.

REFERENCES

Administration on Aging. (2005). *A profile of older Americans: 2005*. Retrieved May 23, 2006, from www.aoa.gov/prof/Statistics/profile/profiles.asp.

Administration on Aging. (2006). *2006 HHS poverty guidelines*. Retrieved May 23, 2006, from www.aoa.gov/prof/poverty_guidelines/poverty_guidelines.asp.

Ambrosino, R., Heffernan, J., Shuttlesworth, G., & Ambrosino, R. (Eds.). (2005). *Social work and social welfare: An introduction* (5th ed.). Southbank, Victoria, Australia: Brooks-Cole/Thompson Learning.

Applebaum, R., & Payne, M. (2005, Spring). How supplemental security income works. *Generations: Journal of the American Society on Aging, 29*(1), 27–29.

Atchley, R. C., & Barusch, A. S. (2004). *Social forces and aging: An introduction to social gerontology* (10th ed.). Belmont, CA: Wadsworth/Thompson Learning.

Austin, C. D., Camp, E. D., Flux, D., McClelland, R. W., & Sieppert, J. (2005). Community development with older adults in their neighborhoods: The Elder-Friendly Communities Program. *Families in Society: Journal of Contemporary Social Services, 86*(3), 401–409.

Axinn, J., & Stern, M. J. (2005). *Social welfare: A history of the American response to need* (6th ed.). Boston: Allyn & Bacon/Pearson Education.

Barnett, R. C. (2005). Ageism and sexism in the workplace. *Generations: Journal of the American Society on Aging, 29*(3), 25–30.

Barusch, A. S. (2006). *Foundations of social policy: Social justice in human perspective* (2nd ed.). Belmont, CA: Brooks-Cole/Thompson Learning.

Binstock, R. H. (2004, Spring). Advocacy in an era of neoconservatism: Responses of natural aging organizations. *Generations, 28*(1), 49–57.

Bush, G. (2005). *Strengthening Social Security for future generations*. Retrieved June 27, 2006, from www.whitehouse.gov/infocus/social-security/.

Butler, R. N. (2006). *Ageism in America: The status reports*. New York: International Longevity Center-USA.

Caro, F. G., Bass, S. A., & Chen, Y.-P. (2006). Achieving a productive aging society. In H. R. Moody (Ed.), *Aging concepts and controversies* (5th ed., pp. 246–251). Thousand Oaks, CA: Sage/Pine Forge Press.

Center for Research and Education on Aging and Technology Enhancement. (2002). *Aging, information technology and the new millennium*. Ithaca, NY: Edward R. Roybal Centers for Research on Applied Gerontology.

Charness, N. (2005, Fall). Age, technology, and culture: Gerontopia or dystopia? *Public Policy and Aging Report*, *15*(4), 20–23.

Cohen, E. S. (2001). The complex nature of ageism: What is it? Who does it? Who perceives it? *Gerontologist*, *41*(5), 576–577.

Coughlin, J. F., & Lau, J. (2006a, Winter). Cathedral builders wanted: Constructing a new vision of technology for old age. *Public Policy and Aging Report*, *16*(1), 4–8.

Coughlin, J. F., & Lau, J. (2006b, March/April). Invention vs. innovation: Technology and the future of aging. *Aging Today*, *27*(2), 3–4.

Cox, D., & Pawar, M. (2006). *International social work: Issues, strategies, and programs*. Thousand Oaks, CA: Sage.

Cox, E. O., & Chapin, R. (2001). Changing the paradigm: Strengths-based and empowerment-oriented social work with frail elders. In E. O. Cox, E. S. Kelchner, & R. Chapin (Eds.), *Gerontological social work practice: Issues, challenges, and potential* (pp. 165–179). New York: Hawthorne Press.

Cox, E. O., & Parsons, R. (1994). *Empowerment-oriented social work practice with the elderly*. Pacific Grove, CA: Brooks/Cole.

Day, P. J. (2003). *A new history of social welfare* (4th ed.). Boston: Allyn & Bacon/Pearson Education.

Dressel, P., Minkler, M., & Yen, I. (1999). Gender, race, class, and aging: Advances and opportunities. In M. Minkler & C. L. Estes (Eds.), *Critical gerontology: Perspectives from political and moral economy* (pp. 275–294). Amityville, NY: Baywood.

Ehrenreich, B. (2002, June/July). Everyday needs consume energy, wages. *Habitat world: The Publication of Habitat for Humanity International*. Retrieved June 23, 2006, from www.habitat.org/hw/june-july02/feature5.html.

Ekerdt, D. J. (2004). Born to retire: The foreshortened life course. *Gerontologist*, *44*(1), 3–9.

Estes, C. L. (2001a). Crisis, the welfare state and aging. In C. Estes (Ed.), *Social policy and aging: A critical perspective* (pp. 95–117). Thousand Oaks, CA: Sage.

Estes, C. L. (2001b). *Social policy and aging: A critical perspective*. Thousand Oaks, CA: Sage.

Estes, C. L., Wallace, S. P., Linkins, K. W., & Binney, E. A. (2001). The medicalization and commodification of aging and the privatization and rationalization of old age policy. In C. L. Estes (Ed.), *Social policy and aging: A critical perspective* (pp. 45–60). Thousand Oaks, CA: Sage.

Friedland, R. B., & Summer, L. (2005, March). *Demography is not destiny, revisited*. Georgetown, DC: Georgetown University, Center on an Aging Society. Retrieved May 12, 2006, from www.cmwf.org/usr_doc/789_friedland_demographynotdestinyII.pdf.

Friedman, T. L. (2005). *The world is flat: A brief history of the twenty-first century*. New York: Farrar, Straus & Giroux.

Gerber, J. (1999). *International economics*. Menlo Park, CA: Addison-Wesley.

Ghilarducci, T. (2006, May). The end of retirement. *Monthly Review*, *58*(1), 12–27.

Gilbert, N., & van Voorhis, R. (Eds.). (2003). *Changing patterns of social protection*. New Brunswick, NJ: Transaction.

Greene, R. R., & Cohen, H. L. (2005). Social work with older adults and their families: Changing practice paradigms. *Families in Society: Journal of Contemporary Social Services*, *86*(3), 367–373.

Gutierrez, L. M., Parsons, R., & Cox, E. O. (Eds.). (1998). *Empowerment in social work practice: A sourcebook*. Pacific Grove, CA: Brooks-Cole/Thompson Learning.

Hart, G. (2006). *God and Caesar in America*. Golden, CO: Fulcrum.

Herd, P. (2005). Universalism without targeting: Privatizing the old-age welfare state. *Gerontologist, 45*(3), 292–298.

Holstein, M. (1999). Women and productive aging: Troubling implications. In M. Minkler & C. L. Estes (Eds.), *Critical gerontology: Perspectives from political and moral economy* (pp. 359–373). Amityville, NY: Baywood.

Hooyman, N. R., & Kiyak, H. A. (2005). *Social gerontology: A multidisciplinary perspective* (7th ed.). Boston: Allyn & Bacon/Pearson Education.

Hudson, R. B. (1997). The history and place of age-based public policy. In R. B. Hudson (Ed.), *The future of age-based public policy* (pp. 1–22). Baltimore: Johns Hopkins University Press.

Hudson, R. B. (2005). The new political environment in aging: Challenges to policy and practice. *Families in Society: Journal of Contemporary Social Services, 86*(3), 321–327.

Hudson, R. B. (2006, Winter). The White House Conference on Aging: No time for seniors. *Public Policy and Aging Report, 16*(1), 1–3.

Jansson, B. (1999). *Becoming an effective policy advocate: From policy practice to social justice*. Pacific Grove, CA: Brooks/Cole.

Karger, H. J., & Stoesz, D. (2005). *American social welfare policy: A pluralist approach*. Boston: Allyn & Bacon/Pearson Education.

Kunkel, S., & Nelson, I. (2005, Fall). Consumer direction: Changing the landscape of long-term care. *Public Policy and Aging Report, 15*(4), 13–16.

Lakoff, G. (2004). *Don't think of an elephant! Know your values and frame the debate*. White River Junction, VT: Chelsea Green.

Leonard, P. (1997). *Postmodern welfare: Reconstructing an emancipatory project*. Thousand Oaks, CA: Sage.

Libson, N. (2006). The sad state of affordable housing for older people. *Generations: Journal of the American Society on Aging, 29*(4), 9–15.

Macarov, D. (2003). *What the market does to people: Privatization, globalization and poverty*. Atlanta, GA: Clarity Press.

Manning, S. S. (1998). Empowerment in mental health programs: Focusing on fields. In L. M. Gutierrez, R. Parsons, & E. O. Cox (Eds.), *Empowerment in social work practice: A sourcebook* (pp. 89–107). Pacific Grove, CA: Brooks-Cole/Thompson Learning.

McMichael, P. (2000). *Development and social change: A global perspective* (2nd ed.). Thousand Oaks, CA: Pine Forge Press.

Medicare and Medicaid (originally known as Health Insurance for the Aged Act of 1965), Pub. L. No. 89-97, 79 Stat. 290 (codified as amended in scattered sections of 42 U.S.C.)

Minkler, M. (2006). "Generational equity" and victim blaming. In H. R. Moody (Ed.), *Aging: Concepts and controversies* (5th ed., pp. 181–190). Thousand Oaks, CA: Pine Forge Press.

Moody, H. R. (2006). *Aging: Concepts and controversies* (5th ed.). Thousand Oaks, CA: Pine Forge Press.

Morrow-Howell, N. (2006, Winter). Civic engagement at the 2005 White House Conference on Aging. *Public Policy and Aging Report, 16*(1), 13–17.

National Association of Area Agencies on Aging. (2006). [Homepage]. Retrieved July 3, 2006, from www.n4a.org.

Novak, M. (2006). *Issues in aging*. Boston: Pearson Education.

Older Americans Act of 1965, 42 U.S.C. § 35-1-3001 [Congressional declaration of objectives]. Retrieved June 30, 2006, from www.law.cornell.edu/uscode/uscode42/usc_sup_01_42_10_35.html.

Older Americans Act (OAA) reauthorization proposal of 2006, H.R. 6179. Retrieved on July 6, 2006 from www.ncoa.org/attachments/OAAReport.pdf.

Palmore, E. (2005, Fall). Three decades of research on ageism. *Generations*, *29*(3), 87–90.

Phillipson, C. (1999). The social construction of retirement: Perspectives from critical theory and political economy. In M. Minlker & C. Estes (Eds.), *Critical gerontology: Perspectives from political and moral economy* (pp. 315–327). Amityville, NY: Baywood.

Robertson, A. (1999). Beyond apocalyptic demography: Toward a moral economy of interdependence. In M. Minkler & C. Estes (Eds.), *Critical gerontology: Perspectives from political and moral economy* (pp. 75–90). Amityville, NY: Baywood.

Rock Ridge Institute. (2006). [Homepage]. Retrieved June 27, 2006, from www.rockridgeinstitute .org.

Rosalynn Carter Institute for Caregiving. (2004). *Caregivers together: Establishing your own care-net—The Community Caregivers Network* [Manual]. Americus: Georgia Southwestern State University.

Rosen, A. L., & Zlotnik, J. L. (2001). Demographics and reality: The "disconnect" in social work education. In E. O. Cox, E. S. Kelchner, & R. Chapin (Eds.), *Gerontological social work practice: Issues, challenges and potential* (pp. 81–97). New York: Haworth Press.

Rother, J. (2004). Why haven't we been more successful advocates of elders? *Generations*, *28*(1), 55–58.

Rowe, J., & Kahn, K. (1997). *Successful aging*. New York: Pantheon.

Schieber, S. J. (1997). A new vision for Social Security: Personal security accounts as an element of Social Security reform. In R. B. Hudson (Ed.), *The future of age-based public policy* (pp. 134–143). Baltimore: Johns Hopkins University Press.

Schultz, J. H. (2001). *The economics of aging* (7th ed.). Westport, CT: Auburn House.

Silverstone, B. (2005). Social work with the older people of tomorrow: Restoring the person-in-situation. *Families in Society: Journal of Contemporary Social Services*, *86*(3), 309–319.

Social Security Act of 1935, Ch. 531, 49 Stat. 620 (1935).

Social Security Administration. (2004). *Income sources of aged units: Percentage with income from specified source, by marital status, sex of non-married persons, and age, 2004*. Retrieved May 14, 2006, from www.ssa.gov/policy/docs/statcomps/income_pop55/2004/sect01.pdf.

Social Security Administration. (2005). SSI federal payment amounts. In *Social Security Online*. Retrieved June 2, 2006, from www.ssa.gov/OACT/COLA/SSI.html.

SPRY Foundation. (2005). *Computer-based technology and caregiving of older adults: What's new, what's next?* Washington, DC: Author.

Stoller, E. P., & Gibson, R. C. (2000). *Worlds of difference: Inequality in the aging experience*. Thousand Oaks, CA: Pine Forge Press.

Stone, R. (2004). Where have all the advocates gone? *Generations*, *28*(1), 59–64.

Takamura, J. (2001). Towards a new era in aging and social work. In E. O. Cox, E. S. Kelchner, & R. Chapin (Eds.), *Gerontological social work practice: Issues, challenges and potential* (pp. 1–11). New York: Haworth Press.

Torres-Gil, F. (2001). Multiculturalism, social policy and the new aging. In E. O. Cox, E. S. Kelchner, & R. Chapin (Eds.), *Gerontological social work practice: Issues, challenges and potential* (pp. 13–32). New York: Haworth Press.

Tout, K. (1989). *Aging in developing countries*. New York: Oxford University Press.

U.S. Department of Health and Human Services. (2006, January 24). Annual update of the HHS poverty guidelines. *Federal Register*, *71*(15), 3848–3849.

Wells, L. M., & Taylor, L. E. (2001). Gerontological social work practice: A Canadian perspective. In E. O. Cox, E. S. Kelchner, & R. Chapin (Eds.), *Gerontological social work practice: Issues, challenges, and potential* (pp. 33–50). New York: Hawthorne Press.

Wilson, K. B. (2005–2006, Winter). Introduction: Where older people live, how needed care is provided. *Generations: Journal of the American Society on Aging*, *29*(4), 5–8.

Chapter 11

EXPLANATORY LEGITIMACY: A MODEL FOR DISABILITY POLICY DEVELOPMENT AND ANALYSIS

Stephen French Gilson and Elizabeth DePoy

In this chapter, we discuss and analyze contemporary disability policy in the United States, with a specific focus on several seminal federal policies. To set the context for our analysis, we begin by providing a conceptual framework, *Explanatory Legitimacy*, through which to examine and analyze disability policy. We then take a brief look back in history to set the context for contemporary disability policy. This glance is a reminder that disability itself is a variable, context-bound construct, and thus definitions have reciprocal relationships with policy. That is to say, disability definitions shape policy and policy shapes conceptualizations of disability. We conclude with the application of the analytic model to disability policy exemplars.

Before we begin our discussion, we pose three definitions:

1. *Policy:* There are numerous definitions of policy, many of which guide the discussions in each of the chapters of this book. Policy definitions range from informal rules that govern conduct and access to resources at multiple system levels, to formal legislation advanced by government bodies. In this chapter, we define policy as the set of explicit statements that guide legitimate status and responses to membership status in the form of resource access, allocation, and other action responses to legitimate category members. Although we do not delimit policy definitions to federal legislation, we focus our analysis on specific federally legislated policy exemplars.

2. *Disability:* As we discuss in detail, we define disability as a contextually embedded, dynamic grand category of human diversity.

3. *Disability policy:* We define disability policy as the set of explicit statements that legitimate membership criteria in the disability category and guide responses to legitimate category members.

EXPLANATORY LEGITIMACY THEORY

Explanatory Legitimacy Theory builds on historical and current diversity analyses and debates. Different from locating disability in a singular domain of the body or the environment, Explanatory Legitimacy analyzes the construct of disability as a contextually embedded, dynamic grand category of human diversity. Thus, who belongs and what policy responses are afforded to category members are based on differential, changing, and sometimes conflicting judgments about the value of explanations for diverse, atypical human phenomena. Explanatory Legitimacy considers the influence of multiple factors (including, but not limited to, natural, chronological, spiritual, and intellectual trends) on value judgments as the key to understanding categorization, the legitimacy of individuals and groups who fit a category, and the policy responses that are deemed legitimate for members.

Explanatory Legitimacy Theory makes distinctions among descriptive, explanatory, and the axiological, or the legitimacy dimensions of the categorization of human diversity and identifies the relationships among these elements. Thus, similar to legitimacy-based analyses of other areas of human diversity, disability, defined and analyzed through the lens of Explanatory Legitimacy, comprises three interactive elements: description, explanation, and legitimacy. This tripartite analytic framework provides a potent platform on which to examine policy responses to members of categorical groups (DePoy & Gilson, in press; Gilson & DePoy, 2002). Let us look at each element now.

Description

Description encompasses the full range of human activity (what people do and do not do and how they do what they do), appearance, and experience. Of particular importance to an understanding of disability definitions and policy responses is the statistical concept of the "norm." Because the understanding and naming of what is normal and thus in contrast not normal are value-based, use of terms such as "normal" and "abnormal" do not provide the conceptual clarity sufficient for distinguishing description from axiology. Thus, in applying Explanatory Legitimacy to disability policy, we use the terms *typical* and *atypical* to depict frequently and infrequently occurring human description, respectively. Disability is located in the realm of the atypical.

Explanation

The second element of Explanatory Legitimacy is explanation. Applied to disability, explanation is the set of reasons for the atypical. With regard to the link between description and explanation, it is important to highlight that explanation is always an inference. Because of the interpretative nature of explanation, this definitional element lends itself to debate, differential value judgment, and diverse policy responses. As we discuss further on in more detail, the current explanatory debate between two explanatory genres (internal and external causes of disability) is a heated one and has great relevance for policy. Internal causes attribute atypical phenomena to a medical-diagnostic condition of long-term or permanent duration (Smart, 2001), whereas the external lens identifies an unwelcoming and even discriminatory environment as causal of disability, in which the atypical is met with barriers and exclusion.

Legitimacy

The third and most important definitional element of Explanatory Legitimacy is legitimacy itself, which we suggest comprises two subelements: judgment and response. Judgment refers to value assessments of competing groups on whether or not what one does throughout life (and thus what one does not do), how one looks, and the degree to which one's experiences fit what is typical have valid and acceptable explanations consistent with both explicit and implicit value sets. Category membership in this case is a value-encased determination about the extent to which the posited explanation for the atypical renders individuals and groups eligible for disability category membership.

Responses are the actions (both negative and positive) that are deemed appropriate by those rendering the value judgments about membership and responses to category members. Disability policy lies in the response element of Explanatory Legitimacy, at multiple points in time, beginning with the decision to consider the need for a category-specific policy, proceeding to the promulgation of the actual policy, continuing with who is legitimately eligible for consideration under the policy, and finally to the response to legitimate category members guided by the content and nature of the policy. Thus teasing apart description, explanation, and values provides the opportunity for understanding and analyzing policy formulation and enactment from a complex, context-embedded perspective.

Now let us look back in history to illustrate the framework and its importance for understanding contemporary disability policy. Unfortunately, in this short chapter we do not have space to visit this rich history in depth. However, we want to draw your attention to selected chronological exemplars to illustrate the diverse, context-embedded understandings and explanations of atypical human characteristics. As you will see, common to all the historical exemplars are the following:

- There are many potential and accepted explanations for a single atypical human characteristic.
- These explanations form the basis for categorization and response to category members.
- The responses proffered provide an analytic window onto the beliefs, values, politics, economics, intellectual trends, and level of technological development of the times necessary for understanding disability policy.

HISTORY

We begin our discussion with ancient civilizations. Although the term "disability" was not documented in the historical literature until recently, there is a record of concern with explaining and responding to "the atypical human" as early as ancient civilizations (Longmore & Umansky, 2001). In Greek societies, despite Aristotle's concern with natural phenomena and the advanced medical knowledge of Hypocrites, individuals with extreme deviations from typical appearance and behavior were not considered human and thus were excluded from communities. Less dramatic departures from the typical were accepted, albeit with differential responses depending on the domain of the atypical feature (Braddock & Parish, 2001; Davis, 1995, 1997; Winzer, 1993). Behaviors consistent with what we label today mental retardation and mental illness were explained as supernatural and were met with both fear and respect (Braddock & Parish, 2001; Davis, 1995, 1997; Winzer, 1993), while, with one exception, those demonstrating atypical activity in mobility, seeing, hearing, and so forth were believed to be sinners whose plight was explained by punishment from the gods. Not surprisingly, the explanatory exception to sin-induced deviation was injury in the line of military duty (Stiker, 2000). When atypical activity was explained in immoral terms, the community was not amenable to providing support. However, when atypical performance resulted from war injury—where the explanation was known and considered heroic—benefits such as pension funds were often put in place to support this elite group. Thus, as far back as ancient civilizations, variations of the human condition were identified in contrast to what was typical, engendered multiple explanations that located individuals in categories of differing worth, and differential responses to the explanations illustrated the values and perspectives of the context (Braddock & Parish, 2001).

In the Middle Ages, the typical pastiche against which the atypical emerged was characterized by poverty and deprivation and human conditions such as blindness, deafness, and lameness that are so often associated with dire living environments (Braddock & Parish, 2001; DePoy & Gilson, 2004; DePoy & MacDuffie, 2004). So, rather than conditions such as blindness or mobility challenges being considered atypical, only the extreme deviations were located in that marginal category and, in concert with the religious and intellectual context of the time, were explained by both spiritual attributions and demonic causes (Braddock & Parish, 2001; Winzer, 1993). However, some accounts also reveal the emerging, albeit minuscule, role of scientific explanations, demonstrated by the distinction between the treatable and the untreatable sick (Braddock & Parish, 2001).

Of particular note in this chronological era are the historical roots of charity and faith healing responses to disability. Christian clergy explained the atypical, despite its immoral nature, as purposively created by God to provide an earthly opportunity for typical laypersons to exhibit tolerance and charitable behavior (Braddock & Parish, 2001). Thus responses such as charitable institutions, faith-based hospitals, and faith healing were created to minister to the atypical and the sick. Not all differences were met with charity, however. In areas where the population believed in demonic explanations for the atypical, people were relegated to begging and persecution depending on the accepted explanation for their atypical condition (Stiker, 2000).

The Enlightenment brought intellectual and value shifts that resulted in supplanting demonic explanations with scientific accounts for atypical human behavior (Stiker, 2000). This is not to say that moral and religious explanations of difference ever disappeared, as philosophers, clergy, and others continued to debate the relationship between God and nature as causal of the human condition (DePoy & Gilson, 2004; Durant, 1991).

As the world and knowledge increased in complexity (Braddock & Parish, 2001), economics and social factors were added to the explanatory repertoire of human atypical phenomena, thereby influencing analysis of all human experience and shaping differential public and private responses to the atypical. And although it is likely that economic status had always played a role in the range of responses to the atypical, prior to the Enlightenment, the primacy of religion may have obfuscated or overshadowed other influences (Braddock & Parish, 2001).

As the Victorian era unfolded, the values of continental Europe, England, and the newly colonized America began to take divergent courses, as did conceptualization and responses to the atypical (Wright, 2001). In the interest of space, we now narrow our focus to the United States.

In colonial America, several trends emerged that provided the foundation for the emergence of contemporary disability definitions and policy responses. First, individuals with atypical conditions explained by illness and aging were valued as worthy of care and family response (Axinn & Stern, 2000). Second was the growth of the American economy. In large part, because the American economy had its roots in the uninvited procurement of land on which indigenous populations lived and on the importation of involuntary labor from other countries (Axinn & Stern, 2000), the existing policies guiding poor relief in colonial America that were based in homogeneous communal values and shared beliefs were ultimately challenged in large part by the geographic proximity of diverse peoples. Thus, the emergence of economic advantage became coupled with social upheaval (Davis, 1995, 1997; Goldberg, 1994) and set the stage for categories of worth that shaped policy responses to people who demonstrated atypical characteristics (DePoy & Gilson, 2004). Third, along with the increase in diverse inherent human characteristics such as race and ethnicity, explanations for what people did and did not do, how people looked, and what they experienced expanded with the burgeoning field of medicine (DePoy & Gilson, 2004; Starr, 1992). Despite the appearance of medicine on the explanatory scene, however, morality and social circumstance remained dominant explanations for the atypical as long as religion was an important factor in American communities. Moreover, with the vast resources available to "everyman" in the New World, tolerance for poverty (and thus acceptance of poverty as a legitimate explanation for the atypical) waned in an environment that allegedly provided a golden opportunity for anyone who was willing to exert some elbow grease (Axinn & Stern, 2000). In response to the increasing social costs and disapproval of poverty, towns and cities began to develop policies that supported segregation of the unproductive, with the result that "undesirables" were remanded to poorhouses (DePoy & Gilson, 2004; DePoy & MacDuffie, 2004).

During this time, in large part due to the juxtaposition of diverse populations resulting from immigration and urbanization, observable diversity, including race, ethnicity, and other intrinsic human differences, began to replace poverty as a major explanatory factor for the atypical (DePoy & Gilson, 2004). The notions of difference and variation provide the segue to a critical conceptual foundation of understandings of disability and thus disability policy responses in the United States.

Note that until now, we have not used the terms "normal" and "abnormal" in our brief history. Remember that we introduced the norm earlier. The concepts of normal and abnormal emerged from the normal curve and measures of central tendency, two mathematical constructs developed by Quetelet (1969) in the late 1800s. The normal or bell-shaped curve depicts observed or measured frequencies in which the apex of the curve represents the most frequent occurrence and the tails represent the least frequent observations. Applying the bell-shaped curve to understanding human variation, Quetelet extrapolated the concept of "the normal man," who was considered to be both physically and morally normal. According to Quetelet's normal man concept and extensive theory based on this concept, *normal* was not only interpreted as the most frequently occurring phenomena but became the basis for what "should be." Observation therefore turned to prescription, and anyone with observed phenomena on the tail ends of the curve was categorized as abnormal. Fields of study that relied on these positivist approaches to inquiry (such as normal and abnormal psychology, medicine, human biology, and clinical social work practice) all distinguished between normal and abnormal and gave birth to explanations and policy responses that met descriptive need on the basis of legitimate abnormal category membership (DePoy & Gilson, 2004).

In the industrial era, the concept of normal became even more hegemonic as mass production, mechanization, and production standards were based on statistical projections of what an average worker should "normally" accomplish within a given set of parameters (Kanigel, 1999). It is critical to note here that the attribution of "not normal," particularly below normal, to observed productivity and contribution to the U.S. economy was and remains an important driver of public policy response (Axinn & Stern, 2000; Longmore & Umansky, 2001; Schriner & Scotch, 1998; Scotch & Schriner, 1997; Stone, 1986).

As we entered the twentieth century, the terms "cripple," "blind," "deaf," and "handicap," used to describe the atypical characteristics of groups of people with permanent medical-diagnostic conditions that affected their daily activity, appearance, and/or experience, were supplanted with broader terms, such as "handicapped" or "disabled," and the category of *disability* emerged. Although this language seemed to be an effort to create publicly respectful and politically correct reference to the undesirable atypical characteristics explained by medical-diagnostic conditions, its vagueness has been problematic. Remember that definitions of disability were important in shaping policy. Who is legitimately included and excluded from the broad category of disability has been and remains unclear and variable and thus confounds that clarity of policy (Heumann, 1993), as we will see later in the chapter.

During the twentieth century, as the medical industry grew in power, medical explanations for the atypical became synonyms for disability types and the primary focus of disability policy responses. Literature now parsed disability into subgroups such as "cognitive disability," "psychiatric disability," and "physical disability," with medical explanatory sets for each subgroup. What each has in common with the other is the observed permanent or long-term limitation in functioning in a particular area assumed to be primarily explained by an intrinsic medical condition. The permanency of the functional deficit led to early twentieth-century policy supporting institutionalization of those individuals and groups who were unable to "function" in environments designed for the "normal" person. Moreover, professionals were at the helm of these institutions and ostensibly organized rehabilitation or restorative practice for persons who resided at the tail ends of the normal curve.

Policy supporting institutionalization proliferated for several reasons. First, as we noted earlier, diagnostic explanations made the prediction of lifelong "abnormality" possible and in need of "treatment." Second, as women entered the workplace, they were no longer able to be the primary supports for atypical family and community members. However, according to Gill (1992), the most important reason for institutional policy responses was the burgeoning care industry through which many professional stakeholders gained significant economic benefit from their work with institutionalized atypical individuals and institutional systems.

Remember the notion of the atypical being placed on the earth to engender charitable responses from laypersons? We see its continuation in the charitable model of disability policy and practice response operationalized as not-for-profit organizations such as Easter Seals, which provided fund-raising and services for worthy individuals whose physically atypical characteristics had worthy medical explanations for disability determination and response.

However, parallel to charity policies was the development of public policy support for a particular disability group, individuals who had to leave the work world because of injury sustained on the job. Clearly, American values on work and productivity were reflected in workers compensation law as early as 1902 (Maryland State Archive, 2005). Thus the importance of economic productivity in shaping policy responses was clearly observed by the turn of the twentieth century. Further illustrating this hegemonic American value on work was the passage of the vocational rehabilitation law in 1920 for veterans of World War I, designed to return to the workplace men whose atypical characteristics were explained by injury in service to their country (Obermann, as cited in Braddock & Parish, 2001, p. 42).

It is important to note that in the middle and even late twentieth century, regardless of the nature of the atypical, explanations were primarily medical. That is to say, the cause of the atypical characteristic is considered to be located internally within an individual's body. It followed that policies focused on supporting care or cure responses to help atypical individuals heal and not place undue financial burden on their families and communities (DePoy & Gilson, 2004).

Although medical explanations remain primary in defining disability even now, the history of disability took an important turn in the second half of the twentieth century that has significantly influenced policy and action responses. Disability rights scholars and activists eschewed the medical explanation of disability, as such explanations of permanent deficit were impotent in creating social change necessary for people with a broad range of atypical circumstances to fully participate in their communities and to actualize their rights as citizens. Rather than accept the disabled as the "work" for the care industry, scholars looked outside the body to explain disability. Early scholars such as Oliver (1992, 1996) and Linton (1998, 2006) proposed the intolerance and rigidity of the social and built environments, rather than medical conditions, as the explanation for disability. Words such as "inclusion," "participation," and "nondiscrimination" were introduced into the disability literature, reflecting the notion that people who did not fit within the central tendencies of Quetelet's normal curve were subjects of stigma, prejudice, marginalization, segregation, and exclusion. Demands for equality of opportunity were anchored on theory and research that documented disabled groups as victims of oppression and discrimination rather than medically abnormal individuals. With the view of disability explained by external factors such as social, economic, political, and even physical marginalization and exclusion, the locus for disability and thus for necessary policy responses has become a moving and complex target.

To briefly summarize, disability has a rich and diverse history. Understandings of disability are embedded in and reflective of their axiological contexts, and thus shape thinking and action responses to the atypical. These factors have intersected to produce two overarching and hotly debated views of disability in the current literature: internal medical-diagnostic and external environmental. Medical-diagnostic definitions locate the causes of the atypical within humans and explain disability as an anomalous medical condition of long-term or permanent duration. Thus, within this conceptualization, the domain of disability definition and response remains within the medical and professional communities. Group-specific policy focusing on special services and resources for disability category members logically follows from medical-diagnostic definitions of disability.

In opposition, however, to what was perceived as a pejorative explanation, the external view of disability was advanced by disability scholar-activists. Within this broad theoretical explanatory rubric, disability is defined as a set of limitations imposed on a full range of individuals with diverse atypical characteristics (with or even without diagnosed medical conditions) from external social, cultural, and other environmental influences. Policies that focus on equality of opportunity through environmental change follow logically from this explanatory approach. Both explanatory genres provide a forum for rich policy debate and response. So now let us move on to the analysis of exemplars of contemporary disability policy, with our thinking and analysis guided by explanatory legitimacy.

EXPLANATORY LEGITIMACY THEORY ANALYSIS OF POLICY EXEMPLARS

Typically, disability policy has been categorized into two areas: policies that guide the provisions of specialized services and resources, such as Social Security Disability Insurance (SSDI; established by the Social Security Amendments of 1956; Berkowitz, 1989), for legitimately disabled populations, and, more recently, those, such as the Americans with Disabilities Act (ADA, 1991; Scotch, 2001), that protect and advance the civil rights of legitimately disabled populations. However, through the lens of explanatory legitimacy, we suggest a different taxonomy, depicted in Table 11.1.

Let us examine this table in more detail. The horizontal axis consists of four divisions of policy on the basis of both content and explicitly intended outcome. As illustrated by our exemplars, these categories are not mutually exclusive.

Policies for nonworkers guide the provision of income and related benefits for the disproportionately high number of legitimately disabled individuals who are not working (and to some extent their family members). Policies that guide the provision of benefits to advance employability direct the provision of training and retraining for disabled individuals with the explicit intended outcome of entry or reentry into the workforce. Policy

Table 11.1   Disability Policy through the Lens of Explanatory Legitimacy

	Benefits for Nonworkers	Benefits to Advance Employability	Legitimacy as Citizens of Disabled Individuals and Groups	Benefits and Privileges
Internal Explanations	SSDI	Rehabilitation Act of 1954 Rehabilitation Act of 1973 Individuals with Disabilities Education Act (IDEA)	Rehabilitation Act of 1954 Rehabilitation Act of 1973 ADA	ADA Golden Access Passport (free entrance into national parks) IDEA
External Explanations		Ticket to Work and Work Incentives Improvement Act of 1999	Rehabilitation Act of 1954 Rehabilitation Act of 1973 ADA	ADA

governing the legitimacy of disabled individuals and groups as citizens is specialized legislation that asserts the group-specific civil rights of disabled populations and individuals. Finally, policies that govern the provision of special benefits to disabled groups include privileges (Stone, 1986) such as designated parking and free entrance into national parks (Golden Access Passport). The policies that we chose as exemplars are not exhaustive by any means, but they offer a range of diverse approaches to disability policy in the United States.

The vertical axis of Table 11.1 contains two divisions, internally and externally focused policy, each responding to its particular explanatory approach to disability. From a simple and linear standpoint, we would expect that the policies that fall under the division of internally focused, on the basis of explaining legitimate disability as an embodied condition, would guide treatment or responses to bona fide category members. Similarly, external policies accept external disability explanations as legitimate and would be expected to address the barriers that exclude disabled groups from participation and rights. However, the divisions are not as simple as they might be.

To understand Table 11.1, we now look at the policy exemplars through the lens of explanatory legitimacy. We suggest that different from analyzing disability policy through its explicit content and intended outcomes, that policy is much more complex than its verbiage. Using the framework of explanatory legitimacy, disability policy is a value-based response to explanations of atypical human characteristics and thus can be understood and changed by laying bare its value stance. Moreover, there are commonalities that unite disability policy that we present in Table 11.2.

Disability policy, though temporarily needed, has long-term consequences of segregation and inequality. First, as we see by the heuristics and consistent with nonrational models of policy analysis (Stone, 2001), Explanatory Legitimacy suggests that because values and context mediate logic, disability policy is not linear and cannot be understood through rational policy analysis approaches. Second, although some policies, as shown in Table 11.1, are targeted at changing the environment, legitimacy for coverage under these policies is restricted to internal explanations of disability. This disjuncture becomes problematic in trying to understand the link between the articulated problem that the policy is designed to remediate and the causal assumption. Third, atypical embodied characteristics that are observable and assumed to be caused by conditions beyond the control of the individual are more legitimate for disability category membership than those that are not directly ascertainable and/or considered to be caused by factors over which individuals have control. Fourth, disability theory and policies are frequently based on assumptions about the

Table 11.2   Heuristics

1. Values and context mediate logic, and thus disability policy is not logical.
2. All policies, even if guiding external action, emerge from an internal causal explanation of disability.
3. Disability policy is organized along a value hierarchy of medical explanations, and not all explanations are acceptable.
4. Disability policy is based on nomothetic assumptions about a group that does not necessarily share commonalities.
5. Disability policy has an economic foundation.

commonalities of a group, which may or may not be accurate (Gilson & DePoy, 2002). Fifth, in a global economic context, disability policy, similar to all federal policy, directly or indirectly addresses resources. We discuss the sixth heuristic toward the conclusion of the chapter. Let us examine several of our policy exemplars to illustrate.

Social Security Disability Insurance

If we analyze SSDI (Berkowitz, 1989), we see that, ostensibly, it is intended to provide income and benefit support for individuals who, because of a long-term or permanent medical explanation, are unable to work. Yet, to legitimately qualify, an individual not only must meet the internally located definition of disability advanced by the Social Security Administration, but also must have previously contributed to Social Security, which one cannot do without working.

Because disability status and response under SSDI are internally situated, the process for legitimacy under SSDI places a medical or human service professional in the gate-keeping role. To be deemed legitimately disabled, a physician (or other specified professional, depending on the explanatory diagnosis for not working) and several other evaluators determine one's fit with the legitimacy criteria. To qualify for benefits, an individual must prove disability legitimacy, which is not assured even if one meets the descriptive eligibility criteria. Explanations such as alcohol dependence, obesity, and chemical sensitivity, which in other policy arenas are explained as medical but often are considered to be under one's personal control, personally excessive, or even hypochondriacal, are not acceptable explanations for legitimate disability status under SSDI policy, even though these explanatory conditions may be consistent with the descriptive outcome of long-term or permanent impairment advanced under the policy guidelines. We have referred to this hierarchy of acceptable conditions as *disability pedigree* to illustrate ranking of worth (DePoy & Gilson, 2004).

A careful examination of acceptable and unacceptable pedigree reveals that SSDI policy values are rooted in notions of personal responsibility, economic contribution, and charity. That is to say, an individual is legitimate only if he or she is not responsible for his or her inability to contribute to the economy. The meager income benefits hark back to the charity model of disability in which disabled individuals were pitied enough for some altruism but not sufficiently valued for support necessary to fully participate in their communities.

While supported on SSDI, individuals can receive Medicaid if their SSDI support is insufficient to elevate recipient income above the state's eligibility guidelines for Medicaid (U.S. Department of Health and Human Services, CMS: Centers for Medicare & Medicaid Services, 2006a). And while SSDI recipients theoretically receive Medicare (the health insurance programs for those in poverty and for elders, respectively), there is a two year waiting period for this benefit putting SSDI recipients at risk for inadequate health insurance (U.S. Department of Health and Human Services, CMS: Centers for Medicare & Medicaid Services, 2006b). Moreover, until the passage of the Ticket to Work and Work Incentives Improvement Act (TWIIA) in 1999 (Gilmer, Personal Communication; Wehman, 2000), an individual who returned to work lost all benefits including all public health insurance. Fortunately, with this newly crafted legislation, health benefits and some income can continue as people return to work. Nevertheless, if an individual is supported on SSDI and/or SSI, it is likely that he or she will be poor.

We also draw your attention to another issue related to health and income support benefits. Although these are most important for recipients of service, don't forget that health insurance pays providers for their work, and the processes through which disabled individuals are qualified as legitimate and then afforded services under SSDI policy constitute a large segment of the labor industry in the United States. Thus, SSDI policy, while benefiting legitimate individuals who cannot earn, contains valued payment systems for those who do earn. The economic value not only for direct policy beneficiaries but also for the labor market is a critically important element to consider in policy analysis and change (DePoy & Gilson, in press). The Ticket to Work and Work Incentives Improvement Act of 1999 policy illustrates this point.

Before its passage, SSDI provided a disincentive for its beneficiaries to work since, as we mentioned earlier, returning to work, often in low-paying positions, eliminated health insurance and income benefits, which often exceeded what a former SSDI recipient could earn in the job market. Thus, rather than enabling individuals to move away from public support, SSDI maintained recipients in the category of public welfare consumer. The Ticket to Work and Work Incentives Improvement Act was enacted to remediate this institutional mistake that rendered SSDI in conflict with its value base of economic self-sufficiency and personal responsibility.

An important exemplar of benefits to nonworkers is provided by SSDI. We contend that policies that establish and support job training and even specialized education fit under the second content category of advancing employability. Several of these policies, such as the Individuals with Disabilities Education Act (IDEA) of 1990 and 1997 and IDEA Regulations of 1999 (Lipton, 1999; Pelka, 1997) and the Rehabilitation Act of 1973 (Barnartt & Scotch, 2001; Scotch, 2001), also fit under the category of benefits and privileges in that they provide specialized accommodations and resources on the basis of legitimate disability membership regardless of the accessibility of the employment or educational arena. These policies, based on nomothetic principles of group commonality, while beneficial to some and necessary for those who have been excluded from participation, do not take into account that all category members may not want or need the resources provided to individuals on the basis of category membership alone. Part of the quagmire in policies that address population categories is that rather than responding to descriptive need, category membership is the mediator and the locus for policy. Consider the Golden Access Passport (National Park Service, U.S. Department of the Interior, 2005), a policy that allows disabled individuals to access national parks without paying. The policy, which assumes financial need on the basis of disability, is targeted at the broad category of disability. Thus, whether or not category members are financially needy, they obtain the privilege of free entrance, unlike individuals who have financial need but are not legitimate members of the disability group. Job training policies and IDEA are similar in that they posit legitimacy for benefits on the basis of assumed need because an individual is legitimately qualified in a category, not because need for the resources and services under these policies is verified. On the other hand, given that specialized education and job training resources are not equivalent to those afforded to the typical population, the paradox of too many and too few resources under categorical policies, such as disability policy based on nomothetic assumptions, continues.

We now move to policies that are designed to assert and advance citizenship. Consistent with civil rights policy for other disenfranchised groups, this genre of legislation fits under the category of protective or antidiscrimination policy. As we address in the sixth heuristic, protective disability policy such as the ADA is both critically needed and extremely limited in promoting long-term equality of opportunity. Let us look to the ADA as an example.

The Americans with Disabilities Act

The 1990 ADA (Scotch, 2001) is protective legislation that applies to disabled individuals. Similar to other protective legislation, the ADA prohibits discrimination on the basis of disability and guarantees equal opportunity for individuals with disabilities in public accommodations, employment, transportation, state and local government services, and telecommunications. Note that we locate the ADA in the internal explanations category of disability policy. Similar to policies that we discussed earlier, although the locus of the problem and its resolution is external, eligibility for protection under the ADA is determined by the pedigree of internal explanations for atypical characteristics. Look at the definition of who qualifies as legitimately disabled under the ADA: "an individual who has physical or mental impairment that substantially limits one or more major life activities, and the individual has a record of such an impairment, or is regarded as having such an impairment" (Public Law 101-336).

Because of its potential not only to provide opportunity where it did not exist, but also to support accommodations and thus special treatment, many groups with internal explanations for atypical function have attempted to seek coverage under the ADA. The court cases and decisions are the evidence of what we refer to as pedigree wars, as groups of individuals seek legitimate disability status in order to obtain rights that they feel they are otherwise denied. Moreover, note that we also locate the ADA under the policy genre of benefits and privileges for this reason.

As we introduced earlier, although protective and nondiscrimination policy is essential to advance inclusion and civil rights, its use as a long-term solution is problematic.

We acknowledge that many individuals with atypical characteristics, particularly those that are observable, have experienced overt and covert discrimination and oppression. As a policy response, the ADA has made significant changes in access to the physical environment, the workplace, the communications and transportation systems, and the educational arena for many people who, without the ADA, would not be able to participate in these domains of daily life. Yet, as a permanent solution, protective policies, which on the surface appear sound, are riddled with value and social action conflicts (DePoy & Gilson, in press). First, rather than assuring that policy for all citizens governs the rights of disability category members, the presence of the ADA implies that disabled individuals need specialized legislation layered on the policy that should already protect their rights. Second, the ADA stipulates that discriminatory practices such as environmental and telecommunication barriers need to be replaced with accessible structures in instances where cost would not be prohibitive. Thus, we see that the legitimate policy responses to discrimination are mediated by cost considerations that diminish civil rights and equality of opportunity of the very group that the policy is ostensibly designed to protect. Third, exactly who fits under ADA policy and what protections are afforded are not clear, and interpretation is thus subject to differential and context-embedded cultural, social, political, and economic value.

CONCLUSION

As we leave specific exemplars to move to general conclusions, we ask you to revisit the historical snippets to set the context for this last part of our discussion on disability policy. If we gaze back in chronological time, we see the roots of contemporary disability policy in the United States in values, context, economy, and intellectual trends.

Framing disability policy in the United States from a population subcategory approach has been both a blessing and a curse. Disability policy has been necessary for and has created safety nets, benefits, and efforts at equalizing opportunity for participation in work, community life, and the economy, yet the maintenance of population-specific policy has the danger of perpetuating separation and differential treatment in the long term. We suggest that because of its structure and focus on values as the drivers for policy, Explanatory Legitimacy provides the framework through which necessary policy change can be informed and enacted. In the twenty-first century we face the challenges and opportunities of an expansive global and virtual environment. We are challenged with the juxtaposition of diverse worldviews and experiences, and gifted with the thinking and action tools to operationalize the values of tolerance and symmetry of opportunity (DePoy & Gilson, in press). Rethinking disability policy and other population-categorical policies on a time continuum as well as on a foundation of celebration for diversity of ideas as well as bodies can move us toward policy that creates universal rights, resources, and privileges on the basis of human description and need rather than on tacit and nomothetic assumptions about individual embodied worth. Our charge is to analyze, rethink, and implement policies that shape our world as one that is welcoming of all.

SUGGESTED WEB SOURCES

Center for Applied Special Technology. (1999–2006). *Universal design for learning.* Retrieved June 17, 2006, from www.cast.org.

Center for Universal Design, College of Design. (2006). *Environments and products for all people.* Raleigh: North Carolina State University, Center for Universal Design. Retrieved June 17, 2006, from www.ncsu.edu/www/ncsu/design/sod5/cud/.

DePoy, E. (2004). *Modular long term care modules.* Orono: University of Maine, Center for Community Inclusion and Disability Studies. Retrieved June 16, 2006, from www.ccids.umaine.edu/hrsaltc/index.htm.

Web Access Subcommittee, University of Maine. (n.d.). *Creating accessible websites.* Orono: University of Maine. Retrieved June 17, 2006, from www.umaine.edu/insider/accessibility.

REFERENCES

Americans with Disabilities Act of 1990, Pub. L. No. 101-336, § 2, 104 Stat. 328 (1991).

Axinn, J., & Stern, M. J. (2000). *Social welfare: A history of the American response to need* (5th ed.). Boston: Allyn & Bacon.

Barnartt, S. N., & Scotch, R. K. (2001). *Disability protests: Contentious politics, 1970–1999.* Washington, DC: Gallaudet University Press.

Berkowitz, E. D. (1989). *Disabled policy: America's programs for the handicapped: A Twentieth Century Fund report.* Cambridge: Cambridge University Press.

Braddock, D., & Parish, S. L. (2001). An institutional history of disability. In G. L. Albrecht, K. D. Seelman, & M. Bury (Eds.), *Handbook of disability studies* (pp. 11–68). Thousand Oaks, CA: Sage.

Davis, L. J. (1995). *Enforcing normalcy: Disability, deafness, and the body*. New York: Verso.

Davis, L. J. (1997). *The disability studies reader*. New York: Routledge.

DePoy, E., & Gilson, S. F. (2004). *Rethinking disability: Principles for professional and social change*. Belmont, CA: Wadsworth.

DePoy, E., & Gilson, S. F. (in press). *The human experience: An explanatory legitimacy approach*. Thousand Oaks, CA: Sage.

DePoy, E., & MacDuffie, H. (2004). *History of long-term care*. Retrieved June 16, 2006, from www.ume.maine.edu/cci/hrsaltc/.

Durant, W. (1991). *Story of philosophy: The lives and opinions of the world's greatest philosophers*. New York: Pocket Books.

Gill, C. (1992, November). Who gets the profits? Workplace oppression devalues the disability experience. *Mainstream, 12*, 14–17.

Gilson, S. F., & DePoy, E. (2002). Multiculturalism and disability: A critical perspective. *Disability and Society, 15*, 207–218.

Goldberg, D. T. (1994). *Multiculturalism: A critical reader*. Oxford: Blackwell.

Heumann, J. E. (1993). Building our own boats: A personal perspective on disability policy. In L. O. Gostin & H. A. Beyer (Eds.), *Implementing the Americans with Disabilities Act: Rights and responsibilities of all Americans* (pp. 251–262). Baltimore: Paul H. Brookes.

Kanigel, R. (1999). *The one best way: Frederick Winslow Taylor and the enigma of efficiency* (Sloan Technology Series). New York: Viking Press.

Linton, S. (1998). *Claiming disability: Knowledge and identity*. New York: New York University Press.

Linton, S. (2006). *My body politic: A memoir*. Ann Arbor: University of Michigan Press.

Lipton, J. (1999). *Individuals with Disabilities Education Act Amendments of 1997 and Idea Regulations of 1999: Summary of changes (with emphasis on IEPs and discipline)*. Berkeley, CA: Disability Rights Education and Defense Fund. Retrieved June 17, 2006, from www.dredf.org/idea10.html.

Longmore, P., & Umansky, L. (Eds.). (2001). *The new disability history: American perspectives*. New York: New York University Press.

Maryland State Archive. (2005, July 22). *State Workers' Compensation Commission origin and functions*. Retrieved June 16, 2006, from www.mdarchives.state.md.us/msa/mdmanual/25ind /html/80workf.html.

National Park Service, U.S. Department of the Interior. (2005). *Entrance pass programs*. Retrieved June 17, 2006, from www.nps.gov/fees_passes.htm.

Oliver, M. (1992). Changing the social relations of research production? *Disability, Handicap, and Society, 7*, 101–114.

Oliver, M. (1996). Defining impairment and disability: Issues at stake. In G. Barnes & G. Mercer (Eds.), *Exploring the divide: Illness and disability* (pp. 39–54). Leeds, England: Disability Press.

Pelka, F. (1997). *The ABC-Clio companion to the disability rights movement*. Santa Barbara, CA: ABC-Clio.

Quetelet, A. (1969). *A treatise on man and the development of his faculties: A facsimile reproduction of the English translation of 1842*. Gainesville, FL: Scholars' Facsimiles and Reprints.

Schriner, K. F., & Scotch, R. K. (1998). Beyond the minority group model: An emerging paradigm for the next generation of disability policy. In E. Makas, B. Haller, & T. Doe (Eds.), *Accessing the issues: Current research in disability studies* (pp. 213–216). Dallas, TX: Society for Disability Studies and the Edmund S. Muskie Institute of Public Affairs.

Scotch, R. K. (2001). *From good will to civil rights: Transforming federal disability policy* (2nd ed.). Philadelphia: Temple University Press.

Scotch, R. K., & Schriner, K. F. (1997). Disability as human variation: Implications for policy. *Annals of the American Academy of Political and Social Science, 549,* 148–160.

Smart, J. (2001). *Disability, society, and the individual.* Austin, TX: ProEd.

Starr, P. (1992). *The logic of health-care reform.* Knoxville, TN: Whittle Direct Books.

Stiker, H.-J. (2000). A history of disability. In W. Sayers (Trans.), *Corporealities: Discourses of disability.* Ann Arbor: University of Michigan Press.

Stone, D. A. (1986). *The disabled state.* Philadelphia: Temple University Press.

Stone, D. A. (2001). *Policy paradox: The art of political decision making* (Rev. ed.). New York: Norton.

U.S. Department of Health and Human Services, CMS: Centers for Medicare and Medicaid Services. (2006a, March 15). *Medicaid.* Retrieved June 17, 2006, from www.cms.hhs.gov/home/medicaid.asp.

U.S. Department of Health and Human Services, CMS: Centers for Medicare and Medicaid Services. (2006b, March 15). *Medicare coverage.* Retrieved June 17, 2006, from www.cms.hhs.gov/center/coverage.asp.

Wehman, P. (2000). Strategies for funding supported employment: A review of federal programs. *Journal of Vocational Rehabilitation, 14,* 179–182.

Winzer, M. (1993). *The history of special education.* Washington, DC: Gallaudet University Press.

Wright, D. (2001). *Mental disability in Victorian England: The Earlswood Asylum 1847–1901.* Oxford: Oxford University Press.

Chapter 12

HEALTH-CARE POLICY: SHOULD CHANGE BE SMALL OR LARGE?

Pamela J. Miller

How does one explain current health-care policies? For educators, students, and practitioners alike, policies that are currently in place in the United States to offer health services are complex, underfunded, disparate, inconsistent, state of the art, miraculous, successful, unjust, illogical, and more. There are too many adjectives, positive, negative, and somewhere in between, that can describe the U.S. approach to health care. This range of successes and failures is described by Enthoven and Kronick (1989) as a paradox of excess and deprivation. Our country has state-of-the-art technology, yet at times, many citizens go without health or medical care. Students often feel completely overwhelmed by health policies, particularly those concerning insurance coverage, unfunded care, and the many different programs embedded in the private and public sectors. Students also need help to remember that policy drives practice. What happens in health systems and what social workers are able to do in their day-to-day work environment are directly linked to the policies that are a part of the institution, the state and federal governments, and the private insurance industry.

Although it can be difficult, if not impossible, to understand all of the policies that have an impact on health care, this chapter discusses a select group of policies that are relevant in today's practice context. Not all of them might be considered mainstream policies, for example, the Radiation Exposure Compensation Act (RECA) or Oregon's Death with Dignity Act. These are offered along with better known policies, for example, the Medicare Hospice Benefit, Medicare Part D, the Patient Self-Determination Act (PSDA), the End-Stage Renal Disease (ESRD) Program, and policies specific to women's reproductive health. These are policies, however, that social workers should know about, that have a huge impact on clients and systems, and, most important, that need to be changed, updated, rewritten, and potentially discarded through advocacy on the part of our profession. Although an examination of these policies in a historical and political framework may not help the practitioner or student feel comfortable with the constraints imposed by current policies, at least some understanding of how the policy developed and how the policy is placed into action may be of benefit. Students and practitioners may have the "ah-ha" experience by understanding the background and political context in which policies evolved. Knowledge is needed for change, and the true motive behind exploration of these policies is to both frighten and inspire students. By examination of multiple health policies, the hope is that just one will spark the student or practitioner to get involved in the change process.

NEEDED BACKGROUND

Before launching into each selected policy, two major elements must be covered: (1) the uninsured and underinsured in this country and (2) health disparities. Both are threads that run through every one of the policies that are explained in more detail in this chapter. Lack of insurance, too little insurance, and health disparities have overarching and far-reaching implications for every facet of the individual policies that follow and for all heath policies in general in the United States.

The Uninsured and Underinsured

The health-care crisis that President Clinton identified in the 1990s is still with us. Our leaders may not be talking about it or working on it, but for those who are in the field and for many of our citizens, the crisis has intensified. The United States is among the few industrialized countries in the world that does not provide health care to all citizens. At the same time, U.S. medical technology is superior and highly utilized by those who can pay for it. The United States spends 13% of its Gross Domestic Product on health, $4,631 per capita, the highest in the world. All of this money, however, does not provide the best measures of health status. Starfield (2000) compared 14 countries and found that the United States ranked on average number 12 across several health indicators. The two most important signals of the health of a country is life expectancy and infant mortality. Among the 13 countries compared, the United States had the highest rate of infant mortality and ranked 11th for life expectancy for females and 12th for males.

Despite our medical miracles and fascination with technology, it is estimated that 18,000 deaths occur in the United States each year due to persons having no insurance or being underinsured (Institute of Medicine [IOM], 2004). With about 15% of the population uninsured, these deaths are a part of the legacy of the U.S. health-care system. The IOM's Committee on the Consequences of Uninsurance has published six in-depth reports that cover in great detail the impact of lack of health insurance in this country. Their overall conclusion is that a lack of health insurance for such a large part of our population "is a critical problem . . . that can and should be eliminated. The Committee believes that leaving 43 million Americans uninsured is costly to the country and should no longer be tolerated" (p. 18). The IOM, part of the National Academy of Sciences, believes that the president and Congress should work to insure all Americans by 2010. They acknowledge the incremental policy changes over the years, yet as a developed country, the United States has a major percentage of uninsured citizens, much like Mexico and Turkey. This group strongly supports an approach that eliminates the $85 billion of uncovered care that happens each year, 85% of which is covered by tax dollars.

There certainly has not been a lack of attempts at health care for all citizens in this country over the past 100 years. The Progressives made an attempt in the early part of the twentieth century, and after women were granted the right to vote, the Sheppard-Towner Act provided tax-supported care to infants and mothers (Siefert, 1983). The New Deal legislation did not cover health care, despite numerous attempts after 1935 to do so. In the Great Society years, two groups of people were given health coverage through the Social Security Act: the poor through Medicaid (Title 19) and the old through Medicare (Title 18). This fit with the War on Poverty and the grassroots efforts by the elderly for relief from medical costs (Katz, 1986). The most recent attempt for a national health program during the Clinton years was dismantled, just like the previous attempts, by insurance companies, organized medicine, pharmaceutical corporations, patriotic and special interest groups, elections, ideological passions, the American people's reluctance to pay for it, and many other diversions (Bodenheimer & Grumbach, 2005).

Health insurance coverage in the United States is tied to work, not citizenship. Again, this grew out of our political history as our country grew and developed. Political stability was not as much of a challenge here as it was in Europe in the 1800s, where socialism emerged as a political force. In this country, as labor unions grew, they did not align themselves with the Socialist Party, so there was not powerful working-class support for social insurance (Starr, 1982). Labor unions demanded health insurance from employers, not from the government. This helps explain why 55% of the population has health insurance through employment-based, private means. Still, many Americans who work do not have health insurance, either because it is not offered or is not affordable. Almost 80% of those without health insurance in the United States work at least part time or have someone in the household who works at least part time (Bodenheimer & Grumbach, 2005). Tying health insurance to employment is not working as it was once envisioned.

States have also made attempts to cover the uninsured. Oregon blazed this trail in 1994 with the Oregon Health Plan, spearheaded by John Kitzhaber, a state legislator and governor. This policy was developed to offer health insurance to *all* poor Oregonians, not just those in the federally defined categories for Medicaid. The plan had three parts: health insurance for all Oregonians with incomes below the poverty level, employer mandates, and the development of an insurance pool for those who could not purchase insurance. The plan was controversial and defined politically by some as rationing. The plan was in a sense illegal and had to be given special consideration by the federal government to be enacted. In fact, the first Bush administration would not approve the waiver needed to allow the plan to go forward. The Clinton administration did approve the Section 1115 waiver in 1993 after Kitzhaber, a Democrat, assisted Clinton in winning Oregon in the 1992 presidential election (Lunch, 2005). In the initial stages, the plan worked well, covering many more Oregonians than typical Medicaid (the uninsured rate fell from 18% to 11%) and reducing charity care at hospitals across the state (Bodenheimer, 1997). Unfortunately, as the state's economy faltered in the recent past, the Oregon Health Plan had to drop many of those who were recently added, and now Medicaid in the state looks much like it did 15 years ago.

Massachusetts's governor recently signed into law legislation aimed at providing health insurance to most of the state's citizens (Commonwealth of Massachusetts, 2006). This plan will require citizens with incomes above 300% of the federal poverty level to purchase health insurance from private companies at reduced rates. Employers, particularly small businesses, will be strongly encouraged to make a contribution toward health insurance premiums as well. The state is making efforts to find and sign up those who are eligible for Medicaid. In the next phase of the legislation, an insurance pool will be developed for the working poor and those citizens who are not employed. Massachusetts has an uninsured rate of about 7%, much lower than many other states (IOM, 2004). It will be interesting to see if the market-based reform plan works and if Governor Romney might use this legislation as a political feather in his bid for the Republican nomination for president in 2008.

Other states have tried to resolve or at least ameliorate the crushing financial and political issue of the uninsured, and most have floundered or failed. The tie to political aspirations has not worked well, and with many states having 15% to 25% of their citizens currently without health coverage, it would seem unlikely that states can do this alone.

Health Disparities

Often health disparities are defined in terms of race. However, gender can also be a barrier when health outcomes are evaluated. Obstetrical and gynecological policies are discussed later. However, women are less likely to receive heart surgeries and kidney transplants, and more women donate kidneys as live donors (Kayler et al., 2002). African American women receive treatment in the later stages of breast cancer and so are more likely to die of the disease than White women. In a study on race and gender, findings suggested that both influenced how physicians treat chest pain, with African American women getting the least intervention (Schulman et al., 1999). There was quite a reaction when this article was published. The American Medical Association wanted to be clear that doctors were not racists, and in the true sense of the word, that may be mostly true. However, there are very clear differences in access to health care, use of resources, and outcomes for our citizens of color. The institutionalization of racism may be more subtle and individuals within health systems may not consciously make racist decisions; however, the effects of disparate treatment are well-documented.

African Americans have far worse health than White Americans. African Americans have lower life expectancy, double the infant mortality rate, and higher mortality rates of cancer, stroke, and heart disease. Native Americans also have poor health outcomes. Other racial groups in the United States have varied health outcomes, and some groups have lower mortality rates than Whites (Bodenheimer & Grumbach, 2005). Immigrants may be healthier than native-born citizens in the early years of living in the country, but acculturation may have a negative impact on health over time (Abraido-Lanza & Dohrenwend, 1999). Health disparities also follow people into the aging process through disparate care in nursing homes (Mor, Zinn, Angelelli, Teno, & Miller, 2005).

In 2002, the IOM released a report titled *Unequal Treatment* (IOM, 2003). One of the tenets of the report is that even when insurance status, income, age, and medical conditions are similar, racial and ethnic minorities tend to receive less quality care than Whites. Many examples are given. Citizens of color are less likely to receive kidney dialysis or transplants, cancer screening, and up-to-date treatments for HIV/AIDS and are more likely to receive amputations. The report is clear that disparities do exist and that there are many reasons for the disparities, and the report also offers ways to reduce disparities. The report puts forth the notion that most health-care providers are not racist. However, due to time pressure, the complexities of the clinical encounter, and previously learned ideas about people of color, stereotyping does occur. These stereotypes then lead to inferior and unequal care.

POLICY TOPICS

The Radiation Exposure Compensation Act

This federal policy is one that most students have little or no knowledge about yet find quite interesting from a historical and political perspective. Congress passed this legislation in

1990 to compensate citizens who may have contracted particular cancers from exposure to nuclear weapons testing that occurred in the 1940s and later. Three groups are eligible to make claims: those who worked at the test sites, those who lived downwind from the test sites, and those who worked in uranium mines. For the downwinders in particular, who have developed 19 kinds of cancer and who live in 21 counties in Utah, Arizona, and Nevada, the compensation is $50,000.

The Institute for Energy and Environmental Research (IEER) analyzed data from a congressionally mandated study conducted by the U.S. Department of Health and Human Services, the Centers for Disease Control and Prevention, and the National Cancer Institute. The IEER (2002) estimates that 80,000 people who lived in or were born in the United States between 1951 and 2000 will get cancer as a result of fallout from nuclear testing and that at least 15,000 of those cancer cases will be fatal.

The Health Resources and Services Administration, which operates the Radiation Exposure Screening and Education Program for RECA, asked the National Academy of Sciences (NAS) to study and make recommendations on three areas of the program: (1) how to improve accessibility to the program and boost the quality of education and screening; (2) whether more recent scientific data could shed light on radiation exposure; and (3) whether more people or more locations in the United States should be added to the eligibility list. During this time, the IEER sent a letter to the NAS chair of the Committee to Assess the Scientific Information for the Radiation Exposure Screening and Education Program, Dr. Julian Preston (Makhijani & Ledwidge, 2004).

The letter states that the United States is a leader in the compensation of those made ill by nuclear tests. The letter asks that NAS consider (a) that persons who live in other parts of the nation should be informed of their potential risk because of exposure; (b) that medical professionals should be educated about the risks and diseases related to fallout; (c) that the definition of downwinder should be expanded to include other locations; (d) that the benefit of the doubt should be given to those exposed, not to the U.S. government, because it caused the harm, particularly since the milk supply appeared to be one of the primary methods for exposure; (e) that many Americans do not have health insurance and some of them are ill because of exposure, including those who were infants or in utero during the 1950s and 1960s; and (f) that the high incidence of thyroid cancer and thyroid disease in the United States may be attributable to radiation fallout.

When the committee released its report in April 2005 (NAS, 2005), they did recommend that RECA eligibility should not be limited to the boundaries that were implemented in the original legislation of 1990. The committee recommended that coverage should be extended to the continental United States, Hawaii, and other U.S. territories. Although the committee did not add to the list of diseases, they did advise that Congress set new eligibility criteria and requested that the screening criteria be made more efficient and inclusive. The committee also recommended more outreach about exposure from fallout through education and communication.

Local or regional communities may also have downwinders, for example, the Hanford downwinders in Washington, Idaho, Montana, and Oregon. This group of concerned citizens maintains that many people have been exposed and made ill by radiation through contaminated food, air, and water from the Hanford site, located in Washington, that manufactured plutonium for nuclear weapons. There has been ongoing litigation since 1990 with DuPont and General Electric, who operated the facility at different times for the

U.S government between 1946 and 1965 (www.downwinders.com). This example and the RECA program highlight the need for policies that attempt to ameliorate problems caused by government. Social workers can be very involved in advocacy and analysis to improve and develop programs that deal with health problems caused by our country's war and nuclear efforts. There is much work to be done here.

Medicare Part D

Many elderly in the United States worry about how to pay for drugs and how to pay for long-term care in their own home or in an institution. The Medicare Prescription Drug, Improvement, and Modernization Act passed through Congress in 2003 and added drug coverage for the nation's elderly and disabled. This was the largest change in the Medicare program since it was first enacted by Congress in 1965. There is a long political and social justice history behind why it took so long to offer this benefit (Larkin, 2004; Oliver, Lee, & Lipton, 2004). There are also politics involved in the passage of the bill in December 2003.

There is certainly no doubt that Medicare beneficiaries needed assistance with drug coverage; from a political perspective, there were many obstacles, particularly from powerful interest groups. However, according to Weissert (2003), several reasons for its passage came together late in 2003 that allowed for passage of the bill: (a) Both political parties needed a drug benefit because their constituents wanted one; (b) the president's poll performance was dropping; (c) there were problems with the war in Iraq; (d) the economy was sluggish; (e) the president had problems with staff leaks that hurt him politically; and (f) because Florida would continue to be a key Republican state for the presidential election in 2004, it would be politically prudent to pass such a bill. Also, it was difficult to oppose the bill because it included increased payments to physicians. So both parties would benefit from passage. There was an "extraordinary political window of opportunity in 2003" (Oliver et al., 2004, p. 289).

Medicare Part D is very complex and remains controversial. All individuals who have Medicare or Medicaid must receive their drug coverage through Medicare. So the poor elderly who normally received drugs through their state Medicaid programs would now receive them from Medicare, as would other poor elderly, at or below 135% of the poverty level ("Gearing Up," 2004). Otherwise, the drug benefit is administered through private firms on a regional basis. The elderly person chooses a plan and then pays a monthly premium and copayments for each prescription. If an individual did not signed up for the program by May 15, 2006, extra charges will be imposed if the person decides to enroll at a later date.

It is interesting to note that the drug industry actually supported this bill in the later stages of its development and movement through Congress. Why is this, since they opposed any and all bills related to government involvement before this? The answer is easy. Drug corporations got a huge piece of business from a group of people who buy lots of drugs; the bill actually prohibits cost control; the government will not be involved in direct administration of the program (that happens in the private and mostly for-profit sector); and the law does not allow the legalization of importing drugs. Just a couple of years earlier, both Maine and Oregon had decided to try to control drug costs in their own states, and the pharmaceutical industry was very opposed to these programs (Palfreman, 2003). So this was a nice package for the drug industry in many different ways. Tucker (as cited in Oliver et al., 2004, p. 319) states:

> The bill pays private insurance companies to take elderly patients. You know how one of the tenets of conservative philosophy is that private companies can always deliver a product better and cheaper? So why does the Medicare bill offer billions in subsidies to private insurers to induce them into the market? That's not competition, that's corporate welfare.

This legislation also fueled reelection campaigns in 2004. The president delivered a campaign promise, and some Democrats who voted for the bill received negative feedback from constituents who saw its passage as a major Republican victory (Mapes, 2003). The American Association of Retired Persons supported the bill, and this prompted 60,000 members who disagreed with this decision to either resign from the organization or refuse to renew membership (Pear & Toner, 2003). There certainly was much to consider, and maybe it was better to have drug coverage for the elderly and disabled now rather than wait several more years for another political point in time to pass such a complex piece of policy. In any case, the price tag for drug coverage under Medicare was estimated at $400 billion; this would cover about one-fifth of the estimated $1.85 trillion that Medicare beneficiaries will spend in the next 10 years (Oliver et al., 2004). However, the true price tag may have been withheld, as a person in the Medicare administration was ordered to withhold cost estimates during the bill's hearings (Pear, 2004).

Social workers are already very involved in helping Medicare beneficiaries sift through the options available through Plan D. It could prove to be unfortunate that the program is basically run through private insurance providers and that the drugs are purchased with no cost controls. The price tag may prove to be unbearable, but who knows? Once again our leaders have enacted a policy that helped some elected officials in the short term yet may have put citizens at risk for little or no benefit. There is much work to be done here.

The Patient Self-Determination Act and the Medicare Hospice Benefit

Although these two policies are different pieces of legislation, they are related in the sense that they are tied to the end-of-life stage. Certainly both are tied to the right-to-die movement that was gaining momentum in the 1970s and 1980s, and it was in 1990 that the PSDA was passed in Congress. The Medicare Hospice Benefit became law in 1982, and hospices began their certification process for the program as soon as the rules were written. Both of these federal policies have had successes, setbacks, and failures. As before, both pieces of legislation have interesting political histories.

The PSDA was passed, in part, by the uproar over the *Cruzan* case. This young woman was injured in a car accident, and although her family believed she would not want to live in a persistent vegetative state, they did not have any of her wishes in writing. This case went to the U.S. Supreme Court and then back to local courts, and so the family requested that the feeding tube be removed (Colby, 2002). Senator John Danforth of Missouri, where the Cruzan family lived, was worried about many other families that were affected by the same dilemmas as the Cruzans. He proposed and pushed the PSDA as a way for citizens to write down their requests for end-of-life treatment, called advance directives, in hopes that situations like the Cruzans' could be avoided (Glick, 1992). The law requires that all health agencies that receive federal funds must inform patients about their organization's polices, state laws, and rights within the PSDA. Each state has different forms and procedures that meet this requirement. There was hope that all Americans would write down their requests, but unfortunately, this has not been the case. Except for a wave of activity after the *Schiavo* case in 2005 (in which government at many levels became very involved), the rate of implementation of advance directives has remained low, somewhere around 18% of the population (Fagerlin & Schneider, 2004).

The Medicare Hospice Benefit became law in 1982 as part of the Tax Equity and Fiscal Responsibility Act. This was the only social program passed during this session of Congress under the Reagan administration. The bill might not have passed if the results of the National Hospice Study had been completed before Congress voted, as it found that hospice care really did not save money, despite how it was pitched to the House and Senate. The hospice benefit is an incremental policy change in that it builds on the home care program already well established in the Medicare program. One major change was the coverage of drugs for terminal illness. This was viewed as quite a landmark at the time. The payment method of hospice was prospective rather than fee-for service, in anticipation of diagnostic related groups that began under the Medicare program in 1983 (Miller & Mike, 1995).

Now the terminally ill in our country had the right to state what they wanted, or more important at times, what they did not want at the end of life. And now a program under Medicare was available to take care of beneficiaries when life was projected to last 6 months or less. As with the PSDA, the hospice benefit is underutilized, and many do not use it at all. The median length of stay in a hospice program nationwide remains 22 days, with 35% of patients dying in 7 days or less after admission (National Hospice and Palliative Care Organization, 2006). There are many reasons given for this problem: denial of death, overtreatment, doctors unwilling to suggest hospice, patients wanting to continue treatment, the inability to predict the time of life left, the complexities of switching into the Medicare benefit, financial concerns, and more. Many who are chronically ill could benefit from hospice-like services but are not eligible, despite a trajectory toward death. Our policies that define life and death, who can receive services and when, and what will be covered by insurance are cutting out a large group of the seriously and chronically ill who become terminal too late to take advantage of the hospice benefit (Abraham, 1993; Bern-Klug, 2004). There is much work to be done here.

Oregon's Death with Dignity Act

Oregon's Death with Dignity Act was approved by voters in 1994 and was rejected as a repeal ballot measure in 1997. Within 8 years of the law's passage, 246 people had used the law to end their lives with a lethal dose of medication (Oregon Department of Human Services, Health Services, 2006). The amount of federal involvement in this case is quite compelling. Congress tried to intervene, and John Ashcroft, attorney general in the Bush administration, tried to stop the law, stating that it violated the Controlled Substances Act (Miller & Werth, 2005). The U.S. Supreme Court ruled in January 2006 that this was not the case. In 1997, the federal government enacted the Assisted Suicide Funding Restriction Act, which orders that federal monies may not be used for a hastened death. This essentially acts like the Hyde Amendment for abortion (Miller, 2000). Oregon is the only state with a law that legalizes a physician to prescribe a lethal dose of medication to end life. Other states may follow (Miller & Hedlund, 2005). At least six other states have some kind of legislation similar to Oregon's that is either pending or in committee (Miller, Hedlund, & Soule, in press). In preparation for the 2006 elections, the Republican Party planned to use Oregon's law (as well as abortion) as a rallying point for voters (Kosseff, 2006).

Because so many who have used the law have been hospice patients, social workers have been involved with many patients and families who have considered the law and/or used it to end their lives. From a policy perspective, this has been an interesting time to observe how policy drives practice and how the guidelines for the law were developed and implemented. All professionals were surprised when the law passed, and most were unprepared for how to deal with the option that now appeared to be legal. Leadership emerged at Oregon's Health and Science University, and many end-of-life practitioners came together, despite their own personal beliefs, and worked to craft guidelines for practice within the law. The policies that were written have changed over time and represent the best practices available to those who choose to use the law and those who work within the Act (Task Force to Improve the Care of Terminally-Ill Oregonians, 2006). There is much work to be done here.

Women's Reproductive Health

This topic brings us to the right to choose and the controversy about life and death. It includes policies about abortion and contraception for all women, young women, and poor women and also whether or not states require insurance coverage of contraception, as well as the availability of emergency contraception. There is much written on this subject from many vantage points, and women's reproductive rights have been a battle for social workers and the American Medical Association for over a century (Haslett, 1997; Wolinsky & Brune, 1994). Feldt (2004) describes the battle over abortion as a "war on choice"; she believes that women's health around the world is in jeopardy as the right to choose is not available or is taken away. Ipas (2006), an international organization for women's reproductive health, estimates that 70,000 women die each year from unsafe abortions, almost half of those in Asia.

The *Roe v. Wade* Supreme Court case established the right of abortion in the United States but did not necessarily guarantee access. The first major legislation to limit access after this famous court case was the Hyde Amendment in 1976. This federal law prevents Medicaid funds from being used for poor women's abortions, and very quickly several states decided to enforce this funding restriction. The Supreme Court even had to rule that the Hyde Amendment was constitutional before it took effect in 1980. Since then, numerous states do not fund abortions for poor women, except in cases of rape, incest, or endangerment of health. Some states will pay for the procedure out of state funds (for a current list of those states, see Guttmacher Institute, 2006).

A study by Jones, Darroch, and Henshaw (2002) looked at the trends and patterns of abortion in the United States. The authors state that the abortion rate fell by 11% between 1994 and 2000. This decline was most notable in young women ages 15 to 17, those in higher socioeconomic groups, and women with college degrees. The rate actually went up for poor women and poor teenagers. This means that the rates went up for women of color, as they are disproportionately poor. Health disparities hit here also. The study emphasizes that all women need access to ways to prevent unwanted pregnancies and that poor women may find it difficult to obtain and use contraception. The authors tie the increase in the abortion rate for poor women to welfare reform at this time. This reform had an impact on Medicaid coverage, coupled with the general increase in the number of women with no health insurance coverage. The authors write that there is a "clear association between poverty status and abortion, the abortion rate being higher among poor and low-income women than among those with incomes greater than 200% of poverty" (p. 234).

The state of South Dakota recently passed a ban on all abortions, even when pregnancy is due to rape or incest; the only exception is when the woman's life, not health, is in danger. Doctors will be fined $5,000 and put in prison for 5 years for violating this law. This is the most restrictive state measure to date. South Dakota already has restrictive policies for abortion and has one clinic that performs abortions by physicians flown in from Minnesota, as no doctors who reside in the state will do abortions (Nieves, 2006). Those opposed to choice want the law to be taken to the U.S. Supreme Court, with the hope that the current Court will overturn *Roe v. Wade*. No court appeals have been filed. However, citizens in the state gathered signatures for a petition requesting that this law not be put into effect until citizens of the state could vote on it in November 2006. Opponents of the law did get a measure on the ballot and voters rejected the restrictive law passed by the state legislature, particularly since abortion could not be accessed even for rape or incest. Now the state legislature is taking another look at the law with this in mind. At least 10 other states have attempted to challenge *Roe v. Wade* by banning all abortions, but none, besides South Dakota, have passed such legislation. Many other states have attempted to reduce access in various ways (Guttmacher Institute, 2006).

Access to abortions for teens is also under great scrutiny, controversy, and change. Parental involvement is required for teens who seek an abortion in 34 states. This could mean parental notification or parental permission; some states require one parent to be involved, and other states require both parents, and sometimes both biological parents to be involved. In January 2006, the Supreme Court ruled that states can require parental involvement in abortion decisions for minors (Ipas, 2006). There is quite a bit of state legislative action on the rights of minors around sexual health, most to restrict rights. Many states have laws about access to birth control and emergency contraception for teens (Guttmacher Institute, 2006).

The American Academy of Pediatrics recently released an update on current trends in adolescent pregnancy (Klein & the Committee on Adolescence, 2005). The authors note that high pregnancy rates for teens in the 1950s and 1960s dropped after abortion became legal; then in 1986 the rates went up, and now the rates have gone down again since 1991. However, at least 4 out of 10 women have been pregnant once before the age of 20. The United States has the highest adolescent birthrate of all industrialized countries, even when compared to countries where sexual activity is higher. The Committee on Adolescence offered many clinical considerations that have an impact on policy. The overarching theme is the need to educate young people about sex and parenting, but also to have contraception, including emergency contraception, available as part of good medical care (p. 284).

Emergency contraception policies are quite complex and differ all over the country. The medication, a high dose of a drug contained in birth control pills, taken within 72 hours after unprotected sex, can prevent a pregnancy up to almost 89% of the time. Some view this as equivalent to an abortion and have many of the same arguments against the use of what has become known as Plan B. At the federal level, the Food and Drug Administration's (FDA) scientific advisors supported the sale of the drug over the counter in December 2003. In an unusual move, in August 2005 the commissioner of the FDA, Lester Crawford, stated that Plan B would not be available over the counter until more research could be obtained about the use of the drug in young teens. The director of the FDA's Office of Women's Health resigned soon after this decision was made; Davidoff (2006) believes that sex, politics, and morality collided in this debate.

When Barr Laboratories agreed to make emergency contraceptives available only to women 17 and older, the FDA still said no, despite data showing that half of all unwanted pregnancies (3 million each year, and 800,000 of those teens), could be cut down by 50% (Advocates for Youth, 2006). There are many state policies about emergency contraception that apply to hospital emergency rooms, selling the drug over the counter, not forcing pharmacists to fill prescriptions (as is allowed for regular contraceptives as well), and whether or not Medicaid should cover this drug (Guttmacher Institute, 2006). Even campus health centers have wrestled with whether or not this drug should be available to college students (August, 2003).

Behind the abortion debate and the ongoing controversy about teens' rights to health care, the coverage of contraceptives by health insurance also rages on. Many private health insurance plans cover prescription drugs, but some do not cover contraception and medical services for such. Take Oregon, for example. There is not a law or mandate or policy that requires private health plans to cover contraception (Guttmacher Institute, 2006). State employees, through policy, do have coverage. There has been an attempt in Oregon, as well as at the federal level, to mandate health insurance for contraception. In 2004, a Catholic social service agency in California was told by the state supreme court that it must provide birth control in its health plan for employees, despite the Church's opposition to contraception (California Catholic Conference, 2006). The questions are: Should women who work for religious organizations have the right to coverage of contraception? Or are women who work for religious organizations to be held to the moral beliefs of the employer?

When discussing women's health, disparities emerge as a problem of access and treatment across many health indicators. Women of color are less likely to receive adequate care for their reproductive health and therefore have higher rates of infant and maternal mortality, late screening for breast and cervical cancer, and higher incidence of HIV/AIDS and other sexually transmitted diseases. Language and cultural barriers may contribute to these problems. Over 16 million women are uninsured, and even when they are insured, some reproductive services are not covered (National Association of Social Workers, 2004). It seems as though women are caught in a loop: President Bush wants to reduce the number of abortions, yet access to birth control is limited. As Davidoff (2006, p. 25) states:

> Like all powerful forces—terrorism, hurricanes, pandemics—the power of sex can seem appalling, terrifying, something that must be controlled at all costs. And since men exert most organized social control, the control over sexuality is asserted primarily by controlling the sexual and reproductive lives of women.

There is much work to be done here.

End-Stage Renal Disease Program

President Richard Nixon signed the ESRD Program into law in October 1972. This program was instituted partly because the technology was available at the time for dialysis (the cleansing of the blood) and kidney transplantation. This program covers the expenses of those with kidney failure who would die without dialysis or transplant through the Medicare program. There is an interesting history behind this federal program, and it is included in this chapter for that reason.

In 1962, *Life* magazine published an article titled "They Decide Who Lives, Who Dies," by Shana Alexander. The story is about a group of seven people who meet a few times a year to decide who can receive dialysis. They were selected as volunteers from the community to serve on this committee at the Swedish Hospital in Seattle. The patients served by this program were in an experiment of sorts to determine if the dialysis treatment, then costing about $15,000 per year, was feasible for the entire country. This group did not make medical decisions; they decided, based on some criteria, who merited the treatment and who did not. Those rejected from the program died.

The article goes on in great detail about the meetings of the committee and the process by which they made decisions over time. There are also quotes from the committee members, identified only by their profession; their names are not used. They did not know the names of the patients until this article was published. The criteria used to consider those who would receive dialysis were the patient's age and sex (those over 45 and children were not considered as a rule), marital status, number of children, income, net worth, emotional stability, educational background, occupation, future potential, and names of references (Alexander, 1962, p. 105). The committee wrestled with the situation of a woman with two children who would have to move to Seattle but did not have the funds, and a man with six children who had a good job. Both needed the treatment and would die if not chosen. One of the members spoke to the problem of remarriage of the surviving spouse of the one not chosen, and the burden to society of a particular person's death. This was truly difficult work, and we can look back on it now and see the snapshot of the social and cultural norms of that time.

Dialysis and transplantation did become more available over time and were seen as ways to save lives and keep people in the workforce. There was still hope that universal health insurance might be a possibility in the near future, particularly because in 1965 coverage for the elderly and poor had been established. Medicare coverage for the disabled was also passed into law in 1972. Congress believed that kidney dialysis and transplantation clearly saved lives and deserved Medicare coverage. Wilbur Mills, a Democrat from Arkansas, actually proposed the idea of the ESRD Program and arranged for a patient to be dialyzed at a House Ways and Means Committee meeting in late 1971 (Iglehart, 1993). When the program passed both the House and Senate in the fall of 1972, there was little discussion about the bill, and it seemed that Congress "implied that the value of life is beyond price" (p. 367).

The ESRD Program provides Medicare coverage for kidney failure to those eligible by disease and by work covered by Social Security. Even children can be covered because their parents have worked enough and contributed to Social Security. The United States has a higher treatment rate than other countries because the criteria used to select those eligible are fairly broad. This means that U.S. survival rates are lower as well (Iglehart, 1993). The intricacies and complexities of this program are enormous. Social workers are mandated to work with patients who come to dialysis centers. The interesting point about dialysis is that almost all of it is carried out in the for-profit sector. The program has also gotten more expensive over the years as more and more people begin dialysis or get a transplant when an organ is available. Although the program serves only .5% of those on Medicare, it uses 6.7% of the Medicare budget. Another way to understand this is that the average Medicare patient uses $6,100 per year, whereas a patient in the ESRD Program uses $41,700 per year (United States Renal Data System, 2005). Those who voted on this so quickly in 1972 truly believed the program would continue to be available to those who had no other health complications and that dialysis would help them get back to work; it would be, in effect, a budget-neutral program.

Students often scratch their heads and wonder why the Medicare system covers only one disease when so many other diseases go uninsured. The politics of the times and the history of the ESRD Program offer a policy that began as a way to save lives based on up-to-the-moment technology and then turned into a program that its founders probably did not expect. Iglehart (1993, p. 371) sums this up well:

> The End Stage Renal Disease Program demonstrates the humane impulse that strikes Americans periodi-
> cally to act on behalf of a vulnerable population. The legislative history of the program suggests that this
> impulse is driven more by emotions, timing, and the political need to expand benefits than by rational
> planning.

There is much work to be done here.

POLICIES AND PROGRAMS WORTH EXPLORING

The National Commission on Prevention Priorities (2006) recently released a study about cost-effective preventive services. The impetus for this research rests with the knowledge that our health system emphasizes cure and treatment of disease rather than working to stop problems before they begin. Couple this with the aging baby boomers and the continued advancement of technology, and health-care spending may grow significantly in the next decade. The study ranked preventive services based on a score of which service produced the most health benefit, added to a score on cost effectiveness. Twenty-five evidence-based clinical preventive services were ranked.

Three services received a perfect score of 10: discussing daily aspirin use with high-risk adults, immunizing children, and tobacco use screening and treatment. Eight services received a score of 7 or higher: adult vaccines for influenza and pneumonia, screening for cancer of the cervix and the colon, vision screening for those over 65, and screening for hypertension, cholesterol, and alcohol intake. Nussbaum (2006, p. 1) explains:

> If colorectal cancer screening were offered at recommended intervals to all people 50 aged [sic] years and
> older, 18,000 deaths could be prevented each year . . . . Colorectal cancer screening costs less than $13,000
> per year of life saved, demonstrating its value as a high-impact, cost-effective preventive service. Yet, less
> than half of the target population uses this service.

People are dying because they do not receive preventive services in a country with some of the most advanced technology in the world. The problem comes back again to lack of health insurance and health disparities and our continued focus on services after disease has taken hold. The finding that screening and treatment for tobacco and alcohol use would be beneficial and cost-effective is also quite interesting. The use of these two substances, in the author's opinion, are often overlooked, denied, ignored, diminished, distorted, or dismissed by health-care professionals. It is so easy to get caught up in the heat of the medical problem at hand and not look at the other factors that are brought into the medical situation. Social workers in health systems must be aware of the need for these screenings and advocate for them with their patients. If our health systems are to survive, prevention must take a lead in how citizens are served in this country. Social workers are trained and educated well to offer some of these services. The problem is that there are no mechanisms for payment, and that is why they are not a priority.

The federal government, through the U.S. Department of Health and Human Services, has launched Healthy People 2010 with two main goals: to increase quality and years of healthy life and to eliminate health disparities. There are 28 focus areas and 10 leading health indicators that are identified as major health concerns: physical activity, overweight/obesity, tobacco use, substance abuse, responsible sexual behavior, mental health, injury and violence, environmental quality, immunization, and access to health care. This project is currently undergoing a period of public comment (Healthy People 2010, n.d.). There are numerous coalitions, businesses, and communities involved in trying to work on the goals and the focus areas. The goals are big, yet very critical.

I would like to share a movement that is small but growing in the state of Oregon. It is called the Archimedes movement and was started in January 2006 by former governor John Kitzhaber (www.archimedesmovement.org). He believes that tension must be created and leadership must emerge to create change in our health-care system. The movement is also based on the ideas that the health programs we have now (in particular Medicare and Medicaid) cannot be updated or upgraded through incremental change and that politics and politicians will not help resolve the health crisis. Communities and coalitions must work together on common goals and values around health care and push our legislators to either defend the current system (which is pretty hard to do) or work on new alternatives and structures for the health care system. Kitzhaber says so eloquently:

> The Archimedes Movement seeks to position Oregon, and hopefully several other states, to request a broad range of waivers (both statutory and administrative) that will force Congress to compare the current system to a comprehensive vision of how we should be providing health care to our people—a vision rooted in traditional and pragmatic values of fairness, inclusion, and quality and promotes health as the fundamental cornerstone of upward mobility in a democratic society.

FUTURE DIRECTIONS

The policies described in this chapter are all part of the health policy course that I currently teach to graduate students. Other important policies and policy topics, which there is not enough room to cover in this chapter, are the Americans with Disabilities Act, transplantation, blood supply, egg donation, funding for and research on stem cells, human subjects research, dilation and evacuation procedures (the Supreme Court, in April of 2007, did uphold the Partial Birth Abortion Act and for the first time allowed for the only exception to be for the woman's life, not her health), preparation for psychological and behavioral consequences of bioterrorism, AIDS, the Ricky Ray Hemophilia Relief Fund, long-term care, the Ryan White Act, the effect of the Tuskegee study on African Americans and research, and RU-486. The list of topics and the political and social history behind each one is rich with the background and politics of the time. Students must understand these histories to be better prepared to focus on the next steps for policy development in health care. Otherwise, we will make the same mistakes and lose the strength and power of what has come before. As stated after each policy topic, there is much to do.

I believe the reader of this chapter has to decide both professionally and personally what matters. Should the focus be on something small, such as revamping a state's Medicaid policy, or large, such as redesigning the entire way health care is delivered? Should we continue the path of market reform of the identified problems or create new ways, outside of the private, for-profit sector, to handle our health crisis? There is certainly much political wrangling both historically and today about how changes should be made and how votes might be garnered by particular stands or ideas. I maintain, somewhat softly, that we appear to have enough data to show that the health system is failing and needs life support of its own. As seen in the policies presented here, many experts, professional groups, scientific organizations, and government agencies have sounded the alarm with solid data about the extreme problems of health-care delivery in our country. We certainly had less hard data before beginning a war on terror. I advocate for a war on uninsured Americans. How do we make this a priority? One small path is to educate about the political past in order to plan for a better future.

CONCLUSION

Policy drives practice, and all of the clinical training in the world cannot change this fact. The lesson plan in my health policy class is to discuss and explore a wide variety of policies in the hope that every student will find one tiny policy that will pull him or her in and get him or her excited about how to be involved—the frightened and then inspired plan for action! Issues of social justice are in every single policy presented here. When students can understand how a policy works, where it came from, whom it concerns, and what politics are involved, they can begin to work for change. The change may come in day-to-day practice awareness or in community involvement for new programs, or logging on to a web site and getting involved in the creation of a new structure for how health care is delivered, or taking leadership on election platforms. The possibilities and strategies are plentiful (Jansson, 2004). The reasons for change are very clear: Too many die due to lack of health coverage and disparities. If we heard about these needless deaths as much as the lives lost in terrorist attacks or hurricanes, maybe some attention to the problem could take hold. We have a natural disaster unfolding every day in the United States through a lack of insurance and disparities. As we say, sometimes in jest and sometimes with great seriousness, What is wrong with this picture? Why are our political leaders not paying attention?

REFERENCES

Abraham, L. K. (1993). *Mama might be better off dead*. Chicago: University of Chicago Press.

Abraido-Lanza, A. F., & Dohrenwend, B. P. (1999). The Latino mortality paradox: A test of the "salmon bias" and healthy migrant hypothesis. *American Journal of Public Health*, 89(10), 1543–1548.

Advocates for Youth. (2006). *Emergency contraception.* Retrieved June 12, 2006, from www .advocatesforyouth.org.

Alexander, S. (1962, November 9). They decide who lives, who dies. *Life*, 102–125.

August, M. (2003, June 2). A battle over the morning-after pill. *Time*, 8.

Bern-Klug, M. (2004). The ambiguous dying syndrome. *Health and Social Work*, *29*(1), 55–65.

Bodenheimer, T. S. (1997). The Oregon health plan: Lessons for the nation. *New England Journal of Medicine*, *337*(9), 651–723.

Bodenheimer, T. S., & Grumbach, K. (2005). *Understanding health policy.* New York: McGraw-Hill.

California Catholic Conference. (2006). *California Supreme Court rules against Catholic charities.* Retrieved June 12, 2006, from www.cacatholic.org/courtdecision.html.

Colby, W. H. (2002). *Long goodbye: The deaths of Nancy Cruzan.* Carlsbad, CA: Hay House.

Commonwealth of Massachusetts. (2006). *Romney launches healthcare reform in Massachusetts.* Retrieved May 17, 2006, from www.mass.gov.

Davidoff, F. (2006). Sex, politics, and morality at the FDA: Reflections on the Plan B decision. *Hastings Center Report*, *36*(2), 20–25.

Enthoven, A., & Kronick, R. (1989). A consumer-choice health plan for the 1990s. *New England Journal of Medicine*, *320*(1), 29–37.

Fagerlin, A., & Schneider, C. E. (2004). Enough: The failure of the living will. *Hastings Center Report*, *34*(2), 30–42.

Feldt, G. (2004). *The war on choice.* New York: Bantam Books.

Gearing up: States face the new Medicare law: Is your state ready for 2006? An introduction to what the new Medicare Part D prescription drug benefit means for Medicaid. (2004). *Families USA: The Voice for Health Care Consumers.* Retrieved June 6, 2006, from www.familiesusa.org/site /DocServer?docID=4401/.

Glick, H. R. (1992). *The right to die: Policy innovation and its consequences.* New York: Columbia University Press.

Guttmacher Institute. (2006). *State facts on abortion, emergency contraception, and insurance coverage for contraceptives.* Retrieved June 12, 2006, from www.guttmacher.org.

Haslett, D. C. (1997). Hull House and the birth control movement: An untold story. *Affilia*, *12*(3), 261–277.

Healthy People 2010. (n.d.). *What is Healthy People 2010?* Retrieved November 4, 2004, from www .healthypeople.gov.

Iglehart, J. K. (1993). The End Stage Renal Disease Program. *New England Journal of Medicine*, *328*(5), 366–371.

Institute for Energy and Environmental Research. (2002). *About 80,000 cancers in the United States, more than 15,000 of them fatal, attributable to fallout from worldwide atmospheric nuclear testing.* Retrieved June 6, 2006, from www.ieer.org/comments/fallout/pr0202.html.

Institute of Medicine. (2003). *Unequal treatment: Confronting racial and ethnic disparities in health care.* Washington, DC: National Academies Press.

Institute of Medicine. (2004). *Insuring America's health: Principles and recommendations.* Washington, DC: National Academies Press.

Ipas. (2006). *The global problem of unsafe abortion.* Retrieved June 12, 2006, from www.ipas.org.

Jansson, B. S. (2004). *Becoming an effective policy advocate: From policy practice to social justice.* Pacific Grove, CA: Brooks/Cole.

Jones, R. K., Darroch, J. E., & Henshaw, S. K. (2002). Patterns in the socioeconomic characteristics of women obtaining abortions in 2000–2001. *Perspectives on Sexual and Reproductive Health*, *34*(5), 226–235.

Katz, M. B. (1986). *In the shadow of the poorhouse.* New York: Basic Books.

Kaylor, L. K., Meier-Kriesche, H., Punch, J. D., Campbell, D. A., Leichtman, A. G., Magee, J. C., et al. (2002). Gender imbalance in living donor renal transplantation. *Transplantation*, *73*(2), 248–252.

Klein, J. D. & the Committee on Adolescence. (2005). Adolescent pregnancy: Current trends and issues. *Pediatrics*, *116*(1), 281–286.

Kosseff, J. (2006, June 12). GOP puts suicide law in spotlight. *Oregonian*, pp. A1, A6.

Larkin, H. (2004). Justice implications of a proposed Medicare prescription drug policy. *Social Work*, *49*(3), 406–414.

Lunch, W. (2005). Health policy. In R. A. Claus, M. Henkels, & B. S. Steel (Eds.), *Oregon politics and government* (pp. 242–255). Lincoln: University of Nebraska Press.

Makhijani, A., & Ledwidge, L. (2004, September 2). *IEER letter to National Academy of Sciences committee that is assessing the Radiation Exposure Screening and Education Program.* Archived at www.ieer.org/comments/fallout/nasltr0904.html.

Mapes, J. (2003, December 5). Wyden, Wu test waters among constituents on Medicare bill. *Oregonian*, A1, A15.

Miller, P. J. (2000). Life after death with dignity: The Oregon experience. *Social Work*, *45*(3), 263–271.

Miller, P. J., & Hedlund, S. C. (2005). "We just happen to live here": Two social workers share their stories about Oregon's Death with Dignity law. *Journal of Social Work in End-of-Life and Palliative Care*, *1*(1), 71–86.

Miller, P. J., Hedlund, S. C., & Soule, A. (in press). Conversations at the end-of-life: The challenge to support patients who consider death with dignity in Oregon. *Journal of Social Work in End-of-Life and Palliative Care.*

Miller, P. J., & Mike, P. B. (1995). The Medicare hospice benefit: Ten years of federal policy for the terminally ill. *Death Studies*, *19*, 531–542.

Miller, P. J., & Werth, J. L. (2005). Amicus curiae brief for the United States Supreme Court on mental health, terminal illness, and assisted death. *Journal of Social Work in End-of-Life and Palliative Care*, *1*(4), 7–33.

Mor, V., Zinn, J., Angelelli, J., Teno, J. M., & Miller, S. C. (2005). Driven to tiers: Socio-economic and racial disparities in the quality of nursing home care. *Milbank Quarterly*, *82*(2), 227–256. Retrieved September 21, 2005, from www.milbank.org/quarterly/8202feat.html.

National Academy of Sciences. (2005). *Assessment of the scientific information for the Radiation Exposure Screening and Education Program.* Washington, DC: National Academies Press.

National Association of Social Workers. (2004). *Reproductive health disparities for women of color.* Retrieved October 15, 2005, from www.naswdc.org.

National Commission on Prevention Priorities. (2006). *Priorities for America's health: Capitalizing on life-saving, cost-effective preventive services.* Retrieved June 7, 2006, from www.prevent.org/ncpp/.

National Hospice and Palliative Care Organization. (2006). *Hospice facts and figures.* Retrieved June 12, 2006, from www.nhpco.org.

Nieves, E. (2006, February 23). S.D. abortion bill takes aim at "Roe." *Washington Post*, p. A01.

Nussbaum, S. R. (2006). Prevention: The cornerstone of quality care. *American Journal of Preventive Medicine.* Available from www.prevent.org/content/view/50/101.

Oliver, T. R., Lee, P. R., & Lipton, H. L. (2004). A political history of Medicare and prescription drug coverage. *Milbank Quarterly*, *82*(2), 283–354.

Oregon Department of Human Services, Health Services. (2006). *Eighth annual report on Oregon's Death with Dignity Act.* Portland, OR: Author. Retrieved March 9, 2006, from www.oregon.gov/DHS/ph/pas/docs/year8.pdf.

Palfreman, J. (Producer). (2003, November 13). The other drug war. *Frontline* [Television broadcast]. Arlington, VA: Public Broadcasting Service.

Pear, R. (2004, May 4). Agency sees withholding of Medicare data from Congress as illegal. *New York Times*, p. A17.

Pear, R., & Toner, R. (2003, November 18). Medicare plan covering drugs backed by AARP. *New York Times*, p. A1.

Schulman, K. A., Berlin, J. A., Harless, W., Kerner, J. F., Sistrunk, S., Gersh, B. J., et al. (1999). The effect of race and sex on physicians' recommendations for cardiac catheterization. *New England Journal of Medicine*, 340(8), 618–626.

Siefert, K. (1983). An exemplar of primary prevention in social work: The Sheppard-Towner Act of 1921. *Social Work in Health Care*, 9(1), 87–101.

Starfield, B. (2000). Is U.S. health really the best in the world? *Journal of the American Medical Association*, 284(4), 483–485.

Starr, P. (1982). *The social transformation of American medicine*. New York: Basic Books.

Task Force to Improve the Care of Terminally-Ill Oregonians. (2006). *The Oregon Death with Dignity Act: A guidebook for health care providers*. Portland, OR: Author. Archived at www.ohsu.edu/ethics/.

United States Renal Data System. (2005). *Annual data report*. Retrieved June 12, 2006, from www.usrds.org/adr.htm.

Weissert, W. G. (2003). Medicare rx: Just a few of the reasons why it was so difficult to pass. *Public Policy and Aging Report*, 13(4), 1, 3–6.

Wolinsky, H., & Brune, T. (1994). *The serpent on the staff: The unhealthy politics of the American Medical Association*. New York: Putnam's Sons.

Chapter 13

SOCIAL DETERMINANTS OF HEALTH: TWENTY-FIRST-CENTURY SOCIAL WORK PRIORITIES

Gary Rosenberg

SOCIAL WORK AT THE END OF THE NINETEENTH CENTURY

The original aims of social work were to link persons in a social context, address economic and social needs, and achieve social justice. As a profession, social work has been considered responsible for assisting the poor, troubled persons, and working families (Morris, 2000a).

Two significant occurrences took place at the end of the nineteenth century that shaped early social work in the Anglo-Saxon countries: the arrival of millions of European immigrants to the United States and the era of the progressive movement. The progressive movement was a middle-class movement advocating for social and political reform against the backdrop of political and economic corruption, the poor living arrangements among immigrants, the rise of socialist ideas, and the conditions adversely affecting women and children. There was a rapid growth of voluntary nonprofit organizations funded by religious communities and leaders in the business world. These agencies allowed social work to grow as an occupation due to the need for dedicated staff. The purpose of the private institutions was to escape the politically controlled government social welfare programs (Austin, 2000). These agencies provided charitable relief to the needy, which included material relief, moral reform, and advice and counseling. As work became more complex, coordinating agencies were formed. Charity organizations were a mix of secular and religious sponsorship (Austin, 2000; Midgley, 1995; Morris, 2000a, 2000b).

At the end of the nineteenth century, the original social workers became advocates for those in need, while considering ways to alleviate daily suffering (Hopps, 2000). The emergence of the social sciences in academia permitted new consideration of applying science to social problems (Austin, 2000).

At the end of the nineteenth and beginning of the twentieth century settlement house workers, family visitors, union organizers, and community workers attacked the negatives, exposed injustices, and advocated for those in need. They wrote with passion and wisdom about the social structures that needed to be changed in order for people to thrive in their daily lives. They believed that social problems were caused by individual malfunctions as well as by social problems affecting the individual and that those social ills could be

A version of this chapter was presented at the 5th International Conference of Social Work in Health and Mental Health, Hong Kong China, December 11, 2006.

remedied by counseling and through social changes in the community and by affecting social policies (Harkavy & Puckett, 1994; Hopps, 2000).

At the beginning of the twentieth century social work faced three main questions in its development: (1) Should the social worker as a motivated, organizational employee be working in voluntary nonprofit organizations controlled by patrons of social work, or work as an independent, educated, career-oriented woman guided by professional principles? (2) Should the social worker address social problems (i.e., poverty) through the individual approach or through public policy initiatives advocated by social scientists? (3) Should the auspices of social work be part of a government social welfare system resembling the European model, or should the concept of social work as a diverse, nongovernmental social welfare system be based on the charitable contributions by wealthy individuals (Austin, 2000; Midgley, 1995)?

THE TWENTIETH CENTURY

The twentieth century was a period of growth of new agencies less interested in social change and the cause and effect of social problems. These agencies functioned to ameliorate an individual's crisis and rarely considered the effectiveness of their services. Health and welfare agencies sought social workers as intermediaries to advocate for their agency and interpret the available services, along with how their clients could use them. Social work's case training made us well equipped for this undertaking; social work did not have the equipment and resources to do all it had aspired to. Very few of the social work jobs required those wanting to make social changes. There was less attention to the reason for social injustices and little attempt at reducing the overall problem. "Half of social work's purpose was disintegrating by the 1930s. One unintended consequence of this emphasis was the slow erosion of professional specialization in group work and community organization" (Morris, 2000b, p. 54). By the 1960s, 85% of social work students chose to concentrate on casework, and only 3% chose community organization. The remainder chose group work or policy/administration. "This reflected what the schools continued to treat as the core or base for their generic approach to the profession and very likely what students preferred for a career" (Morris, 2000b, p. 54). Students' interest in individual casework meant that half of social work's original approach—to improve harmful societal conditions—had lost some of its momentum (Morris, 2000a). Globally, the nation-state became the primary organizing unit for providing help to people (Midgley, 1997, 2001). Health social work became largely based in the health system in hospitals, health agencies, and nongovernmental organizations (NGOs). Residual-oriented practice predominated. Inequities in health services continued, with barriers to access, poverty, homelessness, and hunger affecting world populations, social disorders reaching epidemic proportions, and continued high incidence and prevalence of diseases with known cures.

At the end of the twentieth century social work faced numerous dilemmas:

• "As a profession social work retained a belief in their mission to speak and to work for social change, but that belief was expressed in the articulation of broad objectives by, for example, the National Association of Social Workers, which lacked the technical capability and could not have generated sufficient support to realize them" (Morris, 2000b, pp. 45–46).

- Social work in educational settings reflected a concern for social justice and psychological theories more so than other social sciences. This early focus separated social work from some social sciences, particularly economic theory (Austin, 2000; Haynes, 1998).
- Research is vital to the credibility of the profession. The profession faces challenges to prove that social work interventions are beneficial. It also must provide practice-based research for practice, organizations, and policy makers (McNeill, 2006; Rosen, 2003).

Unanswered questions included:

- Can social work education keep up with the fast-changing social problems and their complexities as they affect individuals and communities (Humphries, 2004; Mohan, 2005; Noble, 2004)?
- How can social work integrate global health and knowledge regarding the effects of globalization (Findlay & McCormack, 2005; Midgley, 2001)?
- How does globalization impact social justice, and does it provide us with an opportunity to respond with new approaches to ameliorate social problems (Midgley, 2004)?

These are some of the issues facing us as we enter the twenty-first century:

- Is it possible for social work to concentrate on helping individuals clinically and also intervene and advocate for more expansive humane social welfare policies (Briar-Lawson, 1998; Buchbinder, Eisikovits, & Karnieli-Miller, 2004)?
- Can social work engage in case and class advocacy (Abramovitz, 1998)?
- What effect will globalization have on social work practice and education (Sewpaul, 2005; Van Wormer, 2004)?
- Can social work define social justice in operational terms?
- Is social justice the organizing value of social work?
- How do we respond to the economic restructuring and radical changes in welfare policy and the increasing dislocation and disadvantage of women, minority populations, and youth (Noble, 2004)?
- How do we reconcile the long-standing problems between the research, education, and practice worlds?
- Can we reconcile and apply practice-based research and research-based practice (Peake & Epstein, 2005)?

Based on these questions and the unresolved issues facing the profession, I offer four hypotheses about the future of social work:

1. The profession of social work will continue to emphasize methodological individualism in practice, research, and education.
2. Social work will align itself with public health efforts, particularly in a global context.

3. A "social development" specialty track will emerge in schools of social work in response to community needs and will successfully link social policies and programs and economic development.

4. Social determinants of health across the life span will unite the profession's knowledge base with the influence of economic and political interests and moral and existential values.

Hypothesis 1: The Profession of Social Work Will Continue to Emphasize Methodological Individualism in Practice, Education, and Research

Social work has not resolved the fundamental conflicts between the remedial approach and its focus on methodological individualism and a focus on social reform and enactment of institutional provisions. Methodological individualism is drawn from epidemiologic studies of populations and has been defined as "the notion that the distribution of health and disease in a population can be explained exclusively in terms of the characteristics of individuals" (Blazer, 2005, p. 8; Diez-Roux, 1998). Throughout social work's history and depending on the theories of social and individual problems and illnesses prevalent at the time, different aspects of individuals and their environment have been considered important in explaining problems and designing interventions to reach solutions to these problems. Group work, community organization, social reform, and public health social work related environmental factors and community characteristics to health and disease. In health care the growing importance of chronic and infectious diseases led to the search for new causal factors, and medical and even public health research shifted to a focus on behavioral and biological characteristics as risk factors for those diseases. Social work, with its emphasis on the person and his or her environment, emphasized individual factors but did look at environmental factors as these affected individuals. The individuation of risk has perpetuated the idea that risk is individually determined. Lifestyle and behaviors are regarded as matters of individual choice and dissociated from the social contexts that shape and constrain them (Blazer, 2005; Haynes, 1998; Swenson, 1998).

Clinical social work health and mental health have developed sophisticated methodology and increasing research evidence of their effectiveness (Proctor, 2002, 2004; Reid, Kenaley, & Colvin, 2004; Rosen, 2003). Social work research in health will, in the future, expand its focus to include group or macro-level variables and epidemiological studies that incorporate multiple levels of determination in health and social work outcomes. By using these types of analyses, we can develop theoretical models that extend across levels and explain how social-level and individual-level variables interact in shaping health and disease. This kind of research can lead to an emphasis on social and economic factors that can focus social work on social change as well as change focused on the individual. For example, we frequently will observe an individual's level of income, but by also looking at mean neighborhood income we may be able to establish markers for neighborhood factors related to health, such as recreational facilities, school quality, road conditions, environmental conditions, and the types of available food, factors that affect everyone in the neighborhood regardless of income. Community unemployment levels likewise may affect all people in a community regardless of whether they are unemployed. To conduct such research and to provide new practice models for health social work, we will develop, refine, and test theories that integrate micro- and macro-level variables and explain these relationships and interactions across levels (Blazer, 2005; Diez-Roux, 1998).

Helpful concepts include structural determination, defined as "the process by which behavior of an individual (that is a person in a social group) is determined by the overall structure of the collection to which it belongs" (Bunge, 1979, as quoted in Diez-Roux, 1998, p. 218). It is also important to think of "cause not as a property of agents, but one of systems in which the population phenomena of health and disease occur and to conceive populations as organized groups with relational properties rather than mere aggregates of individuals" (Loomis & Wing, 1990, as quoted in Diez-Roux, p. 218). This suggestion for future work does not exclude the continuation or appropriateness of testing social influences on the individuals. It is the integration of these levels that is our future task.

The practice of psychotherapy is another example of the belief in methodological individualism. In the United States we project the mood of depression into biological processes, such as a chemical imbalance, and then turn to biology to validate that the mood is natural and unique to the individual. Regardless of biological vulnerability, most first episodes of major depression are closely associated with a stressful life event, such as an economic turndown, job loss, victimization due to crime, or trauma, events often out of the control of the individual. The social origins of health and disease seem to have marginal interest to those proponents of the biological origins of health and disease. Attention to social factors has been restricted to assessing individual social risk factors, such as stressful life events, or individual social outcomes of illnesses, such as loss of employment or disruption of the family, making the target of intervention the individual and not the social problem or pattern. A number of researchers have raised the issue of producing knowledge for control: How does change occur? Does change produce desired outcomes? Can beneficial change be deliberately produced? In a social context, statistical analysis for social intervention will be multilevel, with the use of spatial statistics and econometrics (Diez-Roux, 1998). A community focus in our research will advance scientific knowledge about how and why communities change. With a community focus our practice will move toward a greater understanding of health for all rather than for a single individual and provide the practicing social worker with knowledge about how to strengthen communities for human development and for social justice (Coulton, 2005; Snowden, 2005). Population thinking can inform us about those factors operating at a social and community level: how social capital theory and research can illuminate prosocial norms and how community-level theory and research can inform policy. Prosocial norms combine economic theories of rational action with sociological theories of social structure and anthropological theories of interaction and exchange in social networks (Blazer, 2005; Diez-Roux, 1998; Midgley, 1995).

Social workers are located within the health and public health structures and in nongovernment organizations, whose mission is the improvement of the human condition. It is most unlikely that these structural conditions will change for the vast majority of employed workers or for the schools of social work, which must meet their own admissions projections and economic demands of their universities. Health organizations are provided with economic incentives that focus on effective treatment more than prevention, and the definitions of health are narrow and without understanding of social-level variables. We will develop the knowledge about and programmatic interventions for empowerment and community participation that recognize that how people live and organize their lives because of their social conditions is a target of intervention and that theories invoking and reflecting on the social and relational aspects of social work practice are the core knowledge base of the future (Berkman, 2004; Midgley, 1995).

Hypothesis 2: Social Work Will Align Itself with Public Health Efforts, Particularly in a Global Context

Both social work and public health are concerned with health, prevention, policy formulation, and advocacy and share an ecological practice base. There are numerous existing joint degree programs and an increasing number in the planning stages. Social work and pubic health professionals are struggling with the inclusion and repositioning the importance of social determinants of health. Like social work, the theoretical foundation of public health is based largely on behavioral psychology, biomedical science, and public administration (Potvin & Gendrom, 2005). Both professions are likely to recognize a knowledge base situated more coherently within a theoretical perspective that seeks to understand and guide the contemporary world. Social theory is likely the way that both professions will attempt to reconcile their practitioners, decision makers, and researchers (Hartman, 1990; Potvin & Gendrom, 2005; Ungar, 2002). It is this convergence of interests that a closer relationship and partnership is likely to develop between social work and public health.

Both professions have adopted a practice focus to collectively create the conditions in which people can be healthy. The conditions are the social determinants of health, including but not limited to access to affordable healthy food, potable water, safe housing, and supportive social networks. Social determinants of health, broadly speaking, refer to social, economic, and political resources and structures that influence health outcomes (Berkman & Kawachi, 2000).

Both professions value equity, defined as the absence of avoidable and unfair differences in the determinants and manifestations of good health and longevity between the most vulnerable groups and groups that are well off. Both professions are attempting to adopt a framework for social inclusion to guide the implementation of policies and practices that reduce inequities related to income, race, sex, ethnicity, geographic location, age, ability, and sexual orientation. The convergence of social work and public health is best understood by the following questions, raised by Rose and carried forward by Berkman (2004): "Why do some individuals have hypertension? Is quite a different question from: How come some populations have much hypertension while in others it is rare?" Both are targets of intervention.

Social work will gain from a public health perspective through the use of epidemiology, a focus on prevention, and a focus on populations. Public health will gain a clearly articulated social development perspective and technology, psychosocial perspective and methodology, increased understanding of individual, family, and group behaviors, and methods of change in communities. Working together at local, national, and global levels, we will be able to better identify those broad social, economic, cultural, health, and environmental conditions and look beyond biological risk factors and conduct transdisciplinary research and practice.

Hypothesis 3: A Social Development Specialty Track Will Emerge and Link Social Policies, Programs, and Economic Development

Social workers developed different practice ideologies in part due to the ever-changing social and economic environment and the rapidly changing contexts of practice. Globalization has created new opportunities for international collaboration in the political arena where the potential of governments is to address pressing economic and social problems collectively (Midgley, 2004). If social work is to respond to the global health problems and issues already present in today's world, it will augment its current emphasis on remedial approaches and methodological individualism with a return to its settlement house and community organization roots by adopting an institutional set of practices that link economic and social needs with integrated programs in partnerships with governments, NGOs, foundations, and communities.

Midgley (1997) and others have described how social development seeks to enhance human well-being in the context of an ongoing process of development. Social development is a process of planned social change designed to promote the well-being of the population as a whole in conjunction with a dynamic process of economic development (Midgley, 1997). Social development seeks to create formal organizations and institutional arrangements by which economic and social policies can be better integrated and by ensuring that economic development has a direct impact on the social well-being of all citizens. Reciprocally, social development encourages the formulation of social policies and programs that contribute to economic development. Investments in health care and public health, for example, can increase productivity and obviate the social and economic costs associated with debilitating diseases. Remedial social service programs can enhance and support economic development as a part of social development because they invest in human capital so important to the economic and social development of communities and countries. Social development is characterized by the following:

1. [It is] a link to economic development.
2. It is interdisciplinary/transdisciplinary.
3. There is a defined process.
4. It is progressive in nature.
5. It is interventionalist.
6. It is strategic.
7. It is inclusive and universalistic in scope.
8. Its goal is the promotion of social welfare. (Midgley, 1995, pp. 25–28)

It is beyond the scope of this chapter to more fully describe the processes of social development and its social welfare roots. Its applications to our global economy and the social problems resulting from people and family disruptions, community upheavals, and preventable health problems will provide the profession with another set of methods that strive for social justice in an institutional framework. "Social development is best promoted when governments play a positive role in facilitating, coordinating and directing the efforts of diverse groups of individuals, groups and communities, and effectively utilizing the market community and state to promote social development" (Midgley, 1995, p. 125).

Hypothesis 4: Social Determinants of Health across the Life Span Will Unite the Profession's Knowledge Base with Economic and Political Factors and Moral and Existential Values

By teaching social workers developments from the social sciences, particularly those concepts, findings, and theories that inform about population patterns and variation, we can expand our knowledge base for residual and institutional practice.

Social determinants of health have roots in social epidemiology, particularly those aspects that focus on social inequalities and their contributions to health, disease, and disability (Berkman & Kawachi, 2000). To understand social determinants of health we must use data from

- Global comparisons
- Within-country differences
- Studies of individuals
- Studies from biological processes in animals and humans (Gehlert & Browne, 2006, pp. 252–272)

A number of social factors have been shown to influence the health of individuals and populations:

- Socioeconomic position
- Income distribution
- Discrimination related to race, ethnicity, or gender
- Social network/social support
- Social capital and community cohesion
- Work environment
- Life transitions
- Affective psychological states (Berkman & Kawachi, 2000)

By concentrating on social inequalities social workers will have new knowledge on how society shapes the health of people. The characteristics of social determinants of health include a population perspective that emphasizes the social context in understanding individual behavior and operates on multiple social levels: "The enterprise of understanding the social determinants of health entails an understanding of how society operates, an appreciation of the major causes of diseases, an understanding of psychological processes and how they interact with biological mechanisms, and a readiness to learn from animal models" (Gehlert & Browne, 2006, p. 32–33; McClintock, Conzen, Gehlert, Masi, & Olopade, 2005).

CONCLUSION

The location of social work in hospitals and other health agencies, which currently limits the profession to important remedial work, will be augmented in the future by population-focused, community-based practice and will focus on social determinants of health and illness as a major knowledge base for the profession. The use of transdisciplinary teams of social, behavioral, and biological researchers will work to add to the knowledge base for social work practice by addressing social, behavioral, and biological issues in the same analysis. Through transdisciplinary teams, we will develop a shared language with our colleagues, pool the best disciplinary theories, and develop analyses that include a wide range of social, economic, psychological, and biological factors (Gehlert & Browne, 2006). Support in the United States for this approach comes from the National Institutes of Health Centers for Population Health and Health Disparities Initiatives and studies from their eight centers. Professor Sarah Gehlert leads one such center at the University of Chicago and is interested in health disparities. She hypothesized that social isolation might affect the epigenetic regulation of breast cancer gene expression. She based her hypothesis on three sources: (1) Socially isolated elders living in settings whose social ecology inhibited social interactions were more likely to have died during the 1995 heat wave than nonisolated elderly; (2) in a study of 826 women who received mammograms, those who subsequently developed breast cancer had reported more isolation than those who developed fibrocystic breast disease or remained disease-free; and (3) social isolation was found to be associated with mammary cancer in animal models. She and her colleagues are working on the molecular pathways between social stressors and mammary tumor development, while other social workers are examining community concerns, attitudes, and beliefs about breast cancer and its treatment and are conducting further research on the environmental determinants of social isolation. Efforts such as these will inform the social work practitioner, strengthen the understanding of social variables, and broaden the practice base of social work in its remedial and institutional forms (McClintock et al., 2005).

There are many unsolved issues that will affect our future and the future of those we serve. Many in our world are without basic public health services. How do we reconcile local, national, and global priorities in health? Can schools of social work take on the task of educating social workers for competence in social development? When is it most useful to use evidence-based practice with its roots in logical positivism and/or practice-based research, a reflective practice approach? Can social work organizations maximize the input of clients and workers as a core strategy to achieve organizational effectiveness? Can we contribute to enacting the concept of human rights by helping to restructure health systems so that health for all at a basic level can be achieved? It seems to me that we must find the answers to these questions in this century.

Recently the papers of Martin Luther King Jr. have become public. As King grappled with understanding social issues he wrote:

> On the one hand I must attempt to change the soul of individuals so that their societies may be changed. On the other hand, I must attempt to change societies so that the individual soul will have a change. Therefore, I must be concerned about unemployment, slums and economic insecurity. I am a profound advocator of the social gospel. (as quoted in Jackson, 2006, p. 7)

I hope that this chapter will provide for discussion about the best ways for our profession to proceed into the future. As Goethe said, "Knowing is not enough; we must apply; willing is not enough; we must do" (quoted in Berkman, 2004).

REFERENCES

Abramovitz, M. (1998). Social work and social reform: An arena of struggle. *Social Work in Health Care, 43*(6), 512–526.

Austin, D. M. (2000). Greeting the second century: A forward look from a historical perspective. In J. G. Hopps & R. Morris (Eds.), *Social work at the millennium* (pp. 18–41). New York: Free Press.

Berkman, L. (2004, February 27). *The future of public health in the 21st century: The role of social determinants.* Poster presented at the University of Washington, Seattle.

Berkman, L., & Kawachi, I. (Eds.). (2000). *Social epidemiology.* New York: Oxford University Press.

Blazer, D. G. (2005). *The age of melancholy: Major depression and its social origins.* New York: Routledge.

Briar-Lawson, K. (1998). Capacity building for integrated family-centered practice. *Social Work in Health Care, 43*(6), 539–550.

Buchbinder, E., Eisikovits, Z., & Karnieli-Miller, O. (2004). Social workers' perceptions of the balance between the psychological and the social. *Social Service Review, 78*(4), 531–553.

Coulton, C. (2005). The place of community in social work practice research: Conceptual and methodological developments. *Social Work Research, 29*(2), 73–87.

Diez-Roux, A. V. (1998). Bringing context back into epidemiology: Variables and fallacies in multilevel analysis. *American Journal of Public Health, 88*(2), 216–223.

Findlay, M. & McCormack, J. (2005). Globalization and social work: A snapshot of Australian practitioners' views. *Australian Social Work, 58*(3), 231–243.

Gehlert, S., & Browne, T. A. (2006). *Handbook of health social work.* Hoboken, NJ: Wiley.

Harkavy, I., & Puckett, J. L. (1994). Lessons from Hull House for the contemporary urban university. *Social Service Review, 68*(3), 299–321.

Hartman, A. (1990). Our global village. *Social Work, 35*(4), 291–292.

Haynes, K. S. (1998). The one hundred-year debate: Social reform versus individual treatment. *Social Work in Health Care, 43*(6), 501–511.

Hopps, J. G. (2000). Social work: A contextual profession. In J. G. Hopps & R. Morris (Eds.), *Social work at the millennium* (pp. 3–4). New York: Free Press.

Humphries, B. (2004). An unacceptable role for social work: Implementing immigration policy. *British Journal of Social Work, 34*, 93–107.

Jackson, D. Z. (2006, November 30). A king we never knew. *International Herald Tribune,* p. 7.

McClintock, M. K., Conzen, S. D., Gehlert, S., Masi, C. & Olopade, F. (2005). Mammary cancer and social interactions: Identifying multiple environments that regulate gene expression throughout the life span [Special issue]. *Journals of Gerontology, 60B,* 32–41.

McNeill, T. (2006, April). Evidence-based practice in an age of relativism: Toward a model for practice. *Social Work, 51*(2), 147–156.

Midgley, J. (1995). *Social development: The developmental perspective in social welfare.* London: Sage.

Midgley, J. (1997). *Social welfare in global context.* Beverly Hills, CA: Sage.

Midgley, J. (2001). Issues in international social work: Resolving critical debates in the profession. *Journal of Social Work, 1*(1), 21–35.

Midgley, J. (2004). The complexities of globalization: Challenges to social work. In T. Ngoh-Tiong & A. Rowlands (Eds.), *Social work around the world* (Vol. 3, pp. 13–29). Berne, Switzerland: International Federation of Social Workers.

Mohan, B. (2005). New internationalism: Social work's dilemmas, dreams and delusion. *International Social Work, 48*(3), 241–250.

Morris, R. (2000a). Introduction. In J. G. Hopps & R. Morris (Eds.), *Social work at the millennium* (pp. xv–xix). New York: Free Press.

Morris, R. (2000b). Social work: Century of evolution as a profession. In J. G. Hopps & R. Morris (Eds.), *Social work at the millennium* (pp. 42–72). New York: Free Press.

Noble, C. (2004). Postmodern thinking: Where is it taking social work? *Journal of Social Work, 4*(3), 289–304.

Peake, K., & Epstein, I. (2005). Theoretical and practice imperatives for reflective social work organizations for mental health. In K. Peake, I. Epstein, & D. Medeiros, (Eds.), *Clinical and research uses of an adolescent mental health intake questionnaire* (pp. 23–39). New York: Haworth Press.

Potvin, L., & Gendrom, S. (2005). Social determinants of health inequities: Integrating social theory into public health practice. *American Journal of Public Health, 95*(4), 591–601.

Proctor, E. K. (2002). Quality of care and social work research. *Social Work Research, 26*(4), 195–197.

Proctor, E. K. (2004). Research to inform mental health practice: Social work's contributions. *Social Work Research, 28*(4), 195–197.

Reid, W. J., Kenaley, B. D., & Colvin, J. (2004). Do some interventions work better than others? A review of comparative social work experiments. *Social Work Research, 28*(2), 71–81.

Rosen, A. (2003). Evidence-based social work practice: Challenges and promise. *Social Work Research, 27*(4), 197–208.

Sewpaul, V. (2005). Global standards: Promise and pitfalls for reinscribing social work into civil society. *International Journal of Social Welfare, 14*, 210–217.

Snowden, L. R. (2005). Racial, cultural and ethnic disparities in health and mental health: Toward theory and research at community levels. *American Journal of Community Psychology, 35*(1/2), 1–8.

Swenson, C. R. (1998). Clinical social work's contribution to a social justice perspective. *Social Work in Health Care, 43*(6), 527–538.

Ungar, M. (2002). A deeper, more social ecological social work practice. *Social Service Review, 76*(3), 480–498.

Van Wormer, K. (2004). Globalization, work and social work in the USA. In T. Ngoh-Tiong & A. Rowlands (Eds.), *Social work around the world* (Vol. 3, pp. 48–60). Berne, Switzerland: International Federation of Social Workers.

Chapter 14 ────────────────────────────────

URBAN HOUSING POLICY AND PRACTICE IN THE DEVELOPING WORLD

Sunil Kumar

ARE THE CHALLENGES TO URBAN HOUSING POLICY AND PRACTICE A CHALLENGE OF RESOURCES, TECHNICAL KNOW-HOW, INSTITUTIONAL CAPACITY, OR POLITICAL WILL?

This chapter on urban housing policy and practice in the developing world has three aims. First, I argue that there is an urgent need to focus on urban housing policy and practice in developing and transitional economies. This argument is predicated on several features of life in the contemporary world: (1) The majority of people the world over will be living in cities or urban areas from now on; (2) although in 2006, the number of people living in urban areas in less developed regions was 2.3 billion (43%), this figure is forecast to increase to 3.9 billion (57%) by 2030; (3) although 0.88 billion people (74%) resided in urban areas in more developed regions in 2006 and this figure is forecast to rise to 1.3 billion (82%) by 2030, in comparison with less developed regions' urban population they made up only 33% in 2006, declining to 20% in 2030; (4) poverty in less developed regions, until now largely a rural feature, has begun to figure higher in absolute numbers in urban areas; and (5) urbanization, largely now the result of urban growth rather than migration, will result in a larger number of people living in poor housing conditions with little or no access to water and sanitation. The central argument that this chapter makes in relation to the challenges to urban housing policy and practice in the developing world is the need for a more nuanced and integrated set of policies and practices that link housing to issues of redistribution, labor market opportunities, and social protection in the struggle to reduce poverty.

My second aim is to demonstrate the fragmented nature of housing policy and practice in the developing world. In doing so, I make reference to key housing policy interventions. From the mid- to the late nineteenth century, these sets of housing policy interventions emanated mainly from the World Bank, with each successive phase attempting to make amends to the lacuna of the previous one. However, from the mid- to late 1980s, a number of other actors have taken the stage, resulting in public-private partnerships, the involvement of the private sector in the construction and delivery of housing, the setting up of campaigns and alliances, and the involvement of the not-for-profit sectors and community groups in forming federations with the view to increasing voice. In addition, national governments have sought to learn lessons from their regional neighbors in the design of housing policies. In practice, these policy shifts have resulted in both the state and multi- and bilateral agencies distancing themselves from direct involvement with housing policy and practice, instead assuming a more diffused role in the area of urban development and management. The vacated space for direct housing policy and practice involvement is increasingly becoming occupied by the not-for-profit sector. The ramifications for the fragmented nature of housing policy and practice are clear: Questions of redistribution are rarely on the agenda; the not-for-profit sector is unable to address issues relating to improvements in the labor market opportunities for the poor, focusing instead on savings and microcredit to meet housing costs; and protective as well as promotional social security is being debated but not linked to housing policy. I argue that there is a need to transcend such fragmentation in housing policy and practice and that all actors—the state, the market, the not-for-profit sector, and federations of poor households—have a role to play in such a transformation.

The third and final aim of this chapter is to provide some out-of-the-box thinking on how this fragmentation can be overcome. I do not profess to provide definite answers but rather to reframe the questions that need to be asked, for as the saying goes, it is better to ask the right questions than provide answers to the wrong questions. Three main questions are posed. First and foremost, what should the starting point be in addressing the housing policy and practice challenges in less developed regions? So far it has been housing itself. I argue that this is the wrong starting point. Urbanization, beginning with rural-to-urban migration, is an attempt by the poor to reduce vulnerabilities and enhance capabilities, the latter used in the manner intended by Sen (1993). But what are their prospects in such an attempt? With 48% of North Africans, 72% of sub-Saharan Africans, 51% of Latin Americans, and 65% of Asians of all nonagricultural employment being in the so-called informal economy (self-employed, causal wage employment, and contract and piece-rate work; International Labour Office [ILO], 2002b), with low and precarious wages devoid of even the basic forms of social security and protection—this has to be one of the key starting points. Moreover, if urbanization is now more the result of urban growth than migration, it is not surprising that urban poverty will become a considerable feature of cities. Second, should the exclusive focus of housing policy and practice be on making all those who live in cities owner-occupiers? Although this is a laudable end, the means do not lie in a blind attempt to confer ownership rights, especially to those who are not able to afford it. There is a sizable body of literature on housing tenure that has convincingly argued that housing that provides mixed tenure can act as a ladder of upward mobility (Gilbert, 1991; Gilbert & Varley, 1989b; Kumar, 1996a, 1996c, 2001a, 2001b, 2002; United Nations Centre for Human Settlements [UNCHS], 1993). This second question is not only directly linked to the first, on labor market opportunities, but also has a substantial political dimension which is not helped by a large section of not-for-profits not accepting the diverse tenure argument. The third and final question is whether the current strategies of partnerships between not-for-profit organizations and the state or partnerships between the public and the private sectors are taking the easier path of providing visible progress, to the detriment of holding the state and society to account for the widespread inequality in the size of housing lots that the poor occupy, having to make do with communal water and sanitation rather than services being available at the individual household level, and striving to ensure that the poor actually have a voice in choosing where they live.

AN URBAN WORLD: WHY FRESH THINKING ON URBAN HOUSING PRACTICE AND POLICY IN LESS DEVELOPED REGIONS MATTERS

To make this argument, we must first identify the issues that give rise to the housing policy and practice challenges for the twenty-first century. Because housing is primarily about people, households, and communities, one cannot but begin with the issue of changing population distributions. The first issue of significance is the shift in the distribution of population between more and less developed regions. Of the projected world population of 9.1 billion in the year 2050, only 14% (1.2 billion) will be living in the more developed regions, while the remaining 86% (7.8 billion) will live in less developed regions.[1] Thus, although this represents a 28% increase in the world's population compared to 2006, the staggering fact is that the population in less developed regions will increase by 32%, whereas the population of those living in more developed regions will increase by only 2%. Clearly this has huge implications for the financial, technical, and institutional capacities of developing country governments.

A second significant issue is the change in the distribution of population between rural and urban areas. In 2006, just under half of the world's population lived in urban areas. The United Nations Population Fund (UNFPA, 2007) predicts that sometime in 2007, the majority of the world's population will live in cities, a first in the history of humankind. Although the share of the urban population in more developed regions was 74% and that of less developed regions 43% in 2005, the projections are that the urban population share of the latter will be more than 50% by the year 2020. Of much greater concern here is the prediction that "cities of the developing world will absorb 95% of urban growth in the next 2 decades, and by 2030 will be home to almost 4 billion people, or 80% of the world's population" (UN-HABITAT, 2006, p. viii).

A note on urbanization trends is called for here. It is widely known that each country has its own definition of what an urban area is. Hardoy and Satterthwaite (1986, p. 34) have agued that, for example, if the definition of urbanization used in Peru were to be applied to India, the latter would become the most urbanized region in Asia; it would radically alter statistics for the level of urbanization for South Asia. "It would even alter significantly, the level of urbanization for the Third World and for the world." Having said this, what is of significance is not the issue of comparison per se but the associated economic and political changes that accompany urbanization and the impact of the level of allocated resources and institutional responsibilities that are required to manage it.

Inextricably linked to the changes in the distribution of population and housing is an equally significant issue of poverty and inequality. Poverty is a worldwide phenomenon; for example, it is estimated that in the United States, 37 million people (12.7%) live below the

---

[1] The United Nations Population Fund defines more developed regions as "all regions of Europe plus Northern America, Australia/New Zealand and Japan" and less developed regions as "all regions of Africa, Asia (excluding Japan), Latin America and the Caribbean plus Melanesia, Micronesia and Polynesia" (United Nations Population Fund, 2007, p. 96).

Table 14.1   People Living on Less Than $1 a Day (in Millions)

Region	1981	1984	1987	1990	1993	1996	1999	2002a
East Asia and Pacific	796	562	426	472	415	287	282	214
China	634	425	308	375	334	212	223	180
Europe and Central Asia	3	2	2	2	17	20	30	10
Latin America and Caribbean	36	46	45	49	52	52	54	47
Middle East and North Africa	9	8	7	6	4	5	8	5
South Asia	475	460	473	462	476	461	429	437
Sub-Saharan Africa	164	198	219	227	242	271	294	303
Total	1,482	1,277	1,171	1,218	1,208	1,097	1,096	1,015
Excluding China	848	852	863	844	873	886	873	835

Source: "2006—World Development Indicators: People," by World Bank, 2006, Washington, DC: World Bank. Retrieved February 9, 2007, from http://devdata.worldbank.org/wdi2006/contents/Section2.htm.

official poverty line (DeNavas-Walt, Proctor, & Lee, 2005). In the United Kingdom, poverty figures are based on the concept of relative poverty;[2] 11.5 million (20%) were below the relative poverty line in 2004 to 2005 (Poverty Site, 2007). For some developing countries, the proportion of those in absolute poverty, based on their national poverty lines, is less than the United States or the United Kingdom (China, 4.6% in 1998; Jordan, 11.7% in 1997; Tunisia, 7.6% in 1995). However, for the vast majority of the others, poverty is extensive. According to the World Bank's 2006 World Development Indicators for poverty, for the 56 countries for which national poverty figures are available, 3 countries had more than 70% in poverty, 9 had between 50% and 69%, 24 had between 30% and 49%, and the remaining had below 30%. Tables 14.1 and 14.2 provide changes in the national proportions of the poor according to the international poverty line of $1 per day per person, used by the World Bank.

It must be noted that the poverty figures from the World Bank are being questioned. Researchers have drawn on other data to argue that the number of poor is close to 2 billion, as against the figure of 1 billion used by the World Bank (see the discussion in Townsend, 2007).

Despite the significance of the differences in the estimation of the poor, and although the majority of the poor in developing countries live in rural areas, there is evidence that the proportion of the poor is on the increase in urban areas—a phenomenon a number of commentators have termed the "urbanization of poverty." For example, in 1999, although 64% of rural Latin Americans were poor compared to 34% of their urban counterparts, 64% of all the region's poor lived in urban areas.

Table 14.3 lists some of the countries where the proportion of the rural poor is less than the proportion of the urban poor and three countries—Kenya, Nigeria, and India—where the proportion of the rural poor is only slightly more than that of the urban poor (between 4 and 6 percentage points).

---

[2]The most commonly used threshold of low income is a household income that is 60% or less of the average (median) household income in that year. The latest year for which data are available is 2004–2005. In that year, the 60% threshold was £183 per week for a two-adult household, £100 per week for a single adult, £268 per week for two adults living with two children, and £186 per week for a single adult living with two children. These sums are measured after income tax, council tax, and housing costs have been deducted, where housing costs include rent, mortgage interest, building insurance, and water charges. The money left over is therefore what the household has available to spend on everything else it needs, from food and heating to travel and entertainment.

Table 14.2   People Living on Less Than $1 a Day (in Percentages)

Region	1981	1984	1987	1990	1993	1996	1999	2002a
East Asia and Pacific	57.7	38.9	28.0	29.6	24.9	16.6	15.7	11.6
China	63.8	41.0	28.5	33.0	28.4	17.4	17.8	14.0
Europe and Central Asia	0.7	0.5	0.4	0.5	3.7	4.3	6.3	2.1
Latin America and Caribbean	9.7	11.8	10.9	11.3	11.3	10.7	10.5	8.9
Middle East and North Africa	5.1	3.8	3.2	2.3	1.6	2.0	2.6	1.6
South Asia	51.5	46.8	45.0	41.3	40.1	36.6	32.2	31.2
Sub-Saharan Africa	41.6	46.3	46.8	44.6	44.0	45.6	45.7	44.0
Total	40.4	32.8	28.4	27.9	26.3	22.8	21.8	19.4
Excluding China	31.7	29.8	28.4	26.1	25.6	24.6	23.1	21.1

Source: "2006—World Development Indicators: People," by World Bank, 2006, Washington, DC: World Bank. Retrieved February 9, 2007, from http://devdata.worldbank.org/wdi2006/contents/Section2.htm.

The World Bank's *World Development Report 2000–2001, Attacking Poverty* (2000) acknowledges the work of a number of academics and researchers who have been arguing that neither income nor consumption measures of poverty are in themselves able to adequately capture the multidimensional nature of poverty, which encompasses a range of deprivations and vulnerabilities. There is thus the need to include other dimensions, such as longevity, literacy, and, more recently, asset deprivations, risk, vulnerability, powerlessness, and lack of voice (Baulch, 1996; Moser, 1998; Rakodi, 1995b). Concerns have also been expressed about the need to understand the differences between the causes of urban and rural poverty (Wratten, 1995). Satterthwaite (2001), for example, argues that large cities have particularly high costs of transportation, education, housing, water, sanitation, health care and medicines, and payment of various bribes and fines; the World Bank's international poverty line of $1 per person per day does not capture this additional spending required on nonfood essentials.

Keeping in line with this broader definition of urban poverty, UN-HABITAT (2006, p. x) uses five criteria, as an operational definition of slums, to define shelter deprivation: lack of water, lack of sanitation, overcrowding, nondurable housing structures, and lack of security of tenure. Although the last criterion is more difficult to establish, the first four are physically verifiable indicators of shelter deprivation. The world's slum population has

Table 14.3   Population below the National Poverty Line

Country	Survey Year	Rural (%)	Urban (%)
Georgia	2003	52.7	56.2
Azerbaijan	2001	42.0	55.0
Armenia	2001	48.7	51.9
Mongolia	1998	32.6	39.4
Kenya	1997	53.0	49.0
Nigeria	1992–1993	36.4	30.4
India	1999–2000	30.2	24.7

Source: "2006—World Development Indicators: People," by World Bank, 2006, Washington, DC: World Bank. Retrieved February 9, 2007, from http://devdata.worldbank.org/wdi2006/contents/Section2.htm.

remained relatively constant as a percentage of the entire population, at 31.3% in 1990 (715 million), 31.2% in 2001 (913 million), and 31.2% in 2005 (998 million), yet in real numbers an additional 198 million people became slum dwellers between 1990 and 2001 and a further 85 million were added between 2001 and 2005. Based on the current 2.22% annual growth rate of the slum population, it is estimated that the world's slum population will reach 1.4 billion by 2020 (UN-HABITAT, 2006).

PLANET OF SLUMS: WHY POOR URBAN HOUSING CONDITIONS ARE NOT ALL THAT MATTERS

Urbanization in the developing world, for at least the last half of the twentieth century (in Africa and Asia and much more in Latin America) has been characterized by a strikingly visible form of urban poverty—namely, the juxtaposition of small residential areas of high-quality housing and services with sprawling illegal or quasi-legal[3] residential areas of very poor housing and services. The reality of slums is not new, as the early experience of Europe and North America indicates; what is new is the rate at which squatter and slum formation is taking place. According to *State of the World's Cities 2006–07*, "Asia is already home to more than half of the world's slum population (581 million)—followed by Sub-Saharan Africa (199 million) and Latin America and the Caribbean (134 million)" (UN-HABITAT, 2006, p. viii). This is an astounding 914 million people, or about 14% of the world's total population in mid-2006. The highest annual urban growth rate (4.58%) and slum growth rate (4.53%) is in sub-Saharan Africa (UN-HABITAT, 2006). Slums have received renewed attention as a result of the UN's Millennium Development Goal 7 (Ensure Environmental Sustainability) Target 11, which is to improve the lives of at least 100 million slum dwellers by 2020 (which, if met, would still leave 700 million slum dwellers unaffected; but if the target is not met, the forecast is that there will be 1.4 billion slum dwellers in 2020—just under a fifth of all humanity).[4] The term "planet of slums" has been used by Mike Davis (2004, 2006), first in an article in the *New Left Review* and then in a book by the same name, to bring to the fore the challenges of this burgeoning new urban poor (also see Neuwirth, 2005).

Forces behind the growth of slums vary—in the postindependence years in Africa and Asia due to rural-to-urban migration and weak state action, later due to natural growth and the impact of evictions, and more recently due to the forces of displacement as a result of conflict, particularly in Africa. In addition, the exponential growth of slums is also the result of misplaced interventions, both national (mainly evictions) and international (such as the neoliberal policies of the World Bank and the structural adjustment programs of the International Monetary Fund; UN-HABITAT, 2003a).

---

[3]Settlements of the poor in towns and cities are characterized by two forms of illegality. One is quasi-legal settlements, where the sale and ownership of the residential lots are legal, but the conversion of use, from agricultural to residential, is not legally sanctioned. This form of settlement is most prevalent in Latin America. The other is illegal settlements, where the occupation of either public, private, or institutional land does not have legal sanction. Both types of settlements are called squatter settlements based on a legal classification. Slums, on the other hand, are legal places of human habitation but whose physical conditions—state of the structure, overcrowding, and level of services—are not deemed to be of the minimum standards required for human habitation. Squatter settlements are also slums by this physical definition.

[4]The *State of the World's Cities 2006–07* estimates that only 8 countries are on track to achieve their targets, 15 are stabilizing, 21 are at risk, and a staggering 50 countries are off-track (UN-HABITAT, 2006).

The notion of a planet of slums raises two interrelated challenges to housing policy and practice. The first challenge lies in the physical domain: housing conditions and services. On average in 2003, 6% of all urban households in developing countries lacked a finished main floor (averages mask huge variations, as the figure was 20% in sub-Saharan Africa and 51% in southern Asia);[5] 19% of all urban households lived in overcrowded conditions (15.3% in Southeast Asia, 16.8% in sub-Saharan Africa, and 39.1% in southern Asia); 7.8% lacked access to safe water (27.6% in sub-Saharan Africa and 25.9 in East Asia); and 26.5% lacked improved sanitation (57.2% in southern and eastern Asia; UN-HABITAT, 2006). It is not surprising that these conditions impose social and health costs on those who live in them. Four out of 10 slum children in some low-income countries are malnourished—a statistic comparable to rural areas of those countries; in some cities, the prevalence of diarrhea is much higher among slum than rural children, and child deaths are not so much the result of the lack of immunization as of inadequate living conditions; in sub-Saharan Africa, HIV prevalence is higher in urban areas than in rural areas and is higher in slum than nonslum areas; and slum populations tend to be younger but die sooner than their nonslum counterparts (UN-HABITAT, 2003a, p. ix).

The second interrelated challenge is one of addressing functionings and capability (Sen, 1992). Here, the notion of poverty transcends insufficient income or consumption and instead refers to whether or not one is able to lead a life that one values. According to Sen:

> Living may be seen as consisting of a set of interrelated "functionings," consisting of beings and doings. . . . The relevant functionings can vary from such elementary things as being adequately nourished, being in good health, avoiding escapable morbidity and premature mortality etc. . . . Closely related to the notion of functionings is that of the *capability* to function. It represents the various combinations of functionings (beings and doings) that the person can achieve. Capability is, thus, a set of vectors of functionings, reflecting the person's freedom to lead one type of life or another. (pp. 39–40, emphasis in original)

In such a conceptualization, poverty is represented as "capability deprivation" (Sen, 1997, p. 210). In turn, capability deprivation cannot be reversed without simultaneously addressing deprivations related to livelihoods, political rights, and social protection— deprivations that seriously elude the poor. There is recognition that to overcome urban poverty, policy and institutional reform is needed in the areas of land, housing, and urban services; financial markets; labor markets and employment; social protection and social services (health, nutrition, education, and security); and the environment (World Bank, 2007c). Yet such reforms are rarely put into practice. Part of the problem may lie in the relationship being seen as a one-way street: When urban policy makers and practition- ers attempt to tackle poverty, they acknowledge the multidimensionality of the problem; however, when it comes to housing policy and practice, only some of these dimensions are interlinked—in the main, housing finance and the environment in terms of water and sanitation. Where people live and work has economic, social, and environmental costs; precarious livelihood opportunities influence living conditions; deprivations in the right to earn a livelihood in the city increases risk; and the lack of freedom in being able to find a solution to their housing needs heightens people's vulnerabilities. Housing policy and

---

[5] Only 46.8% of urban households in 13 selected countries lived in housing with durable floors, walls, and roofs (UN-HABITAT, 2006).

practice need to incorporate these capability deprivations and recognize that the means to an all-inclusive housing policy lies in operationalizing a series of measures for the present (accounting for existing constraints and opportunities) that are amenable to improvement in the future.

A BRIEF REVIEW OF HOUSING POLICY AND PRACTICE IN THE URBAN DEVELOPING WORLD

In this section, I highlight the changes in national and international thinking on urban housing and also point out the fragmented nature of the thinking and actions underlying contemporary housing policy and practice. The review is presented as three phases: 1970s to 1983, 1983 to 1993, and 1993 to 2000. Following this, housing policy prescriptions seem to have moved from a "blueprint" approach to one that is specific to each country.

The State as Provider: Conventional Urban Housing Policy and Practice (Before the 1970s)

Cities and urban centers, especially in the postcolonial and postindependence nations of Africa, Asia, and Latin America, have been the locus of rural-to-urban migration. Since the main purpose of migration was economic betterment, it is not surprising that migrants preferred to locate close to places offering the potential of employment and in doing so simultaneously sought to minimize consumption expenditure on housing and transport. Some of them found cheap rental housing in inner-city areas; others squatted on land and built rudimentary shelters with no services such as water or sanitation. As the supply of inner-city rental housing was limited and even decreasing as a result of the conversion of this residential stock to commercial property, more and more migrants were forced into squatter settlements. This growth in squatter settlements did not fit into the modernization projects of the newly independent nations.

The modernization projects of national governments sought to replicate the postwar successes of industrialized nations, using a two-pronged strategy of building highly subsidized housing blocks with high standards for materials and infrastructure and at the same time pursuing a policy of evicting squatters in the name of law and order or urban renewal (Hardoy & Satterthwaite, 1989; Mayo, Malpezi, & Gross, 1986). Large-scale evictions took place in Latin America (Brazil, Venezuela, Chile) in the 1950s, 1960s, and 1970s; in Africa (Nigeria, Tanzania, and Senegal) between the 1950s and mid-1980s; and in Asia (South Korea, Philippines, Thailand, and India) between 1950 and 1975 (Hardoy & Satterthwaite, 1989, pp. 41–43)—destroying even more "existing housing options" than were being built.[6]

---

[6]It is interesting to note that the lessons from the evictions of this period—namely, the loss of shelter options, assets that have been painstakingly accumulated, livelihood options, and social networks—have not been learned ("Evictions," 1994). A few examples: Thousands of families have been evicted between 2001 and 2006 from Luanda, the capital of Angola (Amnesty International, 2007). In China, preparations for the 2008 Olympics is resulting in the forced eviction of thousands (Human Rights Watch, 2004). Thousands are being evicted in urban Cambodia due to pressures from the real estate market (Human Rights Watch, 2006). In the winter of 2005, 700,000 people were forcibly evicted under the banner of Operation Murambatsvina (Drive Out Filth),

The failure of these misplaced and myopic policies is well documented. To briefly summarize: First, the units were very expensive, and few were built compared to need; second, not only did they have to be subsidized, but more important, because they did not match the priorities of the poor, they tended to be occupied by middle- or upper-income families (Hardoy, & Satterthwaite, 1989; Mayo et al., 1986). The end result was a failure of the misplaced modernization dream, the continued destruction of the few housing options available to the poor, and no real progress in meeting housing needs.

The State as Enabler: Nonconventional Housing Policies (Early 1970s to Early 1990)

From the late 1960s to the mid-1970s, research pointed out that squatter settlements were not a problem but an attempt by the poor to meet their housing needs (Turner, 1968). Based on research from Lima, Peru, Turner (1972) argued that the process by which the urban poor gained access to land and built their housing was incremental—leading him to propose the notion that housing should not be seen as a noun but a verb.

According to Turner (1968, p. 356), there are

> three basic functions of the dwelling environment: location, tenure and amenity. For any place to function as a dwelling it must have an accessible location, it must provide secure, continued residence for a minimum period, and it must provide a minimum of shelter from hostile elements.

Based on this line of argument, Turner developed his "bridgeheader—consolidator—status seeker" model of intracity mobility. At the bridgeheader stage of the household life cycle (recent migrants to the city), the most important housing function was proximity to employment. As migrants establish themselves in the city and their employment becomes stable, their housing priorities shift toward securing tenure (consolidator stage).

Turner (1968) argued that the conventional strategies employed by the government were not aligned with the needs and priorities of the poor. Having secured tenure, households in the third stage, status seeking, aspire to modern standards of built housing and services. Contrary to this model of household need, the conventional policy of seeking to provide the poor with housing completed to a high standard (in terms of building and services) with ownership status was a complete mismatch. Turner thus argued that the role of the state should be that of an enabler: providing those elements of the housing process that the poor would find difficult to undertake individually. In the main, governments should ensure the provision of land with minimum levels of infrastructure and some credit, leaving the incremental process of constructing and managing housing to the poor themselves (Turner, 1976, 1978; see also Rodell & Skinner, 1983). This paradigm is also referred to as "aided self-help housing."

This notion of an enabling role for government and active involvement by households and not-for-profit organizations in the construction and management of housing found favor with a number of international development organizations. The first international conference

---

the Zimbabwean government's sudden campaign to purge informal settlements. It is reported that "a year after, the lives of thousands of those affected have not changed. Uprooted last year from homes built illegally in the capital, Harare, families with five or more members have been squeezed into tiny living spaces authorized by the government on the outskirts of the city, with no source of employment and, in some cases, no access to medical facilities."

on human settlements, held in Vancouver, Canada, in 1976, resulted in the creation of the United Nations Centre for Human Settlements (Habitat) in 1978, based in Nairobi, Kenya. UNCHS was renamed UN-HABITAT in December 2001. In its seminal housing policy document, simply titled *Housing: Sector Policy Paper,* the World Bank (1975) outlined its endorsement of the enabling approach—for reasons different from those espoused by Turner. For the World Bank, the opportunity to decrease government spending on housing (serviced land with lower standards rather than high-standard completed housing) as well as reduce subsidies made economic sense. Housing at this time was viewed simply as a consumption good; there were more pressing production areas where scarce resources should be invested. Furthermore, the World Bank saw enabling strategies, based on the principles of affordability, cost recovery, and replicability, as making sound neoliberal economic sense (Pugh, 1997). Two main housing practices emerged from this policy of enabling: upgrading and sites-and-services. Upgrading initially took the form of improving the environment of squatter settlements not situated in hazardous locations—namely, the provision of basic (often communal) water and sanitation, road improvements, and garbage collection. Later on, granting security of tenure was added.[7] The emphasis here was on improving "existing" housing stock and not the creation of new housing stock (see Martin, 1983). In contrast, the aim of sites-and-services was the creation of new housing stock. Governments were urged to make available serviced sites—land with basic physical and social infrastructure—with the view that beneficiaries would manage the construction of their own housing (Rodell, 1983).

These enabling policies had their critics, who in the 1980s were writing from a neo-Marxist structuralist perspective. The most vociferous critic writing in English was Rod Burgess[8] (1977, 1978, 1982, 1985, 1987, 1991). According to Burgess (1985, p. 271), the fundamental question in relation to the low-income housing problem is whether the "economies and practices achieved in the shanty towns can be realized in state self-help housing projects; and if so, are these economies sufficiently large to bridge the growing gap between housing needs and supply?" Burgess (1985) argues that in capitalist social formations, housing has three fundamental dimensions: First, it is a means of subsistence necessary for the reproduction of labor power; second, land for housing is not a reproducible good, and access to land is enshrined in legal rights to property; and third, housing has both a use-value and an exchange-value. Thus, the production of housing in low-income settlements cannot be viewed outside of the process of commodity formation (Burgess, 1978).

Although the merit of this critique lay in its questioning of the structural conditions that gave rise to the poverty of urban people and their housing, it was largely silent in terms of alternative pragmatic policies. Thus in the 1970s and early 1980s, the project-by-project approach of upgrading and sites-and-services became a blueprint housing policy for much of urban Africa and Asia and some parts of Latin America (where the main institution has been the Inter-American Development Bank). Tables 14.4 and 14.5 indicate World Bank spending on urban development between the fiscal years 1972 and 1981.

---

[7] It must be pointed out that in no way was either upgrading or the provision of tenure security applied across the board: Those settlements that were either located on land that has real estate potential or that belonged to influential individuals and groups did not receive any such improvements.

[8] In his critique, Burgess (1977, 1978, 1982, 1985) built on the work of the Colombian architect Pradilla (1976a, 1976b, 1976c).

Table 14.4   Urban Projects: Lending and Costs by Type, 1972–1981

Type	No. of Projects	Amount Lent (U.S. $ millions)	Total Project Costs (U.S. $ millions)	Lending as Percentage of Total
Shelter	36	942.2	1,906.0	49.43
Transport	10	393.5	936.1	42.04
Integrated	13	438.3	1,088.4	40.27
Regional	3	244.0	647.8	37.67
All urban projects		2,018	4,578.3	44.08

Source: "Learning by Doing: World Bank Lending for Urban Development (1972–82)," by World Bank, 1983, Washington, DC: World Bank.

Although enabling policies were successful in places, for example, the large Madras (now named Chennai) Urban Development Projects 1 and 2 in the state of Tamil Nadu, India (Pugh, 1990), the Kampung Improvement Project in Jakarta, Indonesia, and the Tondo Upgrading Project in Manila, the Philippines (Taylor & Williams, 1982), there were also some shortcomings. First, urban development authorities primarily saw sites-and-services projects as large urban projects; thus, the emphasis was on projects with hundreds of residential lots. The scale of these projects meant that land for their location was often on the periphery of cities, far from employment sources. As a result, although beneficiaries applied for and were allotted plots, occupancy rates were very low (Rodell, 1983). Second, and as a result of the scale of sites-and-services projects, their supply fell far short of demand. Third, many urban authorities prescribed high construction standards and set time limits by which the dwellings had to be built (Rodell, 1983)—going against the grain of incremental construction. In sum, "many serviced-site schemes have suffered from exactly the same kinds of problems that public housing projects experienced, being too expensive for poorer groups, in the wrong locations and with plot sizes and site lay-outs which were ill-matched to the needs and priorities of the intended beneficiaries" (Hardoy & Satterthwaite, 1989, p. 127). In relation to upgrading, although the housing and environmental benefits

Table 14.5   Urban Projects: Lending and Costs by Region, 1972–1981

Region	No. of Projects	Amount Lent (U.S. $ millions)	Total Project Costs (U.S. $ millions)	Lending as Percentage of Total
Eastern Africa	10	153.5	251.4	5.49
Western Africa	5	90.0	197.9	4.32
Europe, Middle East, and North Africa	8	170.3	341.4	7.46
Latin America and the Caribbean	18	759.1	1,981.9	43.29
South Asia	6	269.0	588.8	12.86
East Asia and the Pacific	15	576.1	1,216.9	26.58
All urban projects		2,018	4,578.3	100.00

Source: "Learning by Doing: World Bank Lending for Urban Development (1972–82)," by World Bank, 1983, Washington, DC: World Bank.

are secured over a shorter time frame than sites-and-services, the main disadvantage is that it maintains the status quo in terms of land distribution. Rarely are attempts made to increase plot sizes that were originally squatted upon. For instance, upgrading projects in urban India typically contain plot sizes of 20 to 25 square meters.

In the early 1980s, shortcomings of the project-by-project approach to address housing needs was recognized by the World Bank (1983) in a report titled *Learning by Doing*. It identified several problem areas: institutional framework, land acquisition and tenure, and cost recovery, high standards and the implementation of special components such as health, nutrition, and community development (pp. 24–29). Two main challenges were identified: urban growth and the challenge of replicability—the need to recognize the importance of housing markets and "use the comparative advantages of both public and private sectors" (p. 50), the need to strengthen the role of institutional finance and to address urban management and productivity. Similar challenges were noted by the Inter-American Development Bank in its operations in urban Latin America (Rojas, 1995). As a result of these concerns, the focus in the 1980s shifted to housing finance:

> Many developing countries have therefore set up public sector housing finance institutions. These usually provide loans at interest rates below the market or even the inflation rate, using funds from budget allocations and captive savings in the public sector, such as reserves of insurance institutions and pension funds. (UNCHS, 2001, p. 38)

Two decades later, these institutions have not really succeeded in financing housing for the poor. For example, the Government Housing Bank (GHB) of Thailand, set up in 1953 to both fund and produce housing, lay dormant for the first 2 decades, prompting the need to set up the National Housing Authority in 1972 with responsibility for the production of housing, and the GHB becoming solely a financing institution (Kritayanavaj, 2002). Following the 1997 financial crisis in Thailand, it has been argued that the GHB has facilitated the private sector in the provision of housing for the poor. Although the proportion of those on incomes between 10,000 and 1 million baht increased from 88.09% (1997) to 90.91% (2001) in relation to the total number of borrowers, those on very low incomes remained a minority: 12.58% in 1997 and 13.12% in 2001 (Kritayanavaj, 2002). In India, national housing finance institutions have succeeded in lending only to state or regional housing institutions. According to UNCHS (2001, p. 38):

> In a number of developing countries . . . public housing finance institutions or banks have become ineffective or have even collapsed. Insufficient flow of new financial resources to compensate interest rate subsidies, poor management and political interference lead to gradual decline of the value of assets of public funds that are used for this purpose. The number of "nonperforming" loans increase during inflationary periods or economic crises, leading to large-scale default. Attempts to stabilize inflation through interest rate increases (demand management) make it more difficult for public housing banks to serve low-income groups. Barriers to the provision of housing finance to the poor include the mortgage as the lending instrument, the cost of funds and the risk of default. The conventional form of securing a housing loan is through the mortgage loan, a highly formalized legal instrument which requires a clear title to the land, valuation of the property and registration in a land register, all calling for costly professional help that the poor may be unable to afford. Furthermore, regular repayment obligations may be an impediment to moderate-to-low income households without regular incomes.

The year 1987 was designated as the UN International Year of Shelter for the Homeless, and a reaffirmation was made to pursue enabling housing strategies, ensure that the interests and capabilities of women were represented, and recognize that shelter and development are interdependent and that urban development must be environmentally sustainable (United Nations, 1988). The adoption of this resolution was complemented by the New Agenda for Human Settlements (UNCHS, 1988).

If the 1970s was the decade of the oil crisis and sharp increases in the debt burden in Africa, Asia, Latin America, and the Caribbean, the decade of the 1980s saw many people in developing countries suffer the impacts of structural adjustment policies imposed by the International Monetary Fund (see, e.g., Riddle, 1997). Structural adjustment occurred when

> the central objective of macroeconomic policy became the control of inflation through monetary policy, devaluation and the attainment of budgetary balances. Led by Thatcher and Reagan, the policy side of the "counter-revolution" resulted in curbs on trade unions, reduction in taxes and welfare expenditure, the privatization of state enterprises, reduction or abolition of subsidies and price controls, deregulation of key sectors of the economy, and liberalization of exchange restrictions. The solution to the crisis, in the North as in the South, was to allow the market to determine how economic resources can more productively be allocated, and to rely on market forces as the principal determinant of economic decision. (Lapeyre, 2004, p. 4)

Although structural adjustment policies affected the poor in both rural and urban areas (see, e.g., Hellman, 1997; Laurell, 2000), there is evidence that the impacts on the urban poor were more significant. For instance, in a study of the urban informal sector in Nigeria, Meagher and Mohammed-Bello (1996) found four new patterns: (1) Entry into the sector witnesses an intensification from unemployed and low-wage earners; (2) the category of unemployed now included secondary school and university graduates; (3) female participation increased; and (4) an increasing number of employed civil servants were active in the informal sector. Other examples include Harare, Zimbabwe (Potts & Mutambirwa, 1988) Gweru, Zimbabwe (Rakodi, 1995a), Ecuador, Hungary, the Philippines, and Zambia (Moser, 1996), and Mexico (González de la Rocha, 2006).

Structural adjustment policies of the 1980s and the Washington consensus of the 1990s also had a bearing on the forms of housing policy and practice in the urban developing world.[9] This was first heralded by the recognition of the limited impact of the project-by-project approach and the need to consider institutional capacity for housing and finance. By the 1990s, the need to locate housing within the wider functioning of the city was gaining momentum. Several "policy"-type documents are evidence of such a shift. In 1991, the World Bank published *Urban Policy and Economic Development: An Agenda for the 1990s*, with a focus on four key areas: improving urban productivity, alleviating urban poverty through economic and social policies, protecting the urban environment, and increasing understanding of urban issues. In the same year, the United Nations Development Program brought out *Cities, People and Poverty: Urban Development Cooperation for the 1990s*, which contained five areas of action: alleviate poverty, provide the poor with infrastructure and services, improve the urban environment, strengthen local government, and promote

---

[9]For a review of the changes in World Bank involvement—from housing to municipal reform—see Zanetta (2001).

the private sector and not-for-profit organizations. The location of housing within a broader concern for urban development was welcomed by a number of commentators—in particular those who have long argued that although the majority of people in developing countries live in rural areas, cities are the engines of economic growth (Harris, 1989). Furthermore, it is argued that a more holistic approach should replace the narrow sectoral focus on the role of cities in economic development as a result of structural changes resulting from the forces of globalization (Harris, 1997). This shift is reflected in the changes in spending on housing by the World Bank (Table 14.6).

Housing: Enabling Markets to Work as New Urban Housing Practice and Policy experiments (Early 1990s to Date)

The adverse impact of structural adjustment policies, especially on the urban poor, gave rise to many commentators calling for the introduction of safety nets to ease the burdens imposed by adjustment (see, e.g., Cornia, Jolly, & Stewart, 1987a, 1987b). If the priority of the 1980s was "rolling back of the state [and] not making it more effective" (Rodrik, 2000, p. 2), the late 1990s saw a reversal of this trend encapsulated in the title of the World Bank's 1997 *World Development Report: The State in a Changing World*. This recognition of the need for an effective state stemmed from the failures of market-oriented policies in Russia and Latin America; for the latter, the 1990s is often referred to as "the lost decade." The 1997 *World Development Report* recognizes that a two-pronged strategy is necessary for more effective states: "matching the state's role to its capacity" and "rais[ing] state capability by reinvigorating public institutions" (p. 3). The first prong of this strategy was getting "the fundamentals right," recognizing that "the state need not be the sole provider," and "knowing the state's limits" (pp. 4–6).

Although a number of these principles were already part of enabling policies and practices, the need to place housing with a whole sector framework was articulated in the third World Bank (1993) housing policy paper, *Housing: Enabling Markets to Work*. This policy paper acknowledges that "specific housing projects, through sites-and-services, slum upgrading, or housing finance development, has usually been too small to significantly

Table 14.6   Urban Housing Projects Supported by the World Bank and the International Finance Corporation

Focus area	1972–1986	1987–2005	1972–1986 to 1987–2005
Slum upgrading	22.0	4.0	−18.0
Sites and services	49.0	11.0	−38.0
Housing policy	3.0	11.0	8.0
Housing finance	15.0	49.0	34.0
Disaster relief	11.0	25.0	14.0
Total	100.0	100.0	
Total amount loaned (2001 U.S.$ billions)	4.4	10.3	

Source: "Housing and Land," by World Bank, 2007b, Washington, DC: World Bank. Retrieved March 15, 2007, from http://go.worldbank.org/OTO3F852E0/.

affect the housing sector as a whole" (p. 33). It also notes that "the first generation of Bank loans, mainly sites-and-services and slum upgrading projects focused directly on benefiting poorer urban households, and the second generation, mainly loans to financial intermediaries for long-term mortgage finance . . . [have had better results than preexisting policies and programs] . . . although limited in scale" (p. 33). The 1993 policy paper

> explains the rationale for a new housing policy statement, presents a conceptual and analytical framework for understanding the housing sector, and defines the broad characteristics of a well-functioning housing sector. The paper discusses what has been learned about how the housing sector actually works—housing demand, housing supply, the determination of key outcomes in the sector, and the linkages between the housing sector, poverty, the environment, and the broader economy. It outlines the key elements of an enabling strategy, which is necessary for governments to adopt in order to leverage their resources in bringing about a well-functioning housing sector. Seven key instruments of an enabling strategy are discussed—three to stimulate the demand for housing, three to facilitate housing supply, and one to manage the sector in a manner than ensures that markets provide adequate and affordable housing for all. (World Bank, 2007a)

The emphasis on the housing sector as a whole consists of interventions in a range of priority areas: property rights development (titles to land); enhancement of housing finance (supporting competitive and market-oriented institutions); rationalization of subsidies (from general to targeted); infrastructure for residential land development (large-scale trunk infrastructure, infrastructure upgrading in slums and squatter settlements, and infrastructure provision in sites-and-services projects); enhancing the efficiency of the building industry; and supporting regulatory and institutional reform. It also emphasizes the involvement of the private sector wherever possible:

> From 1972 to 1990, the World Bank was involved in 116 shelter projects (sites-and-services and slum upgrading) in 55 countries, with an average project size of U.S.$26 million. These projects achieved some improvements in housing policies in the developing world, mostly in physical design and cost reduction. However, while these projects achieved their physical objectives, they generally failed to meet two other key objectives: cost recovery from beneficiaries to reduce or eliminate housing subsidies, and *replicability by the private sector.* (World Bank, 1993, pp. 5–6, emphasis mine)

Others have also noted the World Bank's emphasis on the private sector:

> [There is a need to] redirect developing-country governments from engaging in building, marketing, financing, and maintenance of housing units toward facilitating *expansion of the private sector's role* in such activities. (Gilbert, 1997, p. 62, emphasis mine)

It is interesting to note that unlike the earlier phases of housing policy development, the interventions suggested in the World Bank's 1993 policy paper have not been put into practice as a blueprint approach but have instead turned out to be policy experiments in which certain elements of policy have been applied in practice. The following subsections focus on three areas representative of this new direction in housing policy: the role of the private sector in subsidized and nonsubsidized housing, housing finance and public-private partnerships.

Enabling Housing Markets to Work in Practice: The Role of the Private Sector and Up-Front Subsidies

Urban Latin America has proved to be the main experimental field for greater involvement of the market and the up-front provision of subsidies as a result of the adoption of neoliberal economic and social policies since the early 1970s, much before the concept of "enabling markets to work" was espoused by the World Bank (Gilbert, 2002b). Chile was the forerunner, with the military government of General Pinochet establishing housing policies that "were directed to eliminate most forms of state control, leaving urban and housing processes to the free play of market forces" (Kusnetzoff, 1997, p. 296). Land was privatized and liberalized and subsidies exclusively provided to private builders who hardly catered to the poor (Navarro, 2005). Illegal settlements were not tolerated, and by the end of 1989, some 40,000 families in the capital, Santiago, had been relocated (Kusnetzoff, 1997). In 1990, the democratic government of Aylwin retained many of the military government's land and urban policies but placed greater emphasis on providing one-off subsidies (Kusnetzoff, 1997). By 2004, 96% of all government housing resources were in the form of subsidies, yet it presented the challenge of ensuring the provision of some 96,000 units per year just to accommodate new demand (Navarro, 2005).

The Chilean model was widely diffused in Latin America by the World Bank, the Inter-American Development Bank, and in particular by USAID because it contained three elements fundamental to the approach of enabling markets to work: explicit targeting of the poor, transparency, and the involvement of the private sector (Gilbert, 2002b).[10]

According to Gilbert (1997), Colombia adopted the Bank's market and rationalized subsidy-based policy prescriptions in 1990. The Institute for Territorial Credit (responsible for the construction of social interest housing) was replaced by a slimmed down National Institute for Social Interest Housing and Urban Reform, which "introduced a policy of giving direct subsidies to poor people, channelled these subsidies toward privately supplied housing options and encouraged the private sector to supply more so-called social-interest housing" (pp. 54–55). Gilbert notes:

> Social-interest housing would be destined mainly for those families earning less than four minimum salaries (U.S.$115 per month), those without their own homes and those whose accommodation was poorly constructed, was overcrowded or lacked a title deed or services. Families earning less than two minimum salaries would be eligible for a subsidy of up to 15 minimum salaries. . . . The units were expected to cost no more than 50 minimum salaries. In practice this meant that little was being provided beyond a serviced site. . . . Those earning between two and four minimum salaries would be eligible for a subsidy to buy houses with a value of between 50 and 135 minimum salaries. . . . To obtain a subsidy, a family should have cash savings of at least five percent of the value of the unit. . . . The beneficiary of the subsidy decided how to use the subsidy *but never received it directly.* (p. 55, emphasis mine)

Gilbert (1997) notes three main challenges of this policy experiment. First, most poor families failed to take up their subsidies either because they had neither "sufficient savings or high enough incomes . . . to buy finished houses . . . [or] had insufficient funds for the down payment . . . [or] had considerable difficulty finding an appropriate housing unit" (p. 58).

---

[10]Costa Rica, Colombia, Ecuador, and Panama adopted Chilean-type subsidy models, and there was interest in Guatemala, Paraguay, Uruguay, and Venezuela to do the same (Gilbert, 2002b).

Second, the policy missed the opportunity to make land available through sites-and-service projects, an argument that is tied to the benefits of subsidizing land and infrastructure rather than the housing unit itself given the rising cost of land and services. Third, the lack of a rental housing policy was shortsighted. Despite these shortcomings, the market-based targeted subsidy policy was successful in other respects: "The new allocation mechanism was more transparent, and more subsidies reached the poor. Private sector investment boosted the resources flowing into social-interest housing. The new approach also recognized the need for more investment in infrastructure and services" (p. 67).

The involvement of the private sector and the provision of one-off up-front subsidies was also reluctantly tried in South Africa, after the fall of apartheid and following the first democratic elections in 1994 (Gilbert, 2002c). One-off capital subsidies of 17,000 rand were to be provided to those with incomes of less than 800 rand and housing delivered through the private sector—the governing instrument being a "social compact" between communities and the provider (Mackay, 1999). Huchzermeyer (2003, p. 600) argues that

> the entitlement, by the poor, to a one-off product linked capital subsidy is a powerful instrument of sociopolitical control. Popular awareness of this individual entitlement leads directly to a demand for standardized delivery, leaving no space for collective reflection on the appropriateness of the individualized product.

She also notes that the requirements of the capital subsidy have led not only to nonprofits competing with developers in delivering the largest houses but also to a focus on those settlements with legal title. There is clearly a need to match housing policy with the politics of South Africa (Huchzermeyer, 2003).

In all three countries there have been shortcomings of the one-off subsidy approach. Two main problems can be identified: the limited resources and thus the limited number of subsidies, and, more important, the lack of credit to supplement the resources needed over and above the subsidies (Gilbert, 2004). In sum, and in line with the thinking on reducing subsidies leading to the adopting of enabling strategies of sites-and-services and upgrading, the use of a one-off capital subsidy meets one principle of the neoliberal agenda: a reduction in government spending on housing.

> The capital subsidy has also permitted each of the governments to limit its spending, perhaps the principal rationale behind the policy. In an environment of neo-liberal economic orthodoxy, a major attraction of the capital subsidy was that it offered a way of helping poor families obtain a house, without letting public expenditure get out of hand. (p. 33)

Enabling Housing Markets to Work in Practice: Private Provision without Subsidies

India has provided fertile ground for public-private partnership experiments. In Mumbai (formerly Bombay), the 2001 census estimated that 54% of households live in slums[11] and in an extremely skewed distribution of land; it is estimated that the poor occupy 10% of the city's land (O'Hare, Abbott, & Barke, 1998). The largest squatter settlement (slum) is

---

[11] See www.censusindia.net/results/slum/slum2.html.

Dharavi, with an estimated population of between 500,000 and one million. In the mid-1980s, a proposal was made to redevelop the slum by relocating some of its residents in four- to five-story apartments built by the municipal government; the costs were to be offset by a 10% subsidy and an interest-free loan for 20% of the construction costs given to beneficiaries and resettling others elsewhere (Mukhija, 2001). The proposal ran into trouble by dividing the community, as a result of which the project was scaled down to a pilot, alerting the municipality to the need to involve the private sector (Mukhija, 2001). The next phase, the Slum Redevelopment Scheme of 1991, took a similar form of redevelopment (households should be relocated in the same site in dwellings of 17 to 21 square meters) but with two differences: involvement of the private sector and cross-subsidies to be provided by the private sector alone. It was anticipated that this would be done by relaxing the laws on the amount of floor space that can be built in proportion to the land. However, the state government's rule that profits could not exceed 25% of the investment dampened the investment spirit of the private sector (Mukhija, 2001). With a change of government in 1995, this scheme was replaced with the slum rehabilitation scheme, with some changes: All families were to be given 25 square meters, the ceiling on developer profits were to be lifted, and although the floor area ratio (FAR) of 1:2.5 was to be retained, the high density of some of the slum areas meant that developers would be allowed to transfer any unused FAR to developments elsewhere. Much of this thinking was built on the high land values at the time; however, the land price crash in 1998 (bringing land values to 1993 levels) seriously impeded progress and interest (Mukhija, 2001). As a result, only 26,000 squatter households were rehoused, against a target of 800,000 (Sharma, 2005). As Mukhija (2001, p. 792) notes:

> Paradoxically, enabling involves not only decentralisation but also some form of centralisation; not only privatisation but also new kinds of public investment; not only deregulation but also enforcement of new regulations; and not only demand-driven development but also supply driven initiatives. In other words, enabling housing provision through market mechanisms requires a different type of state involvement, not necessarily less state involvement.

Enabling Housing Markets to Work in Practice: The Limits to Public-Private Partnerships

Public-private partnerships in housing are a feature of the 1990s. While the previous two sections explored some of the opportunities and challenges relating to the involvement of the private sector in housing practice, this section focuses on public-private partnerships. Often, questions related to public-private partnerships focus on information asymmetries, incentives for the private sector to be involved, the ability to hold the private sector to account, and the legal and institutional frameworks that govern the biparty relationship. A neglected question is one of changes in practices when a private sector organization, previously involved in low-income housing provision, enters into partnership with the public sector. Mukhija (2004) points to a case in the city of Ahmedabad, in the state of Gujarat, India. Here a private sector construction company was providing housing for low-income groups using formal and informal mechanisms in both land development and construction (houses were finished to a very basic wall and roof level with scope for improvement by owners to keep costs low). The company was quite successful in its operation. However, when the public-sector Housing and Urban Development Corporation entered into a partnership with the private company, problems arose, and the company has now pulled out of housing for low-income groups. Mukhija put this down to two main reasons. First, the partnership with the public sector meant that the private company had to adhere to formal rules, thus severely restricting the flexibility offered by the informal mechanisms used in the past. Second, the involvement of the public sector sent the wrong signals to the beneficiaries, who were not content with the notion of making incremental improvements to their housing. These were the two main incentives for the private company to be involved in low-income housing, which, when removed, resulted in its withdrawal from housing for the poor.

THE GOOD AND THE GREAT: INTERNATIONAL DEVELOPMENT ORGANIZATIONS, ALLIANCES, AND CAMPAIGNS

This section briefly presents contemporary development in terms of multisector urban and housing partnerships and campaigns in the late twentieth and early twenty-first century.

The Cities Alliance and City Development Strategies

Cities Alliance (2005),[12] a multidonor coalition of cities and their development partners, was cofounded by UN-HABITAT and the World Bank in 1999 with the view to improve

> the efficiency and impact of urban development cooperation in two key areas: making unprecedented improvements in the living conditions of the urban poor by developing citywide and nationwide slum-upgrading programs; and supporting city-based consensus-building processes by which local stakeholders define their vision for their city and establish city development strategies with clear priorities for action and investments.

Its two main programs are Cities without Slums and the formulation of City Development Strategies. A recent evaluation (Universalia, 2006, p. ii) notes:

> The Cities Alliance has demonstrated effects on the ground, especially considering the generally modest level of resources that it can allocate to cities. Through technical assistance grants for city upgrading or strategic planning initiatives, it has also contributed to taking project experience to a nationwide or city-wide scale of action, reflected in the replication and adaptation of its initiatives and/or new or revised policy frameworks. In the cities that CA has supported, it has had some success in improving the coherence of efforts in development cooperation for urban development. The CA has been able to leverage follow-up investments in the projects that it has supported, although it will need to continuously strengthen this aspect and also help cities to pay increasing attention to domestic sources of capital where possible. The CA has contributed to the development of capacities of project stakeholders, both individuals and organizations, in areas such as strategic city planning, participatory processes, and integrated approaches to slum upgrading.

---

[12]In 1996, the Cities Alliance had 20 members: local authorities, represented by United Cities and Local Governments and Metropolis; Asian Development Bank, Brazil, Canada, Ethiopia, France, Germany, Italy, Japan, the Netherlands, Nigeria, Norway, South Africa, Sweden, United Cities and Local Governments, United Kingdom, UN-HABITAT, United Nations Environment Programme, the United States, and the World Bank.

The Cities Alliance has been less successful in two areas—advocacy and knowledge sharing—that are equally important for achieving its objectives. The CA needs to strengthen its role in generating policy coherence and increasing synergies among the different actors involved, and in influencing national or global development agendas. In a related vein, the CA has not paid sufficient attention to the process of knowledge exchange and transfer among its stakeholders (Members, clients, and other actors in urban development). The Alliance lacks an overall strategy for ensuring that its influencing and knowledge-sharing role helps it to achieve its objectives. Knowledge sharing and advocacy have been constrained by the limited time and resources that Members and the Secretariat can allocate to these areas.

Apart from the challenges outlined in the second paragraph, there is a danger in focusing exclusively on a target-based approach. For example, while the banner of Cities without Slums has the benefit of capturing public attention, the target of improving the lives of 100 million slum dwellers is a fraction of the total number of slum dwellers (close to 900 million by the turn of the century). In addition, there is the question of who is included in this target. Furthermore, such target setting and the emphasis on upgrading can draw attention away from other innovative solutions, such as rental housing and the involvement of nonprofits in social housing. In sum, there is the danger of providing a one-size-fits-all solution to the problem rather than recognizing the need for a "plurality" of housing provision (Keivani & Werna, 2001).

The UN-HABITAT Campaigns on Good Governance and Tenure

In 2000, UN-Habitat launched two campaigns: Secure Tenure and Urban Governance:

[The] overall development objective of the Campaign is to improve the conditions of people living and often working in slum areas and informal settlements in major urban centers of the world by promoting security of their residential tenure and a direct contribution to the realisation of the commitments of the Millennium Declaration, specifically, the goal of improving the lives of 100 million slum dwellers by the year 2020. (UN-HABITAT, n.d.)

An evaluation of the Campaigns on Good Governance and secure tenure notes that:

It is useful to note the distinction between Campaigns and Programs. Campaigns are methods of getting the political, legal and institutional framework right, so that appropriate and effective programs may be delivered. Too often resources have been wasted on programs which are implemented under an inappropriate framework and therefore do not deliver the expected benefits. Campaigns help to create the consensus and agreement necessary for frameworks which encourage and accommodate effective programs. Successful Campaigns precede effective programs. (Fernandes, Fuentes, & Sewell, 2005, p. 9)

Furthermore, the evaluation notes:

Regarding the Governance Campaign, there is a widespread feeling that, much as the topic is important and even crucial, it is somewhat vague and does not lead to any immediate, concrete field of action. As such, it does not easily engender sociopolitical mobilisation and it does not have a straightforward popular appeal. The notion of "good" governance was also criticised, on the grounds that it could easily be construed as a patronising element. (pp. 10–11)

The UN-HABITAT web site[13] speaks of some successes in India (Mumbai), the Philippines (Manila, General Santos, Davao, Iloilo), and South Africa (Durban), but these are minuscule compared to the scale of the challenge. While the intentions of the Campaign for Secure Tenure are to be applauded, unless tenure security for the poor is nationally institutionalized with due recourse to laws protecting the right to shelter, the Campaign is likely to have little clout (see, UN-HABITAT, 2005, on the subject of forced evictions).

The materialization of the Governance Campaign in the diverse countries where the Campaign has been promoted and/or launched has taken different forms with specific issues. In Brazil, for instance, the issues of financing local development and the municipalization of public security were adopted. In Burkina Faso, the emphasis was on capacity building to deliver water and sewage services. However, some feel that the Campaign's general principles of participation, transparency, accountability, and subsidiarity, among others, are not automatically inherent in such specific issues and need to be reinforced.

Regarding the Secure Tenure Campaign, the opposite argument is common: Much as the topic is of fundamental importance, it is perceived as somewhat technical and could easily be reduced to a legalistic question. Moreover, many people believe that the topic does not translate easily—even in linguistic terms—given the different national realities.

Secure Title or an Entitlement to Security

It is often argued that the poor have a preference for ownership. Who would not? However, the pertinent questions to ask are: How will you pay for the costs of legal title? How will you secure housing finance solely on the basis of legal title? How will you use ownership to increase mobility? The importance of these questions is not just related to issues of affordability and finance, but more important to the fact that the institutional framework for mortgage lending does not exist for the poor.

Tenure legalization is not a new concept, having been incorporated into slum upgrading projects in the 1980s. Proponents of secure tenure have argued that a key reason for low housing investments by the poor is the threat of eviction as a result of insecure tenure (Turner, 1972). Providing secure tenure can make a difference in reducing the threat of eviction. It might also provide security from land capture by other individuals and groups (Atuahene, 2006). Nevertheless, whether it is a necessary condition for housing investment is another matter. Some studies have shown that increasing security of tenure has a positive impact on housing investment (see, e.g., Jimenez, 1983; Struyk, & Lynn, 1983), whereas others have argued that although land titles can act as an incentive for investment in housing, the "effects on credit access are modest and there is no effect on labour income" (Galiani & Schargrodsky, 2005, p. 3). In another study, Field (2006, p. 3) notes that in urban Peru

> estimates of early program impact suggest that households with no legal claim to property spend an average of 13.4 hours per week maintaining informal tenure security, reflecting a 14% reduction in total household work hours for the average squatter family. Households are also 28% more likely to work inside of their home. Thus, the net effect of property titling is a combination of an increase in total labour force hours and a reallocation of work hours from inside the home to the outside labour market.

---

[13] See www.unhabitat.org/content.asp?typeid=19&catid=24&cid=2046/.

Two points are worth noting in relation to the Peru. First, the high level of insecurity vis-à-vis land capture by other poor groups is specific to the context; second, although land titling may have freed households to look for work, not much is said about the effects of this freedom on poverty.

Opponents of legalization have cautioned, however, that legalization may be neither a necessary or nor a sufficient condition (see, e.g., Angel, Archer, Tanphiphat, & Wegelin, 1983). Others have argued that legalization can lead to the inclusion of low-income settlements into the land market and to processes of gentrification (Burgess, 1985). To overcome these problems, it has been argued that the installation of services has more of an impact on housing investment (P. W. Strassman, 1980). This leads Varley (1987, pp. 464–465) to conclude:

> The basic problem with the argument concerning legalization and housing improvements is that security of tenure is not a fixed, objective concept, and that it is affected by a variety of other considerations: not only the legality of tenure. Changes in residents' assessment of their security of tenure can also, therefore, be produced by other means. The most important of these is probably the installation of services, which people take as de facto indication of official acceptance of the continued existence of their settlement.

The push for a citywide land titling program only really emerged from the *Housing: Enabling Markets to Work* policy paper, which is explicit on the need to bring about property reforms (World Bank, 1993). Much of this thinking has been influenced by the work of the Peruvian economist Hernando de Soto (1989, 2000). In his book, *The Mystery of Capital: Why Capitalism Triumphs in the West and Fails Everywhere Else* (de Soto, 2000), he argues that "property rights as embodied in titles are an essential mechanism for converting assets to useable wealth" and "he estimates that if developing countries provide secure property rights to residential property, they would effectively 'unlock' $9.3 trillion worth of what he calls 'dead capital'" (Buckley & Kalarickal, 2005, pp. 245–246).

De Soto's claims have received criticism from several academics and researchers (see, e.g., Bromley, 1994, 2004; Buckley & Kalarickal, 2005; Gilbert, 2002a): First, titling is expensive not just due to institutional constraints but mainly because of the cost of adjudicating counterclaims. Second is the question of amnesty to prevent squatting becoming a way of gaining legal ownership; often this takes the form of a cutoff eligibility date for the granting of title, which then results in problems of social exclusion (Woodruff, 2001 cited in, Buckley & Kalarickal, 2005). Third, the value of a title is limited if it cannot be used as collateral (Buckley & Kalarickal, 2005). Fourth, the existence of a continuum of titles means that some may value title more than others (Payne, 2002). There are two other critical issues related to land titling that have received little attention in the literature. First is the fact that land titling is not redistributive; in essence, this means that those who have managed to squat on very tiny lots are going to be eligible only for the land that they currently occupy. This has the danger of maintaining the status quo in terms of the inequities in access to urban land. Second is the displacement of tenants. Given that the occupation of land by the de facto owner is illegal and that land titling would be aimed at all the residents of a given settlement, it is in the interest of the de facto landlord to maximize the amount of land received, resulting in the eviction of tenants before an official visit to verify claims.

In sum, caution needs to be exercised so as not to institutionalize the injustices in the access to land for urban housing that currently exist. Furthermore, although the UN-HABITAT Campaign on Secure Tenure[14] is laudable for its aim of attempting to protect the poor from the vulnerability and risks associated with evictions, it must avoid the danger of being seen as a supporter of legalization through titling.

CIVIL SOCIETY, NOT-FOR-PROFITS, AND OTHERS OF THE SAME ILK BUT WITH A DIFFERENT PERSPECTIVE

The involvement of nonprofits (or nongovernmental organizations [NGOs], as they are known in the developing world) and faith-based groups in housing and human settlements is not a new phenomenon. However, the manner in which they engage with housing and related issues has changed in certain respects.

Project-by-Project Interventions

Early interventions tended to be small-scale, project-based, and focused on helping the poor to build homes using appropriate technology. Cost savings were attained though the use of "sweat equity"—namely, contributions in the form of labor from individual households when it came to building houses and labor contributions from a given poor community for community-level improvements such as water and sanitation. These could take the form of locally based nonprofits or international faith-based nonprofits working in different regions of the world. Perhaps the most well-known example of the former is the Orangi Pilot Project (OPP) in Karachi, Pakistan. Orangi is Karachi's largest *katchi abadi* (squatter settlement) with a population of 1.2 million. The OPP was established in 1980 with the initial aim of enabling its residents to contribute financially and physically to the provision of sanitation within Orangi, based on the notion that although residents do not have the capacity to construct trunk infrastructure (the purview of governments), they could exercise their agency in building sanitation infrastructure lane by lane in their settlement. In 1988, the project was upgraded into four autonomous institutions: the OPP-RTI, responsible for sanitation; the Orangi Charitable Trust, for the Family Enterprise Economic Program; the Karachi Health and Social Development Association; and the OPP Society, which funds housing. In Orangi, people have invested 78.79 million rupees (about U.S.$1.3 million) on internal development (including 405 secondary sewers) in 5,987 lanes consisting of 90,596 houses (there are 104,917 houses in Orangi). The OPP concept has been accepted by the Karachi municipal government and Sindh Katchi Abadis Authority and is being applied to their development plans. Increasingly, the OPP is getting involved in policy issues and promoting macro-level solutions based on its models of sanitation, health, housing, and economic issues (for more details, see Urban Resource Centre, n.d.). Another example is the nonprofit Habitat for Humanity. Their web site notes that "Habitat for Humanity is a

---

[14]The overall development objective of the campaign is to improve the conditions of people living and often working in slum areas and informal settlements in major urban centers of the world by promoting security of their residential tenure and a direct contribution to the realization of the commitments of the Millennium Declaration, specifically, the goal of "improving the lives of 100 million slum dwellers by the year 2020" (UN-HABITAT, n.d.).

nonprofit, nondenominational Christian housing charity whose goal is to eliminate housing poverty and homelessness from the world, and to make decent shelter a matter of conscience and action." Habitat for Humanity states that they have built 200,000 houses all over the world, thus providing safe, decent, affordable shelter to nearly a million people. Habitat for Humanity provides households with interest-free loans for housing and requires them to contribute sweat equity as well as make repayments on the loans. It also uses volunteers from overseas to help (for more details, see Habitat for Humanity, 2006).

Community-Based Housing Finance

Although Buckley and Kalarickal (2005, p. 247) note, "The need to develop a sustainable supply of finance to fund housing continues to be an important part of any set of policy measures to improve housing affordability," access to institutional housing finance for the poor remains largely undeveloped. For example, it has been noted that in India

> resources from the formal [public] system still constitutes a mere 16 percent of the total investment in the housing sector because of its weak financial base attributed to the low household savings.... Furthermore ... most of the finance is extended for house construction rather than for getting access to land. (Durrand-Lasserve & Adusumilli, 2001, p. 17)

The inability to use land as collateral and not having a regular salaried job in the formal sector exclude most of the poor and all of the poorest from institutional access to housing finance—both private and public (see, e.g., Jones, & Datta, 1998; Smets, 1997). It emerged that the only option was to form self-help savings groups. Once again, such mechanisms for saving for emergency consumption loans are not new. Households have also actively used these mechanisms to make housing improvements both for their own use as well as for renting (Kumar, 2001b).

Nonprofits have also had a long history of providing small loans or microcredit for income-generating activities. The involvement of nonprofits in housing finance came about as a result of the realization that microcredit provided for income generation was being invested in housing and services (Jones & Mitlin, 1998). Notwithstanding the benefits of both community-based savings and microcredit, these mechanisms have tended to focus benefits on the individual, thereby restricting the potential for using the savings as collateral to leverage a greater volume of financial resources for housing and services.

The next section explores the development of federations of the poor and the successes and limitations they have had in leveraging institutional finance for housing and services.

Contemporary Activities: Federations of the Poor and Alliances

As noted earlier, although microcredit and savings and credit associations of the poor that provide credit to smooth consumption and production activities have a role to play, they have been limited in leveraging broader institutional support. This is partly because of a narrow focus on the immediate needs of its members, which results in savings groups tending to operate in a fragmented manner.

A realization of the power and voice that can emanate from the coming together of poor groups to form federations and their ability to negotiate and leverage state and private sector resources through partnerships with nonprofits has begun to emerge:

> The federating or networking that results addresses a weakness of many civil society organizations, that of isolation. It is isolation that makes it easy for a leader to dominate, for mis-information to be commonplace, for partnerships to remain unused, because win-win scenarios are not identified, and for groups to give up in despair when land and services are refused. It is also isolation that ensures that many mis-justices are not addressed and that effective lobbying and advocacy is the preserve of the rich. Governments find it easier to ignore the demands of individual isolated communities; it is much more difficult to do so when dozens of community organizations are making their demands through their own federations. ("Editorial," 2001, p. 4)

Federations of the poor can emerge as a result of different threats. For example, the National Slum Dwellers Federation, based in Mumbai, India, was established in 1974 mainly to resist evictions. It is estimated that by 2002, it had a membership of 750,000 people in 52 cities and nine states in India. The largest membership of 250,000 households is in Mumbai (Burra, Patel, & Kerr, 2003). Although the Federation has made some important gains in negotiating resettlement as a result of evictions in Mumbai, its membership is only a fraction of all the urban slum dwellers in India. According to the Census of India 2001, the total slum population of the 640 cities and towns reporting slums was 42.6 million, making the federations membership only 0.02%.[15]

The South African Homeless People's Federation was formed in the early 1990s (Bolnick, 2001). South Africa has had a long legacy of civic struggle against the injustices of apartheid. Following the election of the first democratic government in 1994, proposals were drawn up to channel subsidies for housing for the poor through housing developers and contractors. However, on hearing the negative experience of subsidies from the Indian Federation and the positive experience of the poor forming savings groups and receiving subsidies directly, grassroots organizations of the South African urban poor went on to form local housing savings schemes and networked to create the South African Homeless People's Federation (Patel, Burra, & d'Cruz, 2001). A similar process resulted in the creation of the Zimbabwean Homeless People's Federation, with the support of the South African federation (Chitekwe & Mitlin, 2001).

Scaling Up at the City and National Levels: Partnerships for Sanitation and Housing

One of the criticisms of the past, both of the enabling strategies of sites-and-services and of the activities of nonprofits, has been the limitations to scaling up as a result of the project-by-project approach. Moreover, the latter has not used pilot projects to bring about wider institutional change; rather, the impact has been for the state to assume a position

---

[15] See www.habitatjam.com/webuploads/members/oArpurtham_Jockin_Bio_English.pdf. According to the Census of India 2001, only 26 of the 35 states and union territories reported an incidence of slums. Even within these 26, only 640 cities and towns have reported a slum population of 42,578,150 persons (23% of the total urban population of theses 640 cities and towns). In the 26 cities with a population of more than a million, the slum population in 2001 was 16,565,459 (23% of the total urban population).

of benign neglect because nonprofits were attempting to fill the gaps in shelter and service provision created by state inability or neglect.

Using the example of sanitation provision in Pune and Mumbai, two cities in the state of Maharashtra, India, this section highlights the opportunities and challenges confronting the issue of scaling up nonprofit interventions.

The story of communal toilets designed and managed by the poor and their partners begins in Mumbai. The lack of access to sanitation is most acute for pavement dwellers. In 1985, pavement dwellers, in discussions with the nonprofit Society for the Promotion of Area Resource Centers (SPARC), identified access to water and toilets as a key priority (Burra et al., 2003, p. 16):

> A survey by Mahila Milan/National Slum Dwellers Federation of 151 settlements in Mumbai with 1 million people found that there were 3,433 seats provided by toilets built by the municipality (one for every 1,488 persons), and 80% were not working. Most toilets had broken doors, and many had overflowing septic tanks, latrines clogged with excrement and sites covered with garbage.

With dwellings of less than 10 square meters, individual toilets were not an option, the only alternative being communal toilets. Not being able to convince the municipality of the need for community-designed and -managed toilets, the Alliance, consisting of Mahila Milan (Women Together), a federation of women and their savings group, SPARC, and the National Federation of Slum Dwellers, together with financial assistance from Homeless International, designed and built pilot communal toilets. The innovations were separate areas for men, women, and children, large water tanks to keep the toilets clean, caretakers' accommodation to ensure that the toilets were kept clean, and low pay-as-you-go fees for a household and not an individual.[16] Pilot schemes were also undertaken in Kanpur, Bangalore, and Pune.

The sanitation programs have been scaled up in the cities of Pune and Mumbai in the state of Maharashtra. In Pune, the municipal commissioner recognized that the municipality was failing in its duty to provide sanitation:

> A decision was taken to construct 220 toilet blocks with about 3500 toilet seats through NGOs in 1999 to 2000. This was to be the first phase of the program. On completion of the second phase (planned for another 220 blocks between November 2000 and January 2001), more than 400 blocks or more than 10,000 toilet seats would be constructed... benefiting more than 5 lakh (500,000) slum dwellers. (Burra, 2001, p. 3)

The municipality advertised for nonprofits to bid for the design and management of communal toilets under the condition that the cost had to be less than that estimated by the municipality. The municipality would fund the capital costs, but the collection of user fees and maintenance had to be undertaken by the community. The Pune Mahila Milan and SPARC have constructed in total 114 toilet blocks with more than 2,000 seats and more than 500 seats for children (Burra, 2001). It is interesting to note that it was the municipal

---

[16]The poor level of sanitation and the poor upkeep of communal sanitation provided by the public sector has given rise to the provision of "public" pay-as-you-use toilets by nonprofits. However, these are expensive—1 rupee per use—and could add up to 150 rupees per month for a household when used once a day. See also www.sulabhinternational.org.

commissioner who instigated the program, rather than pressure being placed on the municipality by civil society actors. This shows the importance of political will and a certain level of personal experience.[17]

The success of involving communities in Pune has enabled the Alliance in Mumbai to participate in the Slum Sanitation Program, a component of the World Bank–financed Mumbai Sewage Disposal Project, approved in 1995. An estimated 400,000 slum dwellers have benefited (for more details, see Sarkar & Moulik, 2006). Between 1998 and 2003, the Alliance built 180 toilet blocks, and another 110 are in the process of being completed (Burra et al., 2003). Other community-based models are being tried, for example, in Peru.[18]

These successes are laudable. However, most of the publications describing the projects provide only a picture of their achievements and do not reflect on the wider concerns of sanitation for all. For example, Burra (2001) records the process and the difficulties of the Pune program and notes that only those slums that have been notified—meaning that they have been granted a moratorium from evictions based on a cutoff date of 1995 as the eligibility criterion of the official recognition of their right to exist as a settlement—have been included in the program. He does not question access to sanitation for the rest of the slum dwellers. Similarly, in writing about their successes and challenges in Mumbai, Burra et al. (2003) do not provide a wider picture of the issues: who else was involved in the toilet program, whether there was a cutoff date, and on whose lands the settlements receiving communal sanitation were located. How many households are excluded from access to safe sanitation? Some of these issues are addressed by a recent independent evaluation, but still the question of whether community toilets are the end or only the means to improved individual sanitation remains unanswered (see the evaluation by Sarkar & Moulik, 2006).

On the housing finance front, innovations are afoot to address the issues of lack of collateral by the poor as well as the need to scale up housing finance. For example, Homeless International, an international nonprofit focusing on housing-related issues, has established a program called the Community Led Infrastructure Financing Facility (CLIFF) in India and Bolivia. In short, CLIFF is based on the notion that although the poor are able to save, the lack of physical and income-based collateral excludes the poor. By soliciting donations primarily from a range of UK donors, Homeless International is able to channel through the World Bank's Cities Alliance the 20% to 25% guarantees that national and private banks require to release loans for housing and services. These loans are channeled as block loans (as against the previous practice of individual households seeking loans) to a local nonprofit partner. The savings that the community has made provides the flexibility to begin housing and service improvements.[19]

Homeless International is also developing a Homeless International bond, which will allow it to lend to partners directly in places where the guarantee fund is not likely to work because the banking system is not sufficiently developed even to accept guarantees.[20]

---

[17]In an interview, the municipal commissioner of Pune, who instigated the community-designed-and-built communal toilet program, is reported to have said, "When I first came to Pune, my grandfather used to stay in Vishrantwadi and there used to be long queues before the toilet block there every morning. . . . I used to stand in that queue and so have personal experience of using a public toilet myself" (Burra, 2001, p. 2).

[18]See www.wsp.org/filez/pubs/213200781413_lac_models.pdf.

[19]For more details, see www.homeless-international.org/standard_1.aspx?id=0:27814&id=0:27813/.

[20]See www.homeless-international.org/standard_1.aspx?id=1:30584&id=0:27813/.

Homeless International recognizes the limits to these mechanisms—namely, the need for poor individuals and communities to be organized and represented. Unfortunately, the level of organization that is visible in Mumbai is seen in only a few other urban centers in India. There is also the question of how to replicate the kinds of federations of the poor and their partnerships with nonprofits, seen in Mumbai, in other urban areas in the developing world.

Partnerships: Maintaining the Status Quo or Challenging the State?

The question of whom to partner with is an important one as it essentially questions the role of civil society vis-à-vis the state. As Lewis (2002) notes, there are two civil society traditions. The first is as a desirable social sphere (Ferguson, 1767/1995) and a political sphere, which needs to be ordered by the state to prevent self-interest and a lack of contribution to the common good (Hegel, 1821/1991). Evidence of a move from the social and political spheres to an organizational focus can be found, for example, in the work of Alexis de Tocqueville (1835/1994) on America, who "stressed volunteerism, community spirit and individual associational life as protections against the domination of society by the state, and indeed as a counterbalance which helped to keep the state accountable and effective" (Lewis, 2002, p. 571). The Alliance in Mumbai reflects Tocqueville's approach to a great extent but with a few caveats. For instance, Appadurai (2001) notes that the Alliance in Mumbai is "apolitical," in that it enters into discussions and partnerships with whoever is in power at local or state government levels, irrespective of ideology. This is a pragmatic approach intended to make claims on whoever is in power for the benefit of the members of the Alliance. But it is this membership-based claim making that casts doubt over the extent to which it has been able to hold the state accountable for the common good of all disenfranchised people. Thus, although the sanitation program may have forced the state to extend sanitation to a vast majority of slum dwellers, the same is not the case with the housing relocation program.

This brings us to the second civil society tradition, which, according to Lewis (2002), is the Gramscian sphere. Gramsci (1971) "argued that civil society is the arena, separate from the state and market, in which ideological hegemony is contested, implying that civil society contains a wide range of different organizations and ideologies which both challenge and uphold the existing order" (Lewis, 2002, p. 572). It could be argued that the Alliance, while challenging the state in some ways, also helps uphold some of the existing order in that, for example, it does little to challenge the distribution of land for the poor. In contrast, an example of a nonprofit attempting to stick to its principles and not compromise is provided by Youth for Unity and Voluntary Action (YUVA). A study of an attempt by YUVA to forge a partnership between the municipality of Mumbai, YUVA, and a community group that YUVA supported in its development to deal with landlord tenant issues in one low-income settlement shows how partnerships can be affected by bureaucracy, politicization, and personalization. Furthermore, partnerships can also be affected by a parting of "ways of thinking" between the nonprofit and the community group (YUVA, 1999).

Transnational Alliances and Exchanges

Despite variations in the historical, geopolitical, and socioeconomic trajectories of developing countries, the structural causes of injustices that the poor suffer are not that dissimilar:

They are subject to the same vulnerabilities from eviction and suffer the same deprivations from a lack of water and sanitation across the urban developing world. One way of getting national, regional, and city governments as well as international development organizations to not only recognize the plight of the poor but, more important, to realize that the eradication of poverty and the meeting of housing and service needs can be accomplished only with the active involvement of the poor, was to increase the international profile of the poor. This has culminated in the formation of transnational alliances and the setting up of the Shack/Slum Dwellers International (SDI), which represents member federations of the urban poor and homeless groups in 11 countries in Africa (four), Asia (six), and Latin America (one) (Patel et al., 2001). The origin of this international federation stems from the work (between 1998 and 1991) of the Asian Coalition of Housing Rights (ACHR), a network of grassroots organizations and nonprofits in Asia beginning to link national groups and conduct exchange visits with the view to address issues of urban poverty, form savings and credit groups, and develop leadership among the urban poor. In 1996, a meeting of these national federations in South Africa led to the formation of SDI (Patel et al., 2001).

In Asia, although there was a clearly identified need for nonprofits, professionals, and grassroots groups to "share experiences, tackle the large problem of forced evictions in the region's cities, develop opportunities for organizations of the poor and consider their place in city planning," no forum existed (ACHR, 2001). To fill this gap, the ACHR was established in 1998. Its activities include acting as a pressure group and for crisis intervention in specific problems; disseminating information; providing opportunities for community organizations to facilitate sharing of experiences at the community level and for international members to deepen understanding of the major forces affecting the urban poor; facilitating experience sharing and exchange among groups, especially among the grassroots and NGO groups; providing professional consultation for groups based on needs; coordinating with related agencies, both international and local, especially with regard to regional activities; empowering local organizations and strengthening links among each other; supporting the grassroots struggle for housing with an aim to develop the process that enables people to strengthen their own capabilities; researching key issues and innovative initiatives in the region; providing advocacy at international, national, and local levels; creating space for change and facilitating dialogue on local situations by organizing activities with local groups; and supporting and encouraging young professionals to get involved in community development work and deepen their understanding of the people's process (ACHR, 2001).

Another success was when the alliance of SDI and ACHR advised the municipality of Phnom Penh to set up the Urban Community Development Fund to provide loans for housing, housing repairs, and income-generating activities for the poor of the city. The innovation in relation to the fund is "that it emerged from, and is embedded within, a partnership between the municipality of Phnom Penh and the communities themselves" (Patel et al., 2001).

In a globalizing world, increasingly dominated by transnational capital flows associated with a de-location of old sites of production and a relocation to sites of cheap labor, it is clear that the role of the nation-state is changing, or at least needs transforming. As a result, some have argued that "the contemporary world is characterised by both globalisation and localisation of politics" (Harriss, Stokke, & Törnquist, 2004). Although this discussion of the role of local politics and globalization is at the level of the nation-state and other global actors, much of it applies to the localization of urban politics and the role of global alliances:

> This lateral or horizontal dimension . . . in terms of the activities of Shack/Slum Dwellers International, seeks direct collaborations and exchanges between poor communities themselves, based on the "will to federate." But what gives this cross-national politics its depth is not just its circulatory logic of spreading ideas of savings, housing, citizenship and participation, "without borders" and outside the direct reach of state or market régimes. Depth is also to be located in the fact that, where successful, the spread of this model produces poor communities able to engage in partnerships with more powerful agencies—urban, regional, national and multilateral—that purport to be concerned with poverty and with citizenship. In this second sense, what these horizontal movements produce is a series of stronger community-based partners for institutional agencies charged with realizing inclusive democracy and poverty reduction. This, in turn, increases the capability of these communities to perform more powerfully as instruments of deep democracy in the local context. (Appadurai, 2001, p. 42)

However, such experiments in "deep democracy" also face a number of challenges. Some of these lie in the approach of entering into partnerships with whoever may be in power, despite the fact that they may not share the same moral goals. "Another is that the hard-won mobilization of certain groups of the urban poor may not be best invested as political capital in partnership arrangements, as opposed to confrontation or violence" (Appadurai, 2001, p. 41). Finally, the larger gamble is that "multilateral agencies, Northern funders and Southern governments can be persuaded that the poor are the best drivers of shared solutions to the problems of poverty" (p. 41). This leads Appadurai to conclude that

> this form of a deep democracy, the vertical fulcrum of a democracy without borders, cannot be assumed to be automatic, easy or immune to setbacks. Like all serious exercises in democratic practice, it is not automatically reproductive. It has particular conditions under which it grows weak or corrupt. (p. 43)

PROPERTY FOR PEOPLE OR THE PROPERTY OF PEOPLE: THE POLITICS OF TENURE

One central tendency that has dogged housing policy and practice in the urban developing world is the preoccupation with ownership. Such a preoccupation can be found in almost all the interventions explored so far. For instance, upgrading (even though it was concerned in the early stages with environmental improvement) has in the majority of cases entailed the granting of land title. Sites-and-service projects are inherently based on the notion of ownership and mortgages. As has been seen, the UN-HABITAT Campaign for Secure Tenure (even though it may not claim to be about ownership and land titling) has tended to focus on security of tenure from an ownership perspective. Land titling programs under way in urban Peru, urban Venezuela (Wilpert, 2005), and urban Cambodia, to name a few, have an explicit focus on ownership. Most recently, the relocation of some of the poor from the railway in Mumbai has also focused explicitly on ownership. So, is ownership the only feasible option?

The role of tenure in the life cycle of rural-to-urban migrants has been recognized in the literature since the late 1960s. John Turner (1968, p. 356) noted that the "three basic functions of the dwelling environment are location, tenure and amenity." On the basis of this observation he developed the three-stage "bridgeheader—consolidator—status-seeker" model of residential mobility. For the bridgeheader, proximity to places of employment is a priority. As households established themselves in the city and became consolidated, they sought secure tenure, with amenities being the priority of status-seekers. It could be argued that the poor households in the urban South are not bridgeheaders in the way Turner meant them to be. However, in terms of their poverty they are, and the question is not whether they see ownership as a priority but, more important, what ownership can do for them. The question of the function of the dwelling environment was somewhat ignored as the result of the urgency of the search for an appropriate policy solution to the challenge of slums and squatter settlements, which emerged in the form of settlement upgrading and sites-and-services.

However, the notion that individuals and households "owned" their homes, even if the ownership rights were de facto rather than de jure, gave rise to a focus on ownership. In the 1980s, a number of studies attempted to show that not all the poor were de facto owners, but that a large majority of them were tenants (see, e.g., Coulomb, 1989; Edwards, 1982). A recent study (UN-HABITAT, 2003b) notes that in African cities, tenants accounted for a low of 35% in Pretoria, South Africa (1996), to a high of 63% in Cairo, Egypt (1996); in Asian cities, 28% in Pusan, Republic of Korea (1995), to 41% in Bangkok, Thailand (1998); and in Latin American and Caribbean cities 11% in Monterrey, Mexico (2000), to 52% in Port of Spain, Trinidad (1998). In fact, home ownership has become more difficult for the lowest quintile in some Latin American countries. For example, urban home ownership declined between the early and late 1990s from 82% to 78% in Argentina, 72% to 62% in Chile, 38% to 30% in Colombia, and 73% to 65% in Peru (Fay & Wellenstein, 2005).

Gradually, the much needed focus on tenure began to emerge despite the fact that the attention was on why tenants remained tenants and did not become owners—namely, the constraint versus choice thesis (Gilbert, Camacho, Coulomb, & Necochea, 1993; Gilbert & Varley, 1990). The body of research on tenants has grown substantially since then (Amis, 1984, 1988; Crankshaw, Gilbert, & Morriss, 2000; Gilbert, 1991, 1999; Gilbert et al., 1993; Gilbert & Crankshaw, 1999; Gilbert, Mabin, McCarthy, & Watson, 1997; Gilbert & Varley, 1989a; Gilbert & Ward, 1982; Green, 1988; Kumar, 1989).

It was not until the 1990s that the tenure nexus—ownership, tenants, and landlords—was beginning to become connected. The argument of this literature is that a demand-side exploration of housing in terms of tenants is useful only if one has an equal understanding of the supply side represented by landlords. Much of this literature sought to describe the operation of low-income landlords in terms of their socioeconomic characteristics and the size of their operation (Aina, 1990; Amis, 1984, 1988; Bryant, 1989; Gilbert & Varley, 1989b, 1991; Lee-Smith, 1990; Pennant, 1990). Although this body of research provided much needed evidence of the largely nonexploitive character of low-income landlords—in that they operated on a very small scale and were often as poor or even poorer than their tenants—the research lacked a means of conceptualizing landlordism as a phenomenon (Kumar, 1996a).

A better understanding of the reasons why low-income households become involved in the business of renting can be provided by a production continuum (Kumar, 1996b,

1996c). At one end of the continuum are subsistence landlords who are forced into letting out space even if this entails extreme overcrowding for their own household. In the middle are petty bourgeois landlords, who may be able to survive or cope but find it difficult to make improvements in areas beyond subsistence consumption of their housing. At the other end of the continuum are petty capitalist landlords who do not have either subsistence or consumption needs but nevertheless get involved in the business of renting to reproduce capital. Such a conceptualization moves away from the number of rooms to the underlying cause of why poor households become landlords. Such a framework also provides the basis for a more nuanced understanding of the complex processes of social relations underpinning the development of rental housing at the city level (Kumar, 2001b).

Despite this body of research on tenants and landlords, the existence of tenure mobility (tenant to owner to landlord), a much better understanding of landlordism as an important part of the livelihood portfolio of the poor, and support from UN-HABITAT on the need to have more tenure-neutral policies (UNCHS, 1989b, 1993; UN-HABITAT, 2003b), there has been little movement on the rental housing policy front. Only a few countries—such as South Africa, Chile, Brazil, and Colombia—have attempted to even engage with the idea of either renting or leasing as a supplementary housing policy (UN-HABITAT, 2003b).

Renting is not just a question of affordability, as it would be difficult to explain the high levels of renting in cities in high-income countries. For instance, the proportion of people who rented in selected cities in high-income countries were 54% in Montreal (1998), 42% in Toronto (1998), 89% in Berlin (1998), 80% in Hamburg (1998), 74% in Amsterdam (1998), 49% in Rotterdam (1998), 41% in London (2000), 55% in New York (1998), 53% in Los Angeles (1998), and 38% in Washington, DC (1998). Renting provides tenants with room for maneuver (Kumar, 2005).

TOWARD A CONCLUSION: THE CHALLENGE FOR URBAN HOUSING POLICY AND PRACTICE LIES IN ASKING THE RIGHT QUESTIONS

This concluding section is a critical examination of the urban housing policies and practices outlined thus far. Its main argument is that urban housing policy and practice has suffered three main problems: first, a one-size-fits-all solution (e.g., the focus on ownership); second, a big-bang approach (e.g., earlier upgrading and sites-and-services and now land titling); and third, a fragmented problem-solving approach. I argue that, by and large, this stems from asking the wrong questions. It is not too late to ask the right questions and to seek a more holistic and pluralistic approach to housing policy and practice—one that aims to provide solutions rooted in the realism of the lives of the urban poor and yet incorporates routes that enable poor urban households to gradually move out of shelter poverty.

The Poverty of Resources or the Resources of Poverty?[21] Labor Markets, Urban Poverty, and Housing

With more and more people destined to live in cities and towns, it is not surprising that the locus of poverty is likely to shift to urban areas. In Latin America, although a greater

---

[21] The phrase "the resources of poverty" is borrowed from the title of the book *The Resources of Poverty: Women and Survival in a Mexican City* by Mercedes González de la Rocha (1994).

proportion of the poor live in rural areas, high rates of urbanization have meant that more than half of the poor live in cities (Fay, 2005). This will be the case in urban Africa and Asia sometime in the future.

There is widespread agreement now that poverty is due to more than just income (see, e.g., Amis & Rakodi, 1995; Satterthwaite, 1997; UNCHS, 1996) that it is a multidimensional phenomenon caused by a lack of income, declining access to common property resources, a reduction in state-provided commodities, and a lack of assets, dignity, and autonomy (Baulch, 1996). Although the focus on income poverty was superseded by the basic needs approach of the 1980s—which focused on the provision of health, education, food, water, and sanitation (Stewart, 1985; Streeten & World Bank, 1981) and continues to be applied in the form of settlement upgrading—attention in the 1990s has shifted to a livelihoods approach. A livelihood comprises the capabilities, assets (stores, resources, claims, and access), and activities required for a means of living (Chambers & Conway, 1992). The manner in which the poor use an array of five assets or capitals—human, physical, financial, natural, and social (International Food Policy Research Institute, 2003; Moser, 1998; Rakodi, 1999, 2002a, 2002b; Wood & Salway, 2000)—to address vulnerability has led to a change in focus: from a focus on what the poor do not have (income) to one on how they use what they do have (assets).

Labor Markets, Housing, and Income Poverty

Although the focus on a broader definition of poverty has its merits, there is also the danger in such a line of reasoning that the questioning has shifted from the causes of poverty (the 1970s) to how poverty is managed through a combination of assets. Thus less attention is being paid to addressing income poverty. Income is an important component in the livelihood of the urban poor because transactions in urban areas are highly monetized (Satterthwaite, 1997, 2001; Wratten, 1995). For example, in Latin America, labor accounts for about four fifths of the income of the urban poor (Fay, 2005). As González de la Rocha (2006, p. 85) notes:

> Poor urban households in Mexico face significantly different conditions today. The current situation, characterized by new forms of exclusion and the increasing precariousness of employment, is unfavourable to the operation of traditional household mechanisms of work intensification. Instead of talking about the "resources of poverty," as before, the present situation is better described by the "poverty of resources": a lack of employment opportunities in a context shaped by an exclusionary economic model.

Thus it is crucial that serious attention be paid to improving urban labor markets (Amis, 1995) and giving greater attention to the linkages between urban labor markets and housing. Rural-to-urban migrants have indicated, for several decades, the linkages between employment opportunities and their choice of residential location. In contrast, housing policy and practice has, until now, paid little attention to linkages with the labor market, despite there being evidence to support such linkages (Harris, Rosser, & Kumar, 1996; Kumar, 2001b).

Relocation, Labor Markets, and Livelihoods

It is well known that forced evictions not only destroy the housing of the poor and deprive them of physical assets that they have painfully accumulated over time but also destroy the social networks that the poor have built up to deal with vulnerabilities and crises. There is thus an argument for negotiated resettlement of the poor due to improvements in a city's infrastructure. For example, as part of the World Bank Mumbai Urban Transport Project, some 20,000 households or 60,000 people residing illegally along the railway line had to be relocated. Unlike forced evictions, this was achieved on a voluntary basis through negotiations between the municipal government and the nonprofit acting on behalf of the slum dwellers (Patel, d'Cruz, & Burra, 2002). Although Patel et al. (p. 159) note that this "did not impoverish those who moved (as is generally the case when poor groups are moved to make way for infrastructure development)" and the slum dwellers now live in secure accommodations of 20 square meters, little is said about the differential impact of the resettlement on the livelihoods of the poor: whose livelihoods were improved and whose declined. Because the poor depend on their labor, relocation can result in additional costs of time and transport to the places where they work (Urban Resource Center Phnom Penh, 2002).

Relocation may be necessary in certain cases, for instance when settlements are located in hazardous locations. However, what has been seen in the past 10 years or so are evictions and locations in relation to increasing the efficiency of cities to the detriment of the poor. Two issues need immediate attention. First, the relationship between livelihood and relocation has to take center stage in any discussion of resettlement. Second, there is an urgent need to distinguish and plan differently for livelihood gains that may accrue to some and losses to others. In both the Mumbai and the Cambodia examples, neither of these issues appears to have been considered.

Decent Work Deficits: Limits to Home-Based Enterprise

One of the livelihood strategies open to the poor is that of home-based enterprises or micro-enterprises. Home-based enterprises involving food preparation, small-scale man-ufacturing, and services are to be found in a number of poor urban settlements in Africa, Asia, and Latin America (Gough & Kellett, 2001; Kellett & Tipple, 2000; W. P. Strassmann, 1986; UNCHS, 1989a). In conditions of poverty, the poor explore all means for survival, and home-based enterprises are one of them. Three points, however, are worth noting. First, in many cases home-based enterprises are coping strategies and can provide very little in the form of capital accumulation and therefore an escape from poverty. Second, it is very difficult to distinguish which home-based enterprises are actually "genuine" own-account workers and which are subcontracted and are thus linked to the formal sector. The latter has major implications for wage levels and deprivations in a range of social protection benefits. Third, even in the case of genuine own-account home-based enterprises, the low levels of income generation and vulnerability associated with market guarantees can result in their being categorized as enterprises characteristic of what the ILO (2002a, p. 4) terms "decent work deficits":

> Poor-quality, unproductive and unremunerative jobs that are not recognized or protected by law, the absence of rights at work, inadequate social protection, and the lack of representation and voice are most pronounced in the informal economy, especially at the bottom end among women and young workers.

It is interesting to note, as mentioned earlier, that renting as an "enterprise" is far from being accepted as a form of livelihood for the poor.

Home-based enterprises can make an important contribution to the livelihoods of the poor, and I am not arguing that they should not be allowed. However, attention should be paid to not only the decent work deficits but also the extent to which the planning of low-income settlements can be supportive of the pursuit of such enterprises.

Means or Ends: Short- versus Long-Term Housing Outcomes

In this section I focus on contemporary housing policy and practice in the urban developing world. My main argument is that housing policy and practice should be about means and not ends—thereby distinguishing interventions from outcomes (see, e.g., Moser, 1993, in relation to gender planning).

Upgrading and Land Titling: Ends or Means? Tenure and the Collective versus Individual Provision of Water and Sanitation

Compared to sites-and-services projects, environmental upgrading of low-income settlements is continuing, at times at a very large scale (Riley, Fiori, & Ramirez, 2001), and has included a component of community participation (see, e.g., Imparato & Ruster, 2003). As shown earlier, settlement upgrading has two main advantages. First, it does not alter the relationship between residential location and livelihood opportunities or labor markets. Second, it helps preserve and maintain the critical social networks that the poor have built up over time. However, upgrading also has several disadvantages. First, upgrading often does not allow the individual provision of water and sanitation given the high densities and irregular housing and land development (for the exception of the Orangi Pilot Project in Karachi, see Urban Resource Centre, n.d.). Second, it often maintains the status quo in terms of the extent of land ownership. For instance, in India, the average plot in a squatter settlement is 20 square meters. Upgrading involving the provision of land titles does not attempt to explore issues of redistribution. So if all of the poor of Mumbai—60% of the population—were to be given land titles today, this would maintain the status quo that this population occupies only 6% of Mumbai's land. Third, upgrading (influenced by the belief that all poor households in squatter settlements are de facto owners) often neglects landlord-tenant relationships. Upgrading can often lead to the eviction of tenants as landlords seek to maximize their land holdings. Similar shortcomings are part of land titling policies.

Upgrading and land titling should thus be selectively implemented in relation to the issues raised earlier. At the moment they are being applied as a blueprint solution to the problem of tenure insecurity. Such blueprint approaches need to be replaced with a wider canvas of approaches that are suitable to specific contexts and circumstances.

One or Several Rungs on the Housing Ladder: Ownership and Renting

Ownership may be the ultimate goal of a given society, but it cannot possibly apply to all. The impoverishment experienced by a majority of urban dwellers can make ownership an economic burden. Any attempt at extending ownership has to carefully evaluate the benefits that ownership can bring. It has been shown that infrastructure investments have a greater impact on people's perceived notions of security of tenure than a blanket program of land titling. The lack of tenure security does not preclude individuals and households from either investing in housing improvements or the renting out of rooms (Kumar, 2001b). The reality of urban development is that there will be some for whom ownership has benefits and others for whom renting is either the only option or a choice, such as migrants who do not seek to remain in the city and students and employees who move to cities for short periods of time for either study or work.

The search for a tenure-neutral housing policy is urgent and critical. Politicians as well as civil society organizations have to be convinced of the benefits of a housing market that provides residential opportunities for all rather than lock the poor into a cul-de-sac of few or no benefits from ownership.

A Friendly Critique or a Critical Fiend?[22] *State and Not-for-Profit Partnerships*

Nonprofits and community groups have an important role to play in housing. So far, this has primarily been in the design and implementation of housing projects and programs. Although this is an important contribution, they should also be equally involved in bringing about policy and institutional change that benefit those beyond their immediate membership. It can be said that this has partially been achieved, for example in the Mumbai sanitation program. However, such partnerships have also involved trade-offs, and it is this that needs greater scrutiny. Being involved in partnerships with the state should not preclude nonprofits from being "critical fiends."

Benefits for Some or for All? National and International Goals

In relation to the urban land titling program in Lima, Peru, one commentator notes:

> Although I do agree with the allocation of land titles . . . I also acknowledge that this can lead to further land invasions. However, there are simple ways to circumvent a stampede. For instance, in Peru the government instituted an amnesty of sorts. The government declared that for any invasion that occurred before March 22, 1996, those who presently occupy the land receive title. For any invasion that occurred after the appointed date, occupants would be removed from the land. As long as the Peruvian government adheres to this policy and potential invaders are convinced that there will be no future amnesty, then this is a promising policy for dealing with the brooding threat of future invasions. (Atuahene, 2006, p. 769)

This is a clear indication of closing the door on the potential prosperity that can accrue to those seeking to migrate to cities for economic improvement. There are many other instances in which a cutoff amnesty date is set and the government declares slum and squatter settlements as legal. This is simply not realistic, especially as there is now agreement that urbanization makes an important contribution to economic growth and social development.

A similar problem arises from the UN Millennium Declaration, specifically, the goal of improving the lives of 100 million slum dwellers by the year 2020—100 million slum dwellers for now, sorry to the rest of the 900 million. Targets have their purpose in terms of attempting to ensure that governments commit themselves. However, targets have to be a means to an end and not an end in themselves.

---

[22]This is a Freudian slip, but of the making of my word processor. I meant to type "critical friend" but inadvertently typed "critical fiend." My word processor did not pick up this typo. On rereading and having noticed the error, I decided to let the Freudian slip stay as this makes my argument forcefully. Apologies to my friends who have taken a critical stance against benevolent partnership—I consider them fiends (in the nicest possible sense) who seek to truly empower the poor.

CONCLUSION

This chapter seeks to provoke thought among researchers, policy makers, practitioners, and politicians. It encapsulates current urban housing policy and practice in the developing world, which to a large extent has focused on "property for people." Furthermore, the emphasis has been on ownership through interventions ranging from housing finance to partnerships.

In contrast, the notion of the "property of people" is intended to make various housing and urban development actors cognizant of the fact that despite housing being the most visible manifestation of poverty, it is limited as a starting point for an improvement in the lives of the urban poor. In a highly monetized urban economy, income is an important instrument in negotiating pathways out of poverty. Labor is the single most important asset that the urban poor possess. However, as long as this labor is subject to "decent work deficits," its potential as a lever out of poverty will not materialize. Labor market interventions have a greater capacity to kick-start improvements in housing conditions. Thus, greater recognition should be given to the links between labor markets and housing: They should reinforce one another for mutually beneficial outcomes and not become a simple trade-off, as is the case with many voluntary relocations. Water and sanitation are important contributors to the health of labor. However, housing policy and practice actors must be aware of the dangers of institutionalizing water and sanitation provision too quickly, as this can set a precedent and absolve governments from ongoing responsibilities. The sheer number of the poor in cities and their varied housing needs and preferences require a more nuanced housing policy—one that provides room for maneuver. This calls for not just a mix of ownership and renting, but also the involvement of a greater number of nonprofits in the provision of rental housing. Voice is an important component, as the strategy of organizing the poor and the formation of transnational federations have demonstrated. However, there is a need to go beyond a "benefits for members only" approach. Voice needs to be harnessed and made to work for the wider public good. Although there is recognition that neither the state nor the poor on their own can act in isolation to overcome the magnitude of the poverty, housing, and infrastructure needs of the poor, partnerships between them should be viewed as only a first step. Attempts must also be made to convince employers (direct and indirect) and the wealthy of the overall benefits to be gained from making a contribution to the well-being of their fellow citizens.

Linking the "property of people" to "property for people" requires a flexible and broad-based housing policy framework. Such a framework will enable a range of housing actors, including the poor, to be able to select the most appropriate interventions based on local needs, priorities, and resources. Housing policy needs to be a toolbox rather than a sledgehammer.

REFERENCES

Aina, T. A. (1990). Petty landlords and poor tenants in a low-income settlement in metropolitan Lagos, Nigeria. In P. Amis & P. Lloyd (Eds.), *Housing Africa's urban poor* (pp. 87–101). Manchester, England: Manchester University Press.

Amis, P. (1984). Squatters or tenants: The commercialization of unauthorized housing in Nairobi. *World Development, 12*(1), 87–96.

Amis, P. (1988). Commercialised rental housing in Nairobi, Kenya. In C. V. Patton (Ed.), *Shelter: International perspectives and prospects* (pp. 235–257). Philadelphia: Temple University Press.

Amis, P. (1995). Employment creation or environmental improvement: A literature review of urban poverty and policy in India. *Habitat International, 19*(4), 485–497.

Amis, P., & Rakodi, C. (1995). Urban poverty: Concepts, characteristics and policies. *Habitat International, 19*(4), 403–405.

Amnesty International. (2007). *Angola lives in ruins: Forced evictions continue.* Retrieved February 2, 2007, from http://web.amnesty.org/library/Index/ENGAFR120012007/.

Angel, S., Archer, R. W., Tanphiphat, S., & Wegelin, E. A. (1983). *Land for housing the poor.* Singapore: Select Books.

Appadurai, A. (2001). Deep democracy: Urban governability and the horizon of politics. *Environment and Urbanization, 13*(2), 23–43.

Asian Coalition for Housing Rights. (2001). *About ACHR.* Retrieved March 1, 2007, from www.achr.net/about_achr.htm.

Atuahene, B. (2006). Land titling: A mode of privatization with the potential to deepen democracy. *St. Louis University Law Journal, 50*(3), 761–781.

Baulch, B. (1996). Editorial: The new poverty agenda: A disputed consensus. *IDS Bulletin, 27*(1), 1–10.

Bolnick, J. (2001). uTshani Buyakhuluma (The grass speaks): People's dialogue and the South African Homeless People's Federation. (1994–6). *Environment and Urbanization, 8*(2), 153–170.

Bromley, R. (1994). Informality, de Soto style: From concept to policy. In C. A. Rakowski (Ed.), *Contrapunto: The informal sector debate in Latin America* (pp. 131–151). Albany: State University of New York Press.

Bromley, R. (2004). Power, property and poverty: Why de Soto's "mystery of capital" cannot be solved. In A. Roy & N. Al Sayyad (Eds.), *Urban informality: Transnational perspectives from the Middle East, Latin America, and South Asia* (pp. 271–288). Lanham, MD: Lexington Books.

Bryant, J. J. (1989). The acceptable face of self-help housing: Subletting in Fiji squatter settlements: Exploitation or survival strategy? In D. Drakakis-Smith (Ed.), *Economic growth and urbanisation in developing areas* (pp. 171–95). London: Routledge.

Buckley, R. M., & Kalarickal, J. (2005). Housing policy in developing countries: Conjectures and refutations. *World Bank Research Observer, 20*(2), 233–257.

Burgess, R. (1977). Self-help housing: A new imperialist strategy? A critique of the Turner school. *Antipode, 9*(2), 50–59.

Burgess, R. (1978). Petty commodity housing or dweller control? A critique of John Turner's views on housing policy. *World Development, 9*(9/10), 1105–1133.

Burgess, R. (1982). Self-help housing advocacy: A curious form of radicalism (A critique of the work of J. F. C. Turner). In P. M. Ward (Ed.), *Self help housing: A critique* (pp. 55–97). London: Mansell.

Burgess, R. (1985). The limits of state self-help housing programmes. *Development and Change, 16*(2), 271–312.

Burgess, R. (1987). A lot of noise and no nuts: A reply to Alan Gilbert and Jan van der Linden. *Development and Change, 18*(1), 137–146.

Burgess, R. (1991). Helping some to help themselves: Third World housing policies and development strategies. In K. Mathéy (Ed.), *Beyond self-help housing* (pp. 75–91). London: Mansell.

Burra, S. (2001). *Slum sanitation in Pune: A case study.* Mumbai, India: SPARC.

Burra, S., Patel, S., & Kerr, T. (2003). Community-designed, built and managed toilet blocks in Indian cities. *Environment and Urbanization, 15*(2), 11–32.

Chambers, R., & Conway, G. (1992). *Sustainable rural livelihoods: Practical concepts for the 21st century* (IDS Discussion Paper 296). Sussex, England: University of Sussex, Institute for Development Studies.

Chitekwe, B., & Mitlin, D. (2001). The urban poor under threat and in struggle: Options for urban development in Zimbabwe, 1995–2000. *Environment and Urbanization*, *13*(2), 85–101.

Cities Alliance. (2005). *Charter*. Retrieved January 10, 2007, from www.citiesalliance.org/about-ca /charter-english.html#objectives/.

Cornia, G. A., Jolly, R., & Stewart, F. (1987a). *Adjustment with a human face: Vol. 1. Protecting the vulnerable and promoting growth*. Oxford: Clarendon Press.

Cornia, G. A., Jolly, R., & Stewart, F. (1987b). *Adjustment with a human face: Vol. 2. Ten country case studies*. Oxford: Clarendon Press.

Coulomb, R. (1989). Rental housing and the dynamics of urban growth in Mexico City. In A. Gilbert (Ed.), *Housing and land in urban Mexico* (pp. 39–50). San Diego: University of California, Center for U.S.-Mexican Studies.

Crankshaw, O., Gilbert, A., & Morriss, A. (2000). Backyard Soweto. *International Journal of Urban and Regional Research*, *24*(4), 841–857.

Davis, M. (2004). Planet of slums: Urban involution and the informal proletariat. *New Left Review*, *26*, 5–34.

Davis, M. (2006). *Planet of slums*. London: Verso.

DeNavas-Walt, C., Proctor, B. D., & Lee, C. H. (2005). *Income, poverty, and health insurance coverage in the United States: 2004, U.S. Census Bureau*. Washington, DC: U.S. Government Printing Office.

de Soto, H. (1989). *The other path: The invisible revolution in the third world*. London: I. B. Tauris.

de Soto, H. (2000). *The mystery of capital: Why capitalism triumphs in the West and fails everywhere else*. New York: Basic Books.

de Tocqueville, A. (1994). *Democracy in America*. London: David Campbell. (Original work published 1835)

Durrand-Lasserve, A., & Adusumilli, U. (2001). *Issues and opportunities for the integrated provision of serviced land and credit for progressive housing: Case study India Sector 26, Vashi, Navi Mumbai*. Paris: ACT Consultants and GRET. Retrieved March 1, 2007, from www.iadb.org/sds/doc/IndiaCasestudy.pdf.

Editorial: Transforming opportunities. (2001). *Environment and Urbanization*, *13*(2), 3–7.

Edwards, M. (1982). Cities of tenants: Renting among the urban poor in Latin America. In A. Gilbert, J. E. Hardoy, & R. Ramirez (Eds.), *Urbanisation in contemporary Latin America* (pp. 129–158). London: Wiley.

Evictions. (1994). *Environment and Urbanization*, *6*(1), 3–7.

Fay, M. (2005). Overview. In M. Fay (Ed.), *The urban poor in Latin America* (pp. 1–18). Washington, DC: World Bank.

Fay, M., & Wellenstein, A. (2005). Keeping a roof over one's head: Improving access to safe and decent shelter. In M. Fay (Ed.), *The urban poor in Latin America* (pp. 91–124). Washington, DC: World Bank.

Ferguson, A. (1995). An essay on the history of civil society. In F. Oz-Salzberger (Ed.), *Cambridge texts in the history of political thought*. New York: Cambridge University Press. (Original work published 1767)

Fernandes, E., Fuentes, M., & Sewell, J. (2005). *An evaluation of UN-HABITAT's campaigns for secure tenure and urban governance*. Retrieved February 23, 2007, from www.unhabitat .org/downloads/docs/2200_37204_FINALREPORT%2020Feb2005%20(2).doc.

Field, E. (2006). *Entitled to work: Urban property rights and labor supply in Peru*. New York: Harvard University Press. Retrieved February 29, 2007, from www.economics.harvard.edu/faculty /field/papers/Field_COFOPRI.pdf.

Galiani, S., & Schargrodsky, E. (2005). Property rights for the poor: Effects of land titling. *Centro de Investigación en Finanzas, Documento de Trabajo 06/2005*. Retrieved February 28, 2007, from www.utdt.edu/Upload/CIF_wp/wpcif-062005.pdf.

Gilbert, A. (1991). Renting and the transition to owner occupation in Latin American cities. *Habitat International*, *15*(1/2), 87–99.

Gilbert, A. (1997). On subsidies and home-ownership: Colombian housing policy during the 1990s. *Third World Planning Review*, *19*(1), 51–70.

Gilbert, A. (1999). A home is for ever? Residential mobility and homeownership in self-help settlements. *Environment and Planning*, *31*(6), 1073–1091.

Gilbert, A. (2002a). On the mystery of capital and the myths of Hernando de Soto. *International Development Planning Review*, *24*(1), 1–19.

Gilbert, A. (2002b). Power, ideology and the Washington consensus: The development and spread of Chilean housing policy. *Housing Studies*, *17*(2), 305–324.

Gilbert, A. (2002c). "Scan globally, reinvent locally": Reflecting on the origins of South Africa's capital housing subsidy policy. *Urban Studies*, *39*(10), 1911–1933.

Gilbert, A. (2004, March). Helping the poor through housing subsidies: Lessons from Chile, Colombia and South Africa. *Habitat International*, *28*(1), 13–40.

Gilbert, A., Camacho, O. O., Coulomb, R., & Necochea, A. (1993). *In search of a home: Rental and shared housing in Latin America*. London: UCL Press.

Gilbert, A., & Crankshaw, O. (1999). Comparing South African and Latin American experience: Migration and housing mobility in Soweto. *Urban Studies*, *36*(13), 2375–2400.

Gilbert, A., Mabin, A., McCarthy, M., & Watson, V. (1997). Low-income rental housing: Are South African cities different? *Environment and Urbanization*, *9*(1), 133–147.

Gilbert, A., & Varley, A. (1989a). From renting to self-help ownership? Residential tenure in urban Mexico since 1940. In A. Gilbert (Ed.), *Housing and land in urban Mexico* (pp. 13–37). San Diego: University of California, Center for U.S.-Mexican Studies.

Gilbert, A., & Varley, A. (1989b). *The Mexican landlord: Rental housing in Guadalajara and Puebla*. London: Institute of Latin American Studies.

Gilbert, A., & Varley, A. (1990). Renting a home in a third world city: Choice or constraint? *International Journal of Urban and Regional Research*, *14*(1), 89–108.

Gilbert, A., & Varley, A. (1991). *Landlord and tenant: Housing the poor in urban Mexico*. London: Routledge.

Gilbert, A., & Ward, P. M. (1982). Residential movement among the poor: The constraints on housing choice in Latin American cities. *Transactions of the Institute of British Geographers*, *NS7*, 129–149.

González de la Rocha, M. (1994). *The resources of poverty: Women and survival in a Mexican city*. Cambridge, MA: Blackwell.

González de la Rocha, M. (2006). Vanishing assets: Cumulative disadvantage among the urban poor. *Annals of the American Academy of Political and Social Science*, *606*, 68–94.

Gough, K. V., & Kellett, P. (2001). Housing consolidation and home-based income generation: Evidence from self-help settlements in two Colombian cities. *Cities*, *18*(4), 235–247.

Gramsci, A. (1971). *Selections from the prison notebooks of Antonio Gramsci*. (Q. Hoare & G. N. Smith, Eds. & Trans.). London: Lawrence and Wishart.

Green, G. (1988). The quest for tranguilidad: Paths to home ownership in Santa Cruz, Bolivia. *Bulletin of Latin American Research*, *7*(1), 1–15.

Habitat for Humanity. (2006). *Frequently asked questions: How Habitat for Humanity works*. Retrieved March 1, 2007, from www.habitatforhumanity.org.uk/lea_faqs.htm.

Hardoy, J. E., & Satterthwaite, D. (1986). Urban change in the third world: Are recent trends a useful pointer to the urban future? *Habitat International*, *10*(3), 33–52.

Hardoy, J. E., & Satterthwaite, D. (1989). *Squatter citizen: Life in the urban third world*. London: Earthscan.

Harris, N. (1989). Aid and urbanisation: An overview. *Cities*, (10), 1693–1703.

Harris, N. (1997). Cities in a global economy: Structural change and policy reactions. *Urban Studies*, *34*(10), 1693–1703.

Harris, N., Rosser, C., & Kumar, S. (1996). *Jobs for the poor: A case study in Cuttack*. London: UCL Press.

Harriss, J., Stokke, K., & Törnquist, O. (2004). Introduction: The new local politics of democratisation. In J. Harriss, K. Stokke, & O. Törnquist (Eds.), *Politicising democracy: The new local politics and democratisation* (pp. 1–28). London: Palgrave Macmillan.

Hegel, G. W. F. (1991). Elements of the philosophy of right. In A. W. Wood & H. B. Nisbet (Eds. & Trans.), *Cambridge texts in the history of political thought*. Cambridge: Cambridge University Press. (Original work published 1821)

Hellman, J. A. (1997). *Structural adjustment in Mexico and the dog that didn't bark* (Center for Research on Latin America and the Caribbean Working Paper Series). York University: North York, Ontario, Canada.

Huchzermeyer, M. (2003). A legacy of control? The capital subsidy for housing, and informal settlement intervention in South Africa. *International Journal of Urban and Regional Research*, *27*(3), 591–612.

Human Rights Watch. (2004). *Beijing construction: Forced evictions*. Retrieved February 2, 2007, from http://hrw.org/campaigns/china/beijing08/evictions.htm.

Human Rights Watch. (2006). *Cambodia: Phnom Penh's poor face forced evictions*. Retrieved February 2, 2007, from http://hrw.org/english/docs/2006/08/02/cambod13889.htm.

Imparato, I., & Ruster, J. (2003). *Slum upgrading and participation: Lessons from Latin America*. Washington, DC: World Bank.

International Food Policy Research Institute. (2003). *Jessore and Tongi: Urban livelihoods in the slums*. Washington, DC: Author. Retrieved October 8, 2004, from www.ifpri.org/themes/mp14/profiles/jessoretongi.pdf.

International Labour Office. (2002a). *Decent work and the informal economy*. Geneva: Author.

International Labour Office. (2002b). *Women and men in the informal economy: A statistical picture*. Geneva: Author.

Jimenez, E. (1983). The magnitude and determinants of home improvements in self-help housing: Manila's Tondo Project. *Land Economics*, *59*(1), 70–83.

Jones, G. A., & Datta, K. (1998). From self-help to self-finance: The changing focus of urban research and policy. In K. Datta & G. A. Jones (Eds.), *Housing and finance in developing countries* (pp. 3–25). London: Routledge.

Jones, G. A., & Mitlin, D. (1998). Housing finance and non-governmental organisation in developing countries. In K. Datta & G. A. Jones (Eds.), *Housing and finance in developing countries* (pp. 26–43). London: Routledge.

Keivani, R., & Werna, E. (2001). Refocusing the housing debate in developing countries from a pluralist perspective. *Habitat International*, *25*(2), 191–208.

Kellett, P., & Tipple, A. G. (2000). The home as workplace: A study of income-generating activities within the domestic setting. *Environment and Urbanization*, *12*(1), 203–213.

Kritayanavaj, B. (2002). Financing affordable homeownership in Thailand: Roles of the government housing bank since the economic crisis. (1997–2002). *Housing Finance International*, *17*(2), 15.

Kumar, S. (1989). How poorer groups find accommodation in third world cities: A guide to the literature. *Environment and Urbanisation*, *1*(2), 71–85.

Kumar, S. (1996a). Landlordism in third world urban low-income settlements: A case for further research. *Urban Studies*, *33*(4/5), 753–782.

Kumar, S. (1996b). *Subsistence and petty capitalist landlords: An inquiry into the petty commodity production of rental housing in low-income settlements in Madras*. Unpublished doctorate dissertation, University College London, Development Planning Unit.

Kumar, S. (1996c). Subsistence and petty capitalist landlords: A theoretical framework for the analysis of landlordism in third world low income settlements. *International Journal of Urban and Regional Research, 20*(2), 317–329.

Kumar, S. (2001a). Embedded tenures: Private renting and housing policy in India. *Housing Studies, 16*(4), 425–442.

Kumar, S. (2001b). *Social relations, rental housing markets and the poor in urban India.* London: Department of Social Policy, London School of Economics.

Kumar, S. (2002). Round pegs and square holes: Mismatches between poverty and housing policy in urban India. In P. Townsend & D. Gordon (Eds.), *World poverty: New policies to defeat an old enemy* (pp. 271–295). London: Policy Press.

Kumar, S. (2005). Room for manoeuvre: Tenure and the urban poor in India. In N. Hamdi (Ed.), *Urban futures* (pp. 109–124). London: Intermediate Technology Publications.

Kusnetzoff, F. (1997). The state and housing policies in Chile: Five regime types and strategies. In J. Gugler (Ed.), *Cities in the developing world: Issues, theory, and policy* (pp. 291–304). Oxford: Oxford University Press.

Lapeyre, F. (2004). *Globalization and structural adjustment as a development tool* (Working Paper No. 31). Geneva, Switzerland: International Labour Office, Policy Integration Department.

Laurell, A. C. (2000). Structural adjustment and the globalization of social policy in Latin America. *International Sociology, 15*(2), 306–325.

Lee-Smith, D. (1990). Squatter landlords in Nairobi: A case study of Korgocho. In P. Amis & P. Lloyd (Eds.), *Housing Africa's urban poor* (pp. 175–187). Manchester, England: Manchester University Press.

Lewis, D. (2002). Civil society in African contexts: Reflections on the usefulness of a concept. *Development and Change, 33*(4), 569–586.

Mackay, C. J. (1999). Housing policy in South Africa: The challenge of delivery. *Housing Studies, 14*(3), 387–399.

Martin, R. J. (1983). Upgrading. In R. J. Skinner & M. J. Rodell (Eds.), *People, poverty and shelter: Problems of self-help housing in the third world* (pp. 80–107). London: Methuen.

Mayo, S. K., Malpezi, S., & Gross, D. J. (1986). Shelter strategies for the urban poor in developing countries. *Research Observer, 1*(2), 183–203.

Meagher, K., & Mohammed-Bello, Y. (1996). *Passing the buck: Structural adjustment and the Nigerian informal sector* (Discussion Paper 75). Geneva, Switzerland: United Nations Research Institute for Social Development.

Moser, C. O. N. (1993). *Gender planning and development: Theory, practice and training.* London: Routledge.

Moser, C. O. N. (1996). *Confronting crisis: A comparative study of household responses to poverty and vulnerability in four poor urban communities.* Washington, DC: World Bank.

Moser, C. O. N. (1998). The asset vulnerability framework: Reassessing urban poverty reduction strategies. *World Development, 26*(1), 1–19.

Mukhija, V. (2001). Enabling slum redevelopment in Mumbai: Paradox in practice. *Housing Studies, 16*(6), 791–806.

Mukhija, V. (2004). The contradictions in enabling private developers of affordable housing: A cautionary case from Ahmedabad, India. *Urban Studies, 41*(11), 2231–2244.

Navarro, M. (2005). Housing finance policy in Chile: The last 30 years. *Land Lines, 17*(3). Retrieved February 27, 2007, from www.lincolninst.edu/pubs/PubDetail.aspx?pubid=1042.

Neuwirth, R. (2005). *Shadow cities: A billion squatters, a new urban world.* Routledge: New York.

O'Hare, G., Abbott, D., & Barke, M. (1998). A review of slum housing policies in Mumbai. *Cities, 15*(4), 269–283.

Patel, S., Burra, S., & d'Cruz, C. (2001). Shack/Slum Dwellers International (SDI): Foundations to treetops. *Environment and Urbanization, 13*(2), 45–59.

Patel, S., d'Cruz, C., & Burra, S. (2002). Beyond evictions in a global city: People-managed resettlement in Mumbai. *Environment and Urbanization, 14*(1), 159–172.

Payne, G. K. (2002). *Land, rights and innovation: Improving tenure security for the urban poor.* London: ITDG.

Pennant, T. (1990). The growth of small-scale renting in low-income urban housing in Malawi. In P. Amis & P. Lloyd (Eds.), *Housing Africa's urban poor* (pp. 189–201). Manchester, England: Manchester University Press.

Potts, D., & Mutambirwa, C. (1988). "Basics are now a luxury": Perceptions of structural adjustment's improvement on rural and urban areas in Zimbabwe. *Environment and Urbanization, 10*(1), 55–75.

Poverty Site. (2007). *The UK site for statistics on poverty and social exclusion: The new policy institute.* Retrieved February 6, 2007, from www.poverty.org.uk/01/index.shtml.

Pradilla, E. (1976a, December). *La ideologia burguesa y el problema de la vivienda: Critica a dos teorias ideologicas* [Bourgeois ideology and the housing problem: A critique of two ideological "theories"]. Paper presented at the Idelogia y Sociadad, Rotterdam, The Netherlands.

Pradilla, E. (1976b, December). *Notas acerca de las politicas de vivienda de los estados Latinamericanos* [Notes on the housing policies of Latin American States]. Paper presented at the Idelogia y Sociadad, Rotterdam, The Netherlands.

Pradilla, E. (1976c, December). *Notas acerca del problema de la vivienda* [Notes on the housing problem]. Paper presented at the Idelogia y Sociadad, Rotterdam, The Netherlands.

Pugh, C. (1990). *Housing and urbanisation: A study of India.* New Delhi, India: Sage.

Pugh, C. (1997). Poverty and progress? Reflections on housing and urban policies in developing countries, 1976–1996. *Urban Studies, 34*(10), 1547–1595.

Rakodi, C. (1995a). The household strategies of the urban poor: Coping with poverty and recession in Gweru, Zimbabwe. *Habitat International, 19*(4), 447–471.

Rakodi, C. (1995b). Poverty lines or household strategies: A review of conceptual issues in the study of urban poverty. *Habitat International, 19*(4), 407–426.

Rakodi, C. (1999). A capital assets framework for analysing household livelihood strategies: Implications for policy. *Development Policy Review, 17*, 315–342.

Rakodi, C. (2002a). A livelihoods approach: Conceptual issues and definitions. In C. Rakodi (Ed.) with T. Lloyd-Jones, *Urban livelihoods: A people centred approach to reducing urban poverty* (pp. 3–22). London: Earthscan.

Rakodi, C. (with Lloyd-Jones, T.). (Ed.). (2002b). *Urban livelihoods: A people centred approach to reducing urban poverty.* London: Earthscan.

Riddle, B. (1997). Structural adjustment programmes and the city in tropical Africa. *Urban Studies, 34*(8), 1297–1307.

Riley, E., Fiori, J., & Ramirez, R. (2001). Favela Barrio and a new generation of housing programmes for the urban poor. *Geoforum, 32*(4), 521–531.

Rodell, M. J. (1983). Sites and services and low-income housing. In R. J. Skinner & M. J. Rodell (Eds.), *People, poverty and shelter: Problems of self-help housing in the third world* (pp. 21–52). London: Methuen.

Rodell, M. J., & Skinner, R. J. (1983). Introduction: Contemporary self-help housing programmes. In R. J. Skinner & M. J. Rodell (Eds.), *People, poverty and shelter* (pp. 1–20). London: Methuen.

Rodrik, D. (2000, January). *Development strategies for the next century.* Paper presented at the conference on the Challenges to Globalization, Chiba City, Japan.

Rojas, E. (1995). *The IDB in low-cost housing: The first three decades.* Washington, DC: Inter-American Development Bank.

Sarkar, S., & Moulik, S. G. (2006). *The Mumbai Slum Sanitation Program: Partnering with slum communities for sustainable sanitation in a megalopolis.* Washington, DC: World Bank.

Satterthwaite, D. (1997). Urban poverty: Reconsidering its scale and nature. *IDS Bulletin*, *28*(2), 9–23.

Satterthwaite, D. (2001). *Rural and urban poverty: Understanding the differences, U.S Department of State*. Retrieved February 9, 2007, from http://usinfo.state.gov/journals/ites/0901/ijee /satterthwaite.htm.

Sen, A. (1992). *Inequality reexamined*. New Delhi, India: Oxford University Press.

Sen, A. (1993). Capability and well-being. In M. Nussbaum & A. Sen (Eds.), *The quality of life* (pp. 30–53). Oxford: Clarendon Press.

Sen, A. (1997). *On economic inequality*. Oxford: Clarendon Press.

Sharma, K. (2005, January 22). *Mumbai's demolition marathon: The Hindu*. Retrieved February 27, 2007, from www.hindu.com/2005/01/22/stories/2005012202221000.htm.

Smets, P. (1997). Private housing finance in India: Reaching down market. *Habitat International*, *21*(1), 1–15.

Stewart, F. (1985). *Planning to meet basic needs*. London: Macmillan.

Strassman, P. W. (1980). Housing improvements in an opportune setting: Cartagena, Colombia. *Land Economics*, *56*(2), 153–168.

Strassmann, W. P. (1986). Types of neighbourhood and home-based enterprises: Evidence from Lima, Peru. *Urban Studies*, *23*, 485–500.

Streeten, P. P., & World Bank. (1981). *First things first: Meeting basic human needs in the developing countries*. New York: Oxford University Press.

Struyk, R. J., & Lynn, R. (1983). Determinants of housing investment in slum areas: Tondo and other locations in metro Manila. *Land Economics*, *59*(4), 444–454.

Taylor, J. L., & Williams, D. G. (1982). Upgrading of low-income residential areas in Jakarta and Manila. In J. L. Taylor & D. G. Williams (Eds.), *Urban planning practice in developing countries* (pp. 239–260). Oxford: Pergamon Press.

Townsend, P. (2007). *The right to social security and national development: Lessons from OECD experience for low-income countries: Issues in social protection* (Discussion Paper 18). Geneva: Social Security Department, International Labour Office.

Turner, J. (1968). Housing priorities, settlement patterns and urban development in modernising countries. *Journal of the American Institute of Planners*, *34*(5), 354–363.

Turner, J. (1972). Housing as a verb. In J. F. C. Turner & R. Fitcher (Eds.), *Freedom to build*. New York: Macmillan (pp. 148–175).

Turner, J. (1976). *Housing by people*. London: Marion Boyars.

Turner, J. (1978). Housing in three dimensions: Terms of reference for the housing question redefined. *World Development*, *6*(9/10), 1135–1145.

UN-HABITAT. (2003a). The challenge of slums: Global report on human settlements 2003. Nairobi, Kenya: United Nations Human Settlements Programme.

UN-HABITAT. (2003b). *Rental housing: An essential option for the urban poor in developing countries*. Nairobi, Kenya: United Nations Human Settlements Programme.

UN-HABITAT. (2005). *Forced evictions: Towards solutions? First report of the Advisory Group on Forced Evictions to the executive director of UN-HABITAT*. Nairobi, Kenya: Author. Retrieved February 20, 2007, from www.unhabitat.org/pmss/getPage.asp?page=bookView&book= 1806/.

UN-HABITAT. (2006). *State of the world's cities 2006–07: The millennium development goals and urban sustainability: 30 years of shaping the habitat agenda*. London: Earthscan.

UN-HABITAT. (n.d.). *Global campaign for secure tenure*. Retrieved January 10, 2007, from www.unhabitat.org/categories.asp?catid=24/.

United Nations. (1988). *Global strategy for shelter to the year 2000*. Retrieved January 8, 2007, from www.un.org/documents/ga/res/43/a43r181.htm.

United Nations Centre for Human Settlements. (1988). *A new agenda for human settlements.* Nairobi, Kenya: Author.

United Nations Centre for Human Settlements. (1989a). *Improving income and housing: Employment generation in low-income settlements.* Nairobi, Kenya: Author.

United Nations Centre for Human Settlements. (1989b). *Strategies for low-income shelter and services development: The rental housing option.* Nairobi, Kenya: Author.

United Nations Centre for Human Settlements. (1993). *Support measures to promote rental housing for low-income groups.* Nairobi, Kenya: Author.

United Nations Centre for Human Settlements. (1996). *Urban poverty: A world challenge* (The Recife Declaration, March 1996). Recife, Brazil: Author.

United Nations Centre for Human Settlements. (2001). *State of the world's cities 2001.* Nairobi, Kenya: Author.

United Nations Population Fund. (2007). *Urbanization: A majority in cities.* Retrieved February 5, 2007, from www.unfpa.org/pds/urbanization.htm.

Universalia. (2006). Independent evaluation of the Cities Alliance (Vol. 1). Retrieved February 21, 2007, from www.citiesalliance.org/about-ca/2006-independent-evaluation.html.

Urban Resource Centre. (n.d.). *The Orangi pilot project.* Retrieved March 1, 2007, from www .urckarachi.org/orangi.htm.

Urban Resource Center Phnom Penh. (2002). *Study of relocation of urban poor communities in Phnom Penh.* Phnom Penh, Cambodia: Urban Resource Centre. Retrieved March 1, 2007, from www .citiesalliance.org/cdsdb.nsf/Attachments/Cambodia+-+Phnom+Penh+-+Relocation+of+Urban+ Poor+Communities/$File/PP+CDS+Relocation+Study+-+Final+Draft.doc.

Varley, A. (1987). The relationship between tenure legalization and housing improvements: Evidence from Mexico City. *Development and Change, 18,* 463–481.

Wilpert, G. (2005). *Venezuela's quiet housing revolution: Urban land reform.* Retrieved March 15, 2007, from www.venezuelanalysis.com/print.php?artno=1551/.

Wood, G., & Salway, S. (2000). Introduction: Securing livelihoods in Dhaka slums. *Journal of International Development, 12,* 669–688.

Woodruff, C. (2001). Review of de Soto's "The mystery of capital." *Journal of Economic Literature, 39*(4), 1215–1223.

World Bank. (1975). *Housing: Sector policy paper.* Washington, DC: Author.

World Bank. (1983). *Learning by doing: World Bank lending for urban development (1972–82).* Washington, DC: Author.

World Bank. (1993). *Housing: Enabling markets to work.* Washington, DC: Author.

World Bank. (1997). *World development report 1997: The state in a changing world.* Oxford: Oxford University Press.

World Bank. (2000). *World development report 2000–2001: Attacking poverty.* Oxford: Oxford University Press.

World Bank. (2006). *2006 world development indicators: People.* Retrieved February 9, 2007, from http://devdata.worldbank.org/wdi2006/contents/Section2.htm.

World Bank. (2007a). *Abstract of housing: Enabling markets to work.* Retrieved January 8, 2007, from www.wds.worldbank.org/external/default/main?pagePK=64193027&piPK=64187937& theSitePK=523679&menuPK=64187510&searchMenuPK=64187283&siteName=WDS&entity ID=000178830_98101911194018/.

World Bank. (2007b). *Housing and land.* Washington, DC: Author. Retrieved March 15, 2007, from http://go.worldbank.org/OTO3F852E0.

World Bank. (2007c). *Urban poverty: What are the policy issues?* Retrieved February 2, 2007, from http://web.worldbank.org/WBSITE/EXTERNAL/TOPICS/EXTURBANDEVELOPMENT /EXTURBANPOVERTY/0,contentMDK:20227683~menuPK:341331~pagePK:148956~piPK: 216618~theSitePK:341325,00.html.

Wratten, E. (1995). Conceptualising urban poverty. *Environment and Urbanisation*, 7(1), 11–36.

Youth for Unity and Voluntary Action. (1999). *Our home is a slum: An exploration of a community and local government collaboration in a tenant's struggle to establish legal residency*. Geneva, Switzerland: UNRISD.

Zanetta, C. (2001). The evolution of the World Bank's urban lending in Latin America: From sites-and-services to municipal reform and beyond. *Habitat International*, 25(4s), 513–533.

Chapter 15

CHILD WELFARE POLICY

Richard J. Gelles and Carol Wilson Spigner

Children, especially young children, are dependent on their parents, relatives, communities, and ultimately society for their survival. Children's developmental well-being may be threatened if they become orphans, if they are abandoned by parents or relatives, or if they are maltreated. The maltreatment of children has manifested itself in nearly every conceivable manner—physically, emotionally, sexually, and by forced child labor (Ten Bensel, Rheinberger, & Radbill, 1997). Historians have documented occurrences of various forms of child mistreatment since the beginning of recorded history. In some ancient cultures, children had no rights until the right to live was bestowed upon them by their father. The right to live was sometimes withheld by fathers, and newborns were abandoned or left to die. Although we do not have a means to know how numerous abandonment or killing was, we do know that infanticide was widely accepted among ancient and prehistoric cultures. Newborns and infants could be put to death because they cried too much, because they were sickly or deformed, or because of some perceived imperfection. Girls, twins, and children of unmarried women were the special targets of infanticide (Robin, 1980).

Infanticide was not the only abuse inflicted by generations of parents. From prehistoric times to the present, children have been mutilated, beaten, and maltreated. Such treatment was not only condoned, but was often mandated as the most appropriate child-rearing method. Children were, and continue to be, hit with rods, canes, and switches. Boys have been castrated to produce eunuchs. Girls have been, and continue to be, subjected to genital surgery or mutilation as part of culturally approved ritual. Colonial parents were implored to "beat the devil" out of their children (Greven, 1991; Straus, 1994). Summarizing the plight of children from prehistorical times to the present, David Bakan (1971, p. 3) comments, "Child abuse thrives in the shadows of privacy and secrecy. It lives by inattention."

In many cases of orphans, abandoned children, and even maltreated children, relatives and informal community networks became involved in the caring and protection of dependent children. When kin and community were insufficient, societies developed more formal mechanisms to care for and protect children.

Concern for the rights and welfare of children has waxed and waned over the centuries, but there has always been some attempt to protect children from mistreatment. Six thousand years ago, children in Mesopotamia had a patron goddess to look after them. The Greeks and Romans had orphan homes. A variety of historical accounts mention some form of "fostering" for dependent children. Samuel Radbill (1980) reports that child protection laws were enacted as long ago as 450 BCE. Attempts were made to modify and restrict fathers' complete control over their children. Anthropologists note that virtually all societies have mores, laws, or customs that regulate sexual access to children.

The Renaissance marked a new morality regarding children. Children were seen as a dependent class in need of the protection of society. At the same time, however, the family as an institution was deemed responsible for teaching children the proper rules of behavior. Moreover, this was a period in which the power of the father increased dramatically. This dialectic—concern for children and increased demands and power of parents to control children—has been a consistent theme throughout history.

The Enlightenment of the eighteenth century brought children increased attention, services, and protection. The London Foundling Hospital, founded during the eighteenth century, not only provided medical care, but also was a center of the moral reform movement on behalf of children (Robin, 1980).

This chapter examines child welfare policy specifically in the United States, with attention to the definition of child maltreatment, development of systems for addressing abuse and neglect, and the challenges of foster care. From the founding of the nation until the present, child welfare policies have been molded by efforts at the state level that have influenced the development of policy. In this country, the states retain all powers that are not specifically reserved for the federal government. The federal powers include monetary policy, foreign policy, interstate commerce and transactions, and national taxation policy. Child protection is the responsibility of the states. Thus, there is no single, national child welfare system, nor is there one set of policies in the United States. Because states have the authority to define child abuse and neglect and to develop their own policy responses, there are in fact no fewer than 300 child welfare systems; some are state operated, some county-based, and some are hybrid models. There are 51 sets of child welfare policies, one for each state and the District of Columbia. Most other nations—with the exception of Australia, which has an even stronger federalist system of government—concentrate child welfare policies and programs under a single national policy. In the United States, federal policy formation has followed the development of state policies. However, today there is a federal statutory framework that shapes and is influenced by state policies through the establishment of standards and funding mechanisms.

A second feature of child welfare policy in the United States is the intersection of parental rights and children's rights. The development of parental rights and responsibilities is a derivative of English Common Law and American case law. Parental rights, though not specifically articulated in the U.S. Constitution, are embodied in precedents set by rulings of the U.S. Supreme Court and are heavily influenced by the privacy rights of citizens. Parental rights include the right to custody, control, and decision making for children. With these rights come reciprocal parental responsibilities to protect, educate, support, and care for the child. Children's rights are also developed in case law, in which the doctrines of *best interest of the child* and *parens patria* (the state as ultimate parent; Davidson, 1997) were crafted. The rights of children have been slow to develop, but have been advanced by various advocacy groups seeking to assure that children are protected from acts of omission or commission that threaten children's safety and well-being.

A BRIEF HISTORY OF CHILD WELFARE POLICY IN THE UNITED STATES

The early years of this country were characterized by immigration, internal migration, and the settling of new communities. During the nineteenth century, America was beginning to industrialize and build urban centers (Axinn & Stern, 2004). At the same time there were cycles of economic depression that made it difficult for families to support themselves. Child dependency prior to the nineteenth century was primarily the consequence of children becoming orphans. Maternal death, flu, yellow fever, or other epidemics claimed parents in young adulthood. A second form of dependency came about when parents abandoned unwanted or sickly children or when poverty, homelessness, and alcoholism led parents to desert their children in the hopes that such foundlings would be adopted and raised by individuals with more resources.

Initially, dependent children were cared for in almshouses along with the mentally ill, the cognitively limited, and those with medical conditions. Subsequently, specialized institutions were established for orphaned children (Myers, 2006). Orphanages and foundling hospitals were the primary recipients of orphaned or abandoned children into the beginning of the twentieth century. Lindsey (2004) reports that in 1920 there were approximately 750,000 orphans in the United States. Orphanages, almshouses, or infirmaries (as they were called in Europe) housed children in appalling conditions. Investigations of orphanages produced exposés that portrayed children held in inhumane conditions. Even so, by the end of the nineteenth century there were an estimated 100,000 children housed in 1,000 orphanages (Bruno, 1957; Lindsey, 2004; Myers, 2006). These institutions were primarily funded through private philanthropy.

Well into the nineteenth century there was no official, law-based system of child welfare policy. The child welfare services that existed were the outcome of individual efforts or organized programs advanced by faith-based organizations or reform movements. Three significant events occurred in the mid-nineteenth century that would provide more structure and focus to efforts to protect children.

The first movement was the product of the efforts of a Yale-educated theologian, Charles Loring Brace, who believed that there must be a better way of raising abandoned and orphaned children than in institutions. Moreover, Brace was deeply concerned about the number of children and youth (mostly immigrant children) who appeared to be wandering the streets of New York City (Lindsey, 2004). Brace founded the Children's Aid Society in 1853 and developed a system he called "placing out." Placing out involved taking orphaned or abandoned children from New York City and sending them by train to homes in Ohio, Michigan, Illinois, and Indiana (Brace, 1859). Using a network of Presbyterian ministers to identify appropriate families, Brace placed these children with farm families. In Brace's mind, placing needy children on farms would provide them with a wholesome environment in which they could learn the core values of American culture. Between 1853 and 1890 the Children's Aid Society moved 92,000 children from the streets, orphanages, and almshouses of New York to the farms of the Midwest (Leiby, 1978). However, there was an ongoing debate into the twentieth century about which kind of placement was best for children: institutions or family foster care.

An incident that occurred in New York City in 1874 provided a second opportunity to formalize child welfare policy. The case of Mary Ellen Wilson is usually considered the turning point in concern for children's welfare. In 1874, 8-year-old Mary Ellen lived in the home of Francis and Mary Connolly but was not the blood relative of either. Mary Ellen was the illegitimate daughter of Mary Connolly's first husband. A neighbor noticed the plight of Mary Ellen, who was beaten with a leather thong and allowed to go ill-clothed in bad weather. The neighbor reported the case to Etta Wheeler, a "friendly visitor" who worked for St. Luke's Methodist Mission. In the mid-1800s, child welfare was church-based rather than government-based. Wheeler turned to the police and to the New York City Department of Charities for help regarding Mary Ellen Wilson and was turned down, first by the police, who said there was no proof of a crime, and then by the charity agency, who asserted that they did not have custody of the child. The legend goes on to note that Henry Berge, founder of the Society for the Prevention of Cruelty to Animals, intervened on behalf of Mary Ellen, and the courts accepted the case because Mary Ellen was a member of the animal kingdom. In reality, the court reviewed the case because the child needed protection. The case was argued, not by Henry Berge, but by his colleague Elbridge Gerry, a leader in the charity movement. Mary Ellen Wilson was removed from her foster home and initially placed in an orphanage. Her foster mother was imprisoned for a year, and the case received detailed press coverage for months. In December 1874, the New York Society for the Prevention of Cruelty to Children (SPCC) was founded (Nelson, 1984; Robin, 1980). The SPCC was the first organization that focused on child maltreatment in the United States. Using an "arm of the law" approach, the SPCC accepted reports of abuse and investigated and brought offending parents and caretakers to court for prosecution. Children who were rescued were released to one of the local children's aid societies for care and protection. Protective societies for children appeared and disappeared during the next 80 years.

The third development that helped to formalize child protection was the establishment of the first juvenile court in Illinois in 1899. Until this time, child protection had functioned as primarily a voluntary sector activity. In some instances, the placement of children into institutions and foster care was made by securing surrenders from parents. In other circumstances, the change in custody was informal and lacked legal oversight and protection. The legal system treated children as if they were little adults or as property of their parents. The first juvenile courts were established based on the recognition of the immaturity of children and the need to take action that would further their development. The court that had jurisdiction over dependent and delinquent children was designed to consider the child's social situation when determining what action would meet "the best interest of the child." The court was a civil court that was given the authority to assume protective guardianship, transfer custody, and sever parental rights (Williams, 1980). Eventually, all 50 states established juvenile courts, creating a legal institution that was to become the arbiter of the rights of parents and of children in cases of dependency and delinquency. This development reinforced the notion that the business of protecting children was the responsibility of the state under its *parens patria* power.

By the beginning of the twentieth century, some of the key elements that would shape social policy for abused and neglected children were in place: an approach to investigation and prosecution of abuse and neglect, child placement practices that relied on both social institutions and foster family care, and the juvenile court that had the authority to intervene in the lives of families in order to protect children.

Over the next 50 years the visibility of and concern about child protection as reflected in the protective societies appeared and disappeared. The political scientist Barbara Nelson (1984) notes that by the 1950s public interest in child maltreatment was practically nonexistent in the United States (and much of the world, for that matter). Technology paved the way for the rediscovery of physical child abuse. In 1946, the radiologist John Caffey reported on six cases of children who had multiple long-bone fractures and subdural hematomas. It would take nine more years before the medical profession would begin to accept that such injuries were the direct result of actions by children's caretakers. In 1955, P. V. Wooley and W. A. Evans not only concluded that the X-rays revealed a pattern of injuries, but that the injuries were committed willfully. Wooley and Evans went on to criticize the medical profession for its reluctance to accept the accumulating evidence that long-bone fractures that were seen on X-rays were indeed inflicted willfully.

In 1958, C. Henry Kempe and his colleagues formed the first hospital-based child protective team at Colorado General Hospital in Denver. Kempe, Silverman, Steele, Droegemueller, and Silver would publish their landmark article, "The Battered Child Syndrome," in the *Journal of the American Medical Association* in July 1962. Kempe and his multidisciplinary colleagues' article was accompanied by a strong editorial on the battered child. The article and the editorial were the beginning of the modern concern for child abuse and neglect, a concern that has grown and expanded both nationally and internationally over the past 4 decades.

THE INITIAL INVOLVEMENT OF THE FEDERAL GOVERNMENT

The federal government is a recent arrival in the area of policy for the protection of dependent children, with many of the developments occurring in the second half of the twentieth century. A series of antecedent events that set the stage for active involvement in child welfare policy included the 1909 White House Conference, the establishment of the Children's Bureau, and the development of the federal income maintenance program for poor children and their families. As part of the progressive era, women from the settlement movement lobbied for a federal commission on children. They had lived in urban areas with the poor and had firsthand knowledge of the impact of poverty on children. Out of their advocacy came the 1909 White House Conference on the Care of Dependent Children, which established principles to guide the care of children in the United States. Settling the debate over institutional care versus foster family care, the primacy of family foster care was established, as well as the principle that children should not be removed from their families due to poverty alone. The conference also called for the creation of a unit in the federal government to study the conditions of children (*Proceedings of White House Conference on the Care of Dependent Children*, 1909).

The United States Children's Bureau was founded in 1912 as an agency within the Department of Labor. (The Bureau was later moved to the newly created Department of Health, Education, and Welfare, which was subsequently renamed the Department of Health and Human Services.) The Children's Bureau was founded by an act of Congress with a mandate to

> investigate and report on all matters pertaining to the welfare of children and child life among all classes of our people . . . especially infant mortality, birth rates, orphanages, juvenile courts, desertion, dangerous occupations, accidents, and diseases of children . . . and legislation effecting children. (U.S. Children's Bureau, 1912)

Initially, the Bureau published studies that informed the public and policy makers about key issues. They also published model legislation to help advance the development of juvenile courts (U.S. Children's Bureau, 1961). An important part of their work was in the area of public education on child development issues.

The Children's Bureau has engaged in a variety of activities regarding child maltreatment and participated in the earliest national meetings on child abuse, sponsored by the Children's Division of the American Humane Association. After the publication of Kempe and colleagues' 1962 article, the Bureau convened a meeting in 1963 that drafted a model child abuse reporting law. By 1967, all 50 states and the District of Columbia had enacted mandatory reporting laws based on the Bureau's model. In 1974, Congress enacted the Child Abuse Prevention and Treatment Act (CAPTA) and created the National Center on Child Abuse and Neglect (Nelson, 1984). Today, the Office of Child Abuse and Neglect remains within the Children's Bureau and continues to coordinate the federal effort to prevent and treat the abuse and neglect of children in the United States. In addition to CAPTA, the Children's Bureau is currently responsible for the administration of other federal programs related to child protection, foster care, and special needs adoption.

The third major federal initiative that would impact child welfare policy was the enactment of the Social Security Act of 1935. The Social Security Act, a cornerstone of Franklin Roosevelt's New Deal policies, established a public welfare system for poor, fatherless children and a public welfare system for the purpose of protecting and caring for homeless, dependent, and neglected children who were thought to be in danger of becoming delinquent (Waldfogel, 1998). The Social Security Act included the Aid for Dependent Children program, which succeeded "mother's pensions." As noted later in this chapter, a 1961 amendment to the Social Security Act of 1935 provided funding for children who were removed from their homes for abuse and neglect (O'Neil & Gesiriech, 2005). In 1962, the Aid for Dependent Children programs was changed to Aid to Families with Dependent Children (AFDC).

THE IMPACT OF THE CHILD ABUSE PREVENTION AND TREATMENT ACT OF 1974

The goal of the 1974 CAPTA was to prevent abuse, disseminate information, treat children who were maltreated, and promote the development of a competent workforce. To receive funding under CAPTA, states had to enact the minimum definition of maltreatment and assure that their system for receiving and investigating reports had such provisions as a hotline number, immunity for reporters, mandatory reporting, and confidentiality. The immediate impact of the enactment of CAPTA was an exponential increase in reported cases of suspected child maltreatment. In 1967, Gil (1970) collected information regarding child abuse reporting and found 6,000 confirmed cases of child abuse in the United States. By 1976, 2 years after CAPTA was enacted, states received more than 500,000 reports of *suspected* child abuse and neglect. The number of reports doubled to 1 million by 1979, doubled again to 2 million in 1986, and reached 3 million reports in 1993. Reports of suspected child maltreatment have remained stable at about 3 million per year since 1997 (see Figure 15.1).

The number of reports is significant because it represents the actual number of reports and investigations that state and county child protective service agencies must manage. It is also worth noting that while the number of reports of suspected child maltreatment increased, so too did the rate of reports. In 1977, the rate of children reported as suspected victims of child abuse and neglect was approximately 10 children per 1,000 children in the

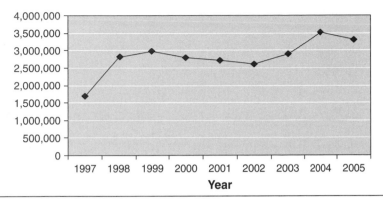

Figure 15.1   Reports of child maltreatment, 1997 to 2005. Based on *Child Maltreatment 2005*, by the U.S. Department of Health and Human Services, Administration on Children, Youth, and Families, 2007, Washington, DC: U.S. Government Printing Office.

United States. The rate doubled to more than 20 per 1,000 children in 1984, and doubled again to more than 40 children per 1,000 in 1996 (see Figure 15.2).

Thus, the initial goal of CAPTA was accomplished, increasing the public identification of children who were being abused and neglected behind closed doors. The assumption behind CAPTA was that if maltreated children could be identified, state and county agencies would be able to take appropriate steps to protect the victims of abuse and neglect and hopefully help the families and caregivers who were maltreating them.

The increase in both the number of children reported and the rate of reporting was not entirely the result of CAPTA. First, CAPTA was followed up by local, and eventually national, public awareness campaigns that were designed to raise the public's (and also specified reporters') awareness of the existence of child maltreatment and the importance of reporting suspected cases. The federal model law (CAPTA) and state legislation provided immunity from prosecution for anyone making a good-faith report of suspected child maltreatment.

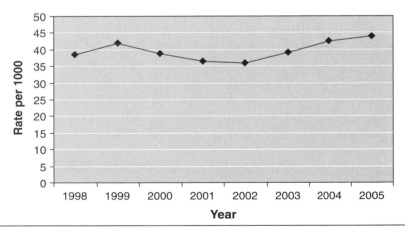

Figure 15.2   Rates of child abuse reports, 1998 to 2005. Based on *Child Maltreatment 2005*, by the U.S. Department of Health and Human Services, Administration on Children, Youth, and Families, 2007, Washington, DC: U.S. Government Printing Office.

Second, the public awareness campaigns were accompanied in some states, and eventually in all states, with technological advances that facilitated the process through which individuals made reports. Even before CAPTA was enacted, Florida developed a public awareness campaign and instituted a toll-free telephone number so that child maltreatment reporters could make a report without incurring a toll charge. In the year after the Florida public awareness campaign and the introduction of the toll-free telephone number (1970), the annual number of reports of child abuse and neglect increased from 17 to 17,000.

A third factor that contributed to the increase in child abuse and neglect reports was the broadening of the definition of what constitutes child maltreatment.

When Henry Kempe and his colleagues (1962) wrote their path-breaking article about child abuse, they labeled the problem "the battered child syndrome." They defined the syndrome as a deliberate act of physical violence that produced diagnosable injuries.

> The Child Abuse Prevention and Treatment Act of 1974 (Public Law 93-247) broadened the definition of maltreatment from Kempe and his colleague's more narrow definition. The definition of child maltreatment included in Public Law 93-247 (Child Abuse Prevention and Treatment Act of 1974) was: the physical or mental injury, sexual abuse, negligent treatment, or maltreatment of a child under the age of eighteen by a person who is responsible for the child's welfare under circumstances which indicate the child's welfare is harmed or threatened thereby.

Unlike Kempe et al.'s (1962) definition, this definition included categories of maltreatment for which there might not be conclusive evidence, such as neglect and emotional injury. In these areas, the standard used to define maltreatment was the "minimum community standard of care." The category was expanded with no specification of what those behaviors or the developmental consequences might be.

In 1984, the definition of child maltreatment was further broadened in the reauthorization of CAPTA (Child Abuse Amendments of 1984). by enacting the following:

> The physical or mental injury, sexual abuse or exploitation, negligent treatment, or maltreatment of a child under the age of eighteen or the age specified by the child protection law of the state in question, by a person (including an employee of a residential facility or any staff person providing out-of-home care) who is responsible for the child's welfare under circumstances which indicate that the child's health or welfare is harmed or threatened thereby, as determined in regulations prescribed by the Secretary.

This refined the definition of maltreatment to cover actions taken by persons responsible for the care of the child and affirmed the role of the state in defining childhood for the purpose of protection. This change recognizes the shared responsibility of the state and federal government in the protection of children. The federal definition was changed in 1988 to indicate that the behavior had to be avoidable and nonaccidental and resulted in a narrowing of the definition by excluding accidents that were not avoidable (Child Abuse Prevention, Adoption and Family Services Act of 1988). This new clause attempted to address the issue of intent; however, it provided no clear guidance as to how to classify or categorize cases based on intent.

The most recent authorization of CAPTA, signed into law in 2003, provides more specificity in the definition of sexual abuse and further defines the Baby Doe provisions related to withholding of medically indicated treatment from infants who are seriously ill (Keeping Children and Families Safe Act of 2003, Pub. L. 108-36). The relevant definitions read:

> the term "child abuse and neglect" means, at a minimum, any recent act or failure to act on the part of a parent or caretaker, which results in death, serious physical or emotional harm, sexual abuse or exploitation, or an act or failure to act which presents an imminent risk of serious harm;

> the term "sexual abuse" includes—

> (A) the employment, use, persuasion, inducement, enticement, or coercion of any child to engage in, or assist any other person to engage in, any sexually explicit conduct or simulation of such conduct for the purpose of producing a visual depiction of such conduct; or

> (B) the rape, and in cases of caretaker or inter-familial relationships, statutory rape, molestation, prostitution, or other form of sexual exploitation of children, or incest with children.

The phrase "withholding of medically indicated treatment" refers to the failure to respond to the infant's life-threatening conditions by providing treatment (including appropriate nutrition, hydration, and medication), which, in the treating physician's reasonable medical judgment, will be most likely to be effective in ameliorating or correcting all such conditions. The phrase does not encompass the failure to provide treatment (other than appropriate nutrition, hydration, or medication) to an infant when, in the treating physician's reasonable medical judgment, the infant is chronically and irreversibly comatose; the provision of such treatment would

> – merely prolong dying;
> – not be effective in ameliorating or correcting all of the infant's life-threatening conditions; or otherwise be futile in terms of the survival of the infant; or
> – the provision of such treatment would be virtually futile in terms of the survival of the infant and the treatment itself under such circumstances would be inhumane. (USC Title 42 Chapter 67 Subchapter I §5106g)

Given the broadening of the definition of child maltreatment, increased public awareness, and technological advances that made it easier to report and respond to cases of suspected child maltreatment, it is not at all surprising that the number and rates of reports have increased. It is important to note that increases in reporting do not indicate an actual increase in the occurrence of child maltreatment.

There has also been an unintended consequence of CAPTA legislation and the goal of increased reporting. By the mid-1980s, the substantiation rate for child maltreatment reports had stabilized at 40%. A founded or substantiated report of child maltreatment generally means that sufficient evidence has been found during the investigation to conclude that a child has been abused or neglected.[1] Thus, one consequence of CAPTA is that more than half of the investigations carried out by state or county child welfare agencies end with a finding

---

[1] The terms vary from state to state, as does the standard for determining what is founded or substantiated and what evidence must be present to determine the outcome of the investigation (Myers, 2006).

that there is insufficient evidence to conclude that abuse or neglect has occurred. Not only does this mean that significant human and financial resources are invested in responding to reports that will end up providing neither protection to children nor assistance to families, but it is also the case that there is less than a 50% chance that someone who makes a report will see that report lead to anything other than an investigation. As the pediatrician Eli Newberger (1983, p. 307) put it 9 years after the enactment of CAPTA, the promise implicit in child abuse reporting laws is an empty promise for many children. Newberger believed that mandatory reporting was a false promise; the law created only intrusive investigations with few actual services offered to the families subjected to the investigations.

FOSTER CARE DRIFT AND THE ADOPTION ASSISTANCE AND CHILD WELFARE ACT OF 1980

It is clear that CAPTA generated substantial increases in the number of children reported for child abuse and neglect. By inference, one might think that this would have also led to an increase in the number of children who were placed into out-of-home care in the United States. However, data on foster care placements (see Figure 15.3)[2] indicate that as early as 1962 there were more than 270,000 children in out-of-home care. The number peaked at 330,000 in 1971, and the next available formal estimate was 302,000 children in foster care in 1980.

Although it appears that the actual number of children in foster care did not increase dramatically during the 1960s and early 1970s, the prevailing professional view of foster care shifted during this time. By the late 1950s, serious questions were raised about the role and function of the foster care system. Until this time, the system was focused on the removal of children from high-risk situations, and the focus of casework practice was on the placement process. Little attention was paid to what happened to children after they entered care. The landmark study *Children in Need of Parents* (Maas & Engler, 1959) documented the status of children in foster care as "orphans of the living," not belonging to their own parents or to any other set of parents. This work and other research indicated that foster care was far from temporary (Fanschel & Shinn, 1978). By the late 1970s, foster care had become a permanent status for many children who entered the child welfare system. Children placed into foster care did not reside in a single foster home; rather, they *drifted* from one placement to another, with little stability or continuity of care. The view of foster care began to shift toward that of a temporary service whose purpose was to reunite children with their families or place them in another family if necessary (Pecora, Whittaker, Maluccio, & Barth, 2000).

As a result of a 1961 amendment to the Social Security Act of 1935, children who were removed from their homes for abuse and neglect could have the costs of their placement funded from the AFDC program of the Social Security Act if they were eligible for the program had they remained at home (O'Neil & Gesiriech, 2005). The funds covered the cost of foster care but provided no funds for services to parents. The composition of the foster care population was shifting to a system that was disproportionately populated by

---

[2]Until 1996, the federal government did not have a formal mechanism for collecting data on children in foster care. Thus, earlier data are estimates derived from various sources and data collection methodologies.

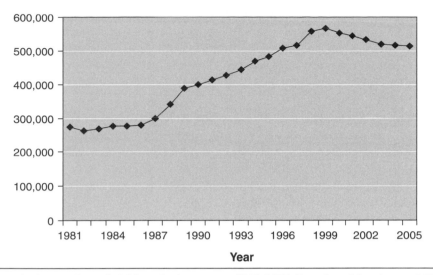

Figure 15.3   Number of children in foster care 1981–2005. Based on Adoption and Foster Care Analysis and Reporting System, retrieved November 15, 2007, from www.acf.hhs.gov /programs/cb/stats_research/afcars/trends.htm.

single-parent families, children of color, and children removed from homes with incomes significantly below the poverty level (Pecora et al., 2000).

In addition to concern over "foster care drift," the paradigm of child abuse and neglect changed in the 1970s. At the time of Kempe and colleague's (1962) first publication on the battered child syndrome, the prevailing causal model was that child abuse was caused by the psychopathology of the caregivers. This model explained abuse and neglect as a function of individual psychopathy. Other models proposed that maltreatment arose out of mental illness or the use and abuse of alcohol and illicit drugs.

By the mid-1970s, the psychopathological model of child abuse and neglect was being replaced with conceptual models that placed greater emphasis on social factors such as income, education, age, marital conflict, stress, and child-produced stressors (see Gelles, 1973; Gil, 1970). Such models were more consistent with an intervention approach that envisioned foster care as a temporary placement while services and resources are directed toward caregivers to provide them means to adequately care for their children. The key assumption behind social-psychological stress models is that all caregivers want to be adequate parents, but there are structural and economic barriers that impede that desire. Children should be kept safe in temporary foster care while the barriers are addressed and removed, or at least lowered.

THE ADOPTION ASSISTANCE AND CHILD WELFARE ACT OF 1980

The Adoption Assistance and Child Welfare Amendments of 1980 (AACWA) were the result of expanded recognition that children in foster care were in social and legal limbo, demonstrated permanency planning programs that documented the ability to move children in foster care back to their own families or on to adoptions, and the need to clearly shift the purpose and operation of the child welfare system.

The Adoption Assistance and Child Welfare Act of 1980 (Pub. L. 96-272) was designed to address the problem of foster care drift. There were *three* major components of this legislation aimed at reducing foster care drift and assuring the right of children to have permanent homes. The first major provision of the legislation was the requirement that states make "reasonable efforts to maintain a family" before they remove a child from the child's birth parents and "reasonable efforts to reunify a family" before establishing a permanency plan of adoption. The reasonable efforts requirement mandated states to provide appropriate services prior to placement and/or services that would allow for a safe reunification of a child who had been removed. The legislation, however, provided no additional funds for such services.

A second provision of the legislation was the requirement that states engage in permanency planning. In brief, permanency planning required each state to have a plan developed within 18 months of a child being placed into foster care that would assure that the child would have a permanent home, either through a safe return to birth parents or through an adoption. To facilitate permanency planning, the law established a set of procedural requirements that included development of case plans, periodic judicial reviews, and dispositional hearings at which the child's permanent plan was established.

The legislation created Title IV-E of the Social Security Act, which provided uncapped entitlement funding for foster care and adoption assistance for children who were eligible for AFDC. The foster care funding was an extension of the old AFDC provision that allowed for payment of foster care costs for poor children. In addition to permanency planning, the major policy innovation was the provision of funds to subsidize the adoption of special needs foster children. Federal funds could be used to support the cost of operating adoption and foster care programs. The funding continued to be linked to placement services—adoption and foster care—with no targeted funding for services to the families of children in need of protection. Further, states were expected to adhere to the spirit of the reasonable efforts provision and to meet the procedural and temporal requirements of the legislation in order to qualify for Title IV-E federal funds for foster care and adoption.

THE IMPACT OF THE ADOPTION ASSISTANCE AND CHILD WELFARE ACT OF 1980

The available data on foster care[3] indicate that in the first few years after AACWA was enacted, there was a decline in the number of children in foster care (see Figure 15.3).

From an estimated 302,000 children in foster care the year AACWA was enacted, the number dropped to 262,000 in 1982, the lowest on record. The number of children in foster care remained under 300,000 until 1987 and then began a significant increase, reaching 400,000 in 1990.

The emphasis on permanency led to the freeing of children for adoption and the subsequent adoption of some of the children. Over 50,000 children were freed for adoption in 1982 as a result of state court action (Maza, 1983). Of the children available for adoption,

---

[3]There was still no official federal effort to collect data on foster care; thus, the numbers cited in the text and Figure 15.3 are from unofficial tabulations.

17,000 had a specific permanency plan for adoption (Maximus Inc., 1984). Of this number 14,400 children were placed for adoption in 1982 (Maximus Inc., 1984).[4]

THE INDIAN CHILD WELFARE ACT OF 1978

Between the time CAPTA was enacted and AACWA became law, a disproportionate number of Native American children were removed from their parents and placed in the foster care system. As many as 25% to 35% of Native American children in certain states were placed in the foster care system between 1974 and 1978 (Myers, 2006). Not only were the children placed in foster care, but the vast majority of the children were placed outside of their tribe with non-Indian families. In response to a multiyear study of the placement of Indian children (Fanschel, 1972), tribal advocacy challenged these practices. In a period in which Congress was actively promoting the sovereign status of tribes, the Indian Child Welfare Act of 1978 (ICWA; Pub. L. 95-608) was enacted (Jones, 1995). The Act established standards for child custody proceedings related to foster care, termination of parental rights, and adoption of Indian children. The standards included tribal court jurisdiction over children who reside on the reservation; the requirement of notification to the tribe of state or local proceedings involving the placement of an Indian child living off the reservation, along with tribal rights to intervene and request transfer of the proceeding to tribal court; an increased standard of proof to clear and convincing evidence; and placement preferences for the extended family or tribe (Pecora et al., 2000).

The intent of ICWA was to limit the placement of Native American children into non–Native American homes. However, ICWA had numerous ambiguities, including the definition of an "Indian child," as well as interpretation of key clauses and terms (e.g., What is "good cause"?). The Act also challenged the tribes to develop or expand their protective services and tribal court capacities.

APPLICABLE SUPREME COURT RULINGS

Before examining federal and state child welfare policy after 1980, it is important to also consider how case law has influenced child welfare policy in the United States. There were three major U.S. Supreme Court rulings in the 1970s and 1980s that established guiding precedents for the child welfare system. In issues of child protection and custody, the Court has been the arbiter of the relationship between parents, children, and the state.

Until the early 1970s, unmarried mothers were deemed the sole custodians of their children. For children entering foster care, the legal proceedings were focused on the relationship between the child and the birth mother. Unmarried fathers were only part of the proceeding in those instances in which their legal relationship to the child was established through cohabitation. This issue was resolved in *Stanley v. Illinois* (1972) when the Supreme Court ruled that unmarried fathers were entitled to a hearing to determine their

---

[4]The remaining proportion of the 50,000 children whose plan was not adoption had permanency plans of long-term foster care or emancipation (reaching the age of a legal adult).

fitness in child protection custody proceedings. This right was based on the due process clause of the 14th Amendment. This landmark decision not only gave unmarried fathers a right to be heard but also gave children access to the resources of their noncustodial, unmarried parent.

U.S. law and tradition grant parents broad discretion as to how they rear their children. In *Smith v. Organization of Foster Families for Equality and Reform* (1977), the U.S. Supreme Court held that the 14th Amendment gave parents a "constitutionally recognized liberty interest" in maintaining the custody of their children "that derives from blood relationship, state law sanction, and basic human right." This interest is not absolute, however, because of the state's power and authority to exercise parens patria duties to protect citizens who cannot fend for themselves. The state may attempt to limit or end parent-child contact and make children eligible for temporary or permanent placement or adoption when parents (a) abuse, neglect, or abandon their children; (b) become incapacitated in their ability to be a parent; (c) refuse or are unable to remedy serious, identified problems in caring for their children; or (d) experience an extraordinarily severe breakdown in their relationship with their children (e.g., owing to a long prison sentence). Cognizant that severing the parent-child relationship is a drastic measure, the U.S. Supreme Court held in *Santosky v. Kramer* (1982) that a court may terminate parental rights only if the state can demonstrate with clear and convincing evidence that a parent has failed in one of the aforementioned four ways. Most state statutes also contain provisions for parents to voluntarily relinquish their rights. In addition, the state has the authority to return a child to his or her parents. Ideally, this occurs once a determination is made that it would be safe to do so and that the child's parents will be able to provide appropriate care.

FAMILY PRESERVATION AND FAMILY SUPPORT ACT

The initial impact of the Adoption Assistance and Child Welfare Act of 1980 (Pub. L. 96-272) was a decrease in the number of children placed into out-of-home care. By 1988, however, the foster care population in the United States had exceeded the previous high of 300,000, reaching 400,000 children (see Figure 15.3). Few policy analysts have commented on why the foster care population began to increase in the late 1980s, but the increase did parallel an increase in the national rates of violent crime (Catalano, 2006), as well as an increase in use of crack cocaine in the northern industrial cities (Blumstein, 1995). Combined with the consequences of deindustrialization and the destabilization of inner-city neighborhoods and inner-city families (Wilson, 1987), the increase in foster care was likely the result of the combined impact of crack cocaine and the deindustrialization of the national economy. In short, the increase in foster care placements was not likely the result of a policy change or policy failure but of changes in the broader environment that impact the ability of parents to adequately care for their children.

While foster care placements were increasing, national policy attention again turned to efforts to decrease the need to place children in foster care. Sensitive about the number of children in out-of-home care and the resulting cost increase, many states implemented family-centered services in the late 1980s and 1990s. Among these was intensive family preservation services, which were designed to be an alternative to the placement of children. The intensive family preservation services model began in Tacoma, Washington, with

Homebuilders, a family service agency. The goal of this model is to provide time-limited intensive intervention with families at imminent risk of placement. The core goal of such programs is to maintain children safely in their homes or to facilitate a safe and lasting reunification.

The Adoption Assistance and Child Welfare Act of 1980 already required that reasonable efforts be made to preserve and reunify families. The belief that intensive family preservation service programs were effective fueled a movement to provide federal funds for such programs. As part of the 1993 Omnibus Budget Reconciliation Act of 1993, the Family Preservation and Support Program was enacted. The bill created a new provision in Title IV-B of the Social Security Act of 1935 and created a $930 million funding stream (over 5 years) to fund family preservation and support programs at the state level. This was the first funding source committed to helping parents address the problems of maltreatment. Focused both on family preservation and family support, the funding addressed diversion from foster care and prevention. The law required that a significant proportion of the funds be invested in each area.

THE MULTIETHNIC PLACEMENT ACT OF 1994 AND THE INTERETHNIC ADOPTION PROVISIONS OF THE SMALL BUSINESS JOB PROTECTION ACT

The most significant event that followed Omnibus Budget Reconciliation Act was the 1993 congressional election. Campaigning under Congressman Newt Gingrich's "Contract with America," Republicans took control of both the House and the Senate in 1994. This political shift marked a more conservative approach to social welfare policy, with a focus on reducing entitlement programs and the role of the federal government. Although child welfare was not a component of the "Contract with America," the fact that Title IV-E was one of the "open-ended entitlements" in the current national welfare system would capture some attention. However, the first child welfare policy issue that was taken up by the new Republican majority was interracial adoption.

As noted earlier, between the 1950s and the 1980s the foster care population became disproportionately children of color (Pecora at al., 2000). One impact of the civil rights era was to move adoption away from the traditional practice of physical matching and infant placement and to increase the acceptance of adoption across racial lines. Prior to the successes of the civil rights movement, some southern states, including Louisiana and Texas, legally banned transracial adoption (Myers, 2006). Such laws were struck down in the 1960s. Subsequently, African-American children began to be placed transracially as Native-American children had been in earlier decades. In the early 1970s, however, concern was raised over the adoption of African-American children by White families. The National Association of Black Social Workers (NABSW) led a campaign against transracial adoption. The NABSW (1974) issued a position paper in 1972 stating that Black children should be placed only with Black families—either in foster care or adoption.[5] They viewed the loss of children through adoption as a major assault on the African-American community. A measure of the depth of concern of the Association was reflected in the statement: "We

---

[5]Conference of the National Association of Black Social Workers, Nashville, Tennessee, April 4–9, 1972.

have committed ourselves to go back to our communities and work to end this particular form of genocide" (p. 159).

The NABSW resolution found a bipartisan audience of post–civil rights conservatives who opposed transracial adoption and liberals who wanted to support the positions of newly empowered minority groups. The resolution increased the awareness of adoption agencies of the need to recruit and develop families in communities of color and led to the development of targeted efforts to extend adoption service to African American and other families of color.

In the aftermath of the NABSW resolution, transracial adoptions declined. In 1976, Black-White placements totaled 1,076 (Silverman, 1993). In 1987, Black-White transracial adoptions were estimated to be 1,169, and adoptions of children of other racial or ethnic groups—mainly Asian and Hispanic—were estimated to be 5,850. It is difficult to ascertain how the preference for within-race adoptions interacts with the racial preferences of adoptive parents who are willing to adopt across racial and cultural lines to produce this result.

Although a small proportion of adoptions, the decline in the number of transracial adoptions contributed to the persistent findings that children of color stayed in foster care longer and were less likely to be adopted (Barth, 1997). From a policy perspective, the fact that the foster care population continued to remain at 500,000 children per year and that children of color remained in foster care longer than White children, were consistently overrepresented in foster care, and were less likely to be adopted interacted with the election of a Republican majority to Congress in 1994. This provided the context for the success of a policy initiative directed at transracial adoption. In addition, a growing body of social science research (Simon & Alstein, 1977, 1987) found no developmental disadvantages among children who were transracially adopted.

The Multiethnic Placement Act of 1994 (MEPA; Pub. L. 103-382, Title V, Part E) had three major goals: (1) decrease the length of time that children wait to be adopted, (2) facilitate the recruitment and retention of foster and adoptive parents who can meet the distinctive needs of children awaiting placement, and (3) eliminate discrimination on the basis of the race, color, or national origin of the child or the prospective parent.

The statutory language of the law included two prohibitions and one affirmative obligation to state agencies and other agencies that were involved in foster care. First, state and private agencies (who received funds under Title IV-E of the Social Security Act) were prohibited from delaying or denying a child's foster care or adoptive placement on the basis of the child's or the prospective parent's race, color, or national origin. Second, agencies were prohibited from denying any individual the opportunity to become a foster or adoptive parent on the basis of race, color, or national origin. Finally, to remain eligible for funding for state child welfare programs, states were required to make diligent efforts to recruit foster and adoptive parents who reflected the racial and ethnic diversity of children in the state who needed foster and adoptive homes.

Congress revisited MEPA in 1996 to address what were perceived to be loopholes in the original law. The Interethnic Adoption Provisions of the Small Business Job Protection Act of 1996 (Pub. L. 104-188) repealed allowable exceptions under MEPA and replaced them with specific prohibitions against *any* actions that delayed or denied placements on the basis of race, color, or national origin. The law also protected children in placements from racial or ethnic discrimination under Title VI of the Civil Rights Act of 1964, creating a right to suc. State and private foster care agencies could be sued by children, prospective parents, or the federal government for delaying or denying placements. States that delayed or denied placements based on race, color, or national origin would also be penalized by a reduction in their federally allocated child welfare funding. Neither MEPA nor the Interethnic Provisions required transracial adoptions, nor did they prohibit same-race adoptions. What the two laws accomplished was to place the foster care and adoption system under the provisions and protections of the Civil Rights Act of 1964.

States were required to modify their statutes and policies to comply with the two laws. Two common provisions in state laws needed to be repealed. First, any provision that allowed for a specified time period to search for a parent of the same racial background as the child was found to be in violation of the law. Second, a provision that established placement priorities modeled on the Indian Child Welfare Act was also a violation and needed to be repealed or revoked. The Department of Health and Human Service's Office of Civil Rights conducted a systematic survey of state statutes and policies to identify the actions states needed to take to achieve compliance. Given that Title IV-E funding was at stake, states moved to statutory and policy compliance within a short period of time. A bigger challenge was shifting the practice of a profession that valued diversity and cultural continuity.

REASSESSMENT OF THE ADOPTION ASSISTANCE AND CHILD WELFARE ACT OF 1980 AND THE ADOPTION AND SAFE FAMILIES ACT OF 1997

Since 1980, federal law has required states, as a condition of eligibility for federal child welfare funding, to make "reasonable efforts" to keep a child in his or her home or reunite the child with his or her caregivers as soon a possible and practical (Pub. L. 96-272, AACWA). The AACWA also required states to make timely permanency decisions for children in out-of-home care that would move the child back to his or her own family or forward to adoption. The balance between reasonable efforts and decision making for children was difficult to establish.

State and local child welfare systems worked hard to meet the goal of family preservation, even in instances when the goal was difficult or impossible to achieve due to intractable family problems and/or lack of resources to meet family needs. The majority of children removed from their homes were ultimately reunited with their parents. Unfortunately, the reunification was very often fragile, and between 20% and 40% of children reunited with their parents were returned to out-of-home placement within 18 months (Barth, Courtney, Berrick, & Albert, 1994). In some instances, family preservation is inadequate and children die—nearly half of the children killed by parents or caregivers are killed after the children come to the attention of the child welfare system (Gelles, 1996; U.S. Advisory Board on Child Abuse and Neglect, 1995). Some children are killed when they remain in their homes; others are killed after a reunification; and an even smaller number die in foster care.

The AACWA was more focused on helping families and working toward reunification than on the decision making related to adoption. As implemented, the legislation did not reduce the length of time in care or move children to adoption in the numbers needed. Prior to 1997, the median length of stay for a child in foster care was 21 months (Child Welfare

League of America, 1999). Approximately 18% of children in foster care stayed longer than 5 years. They remained in foster care while child welfare workers worked toward family reunification, or they remained in foster care because a reunification was not possible and adoption was not achieved for the child. Approximately 100,000 children had a goal of adoption in 1996; only 27,761 were adopted that year (Child Welfare League of America, 1999). At the same time approximately 20,000 children "aged out" of the child welfare system each year not having secured a permanent family; that is, they reached the age of majority in their state and were no longer eligible for foster care or payment of foster parent on their behalf.

An important fact influencing the enactment of the Adoption and Safe Families Act of 1997 (ASFA) was that the number of adoptions of children from the foster care system was about 20,000, and the number of adoptions was in decline (Bevan, 1996). The main adverse consequence for children in out-of-home care was that, though they might spend years awaiting reunification, a reunification might never occur. The longer children waited, the less likely it was that they would secure permanency though adoption.

The legal mandate for child welfare was revised in 1997. First, the ASFA made the child's safety and permanency the paramount goals of the child welfare system. The mandate for reasonable efforts was modified to identify circumstances in which the reasonable efforts requirement was not required. These included "aggravated circumstances," such as when a parent committed a murder of another child, when a parent committed or aided in voluntary manslaughter of another child, when a parent committed an assault that resulted in serious injury to a child, or when a parent has had his or her parental rights involuntarily terminated for a sibling of the child. Second, shorter time lines were established for reunification efforts and permanency decisions to remove barriers to adoption and reduce the time children would stay in foster care awaiting an improbable or questionable reunification. The law required states to seek termination of parental rights in the instance of children being in out-of-home care for 15 of the previous 22 months. The exception to this time line was if children were in the care of relatives or if there was a compelling reason for not terminating parental rights that was in the best interests of the child. Third, states were required to develop a permanency plan for children in out-of-home care within 12 months of the children being placed in care (AACWA required a permanency plan within 18 months of a child being placed in care). Permanency plans could no longer include "long-term foster care." Fourth, states were encouraged to engage in concurrent planning that considered permanency plans that would be used if a safe reunification could not be accomplished.

By making safety of the child the paramount goal of the child welfare system, the ASFA of 1997 changed family preservation from *the* goal of child welfare systems to *a* goal, albeit one of the central and primary goals. The legislation also required states to make reasonable efforts to secure a permanent family for children who could not safely return home and created incentives for states to increase adoptions. The initial impact of the Act has been an increase in yearly adoptions, from 20,000 per year to more than 52,000 in 2005. The number of terminations of parental rights has fluctuated from a high of 73,000 per year in 2000 to a low of 65,000 in 2004, and finally up to 67,000 in 2005. The median length of time children stay in foster care declined to 15.5 months in 2005, while the percentage of children remaining on foster care for 5 years or longer declined to 14%. The number of children of children in foster care dropped from 552,000 in 2000 to 514,000 in 2005 (see Figure 15.4; U.S. Department of Health and Human Services, 2007). It is not clear

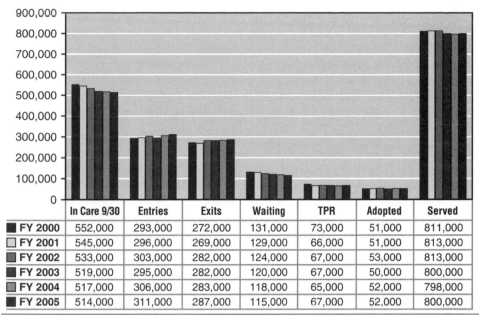

	In Care 9/30	Entries	Exits	Waiting	TPR	Adopted	Served
■ FY 2000	552,000	293,000	272,000	131,000	73,000	51,000	811,000
□ FY 2001	545,000	296,000	269,000	129,000	66,000	51,000	813,000
■ FY 2002	533,000	303,000	282,000	124,000	67,000	53,000	813,000
■ FY 2003	519,000	295,000	282,000	120,000	67,000	50,000	800,000
□ FY 2004	517,000	306,000	283,000	118,000	65,000	52,000	798,000
■ FY 2005	514,000	311,000	287,000	115,000	67,000	52,000	800,000

Figure 15.4   Trends in foster care and adoption, FY 2000–FY 2005 (based on data submitted by states as of January 2007). *Source:* **Adoption and Foster Care Analysis and Reporting System data, U.S. Children's Bureau; and Administration for Children, Youth, and Families, retrieved November 15, 2007, from www.acf.hhs.gov/programs/cb/stats_research/afcars/trends.htm.**

whether these changes are due solely to ASFA, as there were other relevant federal policy changes that occurred in the same time frame, including MEPA, the Interethnic Provisions, and federal welfare reform, that set time lines for the receipt of welfare benefits, as well as work requirements for those receiving welfare benefits.

FOSTER CARE INDEPENDENCE ACT OF 1999

Over the past 2 decades, the national data for foster care documented that approximately 20,000 youth aged out of foster care without a permanent family of their own (U.S. Department of Health and Human Services, 2007). The children who age out are young adults who spent a substantial part of their lives in foster care and are ill-prepared for independent living (Cook, 1991; Kerman, Wildfire, & Barth, 2002). Upon leaving foster care, many had not completed their education and were unable to secure or keep employment. The thousands of "graduates" of the public child welfare system experienced homelessness, depression, arrest, and early parenthood. When this issue was first addressed in 1985, Congress created the Independent Living Program (Pub. L. 99-272). The goal of the program was to assist foster children 16 years and older to prepare for the transition to adulthood. Funding was provided to states to create new programs to support older adolescents in care who were neither going to be adopted nor reunified with their birth families. The initial funding was solely for children eligible for IV-E. However, in 1988 all children 16 years old and older in foster care were covered.

The adolescents were made eligible to receive services for 6 months after the age of emancipation in their state (U.S. House of Representatives, Committee on Ways and Means, 2004). The federal resources were service dollars that were focused on preparation for work and the management of daily life. A few states were creative in trying to assure that adolescents aging out of foster care were supported. These states utilized other funds to create tuition waivers for college, designate a portion of entry-level public jobs for those who age out of foster care, and develop transitional housing. The major inadequacies of the initial independent living legislation was the limit on the age of children that could be served and the lack of any mechanism to meet the need for health care and housing.

In 1999, in response to continuing concerns for the adolescents in foster care who were destined to age out of the system, Congress modified the independent living program to better meet the needs of those aging out of foster care. The Foster Care Independence Act of 1999 (Pub. L. 106-169), extended the age of eligibility for federal funding to 21. Up to 30% of the available funds could be used to cover living costs. The law allowed youth to save up to $10,000 without losing their IV-E eligibility and created an option for states to enroll former foster children in the state medical assistance program until age 21. In a continued effort to create opportunities for former foster children, the law was again modified in 2001 to provide $50 million additional funds for education and training vouchers (Pub. L. 107-133).

CONCLUSION

The federal government has, on average, visited child welfare policy about once every 10 years. The exception was a flurry of federal legislation between 1994 and 2001. The Child Abuse Prevention and Treatment Act is renewable legislation and comes before Congress every 4 to 5 years. The child welfare–related provisions of the Social Security Act of 1935, Title IV, are not renewable, with the exception of funding for Title IV-B, Safe and Stables Families. Thus, the main funding stream and policies for child welfare do not appear on the legislative agenda on a regular basis.

States modify their statutes and administrative procedures on a regular basis. Some modifications are in response to federal mandates (e.g., ASFA); other changes are entirely locally driven. States often modify their definition of child abuse and neglect and procedures for reporting or investigating child maltreatment. Such modifications are usually made so that the state remains in compliance with the Child Abuse Prevention and Treatment Act and continues to remain eligible to receive funding under the provisions of the Act. Some state legislation constitutes significant departures from traditional child welfare policy. In the late 1990s, Florida created legislation that allowed counties to transfer the responsibilities for investigating reports of child maltreatment. Investigations in nearly every state are implemented by an agency under the umbrella of social services or children's services. Florida allowed four counties to shift the funding and responsibility for investigations to the county sheriffs.

Future Policy Issues

As states struggle to secure resources for the child welfare systems, they continue to face the ongoing fact that more than half of child abuse and neglect investigations result in no finding of abuse or neglect. In addition, funding for services for those families and children substantiated for abuse or neglect is primarily provided by local or state funding. Thus, one of the policy issues that may be addressed in the next decade is the legal definition of child maltreatment. One possible policy approach would be to reverse the expansion of the definition of abuse and neglect and create a narrower definition that could result in fewer investigations and the release of more funding for services; or states could create stricter screening procedures and reduce the number of investigations.

None of the federal legislative initiatives in the past 25 years has yielded significant improvements in achieving permanence for children in out-of-home care, assuring stable reunifications, or reducing the number of children waiting for adoption while also reducing adoption disruptions. The pendulum has swung from a concern for family reunification to a concern for child safety, but the issue or permanence remains to be appropriately and adequately addressed.

One overriding issue that impacts child welfare policy is the lack of flexibility of federal funding. The largest federal funding stream is the open-ended entitlement of Title IV-E of the Social Security Act of 1935. Title IV-E provides an open-ended federal match for the costs of children in foster care (provided the children were removed from households that would have been eligible for AFDC funding). In 2007, the funding under Title IV-E was projected to be $4.757 billion for the cost of maintaining children in foster care. Additional matching funds are provided for administration and training. Though there are billions of dollars invested in the child welfare system, those billions are directed primarily for foster care, and states have little to no flexibility as to how to use federal funds. Over the past few years, there have been proposals to make federal funding more flexible (Pew Commission on Children in Foster Care, 2004), but as yet Congress has not engaged in a serious discussion as to how to create more funding flexibility.

Children and families of color have been disproportionately represented in the foster care and child welfare system for the past 30 years. No policy to date has successfully examined or addressed that disproportionality.

REFERENCES

Adoption and Foster Care Analysis and Reporting System. (n.d.). Retrieved November 15, 2007, from www.acf.hhs.gov/programs/cb/stats_research/afcars/trends.htm.

Axinn, J., & Stern, M. J. (2004). *Social welfare: A history of the American response to need* (5th ed.). Boston: Allyn & Bacon.

Bakan, D. (1971). *The slaughter of the innocents*. Boston: Beacon Press.

Barth, R. P. (1997). Effects of age and race on the odds of adoption versus remaining in long-term out-of-home care. *Child Welfare, 76*, 285–308.

Barth, R. P., Courtney, M., Berrick, J. D., & Albert, V. (1994). *From child abuse to permanency planning: Child welfare services pathways and placements*. New York: Aldine De Gruyter.

Bevan, C. (1996). *Foster care: Too much, too little, too early, too late: Child protection: Old problem, new paradigm*. Washington, DC: National Council for Adoption.

Blumstein, A. (1995). Youth violence, guns, and the illicit-drug industry. *Journal of Criminal Law and Criminology, 86*, 10–36.

Brace, C. L. (1859). *The best method of disposing of pauper and vagrant children*. New York: Wyncoop and Hallenbeck.

Bruno, F. J. (1957). *Trends in social work, 1874–1956: A history based on the proceedings of the National Conference of Social Work*. New York: Columbia University Press.

Caffey, J. (1946). Multiple fractures in the long bones of infants suffering from chronic subdural hematoma. *American Journal of Roentgenology, Radium Therapy, and Nuclear Medicine, 58,* 163–173.

Catalano, S. H. (2006). *Criminal victimization, 2006.* Washington, DC: U.S. Department of Justice, Office of Justice Programs.

Child Abuse Amendments of 1984 § 42 U.S.C. § 67 (1984).

Child Abuse Prevention, Adoption and Family Services Act of 1988 §§42 U.S.C. § 67 (1988).

Child Abuse Prevention and Treatment Act of 1974 § 42 U.S.C. § 67 (1974).

Child Welfare League of America. (1999). *Child abuse and neglect: A look at the states* (1999 CWLA Stat Book). Washington, DC: Author.

Cook, R. (1991). *A national evaluation of Title IV-E independent living programs for youth.* Rockville, MD: Westat.

Davidson, H. (1997). The courts and child maltreatment. In M. Helfer, R. Kempe, & R. Krugman (Eds.), *The battered child* (5th ed., pp. 482–499). Chicago: University of Chicago Press.

Fanschel, D. (1972). *Far from the reservation: The transracial adoption of American Indian children.* Metuchen, NJ: Scarecrow Press.

Fanschel, D., & Shinn, E. B. (1978). *Children in foster care: A longitudinal investigation.* New York: Columbia University Press.

Gelles, R. J. (1973). Child abuse as psychopathology: A sociological critique and reformulation. *American Journal of Orthopsychiatry, 43,* 611–621.

Gelles, R. J. (1996). *The book of David: How preserving families can cost children's lives.* New York: Basic Books.

Gil, D. (1970). *Violence against children: Physical child abuse in the United States.* Cambridge, MA: Harvard University Press.

Greven, P. (1991). *Spare the child: The religious roots of punishment and the psychological impact of physical abuse.* New York: Knopf.

Jones, B. J. (1995). Indian Child Welfare Act: The need for a separate law. *ABA General Practice Magazine, 12,* 4. Retrieved April 15, 2007, from www.ABANET.org/genlpractice/magazine/1995 /fall/indianchildwelfareact.html.

Keeping Children and Families Safe Act of 2003, § U.S.C. 42 § 63, (2003).

Kempe, C. H., Silverman, F. N., Steele, B. F., Droegemueller, W., & Silver, H. K. (1962). The battered child syndrome. *Journal of the American Medical Association, 181,* 107–112.

Kerman, B., Wildfire, J., & Barth, R. P. (2002). Outcomes for young adults who experienced foster care. *Children and Youth Services Review, 24,* 319–344.

Leiby, J. (1978). *A history of social welfare and social work in the United States.* New York: Columbia University Press.

Lindsey, D. (2004). *The welfare of children* (2nd ed.). New York: Oxford University Press.

Maas, H., & Engler, R. E. (1959). *Children in need of parents.* New York: Columbia University Press.

Maza, P. L. (1983). *Characteristics of children free for adoption: Child welfare research notes # 2.* Washington, DC: Children's Bureau, Administration for Children, Youth, and Families.

Maximus Inc. (1984). *Child welfare statistical factbook 1984: Substitute care and adoption.* Washington, DC: Office of Human Development Services.

Myers, J. (2006). *Child protection in America: Past, present, and future.* New York: Oxford University Press.

National Association of Black Social Workers. (1974). Position statement on trans-racial adoption (September 1972). In H. Dalmage (2000) *Tripping on the color line: Black-White multiracial families in a racially divided world.* New Brunswick, NJ: Rutgers University Press.

Nelson, B. J. (1984). *Making an issue of child abuse: Political agenda setting for social problems.* Chicago: University Chicago Press.

Newberger, E. H. (1983). The helping hand strikes again: Unintended consequences of child abuse reporting. *Journal of Clinical Child Psychology, 12*, 307–311.

O'Neil, K., & Gesiriech, S. (2005). *A brief legislative history of the child welfare system*. Philadelphia: Pew Commission on Children in Foster Care.

Pecora, P. J., Whittaker, J. K., Maluccio, A. N., & Barth, R. P. (2000). *The child welfare challenge: Policy, practice, and research*. New York: Aldine De Gruyter.

Pew Commission on Children in Foster Care. (2004). *Fostering the future: Safety, permanence and well-being for children in foster care*. Philadelphia: Author.

Proceedings of the White House Conference on Care of Dependent Children. (1909). Senate Document, 60th Congress, 2nd Session, Vol. 13, Document 721.

Radbill, S. (1980). A history of child abuse and infanticide. In R. Helfer & C. Kempe (Eds.), *The battered child* (3rd ed., pp. 3–20). Chicago: University of Chicago Press.

Robin, M. (1980). Historical introduction: Sheltering arms—The roots of child. In E. Newberger (Ed.), *Child abuse* (pp. 1–41). Boston: Little, Brown.

Santosky v. Kramer, 455 U.S. 745 (1982).

Silverman, A. R. (1993). Outcomes of transracial adoption. *Future of Children, 3*, 104–118.

Simon, R., & Alstein, H. (1977). *Transracial adoption*. New York: Wiley.

Simon, R., & Alstein, H. (1987). *Transracial adoptees and their families: A study of identity and commitment*. New York: Wiley Interscience.

Smith v. Organization of Foster Families for Equality and Reform, 431 U.S. 816 (1977).

Stanley v. Illinois, 405 U. S. 645 (1972).

Straus, M. A. (1994). *Beating the devil out of them: Corporal punishment in American families*. New York: Lexington Books.

Ten Bensel, R. L., Rheinberger, M., & Radbill, S. X. (1997). Children in a world of violence: The roots of child maltreatment. In M. E. Helfer, R. S. Kempe, & R. D. Krugman (Eds.), *The battered child* (4th ed., pp. 3–28). Chicago: University of Chicago Press.

U.S. Advisory Board on Child Abuse and Neglect. (1995). *A nation's shame: Fatal child abuse and neglect in the United States*. Washington, DC: U.S. Department of Health and Human Services.

U.S. Children's Bureau. (1961). *Legislative guidelines for the termination of parental rights and responsibilities and the adoption of children*. Publication No. 394. Washington, DC: Author.

U.S. Children's Bureau, § Pub. L. No. 62-116 42 U.S.C. § 191 (1912).

U.S. Department of Health and Human Services. (2007). *Adoption and Foster Care Analysis and Reporting System*. Washington, DC: Author. Retrieved November 15, 2007, from www.acf.hhs.gov/programs/cb/stats_research/afcars/trends.htm.

U.S. Department of Health and Human Services, Administration on Children, Youth, and Families. (2007). *Child maltreatment 2005*. Washington, DC: U.S. Government Printing Office.

U.S. House of Representatives, Committee on Ways and Means. (2004). *2004 green book: Background material and data on the programs within the jurisdiction of the Committee on Ways and Means*. Washington, DC: Author.

Waldfogel, J. (1998). *The future of child protection: How to break the cycle of abuse and neglect*. Cambridge, MA: Harvard University Press.

Williams, C., W. (1980). *Legal guardianship: A minimally used resource for dependent children*. Unpublished doctoral dissertation, University of Southern California, Los Angeles.

Wilson, W. J. (1987). *The truly disadvantaged: The inner city, the underclass, and public policy*. Chicago: University of Chicago Press.

Wooley, P., & Evans, W. (1955). Significance of skeletal lesions resembling those of traumatic origin. *Journal of the American Medical Association, 158*, 539–543.

Chapter 16

PUBLIC FUNDING OF SECTARIAN ORGANIZATIONS FOR THE PROVISION OF HIV/AIDS PREVENTION AND CARE: DISCRIMINATORY ISSUES FOR GAY MALES

Christopher W. Blackwell and Sophia F. Dziegielewski

RELIGIOUS AND FAITH-BASED ORGANIZATIONS PROVIDING SOCIAL SERVICES: CHARITABLE CHOICE

The Personal Responsibility and Work Opportunity Reconciliation Act (PRWORA) of 1996 greatly expanded the accessibility and feasibility of religious organizations and institutions to compete for federal and state funds to provide social services. Lieberman and Cummings (2002, p. 2) provide specific fiscal examples for the General Accounting Office and found "at least 19 states have contracted with FBOs [faith-based organizations] to provide some welfare-related services." The Act contains a provision known as Charitable Choice, which is designed to decrease the barriers of religious organizations in their ability to compete for federal and state funding to provide social services (Bartkowski & Regis, 1999; Cahill & Jones, 2002; Cnaan & Bodie, 2002; Davis, 1996; Glennon, 2000; Kennedy & Bielefeld, 2002; Knippenberg, 2003). The PRWORA provision of Charitable Choice was legislated under the Clinton administration in 1996 and has been largely embraced and expanded by the Bush administration (Cahill & Jones, 2002; Cnaan & Bodie, 2002; Jean, 2002; Rostow, 2003; Yang, 2001).

Charitable Choice is specifically found in Section 104 of PRWORA. Bartkowski and Regis (1999, p. 8) completed an examination of the Charitable Choice policy and some of its legal terminology and concluded the following:

> As outlined in Section 104 of PRWORA, state governments that opt to contract with independent sector social service providers cannot legally exclude faith-based organizations from consideration simply because they are religious in nature. Consequently, the language of "choice" in this legislation is designed to underscore the importance to giving religious congregations the same opportunities that secular nonprofit agencies enjoy in competing for purchase-of-service contracts with state governments. Furthermore, Charitable Choice aims to ensure that state governments cannot censor religious expression—that is, religious symbols or practices—among faith-based organizations that are selected to provide state-funded social services.

Charitable Choice allows religious organizations to compete openly for providing services, yet if organizations that are federally funded can allow their religious beliefs to guide the types of services they provide, it is possible that discriminatory practices can be either intentionally or unintentionally propagated. For example, according to data from the Centers for Disease Control and Prevention (CDC; 2003), men who have sex with men (MSM) represent the largest exposure category of new HIV infections and AIDS diagnoses. As many as 23,153 males were infected with HIV or were diagnosed with AIDS in 2003; 68% of these infections were in males who reported having sexual contact with other men (63% were MSM; 5% represented MSM and injection drug users); and the highest rate of infection was among African Americans (50%), while Whites represented 32% and Hispanics 15% of all infections (CDC, 2003). In addition, while gay men continue to be at highest risk of infection, recent data suggest that infection rates among this population are increasing (Sternberg, 2003). From 2001 to 2002, HIV infections rose more than 7%, with an overall increase of almost 18% since 1999, when the number of infections among gay and bisexual men bottomed out at 6,561 of the 40,000 total HIV infections estimated annually (Sternberg, 2003). The 2003 CDC report *HIV/AIDS among Men Who Have Sex with Men* highlights this finding, thereby emphasizing the need for culturally diverse prevention and education services for these men. This increasing prevalence, coupled with the historic disparity of HIV/AIDS infection in gay men, presents significant considerations not only in the treatment of clients diagnosed with HIV/AIDS, but also in the prevention strategies aimed at lowering infection rates among the general population. In 2005, $15 billion in federal funds were allocated to the prevention and treatment of HIV/AIDS, and 25% of these funds were provided to sectarian organizations (Beamish, 2006). With such large funding allocations to religious organizations that are treating clients already infected, it is certain that gay men who are HIV-positive will need to access services that are provided by such religious organizations. In addition, it becomes necessary to examine the prevention strategies employed by these organizations and the implications these strategies have for gay men.

Religiosity as a Predictor of Homophobia

Religious association is a highly studied and sensitive independent variable related to homophobia (Berkman & Zinberg, 1997; Dennis, 2002; Douglas, Kalman, & Kalman, 1985; Ellis, Kitzinger, & Wilkinson, 2002; Finlay & Walther, 2003; Herek, 1988, 2000, 2002; Herek & Capitanio, 1995; Herek & Glunt, 1993; Hoffmann & Bakken, 2001; Lewis, 2003; Petersen & Donnenwerth, 1998; Plugge-Foust & Strickland, 2001; Wilson & Huff, 2001). Social science researchers have documented the strong positive correlation between religious associations with homophobia (Berkman & Zinberg, 1997; Dennis, 2002; Ellis et al., 2002; Finlay & Walther, 2003; Herek, 1988, 2000, 2002; Herek & Capitanio, 1995; Herek & Glunt, 1993; Lewis, 2003; Petersen & Donnenwerth, 1998; Plugge-Foust & Strickland, 2001; Wilson & Huff, 2001). This linkage, however, is multifaceted, taking into account varying denominations, religious sects, frequency of attendance at religious services, and other independent variables that help to determine overall religious association. Blackwell and Kiehl (in press), for example, failed to capture religious association as a causative factor of homophobia in nurses; the authors concluded that one potential reason for this was the vast difference between spiritual and religious beliefs.

Lewis (2003) compared religious association and differences in overall homophobia among Caucasians and African Americans and found that because African Americans were substantially more religious than Caucasians, the levels of homophobia also were higher.

In addition, heterosexuals that self-identify with a fundamentalist religious denomination typically manifest higher levels of sexual prejudice than do nonreligious and members of liberal denominations (Herek, 2000; Herek & Glunt, 1993). Religious conservatism and liberalism also play a significant role in varying support for gay rights: Jews were the most accepting and born-again Protestants the most disapproving of homosexuality (Lewis, 2003).

This difference in homophobia between conservative and liberal denominations is reflected in the Attitudes toward Lesbians and Gay Men scale (Herek, 1988). Similarly, research utilizing other measurement scales of homophobia, such as the Homophobia Scale (H-Scale), also correlated differences in homophobia among religious denominations (Finlay & Walther, 2003). On this measurement scale conservative Protestants have the highest score, followed by moderate Protestants and Catholics.

There is also a positive correlation between support of lesbian and gay human rights and conservative religious sects (Ellis et al., 2002; Petersen & Donnenwerth, 1998). As measured by the Differential Loneliness Scale, as irrational thought processes increase, so does homophobia. In addition, irrational thought processes tend to be higher among individuals who are Catholic and Protestant. This leads to greater levels of homophobia as measured by the H-Scale in these traditionally classified conservative denominations (Plugge-Foust & Strickland, 2001).

Intensity of religious feeling, frequency of religious service attendance, frequency of prayer, and importance of religion in participants' lives are also highly correlated with homophobia (Berkman & Zinberg, 1997; Herek, 2000; Lewis, 2003). Heterosexuals who rate religion as "very important" are more homophobic than those who rate religion as "somewhat" to "not at all important" (Herek, 2002). Even in disciplines such as social work, where there is great respect for diversity, homophobia tends to be greater among social workers who believe that religion is an extremely important aspect of their lives (Berkman & Zinberg, 1997).

Heterosexuals who attend religious services weekly or more often have higher levels of homophobia than those who attended religious services less frequently (Herek, 2002; Herek & Capitanio, 1995). Specific religious beliefs are also associated with homophobia. Individuals who believe in an active Satan have higher levels of homophobia and have significantly greater intolerance toward gay men and lesbians than those who don't believe in an active Satan (Wilson & Huff, 2001).

For the most part, it appears that liberal Protestants and individuals not affiliated with a religion have significantly lower homophobia scores (Finlay & Walther, 2003). Those least homophobic appear to be individuals who do not self-identify as Christian (Finlay & Walther, 2003).

Although there is a strong religious-associated correlation with homophobia, there does not appear to be a strong correlation between religiosity and gay or lesbian colonization (Dennis, 2002). Thus, regions of the country that have high populations of religious practitioners do not necessarily have smaller populations of gay and lesbian residents (Dennis, 2002). Because religious factors appear to have strong influences in the development of homophobia, gay, lesbian, bisexual, and transgender (GLBT) organizations such as the Human Rights Campaign and the National Gay and Lesbian Taskforce have voiced serious concern about receiving social services through religious organizations (Blackwell & Dziegielewski, 2005).

Practices That Could Lead to Discrimination and Limited Treatment Strategy Related to Substandard Care

A comprehensive report authored by Cahill and Jones (2002) outlined multiple discriminatory and homophobic issues GLBT persons might encounter when seeking social services from faith-based organizations. Among these are proselytizing, direct discrimination and homophobic treatment, lack of access to services, and legislative loopholes that could permit sectarian organizations to exist without proper regulatory response, resulting in substandard care (Cahill & Jones, 2002).

In addition, social scientists have suggested that religious-based homophobia has been coupled with HIV/AIDS prevention efforts since the emergence of the pandemic in the United States in the early 1980s (Lugg, 1998). Lugg found in her literature review that homosexuality was explicitly and repetitiously linked with the ghastly and terminal course of the disease among religious leaders such as Jerry Falwell, Pat Robertson, and Lou Sheldon. The potential impacts of religious organizations in the treatment and prevention of HIV/AIDS among gay males are numerous, including negative and discriminatory aspects of abstinence-only prevention programs, access to care issues, and aversion to religious service providers.

Negative and Discriminatory Aspects of Abstinence-Only Prevention Programs to Gay Men

One of the greatest discriminatory practices is the emphasis on abstinence-only prevention programs that fail to address adult sexuality among gay males. Most professionals agree that human sexuality is a natural and normal part of adult development. Therefore, when working to limit the spread of HIV infection, abstinence, marriage, and the use of condoms are often considered the cornerstones of this type of treatment approach. From this perspective it makes sense that religious-based HIV prevention programs are more likely to promote abstinence-only strategies, and such programs have proliferated under the Bush administration (Rose, 2005). The abstinence-only prevention programs tend to concentrate on stopping sexual intercourse from occurring (Rose, 2005) outside of the context of a loving, stable, and long-term relationship, usually defined as marriage. When using this approach as the foundation of treatment, the focus on marriage as a central aspect of sexual relationships excludes gay men and lesbians, largely due to inequality in marriage policies across the United States and in various religious-based doctrines and practices. The Catholic Church's condemnation of homosexuality, coupled with its ban on the use of condoms and insistence on abstinence, has made it almost "impossible for the Catholic Church to work effectively to suppress the spread of HIV" (Brooks, Etzel, Hinojos, Henry, & Perez, 2005, p. 740).

Brooks et al. (2005) suggest potential areas of discrimination with service provision by primarily African American churches. Often, Black clergy refuse to discuss sexual issues, particularly those behaviors associated with transmission of the virus (anal sex, bisexuality, and homosexuality), and this lack of attention could inadvertently lead to its spread. If sexuality is limited to marriage and gay males cannot marry, this sets up a situation where gay men and women are being told that their desire for human sexual contact is simply not allowed. Although some states allow some of the rights and privileges of marriage through state domestic partner policies and registries, more than 30 states define marriage strictly as between a man and a woman (Meacham et al., 2002); as a result, gay people are marginalized by the invalidity of their relationships.

Researchers have found that the denial and ignorance of sexual relationships and activities between men who have sex with men is largely responsible for the failure of HIV prevention efforts on a global scale (Parker, Khan, & Aggleton, 1998). Researchers assessing prevention efforts in sub-Saharan Africa have discovered an almost complete absence of community-based prevention efforts specifically targeting gay males (Parker et al., 1998). This problem has also been found in many parts of South and Southeast Asia, where HIV infection rates have continued to rise, especially in China, where HIV/AIDS is an emerging epidemic (Giovanna-Merli, Hertog, Wang, & Li, 2006; Parker et al., 1998). India's outreach and prevention efforts have also been deemed largely ineffectual due to a lack of concentration on efforts geared at teaching safe sex practices among MSM (Parker et al., 1998).

Because MSM continue to represent the largest risk group for HIV infection and AIDS diagnoses (CDC, 2003), ignoring this population might actually increase their infection rates as a result of inadequate training and education regarding safe sexual practices, condom use, and avoidance of high-risk behaviors and what constitutes such behaviors. Parker et al. (1998, p. 342) conclude:

> Conspicuous by their absence, the widespread denial of the needs of men who have sex with men in the developing world is another example of the long record of neglect that should bring shame not only to governmental agencies and donors, but to all of us who work not only for an end to the epidemic, but also for a more just and tolerant world.

In addition to the denial of gay sexual relationships perpetuated by abstinence-only prevention programs, abstinence-only interventions are not supported in the literature as effective in stopping the spread of HIV infection longitudinally (Rose, 2005). Religious-based interventions may also be detrimental to the psychosocial well-being of HIV+ individuals. Research conducted by Jenkins (1995, p. 132) found that many seropositive individuals "feel estranged from organized religion because of doctrines that seem unsympathetic and or punitive toward HIV and those who carry the virus." Research suggests that behavior modification and proper training in the correct use and distribution of condoms and the avoidance of high-risk sexual practices are much more effective at reducing the spread of HIV and increasing safer sex, especially among gay males and subsets of gay males (Parker et al., 1998; Ross, Henry, Freeman, Caughy, & Dawson, 2004; Veerman, Tatsa, Druzin, & Weinstein, 1999).

Research has failed to demonstrate the long-term effectiveness of abstinence-only prevention programs (Rose, 2005). Coupled with this lack of evidence, as previously discussed abstinence-only programs tend to marginalize gay men through invalidation of their relationships largely by ignoring behaviors between MSM altogether. Data assert that the most successful interventions aimed at combating the spread of HIV are those that are culturally specific for the individual and those that address disempowering forces in people's lives (Marin, 2003). The emphasis of safer sex practices is seen as an essential component of educational interventions aimed at reducing the transmission of HIV; the most effective and reliable method to reduce HIV infection risk is condom use (Lam, Mak, Lindsay, & Russell, 2004).

A recent increase in the sexual practice known as barebacking (insertive anal intercourse without the use of condoms) among MSM has been seen as a surfacing public health hazard (Wolitski, 2005). Six etiologies for the increase in this unsafe practice have been proposed: (1) improvements in HIV treatment, (2) more complex sexual decision making, (3) the Internet as a means of meeting sexual partners, (4) substance use, (5) safer sex fatigue, and (6) changes in HIV prevention programs (Wolitski, 2005). These etiologies are perhaps interrelated: Improvements in HIV treatment could be leading to fatigue of safer sex as gay men may no longer perceive HIV as a terminal disease, and access to sexual partners who mutually use substances during sexual intercourse could be easier because of increased Internet use to find compatible sexual partners.

Ross et al. (2004) found three environmental variables predictive of safer sex practices among MSM: (1) perceived gay/bisexual men's norms toward condom use, (2) availability of HIV prevention messages, and (3) what one's religion says about gay sex. These findings have major suggestive implications for public prevention policy. Beyond these three predictors, research suggests that lack of consistent use of condoms among a subset of Latino MSM was related to adventurism and impulsivity (Carballo-Dieguez et al., 2005). These findings suggest that educational interventions that empower MSM to identify adventurous and impulsive emotions, partnered with strategic methods to critically think through such situations, may increase the use of condoms during intercourse.

Implications of Access to Care and Aversion to Sectarian Providers among Gay Men

If an HIV+ gay man refuses treatment from a religious-based service provider, serious access to care issues can arise. Charitable Choice legislation contains an alternative provision that requires federal, state, or local governments to ensure that alternative secular programs be available to serve clients who object to receiving services from a religious social service provider (Cahill & Jones, 2002; Glennon, 2000).

However, specifics on how this is accomplished limit this mandate. For example, the regulations, although requiring an alternative service provider, limit choice as they do not provide funding for the nonreligious provider when a religious provider is already available.

In addition, such regulations may be impossible to implement due to distance from such providers and time constraints of devising and organizing such alternatives when they do not already exist (Cahill & Jones, 2002; Davis, 1996). An example might be an AIDS patient living in a rural area who depends on a government-sponsored food pantry to provide sustenance. If the only government-contracted provider is a sectarian one, the client may refuse care because a public service provider not associated with religion is not available. Or, due to loopholes in the legislation designed to maintain the religious identity and integrity of the service provider (Cahill & Jones, 2002), the client may be subjected to homophobic and discriminatory treatment as a result of the religion's condemnation of homosexuality.

While sectarian service providers may cause serious access-to-care issues, the aversion of homosexuals to religion and religious organizations and, subsequently, religious service providers, could also cause HIV+/AIDS clients who are gay men to not seek needed treatments, which may cause an increase in the morbidity and mortality of this population.

As discussed, ever since the dawn of the HIV/AIDS crisis, some religious leaders have claimed that the virus was a punishment handed down from God of those who are sinners or live in "perversity" (Lugg, 1998; Stone, 1999, p. 16).

Although there are few studies regarding the attitudes of gay men toward religion, it could be postulated that gay men are less attracted to Christianity or Islam as a result of their traditional stance against same-sex relationships. The decreased likelihood of gay men to be supportive of religion could pose a severe obstruction to the delivery of services by religious entities to HIV+ gay men or those living with AIDS. Knowing that MSM continue to contribute to the majority of HIV infections and AIDS diagnoses in the United States (CDC, 2003), forcing them to receive care from religious organizations might lead to an even greater disparity in the morbidity and mortality rates endured by this client base.

IMPLICATIONS FOR FURTHER RESEARCH AND POLICY DEVELOPMENT

Exploration of the effects of religious social service providers on HIV treatment and prevention in the gay male population is in its infancy. Data in this area need to be augmented greatly to help meet public health demands and ensure optimal care delivery for those gay men who are HIV+ or suffering with AIDS. Future critical inquiry should assess the role of religion in the life of gay men inflicted with HIV/AIDS and should also qualitatively examine the reactions of persons who have received care from such organizations. This information can then be clearly related to the policy developed and implemented.

In addition, research needs to continue to evolve to discover the best ways to prevent the spread of HIV among MSM. Perhaps of utmost importance, however, is the need for evidence-based policies in the treatment and prevention of the infection. Because sectarian organizations are expected to continue to play a pivotal role in treating and helping to prevent HIV/AIDS, policy makers must closely examine social science research about the pandemic. It is crucial to make informed decisions about policy so that evidence-based treatment strategies are at the root of all decisions. Exploration of how to best stop infection and optimal treatment strategies for those already infected make the best use of allocated funds. Nurses, social workers, public administrators, and all those involved as stakeholders in preventing and treating HIV/AIDS in gay men must play the role of advocate to ensure social justice and equity principles in health care and social service delivery.

Funding in this area is so important, but it is critical that we openly discuss the potential for discriminatory practices that could be encountered by gay men during the prevention and provision of care of HIV/AIDS by religious organizations. Increased homophobia among individuals with strong religiosity was discussed; the focus on abstinence-only prevention strategies and their neglect in addressing sexual relationships between gay men was scrutinized; and possible access-to-care issues associated with gay men's aversion to religious-based interventions were explored. HIV/AIDS is a very real pandemic that continues to threaten the health of the gay male population. Perhaps with future research directives and scholarly inquiry, policy makers can promote an evidence-based approach that can turn the tide and clearly address issues such as disparity, discrimination, and homophobia.

REFERENCES

Bartkowski, J. P., & Regis, H. A. (1999, November). *Religious organizations, anti-poverty, relief, and Charitable Choice: A feasibility study of the faith-based welfare reform in Mississippi.* Arlington, VA: PricewaterhouseCoopers.

Beamish, R. (2006). *Religious groups get chunk of AIDS money.* Retrieved January 30, 2006, from http://news.yahoo.com/s/ap/20060129/ap_on_he_me/aids_prevention.

Berkman, C. S., & Zinberg, G. (1997). Homophobia and heterosexism in social workers. *Social Work, 42*(4), 319–332.

Blackwell, C., & Dziegielewski, S. (2005). The privatization of social services from public to sectarian: Negative consequences for America's gays and lesbians. *Journal of Human Behavior in the Social Environment, 11*(2), 25–43.

Blackwell, C., & Kiehl, E. (in press). Homophobia in registered nurses: Impact on youth. *Journal of Gay and Lesbian Issues in Education.*

Brooks, R., Etzel, M., Hinojos, E., Henry, C., & Perez, M. (2005). Preventing HIV among Latino and African American gay and bisexual men in a context of HIV-related stigma, discrimination, and homophobia: Perspectives of providers. *AIDS Patient Care and STDs, 19,* 737–744.

Cahill, S., & Jones, K. T. (2002). *Leaving our children behind: Welfare reform and the gay, lesbian, bisexual, and transgender community.* Washington, DC: Policy Institute of the National Gay and Lesbian Task Force.

Carballo-Dieguez, A., Dolezal, C., Leu, C., Nieves, L., Diaz, F., Decena, C., et al. (2005). A randomized controlled trial to test an HIV-prevention intervention for Latino gay and bisexual men: Lessons learned. *AIDS Care, 17*(3), 314–328.

Centers for Disease Control and Prevention. (2003). *CDC HIV/AIDS fact sheet: HIV/AIDS among men who have sex with men.* Retrieved January 31, 2006, from www.cdc.gov/hiv/pubs/facts/msm.htm.

Cnaan, R. A., & Bodie, S. C. (2002). Charitable Choice and faith-based welfare: A call for social work. *Social Work, 47*(3), 224–235.

Davis, D. H. (1996). The church-state implications of the new welfare reform law. *Journal of Church and State, 38*(4), 719–731.

Dennis, J. P. (2002). Lying with man as with woman: Rethinking the impact of religious discourse on gay community strength. *Journal of Homosexuality, 44*(1), 43–60.

Douglas, C. J., Kalman, C. M., & Kalman, T. P. (1985). Homophobia among physicians and nurses: An empirical study. *Hospital and Community Psychiatry, 36*(12), 1309–1311.

Ellis, S. J., Kitzinger, C., & Wilkinson, S. (2002). Attitudes towards lesbians and gay men and support for human rights among psychology students. *Journal of Homosexuality, 44*(1), 121–138.

Finlay, B., & Walther, C. (2003). The relation of religious affiliation, service attendance, and other factors to homophobic attitudes among university students. *Review of Religious Research, 44*(4), 370–393.

Giovanna-Merli, M., Hertog, S., Wang, B., & Li, J. (2006). Modeling the spread of HIV/AIDS in China: The role of sexual transmission. *Population Studies, 60*(1), 22–43.

Glennon, F. (2000). Blessed be the ties that bind? The challenge of Charitable Choice to moral obligation. *Journal of Church and State, 42*(4), 825–843.

Herek, G. M. (1988). Heterosexuals' attitudes toward lesbians and gay men: A review of empirical research with the ATLG scale. *Journal of Sex Research, 25,* 451–477.

Herek, G. M. (2000). The psychology of sexual prejudice. *Current Directions in Psychological Science, 9*(1), 19–22.

Herek, G. M. (2002). Heterosexuals' attitudes toward bisexual men and women in the United States. *Journal of Sex Research, 29*(4), 264–274.

Herek, G. M., & Capitanio, J. P. (1995). Black heterosexuals' attitudes toward lesbians and gay men in the United States. *Journal of Sex Research*, *32*(2), 95–105.

Herek, G. M., & Glunt, E. K. (1993). Interpersonal contact and heterosexuals' attitudes toward gay men: Results form a national survey. *Journal of Sex Research*, *30*(3), 239–244.

Hoffman, A., & Bakken, L. (2001). Are educational and life experiences related to homophobia? *Educational Research Quarterly*, *24*(4), 67–82.

Jean, L. L. (2002). Preface. In S. Cahill, (Ed.), *Leaving our children behind: Welfare reform and the gay, lesbian, bisexual, and transgender community* (Sec. 1). Retrieved November 7, 2003, from www.ngltf.org/downloads/WelfRef.pdf.

Jenkins, R. (1995). Religion and HIV: Implications for research and intervention. *Journal of Social Issues*, *51*(2), 131–144.

Kennedy, S. S., & Bielefeld, W. (2002). Government shekels without government shackles? The administrative challenges of Charitable Choice. *Public Administration Review*, *62*(1), 4–11.

Knippenberg, J. M. (2003). The constitutional politics of Charitable Choice. *Society*, *40*(2), 37–47.

Lam, A., Mak, A., Lindsay, P., & Russell, S. (2004). What really works? Exploratory study of condom negotiation strategies. *AIDS Education and Prevention*, *162*(2), 160–171.

Lewis, G. B. (2003). Black-White differences in attitudes toward homosexuality and gay rights. *Public Opinion Quarterly*, *67*, 89–78.

Lieberman, J. I., & Cummings, E. E. (2002). *Charitable Choice: Overview of research findings on implementation* (GAO-02-337). Washington, DC: U.S. Government Printing Office.

Lugg, C. (1998). The religious right and public education: The paranoid politics of homophobia. *Educational Policy*, *12*(3), 267–283.

Marin, B. (2003). HIV prevention in the Hispanic community: sex, culture, and empowerment. *Journal of Transcultural Nursing*, *14*(3), 186–192.

Meacham, J., Scelfo, J., France, D., Underwood, A., Amfitheatrof, E., Blair, R., et al. (2002). Celibacy and marriage. *Newsweek*, *139*(18), 28–29.

Parker, R., Khan, S., & Aggleton, P. (1998). Conspicuous by their absence? Men who have sex with men (MSM) in developing countries: Implications for HIV prevention. *Critical Public Health*, *8*(4), 329–346.

Personal Responsibility and Work Opportunity Reconciliation Act of 1996, Pub. L. 104-193, 110 stat, 2105.

Petersen, L. R., & Donnenwerth, G. V. (1998). Religion and declining support for traditional beliefs about gender roles and homosexual rights. *Sociology of Religion*, *59*(4), 353–371.

Plugge-Foust, C., & Strickland, G. (2001). Homophobia, irrationality, and Christian ideology: Does a relationship exist? *Journal of Sex Education and Therapy*, *25*(4), 240–244.

Rose, S. (2005). Going too far? Sin and social policy. *Social Forces*, *84*(2), 1207–1232.

Ross, M., Henry, D., Freeman, A., Caughy, M., & Dawson, A. (2004). Environmental influences on safer sex in young gay men: A situational presentation approach to measuring influences on sexual health. *Archives of Social Behavior*, *33*(3), 249–257.

Rostow, A. (2003, November 5). *"Faith-based" discrimination suit settled.* Retrieved November 5, 2003, from www.planetout.com/news/article.html?2003/11/05/4/.

Sternberg, S. (2003). *HIV infection rates rising among gay, bisexual men.* Retrieved January 31, 2006, from www.usatoday.com/news/health/2003–07-28-hiv-rate_x.htm.

Stone, K. (1999). Safer texts: Reading biblical lament in the age of AIDS. *Theology and Sexuality*, *10*, 16–27.

Veerman, P., Tatsa, G., Druzin, P., & Weinstein, R. (1999). HIV prevention, children's rights, and homosexual youth. *International Journal of Children's Rights*, *7*, 83–89.

Wilson, K. M., & Huff, J. L. (2001). Scaling Satan. *Journal of Psychology, 135*(3), 292–300.

Wolitski, R. (2005). The emergence of barebacking among gay and bisexual men in the United States: A public health perspective. *Journal of Gay and Lesbian Psychotherapy, 9*(3/4), 9–34.

Yang, C. (2001, July 10). *No deal: White House rejects Salvation Army request to protect anti-gay hiring policy.* Retrieved November 10, 2003, from http://abcnews.go.com/sections/politics/DailyNews/Bush_Salvation010710.html.

Section IV

POLICY FORMULATION AND POSSIBILITIES

The concluding section of this volume addresses creation of policy in a socially, politically, and economically sensitive global environment. Added to this confluence of interrelated elements are the influences of the changing technological world. Somehow within this mix justice-based policies that help move our local, national, and global communities must emerge.

Richard Hoefer, PhD, editor of the *Journal of Policy and Policy Practice*, provides a comprehensive overview of the policy-making process. His discussion, framed by a policy advocacy model, includes possible avenues that social workers can adopt as they look to influence the formation of policy. Dr. Hoefer recognizes that the connections between social welfare policy and the political world are not always well explained or understood. He underscores this observation by exploring the spectrum of political ideologies and then moves into a discussion of politics as process.

Dr. Howard Karger is a nationally recognized expert in public policy analysis, in particular regarding services, or lack thereof, for the poor. He is joined by Peter Kindle, a theologian and social worker, in a critically significant discussion of economics and welfare in a global context. Their premise is that the current welfare state is a relic of the long gone industrial era. Emphasizing three levels of the labor market—primary, secondary, and tertiary—they recommend a new welfare agenda built on policy initiatives reflecting the changing economic landscape of postindustrial America.

The use of technology such as computers, e-mail, access to databases, a variety of software packages, and information available on the World Wide Web are recent phenomena and essentially still in their infancy stage. In a short period of time, about 20 years, technology and its availability to the public has changed how we think and act. Paul Raffoul, PhD, offers critical insight not only into the current technological age but moves us forward into the digital era. He assesses globalization and our ever more penetrable geographic borders, matters related to empowerment, and privacy. Dr. Raffoul cautions us to critically examine the web-based data—just because it's on the Web does not mean it is valid and reliable. Finally, Dr. Raffoul looks to the future and envisions how social justice will be strengthened through technology.

The final chapter in this section centers our attention on welfare reform. Elizabeth Segal, PhD, is well known for her work in this area. Reviewing the history of traditional welfare, in particular for the poor, Dr. Segal advances the concept of "social empathy," which she describes as having insight into other people's lives and realities. Social empathy, according to Segal, results in programs, services, and policies that represent social justice.

Chapter 17

SOCIAL WELFARE POLICY AND POLITICS

Richard Hoefer

The statement "Policy affects practice and practice affects policy" helps educate and remind social workers of the dual role they play: as *practitioners,* working with individuals, groups, organizations, and communities to improve currently occurring difficulties, and as *advocates,* working through political means to alter or remove the causes of current problems. Working both in the present and for the future places social workers in a unique position.

Still, the connections between social policy and the political world are not always well explained or understood. This chapter, after defining important terms, presents a range of political philosophies and shows how their adherents operationalize their view of the "ideal" social policy. A brief description of the process of politics, advocacy, is also provided in the context of the generalist model of social work practice. By showing the range of desired social policies, depending on the philosophy used for justification, it is hoped that readers will see more clearly the need to choose elected officials whose views are in accord with their own and the social work profession's. In this way, the political process of advocacy can be easier. Not having to convince someone with a very different view of what is good and proper in the arena of social policy means that efforts can be made to improve and expand programs rather than to defend what already exists.

DEFINING SOCIAL WELFARE POLICY

Although we might like to have one widely accepted definition of this key term, DiNitto (2007, p. 3) correctly points out that "lengthy discussions of the definition of social welfare policy are unnecessary, often futile, and even exasperating." Despite ambiguity, some parameters are generally accepted and are accepted here. First, social welfare policy relates to enhancing the quality of life of individuals, sometimes acting through groups or communities to do so. Second, social welfare policy can be made by either governmental or private organizations, and it is created by both action and lack of action on the part of decision makers. Finally, social welfare policy is the outcome of a process involving politics.

DEFINING POLITICS

Discussions and definitions of the term "politics" extend far back in time and are used to denote two separate concepts. The first use of the term "politics" is to describe a set of beliefs, as a loose synonym for ideology. The second use describes a process of decision making.

Politics as Ideology

The question "What are your politics?" is clearly understood as a question regarding one's viewpoints, not how one believes policies should be created. It is in this sense that politics and social policy are closely intertwined: The political views controlling a decision-making body determine the social policies that emerge. Political views can be described as falling on a continuum from right (conservative) to left (socialist) and are more or less systematically set forth by political parties. These views and their implications for social policy are described later in this chapter.

Politics as Process

Describing politics as a process has a very long history. Aristotle (2007), who lived in the fourth century BC, wrote, "Man is by nature a political animal." He believed that people naturally congregate and interact with one another. This implies that processes for settling disagreements must be developed. Harold Lasswell (1990, p. 4), an American political scientist, defines politics as the process to decide "who gets what, when and how." Politics, in this view, is a tool much like any tool: It can be used for creative or destructive purposes. It is therefore incumbent upon social workers to understand the ins and outs of the use of this tool so that they can apply it with skill to achieve policy ends in line with their own and the profession's values.

POLITICS AS IDEOLOGIES: ACROSS THE SPECTRUM OF RIGHT AND LEFT

To show the impact of politics as ideology on social policy, this section examines a number of political philosophies and their associated political parties. Each is described, and then the implications of this viewpoint for social policy are discussed.

Ideology usually is described as moving from right to left, a by-product of French prerevolutionary governance, when supporters of the king sat on his right and those desiring change sat on his left. Several other elements besides the desire for change are embedded in the political continuum, however. Baradat (2005) notes that the desire for change helps us differentiate ideologies but that we must also examine the depth of the change desired, the speed of change desired, and the methods to be used to create the change desired to fully describe what makes one ideology different from another. In addition, it is vital to know the values and motivations behind the desire for change in order to fully describe a political view.

The spectrum of views acceptable in a state or country varies tremendously. Some countries have the full or nearly full spectrum represented in their political system, whereas other countries have an extremely truncated spectrum. What is considered far left in one country may be considered middle of the road or even on the right in another country. Some countries may allow only one official political viewpoint. Even within such a uniparty system, however, different factions develop along the lines of how much (if any) change is wanted, how quickly to make changes, and so forth.

Critics of the American political system, for example, argue that there is little true difference between Democrats and Republicans, particularly in an international context. Hard-core American Republicans and Democrats, however, see very large differences between (and even within) their parties. The political spectrum delimited here is purposely wider than what one finds in mainstream American politics and may also be broader than that found in many other countries.

Libertarianism (Neoconservatism)

Description

The key principle for Libertarians is freedom in both social and economic spheres. Libertarians thus desire considerable change from the status quo, seeking to rein in governmental excesses such as high taxes and social programs but also to keep government from interfering in personal matters such as obtaining an abortion or marrying someone of the same sex. By working through the electoral system, Libertarians are willing to endure a slow pace of change, but the amount of change desired is considerable.

Policy Implications

"Libertarians propose to do away with large portions of government" (Murray, 1997, p. 47). This involves eliminating social programs for the poor, the aged, the ill, and almost all other groups. Because taxes would be slashed as an unjustified intrusion into people's lives and livelihoods, little money would be available to pay for social programs in any case. Still, the argument against social programs is based on principled, not pragmatic, considerations. According to this view, social problems are created or exacerbated by government subsidization and protection (Kristol, 2004; Murray, 1997). Libertarians argue that the welfare system, for example, creates problems by allowing people who make poor life choices to remain relatively unaffected by their bad decisions and thus shifts costs from the individual to society. This can only be paid for by taxes taken from people who make better choices and punishes those living "by the rules." Entitlements for benefits would be eliminated: "The general rule has to be: if it is your own behavior that could land you on welfare, then you don't get it, or you get very little of it" (Kristol, 2004, p. 148).

Because an unregulated market allows the most freedom of choice, the principle at work in social welfare policy should be "Let people shop for what they want and pay for what they get" (Murray, 1997, p. 93). Organizations that offer education or health care would compete on both price and service, much as organizations that offer computers or other products do now.

Social problems can be reduced by decriminalizing activities such as alcohol and drug use, pornography, and prostitution. People would still be required to act responsibly, and if they do not, their irresponsible crimes would be punished, but not the use of alcohol or other drugs, the viewing of pornography, or the selling of sex, in and of themselves.

Conservatism

Description

Conservative parties exist in many countries and often have the word conservative in their party name (the United Kingdom, Australia, and Sweden, for example). In the United

States, the Republican Party advances Conservative positions. As the name implies, Conservatives wish to "conserve" what they see as the best policies from the nation's traditions and to rely on a laissez-faire economy. Conservatives advocate for a limited government role in the economy (thus championing the primacy of the market in deciding the distribution of goods and income), low taxes, and little government interference in individual behavior (though some strands of Conservative thought desire government action regarding issues of morality). Conservatives tend to be pessimistic regarding human nature and improvements to the social system, thus they do not expect government action to fix problems. Additional elements of Conservative thought are the importance of property rights and a tendency toward elitism, where "the people" are not fully trustworthy to control the country's fate. This philosophy accepts the need for individuals to have access to social welfare services. Believing that the best government is the government that governs least, however, Conservatives push for assistance to the poor to come from family members and nongovernmental organizations, particularly nonprofits with a faith basis (Olasky, 2000). Decreased regulation of business and a willingness to contract with private organizations to provide services formerly provided by government agencies are additional Conservative positions.

Conservative parties work through parliamentary or democratic methods. Some argue that people of Conservative ideology hold the reins of power through their wealth, social connections, and control of the military-industrial complex (see, e.g., Mills, 1956). Wielding power by controlling what emerges on the governmental decision-making agenda (Bachrach & Baratz, 1962), Conservatives have little to fear from other philosophies, at least in the United States. Conservative forces frequently used violence and threats of violence in the past to thwart unionizing and other left-wing causes, and this use of force continues in some places.

Policy Implications

Conservatives believe that

> the traditional values of hard work, ambition, and self-reliance will lead to individual and family well-being.... Their goal is equity. That is, if everyone is provided with an equal opportunity to compete, conservatives want to minimize policies that are designed to shape the final result. (Dolgoff & Feldstein, 2007, p. 113)

This is not to say that Conservatives are all of one mind in terms of their social agenda. Some who are Conservative on the economic front by wanting to limit government involvement in regulating the economy are also "traditional" Conservatives regarding interference with individual liberty. In other words, they do not advocate for government intervention on behalf of any religious or philosophical view to tell individuals what they can and cannot do. This type of Conservative is close to being a Libertarian. Others, sometimes called cultural Conservatives, who consider themselves strictly Conservative in their economic views, are eager to use government coercion to uphold their religious viewpoints regarding abortion, marriage, sex, and other issues of morality.

Some of the specific policies advocated by Conservative parties are tax cuts for the wealthy, thus reducing government funds for human services; decreased government support for human service programs; and a stronger emphasis and reliance on private organizations (nonprofit and for-profit) to actually provide services to clients. Some Conservatives argue for ending any right to an abortion and for maintaining or strengthening discrimination against sexual minorities.

Religiously affiliated nonprofits have become more important elements of social service provision in recent years, as President George W. Bush's administration specifically allocated money to assist faith-based organizations to receive government funding for the provision of services.

Centrism

Description

Centrists are generally not too upset by the status quo, nor are they unwilling to see opportunities for positive change. By definition, they adopt positions that are between the more extreme views on the right (Libertarian and Conservative) and the left (Liberal and Socialist). They work within the system and tend to be pragmatic (rather than strictly ideological) in terms of proposing possible changes. Slightly adjusting policies in an incremental way to make them better achieve their goals is part of the Centrist perspective. Center parties have established themselves in Nordic countries (Sweden, Finland, and Norway all have a Center Party, for example). In these countries, the Center parties support decentralization of power, small business, pro-environmental policies, and a wary attitude toward the European Union (Wikipedia, 2007a). The flavor of the Swedish Center Party's approach to welfare is found on their website:

> Welfare payments should provide economic security for those who have never been part of the labor market. . . . Welfare should be a safety net which supports these individuals so that their livelihood can be secured. The goal for the individual and society is naturally to move away from dependence on welfare and to become self-supporting through work. It has been shown that it is difficult for people on welfare to enter the labor market. The Center Party wants to make this process easier. Society gains more if people in their working years are involved and complete work duties, pay taxes, and contribute with their knowledge. For the individual it is perhaps even more important. It is not a workable solution to pay people not to work. . . . Therefore, everyone must be encouraged to try to be a part of the labor market. (Centerpartiet, 2007)

An American example of Centrism emerged in the early part of the twenty-first century. Noting the arrival of the Information Age, Halstead and Lind (2001) advocated a new movement, dubbed "radical centrism." It is based on four principles:

- Increasing the amount of choice available to individual citizens.
- Holding citizens to a higher personal standard of self-sufficiency.
- Providing a true safety net model of economic security for citizens.
- Allowing federal jurisdiction to take over from state and local government when the outcome is expanding individual freedoms and choices. (pp. 19–23)

Defined by the amount of change desired and the speed at which they would like to see the change occur, Hallstead and Lind's Centrism does fit the idea of radical. But because they espouse ideas that tend to be between the far right and far left, they are also Centrists.

Policy Implications

Centrist social policy is essentially a point between trusting the common person to do the right thing, given the chance (Liberalism), and not trusting the common person's integrity and desire to work (Conservatism). Centrists thus believe that people want to be responsible but may need encouragement and role modeling to know how to be self-sufficient in a market economy. Services should be available to those who are not able to work, but everyone else should be in the labor force, both for their own good and for the good of society.

Specific policies put forth by Sweden's Center Party are:

- To make it pay to move from welfare to work. This makes the individual even more motivated to look for work.
- To help the person on welfare back to self-sufficiency, through, for example, rehabilitation, education, or seeking a new job.
- To make special efforts with youth and immigrants (the most at-risk groups) so that they can go from welfare dependence to self-sufficiency (Centerpartiet, 2007).

Halstead and Lind (2001) argue that their four principles are more in line with the realities of the twenty-first-century Information Age than are other ideologies and associated political parties. They advocate the following policies:

- Mandatory private health-care system for all Americans that would ensure that the poorest and least healthy are fully covered.
- Progressive privatization of Social Security, based on mandatory retirement savings for all workers.
- Broadened ownership of financial capital so that all Americans can benefit directly from our growing economy.

Liberalism

Description

"Optimism about people's ability to solve their problems is the keynote of liberalism" (Baradat, 2005, p. 27). This relates to the enshrinement of human intellect that emerged during the Enlightenment. Because people are so capable, the reasoning goes, they should be able to assess problems, figure out solutions, and implement their ideas. New ideas have merit and are useful in improving the world. Liberals tend to believe in the importance of achieving equality of opportunity, as well as making strides with government policy to mitigate the excesses of the market because the free market creates high levels of inequality, discrimination, and injury to dispossessed populations.

Modern Liberalism is based on dissatisfaction with the state of the world, a belief in the perfectability of society, optimism, and a willingness to work through the system to achieve its goals. Liberals wish change to be thorough and relatively rapid. In the American system, the Democratic Party is considered liberal.

Policy Implications

Liberal policy positions are in favor of government intervention in the market to improve society and protect human rights (as opposed to property rights), egalitarianism (as opposed to elitism), and personal liberty (as opposed to government intervention into private behavior; Baradat, 2005).

A few examples of specific social policies supported by Liberals are greater equality between racial and ethnic groups, as well as between men and women; livable minimum wage levels; provision of adequate levels of medical care, housing, and nutritious food to all; and sufficient regulation of business to ensure safety in food, medicine, and other products.

Social Democracy

Description

Social Democracy is a view espoused by political parties around the globe (e.g., Australia's, New Zealand's, and the United Kingdom's Labour Parties, and Germany's, Norway's, and Sweden's Social Democratic Parties), although no major party in the United States fits into this category. Social Democracy originally was a strongly Socialist philosophy; now the mainstream of many Social Democratic parties has moved to the right, taking on the title of the "Third Way," a system between pure capitalism and pure Socialism, although still more Socialist than capitalist or Conservative. A common thread for all Social Democratic parties is repugnance concerning the excesses of capitalism, particularly inequality, poverty, oppression of various groups, and strong individualism that negates the importance of solidarity among people and groups.

Policy Implications

Social policy under Social Democrats follows what has been called an "institutional model" in which receipt of social services is considered a normal part of life, so government provides them. While financial realities may prevent governments from providing all services that are desired, the number and scope of services are considerable and reach "from cradle to grave."

Modern Social Democracy takes on a variety of positions, but many national Social Democratic parties belong to the organization Socialist International, which defines Social Democracy as an ideal form of democracy that can overcome the problems inherent in unregulated capitalism (Wikipedia, 2007b). Among other common policies, most Social Democrats support:

- A mixed economy rather than either a totally free market or a fully planned economy.
- Extensive provisions for social security, social insurance, and income maintenance.
- Government-provided (directly or indirectly) education, health care, and child care for everyone.
- Regulations on private businesses to assure worker safety, protection, and fair competition.
- Moderate to high progressive taxes.
- Gay marriage, abortion rights, and a liberal drug policy, although this varies considerably from one country to another (Wikipedia, 2007b).

Socialism

Description

Despite the many variations in philosophy and practice that can be found among Socialists, Socialism has three basic features: public ownership of production, an extensive welfare state, and the desire to create a society in which material want is eliminated (the Socialist intent; Baradat, 2005).

Public ownership of production is needed because private ownership within a mixed or capitalist system assures exploitation of workers and thus must be eliminated. To make a profit, a capitalist must pay a worker less than the income that worker generates; it is the excess of income created by the worker's contribution over the costs of production (including the worker's wage) that is profit. Private owners thus always have an incentive to pay a worker as little as possible to maximize their own income. Nationalizing production or turning production over to cooperatives solves the problem of exploitation, as no one individual benefits from exploiting workers.

An extensive welfare state is used by government to ensure access to the necessities of life. Universal education, health care, pensions, income maintenance, and other programs are instituted. This is in accord with the Socialist intent, the desire to reduce and then eliminate social problems. In this way, Socialism is far superior to capitalism (at least in theory) because hunger, discrimination, homelessness, lack of affordable health care for all, and the other ills seen around the world in capitalist economies can be eliminated.

All Socialists desire radical change in society. Different strands of Socialism have varying ideas relating to the use of violence to achieve radical change. Democratic Socialists eschew violence, believing in the power of democracy to bring about such a large change. Other branches of Socialism, however, believe that the only true power for change comes from "the barrel of a gun."

Policy Implications

Socialist social policy results in the most far-spreading institutional system of all the philosophies described. But it is important to understand that the key element of Socialism is that society is radically transformed by eliminating capitalism. The economic system is radically different from any system where capitalism is allowed to continue, even in Social Democratic countries, which also have extensive social welfare programs.

Socialists have to struggle with the fact that wherever their ideas have been tried, success has been limited. Although the former Soviet bloc countries may not be a true test of Socialist ideas, they are an object lesson in ways that the Socialist theory can be applied with ensuing negative effects. Other experiments in Socialist governance, such as the People's Republic of China and Cuba, have experienced both successes and failures but may not adhere closely to Socialist principles at this time. Still, on a few indicators of national health, they outperform the United States (World Health Organization, 2007). Critics of Socialist ideology focus on the loss of individual freedom that is demanded in return for a promised freedom from material want.

This survey of politics as ideology and the resultant social policies espoused by each political view leads to the conclusion that almost all ideologies are represented by political parties in many countries, particularly industrialized countries, around the world. Further, talk of peaceful change, even if the change desired is radical in scope and speed, is by far more common than are calls for violent revolution. The next section looks briefly at one way to approach the concept of politics as a process of advocating and achieving change in policy.

POLITICS AS PROCESS: HOW TO HAVE AN EFFECT ON SOCIAL POLICY

Jansson (2003) articulates four rationales for conducting policy advocacy:

- To promote the values of social work.
- To promote the well-being of clients, consumers, and citizens.
- To create effective opposition to "bad" policies and to pressure decision makers to adopt or keep "good" policies.
- To alter who the governmental decision makers are.

Elsewhere (Hoefer, 2006), I have described advocacy practice, which I define as a practice model to affect client outcomes in nongovernmental as well as governmental processes. I describe a series of steps that are analogous to the model of generalist practice taught in many schools of social work, thus highlighting the similarity between advocacy practice and other types of social work practice. My model of advocacy practice is described here as a way of understanding the links between politics as a process and social policy. Knowing how to affect policy by engaging in a political process leads to empowerment on the part of social workers and their clients.

Getting Involved

The first step of the advocacy process is to *get involved,* meaning to find a reason and the will to take notice of some situation that challenges one's conception of social justice. Seven variables are important in determining if one is likely to get involved or not: education (level and content), values, sense of professional responsibility, interest, participation in other organizations, skills, and time available. These variables can be altered consciously by anyone and can be shaped by the organizations that employ social workers to promote advocacy by employees.

Understanding the Issue

Understanding should precede action. Sometimes a strong urge to "do something" exists, but it must be resisted. The first step in understanding an issue is to agree on its definition. Advocates next determine who benefits from and who is harmed by the situation. They also assess what some of the causes (proximate and distal) of the situation are.

When this analysis is completed, advocates can move to generating possible solutions to the problem. Often, the way an issue is defined has a strong influence on what the acceptable solutions are, so it is important to have a neutral problem definition statement. Advocates should determine the extent to which social justice is served by any particular proposed solution. Then the proposed solutions can be rank-ordered to determine which, if enacted, would produce the greatest improvement in social justice.

Planning Advocacy

Planning requires detailing the actions needed to make the advocate's preferred solution the one that is eventually chosen by decision makers. First, one must identify what is actually wanted. The overall goal will almost always need to be broken into smaller goals, or outcomes, and the specific actions that are required to make those come true should be laid out. Second, the targets of advocacy, the people who can make the desired decision, are identified, and analysis is done to determine what would convince them to adopt the advocate's desired solution. Planning is also needed to understand how best to negotiate with or persuade the targets. The final planning step is to gather the required information (substantive and contextual) to move forward with the actual advocacy efforts.

Advocating

At this time, the previous work is put to the test as advocates meet with decision makers, make their presentations, and negotiate and persuade. Other advocates can be brought in to speak, or the advocacy attempt can be an individual effort. The decision maker can be a Washington-based legislator or one's supervisor. The change process is usually slow, and advocates must understand the need for patience as well as persistence.

Evaluating Advocacy

Advocacy is often not evaluated in any formal sense, which makes learning from past actions more difficult. Even a minimal effort at evaluation, quickly comparing the advocacy's outcomes against the desired outcomes laid out in the planning stage, yields results in showing what was accomplished and, perhaps, what techniques might work as well or better in the next advocacy effort.

Ongoing Monitoring

What was won (or lost) in the legislative branch can be reversed in the executive or judicial branches of government. Thus, advocates must monitor the actions of additional decision makers in different venues. Understanding the importance of keeping up with new developments is vital, or else gains won by social workers in one arena can be lost to advocates for other views in another.

CONCLUSION

This survey of social policy and politics shows the links between politics as political ideology, politics as a process of change, and the policies that emerge in any jurisdiction. Ruling political parties have the ability to create or destroy programs designed to improve people's lives; in other words, those in power, using their values and ideology, shape social policy to match their interests. In most democratic countries, however, individual people and groups are able to voice their opinions to have their values enacted. This chapter has also provided a brief overview of the steps that can be taken to have an impact on social policy in almost any nation where input exists. It is to be hoped that readers will understand better the range of ideas that exist to be selected from, as well as one basic approach to peaceful change: politics as advocacy.

REFERENCES

Aristotle. (2007). *Politics*. Retrieved February 7, 2007, from www.askoxford.com/results/?view= quot&freesearch=politics&branch=14123648&textsearchtype=exact.

Bachrach, P., & Baratz, M. (1962). The second face of power. *American Political Science Review*, *56*, 947–952.

Baradat, L. (2005). *Political ideologies: Their origins and impact* (9th ed.). Englewood Cliffs, NJ: Prentice Hall.

Centerpartiet. (2007). *Socialbidrag* [Welfare]. (Center Party of Sweden, Trans.). Retrieved February 10, 2007, from www.centerpartiet.se/templates2/Page.aspx?id=33730.

DiNitto, D. (2007). *Social welfare: Politics and public policy* (6th ed.). Boston: Allyn & Bacon.

Dolgoff, R., & Feldstein, D. (2007). *Understanding social welfare: A search for social justice* (7th ed.). Boston: Allyn & Bacon.

Hallstead, T., & Lind, M. (2001). *The radical center: The future of American politics*. New York: Doubleday.

Hoefer, R. (2006). *Advocacy practice for social justice*. Chicago: Lyceum.

Jansson, B. (2003). *Becoming an effective policy advocate* (4th ed.). Pacific Grove, CA: Brooks/Cole.

Kristol, I. (2004). The conservative welfare state. In I. Stelzer (Ed.), *The neocon reader* (pp. 145–148). New York: Grove Press.

Lasswell, H. (1990). *Politics: Who gets what, when and how*. Gloucester, MA: Peter Smith.

Mills, C. W. (1956). *The power elite*. New York: Oxford University Press.

Murray, C. (1997). *What it means to be a libertarian*. New York: Broadway Books.

Olasky, M. (2000). *Compassionate conservatism: What it is, what it does and how it can transform America*. New York: Free Press.

Wikipedia. (2007a). *Nordic agrarian parties*. Retrieved February 10, 2007, from http://en.wikipedia .org/wiki/Category:Nordic_Agrarian_parties.

Wikipedia. (2007b). *Social democracy*. Retrieved February 10, 2007, from http://en.wikipedia .org/wiki/Social_democracy.

World Health Organization. (2007). *Core health indicators*. Retrieved February 12, 2007, from www.who.int/whosis/core/core_select_process.cfm.

Chapter 18

SOCIAL WELFARE AND ECONOMICS: REDEFINING THE WELFARE STATE IN A GLOBAL ECONOMY

Howard Karger and Peter A. Kindle

The American welfare state is driven largely by economics. Specifically, social welfare services in democratic capitalist societies are fueled by tax revenues, which in turn depend on the performance of the larger economy. Although economics plays a major role in modern welfare states, it is not the only variable. Ideology and religion also play significant roles, especially in the American welfare state, and it is reductionistic to overemphasize any one variable, including economics. Social welfare is shaped by an amalgam of forces that exert differential influence depending on the historical period. For example, just as the economic crisis of the Depression formed the basis for the New Deal welfare state, by the 1980s religion and political ideology became equally important influences in shaping welfare policy.

Despite the caveat, this chapter focuses on the role of economics in social welfare policy, especially as it relates to the creation of a viable welfare state in a postindustrial global economy.

THE SOCIAL WELFARE STATE: A LEGACY OF THE INDUSTRIAL ERA

Although rudimentary forms of welfare existed in the United States since colonial times, the modern welfare state was born in the Social Security Act of 1935. When Franklin Roosevelt assumed the presidency in 1933, he faced a country divided between right- and left-wing political factions, a collapsing industrial sector replete with violent labor strikes, a banking system on the verge of collapse, and a class society at its breaking point (Cohen, 1958). FDR's response to the Depression was a massive social experiment with the objectives of relief, recovery, and reform. These New Deal programs formed the basis of the modern American welfare state.

The New Deal shaped the modern welfare state in several ways. For one, federal policy was used to ameliorate some of the more egregious inequities in the labor market by enacting minimum wage laws and establishing the right of workers to strike and collectively bargain. FDR's programs also created important precedents in others areas, including the right of eligible Americans to receive public assistance. The New Deal welfare state took relief from the realm of "we will provide what we have" to an entitlement program whereby resources must be provided to those who qualify.

The New Deal shifted the responsibility for providing public assistance from individual states to the federal government. Consequently, certain public assistance rules and eligibility—but not the determination of cash benefits—were standardized and applied more evenly across states. FDR's New Deal codified a policy directive that established the responsibility of federal and state governments to provide for the needs of citizens deemed worthy of receiving aid. Unfortunately, this important policy precedent was rescinded by the passage of the Personal Responsibility and Work Opportunity Act of 1996 (PRWORA; Karger & Stoesz, 2006).

The New Deal welfare state institutionalized the responsibility of government to assist the jobless and those unable to compete in the labor market. Welfare programs, such as unemployment insurance, assisted displaced workers until they could be reabsorbed into the economy. The New Deal's social compact lasted for more than 60 years.

Despite the disdain of conservatives, the American welfare state grew rapidly from the 1950s to the 1970s. In large part, this was due to the robust growth of the U.S. economy. American innovation had introduced a wide range of products and services, and the productivity of U.S. workers was unsurpassed globally. With this economic dominance, the United States could afford to idle a small percentage of its workforce.

Faced with an expensive war in Vietnam and a sluggish economy mired in stagflation (i.e., a combination of recession and inflation), the U.S. welfare state came under closer scrutiny in the early 1970s. This scrutiny, however, did not translate into the diminution of the welfare state. Even though President Richard Nixon dismantled the Great Society, the welfare state actually grew larger under his administration. Between 1965 and 1975, America's fiscal priorities were reversed: In 1965, defense expenditures composed 42% of the federal budget, while social welfare expenditures accounted for 25%; by 1975, defense expenditures composed 25% of the budget, while social welfare outlays accounted for 43%. Even in Ronald Reagan's conservative budget of 1986, with its large increases in defense spending, only 29% was defense-related compared to 41% for social welfare (DiNitto & Dye, 1987). Despite some ups and downs, the American welfare state was generally in a growth mode from 1935 to the mid-1970s.

The tacit acceptance of welfare programs by Republican leaders did not reflect real support, but a recognition that Americans, despite their outward ambivalence, supported the welfare state. Republicans understood that to be elected at the national level they must appeal to working-class Democrats, many of whom depended on social welfare programs, such as those designed to assist in the purchase of a home (FHA and VA loans), unemployment compensation, and student loans. The challenge was how to psychologically wean these voters away from welfare and, more specifically, how to convince them that welfare programs were actually anathema to their welfare.

A powerful new force emerged in American politics during the 1980s. Fiscal conservatives had been content to snipe at the welfare state since 1935, but by the 1980s they became downright serious about dismantling it. Allied with the religious right, conservatives developed the Contract with America, an agenda designed to replace government responsibility for social welfare with "personal responsibility." One cornerstone of this strategy was the PRWORA, which, among other things, reversed 60 years of federal entitlement by disentitling the needy poor from receiving public assistance. To promote personal responsibility, the PRWORA mandated a tough 5-years-and-out (1 year at state discretion) lifetime cap on welfare receipt, coupled with stringent welfare-to-work requirements.

The 1980s saw a shift toward commodifying what had become social utilities. Services that were formerly free or heavily subsidized, such as mental health services, suddenly became a marketplace commodity for much of the population. Other services provided by government, such as student loans and home mortgages, were now a quasi- or fully privatized marketplace commodity. This change was driven by conservatives who wanted to cut taxes, and one avenue was to dismantle or cut deeply into governmental welfare programs. Through a consummate sales job, a large segment of the American public bought into the idea that their interests were best served by dismantling the welfare state, supporting tax cuts for the wealthy, and purchasing more of their social needs in the private marketplace.

THE POSTINDUSTRIAL ECONOMY

Fiscal conservatives were correct about one thing: The welfare state was a vestige of the industrial epoch. Welfare states emerged in an industrial era marked by relatively strong labor unions and massive capital investment in domestic production. Because unions were relatively strong from the 1940s through the 1970s, universal health insurance was unnecessary for many workers, whose union contracts included health plans. Many nonunionized workers were employed by large corporations that provided health insurance as a normal perk. With the notable exception of low-wage workers and the elderly (covered by the 1965 Medicare act), most full-time workers had health insurance. This is illustrated by the rise in the number of people with health care insurance, from less than 20 million in 1940 to more than 135 million by 1960 (Health Insurance Institute, 1966).

Fueled by the supposed exigencies of the global economy, by the 1990s employers had intensified their race to the economic bottom. In 2004, almost 46 million Americans, or close to 16% of the population—mainly women and children—lacked health insurance coverage. Benefit erosion declined through the early 2000s, and health insurance coverage declined for all wage groups in the 2000 to 2002 period. Pension plans followed the same trajectory: By 2002 only 45.5% of the American workforce had pension coverage, less than the 51% of workers in 1979 (Mishel, Bernstein, & Allegretto, 2005).

Many large employers in the 1950s also provided seniority right; some, such as IBM, even promised lifelong employment. Providing lifetime employment was not altruistic per se, but was based on the belief that investing in workers was a critical factor in increasing productivity. Conversely, high turnover rates hinder productivity because of the expense in replacing and retraining workers. Plus, there was an assumption that corporate loyalty and good morale were important in maintaining high levels of productivity, a concept that fell into disrepute during the later twentieth century.

EMPLOYMENT IN POSTINDUSTRIAL SOCIETY

The modern postindustrial economy is more dynamic and volatile than it was in the industrial era. Modern corporations now make fewer investments in domestic manufacturing, and many prefer to outsource production to foreign producers or set up manufacturing plants abroad. As a result, the promise of lifetime employment has been rescinded by most corporations because employees are no longer viewed as having lifelong value to the company. Instead, employees are viewed as interchangeable and are just one more capital expense.

In the traditional industrial setting, the employer was expected to train the employee. In the postindustrial setting, employees are expected to possess marketable skills before they are hired. Consequently, in the industrial era a high school education was sufficient to ensure that the employee had a knowledge base from which he or she could be trained. In a postindustrial context, the employee is expected to hit the ground running. Those who cannot—or will not—run fast enough are fired. In general, employees are fired the moment they cost more than they earn.

The industrial era welfare state was based on a full-employment model, with social insurance programs, such as unemployment insurance, serving as a temporary stopgap measure for frictional (e.g., people voluntarily moving between jobs) unemployment. However, frictional unemployment has given way to structural unemployment. Middle-age middle managers who are replaced by cheaper workers often end up structurally unemployed or forced to accept a job at a fraction of their previous wages. Those without marketable skills or whose skills do not translate into another employment setting can end up permanently unemployed.

If unemployment is often a consequence of inadequate or obsolete skills, then retraining becomes even more important. But in a postindustrial ownership society, workers own the problem of their obsolete or inadequate skills and are therefore expected to retrain themselves and bear the costs of that retraining. As governmental subsidies for training diminishes—for example, higher tuition costs, cuts in Pell grants and student loans—those most in need of skill training must bear a larger share of those costs.

One major avenue for training and retraining current and future workers has been a college degree. In general, college-educated workers are the only sector of the labor market whose wages have been rising. On average, the annual income for college graduates is 60% higher than for those with only a high school diploma. College graduates with a bachelor's degree earn about $18 an hour compared to abut $10 for high school graduates (see Table 18.1).

Despite the economic benefit of a college degree, the public university system is increasingly transferring more of its costs to consumers. Consequently, it is becoming more inaccessible to larger numbers of people. A general rule of thumb is that tuition rates increase at about twice the general rate of inflation. During the 17-year period from 1958 to 2001, the average annual tuition inflation rate rose between 6% and 9%, ranging from 1.2 to 2.1 times the general rate of inflation (see Table 18.2).

Table 18.1   Median Income for Year-Round, Full-time Workers, 25 and Older, 2001

	No High School Diploma ($)	High School Diploma ($)	Some College ($)	Bachelor's Degree ($)
Men	25,095	34,303	40,337	56,334
Women	17,919	24,970	28,697	40,415

Source: Digest of Education Statistics, by the National Center for Education Statistics, 2002, Washington, DC: U.S. Department of Education.

Table 18.2   The Rate of Inflation for College Tuition

Year	College Inflation (%)	General Inflation (%)	Rate Ratio
1958–1996	7.24	4.49	1.61
1977–1986	9.85	6.72	1.47
1987–1996	6.68	3.67	1.82
1958–2001	6.98	4.30	1.62
1979–2001	7.37	3.96	1.86
1992–2001	4.77	2.37	2.01
1985–2001	6.39	3.18	2.01
1958–2005	6.89	4.15	1.66
1989–2005	5.94	2.99	1.99

Source: "Tuition inflation," by FinAid, 2006b. Retrieved May 8, 2006, from http://www.finaid.org/savings/tuition-inflation.phtml.

Higher education in Texas illustrates this national trend. In 2001, the Texas legislature deregulated tuition and fees. By 2006, tuition and fees at Texas public universities cost $4,857, a 28% increase over 2002 to 2003 after adjusting for inflation. Overall, the average cost of tuition and fees at the nation's public universities cost $5,491 in 2006, a 25% inflation-adjusted increase from 2002 to 2003 (Austin, 2006). The result of this increase is that 60% of undergraduates leave college with student loans, the average being about $20,000. Graduate and professional students borrow even more, with the average debt ranging from $27,000 to $114,000 (FinAid, 2006a).

When John Maynard Keynes (1965) wrote *The General Theory of Employment, Interest and Money* in 1936, the European and U.S. economies were firmly rooted in the industrial era. This partly explains why Keynes stressed the importance of full employment. In fact, the Keynesian welfare states of Europe and the United States were largely based on programs dealing with unemployment or other labor market problems. However, in a postindustrial context, the problem of unemployment is largely related to skill acquisition and the time and resources it takes to acquire the necessary skills to compete in today's global economy.

According to Michael Piore (1977), the modern American economy consists of the primary and secondary labor markets. The primary labor market is composed of workers and managers who occupy stable employment positions, complete with livable wages and perks that include health insurance, retirement benefits, disability and life insurance, and paid vacations. The secondary labor market, which often consists of temporary or part-time work, is characterized by unstable employment, high turnover rates, low pay, and lack of benefits and other employment perks. There may also be a tertiary labor market that is similar to the secondary market, except that the jobs tend to be even more temporary (sometimes daily work), there are no benefits, the pay is even lower, and workers are sometimes paid in cash and off the books. Many employees in the tertiary sector are undocumented workers.

The majority of jobs in the hospitality, light manufacturing, and retail industries are secondary or tertiary labor market jobs. These jobs are often filled by minorities, undocumented workers or immigrants, women, the disabled, older unemployed workers, and others who face job discrimination in their bid to enter the primary labor market. Workers in these positions usually earn less than a livable wage and often work two or more jobs to make ends meet.

The existence of the secondary and tertiary labor markets contradicts classical economic explanations of labor and wages. Many economists view the labor market as a commodities market whereby rational workers seeking to maximize their economic well-being interact with rational employers seeking to maximize their profits. In theory, this supply-and-demand relationship determines employment and wage levels. However, this explanation fails to explain the large differences in wages and employment conditions in the current labor market. Classical economists argue that differences in wages are due to disparities in productivity based on the human capital of differing workers. However, economists such as Jared Bernstein (1995) and others have pointed out that much of this income disparity is related to institutional rather than human capital factors. In other words, it is not productivity alone that determines wages, but also racial, market, technical, organizational, and political factors. Wages may be more determined by good and bad jobs rather than good and bad workers.

Wage problems and income growth are evident when examining recent economic data. In 2005, the economy was strong, having expanded for the fourth consecutive year. Despite this, real hourly wages fell for most workers. For low- and middle-wage workers and those with a high school degree, real wages fell by 1% to 2% in 2004. Those higher on the wage scale experienced marginal gains, although real wages were essentially unchanged even for college graduates. This stagnation in wages occurred despite a strong growth in labor productivity and was especially problematic because inflation was 2.7% in 2004 and 3.4% in 2005, which meant that workers were losing ground (Price & Bernstein, 2006). In contrast, the salaries of chief executive officers exploded. From 1989 to 2000 the wage of median CEOs grew 79%, and their average compensation increased 342%. In 1965, CEOs earned 26 times the wage of the typical worker; by 2003 it was 185 times. American CEOs earn 3 times more than their foreign counterparts (Mishel et al., 2005).

Income growth was strongly correlated to productivity throughout much of the industrial era. Between 1947 and 1973 productivity and income grew by a whopping 104%. Most family incomes benefited from the rapid increase in labor productivity and the concomitant reward of higher incomes. As the global economy matured in the mid-1970s, the relationship between productivity and income growth began to break down. Median family income grew at about one-third the rate of productivity (22% versus 65%) from 1973 to 2002. According to Mishel et al. (2005, p. 3), "While faster productivity growth led to a larger economic pie, growing inequality meant that the slices were divided up such that some income classes—those at the top of the income scale—claimed most of the income growth."

The modern postindustrial economy has ushered in almost unprecedented levels of income inequality. In the 1950s and 1960s real income growth doubled for each household in the five income brackets. This trend was reversed between 1979 and 2000, when the real income of households in the lowest fifth (the bottom 20% of earners) grew by only 6.4% compared to 70% for the top fifth income bracket. The top 1% saw their incomes rise by an astounding 184%. By 2000, the top 1% had claimed 21.7% of the nation's total income. An even starker measure of inequality is the ownership of wealth. In 2001, the wealthiest 1% of all households controlled more than 33% of the national wealth. The bottom 80% of households held only 16% (Mishel et al., 2005).

Although some economists claim that income mobility in America allows the poor to leapfrog to the top, the data tell a different story. Fifty-three percent of those who started out in the lowest fifth income bracket in the late 1980s were still there by the late 1990s.

Another 24% had only climbed to the next fifth. In other words, 77% of those who started out poor remained poor a decade later (Mishel et al., 2005).

Several factors contribute to the decline in real wages: a reduction in the bargaining power of workers, especially the decline of union power; the fall in the real value of the minimum wage; the growing imbalance in international trade; and the exportation of more white-collar jobs offshore. Membership in labor unions—the best security for nonprofessional workers—fell from 30.8% of nonagricultural workers in 1970 to 12.5% in 2005. Union members earn higher wages; in 2005, full-time unionized workers had median weekly earnings of $801 compared to $622 for nonunionized workers (Bureau of Labor Statistics, 2006a). Unionized employees are also 28% more likely than their nonunion counterparts to be covered by employer-provided health insurance (their deductibles are also 18% lower), and they are 24% more likely to have health insurance in their retirement (Mishel et al., 2005).

The global economy is partly responsible for the loss of 4 million manufacturing jobs from 1989 to 2002 (Karger & Stoesz, 2006). Although few hard data exist on the impact of sending white-collar jobs offshore, anecdotal evidence suggests it is having a major impact on the labor force. Specifically, the threat of hiring foreign workers or moving operations offshore is being used to curtail wage growth in the technology and software industries. House Small Business Committee Chairman Don Manzullo (R-IL) summed up the threat:

> U.S. manufacturers contract with engineers from India who send their drawings to workers in Poland who in turn ship their finished products back to America for incorporation into American products. Radiologists in India interpret CT scans for U.S. hospitals. Computer technicians in Ghana process New York City parking tickets. The U.S. economy is growing and creating jobs, but Americans are not filling them. These jobs have been moved overseas where foreigners will work for a lot less. (as quoted in Eskeland, 2003)

IMPOVERISHMENT AND DEBT IN THE POSTINDUSTRIAL ERA

Stagnant wages, structural unemployment, and income inequality have led to increasing levels of absolute and relative poverty. In 2004, the poverty rate was 12.7% (37 million people), up from 12.1% (34.5 million) in 1998. Almost 18% of children under age 18 (13 million) were poor, as were about 12% of the elderly. The poverty rate is even more striking when disaggregated by race: 24.7% of African Americans, 21.9% of Hispanics, and 8.6% of Whites were poor in 2004 (U.S. Census Bureau, 2005).

Absolute poverty thresholds tell only part of the story. About 18% of American house-holds had zero or negative net wealth in 2001. Broken down, roughly 31% of African American households had no or negative wealth compared to 13% of White households. The median wealth for African Americans in 2001 was $10,700, or roughly 10% of the median wealth of Whites (Mishel et al., 2005).

Because of stagnant wages, high levels of consumption, and easy credit, a new class of near-poor or functionally poor households has been born. These functionally poor individuals or families have incomes that are solidly middle class, but they have zero or negative disposable or discretionary income at the end of the month. This group includes home owners who use their property like ATM machines, regularly drawing out equity to finance credit card debt or other purchases. It also includes the middle class with tarnished credit who use high interest rate credit cards or finance purchases through tricky time-deferred payments. This burgeoning sector of the middle class is economically closer to the poor than they are to the traditional middle class.

The ostensible cause of financial hardship among the functionally poor middle class is debt, something endemic to all sectors of our society. In 2006, the federal debt was $8.4 trillion, a $2.1 trillion increase over 1997. This debt is increasing by $1.75 billion a day, with each citizen's share being roughly $28,000 (zFacts.com, 2006).

Consumer spending, much of it fueled by successful advertising and marketing, accounts for two-thirds of the nation's $11 trillion economy and has led to Americans becoming more indebted than ever (Karger, 2005). Excluding mortgages, consumer debt almost doubled from 1994 to 2004, totaling about $19,000 a family. By 2004, Americans owed more than $9 trillion in home mortgages, car loans, credit card debt, home equity loans, and other forms of credit, nearly 40% of which was accumulated in just 4 years. One fifth of the $9 trillion is in variable interest rate loans, such as credit and store cards.

Middle-income consumers are 10 times more likely than upper-income families to devote 40% or more of their income to debt repayment (Uchitelle, 2004). The average household now spends 13% of its after-tax income on debt repayment, the highest percentage since 1986 (Lohr, 2004). (These figures are soft because they fail to take into account forms of predatory lending, such as payday loans, pawnshop transactions, rent-to-own, and tax refund loans.) All told, household debt has increased a whopping 500% since 1957.

Consumer debt is further aggravated by low rates of personal savings. Americans saved about 10% of their disposable income in the 1980s; by 2004, that rate fell to a near record low of less than 1%. (Some estimates put it at –0.5%.) Home equity was also the lowest in recent history due to feverish home refinancing. In 2002, home owners initiated $97 billion in home equity loans, nearly 5 times the amount in 1993 (Karger, 2005; Murray, 2000). Although home refinancing put about $300 billion back into the economy from 2001 to 2003, consumers spent almost all of it (Paul, 2003). Not coincidentally, the foreclosure rate rose 45% from January 2005 to January 2006 ("Foreclosure Rates," 2006).

Credit card debt contributes to the growth of the "new poor." The average credit card balance per household is approaching $12,000, and the average American family spends about $1,100 a year in credit card interest alone (Coalition for Responsible Credit Practices, 2004). Overall, credit card holders carried more than $1.7 trillion in debt in 2002, up from $1.1 trillion in 1995 (Karger, 2005). Debt is now cited as the number one problem facing newlyweds and is fast becoming a major cause of divorce (Coalition for Responsible Credit Practices, 2004).

According to Warren and Tyagi (2003), today's two-income family earns 75% more than their single-income counterpart a generation ago, but has less discretionary income after paying fixed monthly bills. Some of this is attributable to mortgage costs that have risen 70 times faster than an average father's wages (Feran, 2003). In addition, the drop in earnings of non–college graduate males since the 1970s has forced more mothers to work full or part time to make up the difference. This second income has not resulted in families purchasing more; instead, it is used to pay for necessities of shelter, food, clothing, and transportation. Applebaum, Bernhardt, and Murnane (2003) argue that middle- and low-income families have maxed out their earnings capacity through the employment of mothers. Having exhausted their labor reserve, these families are forced to generate additional income by ersatz means, such as mortgage refinancing.

Fixed costs, such as mortgage payments, child care, health insurance, and vehicles and taxes, consume up to 75% of the paycheck of today's two-income family. By contrast, those costs represented about half of a middle-class family's income in the early 1970s. In 2002, American families spent 22% less for food (including restaurant meals), 21% less for clothing, and 44% less for appliances than in 1973. Adjusted for inflation, consumer expenditures are lower than a generation ago (Warren & Tyagi, 2003).

Because second incomes are used to pay for day-to-day living expenses, families are left with no reserve income for emergencies. Moreover, the anemic nature of the modern welfare state does little to ease their vulnerability to privation and bankruptcy if they face life events such as illness, death, desertion, or unemployment.

Although a second income helps pay bills, the effects are diminished by day care costs ranging from $340 to almost $1,100 a month, clothing expenses, and the need for a second reliable car (Runzheimer International, 2004). For many families with young children, half or more of their second wage is consumed by the costs of workplace participation, and after expenses, they see only a small increase in family income. The impact of the second income is further diminished by the gender gap in male and female wages (Economic Policy Institute, 2005).

Indebtedness often leads to bankruptcy. In 2005, there were 2 million personal bankruptcies. Every 15 seconds someone in the United States goes bankrupt, a fourfold increase over 1980. About 1.5 million American households filed for bankruptcy in 2003, 400% more than in 1975 (American Bankruptcy Institute, 2004). In fact, more people file for bankruptcy than graduate from college or file for divorce (Sullivan, Warren, & Westbrook, 2001). In examining bankruptcy filers, Teresa Sullivan, Elizabeth Warren, and Jay Westbrook (1989) found that they crossed all income and occupational levels and were not irresponsible spendthrifts. Instead, they had insurmountable financial problems stemming from a life crisis such as divorce, job loss, or medical problems. The combination of stagnant and low wages plus high debt may lead some middle-class families directly into the path of social welfare programs.

Not every economic problem can, or should, be laid at the doorstep of the global economy. However, certain trends thought necessary to successfully compete in the global economy exacerbate the general economic malaise felt by a growing number of middle-class families. These trends include wage depression and stagnant incomes; the disconnect between increased productivity and wage growth; growing income and asset inequality between classes; the commodification and privatization of public utilities, such as higher education, day care, and health care; regressive tax cuts that deplete the public treasury while benefiting mainly the rich; the reduction of employee benefits; the creation of more part-time jobs without benefits; deep cuts in public services; and financially starving state welfare programs. Taken together, these trends constitute a race to the bottom by industry and government and contribute to the growing Indonesianization of the American workforce.

A NEW WELFARE AGENDA FOR THE GLOBAL ECONOMY

Conservatives argue that welfare state programs are an unaffordable luxury in a competitive global economy. They claim that New Deal welfare programs have outlived their usefulness, if they were ever useful. The demands of the global economy require fewer and more miserly social programs that divert less money from taxes, thereby freeing up more capital for investment. Conservatives argue that market solutions will tackle social problems, and at best, social welfare should be a temporary safety net for frictional unemployment.

The conservative response to the liberal welfare state has been to substitute labor policy for welfare policy (Karger, 2003). For example, the PRWORA was essentially a labor policy clothed in welfare terminology. Passed during a period of strong economic growth (a 2.5% growth rate in the mid-1990s) and low unemployment (4.2%), the 138 million–member U.S. labor force could easily absorb the 4.2 million mothers receiving Aid to Families with Dependent Children (AFDC; just over 3% of the total workforce) without driving down wages or increasing unemployment. The economic giddiness of the mid-1990s reinforced the conservative belief that a job existed for anyone who wanted it.

The passage of the PRWORA represented the culmination of the long-standing conservative goal of deracinating public assistance. When the poor exhaust time-limited public assistance benefits, they become a labor market problem rather than a welfare problem. With that change, public assistance policy was reduced to a short-term transitional step in the march toward the full labor market participation of the poor. Weak federal labor policy, an inadequate minimum wage, the absence of national health-care insurance, and few workplace protections mean that former recipients now occupy secondary labor market jobs and face an even shakier economic future than under AFDC (Karger & Stoesz, 2006). The future of American competitiveness is not based on creating more subsistence-level secondary labor market jobs, but on increasing median-income jobs with full benefits.

Contrary to the conservative perspective, the social welfare state is as necessary in a postindustrial global economy as it was in the industrial era. Perhaps even more so. To ensure global competitiveness, the nation must build and periodically rebuild its stock of human capital, thereby enhancing workforce productivity. It is also necessary to provide subsidized opportunities for workers to retrain to meet the demands of the changing labor market and the higher expectations of employers. Increased productivity is especially important because seven nations in the Organization for Economic Cooperation and Development (OECD) have already surpassed the United States in worker output. In 1950, the average per hour output of OECD countries was 41% of the U.S. average; by 2002 it was 88% (Mishel et al., 2005). The more opportunities society provides its members to enhance their human capital and workplace skills, the more productive its workforce.

Questions abound. How can progressives promote an agenda of prosperity, opportunity, and compassion that will win the hearts and minds of America's affluent, while at the same time addressing the needs of the beleaguered middle class and working poor? Which new industrial relationships will lead to greater global justice? How can policy makers ensure that a fairer portion of the rewards of the U.S. economy flows to the middle and lower classes rather than to corporate profits? These questions beg answers in any new reformulation of the welfare state.

A new welfare agenda must raise the federal poverty threshold. The federal guidelines used to determine poverty were developed 50 years ago and are updated only for inflation. A single parent in 2006 with two children was considered poor if he or she had a yearly income of less than $16,600. The Economic Policy Institute estimates that doubling the poverty threshold would more closely approximate the real costs of meeting a family's basic needs (as cited in Mishel et al., 2005). Because the cost of living dramatically differs in urban and rural areas, and in midwestern versus coastal regions, the poverty threshold should be calibrated on a regional or even a city level (Stoesz & Karger, 1992).

At minimum, a new welfare agenda requires (a) the creation of family-friendly tax policies to reduce income inequality; (b) new legislation that requires everyone, including corporations, to pay their fair share; (c) stronger prolabor laws; (d) universal national health insurance; (e) an increased minimum wage; and (f) a portable, federally guaranteed, non-job-specific benefits package. The remainder of this chapter discusses key components of these proposed policies.

A Welfare Agenda for the Changing Demographics of American Families

A viable postindustrial welfare policy must address the rapidly changing demographics of American family life. For example, about 14% of women who married in the 1940s eventually divorced. A generation later, almost 50% of those married in the late 1960s and early 1970s divorced. Because a second income is required for most families to achieve a middle-class lifestyle, single mothers are inherently disadvantaged economically, which is further aggravated by the gender wage gap. The following illustrates the changing family demographic:

- In the late 1990s more than 10 million women were single parents. Twenty-seven percent of U.S. households include children with one parent; 20 million children under age 18 (28% of all children) live with a single parent, and 23% live only with their mother. One million children are added to the roster of divorced families each year. Disaggregated by race, 74% of White and 64% of Hispanic children live with two parents; 36% of African American children live in two-parent families ("U.S. Divorce Statistics," 2005).
- About 54% of divorced women remarry within 5 years of their divorce. Those with children live on a single income, possibly supplemented by child support.
- About 37% of families maintained by single mothers were poor in 2003, nearly 6 times the rate for married couples with children (U.S. Census Bureau, 2006).

These demographics make it important for government to establish more tax and family-friendly support policies that allow children in single female-headed households to enjoy the same opportunities as those in dual-parent households. Although the Earned Income Tax Credit (EITC) and the Child Tax Credit (CTC) programs help single female-headed families, they are insufficient to close the income gap. For example, the maximum EITC tax credit for a very low-income mother with two children was $4,400 in 2005. The maximum CTC credit she could claim was $2,000, bringing her *maximum* tax refund to $6,400. If the mother earned $7 an hour ($1.85 more than the minimum wage), her yearly income would be $13,440 plus the $6,400 in tax refunds, raising her total income to $19,840, or just $3,440 above the poverty line. This is far short of the $32,800 minimum suggested by the Economic Policy Institute.

Everyone Should Pay His or Her Fair Share

Substituting labor policy for public assistance policy has led to several problems. For one, the absence of worker-friendly labor policies rewards low-wage employers while punishing poor workers forced into low-paying dead-end jobs with few, if any, benefits. There are few consequences for low-wage employers who fail to provide their employees with a minimum number of hours, health-care benefits, or other employment perks. The difference between what these employers pay and the salary needed to support a worker and his or her family is partly made up by publicly funded social welfare programs. In that sense, low-wage employers are parasitic since they rely on these tax and social welfare programs to bridge the gap between low wages and the real cost of living. Hence, the *real* cost of low-wage employment is paid for by taxpayers.

A hypothetical example illustrates the point. In 2005, two family members earning $5.15 an hour would have a combined yearly income of $19,776. If they had two children, that income would be $426 above the federal poverty line of $19,350. The shortfall between wages and the real cost of living is made up by social programs such as EITC, CTC, and food stamps, among others. Specifically, EITC, CTC, and the Food Stamp Program alone (excluding Section 8 housing vouchers, Medicaid, and low-income energy assistance) would provide that family with a maximum yearly supplement of $12,472 ($2,584 more than a third wage at $5.15 an hour). Combined with benefits, the couple's yearly income would rise to $32,248, or $12,898 above the poverty line. If federal poverty programs were abolished, the minimum wage would need to rise to $8.40 an hour to compensate for the loss of governmental benefits. Americans either pay more in taxes to augment low wages (and indirectly subsidize low-wage employers) or more at the cash register. Either way, there is no free lunch.

In free market capitalism, the real costs of production are theoretically incorporated into the price of goods and services. Welfare state programs usurp that requirement. For example, one of the authors recently participated in a panel discussion on increasing the minimum wage. In the final minutes of the debate, a representative from the Houston business community declared that given the EITC, there was no reason to raise the minimum wage. The assumption was that EITC refunds were somehow free money, sidestepping the fact that they come out of general revenue taxes. The money removed from the tax coffers by the EITC and CTC programs is made up by other tax filers. Money removed from the tax base also results in less money for social programs and other human capital investments. In short, the EITC is not free money.

Although virtually everyone pays taxes, significant tax loopholes exist for corporations and the wealthy that are unavailable to the general taxpayer. Consequently, the middle-class taxpayer disproportionately shoulders the tax liability created by low-wage employers. Corporate profits rise as the real costs of wages are offloaded onto the backs of moderate-income taxpayers, who see little tangible benefit from this tax burden. In the end, the burden of higher taxes may outweigh any savings accrued at the cash register.

Instead of spreading the real costs of low wages throughout society, tough new laws should require employers to pay their fair share, either through higher taxes or by a higher minimum wage complemented by the mandate they provide their workers with health insurance and other employment perks. Given the high cost of administering social programs, a front-end approach requiring employers to provide higher salaries and benefits may be cheaper in the long run than trying to close the gap through social welfare programs.

The Need for New Labor Policies

Although EITC effectively supplements family income, the program does nothing for worker protections such as health, disability, and retirement benefits (Karger & Stoesz,

2006). Former beneficiaries and other low-income workers are forced to adapt to a secondary labor market that provides little except low wages. These workers have few workplace protections, and they cannot return to public assistance once they have exhausted their lifetime cap. Hence, the challenge for policy makers is to create a set of labor policies that provide worker protections and facilitate a smooth transition from public assistance to the labor force. These labor policies should protect workers from unscrupulous labor market practices and require employers to provide benefits similar to the primary employment sector. It should also level the playing field between unions and corporations.

Health-Care Reform

The need to compete in the global economy and promote durable labor force attachment requires a national health insurance plan that covers all workers irrespective of their workplace. Whereas many middle- and upper-income workers can count on health insurance as a standard job perk, the working poor are frequently denied this benefit. This is especially true since many low-income workers are employed in part-time service sector jobs that provide health insurance only for middle- or upper-level management. Other low-income workers are employed in jobs where health insurance is provided only to the worker and where family coverage is prohibitively expensive. About 24% of households with yearly incomes less than $25,000 lack health insurance.

Health-care coverage should be delinked from labor force participation because, unless compelled by law, most low-wage employers will not provide it. Several options exist for ensuring that low-income workers receive coverage: (a) Government can provide health coverage directly by expanding Medicaid to cover all adult low-income workers and their spouses, (b) government can design a new program that provides health-care coverage for low-income workers, or (d) government can compel and/or subsidize private sector employers to provide insurance. The last could be accomplished by developing federally subsidized insurance cooperatives (similar to the failed Clinton health-care bill) that would permit small employers to purchase insurance at the same rates and coverage as large employers. Employers who demonstrate that they are financially unable to provide coverage could receive a supplemental health insurance subsidy or voucher.

Upgrading the Minimum Wage

The current minimum wage of $5.85 an hour, a rise of only 70 cents since 1997, has been a bone of contention for decades, with sporadic increases subject to the political mood of the times. The minimum wage is important in determining overall wage structure because many employers use it as a baseline by paying $1 to $2 above it. In 2003, about 2 million hourly workers (2.9% of the workforce) earned the minimum wage (Bureau of Labor Statistics, 2003). In contrast, the Economic Policy Institute estimates that households with one adult and two children require $14 an hour to live barely above the poverty line; 60% of American workers earn less than $14 an hour, and unskilled entry-level workers in many service occupations earn $7 an hour or less (Ehrenreich, 2001). In 2005, the industries with the largest number of minimum wage workers included food preparation- and serving-related services (17.4%), general service occupations (8.9%), and leisure and hospitality services (14.3%; Bureau of Labor Statistics, 2006a).

The declining value of the minimum wage is an important issue to address in a postindustrial welfare context. In 1950, the minimum wage brought a worker to 56% of the median wage. Throughout the 1950s and 1960s, the minimum wage hovered between 44% and 56% of the average wage. By 1980 the minimum wage fell to 46.5% of the average wage; in 1988, it dropped even further to 35.7%. Overall, from 1979 to 1996 the value of the minimum wage declined 29%. Even the increase to $5.15 an hour in 1997 raised it only to 42% of the average wage, bringing a family of three to 83% of the poverty line. To have the same purchasing power as in the mid-1970s, the minimum wage increase in 1997 needed to be $6.07, or almost $1.00 higher (Center on Budget and Policy Priorities, 1997). Moreover, if inflation is calculated at 3% a year, the value of the already low $5.15 minimum wage eroded another 27% from 1997 to 2006.

The minimum wage suffers from several problems: (a) It is low in proportion to the median wage, (b) it is not automatically indexed to the cost of living or the growth in the median wage, and (c) it is not adjusted to reflect regional differences in living costs. The minimum wage does not address the real costs of living or the income needs of the working poor. Nor does it necessarily elevate the worker's mobility. Only 62% of those who earned the minimum wage from 1977 to 1997 rose above it within 1 year (Even & Macpherson, 2000).

Increasing the minimum wage would also have a significant spillover effect for the 10.5 million workers (8.7% of the workforce) who earn up to a dollar more (Rashell, Bernstein, & Boushey, 2001). This increase would raise the wages of all low-income workers by raising the benchmark for all wages. In turn, indexing the minimum wage to the median regional wage would help low-income working families earn enough to bring them above the poverty line and to compensate for gross differences in the costs of living, especially in the more expensive regions of the United States.

Individual states can set a higher minimum wage that overrides the lower federal one. All told, 16 states have adopted a higher minimum wage, including California ($6.75), Washington ($7.63, automatically indexed to the rate of inflation), Oregon ($7.50), Alaska ($7.15), Hawaii ($6.75), Maine ($6.50), Vermont ($7.25), Massachusetts ($6.75), Connecticut ($7.40), Rhode Island ($7.10), Delaware ($6.15), and Washington, DC ($7; AFL-CIO, 2006). In no state does the higher minimum wage equal the poverty line.

More than 100 communities have adopted the concept of a living wage, which is higher than the federal minimum. Typically, city or county living wage ordinances cover only a specific set of workers, usually city or county government workers or those hired by businesses receiving a government contract or subsidy (Karger & Stoesz, 2006). Correspondingly, the 100 communities that have adopted a living wage law represent only a tiny fraction of the thousands of U.S. cities and towns. Moreover, living wage campaigns will likely fail in the more conservative states that typically have the highest concentration of poverty. To ease the burden on the working poor, Congress should raise the minimum wage, automatically index it to inflation, and make it more geographically sensitive.

Portable Benefits Packages

Two important trends exist in the global economy: (1) Corporations are increasingly shedding their responsibility to provide health and retirement benefits to employees, and (2) job tenure has become volatile as lifetime employment has become almost an anachronism.

As employers' needs shift, many find it cheaper and more expeditious to hire new workers rather than retrain existing employees.

The widespread reduction of benefits is obvious when examining the share of workers covered by employer-provided health and pension plans. From 1979 to 2003, the numbers of employees covered by employer-provided health insurance plans shrank from 69% to 56.4%. Although this drop was the steepest in the bottom two income tiers (representing a 13% drop in health-care coverage), it cut across all income classes, and even the top fifth experienced an 11.7% cut. Pension plan coverage followed a similar trajectory, dropping from 50.6% of the workforce in 1979 to 47.2% in 2003. Although this cut affected all income brackets, the lowest fifth was the least affected, dropping from 18.4% of workers in 1979 to 14.3% in 2003. By 2003 fewer than half of middle-income workers had pension plans (Mishel et al., 2005).

Benefits commonly provided in the primary labor sector, such as family health insurance, life and disability insurance, and supplemental retirement plans, are rare in the secondary labor market and virtually nonexistent in the tertiary and temporary employment sectors. Encouraging steady labor force attachment requires not only higher wages, but also replicating a system of employment-based benefits similar to those currently enjoyed by most primary sector workers.

It is unlikely that job security will resurface as an important workplace issue in the near future. Equally unlikely is the hope that the majority of low-wage employers will voluntarily choose to offer benefits similar to those in the primary labor sector. What is likely is that the volatile nature of secondary labor market jobs will continue and that tenure and job security in the primary labor sector will become even more unpredictable.

One solution is for the federal government to subsidize a comprehensive, non-job-specific portable benefits package (Stoesz & Karger, 1992). As low- and moderate-income workers change jobs or are terminated, their benefit package would follow them. If a low-wage worker later moves into a primary sector labor market job with benefits, the portable benefits package would be discontinued and the worker given the option to cash out his or her contribution. A viable portable benefit package could include life, disability, and health insurance; supplemental unemployment insurance; and a supplemental retirement plan. Low-income workers would be given the choice of picking specific benefits from a list of options, utilizing cost sharing among the federal government, the employer, and the employee.

Another important component of a portable benefits package would be the requirement that all employers provide unemployment insurance (UI) coverage for their workers, regardless of their full- or part-time status. Employers unable to financially shoulder added UI costs could receive governmental assistance. To maintain a social insurance feature, the modified UI benefit system would continue to incorporate eligibility and time standards, but these would be calculated on the time spent in the workforce rather than in a particular job. Like Social Security, time spent in the workforce would be portable and could be moved from job to job.

Still another key feature of a portable benefits package could include supplemental retirement benefits, which most low-wage employers fail to provide for their workers. Social Security replaced about 57% of a low-wage earner's income in 1999 (TIAA-CREF, 2001). In 2002, a worker with steady low earnings (defined as 45% of the national average wage) since age 22, and who retired at age 65, received $682 a month or $8,184 a year in Social Security benefits. In contrast, a high-income earner who retired that same year received $1,660 a month or $19,920 a year (Social Security Administration, 2002).

There are several ways the federal government can remedy the pension problem. One is for the government to supplement the Social Security tax paid by low-income workers, thereby bringing their taxable Social Security income up to the national average wage. That same low-income worker could then retire at age 65 with a monthly Social Security benefit of $1,127, or $13,524 a year (Social Security Administration, 2002). Alternatively, the federal government could supplement a low-wage earner's income by contributing to an individual retirement account (IRA) or a Keogh fund. In either case, subsidizing a low-income worker's retirement benefits would help solidify labor force attachment and mitigate against the prospect of extreme poverty in old age and the subsequent need for public assistance.

Especially in the retail trades, corporations cut costs by relying on non-benefit-eligible part-time workers. This trend hampers the income growth, career path, and employment security of workers. Moreover, part-time workers remain at the minimum wage longer than full-time workers (Even & Macpherson, 2000). A government-subsidized benefits package would discourage employers from hiring part-time workers to avoid paying benefits. For instance, if all employers were required to contribute to a federally subsidized portable benefits package, there would be little incentive to hire only part-time workers. Corporations would also benefit by lowering turnover rates, resulting in less training time. Full-time workers also typically learn their jobs better than part-time workers.

CONCLUSION

The global economy poses powerful challenges for social workers and other welfare advocates. On the one hand, social workers can continue to mount a futile rearguard effort to defend a New Deal welfare state tethered to a quickly disappearing industrial context. On the other hand, they can propose a bold new welfare system that addresses a postindustrial global economy, which in many ways is more obdurate than the industrial economy it is replacing. Welfare state programs are needed now more than ever given the trend toward increased income inequality, stagnant wages, unstable employment, declining union strength, a growing number of medically uninsured Americans, and the rapid growth of low-wage secondary labor market jobs. To address these problems, this chapter has outlined some specific policy initiatives relevant to the changing economic landscape of postindustrial America.

The early 2000s is a time of challenges, but it is also a time of great opportunities for change. For example, some welfare advocates believe that corporations are opposed to social welfare. While that may have been true in the past—and in some cases still is true—many corporations are beginning to reevaluate their position on social welfare. Buckling under the demands to provide expensive health and welfare benefits to their current and former workers, many corporations are now more open to change, especially in health care.

Like consumers, corporations are also victimized by the avarice of the health care industry. For instance, HMOs nearly doubled their profits from 2002 to 2003, adding $10 billion to their bottom line. Top executives at the 11 largest health insurers made a combined $85 million in 2003. In 2004, the four largest health insurance companies reported

$100 billion in revenues, or $273 million a day (Sirota, 2006). The sheer scope of these revenues allowed the health-care industry to spend more than $300 million on lobbying in 2003, plus another $300 million in campaign contributions to politicians from 2000 to 2005 (Sirota, 2006).

Despite intense lobbying by the health-care industry, a 2003 ABC/*Washington Post* poll found that Americans prefer a universal health insurance program over the current employer-based system by a 2 to 1 margin (62% versus 32%). In 2003, the *Journal of the American Medical Association* published a proposal for a government-sponsored universal health-care program that was endorsed by more than 8,000 physicians, including two former surgeon generals (Sirota, 2006). Due to the high costs of health insurance, Ford, GM, and Chrysler have endorsed Canada's universal health-care system. One poll found that 63% of small Michigan businesses favored creating a universal health-care system, even if it required a small tax increase (Sirota, 2006). Welfare advocates may find strange bedfellows in their attempt to create a viable postindustrial welfare state. In fact, it would be no small irony if a successful health-care reform proposal came about through the efforts of large corporations.

The vigor and durability of the American welfare state has surprised even its staunchest critics. At some level, most Americans know the private marketplace is too volatile and cold-hearted to entrust it with their health, welfare, and retirement. This partly explains why the Bush administration's attempt to privatize Social Security was moribund almost from the point of inception. Although Americans want to change social welfare policy, they are apparently not ready to throw out the baby with the bath water. That alone opens up exciting possibilities to create a viable and robust welfare state to meet the challenges of the new global economy.

REFERENCES

AFL-CIO. (2006). *Living and minimum wage, state minimum wage rates.* Retrieved May 11, 2006, from www.aflcio.org/issues/jobseconomy/livingwages/staterates/.

American Bankruptcy Institute. (2004). *Facts.* Retrieved March 15, 2005, from www.abiworld.org.

Applebaum, E., Bernhardt, A., & Murnane, R. (Eds.). (2003). *Low-wage America.* New York: Russell Sage Foundation.

Austin, L. (2006, April 23). Increases after tuition deregulation mirror those seen nation-wide. *KVUE.com* Retrieved November 6, 2007, from www.kvue.com/news/local/stories/042306 cckrKvuetuition.645651e6.html.

Bernstein, J. (1995). *Where's the payoff?* Washington, DC: Economic Policy Institute.

Bureau of Labor Statistics. (2003). *Characteristics of minimum wage workers: 2003.* Retrieved October 23, 2005, from www.bls.gov/cps/minwage2003.htm.

Bureau of Labor Statistics. (2006a). *Household data, annual averages.* Retrieved May 10, 2006, from www.bls.gov/cps/cpsaat45.pdf.

Bureau of Labor Statistics. (2006b, January 20). *Union members in 2005.* Retrieved May 9, 2006, from www.bls.gov/news.release/union2.nr0.htm.

Center on Budget and Policy Priorities. (1997, March). *Assessing the $5.15 an hour minimum wage.* Retrieved September 24, 2004, from http://epn.org/cpbb/cbwage.html.

Coalition for Responsible Credit Practices. (2004). *The crisis of growing consumer debt.* Retrieved October 15, 2005, from www.responsiblecreditpractices.com/issues/growing.php.

Cohen, N. (1958). *Social work in the American tradition.* New York: Holt, Rinehart and Winston.

DiNitto, D., & Dye, T. (1987). *Social welfare: Politics and public policy*. Englewood Cliffs, NJ: Prentice Hall.

Economic Policy Institute. (2005, January 5). *Slowdown in male earnings leads to smaller gender wage gap*. Retrieved May 14, 2006, from http://www.epinet.org/content.cfm/webfeatures_snapshots_20050105.

Ehrenreich, B. (2001). *Nickel and dimed*. New York: Owl Books.

Eskeland, P. (2003, June 20). *Chairman Manzullo: America's white-collar workers latest victims of overseas jobs migration* (Small Business Committee notes, No. 108-20). Retrieved May 11, 2006, from www.wipp.org/press/200306_press/20030620_notes.html.

Even, W., & Macpherson, D. (2000). *Rising above the minimum wage*. Washington, DC: Employment Policies Institute.

Feran, T. (2003, September 22). Two incomes don't add up. *Houston Chronicle*, p. 3E.

FinAid. (2006a). *Student loans*. Retrieved May 14, 2006, from www.finaid.org/loans/.

FinAid. (2006b). *Tuition inflation*. Retrieved May 8, 2006, from http://www.finaid.org/savings/tuition-inflation.phtml.

Foreclosure rates across the U.S. (2006). *MSN Real Estate*. Retrieved May 9, 2006, from http://realestate.msn.com/buying/Articlenewhome.aspx?cpdocumentid=340866/.

Health Insurance Institute. (1966). *Source book of health insurance data, 1965*. New York: Health Insurance Institute.

Karger, H. (2003). Ending public assistance: The transformation of U.S. public assistance policy into labor policy. *Journal of Social Policy, 32*(3), 383–401.

Karger, H. (2005). *Shortchanged: Life and debt in the fringe economy*. San Francisco: Berrett-Koehler.

Karger, H., & Stoesz, D. (2006). *American social welfare policy: A pluralist approach* (5th ed.). Boston: Allyn & Bacon.

Keynes, J. M. (1965). *The general theory of employment, interest and money*. New York: Harcourt.

Lohr, S. (2004, December 5). Maybe it's not all your fault. *New York Times*, p. 8.

Mishel, L., Bernstein, J., & Allegretto, S. (2005). *The state of working America 2004/2005*. Ithaca, NY: Cornell University Press.

Murray, T. (2000, November 4). Experts warn against milking home equity to extend debt. *Minneapolis St. Paul Star Tribune*, p. B-5.

National Center for Education Statistics. (2002). *Digest of Education Statistics*. Washington, DC: U.S. Department of Education.

Paul, N. (2003, June 12). Culture of consumption. *Christian Science Monitor*, p. 18.

Piore, M. (1977). The dual labor market. In D. Gordon (Ed.), *Problems in political economy* (pp. 65–83). Lexington, MA: D. C. Heath.

Price, L., & Bernstein, J. (2006, January 27). *The state of jobs and wages*. Washington, DC: Economic Policy Institute. Retrieved May 6, 2006, from www.jobwatch.org.

Rashell, E., Bernstein, J., & Boushey, H. (2001). *Step up, not out: The case for raising the federal minimum wage for workers in every state* (Issue Brief No. 149). Washington, DC: Economic Policy Institute.

Runzheimer International. (2004). *Daycare costs nationwide*. Retrieved December 21, 2005, from www.runzheimer.com.

Sirota, D. (2006). *Hostile takeover: How big money and corruption conquered our government—And how we can take it back*. New York: Crown.

Social Security Administration. (2002). *Benefit examples for workers with low earnings*. Washington, DC: Retrieved March 16, 2005, from www.ssa.gov/OACT/COLA/exampleLow.html.

Stoesz, D., & Karger, H. (1992). *Reconstructing the American welfare state*. Savage, MD: Rowman & Littlefield.

Sullivan, T., Warren, E., & Westbrook, J. (1989). *As we forgive our debtors*. New York: Oxford University Press.

Sullivan, T., Warren E., & Westbrook, J. (2001). *The fragile middle class*. New Haven, CT: Yale University Press.

TIAA-CREF. (2001). *Making sense of Social Security: Your retirement benefits*. Retrieved February 22, 2004, from www.tiaa-cref.org/wc_libser/mss/benefits.html.

Uchitelle, L. (2004, June 28). Families, deep in debt, facing pain of growing interest rates. *New York Times*, p. 15.

U.S. Census Bureau. (2005, August 30). *Income stable, poverty rate increases, percentage of Americans without health insurance unchanged*. Retrieved May 9, 2006, from www.census.gov /PressRelease/www/releases/archives/income_wealth/005647.html.

U.S. Census Bureau. (2006). *American community survey*. Retrieved May 12, 2006, from www.census.gov/acs/www.

U.S. Divorce Statistics. (2005). *Divorce Magazine*. Retrieved May 11, 2006, from www .divorcemag.com/statistics/statsUS.shtml.

Warren, E., & Tyagi, A. (2003). *The two-income trap*. New York: Basic Books.

zFacts.com. (2006). *National debt clocks and savings clocks*. Retrieved May 31, 2006, from http://zfacts.com/p/461.html.

Chapter 19

DIGITAL TECHNOLOGY AND SOCIAL POLICY: SOCIAL JUSTICE IN A WORLD OF ANYWHERE ACCESS?

Paul R. Raffoul

While there is a lot of discussion about the new digital revolution that has been taking place since the early 1980s, when the Information Age began, little has been written about its impact on social policy and social justice. The latest slogan, at least as stated recently by Bill Gates, is "a world of anywhere access." This comes on the heels of Thomas Friedman's best-selling book, *The World Is Flat* (2005), in which he traces the recent history of the twenty-first century using the developments in technology as the model for moving from the information revolution to the digital revolution. He identified 10 information "flatteners," beginning with the release of Microsoft Windows, version 3.0 (1990), to make the world of information flat: "The diffusion of the PC, fax machines, Windows and dial-up modems connected to a global network all came together in the late 1980s and early 1990s to 'create the basic platform that started the global information revolution' "(Craig J. Mundie, chief tech officer for Microsoft, in Friedman, 2005, p. 53).

How has this burgeoning technology influenced social policy? What are the implications of this technological revolution for the future of social policy? As the title of this chapter suggests, the big question is this: Can social justice exist (or be increased) in a world of anywhere access? I address this question by reviewing where we have come from with technology and how technology has influenced social policy. The challenge concerns the development of social polices that ensure the enhancement of social justice while maintaining the balance between privacy and society's need for shared information. The final section addresses this question about social justice and technology over the next 15 years.

Fifteen years ago people did not have cell phones, PDAs, or iPods. The Internet was just beginning to change the way people access information. E-mail was beginning to alter the way people communicated both at work and at play. The business community was still struggling to find a standard combination of hardware and software (remember WordStar and Word Perfect?) to fit their particular work environment. The policy issues of privacy, confidentiality, and security of information had yet to become a reality. Personal identity was not at risk of theft or misrepresentation.

Today, these devices have become ubiquitous. A large majority of those under the age of 35 own an iPod or have some chord dangling from their ears or something hanging onto the outside of one ear. Cell phones have become so widely used that some states are now considering laws to ban their use in automobiles or to limit their use to hands-free operation while driving a motor vehicle. We are still seeking a social balance as to where and when cell phones are acceptable. For example, many courthouses ban cell phones and force you to forfeit it on the way in. Many companies have policies on where, when, and what type of devices can be brought through security because of privacy and security concerns. People complain that they cannot work as effectively if their e-mail or business network is not working. More important, the productivity of individuals decreases considerably when the technology they rely on to do their work or conduct their lives is not working. A recent test by a newspaper editor revealed that he could not go without his cell phone for more than a couple of days. He lost his temper, his productivity decreased, and eventually he succumbed to tears because he could not be contacted on his cell phone by people he deemed important.

The issues of privacy and security are uppermost in the minds of employers. Personal identity theft has become a major source of illicit revenue. Identity theft is no longer an unusual occurrence. According to a 2005 survey released jointly by the Better Business Bureau and Javelin Strategy and Research, although identity fraud no longer seems to be increasing, 9.3 million American adults became victims of identity fraud in 2004. The total U.S. annual identity fraud cost was $56.2 billion, a figure that has remained essentially unchanged since a Federal Trade Commission survey in September 2003 (Better Business Bureau, 2003). If this trend in the use of technology and the products derived from technology continues, what will happen in the next 15 years? How will technology influence social policy, and will social justice be any more attainable than it is today? Several critical themes will begin to answer these questions in this chapter.

GLOBALIZATION

Globalization is advancing today throughout our society, both in the workplace and in our personal lives, at a very rapid rate. With the increased use of digital technology the world has become a smaller place, with fewer barriers to communication and greater access for everyone, wherever they are in the world, for whatever information they want to know. Geography is no longer a barrier to communication; people from all over the world can organize around issues of mutual interest and have access to information that is available to all.

> A revolution in technology has enabled any work that can be digitized to be performed virtually anywhere on the globe. Today highly skilled employees in Bangalore, Beijing, and other distant places on the planet can communicate with colleagues in American companies almost as easily as if they were working down the hall. (Bok, 2006, pp. 4–5)

Social justice takes on a new meaning when the common frame of reference is humankind and not just our own society. Will this globalization trend make the achievement of social justice more possible, or will it make for increased discrepancies and injustices?

SOCIETAL ACCEPTANCE AND UTILIZATION OF TECHNOLOGY

With this diffusion of technology throughout the world has come the societal acceptance of technology as enabling more of our behavior to be visible, albeit in digital form. We have become accustomed to being recorded when speaking on the telephone, being videotaped while shopping or using a financial institution, and being told to go to the Internet for further information.

The creation of the search engine Google and its phenomenal growth is a good example of our acceptance and utilization of technology. It is reported that Google is now processing 1 billion searches per day, up from 200 million just 2 years ago. Who are the people asking these questions? What are they using this information for?

The evolution of Google is Friedman's (2005, pp. 152–159) ninth flattener:

> Never before in the history of the planet have so many people—on their *own*—had the ability to find so much information about so many things and about so many other people. . . .
>
> There is no bigger flattener than the idea of making all the world's knowledge, or even just a big chunk of it, available to anyone and everyone, anytime, anywhere. . . .
>
> In the age of the superpower search, everyone is a celebrity. Google levels information—it has no class boundaries or education boundaries. Google is like God. God is wireless, God is everywhere, and God sees everything. Any questions in the world, you ask Google.

EMPOWERMENT

With the availability of information to everyone comes personal empowerment and community development. All participants share equally in information, which leads to more informed decision making and, hopefully, better planning. Although the validity and reliability of information is not always known, it is equally available to all and provides a shared beginning for groups with similar and special interests. It also establishes, builds, and maintains relationships without geographic, ethnic, or social boundaries. The so-called digital divide no longer refers to access to information, but to the divide between credible information and bogus or spurious information. The challenge for policy makers is to ensure that credible information is made available as soon as possible to all constituents.

PRIVACY ISSUES

Personal identity, confidentiality, and security issues have become especially important as we have moved into a digital world. Potential violations of personal freedoms have led to many inconveniences and delays in implementing a truly digital environment in all areas of our lives. Even with passwords required to gain access to your personal computer, your network, your work computer and work network and to access a variety of sites on the Internet, all access points have become vulnerable to hacking by unauthorized persons and created numerous security risks, often with considerable financial consequences. It has become the norm to have to register, select a password, and authenticate yourself in order to conduct business in any way on the Internet. Financial institutions, with the prodding of the federal government to develop mandatory identity management systems, will be making it even more difficult in the future for unauthorized users to gain access to accounts and information.

From a social policy standpoint, the question is where to draw the line between freedom of information and individual information confidentiality and identity security. For example, how can we provide information about human needs without losing an individual's privacy rights? How can we identify individuals in need without taking away their privacy?

INFORMATION ACCESS AND AUTHENTICITY

Just because information is universally available doesn't make it accurate (valid), consistent (reliable), or useful, especially to those underserved and underrepresented populations who do not have a strong political voice with which to influence social policy. Being able to access information through the use of technology, which today is primarily the Internet, does not mean it is automatically useful and meaningful to the user. Critical analysis, reading, and synthesis are often required to access the most useful, current, and accurate information available on the Web. This is not an innate skill but rather one that requires learning and practice to maximize one's efficiency in terms of time and effort. Even learning how to fully use a search engine (e.g., Google, Yahoo, MS Search) requires a basic understanding of Boolean logic, named after the Irish mathematician George Boole, to use the three logical operators *or, and,* and *not.* Such skills are now being taught in elementary and middle schools across the country.

It is important to remember also that once information is on the Internet it takes on a life of its own, which means that it lives on, sometimes much longer than anyone could imagine, and remains a source of outdated information that is unchanged by time. It is relatively easy today to enter a person's name on a web site and find that person's local address, phone number, and e-mail alias. For less than $20, a background check can be obtained, criminal records can be checked, credit reports generated, as well as motor vehicle registration, marriage licenses, and divorce decrees. While there are clearly unanswered ethical issues around the use of this personal information, once it is on the Internet it is publicly available and beyond the control of the individual user.

A recent letter to the *New York Times Sunday Magazine* ethicist, Randy Cohen, highlights the ethical dilemma yet to be resolved. A college admissions reviewer had read on the Internet the personal information of a high school graduate seeking admission and asked about the ethics of including this information in his admission review materials. Cohen's answer was,

> You would not read someone's old-fashioned pen-and-paper diary without consent; you should regard a blog similarly. Your reading this student's blog is legal—he posted it voluntarily, and in that sense it is public information—but not every young person grasps this. Many unwisely regard their blogs as at least semiprivate. You should not exploit their youthful folly. Indeed, so befogged are students about online postings—especially to FaceBook, MySpace and the like—that universities commonly devote a portion of freshman orientation to wising them up. . . . Because such material will not be considered for most students, it is unfair to subject your interviews to this additional scrutiny. What's more, such online info is unreliable, even when posted by the person himself, as many an Internet dater has learned to her peril. Not every six-foot guy with a head of rich luxuriant hair would be recognized as such. Not in person. Not by his wife. (www.nytimes.com/2007/03/11/magazine/11wwlnethicist.t.html?_r=1/)

An example of how information can be changed on the Internet is the user-contributed online encyclopedia Wikipedia. Wikis are web sites that allow users to directly edit any web page on their own from their home computer. This allows the reader the ability to track the status of articles, review individual changes, and discuss issues and functions as "social software." "Wikipedia works by consensus, with users adding and modifying content while trying to reach common ground along the way" (Friedman, 2005, pp. 92–93).

Again, however, the validity and reliability of such information is inconsistent, subject to change over time, and at the mercy of the online readers who contribute. Some colleges and universities have recently prohibited students from using such web sites for these reasons.

ENSURING DIVERSITY AND CULTURAL DIFFERENCES

As we become one with the world, it is important to retain our individual identities, including the cultural, ethnic, and geographic differences that make up our global society. Just because we all have access to the same information doesn't mean that we will all use it in the same way. There is a tendency to assume that with everyone having access to the same information there is one big digital melting pot of information that is available and applicable to everyone in the same way.

> There is another side to in-forming that people are going to have to get used to, and that is other people's ability to in-form themselves about you from a very early age. Search engines flatten the world by eliminating all the valleys and peaks, all the walls and rocks, that people used to hide inside of, atop, behind, or under in order to mask their reputations or parts of their past. In a flat world, you can't run, you can't hide, and smaller and smaller rocks are turned over. Live your life honestly, because whatever you do, whatever mistakes you make, will be searchable one day. The flatter the world becomes, the more ordinary people become transparent—and available. (Friedman, 2005, p. 158)

INFLUENCING THE DEVELOPMENT OF SOCIAL POLICY

Technology provides the means for greater participation of more people in the development of social policy than ever before. With the availability of information, increased access and communication and consensus building comes the potential to have an increasingly greater impact on the development of new social policies that can benefit more people. The means to achieve greater social justice for everyone is now available to more people than ever before. Whether people are willing to take advantage of this technology remains unanswered.

In the first empirical report of the extent of e-mail use by agency-based direct service social workers, Finn (2006) found that although e-mail use was common practice among 75% of the social workers in his convenience sample ($N = 384$), policy and practice on the use of e-mail in social work agencies is not uniform. Only 50% reported that their agency has a written e-mail policy, and only 33% indicated that the agency attaches a confidentiality statement to their e-mails. "It appears that practice has outpaced policies and infrastructure at many social work agencies that use e-mail" (p. 15).

UNINTENDED CONSEQUENCES OF TECHNOLOGY AND SOCIAL POLICY

Major societal change due to the influence of technology will take time. Some changes began 15 years ago. Some changes have occurred relatively quickly, as seen in the way the younger generation has taken to the Apple iPod and made it the world's best-selling range of digital audio players and how its worldwide mainstream adoption made it one of the most popular consumer brands. The changes yet to come in the next 15 years will depend, in part, on the development of social policies that control how technology will be defined and utilized. A major variable in the use of technology and the development of social policies for them is the people who use them.

One example has to do with people's attitudes and beliefs about using technology in their professional practice. Take direct service social workers, for example. Jerry Finn's (2006, p.18) study suggests that

> e-mail is becoming common among social workers, and is beginning to be used between social workers and consumers as well. As electronic communication becomes increasingly integrated into agency life, new opportunities for providing efficient, effective, and convenient services will arise. These opportunities may be underutilized or undermined, however, by social worker's negative attitudes and lack of information about the therapeutic and supportive use of e-mail with consumers. Social workers are concerned about the quality of their relationship with consumers of services. If they believe that e-mail is not an effective therapeutic medium and that lack of confidentiality can occur when e-mail is used, they are not likely to support online services. Policies and infrastructure that promote e-mail safety and confidentiality will need to become standard practice. Attitude change and policy development will require well-conceived and comprehensive research efforts to further define, assess, and examine e-mail use in order to inform agency training and practice.

Who will be the master, technology or social policy designed to enhance social justice? How we define social policies about technology in the future will determine how quickly societal changes will take place. It will also determine, in large part, how attainable social justice will become in the future. Technology is a double-edged sword: It can be the motivator to change for the better for everyone, or it can be the divider between the haves and the have-nots creating more social injustice.

Looking back over the past 15 years, it would appear that technology has led in the reformulation of social policies. That is, policies have been developed in response to technology rather than in anticipation of technological changes. Identity theft, loss of personal information, spamming, phishing, and so on have created the need for new policies and procedures for protecting personal information from being exploited by others. Laws have been passed to control these activities as technology has made information more available. Social policies have been developed to maintain social justice at the boundary between personal privacy and society's need to know. Vigilance in monitoring this interface will insure that social justice can be maintained in a world of anywhere access.

A LOOK AHEAD TO THE YEAR 2022

What will the social work workplace look like when the world of anywhere access has been around for some 15 years? Will we be inside a central office building? Will we have the same regular 9 to 5 office hours? Will all our client contacts be face-to-face? All our therapy? All our work? I don't think so.

Given the rapid deployment of technology throughout our society and the world, it is highly likely that in the next 15 years, we will move away from a centralized, single, unitary workplace. Social workers will probably be working wherever they are physically located, with access to their office databases, clients' records, and the clients themselves via digital technology, either in real time (live video) or in recorded time. Just as centralized, stationary, desktop computing in universities is being transformed today into a learning commons with access to multiple forms of computing (i.e., from desktops to laptops, with digital media equipment, photographic equipment, graphics, images, all available in a common environment), so too will the workplace of social workers be transformed. Social workers will most likely be where their clients are (both geographically and emotionally) with the ability to communicate instantly with them in real time. Clients will no longer have to come to the office to initiate contact and complete applications, but will have access, via the Internet, to all the forms they need to complete the application process before meeting, probably face-to-face, with an intake worker.

Online therapy (e-therapy) has already begun to appear on the Internet; a recent Google search found over 32 million web sites under that category alone. While e-therapy is not psychotherapy and should not be compared to traditional, face-to-face therapy, it is viewed by many as an alternative source of help when traditional therapy is not accessible. It may be conducted as a single consultation to answer a question or as an ongoing conversation via e-mail, chat, video, or even Internet phone (voice-over-IP). To support their belief in online therapy, some cite the surgeon general's report on *Mental Health* (1999), which states that while 20% of Americans have a diagnosable mental illness, nearly two-thirds reportedly never seek treatment for their illness. The use of online therapy will most certainly continue and expand as the demand for services continues to increase faster than the supply of qualified practitioners. Research is needed to monitor, evaluate, and develop best practice strategies for online therapy, particularly in relation to hidden or underserved (especially in rural areas) populations.

Another exciting use of digital technology has been the creation of virtual reality (VR) software that can be used to simulate a variety of clinical and behavioral situations. Such software is being used to educate children with disabilities, parents of children with disabilities, persons with dependency issues, smoking cessation interventions, and the like. Online, there are some 12 million VR web sites now identified. Anywhere that a digital image can be utilized there is a software program to enable this image to be viewed in a VR environment. The convenience of being able to transport to the person in need such a variety of clinical, educational, and behaviorally specific programs has expanded the use of VR software from business applications ("How do I build this product in the right way?") to clinical applications ("How can I quit smoking in a room full of smokers?") to parental training programs.

The demand for such programs will only increase as more and more people become comfortable with the use of digital media and as the cost of digital equipment continues to decrease. It won't be too long before printed owner's manuals will be replaced with digital media showing how to assemble any product you buy. On the clinical side, it will be possible, I suspect, to purchase your own VR software to lose weight or quit smoking without having to go to a clinic or find a therapist. The number of possible applications of this technology seems unlimited. Who should be responsible for educating our children in the use of this technology? What responsibility should public schools have for teaching our children about the use of technology? Can we increase the use of technology, and increase social justice, by making such education available to all? I think so.

So, where we will be in 15 years with technology and social policy is difficult to say with certainty, but it surely will be a different place than where we are today. Few people 15 years ago could imagine how much would have changed by now. Who is brave (or stupid) enough to predict where we will be 15 years from now? Suffice it to say that if we keep our views of social justice clearly in mind, our future social policies will provide opportunities to increase social justice for all in the world.

REFERENCES

Better Business Bureau. (2003). *Identity theft*. Retrieved March 2, 2007, from www.bbbonline.org /idtheft/consumers.asp.

Bok, D. (2006). *Our underachieving colleges: A candid look at how much students learn and why they should be learning more*. Princeton, NJ: Princeton University Press.

Cohen, R., (2007, March 11). *Online extracurriculars*. Retrieved March 13, 2007, from www.nytimes .com/2007/03/11/magazine/11wwlnethicist.t.html?_r=1.

Finn, J. (2006). An exploratory study of email use by direct service social workers. *Journal of Technology in Human Services*, *24*(4), 1–20.

Friedman, T. (2005). *The world is flat: A brief history of the twenty-first century*. New York: Farrar, Straus and Giroux.

Mental health: A report of the surgeon general. (1999). Available from www.surgeongeneral.gov /library/mentalhealth.

Chapter 20

WELFARE REFORM: THE NEED FOR SOCIAL EMPATHY

Elizabeth A. Segal

The history of welfare in America parallels public opinion and reflects values and beliefs that are deeply held. As a public policy, welfare today is typically regarded as limited to the cash assistance program of Temporary Assistance for Needy Families (TANF), which evolved from the 1935 Aid to Dependent Children (ADC) and the 1962 Aid to Families with Dependent Children (AFDC) provisions of the Social Security Act. However, TANF is actually a very small part of the social welfare programs and services provided through government. Federal, state, and local efforts to provide for social well-being are vastly greater than TANF. In the context of our entire social well-being, government involvement in programs such as Social Security and Medicare far outweigh the contributions to TANF. Consider that in 2006 the federal financial effort for Social Security and Medicare was $918 billion, or 34% of the entire U.S. budget, while expenditures for TANF were $17 billion, or .6% of the budget (Congressional Budget Office, 2007). In spite of its very small size, TANF and its predecessors ADC and AFDC have been the focus of welfare reform. We can conclude that this emphasis defines welfare in America as cash assistance to the poor, not government interventions for social well-being. Thus, the policy discussions and changes regarding cash assistance for the poor are the focus of this discussion on welfare reform.

The ADC program was designed to be temporary, an emergency response to the needs of poor widows and their children in the wake of the Great Depression. It was thought that once the major part of the program, the social insurance provisions that have come to be known as Social Security, had time to take hold, there would no longer be a need for cash assistance to poor women and children. The view at the time was that these needy families were deserving of help, and "by devoting themselves to mothering, the female recipients were performing what God, nature, and society intended women to do and doing so, moreover, under difficult circumstances" (Gordon, 2001, p. 17). So what happened over the next 60 years? Why, by 1996, were politicians and the public calling for welfare reform to "end the dependence of needy parents on government benefits by promoting job preparation, work and marriage . . . to enable them to leave the program and become self-sufficient" (Pub. L. 104-193, sections 401 and 402)?

How did the nation move from wanting to care for poor families by using government support to keep women in the home, to insisting that these mothers go to work and stop receiving government support? The years 1935 to 1996, and the more than 10 years since the latest experiment in welfare reform, reveal a journey in societal policies and programs that reflect shifting values and beliefs and call for a new approach that is truly kinder and gentler, one that reflects social empathy.

Social empathy is based in personal empathy, the ability of a person to understand what life is like for another person. It is nonjudgmental and not sentimental, as is sympathy. Sympathy is feeling bad for someone and may even evoke thoughts of irresponsible behavior on the part of the person for whom we feel bad. Empathy is imagining yourself in another person's situation, imagining what that would feel like and what you would wish to be done. It does not deny personal responsibility, but responsibility is not the focus. Social empathy in regard to poverty places empathy in the larger societal context and asks those who are in power and with resources to imagine what life would be like if they did not have those resources. It requires an ability to view others' life circumstances as if they were your own. The evolution of welfare from 1935 to the present reflects a great deal of sympathy and blame, but little social empathy.

A BRIEF HISTORY OF WELFARE REFORM

The Great Depression was the catalyst for federal involvement in personal well-being, a course that continues today. Social Security has become an institutionalized social welfare program that has widespread support and is considered the right of every working man and woman in America. Its counterpart, welfare, does not enjoy such support. In 1935, President Franklin Roosevelt did not want the federal government to become entrenched in providing relief, and he knew that direct relief was not enough to correct the economic problems brought on by the Depression:

> The Federal Government must and shall quit this business of relief. . . . I am not willing that the vitality or our people be further sapped. . . . We must preserve not only the bodies of the unemployed from destitution but also their self-respect, their self-reliance and courage and determination. (Roosevelt, 1935)

The Depression disproved the concept that poverty was due to personal laziness and unworthiness. The evidence was that millions of hard-working, responsible, and previously economically stable workers were unemployed and could not find work. The overall failure of economic institutions lessened the resistance toward adopting a national welfare policy (Trattner, 1999). Those in power could see the impact of the Great Depression in ways that were understandable, to people they could relate to, hard-working people who were part of the economic system. Although the Social Security Act of 1935 contained both the long-term social insurance provisions of Social Security and the short-term cash assistance provisions of welfare, the two parts were anything but equal. Even the early founders were not invested in both programs:

> The Bureau of Public Assistance was in charge of a despised program, which, at least in theory, the Social Security Boards intended should wither away, whereas the Bureau of Old Age and Survivors Insurance was in charge of a preferred program that was expected to grow until, again in theory, it virtually supplanted the first. (Derthick, 1979, p. 160)

Thus, the two parts of public economic support—social insurance and public assistance—evolved in very different directions. Although the original ADC program seemed to embrace poor families, this has not been the typical policy response. Welfare historically faced reform when the need for cheap labor arose, when patriarchal arrangements were challenged, or when public perception held that welfare interfered with social expectations (Abramovitz, 2000; Axinn & Hirsch, 1993; Piven & Cloward, 1971).

The original ADC program was passed as Title IV of the Social Security Act in 1935. Although originally anticipated as a temporary response to poverty that would, in time, be unnecessary due to the expansion of Social Security, ADC instead expanded. In 1935, only needy dependent children were covered. The federal program did not cover a parent or relative in the household. However, in 1950 the program began to include the coverage of a caretaker relative. The program was expanded again in 1961 to include unemployed parents, and in 1962 the coverage of a second parent was included and the program was changed to Aid to Families with Dependent Children (U.S. Department of Health and Human Services, 1998).

Sentiment toward the poor shifted following the perceived failures of the War on Poverty. In spite of the growth and permanency of the AFDC program, families were still poor and seemed to linger on the program. By 1988, AFDC was under scrutiny and amended significantly through the Family Support Act (FSA) of 1988. The core of the FSA was to bolster parental responsibility through enforcement of child support, as well as education and training to prepare AFDC recipients for employment (Segal, 1989). These policy changes reflected the shift from the 1930s ideology of supporting young widows to stay at home with their children, to the 1980s ideology of pushing parents out of the home and into taking responsibility for children born outside of marriage. While the FSA amendments to AFDC impacted families through greater emphasis on child support enforcement and more employment activities for adult recipients, they did not change the original structure of the program. It was still an entitlement social welfare program—as long as a family was eligible, it received benefits and states received matching federal funding to cover all recipients.

The original design of the social welfare system was to maintain women in roles supportive of the nuclear family (Miller, 1992), which in turn supports an economic system with a wage earner outside the home and a homemaker caring for children inside the home. This structure reflected the demographics of the times; the majority of poor single women headed households due to the death of a husband. However, over the next 50 years, families changed, and the majority of families receiving AFDC were headed by single women who were divorced or never married. By 2002, only .8% of adult recipients were widowed, compared to 67% who were single and 21% who were divorced or separated (Administration for Children and Families, 2004). The FSA of 1988 tried to deal with this changing demographic by enforcing the responsibility of the noncustodial parent through child support enforcement. However, the impact of these changes were not apparent to policy makers. It seemed that the federal government was supporting illegitimacy. As Senator Lauch Faircloth, one of the key sponsors of 1996 welfare reform, stated, "The federal government has paid people to have children out of wedlock" (as quoted in Youth Policy, 1994, p. 44). So members of Congress once again focused on welfare reform.

The efforts of 1996 followed the pattern set during the 1980s to limit government involvement. Welfare reform of 1996 was embodied in the Personal Responsibility and Work Opportunity Reconciliation Act (PRWORA; Pub. L. 104-193), which was designed to do three things: enforce work, promote marriage, and reduce the role of government in social welfare (Abramovitz, 2006). The major policy goal was to decrease people's dependence on welfare. Another of the overall goals behind welfare reform during this period was to not only "end welfare as we know it," the comment made popular by President Bill Clinton, but to end the growth in welfare state spending. One of the key proposals circulating during this time called for capping the growth of welfare spending on programs for family support, particularly cash assistance programs. The final law included caps on monies to the states for public assistance benefits and tightened eligibility for cash assistance programs.

TEMPORARY ASSISTANCE FOR NEEDY FAMILIES

Public cash assistance, or welfare as we commonly refer to it, was the target of 1996 welfare reform. Those reform efforts created the TANF program out of the AFDC program. This reform shifted the emphasis of the program from income support to welfare-to-work. The ostensible goal of the program was to emphasize economic self-sufficiency and decrease the number of people receiving assistance by emphasizing employment. Specifically, one of the primary goals outlined by the law states that the purpose of creating TANF was to "end the dependence of needy families on government benefits by promoting job preparation, work, and marriage" (Sec. 401 (a) (2)). The expected outcome was that fewer people would receive welfare, they would become employed and self-sufficient, and there would be a savings of federal money due to less being spent on welfare assistance.

Today, TANF is a time-limited, no-guarantee program. It provides temporary cash assistance, up to 2 years consecutively, with a total lifetime maximum of 5 years, and requires work efforts of all participants. Recipients must participate in at least 30 hours a week of unsubsidized or subsidized employment, on-the-job training, community service, vocational training, or child care for other parents involved in community service. In addition, states must achieve a 50% rate of work participation for families with an adult. This approach greatly deviated from the 60-year-long policy of AFDC. The substitution of TANF for AFDC changed the way public assistance had been provided to poor families. No longer was there unlimited enrollment as long as a family qualified, nor could mothers stay at home; instead, work was the ultimate goal.

The welfare reform of 1996 has stood, with only minor changes. The latest revisions came in 2005 as part of the Deficit Reduction Act (Pub. L. 109-171). With the program set to expire in 2002, Congress debated the legislation, but could not reach consensus on reauthorization. For 3 years, stopgap extensions were passed until reauthorization was agreed on in 2005. The new legislation reauthorizes TANF through fiscal year 2010 at the current level of $16.5 billion per year, funds marriage promotion grants, increases child care funding, and extends transitional medical assistance for 1 year. There were efforts to increase the work participation rate, but these proved to be unsuccessful. However, the new legislation mandates regulations that clearly define what constitutes work activities and sets standards for verifying work participation (Falk, Gish, & Solomon-Fears, 2006). The end result of the new, tighter work standards will likely have the effect of increasing the work participation rate. These latest efforts simply reinforce the goals of the 1996 reform and maintain the emphasis on work, marriage, and decreasing the role of government in supporting poor families.

Since its inception in 1996, TANF has been successful in decreasing the number of recipients. By 2004, TANF roles dropped from more than 12 million participants, of whom 8.5 million were children, to fewer than 5 million, of whom 3.6 million were children (Social Security Administration, 2006). The goal of reducing the number of public cash assistance recipients was achieved by welfare reform, yet how successful has TANF and the welfare reforms of 1996 been in promoting work and marriage? And more important to social welfare advocates, how well has TANF done in alleviating poverty and improving life outcomes for poor children? Finally, in terms of reducing social welfare expenditures, how successful has welfare reform been in capping federal expenditures?

THE SUCCESS OF WELFARE REFORM

Research findings on the impact of TANF are mixed. Although more women left TANF for employment, they do not seem to be better off financially. They have full-time jobs that pay $7 to $8 an hour, and even though they may have transitional support, they eventually lose health-care coverage from Medicaid (Acs & Loprest, 2004). Other researchers found similar results: "Welfare recipients tend to have unstable, short-term jobs, with few benefits and low wages" (King & Mueser, 2005, p. 2).

Data reveal that although the numbers on TANF have declined, there are more families today that qualify but do not receive support. In 1995, 84% of families that met the eligibility requirements of the AFDC program participated; by 2002, only 48% of eligible families were enrolled in TANF. The drop among poor children was even more severe. The share of children living in poverty who received AFDC/TANF dropped from a high of 62% in 1995 to a low of 31% in 2003 (Parrott & Sherman, 2006). This trend occurred in spite of growth in the numbers of poor children. There were almost 1.3 million additional children living in poverty from 2000 to 2003 (DeNavas-Walt, Proctor, & Lee, 2006).

This means that today many eligible families are not receiving support, and fewer poor children are covered by the program. Thus, the "success" in decreasing the caseloads of public cash assistance programs seems to be a result of factors that do not include reducing poverty or decreasing need for the program. The decline in coverage of eligible families leaves an estimated 2 million children living in poor households with a jobless adult and no income assistance from TANF. Even before the current data revealed the decline in TANF coverage, welfare advocates were alarmed by the impact of the 1996 welfare reform:

> As currently implemented, the welfare-to-work solution is a match made in hell. It joins together poor mothers with few resources whose family responsibilities require employment flexibility with jobs in the low-wage labor market that often are the most inflexible, have the least family necessary benefits (vacation time, health care, sick days), and provide levels of pay that often are insufficient to support a single person, let alone a family. (Albelda, 2001, p. 68)

Poverty among children in the United States is still prevalent, especially considering the wealth and recent economic growth in the nation overall. Concurrent with this trend is the decline in TANF, the primary antipoverty program for poor households. With declines in low-income families' earnings accompanied by declines in public programs, the persistence of poverty among children worsens. With deeper poverty comes diminished opportunities for positive development and life outcomes.

WHO RECEIVES WELFARE?

When policy makers focus on welfare reform, who are they really targeting? To the public, reform sounds like major overhauls of our social welfare system. However, welfare reforms, particularly the changes of 1996, have historically been focused on public assistance recipients of the AFDC/TANF programs. As discussed previously, this represents a very small part of the national budget. Two-thirds of the recipients of AFDC/TANF programs have been children, most of whom are under the age of 12. The one-third of the program recipients who are adults are primarily single women, most of whom are lacking sufficient formal education or work experience. They are the poorest families in this country.

According to the Administration for Children and Families (2004), 47% of TANF families had only 1 child, and 28% had 2, with 74% of the children under 12 years of age. Only 3% of the adult recipients had an education level beyond high school completion. Almost 75% are families of color: 38% African American, 25% Hispanic, 2% Asian, and 1% Native American; 52% of the adult recipients were under the age of 30. The average family monthly benefit in 2004 was $397 (Social Security Administration, 2006). The demographics reveal that TANF consists of very young families of color with single, never-married mothers, who have minimal formal education. These families represent those on the edge of our social system in terms of economics, family composition, race, age, and education.

WHY WELFARE REFORM HAS FAILED

How do we determine if welfare reform has been successful? That depends on our perceptions and expectations of the program. If the goal was to reduce the number of people receiving TANF, then welfare reform has been very successful, reducing the numbers by almost 58%. If the goal was economic self-sufficiency, then the changes have failed. What welfare reform did not change, and actually never addressed, was poverty. In fact, in congressional discussions preceding the vote on the 1996 welfare reform, poverty was not addressed as a social issue, only as a personal responsibility (Segal & Kilty, 2003). So it is not surprising that PRWORA barely addresses barriers to economic success. Other than child care, no other resources to support self-sufficiency, such as health care, transportation, job availability, or education, are addressed. The only social programs that are included are promotion of marriage and discouragement of out-of-wedlock births.

No one wants to deal with the structural problems that face our nation—the budget deficit, a market economy that does not support full employment, a substandard minimum wage, the lack of universal health care, unequal access to quality education, and disregard for the future well-being of all children. Focusing on the poor person and his or her behavior rather than the systemic causes of poverty is not new and has been reflected throughout our modern history (Katz, 1989; Patterson, 2000; Wilson, 1987).

As has been done with other difficult public policy issues, deconstructing services has great appeal. Welfare has not worked, there are still poor people, so momentum rises to dismantle the system. For advocates of programs for the poor, the result of this dismantling, or "dewelfarization," would be millions of families, most of whom included young children, receiving less government support. Their analyses foretold that

> the bill would make deep, often indiscriminate, cuts in basic support without including strategies for improving employability or making work pay. Increases in poverty, homelessness, and hunger for millions of children would almost certainly result, and states would likely end up paying a greater share of the costs of programs for the poor. (Bloom, Parrott, Shapiro, & Super, 1994, p. xxi)

Very recent research points to this outcome, 10 years later. According to an Associated Press analysis in 2007:

> The welfare state is bigger than ever despite a decade of policies designed to wean poor people from public aid. The number of families receiving cash benefits from welfare has plummeted since the government imposed time limits on the payments a decade ago. But other programs for the poor, including Medicaid, food stamps and disability benefits, are bursting with new enrollees. (*New York Times*, 2007)

While cash assistance spending dropped, expenditures on noncash assistance grew significantly. Table 20.1 outlines the changes in a nine-state sample conducted by the U.S. General Accounting Office (2006). Welfare-related health-care costs grew the most, only marginally offset by reductions in cash assistance. In the nine-state sample, while the states cut back $8.4 billion in cash assistance, they spent an additional $25 billion in health care and $17.4 billion in noncash assistance programs, all in constant dollars controlling for inflation. Thus, though people were leaving the welfare rolls and no longer receiving a monthly cash assistance check, they were accessing other social support programs targeted for low-income families. This raises two questions: Did the loss of cash assistance create more hardships for which families needed support? And does trying to assist poor adults in gaining employment and self-sufficiency cost more than providing monthly cash assistance payments?

What we do seem to know is that the efforts at welfare reform did not address poverty and true economic self-sufficiency for families receiving public assistance. Instead, we witnessed the frustration and anger of a society struggling with structural changes that are not easily addressed. Single-parent families are a reality at all economic levels, but the impact is especially felt among low-income families.

Table 20.1   1995–2004 Changes in Welfare-Related Expenditures

Categories of Change in Real Spending	Median (%)	Total Dollars (in Billions)
Noncash assistance (employment services and training, work, other supports, and aid for at-risk families)	+45	+17.4
Welfare-related health care	+61	+24.9
Cash assistance	−62	−8.4

Note: Nine-state sample—CA, CO, LA, MD, MI, NY, OR, TX, WI.
Author calculations based on data in *Welfare Reform: Better Information Needed to Understand Trends in States' Uses of the TANF Block Grant*. GAO-06-414. U.S. General Accounting Office, 2006, Washington, DC: Author.

INHERENT CONTRADICTIONS IN WELFARE REFORM

The TANF program was designed to end welfare as we know it. It was enacted to promote economic self-sufficiency and promote the nuclear two-parent family. It does this by limiting the amount of time a family can receive assistance and by mandating work efforts. It created rewards for marriage and penalized a woman for the birth of an additional child out of wedlock. These efforts, while touted as reform, raise a number of contradictions.

If the best people to raise a child are his or her parents, then support of them to be *with* their child would be imperative—hence the legislative incentives for marriage, pushing father involvement through child support enforcement, and deterring out-of-wedlock births. However, if those parental roles are not met, then the one parent who *is* willing and able to be with the child is mandated to *leave* her child during the day with someone else and is not supported to stay at home to care for her child. This position deviated from the original intent of the program, which was to keep a mother at home to raise her children in the event that the father was gone. The new welfare reform does not address the contradiction that a child's own parent is the best caretaker, but if that parent does not conform to the one model of two parents, one male and one female, and married, then public support will not be provided.

The outcome is not at all focused on the well-being of the child nor on the support of the caretaking parent, but only on perpetuating one and only one option of family structure, a structure that has declined in the overall society anyway. From 1950 to 2002, the rate of divorce in the United States increased 54% and the rate of marriages declined 30% (U.S. Census Bureau, 2005). It is difficult to mandate family constellations for those who are not dependent on government programs, but we do so for those who are.

VALUES CONFLICTS

Poverty is related to both individual behaviors and structural conditions. However, the continued existence of poverty in the United States goes beyond these two reasons. Why do Americans accept poverty as a perpetual part of the economy and social fabric? Why are we not distressed that in the wealthiest nation in the world there are millions of people who are living without enough food and clothing and with inadequate shelter?

People are not opposed to the principle of government support for the needy, but there is a very strong perception that most people who receive welfare are undeserving. In a comprehensive study of public attitudes toward welfare, Gilens (1999) concluded that a major reason why higher income people oppose welfare is because they lack personal experience with welfare and thus have different perceptions of how it impacts the lives of people who are poor. The reason for our disconnect between social well-being and poverty is our inability to relate, and in turn understand, what it is to live in poverty and why people seem to be stuck there. In researching attitudes toward public assistance, Gilens found that "well-off Americans are more likely to want welfare spending cut, but this desire is not motivated by self-interest; rather, it reflects the different experiences with and perceptions of welfare that characterize Americans of different social classes" (p. 31).

We are a conflicted nation when it comes to need and responsibility. Nearly 66% of the public believe that "the government should guarantee every citizen enough to eat and a place to sleep," yet 78% believe that "people should take responsibility for their own lives and economic well-being and not expect other people to help" (Bostrom, 2001, p. 12). There are a number of conflicting values that reflect the split between believing in government support and expecting individuals to be personally responsible for their well-being (Segal, 2007). The following key areas where people's values and beliefs split compound the difficulties we face in trying to create social policies that address poverty and in turn welfare reform.

Undeserving versus Deserving

The concept of who deserves to be helped and who does not officially dates back to colonial times and the adoption of the Elizabethan Poor Laws. Although public awareness grew that some people simply need help, the standard was that they should be deserving of that help. "Deserving" was translated into "needing" through no fault of one's own. Thus, widows, orphans, people with physical disabilities, and the elderly fit into legitimate categories of need. Able-bodied adults not working were seen as undeserving. These differentiations continue today. But what about the individual who might want to work, but who dropped out of school at 16? Do we hold that young person responsible for the rest of his or her life for the decision to leave school, or do we try to intervene to assist that person? And if we do intervene, do we do it with a monthly cash assistance check, do we enroll him or her in a work program, or do we send him or her back to school? We tend to make that decision based on the next set of conflicting values.

Self-Sufficiency versus Social Support

How much is each individual responsible for having enough to eat, a safe place to live, and an education? To what extent is it our collective social responsibility to ensure these things? If we view poverty as the result of a person's unwillingness to work hard enough or mistakes the person has made in his or her life, then we are most likely going to focus on individual responsibility. If we view poverty as a consequence of social conditions, then we are most likely going to call for public policies and programs that address poverty through government and societal efforts. For some of us, the value of social responsibility is so strong that it may not matter who is at "fault" for poverty, the individual or society. Rather, our responsibility to others is greater than our focus on individualism. Thus we believe it is important to take care of all people, regardless of the cause of their need. Yet even when we are willing to provide support, there is a value conflict over how to do so.

Entitlement versus Handout

Being entitled implies an earned right to something. The sense is that for previous efforts one has made, one is now rewarded. The Social Security program falls under this model. A handout implies that a person is getting something yet doing nothing in return. In the early years of ADC, women heads of households were seen as doing a social good; they were raising their children in spite of having lost their husband. Over time that perception changed as the type of women receiving assistance changed. No longer widows but divorced or never-married mothers, these women were perceived as getting something for doing nothing. By 1996, this belief was so strong that it was a major impetus behind welfare reform.

Sympathy versus Empathy

In spite of what may have seemed to be callousness in welfare reform policy, there was a great deal of talk about helping and caring. A few years later, the phrase "compassionate conservative" was coined and used by George W. Bush in his presidential bid. It captured the sentiment behind welfare reform. Many welfare advocates were confused by this concept, viewing the changes as anything but compassionate. The confusion lies in the distinction between sympathy and empathy. Both call for examining what others have experienced, but the concepts differ in application. Sympathy, like compassion, involves feeling bad for people and hoping to help them. Empathy requires understanding the situation and circumstances around another person's situation and imagining what it would be like to be in those same circumstances. Empathy tends to consider the environment and outside factors, whereas sympathy typically focuses on the individual's role and responsibility. Welfare reform has displayed a great deal of sympathy, but very little empathy.

THE GAP IN EXPERIENCING AND UNDERSTANDING POVERTY

Contributing to welfare reform failure is the gap between those who experience poverty and those who decide what to do about it. Policy makers today are educated people of substantial economic means far removed from poor people for whom they create social programs. Table 20.2 outlines the differences between the recipients of public assistance through the TANF program and the policy makers who enacted welfare reform legislation that created the TANF program (Segal, 2006). The members of Congress who crafted and enacted welfare reform were predominantly older, married, White men with high levels of income and education. They were developing a program for unmarried young women, a majority of whom were women of color, with low levels of education and no income. The divide between the rich and the poor is not just in lifestyles; it is also about who makes decisions about and for people vastly different from themselves.

Although we are not often privy to the personal experiences or beliefs of policy makers and their families, President Bush's mother revealed the distance between herself and those who are poor, while doing so with great sympathy. In the fall of 2005 following Hurricane

Table 20.2 **Comparison of Temporary Assistance for Needy Families Adult Recipients and Members of Congress**

	TANF Adults	Members of Congress
Average Age	31 years	55 years
Female	90%	14.4%
White	31.6%	87.1%
Black	38.3%	6.9%
Hispanic	24.9%	4.5%
More than a high school education	3.3%	92.7%
Employment rate	25.3%	100%
Millionaires	0	29.2%

From "Welfare as We *Should* Know It: Social Empathy and Welfare Reform" (p. 271), by E. A. Segal, in *The Promise of Welfare Reform: Political Rhetoric and the Reality of Poverty in the Twenty-first Century*, K.M. Kilty, and E. A. Segal, 2006, Binghamton, NY: Haworth Press. Adapted with permission.

Katrina, former first lady Barbara Bush toured hurricane relief centers in Houston. After her visit, she stated, "So many of the people here were underprivileged anyway. This is working very well for them" (Editor & Publisher, 2005). This was her response to the conditions of people who lost their homes and all their possessions and were likely to have been poor before the hurricane. Barbara Bush is not a mean person. However, she lives far removed from the average person's life, and even farther removed from someone in poverty. She did not lack sympathy or compassion, but she did lack empathy.

SOCIAL EMPATHY

What Is Social Empathy?

Social empathy describes the insights one has about other people's lives that allow one to understand the circumstances and realities of other people's living situations (Segal, 2007). Why is empathy important? Empathy for individuals is key to personal growth (Watson, 2002). Research suggests that people with empathy are more likely to be civic-minded and become responsible citizens (Loeb, 1999). In 1994, Daniel Goleman wrote about emotional intelligence and its importance for personal and social development. He outlined five key domains of emotional intelligence; empathy serves as one of the key components. Without empathy, people tend to behave in ways that are less socially productive. A lack of empathy is strongly correlated with destructive tendencies (Hoffman, 1984), the worst of which may be sociopathic behaviors (Stout, 2005). For the most part, research has focused on empathy and individual behaviors. What is the impact on society when empathy is used in policy making, or the converse, when it is not?

Empathetic individuals, if they are in decision-making positions, can use their empathy to guide their course of action. But relying on empathetic policy makers can be hit or miss, and more miss today as the experiences of those at the top are so distant from those at the bottom. So although we can hope for empathetic individuals to come forward and serve in policy-making positions, we can also work to create a culture of empathy that focuses on social issues. That is the goal of social empathy: to use insights about the circumstances of people's lives to develop public policies and programs that are appropriate and responsive to those in need.

The Benefits of Social Empathy

When we have social empathy, we are more likely to develop practices, services, programs, and policies that promote social justice. Social empathy provides a framework for addressing the key social inequality of poverty. This perspective has been absent from welfare reform policy making in recent years. What difference might it make if we had a deep understanding of what it is like to be a young single mother, with perhaps only a high school education, living each day full of uncertainties about where to sleep, if there is enough to eat, where to go to get medical care, how to get clothing, where to leave our young child while we go out and look for a job, and what to do if all these basic needs are unmet? The difference it makes is that if we truly understand, if we can truly imagine ourselves in that situation, we can better respond to those needs.

The foundation of TANF was the Great Depression. It is interesting to note that the piece of social legislation in the United States that gave rise to the ADC program, the

Social Security Act of 1935, was sponsored by two members of Congress who intimately understood the limitations of poverty and social inequality:

> On January 17, 1935, President Roosevelt asked Congress for social security legislation. That same day, the administration's bill was introduced in both houses of Congress by men who had felt keenly the meaning of social insecurity. Robert Wagner, who steered the social security measure through the Senate, was the son of a janitor; as an immigrant boy, he had sold papers on the streets of New York. Maryland's David Lewis, who guided the bill through the House, had gone to work at nine in a coal mine. Illiterate at sixteen, he had taught himself to read not only English but French and German; he had learned French to verify a translation of Tocqueville. The aged, Davy Lewis declared, were "America's untouchables.... Even under slavery, the owner did not deny his obligation to feed and clothe and doctor the slaves, no matter what might happen to crops or to markets." (*Congressional Record,* 74th Congress, 1st session, p. 5687, as cited in Leuchtenburg, 1963, p. 131)

These members of Congress drew from their personal experiences with poverty. They supported legislation that addressed structural poverty, rather than focus solely on individual failures. Today there are very few policy makers who themselves grew up impoverished. How can we expect today's privileged politicians to understand poverty firsthand? Because policy makers and those in positions of economic and social power are so far removed from the day-to-day experiences of people who are poor, it is necessary to help them to understand what it means to live in poverty. Developing social empathy is the key to creating social policies and programs that go much deeper in ameliorating the contributing factors to poverty.

WHERE DO WE GO FROM HERE? THE FUTURE OF WELFARE IN AMERICA

In spite of ongoing efforts to eradicate public welfare, dating back to even before passage of the Social Security Act in 1935, the program is still here. The reauthorization of TANF in 2005 demonstrates that although the program has been pared back, it appears to be entrenched in the social welfare landscape of America. The social value of regarding the program from the perspective of individual responsibility also seems to be entrenched. This perspective, however, misses what may be the most important element of the TANF program, yet is rarely addressed: the children. Two-thirds of TANF recipients are young children. Demanding a change in their family structure ignores the day-to-day life of these children. To not promote healthy development of the children, regardless of what choices their parents made, is shortsighted. Recent research by a panel of national poverty experts highlights how shortsighted our social welfare policies are in terms of childhood poverty:

> Our results suggest that the costs to the United States associated with childhood poverty total about $500B per year, or the equivalent of nearly 4% of GDP. More specifically, we estimate that childhood poverty each year:
>
> - Reduces productivity and economic output by about 1.3% of GDP
> - Raises the costs of crime by 1.3% of GDP
> - Raises health expenditures and reduces the value of health by 1.2% of GDP. (Holzer, Schanzenbach, Duncan, & Ludwig, 2007, p. 1)

Children are not capable of finding jobs that pay decent wages or securing adequate housing or health care or education. If we think those are necessities for poor children, then we need to reexamine welfare reform. And we need to do so from the perspective of what it means to be in that situation, using social empathy to construct effective public programs.

REFERENCES

Abramovitz, M. (2000). *Under attack, fighting back: Women and welfare in the United States.* New York: Monthly Review Press.

Abramovitz, M. (2006). Neither accidental, nor simply mean-spirited: The context for welfare reform. In K. M. Kilty & E. A. Segal (Eds.), *The promise of welfare reform: Political rhetoric and the reality of poverty in the twenty-first century* (pp. 23–38). Binghamton, NY: Haworth Press.

Acs, G., & Loprest, P. (2004). *Leaving welfare: Employment and well-being of families that left welfare in the post-entitlement era.* Kalamazoo, MI: W. E. Upjohn Institute for Employment Research.

Administration for Children and Families. (2004). *TANF sixth annual report to Congress.* Washington, DC: U.S. Department of Health and Human Services.

Albelda, R. (2001). Fallacies of welfare-to-work policies. *Annals of the American Academy of Political and Social Science, 577,* 66–78.

Axinn, J. M., & Hirsch, A. E. (1993). Welfare and the "reform" of women. *Families in Society, 74*(9), 563–572.

Bloom, D., Parrott, S., Shapiro, I., & Super, D. (1994). *The Personal Responsibility Act: An analysis.* Washington, DC: Center on Budget and Policy Priorities.

Bostrom, M. (2001). *Achieving the American dream: A meta-analysis of public opinion concerning poverty, upward mobility, and related issues.* New York: Ford Foundation.

Congressional Budget Office. (2007). *The budget and economic outlook: Fiscal years 2007–2016.* Washington, DC: U.S. Government Printing Office.

DeNavas-Walt, C., Proctor, B. D., & Lee, C. H. (2006). Income, poverty, and health insurance coverage in the United States: 2005. In *Current Population Reports,* P 60–231. Washington, DC: U.S. Census Bureau.

Derthick, M. (1979). *Policymaking for Social Security.* Washington, DC: Brookings Institution.

Editor & Publisher. (2005, September 5). *Barbara Bush: Things working out 'very well' for poor evacuees from New Orleans.* Available from www.editorandpublisher.com/eandp/news/article/.

Falk, G., Gish, M., & Solomon-Fears, C. (2006). *Welfare reauthorization: An overview of the issues.* Washington, DC: Congressional Research Service, Library of Congress.

Gilens, M. (1999). *Why Americans hate welfare.* Chicago: University of Chicago Press.

Goleman, D. (1994). *Emotional intelligence.* New York: Bantam.

Gordon, L. (2001). Who deserves help? Who must provide? *Annals of the American Academy of Political and Social Science, 577,* 12–25.

Hoffman, M. L. (1984). Empathy, social cognition, and moral action. In W. Kurtines & J. Gerwitz (Eds.), *Moral behavior and development: Advances in theory* (pp. 283–302). New York: Wiley.

Holzer, H. J., Schanzenbach, D. W., Duncan, G. J., & Ludwig, J. (2007). *The economic costs of poverty in the United States: Subsequent effects of children growing up poor.* Washington, DC: Center for American Progress.

Katz, M. B. (1989). *The undeserving poor: From the war on poverty to the war on welfare.* New York: Pantheon Books.

King, C. T., & Mueser, P. R. (2005). Urban welfare and work experiences: Implications for welfare reform. *Employment Research, 12*(3), 1–4.

Leuchtenburg, W. E. (1963). *Franklin D. Roosevelt and the New Deal*. New York: Harper & Row.

Loeb, P. R. (1999). *Soul of a citizen: Living with conviction in a cynical time*. New York: St. Martin's Press.

Miller, D. C. (1992). *Women and social welfare*. New York: Praeger. Retrieved February 26, 2007, from www.nytimes.com/aponline/us/AP-Welfare-State.html.

New York Times. (2007, February 26). Available from www.nytimes.com/aponline/us/AP-Welfare-State.html.

Parrott, S., & Sherman, A. (2006). *TANF at 10: Program results are more mixed than often understood*. Washington, DC: Center on Budget and Policy Priorities.

Patterson, J. T. (2000). *America's struggle against poverty in the twentieth century*. Cambridge, MA: Harvard University Press.

Piven, F. F., & Cloward, R. A. (1971). *Regulating the poor: The functions of public welfare*. New York: Random House.

Roosevelt, F. D. (1935, January 4). Annual message to Congress. Available from www.presidency.ucsb.edu/ws/print.php?pid=14890/.

Segal, E. A. (1989). Welfare reform: Help for poor women and children? *Affilia, 4*(3), 42–50.

Segal, E. A. (2006). Welfare as we should know it: Social empathy and welfare reform. In K. M. Kilty & E. A. Segal (Eds.), *The promise of welfare reform: Political rhetoric and the reality of poverty in the twenty-first century* (pp. 265–274). Binghamton, NY: Haworth Press.

Segal, E. A. (2007). *Social welfare policy and social programs: A values perspective*. Belmont, CA: Thompson/Brooks/Cole.

Segal, E. A., & Kilty, K. M. (2003). Political promises for welfare reform. *Journal of Poverty, 7*(1/2), 51–67.

Social Security Administration. (2006). *Annual statistical supplement, 2005*. Washington, DC: Author.

Stout, M. (2005). *The sociopath next door*. New York: Broadway Books. (Supplement. Washington, DC: U.S. Government Printing Office.)

Trattner, W. I. (1999). *From poor law to welfare state: A history of social welfare in America* (6th ed.). New York: Free Press

U.S. Census Bureau. (2005). *Statistical abstract of the United States* (125th ed.). Washington, DC: U.S. Government Printing Office.

U.S. Department of Health and Human Services. (1998). *Aid to Families with Dependent Children: The baseline*. Washington, DC: Office of Human Services Policy.

U.S. General Accounting Office. (2006). *Welfare reform: Better information needed to understand trends in states' uses of the TANF block grant* (GAO-06-414). Washington, DC: Author.

Watson, J. C. (2002). Re-visioning empathy. In D. J. Cain & J. Sieman (Eds.), *Humanistic psychotherapies: Handbook of research and practice* (pp. 445–471). Washington, DC: American Psychological Association.

Wilson, W. J. (1987). *The truly disadvantaged: The inner city, the underclass, and public policy*. Chicago: University of Chicago Press.

Youth Policy. (Ed.). (1994). *Creating a Successful Transition from Welfare-to-Employment System, 16*(2/3).

Author Index

Subject Index